A BIRD-FINDING GUIDE TO CANADA

A
BIRD-FINDING

GUIDE TO

CANADA

REVISED EDITION

Edited by J. Cam Finlay

M&S

Canadian Cataloguing in Publication Data

Main entry under title:

A bird-finding guide to Canada

Rev. ed.
ISBN 0-7710-3219-6

1. Bird watching – Canada – Guidebooks.   2. Birds – Canada.
I. Finlay, J. C. (James Campbell), 1931– .

QL685.B57 2000   598'.07'23471   C99-933025-X

We acknowledge the financial support of the Government of Canada through the Book Publishing Industry Development Program for our publishing activities. We further acknowledge the support of the Canada Council for the Arts and the Ontario Arts Council for our publishing program.

Design: Ingrid Paulson
Illustrated by Terry Thormin
Typeset in Bembo by M&S, Toronto
Printed and bound in Canada

McClelland & Stewart Inc.
The Canadian Publishers
481 University Avenue
Toronto, Ontario
M5G 2E9

1 2 3 4 5   04 03 02 01 00

1984 Edition

For Joy, whose ideas, encouragement, faith and support ensure dreams become reality.

For Brett, Warren and Rhonda, who have supported and encouraged their father to do his project.

For Muriel and Hugh Finlay, who encouraged their son to keep his enthusiasm and to grow in the direction of his choice.

2000 Edition

For Joy who continues with ideas and support.

Now sixteen years later for our grandchildren Chris, Jessica, Paul, Jenise, Liam, Cassia and Annika, who we hope will be encouraged to further explore our great country.

CONTENTS

PREFACE 1984

Joy and I, in our travels, have tried to search out those special places where nature is at its best. Many people have helped us to find those spots. In the same spirit of cooperation, and with the same willingness to share their knowledge, individuals across the country have helped to make *A Bird-Finding Guide to Canada* a reality.

Recognizing that no one person could know of all the places to find birds in Canada, Terry Thormin and I decided to use the same approach as we had in preparing *A Nature Guide to Alberta*, that is, to contact people and request their assistance. The response was both swift and astonishingly enthusiastic. Individuals from each province and territory agreed to coordinate their regional material: R. Yorke Edwards and Wayne Campbell in British Columbia; I handled Alberta; Dr. C. Stuart Houston and Dr. J. Bernard Gollop in Saskatchewan; Rudolf F. Koes and associates in Manitoba; Dr. Chip Weseloh, Linda Weseloh, and Arnet Sheppard in Ontario; Mabel McIntosh and Réal Bisson in Quebec; David Christie looked after New Brunswick; Jim Wolford saw to Nova Scotia; Winifred Cairns in Prince Edward Island; John Pratt and Bruce McTavish oversaw Newfoundland material; Dave Mossop and Robert Frisch in the Yukon; and Dr. Tom Barry in the Northwest Territories. A special thanks to all of you for the many hours spent obtaining and writing contributions, revising and upgrading material, and then cheerfully undertaking that final major edit in early 1983.

Many others willingly provided specific material for selected sites. Their names appear at the ends of their contributions. Others did not want to be listed in the text but provided excellent data, or helped in the provincial editing in the last round, including: Manley Callin, M. Cobus, Joyce and Bill Anaka, Mary Gilliland, Bruce Linegar, C. A. Wallis, John Wells, C. R. Wershler, and Al Wiseley. Several other people have provided information that I have not been able to use, but which was certainly appreciated, including: from Alberta, Greg Wagner; from Ontario, Christopher Harris; from New Brunswick, Stanley Gorham, Don Kimball, Louis Lapierre, Ron Weir, and Doug Whitman. Thanks to all of you, including Wayne Harris, who had to redo his material because Canada Post lost the originals.

To those who encouraged me near the start, including Diane Griffin, Arnet Sheppard, Dr. Robert Nero, Bob Carswell, and David Christie, I say a special thanks.

Thank you to friend, adviser, and colleague Terry Thormin, who prepared the drawings for the book, and to those who provided slides to assist him: Yorke Edwards sent one by David MacKenzie; Terry Pratt sent one taken by J. R. Graham; Réal Bisson supplied some, including those by J. R. Coulouche; David Christie contributed several; and also Richard Fyfe and Bob Gehlert, who supplied slides to assist Terry, plus pictures for the cover of the book.

Thanks to Stephanie Kucharyshyn and Inge Wilson, of the cartographic staff at the University of Alberta Department of Geography, who drew the maps.

Many of the historical items, natural history notes, special activities and other gems of particular interest have been taken from that excellent book *Canadian Book of the Road*, by the Canadian Automobile Association and The Reader's Digest Association (Canada) Ltd., 1979.

Thanks to ornithologist and good friend Dr. Martin McNicholl for reviewing the manuscript in its early stages, though I, of course, take full responsibility for any errors and omissions.

Anita Moore spent many hours, including weekends and evenings, typing the draft and several revisions. Thanks Anita. To my mother-in-law, Marie Barton, whose gifts over the years of reference books on birds and other natural history subjects have been invaluable as I wrote this one, a special thanks.

To Mel Hurtig and the entire staff at Hurtig Publishers I say thank you for making the production of this book possible. A very special thanks to Anne Leobold, my editor, who tightened up the manuscript, did the necessary cross-checking, and finally picked up those gremlin-caused errors that always seem to creep in. And finally, I appreciate the cordial and helpful relationship established with Ms. José Druker of Hurtig, who worked with me to ensure this book would meet the high standards of the trade.

Joy and I have been married nearly thirty years. She has continually encouraged me to develop and broaden myself. It was she who gave me the necessary moral support when I left my job as a geologist to become a naturalist. Without her ideas, enthusiasm and, most of all, her special consideration and commitment to each of our children and myself, we could not be doing the things that we are. Thank you, Joy.

And all you keen birders out there, send me corrections and additions to the choice spots that have been missed, to be included in the revised edition within the next five years. Let's make the second edition more complete.

J. CAM FINLAY

Edmonton, Alberta
December 1983

PREFACE 2000

Wildlife watching has become big business. Over $11 billion was spent in Canada, one-tenth the amount spent in the United States, on nature-related activities such as trips, on equipment such as binoculars, on bird feed, on the purchase of lands for wildlife and other related items, according to a Statistics Canada study in 1996. Bird-watching has become the fastest-growing hobby, besides gardening, on the continent. To meet the ever-increasing needs of these nature lovers, numerous books and publications have come out since our first edition in 1984. Thus when Doug Gibson, publisher for McClelland & Stewart, approached me last spring to update the book I said, "No!" as I considered there was no need, the gap being filled by local and regional guides. Finally after several phone calls from him, his trip here on business and "arm twisting" me while we attempted to bird-watch at Esquimalt Lagoon, I agreed.

I am really pleased that Doug's persuasion worked, as it has been fun (much work, too) contacting old friends, colleagues and associates, many of whom I had not talked to for fifteen years, as well as several new people I had heard of or who came from nowhere to enthusiastically assist in this big project. Once more the efforts by all of you reinforced my conviction that the Canadian naturalist community (many of them birders) is made up of wonderful helpful people.

As in 1983, I recognized that no one person could know all, or even a very small segment, of the many great birding sites in Canada. I went to the phone and later e-mail and fax to make, and follow up, my contacts. It worked! Birders came from everywhere to assist. In a relatively short time, we built up a team of enthusiastic people from across the country who agreed to collect and organize provincial and territorial chapters. Several even took on the huge task of rewriting their whole chapter. A big job! These coordinators include Gary Davidson for British Columbia; Jocelyn Hudon, who did Alberta; Martin Bailey did Saskatchewan; Rudolf F. Koes, as in the previous edition, produced the Manitoba chapter; Margaret Bain of *Birders' Journal* pulled Ontario together and provided the original checklist on which we built the enclosed list; Pierre Bannon, coming on somewhat late, still kept the deadlines for Quebec; David Christie, a colleague from over thirty years ago, again handled New Brunswick; Nova Scotia once more was looked after by Jim Wolford, a grad student with me eons ago and a close friend of Joy and me; Prince Edward Island was overseen by Dan McAskill, another close friend of Joy and me; John Pratt again oversaw Newfoundland, and this time added Labrador; Cathy McEwen brought on a team for the Yukon, including Cameron Eckert, who supplied most of the material; Cathy also provided me with Northwest Territory contacts; Craig Mathans wrote almost the complete Northwest Territories and the new section on the territory of Nunavut.

To all of you, this book could not have been written without your many hours of hounding for copy, often writing and rewriting, revising and upgrading manuscripts, plus giving me a very comprehensive up-to-date checklist for each province and territory. A very sincere special thanks to all of you and to those from whom you obtained data and who are named at the end of appropriate sites.

As the site texts began to arrive, it was soon apparent that I had to either upgrade my 1993 computer system or get help. Fortunately, our very good friend and colleague Tom Gillespie, who works closely with me on the study of Western Purple Martins and banding Rufous and Anna's Hummingbirds, is a computer whiz. He came to my aid. As the copy arrived in document form by e-mail in various formats, he converted it into files that I could use on my outdated system. A very special thanks to you, Tom, for the many hours, at times frustrating, you worked over material so that it was usable on my system.

As the final copy began to appear, we realized that line drawings should be in the text as in the previous edition. Our friend Terry Thormin, who was instrumental in getting the first edition up and running, very generously agreed that we could again use his artwork for this new edition. Thanks ever so much Terry.

J. CAM FINLAY

270 Trevlac Pl., R.R. 3
Victoria, B.C.
V8X 3X1

December 10, 1999

THE PLAN

The book covers Canada from offshore Vancouver and the Queen Charlotte Islands on the west coast to St. John's, Newfoundland, on the east; from Point Pelee in southern Ontario to Ellesmere Island in the high Arctic. The text is designed to help the beginner, the average naturalist and the keen "lister" to find new and not-so-new species while visiting interesting places. An attempt was made to select the best birding areas, most national and many provincial parks, and nearly all major urban centres.

The arrangement of chapters by province and territories overlaps ecological boundaries and is not very scientific. However, such divisions worked in similar guides done for the United States, and we hope the arrangement works well here too.

Birds covered (over 600 species) include those of general and specific interest for an area. The more common species, such as American Robin or White-throated Sparrow, are seldom mentioned. Colour phases or races are noted where they are known to be present. The most recent checklist from *Birders' Journal* has been followed for terminology. Certain terms are used as follows:

waterfowl: swans, geese and ducks
water birds: all species associated with water and marshes
waders and *shorebirds*: those with longer legs found on beaches and shores
alcids: seldom used, but when it does occur includes Razorbills, Dovekies, murres, guillemots and puffins
pelagic species: mainly shearwaters and petrels
land birds: those not usually associated with water

To find a specific species, look it up in the checklist, then turn to the text to determine how, when and where to find that and other species in the region you plan to visit. The introductions to each chapter provide highlights. It would be useful to read the text with a provincial road map in hand. These maps usually provide information about parks, campsites and other recreational opportunities. When writing for a map, request a complete tourist package for that province. You can often dial toll free for this information (see text).

HELPFUL SUGGESTIONS

Clothing and Safety Equipment

In parts of Canada the temperature can change in a few hours from above freezing to −20°C. In spring and fall you can encounter anything from temperatures of 20°C to a snowstorm. Carry a wool pullover sweater at all times. A light jacket or windbreaker is useful. Bring a light parka, mitts and warm headgear (about one-half of your heat loss is from the top of your head).

In summer, from June through August, the weather is generally warm with some rain showers. Bring a light rain jacket and that wool pullover sweater. Also, make sure you bring insect repellent.

Winter brings the cold. Freezing temperatures occur from central British Columbia to Newfoundland. In Victoria, Vancouver and the southern tip of Ontario, and the southern Maritimes (N.S., P.E.I., N.B.), the cold temperatures are not too extreme. To go birding during the winter in most of the country, make sure to carry in your car, at all times, lined parka and boots, wool pullover sweater, warm headgear, woollen mitts with an outside shell, warm trousers and long underwear (pyjamas will do), matches, a candle in a can to use as a stove for heat and to melt ice or snow, a sleeping bag, food, a flashlight, a shovel and a heavy rope or tow chain. If possible, all equipment should stay in the back seat. Trunks freeze up! And always carry a first-aid kit in your car.

Special Equipment

Special equipment is not necessary to enjoy watching birds, but it does help. Three items that will add to your enjoyment include field guides, binoculars and backpack.

Field Guides. Several guides are available in most bookstores. The ones recommended below are all compact and available in paperback. I prefer *Field Guide to the Birds of North America*, Third Edition (National Geographic Society). Two other guides, both by Roger Tory Peterson and published by Houghton Mifflin in Boston, are *A Field Guide to the Birds of Eastern and Central North America* (4th ed. and completely revised, covering areas east of the 100th meridian, the Manitoba-Saskatchewan boundary) and *A Field Guide to Western Birds* (areas west of the 100th meridian).

Binoculars. There are many styles, makes and models on the market, with prices ranging from $50 to over $1000. I suggest you avoid the very inexpensive pairs, as these will reduce rather than increase your enjoyment. Check with your local bird-supply and/or camera store for help in selecting a pair to suit your eyes and pocketbook.

Backpack. We all need something to carry our lunch, water bottle, rainwear, tuque, pullover sweater, mitts, extra film, camera, insect repellent and field guides. There are many good day packs on the market. The size of pack depends on how much you carry. I usually have quite a bit of material and so one Christmas our three children gave me an excellent backpack, Outbound by Taymor. It has side pockets, back pockets and top cover in which to stuff a jacket.

Attracting Birds

Most of us want to bird-watch all year. There are three main points to consider if you wish to bring birds to you: water, food and shelter.

Water. Dripping and/or running water does wonders. Even a plastic pail with a small hole that allows water to drip into an upside-down garbage can lid will bring birds. Another technique is to place a garden hose with a slow drip above a birdbath or lid. A spraying fountain is, of course, much better (and more work to build) as are small waterfalls.

Food. Feeding birds can bring its rewards (and expense if you go overboard). Eastern Canadians usually prefer a mix to attract a wide variety of species. Those of us in the west generally feed sunflower seeds; even House Sparrows love them. Hummingbirds occur across southern Canada and can be brought in with a simple feeder. Use one part (or less) sugar to four parts water, no colouring added. Carry a hummingbird feeder when you travel and set it up in a campground. You will be surprised at how often you attract hummingbirds, June through August. Carrying a small bag of birdseed to put on a plate at your campsite also brings in the sparrows and finches.

Shelter. Birds require a place to hide, nest and rest. In landscaping your yard, try to balance open sites with small clumps of bushes. Such a plan provides "edge effect" which the majority of birds prefer. If you are travelling, look for such edges and carefully check them out. They are usually the most productive.

Further Information

Lists of references for each province have been incorporated into the appropriate chapters. A Canada-wide publication, *Birders' Journal*, is available by subscription; write to 8 Midtown Drive, Suite 289, Oshawa, Ontario L1J 8L2.

For those of you interested in birds and broader natural history subjects, the Canadian Nature Federation is by far the best organization to join. They put out a beautiful magazine quarterly, *Nature Canada*. Further information and a subscription may be obtained by writing: Canadian Nature Federation, 1 Nicholas Street, Suite 606, Ottawa, Ontario K1N 7B7; phone 1-800-267-4088; or e-mail cnf@cnf.ca

Several provinces have their own publications. Refer to the text for these.

A CODE FOR USING THE OUT-OF-DOORS

Make all visits to a site instructive and productive, not destructive.

The birds, mammals, insects and other natural objects are for all to enjoy – in place. Take notes and photographs; refrain from breaking branches for a better look or picture; don't collect.

Nests, eggs and young are to be left alone; it is an offence under law to remove them.

Avoid approaching colonial nest sites too closely. Disturbance of these birds prevents them from defending eggs and young from predators.

Stay well away from nests of birds of prey during the early and mid stages of the nesting cycle. These species, if disturbed before the young are partially feathered, often abandon the site.

Leave family groups of young waterfowl and game birds alone. Splitting them up could result in losses.

Avoid use of powerboats to explore marshes and lakes. A canoe causes much less disturbance.

Observe dancing grounds, or leks, of grouse from a distance. Place your photographic blind on the edge the night before and enter well before dawn; depart after all birds have left about midday.

Avoid the use of a tape recorder to attract singing males on territory in city parks and other urban sites. Heavy use of tape recordings by birdwatchers can substantially reduce breeding success.

Trails are for your use; stay on them when on foot or in a vehicle. Alpine and arctic tundras and even very dry prairie vegetation are particularly fragile. Such environments will take hundreds of years to recover (if ever) from one passing of a set of vehicle tires.

Tens of thousands of dollars are spent each year to pick up trash and litter. What you bring in you can take out!

Carry your own lightweight tent and sleeping mat. Building of a lean-to, or cutting spruce branches for a mattress, was useful 50 years ago when few people camped and equipment was heavy.

Parks and other public areas have special sites for open fires. Use the wood provided. Dead upright trees provide homes for chickadees. Practise axemanship in the woodpile! Bring your own wiener sticks (wire coat hangers make excellent ones).

Ask permission to enter private land. These landholders are often very helpful and will show you their private birding spots.

Close and fasten all gates. They are there to keep valuable livestock from wandering.

Safeguard all water supplies. Avoid dumping scraps and rubbish into streams, ponds and lakes. Don't drive through streams if it can be avoided, as you could disturb fish spawning grounds.

Keep dogs and cats under control at all times. These urban pets have become the most ruthless of city predators upon small wildlife.

Leave wild plants for others to enjoy. A picked flower wilts in a few hours and the plant will not be able to reseed. Transplanted flowers usually require special soil and conditions not found in your yard.

A BIRD-FINDING GUIDE TO CANADA

BRITISH COLUMBIA

Our most westerly province contains more life zones and bird species than any other political unit in Canada. The variety results in birders from east of the Rockies adding dozens of species to their life lists per day upon first arriving. Where else can you find huge colonies of petrels, murres, auklets and puffins; Gyrfalcons, large numbers of Bald Eagles, the largest concentration left in North America of Peregrine Falcons; White-tailed Ptarmigans, Heermann's Gulls, White-throated Swifts, Canyon Wrens, White-headed Woodpeckers, several species of hummingbird, Crested Mynas and Eurasian Skylarks.

Covering 948,596 km², the lands range from sea level to 4663 m at Mount Fairweather. Habitats and birds to search for include:

Boreal forest with spruce and Balsam Fir, cold; in the north and east, with the usual cross-Canada birds, including Spruce Grouse, Boreal Owl, both three-toed Woodpeckers, Blackpoll Warbler and Dark-eyed Junco.

Subalpine forest similar to above; occurring in all southern ranges of the mountains, with many boreal species and others including Gray Jay, Hermit Thrush, Varied Thrush and both species of crossbills.

Alpine meadows, dry tundra, rock barrens, cold; found at different elevations dropping as you proceed north, with Golden Eagle, White-tailed Ptarmigan, American Pipit, Gray-crowned Rosy Finch and Golden-crowned Sparrow.

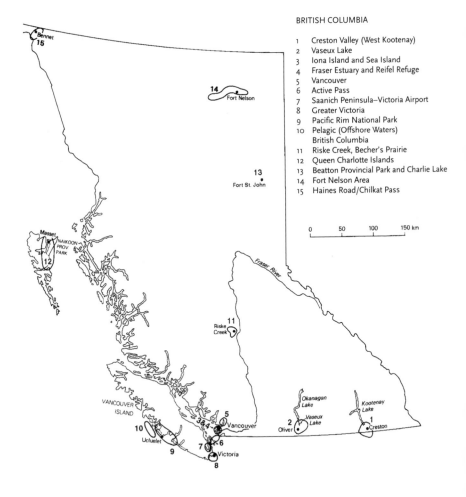

BRITISH COLUMBIA

1   Creston Valley (West Kootenay)
2   Vaseux Lake
3   Iona Island and Sea Island
4   Fraser Estuary and Reifel Refuge
5   Vancouver
6   Active Pass
7   Saanich Peninsula–Victoria Airport
8   Greater Victoria
9   Pacific Rim National Park
10 Pelagic (Offshore Waters)
    British Columbia
11 Riske Creek, Becher's Prairie
12 Queen Charlotte Islands
13 Beatton Provincial Park and Charlie Lake
14 Fort Nelson Area
15 Haines Road/Chilkat Pass

Montane forest with Douglas-fir, Ponderosa Pine, dry; featuring Swainson's Hawk, Black-billed Magpie, Clark's Nutcracker, Lewis's Woodpecker, Mountain Chickadee and Lazuli Bunting.

Grassland/steppe consisting of Bunchgrass, bitterbrush and sage areas, very dry; with Sharp-tailed Grouse, Long-billed Curlew, White-throated Swift, Rock Wren, Canyon Wren and Western Meadowlark.

Dry coastal forest with Douglas-fir and Garry Oak, dry/moist; home to California Quail, Common Bushtit, Bewick's Wren, Black-throated Gray Warbler and House Finch.

Wet coastal forest with Hemlock and Red Cedar, wet; hosting Pileated Woodpecker, Steller's Jay, Swainson's Thrush, Chestnut-backed Chickadee and Townsend's Warbler.

The sea and its shores, impossible to generalize, contain a variety of birding habitats. The Queen Charlotte Islands offer huge seabird colonies (petrels, puffins, murres, auklets, etc.). Offshore cruises usually produce albatross, shearwaters, phalaropes, Sabine's Gulls and members of the auk family. Seashores can be very productive in rich areas such as some right in Victoria, where wintering water birds include Harlequin Duck; California, Mew, Heermann's and other gulls; Common Murre; Pigeon Guillemot; Marbled and Ancient Murrelets; and Rhinoceros Auklet.

To watch seabirds, come in spring (May/June) to the nesting colonies. Since many of the colonies are on islands, access is by boat. Furthermore, access to many of the colonies is restricted during the breeding season. These birds are often numerous along the coast in fall and winter. Shorebirds are best observed in May and again in August/September. Most lowland species nest from late May to mid-July. Mountain birds usually nest from mid-June into July. A caution: snow may be deep in mid-June and July in the high country.

There are a number of "hot spots" in British Columbia. The south end of the Okanagan Valley offers a great variety of habitats, and therefore a large mix of birds, in a relatively small area. Since it also includes the northern portion of the Great Plains Desert, you can find such species as White-throated Swift, Sage Thrasher and Canyon Wren. The Queen Charlotte Islands are an excellent place for seabird colonies and Peregrine Falcons, but watch the weather. Victoria is home to the introduced Eurasian Skylark on the Saanich Peninsula and a good variety of other water and land birds. Iona and Sea Islands and the Fraser River delta offer large concentrations of shorebirds during migration and waterfowl during winter. The northeast corner of the province is actually east of the Rocky Mountains, giving the western birder access to eastern species. Several of the national and provincial parks allow relatively easy access to alpine regions for species like White-tailed Ptarmigan and Gray-crowned Rosy-Finch. All these hot spots are covered in more detail in the upcoming sections.

For the rushed visitor with a week to spend, the following itinerary will likely be the most productive. Spend two days in the south Okanagan, a day in Manning Provincial Park (after mid-June when the timberline road is open), two days in the Fraser River Delta, and two days in Victoria.

The Vancouver rare bird alert telephone number is (604) 737-3074, the Victoria number (250) 592-3381 and the one in Nanaimo (250) 390-3029. These numbers will alert you to interesting birds in the region and also give you names of local birders who might help. An overall birding Web site for B.C. provides additional help at http://birding.bc with subsets for
Victoria at http://birding.bc.ca/victoria
Nanaimo at http://birding.bc.ca/nanaimo
Prince George at http://birding.bc.ca/princegeorge
The general e-mail for such information is info@birding.bc.ca The site for Vancouver is http://naturalhistory.bc.ca/vnhs/

Further information about birding and birders in B.C. may be obtained from the British Columbia Field Ornithologists at Box 8059, Victoria, B.C. v8w 3R7 with their Web site http://birding.bc.ca/bcfo/
For B.C. bird highlights contact http://www.visionfoundation.org/ B.C. Fish and Wildlife has a Web site for Watchable Wildlife at http://www.birding.bc.ca/victoria
Their Wildlife Watch site is http://www3.bc.sympatico.ca/driftwood/bcwwhome.htm

A few communities host wildlife festivals with special emphasis on birds including the Brant Festival at Parksville/Qualicum Beach. For information, go to http://www.island.net/~bfest/
The Columbia Valley Bird Festival is at http://www.adventurevalley.com/wings/
The Meadowlark Festival is at Penticton http://www.meadowlarkfestival.bc.ca/.

In addition to all the Web sites listed, for further information contact http://birding.bc.ca/links.htm

Lists of natural history clubs around the province can be obtained from the Federation of B.C. Naturalists at 425 – 1367 West Broadway, Vancouver, B.C. V6H 4A9. Their Web site is http://members.xoom.com/fbcn/

As you travel around B.C., you will find that most communities have tourist information centres (many with museums) that are good sources of local information. Vancouver has several nature centres operated by the various municipalities and many of the national and provincial parks have naturalist programs. The Royal British Columbia Museum in Victoria has some of the best natural history displays in Canada; the Web site is at http://rbcm1.rbcm.gov.bc.ca Their Grace Bell collection is at http://www.rbcm.gov.bc.ca/nhpapers/gracebell/english/index.html

For more general information on travel in B.C., contact Tourism B.C., Parliament Buildings, Victoria, B.C. v8w 2z2; phone 1-800-435-5622. Their Web site is http://www.snbc/res.com

YORKE EDWARDS
Revised by Gary Davidson

Birds Found in Mountain National and Provincial Parks

Almost 12 per cent of British Columbia's land area is protected in either provincial or national parks, mainly in the mountains. Many of them contain some excellent birding sites. While it is impossible to deal with all of them here, some of the more accessible parks warrant mention. Four national parks occur in the southeastern portion of the province: Kootenay, Yoho, Glacier and Mount Revelstoke. The Trans-Canada Highway passes through three of them on the east side of the province. One, Yoho, is one of the few locations in B.C. where a Yellow Rail has been recorded.

The interior provincial mountain parks include Kokanee Glacier, Cathedral and Manning. Coastal regions have Mount Seymour and Garibaldi.

Both these national and provincial parks provide relatively easy access to alpine and subalpine areas. A number of species are restricted to these high-elevation zones. In the Birding Features section below, sample locations are mentioned for most species; however, occurrence is not limited to those sites. Contact the various park offices ahead of time to obtain hiking trail guides, checklists and possible leads on specific species.

Birding Features

For species listed below, locations given are merely example sites. All species could occur in most or all of the parks mentioned above, as well as in other mountainous regions.

Prairie Falcon. There are one or two lowland locations to look for this species, (e.g., the cliffs near the north end of Osoyoos Lake), but it can also be found in the alpine. Cathedral Provincial Park is a good place to start.

White-tailed Ptarmigan. In some alpine areas it can be quite common and seems to favour rocky meadows. Find spots with plenty of grasses and wildflowers, but with frequent rock outcroppings. Look for it in Kokanee Glacier Provincial Park.

Rock and Willow Ptarmigan. Though not common, both of these birds have been reported from Garibaldi Provincial Park.

Northern Hawk Owl. This bird is an irregular winter visitor to southern B.C., and much more common in northern regions. It has been reported as breeding in Mount Revelstoke National Park.

American Pipit. A common migrant through B.C., the American Pipit is also a common breeder in the mountains and can be found breeding in almost any alpine region that features small lakes and tarns. All of the above-mentioned parks likely have these pipits.

Boreal Chickadee. In southern B.C. this is a subalpine species. Almost any road or trail that reaches up into the subalpine zone will produce this bird. In the southern interior mountains, the subalpine is reached at 1700 to 1800 m and lower as you go north. The road to the top of Mount Revelstoke National Park is a good place to find this species together with the other three B.C. chickadees.

Horned Lark. Three subspecies of Horned Lark occur in B.C. The "Dusky" Horned Lark (*Eremophila alpestris merrilli*) breeds regularly in the interior grasslands. The "Streaked" Horned Lark (*E. a. strigata*) is found in the extreme southwestern corner of B.C. The "Pallid" Horned Lark (*E. a. articola*) breeds sporadically in alpine regions across the province.

Golden-crowned Sparrow. In interior B.C. this bird occurs infrequently during migration. It also breeds in the subalpine zone of the southern mountains. Try Garibaldi and Manning Provincial Parks.

Timberline Sparrow. As of the writing of this book, the bird has not yet been split from the Brewer's Sparrow as a separate species, but presumably will soon be, so we have included it here. Its distribution is not well documented but has been reported from Yoho National Park.

Gray-crowned Rosy Finch. It can appear almost anywhere in the province, particularly in the interior, during migration and winter, but it's quite irregular and can be hard to find. It may be easier to locate in summer in one of the alpine regions. Look for this bird in Kokanee Glacier and Garibaldi Provincial Parks and Yoho National Park.

White-winged Crossbill and Pine Grosbeak. Both of these species occur irregularly at lower elevations but may be more easily found at higher elevations. Both occur in Kokanee Glacier Provincial Park and Kootenay and Mount Revelstoke National Parks.

GARY DAVIDSON

Creston Valley (West Kootenay)

The wetlands immediately west of Creston, surrounded by dry hills, provide opportunities to see over 260 species of birds. Even in the coldest month, January, a diligent search could furnish up to 80 species. Good all-weather roads, a recently revised checklist, Elk, White-tailed Deer and Coyote all add to the experience. The Wildlife Interpretation Centre provides an excellent base from which to operate. The facility, operated by the Creston Valley Wildlife Management Authority, is adjacent to 6480 ha of wetland set aside by the Creston Valley Wildlife Management Authority Act of B.C. The federal government, in cooperation with the B.C. government, erected the building and put in the initial displays. Centre staff lead regular walks and canoe trips into the marshes and onto the surrounding slopes. Good trails and a viewing tower enhance wildlife viewing.

The facility lies about 10 km west of Creston on Highway 3, the Crowsnest Pass route. Daily Greyhound bus service passes through Creston. Visitors can also be dropped off on Highway 3, 0.5 km north of the Wildlife Centre. Accommodation, with a good selection of visitor services, is available in Creston. Several campgrounds exist in the vicinity, the closest being at Summit Creek, 2.5 km north of the centre on Highway 3. If staying at this campground, be sure to remember insect repellent! (Note: This campground is in operation only from May through September.)

For further assistance, drop into the centre to obtain copies of "Creston Valley Checklist of Birds" and "Checklist of West Kootenay Birds." You can also write to Creston Valley Wildlife Centre, Box 640, Creston, B.C. V0B 1G0; phone (250) 428-3260.

Birding Features
In the early spring, from late February through March, waterfowl are abundant. They occur on the open water at the centre, in marshes off the Creston-Summit Creek Road, in Leach and Duck Lakes, and at the south end of Kootenay Lake. These sites contain dark vegetation and circulating underwater springs, both of which speed up the melting of ice. Shorebirds arrive later at these spots on spring and fall migration.

From mid-April to late June, driving the roads in West Creston and in the vicinity of Duck Lake and Wynndel may provide good viewing of migrating land birds. For optimum birding allow at least half a day to tour these roads. At Summit Creek Campground, Pileated Woodpeckers live in the forests along with Hammond's Flycatchers, Winter Wrens, Chestnut-backed Chickadees and many others. At the Wildlife Centre, look for a variety of waterfowl and marsh birds like Sora and American Bittern. Upland birds nearby include Black-headed Grosbeak and Blue Grouse. On Lone Pine Hill and Corn Creek Dike, both Rufous and Calliope Hummingbirds may be found, along with Lazuli Buntings. Driving farther south from the centre on Reclamation Road, watch for Bobolinks in the fields. Farther east, at the Wynndel turnoff, Turkey Vultures may be observed. Proceeding on, be prepared to spend some

Flammulated Owl

time at Duck Lake, one of the better birding spots in the valley. A primitive road on the south side of the lake provides excellent viewing over the lake and adjacent marshes. Birds of particular interest include Cinnamon Teal and Forster's and Black Terns. There is also a Western Grebe colony on the lake. Marsh Wrens are easily viewed here. Challenges to birders in the area are locating Indigo Bunting and Yellow-breasted Chat.

Birds gather here from August to late November. As the ice begins to form near the end of the year, freezing is delayed in several places by dark vegetation, underwater springs and moving streams. Birds concentrate at the open water, making them quite productive for the birdwatcher.

In winter, from December through February, the key to finding birds is to locate shelter and feeding sites. Open water is often teeming with birds. Other areas to search include livestock feedlots, orchards and back yards with trees and shrubs bearing fruit and seeds or bird feeding stations. In the coldest month, January, there is still good birding on Highway 3A up to the south end of Kootenay Lake; on the road to Duck Lake; along the Creston-Summit Creek Road south to Twin Bridges (Peterman Road); and north on Nick's Island Road. Observations from the Canyon-Lister Road, Highway 21, South Creston circle route are worthwhile, too. Wild Turkeys are often seen in this area at any time of year. Short-eared (occasionally) and Northern Pygmy-Owls (often) may be seen in the winter. Mountain, Chestnut-backed and the more common Black-capped Chickadees are usually present.

Other birds found in the valley include Bald Eagle, which remain all year and nest locally. Virginia Rail are sometimes seen in summer. Vaux's Swift at times hawk for insects. Three of the four hummingbird species found locally have nested, including Black-chinned, Rufous and Calliope; the fourth, Anna's, has been reported in the winter. The area is great for swallows, with six species known to nest: Violet-green, Tree, Bank, Northern Rough-winged, Barn and Cliff.

ROBERT BUTLER AND ED McMACKIN
Revised by Ed McMackin

Vaseux Lake

The Vaseux Lake area, south of Penticton, has been known for over half a century as one of the prime birding areas in Canada. It has a high species diversity including migratory waterfowl. In addition, birds of the intermontane Great Basin to the south, such as White-throated Swift, White-headed Woodpecker and Canyon Wren, rare or unknown in other spots in Canada, may be seen here. This is one of the best places in B.C. to see Yellow-breasted Chat. The nearby cliffs are home to California Bighorn Sheep and the Western Rattlesnake.

A good spot to begin your exploration is the Vaseux Lake Wildlife Centre parking lot at the north end of the lake. From the parking lot, a trail leads to a boardwalk across two old river channels to a waterfowl viewing blind. The east shore, from Vaseux Lake Provincial Park south, is privately owned, together with some of the area south of the gravel road that leaves the park heading southeast. The island at the south end of the lake is also private property. The remainder of the shoreline belongs to the federal government and is administered by the Canadian Wildlife Service (CWS) as a wildlife sanctuary. The cliffs to the east are also administered by the CWS as California Bighorn Sheep range. There are no restrictions to hiking on the cliffs. Motorboats are prohibited on the lake.

The first settlers arrived around the turn of the century, including the well-known naturalist and writer H. J. Parham. Early ornithologists, including Taverner and Brooks, led collecting expeditions to the area in the 1920s. The lake and adjacent shoreline were made a wildlife refuge in 1923. The Okanagan River was channelled in the 1950s resulting in a lowered water table and a reduction in the size of the marsh at the north end of the lake.

Good birding areas include about 12 km² around the lake, which is 4 km long and 1 km wide. The lake and park lie about 16 km south of the Penticton International Airport and 6 km south of Okanagan Falls, on Highway 97.

There is one motel, Vaseux Lake Lodge, at the south end of Vaseux Lake, with others nearby on Highway 97 and in Okanagan Falls. Vaseux Lake Provincial Park contains nine camping sites. Okanagan Falls Provincial Park, 6 km to the north, contains 20 spots. There are seven camping spots at Inkaneep Provincial Park, 5 km south of the lake. The nearest gas and service stations are at Okanagan Falls and Gallagher Lake to the south. Specific tourist information on the region may be obtained from Oliver Chamber of Commerce, P.O. Box 460, Oliver, B.C. V0H 1T0; phone (250) 498-6321; e-mail address is info@oliverchamber.bc

Pygmy Nuthatch

Additional reading on the area is available: H. J. Parham, *A Nature Lover in British Columbia*, 1937; R. A. Cannings, R. J. Cannings and S. G. Cannings, *Birds of the Okanagan Valley, British Columbia*, Occasional Paper, Royal British Columbia Museum, Victoria B.C. (1987).

For a checklist of birds of the Okanagan Valley, or for additional birding information, contact Dick Cannings, 1330 Debeck Road, S11, C96, R.R. 1, Naramata, B.C. V0H 1N0; phone (250) 496-4019; e-mail address is cannings@vip.net

Birding Features

Habitat for birds includes *Typha/Scirpus* marsh and wet meadows at the north end of the lake; birch, alder and willow thickets at the northeast corner, along the west shore and at the southwest corner; dry Ponderosa Pine forests with grassland on the northeast side below and above the cliffs near Vaseux Lake Provincial Park; and the cliffs overlooking the park. The most productive birding can be done in a day or less on the northeast side of the lake where all habitats are readily available to a hiker. The gravel road that goes southeast from the park provides easy access to the cliffs and dry forest. Climb up the cliffs via the powerline right-of-way at the point where the gravel road crosses Irrigation Creek.

A number of birds are year-round residents. For Canada Geese this lake is a major breeding site; Golden and Bald Eagles are often seen; California Quail and Chukar are common; White-headed Woodpecker is rare but can be found; Black-billed Magpie, Clark's Nutcracker, Mountain Chickadee and the three nuthatches (Red-breasted, Pygmy and White-breasted) are all common; Marsh Wren are common in summer, uncommon in winter; Canyon Wren are fairly common along the cliffs; Townsend's Solitaire and Cassin's Finch are common; Red Crossbill are irregular but fairly common.

Winter visitors include a great variety of waterfowl if all or part of the lake remains open. Tundra Swan are fairly common and Trumpeter Swan are uncommon. Bohemian Waxwing are uncommon; Northern Shrike are fairly common; Gray-crowned Rosy-Finch and Snow Bunting are rare and irregular visitors.

During the peak times of migration in April and November, large numbers of most fresh-water Pacific Flyway waterfowl pass through. There are no mudflats and thus few migrating shorebirds stop. American White Pelican rarely pass through. Snow Geese are casual visitors, as are Harlequin Duck, which sometimes overwinter.

Summer birds arrive in late March and April to breed. They include American Bittern and Osprey; Caspian Tern are sometimes casual visitors; Common Poorwill appear along the gravel roads near the cliffs and White-throated Swift are common here. Four hummingbird species occur: Calliope is the most common; Rufous is fairly common; Black-chinned is uncommon and Anna's is rare. All hummingbirds are best observed along Irrigation Creek. Lewis's Woodpecker are fairly common and Williamson's Sapsucker occur in the larch forests to the east at higher elevations. To see the latter species, travel the gravel roads either to the north or south of Shuttleworth Creek canyon, which lies east of Okanagan Falls. The south road from the canyon is usable with permission from the logging company; the office is located at the base of the road. Say's Phoebes are fairly common; Dusky Flycatchers are common. Look at the base of the cliffs for the fairly common Rock Wrens. Veerys are fairly common in the thickets along the lakeshore. Both Western and Mountain Bluebirds are fairly common. Yellow-breasted Chat may be found in the dense thickets, especially along the old river channels at the north end of the lake. Bobolink are sometimes seen in the meadows at the south end of the lake. Black-headed Grosbeak inhabit the thickets along the lakeshore. Lazuli Bunting and Lark Sparrow are fairly common in shrubs in the dry grasslands below the rock cliffs.

ROBERT A. CANNINGS,
RICHARD J. CANNINGS AND SYDNEY G. CANNINGS
Revised by Richard J. Cannings

Iona and Sea Islands

These islands, north of Vancouver International Airport, hold the record for the site with the largest numbers of rare birds seen in B.C. Their diversity of tidal marshes, upland fields and sewage lagoons are the draw. Bring a spotting scope as some birds will be far out on the water, and when the tide goes out, shorebirds follow.

Once two islands in the mouth of the Fraser River, they are now joined by a causeway. Most of Sea Island on the west has been developed into the Vancouver International Airport. Iona Island, owned by Greater Vancouver Regional District (GVRD), holds a sewage treatment and settling pond. GVRD has constructed a 4 km causeway projecting northwest into the sea, which serves to divert the flow of effluent into the Strait of Georgia. There is no access to or from the airport grounds. Birdwatchers are encouraged to explore the sewage lagoons. The sightings book at the kiosk will tell you what new birds are present.

The extensive mudflats on the causeway and islands are covered completely twice each day by the tide so check the tide tables before visiting. The 0.8 to 1.2 km accessible waterfront is all coastal wetland and mud and contains some great shorebird numbers during low tides.

Access from the U.S.A. or from Surrey, White Rock or North Delta is by Highway 99. Use a Greater Vancouver road map to find your way. Take Highway 99 north, across the Alex Fraser Bridge and turn left at the first light. Travel along this "Richmond Connector" to Shell Road, turn right and drive north to Bridgeport Road. Turn left towards the airport; proceed over the Sea Island swing bridge and immediately turn right onto Grauer Road and then under the Arthur Laing Bridge. Do not take the road over this bridge as it leads to Vancouver and the airport. Grauer turns right and becomes Macdonald; drive north for a short distance and then west onto Ferguson Road; follow the GVRD signs to Iona Regional Beach Regional Park. The airport will be on your left.

Coming south from Vancouver, take Highway 99 to the first exit to the airport. Drive west on Sea Island Way over Sea Island swinging bridge and immediately turn right onto Grauer Road; continue as above to the park.

Alternatively from Vancouver, travel southbound onto the Arthur Laing Bridge and take the Richmond exit. Turn left at the first traffic light and then immediately turn left again. At the stop sign, proceed straight onto Grauer Road and continue as above.

If you are coming from Vancouver across the Arthur Laing Bridge watch for Crested Mynas (an introduced species) on the west side by the old buildings. While on Grauer Road during fall and winter, look for raptors such as Rough-legged and Red-tailed Hawks, Northern Harrier and Bald Eagle. At dusk, and later, Short-eared and Barn Owls can be found along here.

As you drive west on Grauer, where the road turns north onto Macdonald, stop and scan the airport field for raptors. Trails radiate through the old overgrown military complex, the Cora Brown Subdivision, just off MacDonald Road. This and the airport field are usually good for passerines, Northern Harrier, Northern Shrike and Short-eared and Barn Owls at dusk. As you drive, check the fence and fields for American Kestrels, Brewer's Blackbirds, Canada and Snow Geese in the fall.

With no car, take the bus to the airport and disembark at the Delta Inn. Start walking in. You may be given a lift by one of the numerous birders who come regularly to the site.

Iona Island has a Bird Banding Station operated through spring and fall. If you would like to volunteer or visit the site, contact the Canadian Wildlife Service, 5421 Robertson Road, Delta, B.C.; phone (604) 946-8546 or Libor Michalak at (604) 274-2231.

Birding Features

As the best-known birding spot in the lower mainland, the site has recorded 305 species, of which 64 were breeding, and 104 were seen less than once per year. Special birds found include shorebirds such as Spoonbill Sandpiper, Hudsonian Godwit, Great Knot, Curlew Sandpiper, Red-necked Stint, Little Stint, Bar-tailed Godwit and Sharp-tailed Sandpiper. Each year look for Wandering Tattler, Black Turnstone, Surfbird, Pacific- and American Golden-Plovers, Red and Red-necked Phalaropes and other Siberian and Eurasian species. Rare water birds seen include Common Moorhen, Laughing and Common Black-headed Gulls; Common Eider shows up too.

The sewage lagoons attract hundreds of regulars like Glaucous-winged Gull and many hybrid gulls in fall and winter. Mew, California and Glaucous-winged Gulls are present all year. Bonaparte's, Thayer's, Heermann's, and still rarer Sabine's Gulls and Black-legged Kittiwakes, are best observed later in the fall off the tip of the south jetty. It's a great place to compare Ring-billed Gull with Mew Gull. The mudflats provide feeding and roosting sites for hundreds of shorebirds. On high tide nights, over 1000 peeps can be seen settling in to roost.

Sanderling and large numbers of wintering Dunlin are at their northern limit. This is also the southern breeding limit for Semipalmated Plover. The marsh to the west of the ponds has the most western record for regularly seeing Yellow-headed Blackbirds from May through the end of August.

Fall migration begins with shorebirds returning in early July and continues through October. Passerines passing through are most plentiful from the end of August into October. The most abundant are large numbers of Orange-crowned Warblers, Fox Sparrows, Lincoln's Sparrows, White-crowned and Golden-crowned Sparrows and Song Sparrows. Rare ones have included Brewer's and Lark Sparrows, Gray-crowned Rosy Finch, Scissor-tailed Flycatcher, Yellow Wagtail and Red-throated Pipit.

Iona has two jetties extending into Georgia Strait. The north one has scanty vegetation and is accessible along a beach extending approximately 10 km out. The south jetty with its gravel trail is accessible by foot and extends 4 km out, so be ready for a long walk – or you can bike it! Along the trail a variety of ducks can be seen year-round together with other water birds such as Western Grebe, Double-crested Cormorant and Common Loon. As you walk, look for Lapland Longspur, Bald Eagle or Horned Lark in winter or during migration. The tip of the south jetty has produced some good birds, particularly during spring or fall migration after a weather frontal system and/or during high tide. Birds seen here regularly during this time include Western Grebe; Pelagic and Brandt's Cormorants; Brant; Parasitic Jaeger; White-winged and Surf Scoters; Red-throated, Pacific and Common Loons; Caspian and Common Terns; Common Murre; Pigeon Guillemot; Marbled Murrelet; and Rhinoceros Auklet. Rarities like Fork-tailed Storm-Petrel, Sooty Shearwater, Yellow-billed Loon, Cassin's Auklet, and even Tufted Puffin have been recorded.

Winter is good for raptors, including Rough-legged Hawk, Northern Harrier, Peregrine Falcon, Gyrfalcon, Red-tailed Hawk, American Kestrel and Short-eared, Saw-whet and Barn Owls. Also, watch for Northern Shrike and flocks of Lapland Longspurs with Snow Buntings in the adjacent fields. The sewage and marsh ponds can be good for overwintering ducks. Tufted Duck has turned up a number of times.

The most common birds throughout the year except summer (June/July) include Northwestern Crow; Double-crested Cormorant; Sanderling; Black-bellied Plover; Barrow's Goldeneye; many North American ducks; Dunlin; Western Sandpiper; Mew, California and Glaucous-winged Gulls; Caspian Tern; Golden-crowned, Fox and White-crowned Sparrows.

WAYNE CAMPBELL AND D. MARKS
Revised by Libor Michalak

Fraser Estuary and Reifel Refuge

The Fraser Estuary, south of Vancouver, provides the most important wintering waterfowl habitat on the West Coast. The area also supports the largest number of wintering waterfowl in Canada. Birds come from three continents: Asia (Russia) and North and South America. The marshes host over 50,000 wintering Snow Geese and 100 Tundra and Trumpeter Swans. In November come to the annual Snow Goose Festival. Over 20 species of birds of prey have been reported. Many are attracted to the George C. Reifel Migratory Bird

Sanctuary (Reifel Refuge), which is part of the Alaksen Migratory National Wildlife Area of over 400 ha. Over 260 species have been recorded at the refuge. Both properties, part of the Westham Island, sit on the Fraser River Estuary, just west of the South Arm Marshes Wildlife Management Area.

Habitats on the sanctuary are important for migrating birds and include tidal salt-water mudflats, fresh-water, brackish and salt marshes and upland fields, attracting a wide range of birds.

Most of the estuary, including Westham Island, is privately owned, dyked and farmed. The extreme northwest end of the island, including Reifel Island, is owned by the federal government. Parts of these holdings are leased to the British Columbia Waterfowl Society, which operates the public area within the refuge. The sanctuary, open from 9 A.M. to 4 P.M. every day, charges an admission to help offset maintenance costs. The Alaksen National Wildlife Area is open to visitors during business hours Monday to Friday (except holidays). Please check in and out at the Canadian Wildlife Service office before proceeding.

To reach the sanctuary drive south from Vancouver to the junction of Highways 10 and 17, follow Highway 10 (Ladner Trunk Road) west; it becomes 48th, then 47A Avenue and then River Road West. Look for the sanctuary sign at Westham Island Road and turn right, crossing the Canoe Pass Bridge. The road beyond the bridge, in fall and winter, can be very good for raptors – some days up to 40 Bald Eagles can be seen from the bridge along the water's edge! Follow this road for 4.8 km to the sanctuary entrance. If coming from the east, proceed west off Highway 99 to Highway 10; follow it to River Road and continue as above. Watch for a Barn Owl in the barn to your left as you turn onto the gravel road to the parking lot. Ample parking is provided. You'll find a nature interpretation house, waterfowl feeding stations, easy walking trails with bird blinds and a viewing tower. Be sure to ask at the gift shop for current unusual sightings, which may include a roosting owl.

Bus service from downtown Vancouver bus station (with pick-up along the route) takes passengers to the Tsawwassen ferry landing. You can be dropped off at the intersection of Highways 10 and 17, which is about 14 km from the refuge.

All services, including a hospital, are available in Ladner, 11 to 16 km away. There are several campgrounds along Highway 17 near the ferry dock site. Environment Canada has produced an excellent booklet on the estuary, "Explore the Fraser Estuary!" by Peggy Ward. The book is available from most bookstores and the Canadian Government Publishing Centre, Supply and Services, Hull, Quebec K1A 0S9. Information on the refuge and trail maps may be obtained by writing to Interpretive Section, Canadian Wildlife Service, Box 340, Delta, B.C. V4K 3Y3; phone (604) 666-0143, or British Columbia Waterfowl Society, George C. Reifel Migratory Bird Sanctuary, 5191 Robertson Road, Delta, B.C. V4K 3N2; phone (604) 946-6980.

Birding Features
The variety and abundance of suitable food at the mouth of the Fraser River attract millions of waterfowl and shorebirds each year. Staff at the refuge feed

them, making the spot a veritable hive of activity in winter. Common birds include Golden-crowned and White-crowned Sparrows, Spotted Towhee, Northern Shrike, Dark-eyed Junco and Song Sparrow. In the spring and fall shorebirds are numerous and raptors winter in abundance.

Visiting the extensive ponds, dykes and marshes in peak season may produce many shorebirds at high tide. Sharp-tailed Sandpiper is regular in September and October. Rare sightings have included Smew and Spotted Redshank. The influx begins in late August, increases through September and October, and peaks in November and December through till March when the birds begin to leave for their breeding grounds.

Tundra and Trumpeter Swans are the highlights for the area. In addition, on some fall days you can stand on the road entrance to the refuge, look up and see the many hundreds of Snow Geese take off from the fields and blanket the sky! It is best to come for swans in later October and November when they settle into the fields for feeding and roosting. They like to use the marshes off Brunswick Point, immediately south of Westham Island and Canoe Passage. The Snow Geese feed all along the Fraser Delta and can be found in groups almost everywhere where there are bulrushes, sedges (their favourite) and agricultural lands. These birds begin arriving in October with peak numbers of 20,000 or so by late December and depart in March-April for Wrangle Island, off the coast of northeastern Siberia. In spring Brant can be seen in groups (over 20,000) off the shoreline and flying near the shore in the Strait of Georgia. Other geese such as the Emperor, Ross's and Greater White-fronted have been seen.

Ducks are by far the most abundant birds. Dabblers, divers and some sea ducks include Oldsquaw; Black (one of the only places to see it on the lower mainland); Red-breasted, Hooded and Common Mergansers; White-winged and Surf Scoters; Common and Barrow's Goldeneye; and Greater and Lesser Scaups. Harlequin Ducks are often noted in numbers. Several duck species breed in the estuary including Mallard, Gadwall and Cinnamon Teal. Wood Duck, common on the refuge but seldom seen outside, can be found here. The dabbling ducks are attracted to the tidal marshes for abundant food in early fall. During the winter you can locate hundreds of Eurasian Wigeons along the estuary, probably one of the best places in western Canada to see them. Tufted Ducks can even be found here most years. Watch for patrolling Bald Eagles. During the hunting season in October to January, waterfowl use the estuary, particularly the refuge, for loafing sites in the daytime. At dusk the movement begins, with thousands of ducks sometimes blanketing the sky as they fly inland to feed on unharvested crops in the flooded fields.

Over 20 species of raptors are present. This is one of their few wintering sites in B.C. Bald Eagles congregate in large numbers from November through February prior to moving inland in April. One or more pairs nest in the refuge. Abundant hawks, best seen over the fields, are Red-tailed, Rough-legged and Northern Harrier. The falcons include Peregrine, Merlin and American Kestrel. You may locate a Prairie Falcon, which frequents the area. Accipiters are found where feeders and small passerines are present. In these areas watch for Sharp-shinned and Cooper's Hawks or maybe even the rarer Goshawk.

Owls are found throughout the area because of extensive agriculture. Mice and voles in the fields and riparian corridors between the agricultural fields provide them with prey. Northern Saw-whet, Long-eared, Western Screech-, Barred and Great Horned Owls have been found around the refuge. Snowy Owls often sit on fence posts in fields along with Short-eared Owls at dusk. This is the best time to stop at old barns to search for Barn Owls. They breed throughout the area, making the lower mainland of B.C. the most concentrated location in Canada for this bird.

The extensive mudflats on the estuary provide feeding sites for an estimated 5 million migrating shorebirds of over 38 species each fall and spring. The best time to see the rare Sharp-tailed Sandpiper is in September and early October as it feeds with other shorebirds on one of the many flats.

Nesting marsh birds such as Virginia Rail, Sora, American Bittern and Marsh Wren are best spotted from May through July.

WAYNE CAMPBELL
Revised by Libor Michalak

Vancouver

A metropolitan community of about 2 million people, Greater Vancouver contains parks, forests, beaches and lakes, all close to mountains and the sea. This diversity of habitats attracts at least 406 species of birds. Of these, at least 164 nest. An additional 36 species are sighted once per year. The maritime climate allows a birder to list over 50 species quickly at any time of the year. Wintering water and shore birds include Western Grebe, Pelagic Cormorant, Harlequin Duck, Barrow's Goldeneye, Black Turnstone and Pigeon Guillemot.

Founded in 1862 as Gastown (after "Gassy Jack" Deighton, who built a saloon in 24 hours with the help of lumberjacks), the ramshackle frame-building settlement prospered. Incorporated in April of 1886, the community was wiped out by a forest fire in June of that same year. By the end of 1886, citizens were erecting more permanent brick and stone structures. The large influx of Europeans after World War II turned the city into a cosmopolitan community. Botanic gardens, art galleries, museums and spectacular scenery, in combination with birdwatching, make a three-day visit memorable.

The major international airport on the southern fringe, and the western terminus of VIA Rail and international bus service, all provide easy access to the city.

Vancouver contains a variety of accommodations. See the local tourist centres for the *B.C. Accommodation Guide.*

The Wild Bird Trust and Vancouver Natural History Society (VNHS) have Web sites that can be reached through www.naturalhistory.bc.ca VNHS posts current bird sightings and the *Wandering Tattler* newsletter on the Web, along with field trip and meeting details. They also have a Bird Alert report at (604) 737-3974.

Major contacts are Al and Jude Grass, 103-7065 Stride Avenue, Burnaby, B.C. V3N 1T3; phone (604) 520-3706.

Birding Features

Stanley Park. Named after Lord Stanley of Stanley Cup hockey fame, the park is owned and operated by the City of Vancouver. Stanley Park Nature House is located at Lost Lagoon, near the concession and bus loop at the Georgia Street entrance to the park – check there for bird information. The 400 ha (1000 acre) park is located on a peninsula at the mouth of Burrard Inlet. A half-hour walk northwest from the downtown core will get you there. By bus, catch the Stanley Park bus from downtown and disembark at the entrance near Lost Lagoon. By car, take Highway 1A and 99 and watch for the turnoff on the right from the freeway at the main entrance on the south end of the park. Be careful that you leave at this park entrance or you'll get onto the causeway – there is no getting off until you are over the Lions' Gate Bridge.

The park was logged selectively in the early part of the century, and hazardous trees are still being removed. Logging has resulted in the creation of forest-edge habitat. Extensive areas are cleared for gardens, which attract urban birds. Habitats include rocky shores, sandy beaches, offshore waters, forests, gardens and a lake. The best birding walk (two to three hours) is from the bus loop at the park entrance, along the south side of Lost Lagoon, over the stone arch bridge, then to the sea wall on the edge of English Bay; take the sea wall north, about halfway to the lip of the peninsula to Ferguson Point, then cut east via the forest trail, back to Lost Lagoon and the park entrance. This walk usually produces 60 to 70 bird species with no trouble. You may wish to continue beyond Ferguson Point, right around the tip (a total of 11 km) to Lumberman's Arch on the east side, then back through the former zoo to the entrance. Take another shorter walk east from the main gate along Burrard Inlet to Brockton Point, then northwest to Lumberman's Arch and again back to the main entrance. You can drive around the periphery of the park, stopping for a short stroll. There is a charge for parking, so be sure to pick up a ticket when you enter the park.

Other trails crisscross through the forest. A good inland hike may be taken to Beaver Lake, then around the shore. The lake is reached by road or pathway from the sea wall about halfway between Lumberman's Arch and Lions' Gate Bridge to the north. Beaver Lake contains the only bit of real marsh in the park.

Stanley Park is probably the best birding area for wintering waterfowl around the lower mainland of B.C. Look for Western Grebe, Pelagic Cormorant, Harlequin Duck, Barrow's Goldeneye, Black Turnstone and Pigeon Guillemot. Nearby forests contain Red-breasted Sapsucker, Winter Wren, Brown Creeper and Black-throated Gray and Townsend's Warblers. Species diversity is best from mid-November to mid-March. Summer is fairly quiet. Rarities are showing up continually, including Ruddy Turnstone, Tufted Duck and Black Phoebe. Great Blue Herons are common, as they nest in the area of the former zoo. Look for these birds on the mudflats at low tide. Lost Lagoon has a good variety of wintering waterfowl, including Redhead, Canvasback, Ring-necked Duck, Lesser and Greater Scaups, Wood Duck, Common and Barrow's Goldeneyes, Mallard and Red-breasted and Common

Mergansers. Double-crested Cormorants rest on the fountain. Gulls include Ring-billed, California, Herring, Glaucous-winged, Mew and Bonaparte's.

Burnaby Lake Regional Park. Located east of downtown Vancouver, between Highways 1 and 7, off Kensington Avenue (on the west side of the park) or off Cariboo Road (on the east side), the lake and surrounding park have been known by birders for many years. The area became a regional park in 1972. The nature house sits on the north side (from Winston Avenue, turn south on Piper Avenue) and is open weekends in summer. To get a brochure or a bird checklist for the park, contact GVRD Parks, 4330 Kingsway, Burnaby, B.C. V5H 4G8; phone (604) 432-6350.

This is one of the few fresh-water lakes and marshes near Vancouver in which large concentrations of waterfowl are observed. During the fall, hundreds of Green-winged Teals overwinter. American Coots and Mallards are there in large numbers with some Northern Shoveler, Gadwall and Wood Duck.

Mount Seymour Provincial Park. The 3508 ha park lies east and immediately adjacent to Vancouver. Take Highway 1 north over the Iron Workers Memorial Bridge (formerly Second Narrows). Turn east shortly after the bridge and follow signs for 3 km to the park entrance. Ask for a bird checklist, park brochure and other material at the park office at the entrance. Elevation rises from 100 m at the gate, up the twisting and turning road to 1000 m at the base of the chair lift to the top. Lower slopes of the park were logged in 1920s, with a resultant present growth of cedars, mixed with Western Hemlock forest below 900 m. Above this height, Mountain Hemlock prevails.

The excellent checklist and park brochure provide good information about birds to see at several stops, and about trails to walk along the road to the top. The area provides ready road access to coastal subalpine habitats adjacent to the city. Snow usually does not leave the higher elevations until mid-June. Lower elevations are therefore the best sites in spring, from mid-May to mid-June. You should spot a Gray Jay, Gray-crowned Rosy-Finch, and Red and White-winged Crossbills. You may also sight a Blue-headed Vireo and several warblers, including Black-throated Gray, Townsend's and Wilson's. The park is also home to Northern Pygmy-Owl and Western Screech-Owl. At the Deep Cove roadside lookout at the start of the Perimeter Trail, in summer look for Black and Vaux's Swifts. Watch along the way for a Red-breasted Sapsucker.

If you are in the area from November through May, try exploring on snowshoes or cross-country skis. Check at the park office for recreation brochures.

Deer Lake. Burnaby's Deer Lake Park provides excellent birding, especially at its west end. Habitat includes marsh, old field and forest. This is an excellent location for raptors such as Cooper's Hawk and Sharp-shinned Hawk. Hutton's Vireo is resident here. Good waterfowl diversity is also found.

Maplewood Flats Conservation Area. Found in North Vancouver (east on Dollarton Highway), this conservation area is a "must" visit for birders, any time of the year. Good habitat diversity makes for fine birding. The western subspecies of Purple Martin nests here (one of only a few locations in B.C.). Ospreys nest on a piling offshore and are seen off Osprey Point during summer. Good waterfowl concentrations are found in winter – Harlequin Duck, Surf Scoter, Barrow's Goldeneye and large rafts of scaup. The site is managed by the Wild Bird Trust of British Columbia, whose office and information centre are located on site. A bird sighting board is found outside the office.

AL AND JUDE GRASS
Revised by Al and Jude Grass

Active Pass

Active Pass, a channel of public, navigable sea, lies between Galiano and Mayne islands on the ferry trip between Vancouver and Victoria (Tsawwassen to Swartz Bay). Waters often race and boil through the pass, influenced by the tides. These upswellings make the pass a place of outstanding biological richness, attracting spectacular concentrations of water birds. The entire channel is worthwhile; however, the western third is usually the most prolific. There can also be significant concentrations of birds up to 500 m beyond the mouths of the channel.

California and Northern Sea Lions are often spotted in the water on the south side just as you enter the pass from the west or coming from the east. The California Sea Lion has increased in this area over the years.

The pass is most easily accessible by the car ferry. Ride the windy bow through the pass. Dress warmly from September to May. Local island ferries also ply the channel to visit the many islands. Seasonal timetables are available from the B.C. tourist offices along the highways or by writing to their headquarters in Victoria. The more leisurely approach is to rent or charter a small local boat from people in the small communities on either side of the pass at Saltspring Island or near Swartz Bay. However, watch carefully, as these are dangerous waters, both from the churning tides and the big ships that regularly ply the channel. These big boats cannot stop or turn quickly!

Visitors usually stay in Vancouver or Victoria. However, the B.C. Ministry of Tourism publishes an annual list of motels and hotels in the province. Accommodation on Mayne and Galiano Islands is detailed in this tourist booklet. Tiny communities on these islands also offer most village services, such as groceries and gasoline.

For further help, refer to a weekly study from September to May on the area: "Birds Seen in Active Pass, British Columbia," by R. Y. Edwards, in the British Columbia Provincial Museum Annual Report for 1964, pp. 19–23, now out of print.

Birding Features

The best birding occurs when ebbing or flooding tides produce strong currents. Few birds feed during slack water, appearing to scatter to other sites. The area is a favoured wintering location for a number of species. The dominant species, in season, are Arctic Loon; Western Grebe; Brandt's Cormorant (fewer than 15 years ago); Glaucous-winged, Bonaparte's and Mew Gulls; and

Common Murre. The Brandt's Cormorants are especially interesting, since almost all of these birds nest south of British Columbia, some as far away as California. Storms bring in and hold occasional pelagics, including Sooty Shearwater, Fork-tailed Storm-Petrel, Sabine's Gull and others.

In summer, June and July, there are few birds. Pigeon Guillemots are resident throughout the year. Bald Eagles nest locally and are seen in numbers later on in winter, with a dozen or more resting on trees or fishing in concentrations of feeding seabirds.

The greatest numbers of seabirds occur from September to May, with March the best month. In September and October, Bonaparte's Gulls peak in abundance (as many as 5000); Heermann's Gulls arrive from Mexico and are most numerous. As fall moves into winter, other birds come to feed. White-winged Scoter is there; Glaucous-winged and Mew Gulls remain high in numbers (200 to 400) all season. Pigeon Guillemots are numerous. With luck, you can also see Parasitic Jaeger, Marbled Murrelet, Rhinoceros Auklet and other pelagic species. If you are good with gulls, try for Thayer's; they are sometimes numerous in winter. By February, Brandt's Cormorants reach maximum numbers of up to 4000, as do Common Murres, with up to 1500 seen. By April, Arctic Loons climax in abundance (1000 to 2500), as do Western Grebes, with as many as 1000. Bonaparte's Gulls reach their record peak in April and May.

YORKE EDWARDS
Revised by David Stirling

Saanich Peninsula – Victoria Airport (Skylarks)

The Saanich Peninsula, on Vancouver Island, is the only place in North America where Skylarks can readily be found. Transported from Great Britain near the turn of the century, the birds quickly adapted and were once much more common than today. However they still can be seen in numbers, especially at the Victoria International Airport. Human activity has modified the landscape somewhat over the past 100 years, but the impact has not been excessive. Haying and mowing are the only disturbances within the airport property. Nearby farmland is mainly pasture and hayfields. Thus the whole area is good habitat for upland birds.

Victoria International Airport lies just west of Sidney and 24 km north of Victoria on Highway 17 (Pat Bay Highway). Drive north from Victoria on this highway to the traffic light at Beacon Avenue (Sidney). Turn left (west) to the loop road around the airport (see below). Those arriving from Vancouver and the lower B.C. mainland arrive at the Swartz Bay ferry terminal; proceed south on Highway 17 for about 4.5 km to the traffic light at Beacon Avenue and turn right (west) to drive around the airport. If arriving on Washington State Ferries from Anacortes or the San Juan Islands, disembark in Sidney. Drive a short distance north to Bevan Avenue; turn west to drive the few blocks to Beacon Avenue and Highway 17; cross the highway and continue west on the circuit around the airport.

Victoria and the Saanich Peninsula are serviced by car and/or passenger ferry from Vancouver (B.C. Ferries), Anacortes (Washington State Ferries), Port

Angeles (Black Ball Ferries) and Seattle (Clipper Navigation). Public buses operate to within a moderate walking distance of the airport. Airport buses call at the major downtown Victoria hotels. Air travellers may come in on scheduled flights via Air Canada, Canadian Airlines, Horizon Air or WestJet.

To locate other sites, hear of current unusual species or even contact local birders, dial the Victoria Rare Bird Alert at (250) 592-3381. For assistance in finding Skylarks, phone Barbara Begg (250) 656-5296.

Birding Features

To see Skylark throughout the year, take the roads that circle the airport. Turn west off Highway 17 on Beacon Avenue; continue to the end of Beacon and turn north to Mills Road; travel west along Mills through the good Skylark habitat that persists to West Saanich Road. Make frequent stops on this stretch of Mills; get out and look and listen. A particularly good viewing area, especially in breeding season, is off Mills Road opposite Meadland Road. A short stroll here to the airport fence provides you with a relatively quiet listening post at an elevated vantage point. Continue west to the end of Mills; turn south for a short distance on West Saanich Road; turn left on Willingdon Road. After exploring the area, continue on southeast past the terminal, then swing north on Canora Road; proceed to the far north end of Canora. The end of Canora, at the airport fence, is probably the best single spot to see and hear Skylarks year-round.

Other birds to be seen are seasonal. In summer, Killdeers and Savannah Sparrows are common. At the southwest corner of the airport, look in marshy places for Mallards and Red-winged Blackbirds, which are here all year. The woods to the south of the creek, outside the airport, are good for Yellow Warblers and White-crowned Sparrows in summer, and Golden-crowned Sparrows in winter. In suitable habitat around the perimeter of the airport be on the lookout for other western or northern specialists such as California Quail, Rufous Hummingbird, Northern Shrike, Steller's Jay, Northwestern Crow, Violet-green Swallow, Chestnut-backed Chickadee (the only chickadee on Vancouver Island), Bushtit, Bewick's Wren and Spotted Towhee.

In winter the airport can be productive for raptors and owls. Watch for Red-tailed Hawk, Northern Harrier, Peregrine Falcon, Merlin, American Kestrel and Bald Eagle. Short-eared and Snowy Owls are seen in some years.

On both sides of the Saanich Peninsula, the nearby ocean provides good birding in winter. On the west side, at Patricia Bay, White-winged, Surf and Black Scoters may be seen. The bay is also good for Common Loon, and perhaps Pacific and Red-throated. Look for alcids, Red-necked, Horned and Western Grebes and a variety of ducks including Eurasian Wigeon, Common and Barrow's Goldeneyes. On the east side of the Peninsula, at Bazan Bay, most of the above birds may be spotted as well as an uncommon Eared Grebe. From late March through April, Bazan Bay is good for Brant.

Another popular birding location on the peninsula is Martindale Flats. It is east off Highway 17, which is crossed by Island View and Martindale Roads. Turn east off Highway 17, at the traffic lights, onto Island View Road; drive a short distance, park just east of the big red building and walk south down the private dirt road. Alternatively, leave Highway 17 south of the Island View traffic light at Martindale Road and drive east to park along Lochside Trail and walk north. The open fields have a small population of breeding Skylarks here. In fall and winter there are occasionally large flocks. The hedgerows and trees along Lochside can be interesting for sparrows and other perching birds, particularly during migration. The site is probably Victoria's best location for Peregrine Falcons and winter vagrants. Shorebirds migrate through in fall as well as thousands of American Pipits.

Many uncommon and rare-to-the-region species have been discovered in the valley over the years: Black-crowned Night-heron; Swainson's Hawk; Yellow Wagtail; Loggerhead Shrike; Palm Warbler; Indigo Bunting; American Tree, White-throated and Harris's Sparrows to name a few.

In winter Martindale Flats is perhaps at its best when partially flooded by winter rains. At this time look for a flock of Trumpeter Swans, many dabbling ducks and a small number of shorebirds. These in turn attract raptors, including Gyrfalcons during a lucky year. Annual Christmas Bird Counts for Martindale Flats can fetch over 70 species. Rare birds that show up here can include Sandhill Crane, Red-throated Pipit, Swamp Sparrow, Upland Sandpiper and Buff-breasted Sandpiper.

While here, you may wish to continue east on Island View Road to the beach. In winter there is a small, but dependable, flock of Black Scoter present. It is usually worthwhile to park and walk the trails north into the bushy sand dune areas in the park for other birds.

HAROLD HOSFORD
Revised by Barbara Begg

Greater Victoria

Set on the southern tip of Vancouver Island, Victoria is the capital city of B.C. The region has one of the mildest and most temperate climates in Canada, which draws many people (and birds) from across the country, particularly in winter. Greater Victoria, with a population of over 300,000 and made up of over 10 incorporated municipalities, has hosted nearly 350 species of birds and holds the Canadian record for the largest number of species (152) on a Christmas Bird Count. Southward-flowing cold water currents along the west coast of Vancouver Island combined with unique properties of the Inside Passage on the east side of the island bring several pelagic species into the Strait of Juan de Fuca, south of Victoria and north of Port Angeles in Washington State. August to December is the best time to search for seabirds. Go down to the shores, take a ferry trip across the strait or charter a vessel for possibly spotting South Polar Skua, Black-vented Shearwater and Sabine's Gull. At that season, summer migrants may linger, vagrants and juveniles wander west, Asian species move south and pelagic species move into the strait. In addition, particularly in early fall or spring, the rich offshore waters bring in shorebirds and accompanying birds of prey. In summer the area lies at the northern nesting limits of several species and in winter, for others, the extreme northern and southern limits of their wintering ranges.

Late spring (March and April) offers some prime birdwatching as southern nesters move north (Brant) and eastern and southern migrants fall out after crossing the strait. Recent rare spring migrants recorded include Costa's Hummingbird, Indigo Bunting, Lazuli Bunting, Magnolia Warbler, and Ash-throated Flycatcher.

Victoria hosts Anna's Hummingbird near its northern breeding limit. These birds raise two sets of nestlings, laying the first clutch in late January or early February and the second in late March.

Skylarks are found on the Saanich Peninsula just north of Victoria proper (refer Saanich elsewhere).

The Victoria Rare Bird Alert at (250) 592-3381 gives special sightings and updates. The Naturalist Events line lists field trips, special talks and related activities on (250) 479-2054. Their Web site is at http://www.birding.bc.ca/victoria

The Victoria Natural History Birders Night is at 7:30 P.M. on the last Wednesday of each month from September to May at the Begbie Building on the University of Victoria Campus.

Access to Vancouver Island is by plane or ferry. The main airport lies just north of the city. Regional airlines have services to the mainland with some direct cross-country flights originating in Victoria. B.C. Ferries cross to and from the mainland every hour during the summer and on the odd hours the rest of the year. These car and/or passenger ferries arrive from Vancouver (B.C. Ferries), Anacortes (Washington State Ferries), Port Angeles (Black Ball Ferries) and Seattle (Clipper Navigation). Other B.C. Ferries service Nanaimo, two hours by car north of Victoria.

The Royal British Columbia Museum in Victoria has some of the best bird and other natural history displays in Canada; Web site http://rbcm1.rbcm.gov.bc.ca; their Grace Bell collection is at http://www.rbcm.gov.bc.ca/nhpapers/gracebell/english/index.html

As a major city, Victoria has many services, including several excellent camping sites such as Goldstream Provincial Park set in a rain forest just outside the city.

For information on travel in the Victoria area, phone (250) 953-2033; e-mail info@tourismvictoria.com or visit their Web page at www.tourismvictoria.com

The main tourist office providing information for the province is also in Victoria in the downtown Parliament Buildings. Phone them at 1-800-435-5622; their Web site is at http://www.snbc/res.com

Birding Features

Island View Beach. This is one of the best year-round birdwatching spots in Greater Victoria. Habitats include marshland, sand dunes, grassy fields, sloughs, hawthorn and rose thickets and conifer stands. To reach it, drive north from Victoria proper on Highway 17 (Pat Bay Highway) for about 15 minutes outside of the city and watch for the traffic light at Island View Road (look for a big red building just east, right, of this intersection). Turn right, or east, on Island View and drive to the parking spot adjacent to the beach. As you

Black Turnstone

Harlequin Duck

drive east, past the red building, you are moving through Martindale Flats (private property). On these flats (refer Saanich elsewhere), check both right and left for a variety of birds including Skylarks.

Offshore at the beach, in winter watch for loons, including Pacific, Common and Red-throated, as well as all three scoters; Oldsquaw; Horned, Eared, Red-necked and Western Grebes; Red-breasted Merganser; Bufflehead; various gulls; and other seabirds. Brant are seen during spring migration. Shorebirds can be found in low numbers during spring and fall migrations; look for Black Oystercatchers in winter as well as grebes, bay ducks and various gulls. The fields and hedgerows shelter various sparrows including American Pipits, Bushtits and warblers. Watch for Short-eared Owls and Northern Shrikes also in winter.

Mount Tolmie. An excellent location for spring migration fallouts. From downtown, take Johnson Street, which turns into Begbie Street, which in turn becomes Shelbourne Street until you reach Cedar Hill X Road. (Look to the right; you should see Mount Tolmie – that's where you want to go; you're going to take the north entrance.) Turn right at Cedar Hill X Road. Stick to the left at the split in the road. At the top of Cedar Hill X Road, turn right onto Glastonbury, which becomes Mayfair Drive and on up Mount Tolmie. Park at the top or off Mayfair Road.

This Garry Oak forest hill has attracted Lazuli Bunting, Ash-throated Flycatcher, Eastern Kingbird and many other accidentals. Trails lead all over this small hill. Try the thicker Garry Oak meadow (sheltered area) to the east of the parking lot (below the concrete reservoir) for special birds. A walk over the mid-hill northwest slopes can also be productive. Anna's Hummingbird is a year-round resident. Anna's may also be found all year at Rithet's Bog Park; leave Highway 1 at Quadra Street, go north off Quadra to Chatterton Way and then right on Dalewood, where you can park and walk down to the trail along the edge of the bog.

Victoria Waterfront: Clover Point to Ogden Point Breakwater. Located on the southern tip of Vancouver Island along Dallas Road, this drive has several parking spots where you can get out and look for sea and shore birds. With a scope, you may spot offshore species such as Caspian Tern and Red-necked Phalarope. Closer in, from September to March, look for Heermann's and Western Gulls, Harlequin Duck, Black Oystercatcher and Black Turnstone. Clover Point is great for gulls and watching for special birds that fly past. Lapland Longspurs gather here in fall. Ogden Point Breakwater offers an elevated vantage point close to deep water and a possible sighting of many open water alcids in close. Check the breakwater itself for Black Turnstones and anything else that might turn up "right below." Brown Pelicans and Tufted Puffins are occasionally seen as they fly by anywhere along this shore.

For those interested in walking the route, try starting from the Ogden Point Breakwater and walking the full distance to Clover Point. Stay close to sea side and watch at the many rock reefs and small bays, which can turn up a new bird or two. On the way back, detour into Beacon Hill Park for Bushtits,

Chestnut-backed Chickadees (the only chickadee species on the island), Red-breasted Nuthatches, Spotted Towhees and Great Blue Herons (with a small rockery on the west side of this park). A pair of Bald Eagles nests on the west side of the park, but their nest is hard to see as it is buried in heavy foliage.

Esquimalt Lagoon. This is a great spot to look for the shorebirds and Brant, as well as a variety of gulls that use both sides of the Lagoon Road during migration. To find this road, take Highway 1 west from Victoria and exit at the Colwood turnoff onto Highway 1A. Drive west a few blocks to the Ocean Boulevard turnoff on the left, and follow the signs to Fort Rodd Hill. Continue on past Fort Rodd to Lagoon Road, which crosses the bridge (inlet and outlet to the lagoon) and park on the outer or inner bank. You may check out the birds near the bridge on both sides where Brant are often found. Then drive farther down the road with more checks at several spots along the way.

Wintering waterfowl, gulls, seabirds and shorebirds are plentiful, including Red-necked Merganser, Barrow's Goldeneye, Lesser Scaup, Canvasback, Black Turnstone (some of which are very tame), Black-bellied Plover, Sanderling and Dunlin. Walk the inner bank to find shorebirds and scope the lagoon as well as offshore. The site is best on an incoming tide. Caspian Terns can be found here in late spring. Great Blue Herons feed all along the shore in good numbers. The other end (southwest) of the lagoon holds a different mix of birds and is worth a drive.

Goldstream Provincial Park. The site contains temperate old-growth rain forest habitat and lies at the mouth of Goldstream River with a salt-water estuary. To find this gem of a park, follow Highway 1 towards Duncan. Just before the highway starts to climb up the Malahat Pass, look for signs on the right directing you to the Goldstream parking lot. From here, walk to the Goldstream Nature House to pick up a park map and check for any special birds. In summer, up to 50 Rufous Hummingbirds are attracted to the feeders at the Nature House. A video camera relays live action of the hummingbirds from late March to June. At appropriate times the camera is pointed at other birds of interest, such as Bald Eagles feeding on fish in late fall and winter.

During the fall and winter spawning season (mid-October until about February) various gulls, American Dippers and Bald Eagles feed on hundreds of spawned-out salmon and their eggs in the thousands. In spring, Red-breasted Sapsucker, Pileated Woodpecker, Swainson's Thrush and Willow and Pacific-slope Flycatchers are common. Adjacent Mount Finlayson can be a good spot for Ruffed Grouse, raptors, warblers and flycatchers. Be careful on the climb up and down, as the trail can be dangerous in wet weather and can also fog up very quickly.

Witty's Lagoon. This site is also a good all-round location and one popular with many local birders. The variety of habitats from sandy beach and rocky shore to thick woods and a salt-water lagoon offer great birding potential. Take Highway 1 west and exit at the Colwood (1A) turnoff. At the Metchosin Road traffic light, turn left and follow Metchosin for some distance, watching for the Park sign on the left leading to the parking lot at the small Nature House.

The woods, shore and lagoon feature shorebirds, raptors, gulls, warblers, flycatchers, seabirds, sparrows and migrant fallouts. It is best on an incoming tide.

KEVIN SLAGBOOM

Pacific Rim National Park

The first national marine park to be established in Canada, Pacific Rim, is located on the west coast of Vancouver Island, and includes islands, seacoast, long beaches, deep forest, bogs and muskeg. Nearly 260 species of birds have been reported either in the park or in the offshore waters, with at least 80 breeding residents. An additional 17, including all three scoters, Harlequin Duck, Black-footed Albatross, and Northern Fulmar, are present throughout the year. Spot the Northern Sea Lions at the Sea Lion Rocks and watch a Gray Whale as it feeds in the bays.

The Nuu-chah-nulth people, then known as Nootka, were here when James Cook landed at Nootka Island about 90 km north of Long Beach in 1778. These peoples were wealthy compared to inland tribes and had established more or less permanent villages that changed with the season. The forests, and particularly the sea, provided an abundance of food. The excess of food allowed time for them to become skilled at basket-weaving and design. Warfare was common between villages, revenge often being the motive, but slaves, booty and a measure of prestige were also gained.

Along this coast in 1778, Cook found Sea Otter and took a few pelts to China. The rush was on to obtain these silken trophies that could be had for a few pennies and sold in the Orient for $120 (in 18th-century dollars). Eventually, the otters were gone. Then came the whalers, who nearly exterminated the Gray Whale and others. In the 1870s, sealskin became fashionable. The huge herds of Fur Seal migrating from California to the Pribilof Islands, in the Bering Sea, were decimated. At about the same time, smallpox and other white man's diseases took most of the native people. White settlers moved in to use the salmon, and a major fishing industry was begun and continues today. It should be noted, however, that today salmon stocks are dangerously low. It would seem that man has again decimated a valuable natural resource.

Tofino and Ucluelet, both just outside the park, developed as salmon fishing centres. The road between these two communities was completed in 1942. Then in 1959 Highway 4 linked the two communities to the main traffic artery on the east side of Vancouver Island. The sandy beaches were now accessible and quickly became very popular. Public pressure was exerted for a national park, culminating in the establishment of Pacific Rim National Park in 1970.

The park comprises three sections of land and sea. The Long Beach unit consists of 55 km², with two major beaches, one stretching 16 km and the other 6.4 km. The Broken Islands Group has about a hundred islands and rocks located within Barkley Sound. They and the adjacent waters make up about

58 km². The third unit, the West Coast Trail, is primarily a challenging hiking trail, 73 km long. This is the historic Lifesaving Trail, built for use by ship-wrecked sailors who survived the "Graveyard of the Pacific" just offshore. Over 40 ships have sunk near here.

The park is reached via Highways 4 and 105, west of Port Alberni, or by boat or plane. Bus service runs from Port Alberni to Ucluelet and Tofino year-round. The Alberni Marine Transport Company in Port Alberni runs the MV *Lady Rose*, a 100-passenger mail and cargo vessel, from Port Alberni to Ucluelet from June 1 to late September (a great ride in summer). The Ministry of Transport operates an airfield with three 1525 m concrete runways at Tofino, behind the north end of Long Beach. The field is not lit for night flying. Aviation gas is available. Floatplanes can obtain aviation gas and mooring at Ucluelet and at Pacific Rim Airline dock in Tofino. Several firms provide sea charters from Tofino and Ucluelet.

Telescopes are available at various locations for free public use at the Long Beach Unit. Naturalists are stationed at this site throughout the year, with formal programs offered from June to September. The rest of the year, they may be booked by groups as requested.

The 92-unit campground at Green Point is the only serviced one in the park. Both Tofino and Ucluelet have a variety of commercial accommodation and most other amenities. A hospital is at Tofino.

The park has produced a wide variety of material, including a bird check-list, brochure, and pamphlets on hiking. *West Coast Trail, Rainforest Trail, The Gray Whale* and *Geology of Pacific Rim* are all available free from the information centre on Highway 4, year-round at the park office on Ocean Terrace near Wickaninnish or by writing The Superintendent, Pacific Rim National Park, Box 280, Ucluelet, B.C. V0R 3A0; phone (604) 726-7721.

The British Columbia Provincial Museum has published *Birds of Pacific Rim National Park*, Occasional Paper No. 20. This is a very complete work, and material from it has been used in the preparation of this section. Unfortunately, this excellent work is now out of print.

Birding Features

Pacific Rim is the only readily accessible part of the Pacific Ocean with long stretches of hard-packed sandy beaches and huge breaking waves, on the west coast of Vancouver Island. Birding highlights are seabirds, shorebirds and water birds. Notable species include Red-throated Loon, Brandt's and Pelagic Cormorants, Great Blue Heron, Bald Eagle, Black Oystercatcher, and Glaucous-winged Gull. Several forest species to locate include Steller's Jay, Hermit Thrush and Townsend's Warbler. The population of Pileated Woodpeckers is denser here than in any other national park in Canada. Chestnut-backed Chickadee, Golden-crowned Kinglet, Winter Wren, Brown Creeper and Red Crossbill are present year-round. Notable species that winter elsewhere but move into the park to breed include Fork-tailed and Leach's Storm-Petrel, Marbled Murrelet, Rhinoceros Auklet, Tufted Puffin, Band-tailed Pigeon, Rufous Hummingbird, Swainson's Thrush and Orange-crowned Warbler. Four species of shearwaters and Caspian Terns appear in summer but do not breed here.

There are 23 species of primarily winter birds that use the waters, including 3 species of grebe, 8 of diving ducks, Double-crested Cormorant and Trumpeter Swan.

The islands off Long Beach support breeding populations of Pelagic Cormorant and the only Canadian colony of Brandt's Cormorant. Also found breeding are Black Oystercatcher, Pigeon Guillemot and Glaucous-winged Gull. Sometimes boat trips are made available to see the birds, Gray Whales and Northern Sea Lions. These mammals may be observed by using the telescopes at Green Point on Long Beach.

In winter, from November to the end of February, look for loons (especially Yellow-billed), grebes, scoters, scaup and Bufflehead just offshore. In the woods, search for Steller's Jay and a rare Blue Jay, Winter Wren, Dickcissel (rare), Song Sparrow and Dark-eyed Junco. By March Varied Thrush and Song Sparrow are singing on territory and juncos seem to be everywhere. The numbers of gulls and diving ducks also peak in March. They come to feed on the herring that spawn in the local bays.

Spring migrants peak in numbers during April and May. Look for shorebirds, including Snowy Plover (only accidental), Buff-breasted Sandpiper and Hudsonian Godwit. June is the slowest month. Caspian Terns appear in summer. The fall movement of shorebirds begins in early July and peaks in August. This latter month is also good for migrating geese and dabbling ducks, especially offshore, and for Heermann's Gulls at Long Beach. Fall migration continues through October. Look for Brown Pelicans then. The last to arrive near the end of the year are the Trumpeter Swans and goldeneyes.

Specific spots worth visiting include McLean Point near the northern tip of the Long Beach Unit. Here you can find Common Loon, which is a resident; a possible Red-throated Loon; in the fall look for hundreds of Greater Scaup. Spring brings many Buffleheads. The above-mentioned publication, *Birds of Pacific Rim National Park*, describes in some detail a transect on McLean Point Road taken throughout the year. There are 78 species listed. Watch for Common Yellowthroat in the pine bogs here.

Several good forest trails occur in the park. Some have been used as transect study areas and have been reported in the publication mentioned above. On these trails watch and listen for the cooing of Band-tailed Pigeons from June through August. Western Screech-Owl is a frequently heard bird. Look for it on the highway in winter near Long Beach. Of course Rufous Hummingbirds will challenge you on these woodland walks from April through August. When you reach the shores of water bodies, check for Belted Kingfishers. Western Flycatchers are the most conspicuous of its family from June through August. Also listen for the "quick-three-beers" of the Olive-sided Flycatcher, which becomes a familiar summer sound in the park. When you come to a shrub site, check carefully for Orange-crowned Warblers, the most frequently seen warbler. Golden-crowned Sparrows are spotted from mid-April to mid-May and mid-September to mid-October. In recent years, Palm Warblers, Baltimore Orioles and Harris's Sparrows have shown up in the fall.

Barkley Sound, with approximately 100 islands in the park, has also been surveyed carefully in the above-mentioned book. Look for a variety of seabirds, including the regular but uncommon Buller's Shearwater; Sooty Shearwater; a breeding colony of Leach's Storm-Petrels on Seabird Rocks and Cleland Island; the northernmost colony of Brandt's Cormorants on Sea Lion Rocks, Starlight Reef and at times other spots. Pelagic Cormorant is a common resident on the islands. Bald Eagles are everywhere and stay all year. They are most abundant at the northeast end of Barkley Sound. Ospreys are seen most easily at Long Beach and nest on Vargas Island, near the north end of Yarkis Beach on the east side of the island. Also look for this bird in the Grice Bay area. Surfbird is an abundant migrant through these islands, particularly in April and from mid-July through August. Heermann's Gull is a likely bird on the offshore reefs and islets. Look for small flocks of Common Murres in protected waters from October to April. Pigeon Guillemots nest on Seabird Rocks and Florencia Island. Marbled Murrelets occur in pairs along the islets from April through September. Rhinoceros Auklets have a small colony on Seabird Rocks, as do Tufted Puffins. Listen for Western Screech-Owl on Turtle Island from May through July. Nearby islands may also contain breeding birds. Rufous Hummingbird probably breeds on every vegetated island and islet in Barkley Sound. Search for clumps of *Rubus*, which supply it with nectar.

The park is an important wintering area on Vancouver Island for Trumpeter Swan. They are best seen from late November through early January in several spots including Grice Bay, Sandhill Creek, Swan Lake, Kichla Lake, Kieha Meadows, Hobiton Lake and Cheewhat Lake. Swan Lake appears to be the best site from mid to late November. Areas to search close to the park include Megin Lake, the estuaries of Tranquil Creek, and the Cypre, Moyeha and Bedwell Rivers, all draining into Clayoquot Sound; several locations in the Kennedy Lake area may have these birds too.

Peregrine Falcons usually appear in the park in August when shorebirds are passing through and begin to decrease from January onward. The best site to look for these falcons is among the waterfowl wintering areas in Clayoquot Sound.

WAYNE CAMPBELL
Revised by Adrian Dorst

Pelagic (Offshore Waters) British Columbia

Oceanic birds such as albatrosses, storm-petrels and shearwaters are often the most inaccessible birds to all but the very keen searcher. To attain the goal of more new species, British Columbia birdwatchers began to take organized trips off the west coast of Vancouver Island in spring and fall of 1979. In addition to birds, Northern Sea Lions, Gray Whales, sharks and marine fish are all good possibilities.

At present, trips are not regularly scheduled but can be organized at relatively short notice by Victoria and Vancouver birders. Your best bet is to call the Victoria Bird Hot Line at (250) 592-3381 and ask if an excursion is available. Recently, most trips have left from the west coast of Vancouver Island at Ucluelet or Port Renfrew. The most productive times for a pelagic trip tend to be May, and August through early November. Just north of Tofino, west of Gold River, Captain James Cook first landed at Friendly Cove in Nootka Sound in 1778. Fourteen years later, Captain George Vancouver, who had been a 20-year-old midshipman on the Cook expedition, returned and gave the large island his name.

Birding Features

Pelagic species frequently encountered on these trips include Black-footed Albatross, Sooty Shearwater, Pink-footed Shearwater, Buller's Shearwater, Fork-tailed Storm-Petrel, Pomarine Jaeger, Sabine's Gull, Cassin's Auklet and Tufted Puffin. With a little luck, you'll see some of the rarer ones such as Laysan Albatross and South Polar Skua. A choice selection of marine mammals inhabit the area – great views of Northern and California Sea Lions; Gray, Humpback and Killer (Orca) Whales; and Dall Porpoises can be had.

If you are desperate to find some of the pelagic species, but can't find a scheduled trip, try the following:

a. Charter a boat yourself from Port Renfrew, Bamfield, Tofino or Kyuquot. You need to get out at least 20 km offshore and preferably farther for the best birding.

b. Charter a floatplane from Tofino for an aerial view. You need to be quick at identification; however, you will be quite close to the birds if you are flying at an altitude of 300 m or so.

c. Try the ferry route between Victoria and Port Angeles, Washington – best from September through November; the Hecate Strait crossing between Prince Rupert and Skidegate on the Queen Charlottes – variable but can be excellent at any time of year; or the Inside Passage between Port Hardy and Prince Rupert or Bella Coola – the best areas in the south, so make sure you select a sailing that leaves Port Hardy in the morning or arrives there in the evening.

d. Take a whale-watching trip from Victoria or charter a boat to bird Juan de Fuca Strait. The best area is usually between Discovery Island and Race Rocks, with the largest number of birds and greatest variety occurring September through mid-December. The area can be fantastic for close-up viewing of gulls, alcids, shearwaters and phalaropes.

WAYNE CAMPBELL
Revised by Michael Shepard

Riske Creek, Becher's Prairie

Becher's Prairie near Riske Creek in south-central B.C. contains the best mix of dry plateau grasslands and pothole marshes in the province. The wetlands provide habitat for high concentrations of migrating and nesting waterfowl. The area lies in the Caribou-Chilcotin region, which contains the highest concentrations of breeding Barrow's Goldeneye and Buffleheads in the world. Riske Creek is also the northern limit of Long-billed Curlews in B.C.

Becher's Prairie is mainly Crown owned; the northern half is a military reserve used occasionally in summer as a training ground by the Department of National Defence. The whole area, including the military reserve, is under a grazing lease. Vehicles must stay on the roads, as the grasses are easily damaged by automobile traffic.

The area was originally settled by cattle ranchers and has been grazed for decades. Lands are relatively flat-rolling and covered with grasses interspersed with scattered clumps of Trembling Aspen, Lodgepole Pine and Douglas-fir. The lakes show a wide range of salinity; some of their margins have extensive bulrush stands, others are bare and salt-encrusted.

The Riske Creek site, of approximately 100 km², lies 40 km southwest of Williams Lake on Highway 20. Greyhound Bus, British Columbia Rail and Canadian Airlines all regularly service Williams Lake. Travel from there to the birding site by automobile; rentals are available at Williams Lake. A short day's driving time is sufficient to cover the loop. Be sure to make regular stops for exploratory hikes at potholes, open fields and woods. Begin at Riske Creek Store-Post Office; take the gravel road north for about 7 km; bear right, or northeast, to the dirt track for another 2 km or less; turn sharply south to the gravel road and angle southeast for about 11 km to Highway 20, then back to Williams Lake.

The closest commercial accommodation is at Chilcotin Lodge and trailer park at Riske Creek. There are several hotels and motels at Williams Lake. B.C. Forest Service campsites are nearby, a gas station, telephone, store and post office are at Riske Creek, and there is a hospital at Williams Lake. Additional tourist information on the area is available from the Visitor Information Centre, 1148 S. Broadway Ave., Williams Lake, B.C. V2G 1A2. Their office is located at the junction of Highways 97 and 20 on the south entrance to Williams Lake. Ask them for directions to the local nature centre.

Further birding help can be provided by Anna Roberts, 2002 Grebe Drive, Williams Lake, B.C. V2G 1M3; phone (250) 392-5000.

Birding Features

The mix of dry plateau grasslands and pothole marshes provides a wide diversity of bird habitat. Uncommon residents include Northern Goshawk, Sharp-tailed Grouse and Three-toed Woodpecker; Red Crossbill is fairly common, but White-winged is irregular.

Winter visitors include Great Gray, Boreal and Northern Hawk-Owls, all of which are rare but possible; Gray-crowned Rosy-Finch and Snow Bunting are irregular.

On migration most Pacific Flyway waterfowl are common; Sandhill Crane uses the prairie as a staging area and many shorebirds stop on their way through.

Summer species start arriving in late March to early April. Birds found from then until September include four species of grebe, Red-necked, Horned, Pied-billed and Eared, which are abundant and have a colony at the north end of Rock Lake (south of the back road, about 2 km north of Highway 20 on the east leg of the loop). Mallard and Northern Pintail are present, as are Gadwall and three species of teal, Green-winged, Blue-winged and Cinnamon. American Wigeon nests, as do Redhead and Canvasback. Ruddy Duck, Lesser Scaup, Barrow's Goldeneye and Bufflehead are common (see above for comments on abundance). Golden Eagles are uncommon; Bald

Eagles nest nearby and are fairly common. Sandhill Cranes nest in very small numbers in the marshes. This is the northern limit for Long-billed Curlews in B.C. Greater Yellowlegs are fairly common breeders and are near the southern limit of their breeding range in the province. Long-eared Owls are found in conifer groves; Flammulated Owls are locally common in the Douglas-fir woodlands along the Fraser River. Common flycatchers include Willow, Least and Dusky. Horned Lark is a common breeder on the grasslands. Mountain Chickadees occur in the woodlands, and Mountain Bluebirds nest along fence rows. Yellow-headed Blackbird is abundant in the *Scirpus* marshes. Savannah and Vesper Sparrows appear in number on the grasslands.

ROBERT A. CANNINGS,
RICHARD J. CANNINGS AND SYDNEY G. CANNINGS
Revised by Richard J. Cannings

Queen Charlotte Islands

The rugged mountains and lush forests on the Queen Charlotte Islands are often shrouded in rain and mist. These lands sit on the edge of the continental shelf. To the west, the drop-off is over 3000 m to the ocean floor; to the east, the floor of Hecate Strait is in places only about 15 m below sea level.

Peregrine Falcons breed here in larger numbers than anywhere else in the world. Subspecies of the darker Northern Saw-whet Owl, Hairy Woodpecker, Steller's Jay and Pine Grosbeak add to the interest. Two hundred seabird breeding sites have been identified. Mammal species are few. The Western Toad is the only native amphibian; no reptiles are present.

Weather is very unpredictable and can be severe. Don't venture out to the islands without some advance planning. Commercial accommodation is limited and should be prearranged.

These islands are the ancestral home of the Haida people. Their carvings were, and still are, beautiful pieces of art. After the Europeans arrived in 1774, the Haida, very susceptible to white man's diseases which devastated their numbers, abandoned their ancestral villages and moved first to missions and later to reserves. By the 1820s, they had discovered argillite, a soft rock found only at Slatechuck Mountain on Graham Island. By combining argillite and their carving skills perfected earlier on cedar, they made beautiful pieces of art which live today in the fine pieces still being produced.

The two main islands, Graham to the north and Moresby to the south, are separated by a narrow channel. The island's airport is located at Sandspit, at the north end of Moresby. Regular air service to the mainland is available. Bus and ferry services take you from the airport to Skidegate, on Graham Island. B.C. Ferry Corporation also runs a regular ferry service between the islands and Prince Rupert on the mainland. Car rentals are available at Sandspit, Massett, Queen Charlotte City and Port Clements. A paved road connects Massett, Queen Charlotte City and Port Clements. Numerous logging roads provide access to other areas.

One provincial park, Naikoon, 707 km², preserves a large block of wilderness on the northeast corner of Graham Island. A road leads from Massett into the park and Tow Hill, a lookout where Peregrine Falcons often bring prey to pluck and consume. Camping is available in Naikoon Provincial Park.

Information on the wildlife of the Charlottes is limited, but increasing all the time. *Islands of Discovery: An Outdoor Guide to the Queen Charlotte Islands*, by Dennis Horwood and Tom Parkin, would be a useful book to have before travelling to the islands.

Several of the seabird colonies are ecological reserves that require special permission and a permit. To obtain one, write to Director, Ecological Reserves Unit, Ministry of the Environment, B.C. Provincial Government, Victoria, B.C. V8V 1X4.

Birding Features

Historically, the islands have not been well birded. A visitor has a good chance of adding new species for the islands, B.C. and even Canada. These islands have been close to Siberia and Alaska for a long time; you can expect the unexpected. Spectacled Eider, Steller's Eider, Red-faced Cormorant, Magnificent Frigatebird, Wood Sandpiper, Red-legged Kittiwake, Skylark, Rustic Bunting and Great-tailed Grackle have all been found. It is the best place in the province to see Brambling, Aleutian Tern and Yellow-billed Loon, all of which are seen annually. Stragglers from more northern seabird colonies include Parakeets and Least Auklets.

The islands provide habitat for large numbers of breeding seabirds, the most numerous being Ancient Murrelet. The majority of the world's population of this species nests on the Queen Charlotte Islands. They are common to abundant in late May and early June. Other breeding seabirds include Cassin's and Rhinoceros Auklets and Horned Puffin. With this abundance of seabirds, Peregrine Falcons reap a rich harvest. Falcons and Bald Eagles are at their peak of breeding abundance for B.C. here. Because of their proximity to the continental shelf, the islands are an excellent place for pelagic species. Laysan Albatross, South Polar Skua and three species of jaeger are all present.

Birding on the Charlottes depends so much on the season, and on the weather. Rain, wind and fog are very common in certain seasons. Prediction of weather conditions and consequent bird abundance is very difficult. For example, thousands of turnstones can be seen in the fall off Sandspit some years; in others they are rare or absent. However, you can always count on the regularity and abundance of seabirds at their breeding colonies.

The seabird colonies are best from May to July. In winter, waterbirds can be found around the entire islands in protected waters. Skidegate Inlet is often a good spot. The main, easily accessible, areas are as follows:

Delkatla Slough at Massett. In spring and fall watch for Short-billed Dowitchers, Least Sandpipers, Sandhill Cranes and Canada and Greater White-fronted Geese. The latter can occur in flocks of a thousand or more. Peregrine Falcons hunt here.

Rose Spit, at the northeast corner of Graham Island, is an excellent spot to observe migrating waterfowl, shorebirds and seabirds.

Port Clements, at Massett Inlet on Graham Island, is good for water birds. It is the best place in the Charlottes for Northern Goshawk.

Skidegate Inlet, between Graham and Moresby Islands, should be carefully examined from both sides, and while crossing on the ferry, for seabirds, all year. In particular, watch for Pelagic Cormorant, Black Oystercatcher, Glaucous-winged Gull and Pigeon Guillemot.

Sandspit, on Moresby Island, at the end of the road is another good spot to watch for shorebirds in spring and fall.

Langara Island, about 8 km long and 6.5 km wide, lies off the northwest corner of Graham Island. The shores are steep, with the interior partly forest and partly muskeg. Bald Eagles are abundant year-round residents. The island is reached by boat; it can be a tricky trip, so be cautious. Peregrine Falcon nests on Cox Island, on the southeast side of Langara Island. At the south end of Langara, north of the aboriginal village of Dadens, Ancient Murrelets have riddled the ground with burrows.

The 200 seabird breeding sites on the Queen Charlotte Islands include 1.5 million pairs of birds of 12 different species. Ancient Murrelet and Cassin's Auklet are the most numerous. Other species include Leach's and Fork-tailed Storm-Petrels, Pelagic Cormorant, Glaucous-winged Gull, Common Murre, Pigeon Guillemot, Rhinoceros Auklet and Tufted Puffin.

WAYNE CAMPBELL AND YORKE EDWARDS
Revised by Gary Davidson and Wayne Campbell

Beatton Provincial Park and Charlie Lake

Beatton Provincial Park is an excellent place to begin exploring the Peace River region of British Columbia. Located east of the Rocky Mountains, the region is a mix of aspen parkland, prairie grain farms and boreal forest, all of it biologically more similar to the prairie and eastern provinces than to typical mountainous forests of most of B.C. A number of "eastern" birds such as Eastern Phoebe are restricted within B.C. to the Peace country and the north-eastern corner of the province. Beatton Provincial Park is home to several such species, which can be seen without too much trouble.

Beatton Park is a block of aspen and White Spruce woodland surrounded by grain farms on three sides and Charlie Lake on the fourth. It contains a campground (37 sites), a boat launch, a picnic area and a small playing field. Trails provide easy access to the forest. The beach can attract shorebirds during insect outbreaks in May and again in mid- to late August, though this doesn't happen every year. Offshore, a wide diversity of loons, grebes, ducks, gulls and terns use Charlie Lake as a migratory rest stop, making the lake one of the most important staging areas in the Peace region.

To reach Beatton Provincial Park, drive about 6 km north of Fort St. John along the Alaska Highway towards Charlie Lake. The turnoff, to the right on 271 Road, is well marked. Drive about 7.5 km along 271 Road to the entrance road on the left which runs due west along the northern edge of the park and enters the park near its northwest corner. The campground is a few hundred metres farther.

Birding Features

The park's Trembling Aspen forests are home to Yellow-bellied Sapsucker, Least Flycatcher, Red-eyed Vireo, Ovenbird, Yellow Warbler and Rose-breasted Grosbeak from mid-May through August. The aspens around the campground are excellent for Baltimore Orioles. The picnic parking lot has willow thickets and is often alive with songbirds, including Western Wood-Pewee, Blue Jay, American Redstart and White-throated Sparrow. Check the cook shack on the lawn above the beach for a pair of nesting Eastern Phoebes. The beach has summer resident Spotted Sandpiper, and in low-water years has also attracted small numbers of other shorebirds including Lesser Yellowlegs, Least Sandpiper and Semipalmated Sandpiper, as well as less common species including Stilt Sandpiper.

The spruce stand south of the playing field is the summer home of Golden-crowned Kinglet, a few Boreal Chickadees, Yellow-rumped Warbler (Myrtle subspecies), Chipping Sparrow, Dark-eyed Junco (Slate-colored subspecies), and usually a pair or two of Black-throated Green Warblers, which, in B.C., occur only in the Peace Lowlands from Fort St. John and Dawson Creek west to about Chetwynd. Occasionally one or two Cape May Warblers also spend the summer and have bred. Since they forage very high in the canopy and have very high-pitched songs that are easily confused with Golden-crowned Kinglets, or not heard at all, Cape Mays are difficult to see. After their arrival in mid-May and throughout June, look for singing males in the very tops of the spruce at dawn. A telescope helps. Even less regularly occurring are Bay-breasted Warblers, which appear in the park every few years. They may be seen either in old spruce or in mature aspen surrounding the grove. Also in the mixed forest along the spruce edges look for Blue-headed Vireo, Yellow-bellied Sapsucker, and Tennessee Warbler. Follow the trail due south (parallel to the lakeshore) through willow thickets. Black-and-white Warblers are frequent here.

During songbird migration, mid-May to early June and early August to very early September, look for mixed flocks of vireos, warblers, kinglets and chickadees. These may include rarer species such as Philadelphia Vireo, Townsend's Warbler (here, a western stray from the Rockies), Mourning and Canada Warblers.

In winter the park has far fewer birds, but with diligence you might find Ruffed Grouse; Northern Goshawk; Great Horned Owl; Three-toed, Downy and Hairy Woodpeckers; Boreal Chickadee; Northern Shrike; Pine Grosbeak; Common and Hoary Redpolls. In late March and April, listen for the monotonous "tooting" of Northern Saw-whet Owl.

Beatton Park is also a good vantage point from which to scan Charlie Lake. Once the lake thaws, usually between May 1 and 10, waterfowl can be plentiful. Look for diving ducks, including Lesser Scaup, White-winged and Surf Scoters, and Oldsquaw, resting on the centre of the lake. In late May and early June a few Sabine's Gulls usually appear on their northbound migration.

Common Terns also appear, with smaller numbers of Arctic Terns, and occasional stray Forster's Terns, probably from colonies in west-central Alberta. Up to 2000 Bonaparte's Gulls appear in late July some years, and flocks of a few hundred Franklin's Gulls are a feature of spring and early summer.

Another vantage point on the other side of the lake is at the Charlie Lake Provincial Park boat launch. To get to it, return to the Alaska Highway, continue about 5 km past the south end of Charlie Lake and turn right down Lakeshore Drive. In a couple of kilometres, the drive ends at the boat launch. Charlie Lake also has camping (58 sites) but is covered by a younger aspen forest without much spruce, and thus without "spruce" warblers like the Black-throated Green.

CHRIS SIDDLE

Fort Nelson Area

Travelling north from its beginning at Dawson Creek, B.C., the Alaska Highway begins its descent from the foothills into the lowlands near the abandoned community of Trutch, passing through 140 km of flattish country to Fort Nelson, before turning west and once more ascending the eastern foothills of the Rocky Mountains. Basin elevations are around 370 m with surrounding plateau elevations of around 680 m. A visitor often speeds through these lowlands without stopping to check for birdlife. This would be a mistake, since it is rich in birds.

Biogeographically, the Fort Nelson Lowlands are near the northwestern edge of the aspen parklands that stretch across the Prairie provinces from the Canadian Shield. Many species more common in eastern Canada are found here including Common Grackle, Rose-breasted Grosbeak and several warblers, including Black-and-white, Cape May, Bay-breasted, Connecticut, Mourning and Canada.

From the age of the dinosaurs onward to the start of the last ice age, the lowlands were a lush tropical jungle. Later, as the ice melted, they became a post-glacial lakebed. The geological substrate is thus largely sedimentary, resulting in the rivers all running muddy, and vast gas deposits lie beneath the surface. Above ground, both the Aboriginals and Europeans that followed found bountiful wildlife and fur-bearing animals such as Beaver in the lowlands. In modern times, the area opened up with the building of the 2436 km long Alaska Highway during World War II. Today the highway serves as the tourist route, access point to gasfield exploration, and link between Alaska, the Yukon and points south.

Greyhound runs a daily bus service in summer from Edmonton to Whitehorse. Service is reduced to three times a week from late fall to spring. The town of Fort Nelson maintains a major airport 11 km to the northeast. Motels and campgrounds occur at scattered communities along the highway with several to choose from in Fort Nelson. The highway is paved or seal-coated for most of its length, with occasional long distances between service stations. As a precaution, carry an extra spare tire, emergency rations, lots of warm clothing and a sleeping bag.

There are frequent summer showers and some heavy rains under easterly upslope winds. Long summer daylight hours lead to warm days and nights allowing lush vegetation growth. Some of the world's largest aspen stands are found here. Be warned, however, that mosquitoes and black flies abound!

The British Columbia Provincial Museum published a relevant paper "Birds of the Fort Nelson Lowlands of Northeastern British Columbia," by A. J. Erskine and G. S. Davidson, *Syesis*, Vol. 9, 1976:1–11. At that time, 157 species of birds below 610 m were recorded. This included 30 breeding species with an additional 76 probably breeding. In the ensuing 23 years, efforts by hundreds of observers have boosted the four-season total to 216 species with 124 confirmed or probable breeders.

Birding Features
The lowlands are largely forested with White and Black Spruce. Trembling Aspen forms pure stands on the warmer south-facing slopes and grows to impressive size, especially on the Poplar Hills from Fort Nelson west to Kilometre 548. Balsam Poplar is the pioneer tree on river gravels, where it can attain huge size. Black Spruce muskegs are common at the poorly drained lower elevations and there are many raised spruce bogs at higher elevations.

Birds that are near their range limits on these lowlands include:

Northern limit: Broad-winged Hawk, Osprey, Black Tern (breeding), Barred Owl (breeding), Yellow-bellied Flycatcher, Blue-headed and Philadelphia Vireos, Canada Warbler (breeding), and Rose-breasted Grosbeak (breeding).

Southern limit: Surf Scoter (breeding), and Rough-legged Hawk (summer).

Western limit: Broad-winged Hawk; Cape May, Black-throated Green, Bay-breasted, Connecticut, Mourning and Canada Warblers; Rose-breasted Grosbeak.

Spots to visit include:

Fort Nelson community. There is good mixed wood habitat behind the landfill, which is a fine place to check for Canada Warblers. Look for Herring, Ring-billed and Mew Gulls, as well as American Crows and Common Ravens at the landfill itself. Crows have only recently moved into the lowlands as more or less permanent residents. The gulls also frequent the large water treatment lagoons on the southern edge of the community – keep watching for a stray California Gull. In town, look for Common Nighthawk, Western Wood-Pewee, Tree Swallow, as well as a Cliff Swallow colony on the high school; also House Wren, American Robin, Brewer's Blackbird, Western Tanager, Purple Finch and Savannah, Clay-colored and White-crowned Sparrows can be found. Be on the watch for Blue Jay, which has recently moved into the area. The newly developed Community Forest atop the hill in town has many kilometres of trails, which lead through mixed wood, open logged areas and Black Spruce bogs. Here you will find Three-toed Woodpecker, Winter Wren,

Ovenbird and Rose-breasted Grosbeak in the woods, Lincoln's and White-throated Sparrows in the regenerating areas, and Fox Sparrow, Rusty Blackbird and maybe Palm Warbler in the spruce bogs. Crossbills may or may not be present depending on cone crops. The golf course atop Radar Hill west of town is a reliable spot for Common Nighthawk.

Parker Lake. To reach this site, go 11.2 km west of Fort Nelson on the Alaska Highway and then left on an unmarked dirt road for 1.3 km. This access road is directly across from where the Old Alaska Highway joins the current Alaska Highway. From late May to July, you may find Red-necked and Horned Grebes, a variety of ducks including Barrow's Goldeneye, Lesser Scaup, White-winged and Surf Scoters, Sora, Common Loon, Bonaparte's Gull, Sandhill Crane, Black Tern, Marsh Wren, Western Wood-Pewee, Alder and Yellow-bellied Flycatcher, Palm Warbler, Common Yellowthroat, and LeConte's and Swamp Sparrows. This is also the best spot for spring and fall migrant waterbirds.

Fort Nelson River and east to the gasfields. Eight kilometres south of Fort Nelson near the prominent service station at Kilometre 468.8, take the Sierra High Grade road to the east about 3 km. Here you will cross a bridge spanning the Fort Nelson River. This is the most northerly one-lane dual train/car bridge in Canada so watch for oncoming locomotives. Past this bridge, the road continues eastward for at least 130 km, with a maze of dirt roads servicing the innumerable gas wells. Be aware that all gas wells are capable of giving off potentially fatal fumes! When exploring this area, be careful that you remember your return route. As with all dirt roads in this area, prolonged rainfall will turn the road surface into a mudbath! There are no services so travel with a full gas tank. Look for American Kestrel, Red-tailed Hawk and the furtive Northern Goshawk; Swainson's, Hermit and Varied Thrushes; Black-and-white, Tennessee, Orange-crowned, Magnolia, Connecticut, Mourning and Palm Warblers; Ovenbird; Rose-breasted Grosbeak; and Savannah, Lincoln's, Fox and White-throated Sparrows. The many beaver ponds provide breeding habitat for Sora, Solitary Sandpiper, Greater and Lesser Yellowlegs, Northern Waterthrush, Swamp Sparrow, Rusty Blackbird and Common Grackle. Le Conte's Sparrow can sometimes be found in the grasses lining the roadside ditches, and you may be lucky enough to happen upon a Nelson's Sharp-tailed Sparrow in the reeds.

Muskwa River. Follow Airport Road north from the town of Fort Nelson 11 km to the airport but continue straight on instead of turning right into the airport terminal. This road leads you down to the poplar bottomlands near the confluence of the Muskwa and Fort Nelson Rivers. Here you'll find an excellent mixture of seral deciduous and mature coniferous vegetation, as well as a few open areas, which provide prime habitat for many birds. Expect to find all the species listed in the previous paragraph, as well as Great Horned Owl and Hammond's Flycatcher in the taller poplars and spruces; Philadelphia Vireo in the regenerating willows; Cape May and Bay-breasted Warblers in the taller spruce; Canada Warbler in the moister brushy creekside draws; and the widespread American Redstart.

Fort Nelson Airport. The wide-open airport property provides an ideal staging area for many migrants, including American Golden-Plover, Sandhill Crane and Say's Phoebe from late April through May. Raptors such as American Kestrel, Merlin and Red-tailed Hawk breed in the surrounding woods and forage on the airport lands. Upland Sandpipers have recently been discovered in June and July here, suggesting that nesting may be occurring. There is a reliable southward migration of Upland Sandpipers through the airport the middle two weeks of August. Crows, ravens, blackbirds, starlings and many other birds flock to the airport clearing during the mid-summer locust hatches in late July through mid-August. Lapland Longspur and American Pipit swarm through in late April to early May and again in September.

Kilometre 512. At the mature aspen forest around Kilometre 512, look for American Kestrel, Common Snipe, Pileated Woodpecker, Yellow-bellied Sapsucker and Philadelphia Vireo; warblers, including Black-and-white, Orange-crowned, Magnolia, Blackpoll, Ovenbird, Mourning, Wilson's, Canada and American Redstart; Rose-breasted Grosbeak and Swamp Sparrow.

Kilometre 538. In the bottomland White Spruce forest around Kilometre 538, search for Sharp-shinned Hawk, Bald Eagle, Red-tailed hawk; Ruffed Grouse, Barred and possibly a late Boreal Owl calling in the middle of the night; Belted Kingfisher near the Muskwa River, southeast of here; Pileated Woodpecker, Three-toed Woodpecker, the difficult flycatchers of the Empidonax group, Western Wood-Pewee, Gray Jay, Boreal Chickadee, American Robin, Varied and Swainson's Thrushes, Golden- and Ruby-crowned Kinglets, Bohemian Waxwing, Blue-headed Vireo, warblers (including Black-and-white, Yellow, Orange-crowned, Magnolia, possibly Chestnut-sided, Bay-breasted, Blackpoll, Ovenbird, Northern Waterthrush, Mourning, Wilson's and American Redstart), Western Tanager and Rose-breasted Grosbeak.

Kilometre 542. In the Black Spruce muskeg at Kilometre 542 and at Kledo Creek, a short distance farther west, check for Sharp-shinned Hawk, Spruce Grouse, Common Nighthawk overhead, Hermit Thrush, Palm Warbler, White-winged Crossbill and Chipping Sparrow.

Near Kledo Creek. The old gravel pit area 2 km downstream from the Kledo Creek Bridge is a good location for Greater Yellowlegs, sometimes Black-backed Woodpecker, Bank Swallow in the sand and gravel piles and Dusky Flycatcher. Blackburnian Warbler was found near here recently. Check under the Kledo Creek Bridge for Eastern Phoebe.

Kilometre 614. In the hillside Black Spruce forest at Kilometre 614, explore for Ruffed Grouse, Gray Jay, Red-breasted Nuthatch, Brown Creeper, Winter Wren, Varied Thrush, and Golden- and Ruby-crowned Kinglets.

WAYNE CAMPBELL
Revised by Jack Bowling

Haines Road/Chilkat Pass

The Chilkat Pass crosses the mountains from Haines, Alaska, to Haines Junction, Yukon. This pass in the extreme northwest corner of B.C. is one of the few accessible places in Canada where all three species of ptarmigan occur. The area is adjacent to one of the largest gatherings of Bald Eagles in North America. Gyrfalcons are year-round residents and Wandering Tattlers are rare breeders.

You reach this area by road. Travel to Whitehorse in the Yukon and then take Yukon Highway 1 west from Whitehorse, for 158 km to Haines Road No. 3 and south to B.C. At the border the road becomes B.C. No. 4 over the Chilkat Pass. This is Crown land with some seasonally operated guiding settlements, mostly used in the fall hunting season by guided groups.

A highway maintenance camp is situated on the west side of the road, about halfway down the B.C. stretch on the way into Haines, southwest of Kelsall Lake. There are no really good roads off the highway, but there are some crude trails into such places as Kelsall Lake and Three Guardsmen Mountain.

No motel or camping facilities are present in the pass and no services. Food, gas and sleeping accommodation can be found at Kathleen Lodge located at Kilometre 220. Groceries and other supplies should be acquired before leaving Whitehorse, at Haines Junction or down at Haines, Alaska. The closest hospital and medical services are at Haines Junction. For help or a telephone in case of such emergencies as illness or accident, contact the road maintenance camp mentioned previously, about midway through the pass. The highway has fairly heavy traffic because of the movement to and from Haines. A ferry service at Haines will take you down the straits, with regular service to Prince Rupert, B.C. This ferry trip is well worth the money for the scenery alone, not to mention the dozens of Bald Eagles seen en route.

For road conditions, services and other information contact Yukon Government Travel Information at (867) 667-5340.

The nearest naturalists or contact people are at Kluane National Park in the Yukon. For more information, obtain the article by Robert B. Weeden, "The Birds of Chilkoot Pass, British Columbia," in *Canadian Field-Naturalist* 74(2) 1960: 119–29.

Caution: Carry winter clothing and a warm sleeping bag at all times. There are regular unseasonable snowstorms. The low areas are very damp, so wear rubber boots. Carry a full five-gallon can of gasoline.

Birding Features

The landscape is covered with Alpine Willow and in places is difficult to walk through. The real alpine areas are about one-half to one hour's walk from the lower elevations. However, you are in the alpine area at the summit of the pass. The views are magnificent, with snow-covered mountains and glaciers dominating. Much of the area around the smaller lakes is very damp and wet, typical of shallow bog sites.

Because of the high elevations, birding visits should take place from May through September. In early May, and again in September, the birds pass through in great numbers. Blizzards occur regularly and happen very suddenly.

There are three major routes along which birds pass through the coastal mountains from the Pacific to the interior of the Yukon and eastern Alaska. The Chilkat Pass is the largest and most northerly of these. Birds in large numbers are often seen flying very low through the pass because of the adverse weather so often encountered.

The chief attraction during the nesting season is the Golden Eagle and a possible nesting Gyrfalcon. These falcons are more common in the fall (October). There is a large concentration of Bald Eagles at the mouth of the Klukwan River and Chilkoot River in Alaska. This is one of the largest groupings of these birds left anywhere in North America. They feed on the salmon. This region is the southern limit of nesting by American Golden-Plover, Wandering Tattler, Least Sandpiper, Short-billed Dowitcher, Arctic Tern, Smith's Longspur and Snow Bunting. Common and Red-throated Loons also nest here. Gray-cheeked Thrushes are fairly common throughout the area. Smith's Longspurs nest near Kelsall Lake. As mentioned above, all three species of ptarmigan are observed easily. The most abundant, Willow, has a range that almost exactly coincides with the shrub-tundra zone. Northern Hawk-Owl is a frequent visitor in the fall. Redpolls and White-crowned and Golden-crowned Sparrows breed here. Scan the hills for Stone Sheep, Grizzly Bear and Caribou.

WAYNE CAMPBELL AND DAVE MOSSOP
Revised by David Stirling

ALBERTA

From mountain peaks through parkland to prairie, Alberta is home to everything from Trumpeter Swan, Willow Ptarmigan, Northern Pygmy-Owl, Gray-crowned Rosy-Finch, through Three-toed Woodpecker, to Sage Grouse, Ferruginous Hawk, Burrowing Owl and Mountain Plover.

The province has an area of 661,185 km², but its population is mainly in the two cities of Edmonton and Calgary. The Rocky Mountains, which dominate the western side, are capped with tundra and home to ptarmigans, Gray-crowned Rosy-Finch and other upland species. In the northeast corner of the province, a small piece of Canadian shield is home to Peregrine Falcon. Boreal forest, with Black Spruce bogs and appropriate birds, makes up the northern half of Alberta. A piece of prairie, with nesting Trumpeter Swan, is inserted into this boreal forest in the Peace River Country in the northwest. Farther south, aspen parkland with interspersed bluffs (prairie word for clump) of Trembling Aspen and open grasslands are found around Edmonton. Continuing south, the prairie appears from about Red Deer

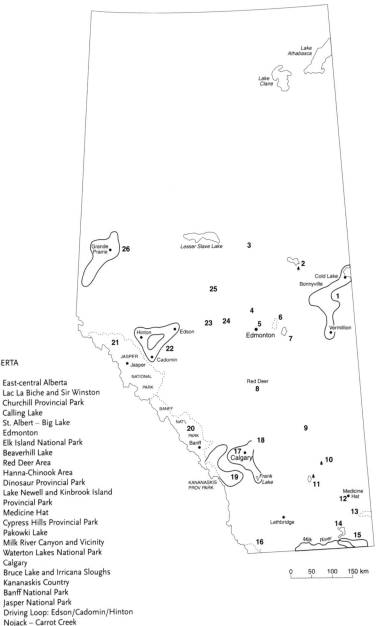

ALBERTA

onward. The remaining southeast of the province consists of short grass, very dry country where a few pairs of Mountain Plover nest on the uplands along the Milk River, the only place they're found in Canada.

The top birding site in Alberta, in most seasons, is Beaverhill Lake. Within an hour of Edmonton, you can see thousands of geese in spring and a wide variety of shorebirds from April to October. Dinosaur Provincial Park offers prairie birds. East-central Alberta provides boreal nesting species and many birds on migration. Pakowki Lake, south of Medicine Hat, hosts the more southern species and contains a few White-faced Ibis each year. Waterton Lakes National Park often has western birds that slip over the low passes from B.C., together with mountain species and prairie birds.

There are two birding hotlines: southern Alberta at (403) 237-8821 and northern Alberta at (780) 433-2473. The Federation of Alberta Naturalists (FAN), Box 1472, Edmonton, Alberta T5J 2N5 will provide a list of natural history clubs in Alberta and other information (also check their Web site at http://www.connect.ab.ca/~fan/ or the following site http://www.interlog. com/~gallantg/canada/society.html)

Succinct accounts on significant wildlife (and birding) areas in the province can be found on the Alberta Wildlife Viewing Guide at http://www.gov. ab.ca/env/fw/view/index_java.html (also in book format by Lone Pine Press, 1990), and the Important Bird Areas site at http://www.bsc-eoc.org/Iba/ albmain.html (Alberta site). Alberta hot spots at http://www.camacdonald. com/birding/caalberta.htm is also worth a look. For a list of checklists, contact the Provincial Museum of Alberta at (780) 453-9179 (or e-mail jhudon@ mcd.gov.ab.ca). For a listing of Alberta's special places, see http://www.gov.ab. ca/env/parks/sp_places/newsp.html

Maps and information on the Natural Regions and Subregions of Alberta can be found at http://www.gov.ab.ca/env/parks/anhic/anhic.html

Finally, camping reservations can be made at http://www.gov.ab.ca/env/ parks/camping/campres.html

Detailed maps of the province can be obtained from several specialized map stores, like Map Town in Edmonton (10344 – 105 St. NW, Edmonton, Alberta, T5J 1E6; phone [780] 429-2600). Non-Alberta residents may obtain a good road map by writing to Travel Alberta, Box 2500, Edmonton, Alberta T5J 4G8, or by calling toll free 1-800-661-8888 (outside of Alberta) or (780) 427-4321 (within the province).

Birdwatchers intending to spend much time in the province should purchase a copy of either the Federation of Alberta Naturalists *Field Guide to Alberta Birds*, by W. Bruce McGillivray and Glen P. Semenchuk (Edmonton: Federation of Alberta Naturalists [FAN], 1998) or *Birds of Alberta*, by Chris Fisher and John Acorn (Edmonton: Lone Pine Press, 1998). Those with a special interest in the distribution of Alberta birds will be well served by *The Atlas of Breeding Birds of Alberta*, edited by G. P. Semenchuk (Edmonton: FAN, 1992).

JOCELYN HUDON

East-central Alberta

The area is diverse in character and boasts a list of well over 300 species. The northern portion is transitional between boreal forest and aspen parkland, while the southern part features grasslands and prairie potholes (sloughs) blended with extensive pure aspen stands and agricultural lands. The key attractions are the woodland warblers, owls, rails and a number of other species which reach the western edge of their breeding range in the eastern portion of the province, and a number of vagrants. The birding potential is so great that a book could easily be devoted to the area, so only brief highlights are provided.

The majority of the key species can be found near Cold Lake. Cold Lake can be reached by bus (three times daily from Edmonton), but the area requires a vehicle to be thoroughly explored. It is 292 km northeast from Edmonton on Highway 28. Other places of interest to the south are around Bonnyville, the Whitney Lakes Provincial Park east of Elk Point, Vermilion Provincial Park near Highway 16 (Yellowhead) and around St. Paul (see below).

A number of campgrounds can be found around Cold Lake, with Cold Lake Provincial Park offering the best birding potential and the greatest comfort (showers). For those preferring motel/hotel accommodation, there is no shortage of facilities. To adequately check the Cold Lake area requires at least two days.

Published checklists for Cold Lake, Whitney Lakes and Therien Lakes area are available from the Recreation Park & Wildlife Foundation in Edmonton, or can be obtained by writing to Cold Lake Provincial Park, Box 8208, Cold Lake, Alberta T0A 0V0; Whitney Lakes Provincial Park, Box 39, Elk Point, Alberta T0A 1A0; or Fish and Wildlife District Office, Box 1450, Eldorado Building, St. Paul, Alberta T0A 3A0. Checklists may also be available at Cold Lake Park and Whitney Lakes Park offices. The Bonnyville Wetlands Society (Box 5257, Bonnyville, Alberta T9N 2G4) has published a checklist for Jesse Lake area, and a checklist for Vermilion Provincial Park may be obtained at the park office (or Box 1140, Vermilion, Alberta T0B 4M0). For further information, contact the rangers-in-charge at the respective parks. Phone numbers for some of these offices can be taken from the Alberta Wildlife Viewing Guide at http://www.gov.ab.ca/env/fw/view/index_java.html.

A week-long trip to the area with stops at the sites below in late May or early June would easily provide at least 200 species and give some of the best birding in the province, since one-day counts of 160 species have already been accomplished.

Birding Features

Cold Lake Area. Cold Lake Provincial Park is about 400 ha in size and has an excellent trail system that explores most of the habitats. The park can be reached by driving east from Cold Lake or from Grand Centre. Drive east from the traffic lights at Cold Lake for about 5 km on a paved road and turn north on a good gravel road to get to the park. Shortly after turning north, find a willow swamp, sedge/grass fen where rails and Sedge Wrens can usually be found. English Bay campground, located north of Cold Lake on the west side of the lake, is another spot which has great potential, especially the marshy beaver pond found before reaching the campground.

Cold Lake Provincial Park has long been known as the warbler capital of Alberta. May 23 to June 10 is the best time, after which many of the birds sing less, become more secretive and are much harder to find. Sabine Gulls and Gray-cheeked Thrushes have also been seen during this time.

Prior to the warbler period, from the third week in April to early May, the area can be very good for migrating flocks of Sandhill Cranes, which may include one or two of their rarer cousin, Whooping Crane. Sometimes large numbers of accipiters fly along the edge of Cold Lake, together with Broad-winged Hawks and many sparrows including (Eastern) Fox Sparrow and Harris's Sparrow – two species generally uncommon to rare in other parts of the province. Waterfowl are not usually very abundant right at the lake, but many birds fly through or over the area. Species of note which have been recorded are Greater Scaup (can be more common than Lesser Scaup at this time), Hooded Merganser and even Eurasian Wigeon and Harlequin Duck. Rare gulls are sometimes encountered at this time but can be found with luck at almost any time of the year outside of midsummer. Shorebirds are only rarely recorded at Cold Lake itself but other sites (see Jesse Lake under Bonnyville area below) not too far away can be excellent.

Warblers most sought after and which can be found in the provincial park are the Chestnut-sided, Blackburnian, Black-throated Green, Bay-breasted and Cape May. The most difficult of these species, the Chestnut-sided, can usually be located in fairly open but mature deciduous sections (for example, along the road between the campground and the boat-launching facility). The other four species are usually heard or seen in mature mixed-wood stands with tall spruce predominating, especially the sections of the park adjacent to campground loops E and F. Winter Wrens can be found here too. Other warbler species which are here and seen more easily than at other locations are Magnolia and Canada. To find some of these warblers, it helps to be able to hear high-frequency sounds and to be able to locate their source since these birds often sit motionless near the tops of very high trees when singing, where even their conspicuous colours are lost among moving leaves and a tangle of foliage. To find Connecticut, Palm and Nashville Warblers, visit spots away from Cold Lake Provincial Park. A drive north along the west side of the lake to English Bay passes some wetlands and a fairly extensive Black Spruce bog. Both habitats can be very productive. Bonaparte's Gull nests in the bog. The shoreline of the lake at English Bay can be very good for loafing gulls, shorebirds and other waterfowl. The water of the bay often has rafts of scoters, mergansers and grebes. Late in the fall watch for Black Scoter and Pacific Loon here. Palm Warbler and Yellow-bellied Flycatchers can sometimes be found along the bog edges but are generally more common in similar habitats along the road north to Primrose Lake. Yellow-bellied Flycatcher usually do not arrive or at least do not vocalize before early June, and even then are generally very inconsistent in their calling. Nashville Warblers (eastern race) have been found a number of times in the willow borders along English Bay, near the English Bay Campground and along the road north to Primrose Lake and is suspected of nesting. Connecticut Warblers are found in mature deciduous stands near English Bay and along the road to Primrose Lake. Three-toed and Black-backed Woodpeckers have been recorded in the area, more so in winter than in summer, with the English Bay Campground being a better bet in the summer (have nested). Boreal Chickadees, Winter Wrens, Blackburnian Warblers and White-winged Crossbills are usually found in the campground area at English Bay.

To find Yellow and Virginia Rails and Sedge Wrens as well as Nelson's Sharp-tailed Sparrows, check sedge and grass fens with scattered willows, especially at dusk or early in the morning when these birds are more active. One area close to the provincial park that is usually good for all these species is the fen area south of Centre Bay, reached by going south on the first road after leaving the park entrance. Virginia Rails are somewhat irregular in occurrence and cannot be found every year.

To find owls you have to listen in March or early April. The best spots are along the road to Primrose Lake. The mature mixed-wood forests just before and adjacent to the weapons range gate are usually productive for Boreal and Barred Owls. Northern Saw-whets are more common in the straight deciduous forests closer to Cold Lake. Great Gray Owls are very rare and even in the winter are not easily found. Barred Owls have also nested in Cold Lake Provincial Park but on only a few occasions. Turkey Vulture, another species which is a regional specialty, can often be found flying above Cold Lake Provincial Park or in the vicinity of other lakes to the west of Cold Lake (like Moore Lake).

The Cold Lake area has also become famous for vagrant waterfowl and gulls, which show up from late September to mid-December. Because it does not often freeze until the end of December, many unusually late birds have been recorded here. Rarities include Yellow-billed Loon, Common Eider (only provincial record; yet to be adjudicated), Black Scoter, Barrow's Goldeneye, Harlequin Duck, Red Phalarope, Parasitic Jaeger, Mew Gull, Glaucous-winged Gull, Great Black-backed Gull and Ancient Murrelet. Thayer's Gulls, Glaucous Gulls and Pacific Loons are regular and sometimes even numerous. Oldsquaws are also regular in small numbers but are usually far from shore and can easily be missed. The best areas for the gulls are the Grand Centre Dump found on the east side of Highway 28 at the southern edge of the town, the lakeshore in the town of Cold Lake itself (especially the town beach and the area east of the Marina) and Centre Bay, visible from the boat-launching area in the provincial park. If you have more time, French Bay, east of Cold Lake (almost on the Saskatchewan boundary), and English Bay on the west side of the lake can be very rewarding. A scope is almost a necessity to scan the lake for the rare ones. Warm clothing is definitely required, especially on windy days and later in the season. At this time, try to avoid days when temperatures are very cold, not only for your own comfort but also to avoid the notorious fog which develops and sometimes persists all day because of the warmer water temperature.

Another place having good birding potential, the Martineau River delta at the northwest corner of Cold Lake, is not accessible by road but requires a boat. The east side of the lake, located in Meadow Lake Provincial Park, Saskatchewan, can be accessed via a gravel road from Pierceland, Saskatchewan, but does not offer any species which cannot be found on the Alberta side. For those travelling by car with time to spare, there are a number of places to explore on the way to and from Cold Lake that offer opportunities to find species not usually found at Cold Lake. At least two days are needed to adequately check the Cold Lake area.

Bonnyville Area. Close to Bonnyville a number of locations offer excellent opportunities to observe wetland birds. Jesse Lake, located on the southern edge of the town, has an excellent trail system with a viewing tower. Waterfowl are abundant from late April to mid-September, and shorebirds can be plentiful when water levels are ideal. Rarities which have been found here include Cattle Egret, Black Duck, Western, Sharp-tailed and Buff-breasted Sandpipers. Muriel Lake to the south of Bonnyville can be worthwhile. Explore the area from the campground located on the east side of the lake, the road along the south side of the lake or from the Muriel Lake Campground located on the north shore. Pelicans, cormorants, Western Grebe and a number of gull species, terns and waterfowl are all plentiful. Shorebirds may occasionally include some surprises such as Ruff, and late fall can be good for Pacific Loon. For woodland birds, Moose Lake Provincial Park with its predominant Jack Pine forest and Franchere Bay area offer a chance to find species such as Spruce Grouse, which can be difficult elsewhere in the area. Kehiwin Lake (also known as Long Lake) located on Highway 41 southwest from Bonnyville and on the road south to Elk Point and Whitney Lakes Provincial Park is surrounded by deciduous forest. The west side of the lake is a good location for Great Crested Flycatcher, a local specialty. Drive to the south end of the lake and look for a road marked Elks Wilderness Park. Follow it to the campground and proceed up a fairly steep hill. Park at the top and listen for the distinctive "wheep" call. Most other parkland species can be found in the general area. Philadelphia Vireo, Veery and Gray Catbird are only some of the birds which may be here that are generally not easy to find at Cold Lake. Waterfowl is plentiful at the south end of Kehiwin Lake and includes Ring-necked Duck. Sabine Gulls stop at this location both in the spring (May 20 to June 5) and fall migration (early September) but only a few birds are involved, so luck is needed to find one. Turkey Vultures are sometimes seen, and an active Osprey nest sits on a telephone pole along the east side of Highway 41 north of the campground. (See http://www.town.bonnyville.ab.ca/birdwatching.html)

Whitney Lakes Provincial Park. Whitney Lakes Park, located about 32 km east of Elk Point on paved Secondary Highway 646, has a campground at Ross Lake. The area features a wide mix of habitats from Jack Pine forest and Black Spruce bog to mature deciduous stands, lakes and small wetlands. Laurier Lake is the largest and is known to have Oldsquaw, Surf Scoter and Pacific Loon stop on migration. Some years large numbers of Hooded Mergansers stage on Whitney Lake in the fall.

Virginia Rails have been found in the wetland complex at the north end of Laurier. Turkey Vultures have nested in the area for years and are often seen flying over. Another specialty, the Great Crested Flycatcher, can sometimes be found near Ross Lake Campground. There are few good roads through, most being gravel, but access points can be attained from Secondary Highway 646 to Whitney Lake, to Laurier Lake from the south, and a road which follows the east side of Laurier Lake to the north of the lake.

Vermilion Provincial Park. Vermilion Park, 769 ha in size, lies along Vermilion River, at the northwest corner of the town of the same name, 189 km east of Edmonton just north of Highway 16. The south side of the park is wooded with aspen and contains breeding birds typical of parkland. A number of trails traverse this section of the park. Extensive marshland occurs at the west end. Migrants of many species stop in spring and fall to feed and rest briefly in this wooded oasis surrounded primarily by agricultural land. With luck Great Crested Flycatchers can be found here during the summer. The north side of the park features exposed grasslands where birds of this habitat, including Sprague's Pipits, may be found. Marshes and numerous sloughs are good locations for waterfowl and other birds associated with wetlands. Large numbers of geese, including Ross's, pass through during spring and fall. Albert Lake, a smaller alkali lake south of Islay on Secondary Highway 893 and then east along Secondary Highway 619, can be very productive for shorebirds. Small numbers of Smith's Longspurs pass through the area in mid-May.

St. Paul. At the southern edge of town, located along Highway 28, sits Upper Therien Lake. This shallow lake is teeming with waterfowl, grebes, gulls and terns. Pelicans and cormorants are regular. In spring (late April) it is one of the most reliable spots in the region for Greater Scaup. In late May to June 7 look for Sabine Gulls. Other rarities include Black Duck (late fall), Hooded Merganser, Barrow's Goldeneye, Red Phalarope, Black-necked Stilt, Parasitic Jaeger and Glaucous, Glaucous-winged and Thayer's Gulls. The lake can be viewed from Parc Legasse at the northeast corner of the town or along portions of the road which skirts the eastern edge of the lake. Aspen forests to the south of the lake contain birds typical of parkland. The only record of Summer Tanager for the province was found here; Black-billed Cuckoos have been recorded in years when tent caterpillars were plentiful. A number of other lakes in the area can be productive for shorebirds; lakes such as Lower Therien Lake have even produced Ruff, but most are not easily accessible to the general public. In the area surrounding St. Paul, small numbers of Sedge Wren and Nelson's Sharp-tailed Sparrow can be found if you locate grass or sedge fens with scattered willows. Connecticut Warbler and Great Crested Flycatcher are seen east of St. Paul closer to Kehiwin Lake. Try the first 3 km on the Shamrock Valley road north of Highway 28 approximately 15 km east of St. Paul. In the winter the occasional Gyrfalcon and Northern Hawk Owl are recorded in the area.

RICHARD KLAUKE

Lac La Biche and Sir Winston Churchill Provincial Park

East and north of Lac La Biche in north-central Alberta there is a rich diversity of boreal habitats, including spruce forests, abundant lakes, fen and bog systems, south-facing open slopes and ravines with aspen. This is an excellent location for numerous summer resident boreal birds and migrants which utilize the lakes for staging to and from their northern breeding grounds. Over 250 species have been reported.

From Edmonton, drive north on Highway 2 to Athabasca, then east on Highway 55 to Lac La Biche (a total of 220 paved kilometres from Edmonton), where all services are available. Adequate camping facilities occur at nearby Sir Winston Churchill Provincial Park.

Information is available from the Lac La Biche Birding Society (P.O. Box 1270, Lac La Biche, Alberta T0A 2C0), the Lac La Biche tourism booth (on Highway 55 at the west end of town) and the regional office of Alberta Recreation and Parks, and Fish and Wildlife located in the Provincial Building off Beaver Hill Road on the east side of town. A bird checklist is available for Sir Winston Churchill Provincial Park, which is being updated. New bird-finding guides for Sir Winston and nearby Lakeland Provincial Park and Provincial Recreation Area are in preparation.

Birding Features

The larger lakes in this area support diving ducks, such as Common Goldeneye, Lesser Scaup and White-winged Scoter. Surface-feeding ducks, such as teals, Mallard and American Wigeon, are also common in the bays and on the smaller water bodies. In May and June, and August and September, these water bodies are important staging areas for hundreds of migrating water birds. Lac La Biche, Alberta's seventh largest lake, and Sir Winston Churchill Provincial Park are the recommended spots (the former for water birds and the latter for land birds, including boreal warblers – 23 species of which have been found). For other sites, ask the staff at the park.

WAYNE NORDSTROM
Revised by Richard Thomas

Calling Lake

A two-hour drive from Edmonton, the area sits in boreal mixed-wood forest and boasts some of the highest species counts of any North American Breeding Bird Survey routes. Peak activity occurs in June, during the breeding season. April-May has waves of migrants passing through. Calling Lake itself is 138 km² in size, with a maximum depth of 18.3 m, and is well known in the sport fishing community for its northern pike and walleye. An American White Pelican colony occurs at the north end of the lake, accessible only by boat.

Head north from Edmonton on Highway 2, 145 km to Athabasca. From there, follow Secondary Highway 813 farther north for about 65 km. The most accessible birding area is Calling Lake Provincial Park. The lakeshore can be approached from the park's day-use area. The sandy, pebbled shoreline provides easy walking to see waterfowl and shorebirds. A trail heads west from the campground, through a forest of varying age and composition, where many boreal birds may be observed. Another trail can be accessed 1 km north of the park, across from the Trailer Inn. This route passes through Jack Pine sand dunes and mature mixed-wood forest.

The park provides a good base for day trips, with 25 campsites. The campground is open from the first of May through Labour Day (early September). Groceries and camp supplies are available at the Moosehorn Market, 7 km north in the hamlet of Calling Lake. Be sure to stop at the Calling River outflow and explore the surrounding wetlands.

In dry weather and with a good vehicle, drive 2 km south of the park and head west on the "1000 Road" for a great birding experience. This road leads into a study area, where researchers have been examining the effects of forest harvesting on the resident winter and breeding bird communities. If the road is dry, you can travel at least 40 km. If road conditions are not so favourable, there are still many good birding opportunities to be had within an easy hike off the highway.

The Rock Island Fire Tower Road, located approximately 9 km north of Calling Lake, is usually in better condition than the 1000 Road and provides access to many of the same habitats. Stop at the Calling River inflow and look for Pelican flying over in late afternoon and evening. On this sideroad, stop and walk down some of the seismic trails or roads or pipeline rights-of-way for several kilometres to find old-growth aspen or White Spruce-dominated forest, Black Spruce bogs, sedge willow fens, pockets of Jack Pine, as well as recent cuts and regenerating forest. If walking, make sure you have a compass and first-aid kit. Be aware that Black Bears abound.

A number of scientific publications have been written on this area highlighting research. For more information, contact Dr. F. Schmiegelow, Department of Renewable Resources, University of Alberta, Edmonton T6G 2H1.

Birding Features

The boreal forest in winter supports a small but diverse resident bird community. Days are short, and often very cold, but observers, on a sunny afternoon, may be rewarded with up to five species of woodpecker (Hairy, Downy, Black-backed, Three-toed and Pileated), flocks of Common Redpolls, Red Crossbills, Pine Grosbeaks, Spruce and Ruffed Grouse, and roadside encounters with Snow Bunting and Great Gray Owl. By late winter, look for Lapland Longspur in roadside open areas, Northern Shrike perched in a remnant snag in recent clearcuts, and Northern Hawk Owl in the extensive, open Black Spruce stands. After dusk, listen for owls: Barred, Northern Saw-Whet, Boreal, Great Gray, Great Horned, and Northern Hawk Owls. Even Northern Pygmy-Owls occur in the area.

From mid- to late April, watch for waves of migrating waterfowl and shorebirds, flocks of Greater White-fronted, Snow and Canada Geese, Sandhill Cranes and Tundra Swans. Red-breasted Merganser and Oldsquaw can also be observed. Bald Eagles show up too on snags. Watch the shores for Sanderling;

Short-billed Dowitcher; Spotted, Least and Semipalmated Sandpipers; American Golden-Plover and Black-bellied Plover; and Ruddy Turnstone.

In late May and June, in the forest, find (in order of abundance) Tennessee Warbler; Ovenbird; Red-eyed Vireo; Least Flycatcher; Mourning, Black-throated Green and Connecticut Warblers; and American Redstart. The much sought-after Connecticut Warbler is found in mature aspen stands. Sightings of Western Tanager, Rose-breasted Grosbeak, Swainson's and Hermit Thrushes, Winter Wren, Blue-headed and Philadelphia Vireos are also a good bet. Seek out the older, White Spruce dominated stands for glimpses and the songs of Bay-breasted, Cape May and Blackburnian Warblers. In the lower branches find Magnolia Warbler.

A stroll through one of the numerous Black Spruce bogs will yield Dark-eyed Junco, Gray Jay, Ruby-crowned Kinglet, and possibly Olive-sided Flycatcher, Palm Warbler, Black-backed Woodpecker and Spruce Grouse. Extensive wetlands are often interspersed with these stands and some open areas, supporting Common Yellowthroat; Sora; Common Snipe; Wilson's Warbler; Yellow-bellied, Alder and Willow Flycatchers; Greater and Lesser Yellowlegs; and Marsh Wrens. Some open areas and clearcuts have Le Conte's, Savannah, Clay-colored, Lincoln's and Song Sparrows.

Raptors to be found include regular sightings of Red-tailed and Broad-winged Hawks (many dark-phased), Northern Harrier and Osprey (the latter two along lakeshores and open marshes). Northern Goshawk and Cooper's and Sharp-shinned Hawk can also be found here in reasonable numbers.

Among the more unusual sightings for this region are Lark Sparrow, Varied Thrush, Harris's Sparrow (during migration), Mountain Bluebird, Say's Phoebe, Calliope Hummingbird, Gray Catbird, Northern Pygmy-Owl and Sharp-tailed Grouse.

ROGER BROWN AND FIONA SCHMIEGELOW

St. Albert – Big Lake

St. Albert is about 15 minutes north of Edmonton on Highway 2. St. Albert has on its doorstep Big Lake to the west and River Lot 56 Natural Area to the east. The Sturgeon River and its Red Willow Trail connect the two with trails along the river. Big Lake has been proclaimed an Alberta Special Place and is being considered as a candidate as an Important Bird Area for Canada. At the outlet from Big Lake, a local environmental group called BLESS (Big Lake Environmental Support Society) has constructed a viewing platform and a shelter. The platform may be reached by walking from the south end of Riel Drive (park at the Canoe and Kayak Club or the Soccer Club) or from the BLESS shelter accessed from Rodeo Drive and the R.V. Park/Rodeo Grounds.

Viewing opportunities are particularly good in early spring and late fall when migrating waterfowl concentrate on a relatively small area of open water. In summer, views tend to be more distant, although the adjoining storm-water lagoon (just south of the viewing platform) usually holds a variety of species within viewing range. Most local species of waterfowl and raptors are encountered here during the course of the year, while sparrows frequent the brushy edges of the trail. Big Lake is an important spring staging area for ducks, geese and swans, while Sandhill Cranes pass high overhead in large numbers in both spring and fall.

A recent viewing development on the north shore of Big Lake potentially offers the best opportunity for sighting rarities. The St. Albert Rotary Club and Ducks Unlimited have cooperated in setting up an interpretive trail which ventures out into the Big Lake marshes and half-circles a shallow lagoon. Access is off Meadowview Road, approximately 7 km west of the St. Albert Grain Elevators (look for roadside signs). Already, it has proven one of the best sites locally for viewing migrating arctic shorebirds while sightings of hunting Peregrine Falcons (breeding on buildings and structures in Edmonton) are frequent.

A White Spruce wood lot, 1.5 km west of the grain elevators on the south side of Meadowview Road, is a good area for winter residents and migratory warblers.

At the other end of Red Willow Park, accessed from the Kingswood Day Use Area (off Sturgeon Road), River Lot 56 is a mixed aspen wood lot alongside the Sturgeon River. Careful early-morning listening can be rewarded by good numbers of boreal warblers and sparrows during migration. Similar sightings may also be made by walking the trails in the vicinity of Lacombe Park Lake (accessed off McKenney Avenue). In both cases, migrants appear to "funnel" along watercourses or follow small ravines and shelterbelts as they slip through on migration.

All services are readily available in both St. Albert and Edmonton.

Birding Features

Big Lake is considered one of the 10 best staging areas in Alberta. Spring and fall, see large numbers of Canada Geese, Mallards, Northern Pintails, American Wigeons, Green-winged and Blue-winged Teals, Canvasbacks and Lesser Scaups. It is also a good place to look for the rarer Greater Scaup, which can often be seen with the earliest spring arrivals in April. Tundra Swans congregate in the thousands in migration, and colonies of Eared Grebes nest throughout the lake. The west end of the lake supports very large colonies of Franklin's Gulls, Black Terns and Forster's Terns. The adjoining storm-water lagoon at the southeast corner of the lake sees Common Loon, Common Merganser, White-winged and occasionally Surf Scoters, Double-crested Cormorant, Red-necked Grebe and, in the fall, Hooded Merganser along with the more common waterfowl. From the viewing platform, a careful search of the reed beds on the lake will often turn up several Pied-billed Grebes. The damp sedge meadows to the east of the lagoon often produce both Le Conte's and Nelson's Sharp-tailed Sparrows.

The interpretive trail on the north shore of Big Lake gets a wide variety of ducks and shorebirds in migration and has the potential of turning up rarities. Nesting shorebirds include the usual prairie birds such as Killdeer, Common Snipe, Willet, Marbled Godwit, American Avocet and Wilson's Phalarope. The marsh also has nesting Le Conte's and Nelson's Sharp-tailed Sparrows. Northern Harrier regularly quarters the marsh and Peregrine Falcon hunts the shorebirds and ducks. In fall Short-eared Owls course the area, as do Snowy Owls in winter.

The spruce lot has resident Great Horned Owls and in winter has good numbers of Black-capped and Boreal Chickadees, Red-breasted and White-breasted Nuthatches, Pine Siskin and Hairy, Downy, and occasionally Three-toed and Black-backed Woodpeckers. In years when they are around, this is a good place to find White-winged and Red Crossbills. River Lot 56 on the east side of town is particularly good for migrating warblers and sparrows, both in spring and fall. In summer it has resident Great Horned Owl and woodpeckers, including an occasional Three-toed or Black-backed.

ALLAN HINGSTON AND PETER DEMULDER

Edmonton

Edmonton, the capital of Alberta, straddles the North Saskatchewan River valley. The south-facing slopes of the river bank contain some prairie vegetation, while the north-facing ones have boreal forests. Several deep ravines containing a mixture of Trembling Aspen and White Spruce cut through the city. About 100 pairs of Merlins nesting in the Greater Edmonton Area (including St. Alberta and Sherwood Park) make for the highest density of this species known in the world.

Edmonton began as a fur-trading post in 1795. Settlement started in 1870. With the arrival of the railroad in 1891, agriculture became the main business. Oil was discovered just south of Edmonton, at Leduc, in 1946. Edmonton then became the field headquarters of the oil industry. Today Edmonton and the nearby dormitory communities have about 890,000 people. Of these, nearly two-thirds are relative newcomers or were born after the discovery of oil – a city of young, aggressive people!

Several national and international airlines service Edmonton. Buses come from both east and west on Highway 16 and south from Calgary on Highway 2. Trains arrive from Calgary on the main CPR line. Hotels and motels are spread throughout the city, but mainly on the south side on Highway 2 and west side on Highway 16. A campground is found at Rainbow Valley, off the Whitemud Freeway, in the southwest sector. Provincial highway campsites are placed on the east side along Highways 16 and 14, and on the west end along Highway 16. There are several hospitals, with the university the main research, patient and outpatient centre.

The Edmonton Natural History Club has published several books on the natural history of the city. These include *Nature Walks and Sunday Drives Around Edmonton*, by H. Saley, H. Stelfox and D. Ealey (1995) and *A Winter Birding Guide for the Edmonton Region*, by H. Stelfox and C. Fisher (1998). A checklist for the Whitemud Creek Ravine is available. For copies or help contact the John Janzen Nature Centre, P.O. Box 2359, Edmonton, Alberta T5J 2R7; phone (780) 496-2910, or look in any of the major bookstores. The Edmonton Natural History Club and the Edmonton Bird Club offer various field trips throughout the year; those interested in participating can find the trips listed at http://www.connect.ab.ca/~snowyowl/nn.htm

Birding Features

The city has several good birding spots. The ravines are the best places, with Whitemud Creek the outstanding spot for diversity and numbers of birds. Two easy access points are near the mouth, where Fox Drive crosses the creek, and at Rainbow Valley, where Whitemud Drive passes over the creek. From Rainbow Valley one can walk either upstream or downstream. A number of city buses provide access to these locations. Other city ravines contain fewer birds but are still often very good. Check the city map for locations.

The woodlands along the river banks serve as major stopover sites during migration. The north-south alignment of Whitemud Creek Ravine funnels many birds through, particularly in the fall. The area below the University of Alberta on the south side of the river is another good spot for fall migrants, often producing a dozen or so warblers in a morning, including such rarities as the Chestnut-sided. The numerous fruiting trees planted in the city, mainly Mountain Ash and small crabapples, attract thousands of overwintering Bohemian Waxwings. In winter the Waxwings are the favourite prey of Merlins.

Spring begins in late February, with Great Horned Owls on eggs in the Whitemud Valley. Various waterfowl and occasional grebes turn up on the river as it breaks up in March or April. Golden and the more common Bald Eagle use the river as a main route on their way to nesting territories. Gulls start congregating on the river in late March. Juncos and sparrows move through by mid-April. The main migration of land birds takes place in mid-May. Watch for flycatchers, thrushes, vireos and warblers.

A number of wetlands can be found within city limits, but probably the best is the Edcon Ponds on the corner of 170th Street and 137th Avenue. Here spring migration can produce a variety of waterfowl, grebes and shorebirds and even an occasional rarity like Snowy Egret. From late May to mid-July, some ducks, including Blue-winged Teal, Common Goldeneye and Mallard, are around. They nest in the less frequented parts of Whitemud Creek Ravine, as occasionally does the Common Merganser. For some years, Peregrine Falcons have been released in the city from captive research stock. The first pair of these now-wild birds raised young on a shelf placed on a high-rise building in the downtown core in 1981. In 1999 the downtown pair was retrofitted with satellite transmitters, which will permit researchers to continuously follow their whereabouts. At least three (occasionally four) pairs of Peregrine Falcons are now in various locations throughout the city, making Edmonton the Peregrine Falcon capital of Canada. The pair nesting on the Clinical Science Building on the University of Alberta campus can easily be observed from the picnic area on the east side of the Mackenzie Health Science Centre (best in the morning; in the spring; or when young are in the nest in August).

Merlins raise young in old magpie or crow nests throughout the city, in most of the larger developed and manicured parks, in the main cemeteries, and all along the river valley and ravines. American Kestrel nests at several additional sites in the city. In open fields around the edges of the city, one can find Red-tailed and Swainson's Hawks and Northern Harriers. Great Horned and even a few Northern Saw-whet Owls nest in various ravines.

Common Nighthawk nests on the roofs of downtown buildings and a few flat-topped suburban homes, although not as commonly as in the past. A variety of land birds rear their young in the ravines and city parks. These include Cooper's Hawk; Belted Kingfisher; Hairy, Downy and Pileated Woodpeckers; Least Flycatcher; Eastern Phoebe; Western Wood-Pewee; Black-capped Chickadee; Ruby-crowned Kinglet; and, more recently, Common Raven. The Purple Martin is near the northern limits of its breeding range. Black-billed Magpie existed in small numbers until the late 1950s, when their numbers exploded. Today these birds are very common. Edmonton has the distinction of having magpies whose black plumage is replaced by grey. The occurrence of these dilute magpies goes back at least 50 years. Both White-breasted and Red-breasted Nuthatches nest in the city. The White-breasted first arrived from the southeast in the mid-1950s. Other birds to watch for as they raise nestlings are the Cedar Waxwing, Gray Catbird, Veery, Red-eyed and Warbling Vireos, Yellow and Mourning Warblers, Ovenbird, Pine Siskin, and several sparrows, including White-throated, Chipping, Song and Clay-colored, and Dark-eyed Junco. The Western Tanager is easily found in Whitemud Ravine, together with Purple Finch and the occasional Boreal Chickadee and Rose-breasted Grosbeak.

From early August through October, many water birds are on the river. Both species of eagle move through going west along the valley. Huge flocks of Sandhill Cranes pass over in September. The movement of land birds, including some of the rarer warblers, is spectacular in August, particularly in

Great Horned Owl

Black-billed Magpie

Whitemud, and below the University of Alberta on the south side of the river between Groat Road Bridge and the High Level Bridge. In September flocks of sparrows move through the city, including some of the more unusual ones such as Harris's.

In winter, fewer species of birds are around Edmonton (the maximum record for a single year is 57 on the Christmas Bird Count, but as of 1997 the total number of species recorded was 108). Mallard, Common Goldeneye and the occasional Common Merganser stay on the open water below the 105th Street Bridge and nearby Rossdale Power Plant. Even larger concentrations of ducks congregate on the ice-free water between the Goldbar and Clover Bar Water Treatment Plants in east-central Edmonton. These have been known to attract good concentrations of Bald Eagles (up to 15) and Gyrfalcons (up to 5) from November to December some winters. Good views of Gyrfalcon kills may be made at a farming operation at the intersection of Highways 16 and 21, where ducks attracted to silage fed to cattle fall prey to these majestic birds. Merlins successfully pursue the thousands of Bohemian Waxwings. The occasional Northern Saw-whet and Snowy Owl enters the city. The Three-toed and, less commonly, Black-backed Woodpeckers spend the winter in the ravines. Whitemud Park is one of the best places in Alberta to look for both in winter. Another good area lies north towards Bon Accord, alongside roads in "islands" of boreal forest among open fields. Boreal Chickadees move into the western ravines when the snow flies. The White-breasted and, less commonly, Red-breasted Nuthatches are at feeders. Brown Creepers are around but uncommon. Golden-crowned Kinglets are often found on the university campus. Bohemian Waxwing numbers have been over 25,000! Common and Hoary Redpolls are present, as are Evening and Pine Grosbeaks, and Red and White-winged Crossbills. Rarities, but still seen fairly regularly in winter, are Townsend's Solitaire, Varied Thrush, Gray-crowned Rosy-Finch and Steller's Jay. The grain elevator on the north side of the Yellowhead Highway between 127 and 142 Streets has, in recent years, been excellent for overwintering Gyrfalcon and Prairie Falcon. Probably the best observation point is the parking lot of Cronkhite Supply at 13030 Yellowhead Trail at the south end of the grain terminal.

Thousands of gulls are found from mid-April to the end of October at the Clover Bar disposal site. Ring-billed and California are the most numerous, with Herring and Franklin's present in smaller numbers. Early morning, before the garbage trucks arrive, is the best time. The site is located on the east side of the city, east of the Clover Bar bridge, north on 1st Street for about 3.2 km to the spot. Make sure to stop at the gate to ask permission to enter specifically for birding purposes. Rarities like Glaucous, Iceland, Glaucous-winged, Mew and Thayer's Gulls have been recorded during migration, but it usually takes some dedicated searching to find any of them.

TERRY THORMIN
Revised by Terry Thormin and Jocelyn Hudon

Elk Island National Park

The park consists of lower boreal mixed-wood forest, interspersed with groves of aspen and grasslands to the south, laid on a rich mosaic of wetlands. It is encircled by farmland, providing a variety of habitats for over 250 species of birds. The park is surrounded by a 2.4 m page wire fence and is the home of a large herd of Plains Bison, another of Wood Bison and numerous Elk (Wapiti), White-tailed and Mule Deer, Moose and Coyote. Beavers can be found throughout the park.

It was established in 1899 when land was set aside as a federal timber reserve. In 1906, the northern part became an Elk preserve. Since then, the descendants of these initial mammals have never been crossed with other subspecies. Thus they are one of the few pure herds of Elk in existence. The park also played a key role in preserving and housing the last herd of Plains Bison left in existence in those early years. In the mid-1960s one of the last two remaining small herds of the largest North American mammal, the Wood Bison, was transferred to Elk Island.

The 194 km² park lies 35 km east of Edmonton on Highway 16. The Greyhound bus will stop at the south gate on the highway, if you ask. Another company also runs a bus from Edmonton through Lamont, a town 5 km from the north gate. There is an extensive system of hiking trails through rolling

country, in the northern two-thirds of the park. These trails and other amenities are illustrated on the park map-brochure, which is available from the information centre.

A campground is open in summer on a first-come basis. A more primitive
group tenting area is provided for nonprofit organizations by reservation.
Winter campers may use the boat launch area and the group tenting site.
Commercial accommodation and other services may be obtained in
Edmonton; Fort Saskatchewan, 25 km northwest; or Lamont, 5 km north.

Information on the park, including a bird checklist, is available from The
Superintendent, Elk Island National Park, Site 4, R.R. 1, Fort Saskatchewan,
Alberta T8L 2N7; phone (780) 992-2950. Park naturalists can assist you
throughout the year at the main headquarters, 16 km north of the main gate
on Highway 16. Reference books include *Island Forest Year: Elk Island National
Park*, by D. E. Griffiths (Edmonton: U. of A. Press, 1979), *Walk on the Wild
Side: An All-Season Trail Guide*, by Jean Burgess (Fort Saskatchewan: Friends of
Elk Island Society, 1986), and *Finding Birds in Elk Island National Park*, by Judith
Cornish (Friends of Elk Island Society, 1988).

Birding Features

The park, surrounded by grain and cattle farms, contains a variety of habitats,
some of which normally are found only much farther west and north. The
interspersion of boreal forests and aspen parkland provides opportunities to
birdwatch in White Spruce groves, Trembling Aspen clones, mixed-wood
forests, Black Spruce bogs, wetlands, eutrophic lakes and man-made grass
meadows. During the breeding season see Common Loon; five of the six
Alberta grebe species; Black-crowned Night-Heron and Great Blue Heron;
Double-crested Cormorant and American White Pelican; almost all the ducks
of the prairies; Great Horned and Great Gray Owls, and possibly Barred Owl.
Elk Island is one of the few places locally to find Sedge Wrens, as this is near
their northern limit.

Some common forest breeding birds include Yellow, Connecticut and
Tennessee Warblers; Ovenbird; Common Yellowthroat; Red-eyed Vireo;
Baltimore Oriole; and Hermit Thrush. You can also see some of the park's
breeding flycatchers such as Least and Alder, and the elusive Great Crested and
Olive-sided Flycatchers. The park has a rich diversity of breeding sparrows
such as the White-throated, Clay-colored, Chipping, Le Conte's, Lincoln's,
Savannah, Song and Nelson's Sharp-tailed. Northern Rough-winged Swallow
reaches its northern limits here.

During fall and winter, look for Common Raven, Northern Goshawk,
Ruffed Grouse, Great Horned Owl, both Boreal and Northern Saw-whet
Owls, Northern Hawk Owl, both three-toed woodpeckers, Boreal and Black-
capped Chickadees, Evening and Pine Grosbeaks, Brown Creeper and
Golden-crowned Kinglet, and possibly Bald and Golden Eagles.

During spring (late April to early June) and fall (August and September)
migration, the numerous water bodies attract and hold a large number of water
birds with some shorebirds. The mix of woodlands also makes the park an

excellent source of land birds passing through. Look for American Tree and White-crowned Sparrows, particularly in early spring.

The best water-bird locality is the northwest end of Astotin Lake, accessible by trail and canoe. Astotin Lake is one of a very few areas outside of the mountains where Barrow's Goldeneyes breed. A few Trumpeter Swans return annually to the park and Beaverhills area as part of a restoration project coordinated by the Canadian Wildlife Service and Parks Canada. The interspersed spruce and aspen north and northeast of the park's recreation area are the best spots for land birds.

BILL FISHER AND STAFF OF ELK ISLAND NATIONAL PARK
Revised by Norm Cool, Conservation Biologist,
Elk Island National Park and Bob Carroll

Beaverhill Lake

Hosting huge concentrations of waterfowl and shorebirds each spring and fall, this large shallow body of water serves as a launching pad for arctic birds. Over 280 species have been reported here. You can experience wave upon wave of Canada, Snow and Greater White-fronted Geese passing overhead, while nearby fields are covered with tens of thousands of them. Over 40 species of shorebirds have been recorded at the lake. The first confirmed record of nesting Black-necked Stilts in Canada was a pair at Beaverhill Lake. Peregrine Falcon can be observed during migration, hunting shorebirds and waterfowl. Early spring and late fall bring tens of thousands of Tundra Swans.

The water level at Beaverhill Lake (sometimes called Beaverhills Lake) has fluctuated from lows in the mid-1800s when buffalo walked across the dry bed, to highs in the early 1900s when cartloads of suckers and Northern Pike were harvested. This perpetual interplay of high and low water levels is the key to creating mudflats, which provide large food supplies for birdlife. Early ornithologists made major collections here, particularly in the 1920s.

With the constant change in water level, local farmers pressed for drainage and/or damming. Finally, in 1972, a bay at the southeast corner was dammed off by Ducks Unlimited to create Robert Lister Lake. This small body of water now provides excellent breeding habitat for birds.

The status of the Crown land around the lake has changed from a public shooting ground in 1925 to a national nature viewpoint by the Canadian Nature Federation in 1981. It is now also designated as a Ramsar site, internationally recognized as a special place for migratory birds.

The approximately 16×12 km lake lies about 65 km east of Edmonton between Highways 14 and 16. An access map is found on the Web at http://www.connect.ab.ca/~snowyowl/map.htm or can be obtained from the John Janzen Nature Centre in Edmonton (see above). From Highway 14 turn north into Tofield and then sharply east just across the railway tracks to gain access to two different locations. The first, about 4 km from town, is Francis Viewpoint. A sign marks the road going north to a parking area, and from there it is an easy walk to the blind on the shore. Another 4 km along the

Willet

same road going east, you arrive at a parking lot north of the road and a trail that goes in past a marsh to the Natural Area at the southeast end of the lake. This is where the Beaverhill Bird Observatory is located at the edge of the woods (Web site: http://www.ualberta.ca/~jduxbury/BBO/bbopage.htm). To reach the east shore, proceed east from Tofield for 6.4 km; south 1.6 km and east around the marsh for 4 km; north 1.6 km and then east 5.6 km; north 6.4 km and west to the end of the trail. Walk down to the shore. Another east access point lies 3.2 km north of the above west turn into the lake. The north end of the lake is reached from Highway 16, 20 km east of the main entrance to Elk Island National Park. To reach this north end, drive south from Highway 16, 3.2 km to the stone house and either hike or drive south on the primitive trail to the lake. The northwest end is reached 3.2 km west of the above stone house corner and 3.2 km south. The northwest side is the spot where we have watched wave after wave of geese leaving the lake to feed on nearby fields. The west side may be approached by driving 8 km north of Tofield and then east about 2 km to the end of the trail. All trails leading down and along the lakeshore are often not passable by car in early spring or after heavy rain.

The town of Tofield, with help from the Canadian Wildlife Service and the birding community, holds a Snow Goose Festival every year on the third weekend of April (Web site: http://www.tcnap.tofield.ab.ca/snowgoos.htm). This includes regular bus trips out to see the thousands of Snow Geese and other birds present at this time. For more information, contact the Beaverhill Lake Nature Centre in Tofield at (780) 662-3191.

The Greyhound bus goes through Tofield from Edmonton daily. A taxi may be rented in town to drive you out the 4 km to the south end of the lake.

All services are available in Tofield or Edmonton. Provincial roadside camp-sites are located on both Highway 14 to the south and Highway 16 to the north of the lake.

Reference material includes a superb book with lots of illustrations, *Prairie Water, Wildlife at Beaverhills Lake, Alberta,* by Dick Dekker (Edmonton: U. of A. Press, 1998). Much of the ornithological history of the lake has been doc-umented in the book *The Birds and Birders of Beaverhill Lakes,* by R. Lister (Edmonton: Edmonton Bird Club, 1979). The Edmonton Natural History Club's publication *Nature Walks and Sunday Drives Round Edmonton* (see above) contains a write-up on Beaverhill Lake. A Web site on the birds of Beaverhill Lake can be found at http://www.connect.ab.ca/~snowyowl/beaver~1.htm, and the list of species observed at Beaverhill Lake is found at http://www.connect.ab.ca/~snowyowl/checklist.htm

Birding Features

This shallow lake, surrounded by grassy and often wooded shorelines, with a fluctuating water level, is a major feeding and staging area for waterfowl and shorebirds. Years of high water kill off the encroaching vegetation, widening the mudflats in late summer as the water drops. High water also inundates the colony of cormorants and pelicans. Upon the return of low water levels, these island nesters come back, as do other birds such as American Avocet, which feeds and nests on the extensive mudflats during the summer.

Wind is also a major factor in the creation and maintenance of shorebird habitat. The prevailing winds from the northwest push the shallow waters up on the south end of the lake. This almost tidal action causes alternate flooding and drying of the shoreline, enhancing the mudflats.

The third factor important to the massive population of shorebirds is food – the countless midges hatching each year around mid-May. In calm periods these insects hang like low clouds, almost obstructing the view. When the wind picks up they seek shelter in the emergent and shoreline vegetation, and the shorebirds move in to feast. Dick Dekker, in an article in the *Alberta Naturalist,* reports that in 1978 he estimated Pectoral Sandpipers in excess of 10,000 and 1500 Buff-breasted Sandpipers congregated in fields on the east side. Nearby pastures held 300 Black-bellied Plovers, 200 Red Knots and 150 Sanderlings. Several other species of shorebirds were also present in scattered flocks. If it is a late spring, with the midges hatching at the end of May, many sandpipers and plovers linger well into June.

This site is one of the best spots in Alberta to look for rarities. Over the years such birds as Red-throated Loon; Great and Snowy Egrets; Brant; Wood Duck; Gyrfalcon (Peregrine Falcon is regular); Snowy Plover; Surfbird; Wandering Tattler; Western and Sharp-tailed Sandpipers; Black-necked Stilt; Red Phalarope; Parasitic and Long-tailed Jaegers; Glaucous, Thayer's, Mew, Little and Sabine's Gulls; and Caspian Tern have been reported. Prairie birds that have been observed include Ferruginous Hawk, Prairie Falcon, Piping Plover, Long-billed

Curlew, Sprague's Pipit (occasional breeder), Bobolink (regular breeder), Lark Bunting, Lark Sparrow, Baird's Sparrow (occasional breeder) and McCown's and Chestnut-collared Longspurs (occasional breeders). The lake, lying near both the Pacific and Central flyways, should attract other species.

If the season is early, the first Canada Geese appear in mid-March. They are followed by Greater White-fronts and finally Snows and Tundra Swans. The Snow Geese usually build to a peak by the third week of April, when their numbers may be as high as 50,000. Early springs tend to hold birds at Beaverhill for a week or more, while in late years, these tens of thousands, often up to 100,000, move through very quickly. At the same time, ducks are building up in numbers. Rough-legged Hawks, eagles, Snowy Owls and Snow Buntings are going north. By early to mid-April the first shorebirds show up, usually the yellowlegs. The first large flocks of Lapland Longspur also appear. By the end of April all waterfowl, as well as grebes, cormorants and pelicans, will be back. Most shorebirds will also have appeared. By this time Red-tailed and Swainson's Hawks and Northern Harriers occur regularly. There is a good possibility of spotting a Peregrine Falcon or even a Prairie Falcon. During the last few days of April and early May, watch for masses of Sandhill Cranes going over in flock after flock, hour after hour. Late April and early May will often produce small numbers of Cinnamon Teals, or perhaps even a Wood Duck or Hooded Merganser. By early May, many passerines are filtering through the nearby woods. May is the shorebird month. The best spots fluctuate from year to year, depending on water levels and shoreline vegetation, or even daily, depending on wind conditions, so it is best to ask local birders for recent information before venturing forth. Before the lake is ice-free, check nearby flooded fields and wet meadows for yellowlegs, Pectoral Sandpiper, dowitchers and Hudsonian Godwit. If the spring is cold, the flocks go through in quick succession. In warm weather, with lots of food, their numbers are often large but spread out. The best seasons are those after a winter with little snow, followed by an early and warm spring. As the minimal meltwater pools in fields dry up, the birds congregate on the shore, where there is plenty of mudflat habitat. In early May, scan for groups of Hudsonian Godwits. Piping Plover and Long-billed Curlew occasionally straggle this far north. Large flocks of Red-necked Phalaropes can often be seen. In mid-May, look for the occasional flock of Ross's Geese or Smith's Longspurs. The fields on the west side are the best for longspurs. The last three weeks of May will often produce small flocks of American Golden-Plovers and Buff-breasted Sandpipers, especially in the fields just north of the north shore and in the fields along the east and west shores. This is midge time. The variety of shorebirds is surpassed only by their sheer numbers, with up to several thousands in the fields or along the shore. Examine each flock for Ruddy Turnstones, and Pectoral, Least, Semipalmated and Buff-breasted Sandpipers. This is also the time to look for Whimbrel, particularly in the fields on the west side. The shorebird migration continues into June, gradually petering out by the middle of the month.

The nesters include Killdeer, Common Snipe, Willet, Marbled Godwit,

American Avocet and Wilson's Phalarope. These species continuously call, so the symphony remains until mid- to late July. Nesting waterfowl include the normal complement of prairie-pothole species. Eared and Western Grebes also raise young. The Great Blue Heron colony lies near the north end. Small rocky islands are home to American White Pelican and Double-crested Cormorant. Several colonies of California and Ring-billed Gulls and Common Terns occur. Nesting marsh birds to ferret out include Pied-billed Grebe, Black-crowned Night-Heron, Marsh Wren, Yellow-headed and Red-winged Blackbirds and Le Conte's Sparrow. Yellow and Virginia Rails, Sedge Wren and Nelson's Sharp-tailed Sparrow are regularly reported. Try Robert Lister Lake at the southeast corner of Beaverhill Lake for these marsh species and water-fowl. Nearby open fields should be scanned for prairie birds, including Sprague's Pipit, Bobolink and Chestnut-collared Longspur.

The fall movement is considerably more prolonged than spring migration. By mid-July, the first shorebirds are back and by the end of the month most species are in. These early returnees consist of flocks of adult non- or unsuc-cessful breeders. Fall is also the best time for rarities and accidentals. By mid-August, the shorebird migration has swelled to a tide of hundreds to thousands of individuals, including yellowlegs, Pectoral Sandpiper, dowitchers, Stilt Sandpiper and many others. Dowitchers are in the greatest numbers, but a good day can produce 15 to 20 species of waders. The numbers persist into September, and even early October some years, before a gradual decline occurs. The last shorebirds are gone by early November. Mid- to late August usually sees a buildup of geese and Sandhill Crane numbers. Predatory birds, too, return to harass the shorebirds. Look for Peregrine Falcon and Parasitic Jaeger, maybe even a Long-tailed Jaeger. By early to mid-September, Tundra Swans line the shores in thousands and remain numerous until late October before diminishing in November. September is the time to study each flock of waders carefully in search of one of Canada's rarest shorebirds – the Sharp-tailed Sandpiper. During the late 70s and early 80s it was a regular visitor in numbers from one to six with most sightings just west of the dam at Robert Lister Lake, but in recent years the records have been very few. In October, check the fields for large flocks of longspurs and buntings. The south shore collects large numbers of ducks at this time, attracted by the feeding station lure programs. Scrutinize tall snags for Bald Eagle, which regularly pick off crippled ducks until after freeze-up. By early to mid-November the lake starts to freeze and most birds disappear.

In winter, try open fields and nearby woodlands. Snowy Owl can be very common, particularly in the northwest corner. A few Rough-legged Hawks are sometimes present, and there are often one or two Northern Shrikes around. Hoary Redpolls usually occur among the flocks of Common Redpolls. Snow Buntings may be fairly common. By late February to early March, the first Great Horned Owl has started to nest and spring has returned.

TERRY THORMIN
Revised by Terry Thormin

Red Deer Area

Nestled between boreal forest of the north, montane forest on the west and southern prairies, the parklands of Red Deer provide a mixture of birds. The city sits on Highway 2, midway between Calgary and Edmonton.

The settlement sprang up in 1882 as a place to ford the Red Deer River (early fur traders noted the similarity of Wapiti to European Red Deer). A stopping house was built and later fortified to serve as a barrack during the Northwest Uprising. The arrival of the railway expedited growth, and in 1913, Red Deer was incorporated as a city. Today, the local economy is driven by agriculture, petroleum and manufacturing.

All the amenities of a big city are found here. For more information, contact the Red Deer Visitor & Convention Bureau at 1-800-215-8946 or visit their Web site at http://www.visitor.red-deer.ab.ca; write them at Box 5008, Red Deer, Alberta T4N 3T4. A bird checklist for nearby Dry Island Buffalo Jump Provincial Park is available from Midland Provincial Park, P.O. Box 208, Drumheller, Alberta T0J 0Y0.

Birding Features

Numerous trails meander through the Red Deer River valley. Habitats range from marsh to meadow, to old-growth spruce forest. This diversity is most evident in the 118 ha Gaetz Lakes Sanctuary, established in 1924. Access is via the Kerry Wood Nature Centre, a 1.2 km drive or 20-minute walk north from the nearest bus stop at 55th Street and 45th Avenue. The centre provides a sanctuary checklist and other information. The two Gaetz Lakes are the remnant of an oxbow in the Red Deer River and host several Red-necked Grebe pairs and a Common Grackle colony. The mixed-wood forest includes Ruffed Grouse, Blue Jay and Boreal Chickadee. In spring, they are joined by Western Wood-Pewee, Least Flycatcher and Blue-headed Vireo, while early successional habitats become occupied by Clay-colored Sparrow and Baltimore Oriole. In some years, Olive-sided Flycatcher and Rose-breasted Grosbeak are found. The labours of Yellow-bellied Sapsucker and Pileated Woodpecker are evident. In winter, the sanctuary attracts Three-toed and Black-backed Woodpeckers, both of which frequent the south end. Common and Hoary Redpolls are other winter visitors that occur in variable numbers. A sighting of Trumpeter Swans or Gyrfalcons is possible in season.

Winding its way eastward out of the city, the Red Deer River nourishes the riparian habitat of Dry Island Buffalo Jump Provincial Park, a contrasting wilderness of prickly-pear cactus and fossil-laden badlands interspersed with marshes and fingers of boreal forest. To reach the park, drive south on Highway 2 to Highway 42, proceed east to Highway 21, continue south, and follow the signs. The park remains one of Alberta's best sites for Turkey Vultures. Although the species has nested in the area, most of the dozen or more birds that summer in the valley are thought to be nonbreeders. Baird's Sparrow and Western Meadowlark occur near the park entrance. Prairie Falcon breeds and Peregrine Falcon, having reoccupied several aeries both up- and downstream of the park, are to be expected. Badlands are home to Say's Phoebe, Mountain

Bluebird and, in some years, Rock Wren. Orange-crowned Warblers and Spotted Towhees are found. Veery is reliably located at the picnic area.

Travelling west from Red Deer you enter boreal forest and its associated fauna. Here, the Medicine River Wildlife Rehabilitation Centre maintains an interpretive trail and observation tower at Sandhill Slough. The site is accessed by taking Highway 2 south to Highway 54 and continuing west to Raven. From there, drive 4 km south and 1.5 km east. Parking and the trailhead are on the left. The marsh hosts a breeding pair of Sandhill Cranes each year. By mid-May, the birds are tending young. Their neighbours include Great Gray Owl and Yellow-headed Blackbird. Low-lying areas to the east and west support populations of Yellow Rail, Alder Flycatcher and Le Conte's, Nelson's Sharp-tailed and Swamp Sparrows. Sedge Wren is heard singing in some years. Northern Goshawks and Gray Jays are resident, while Tennessee Warblers and, occasionally, Connecticut Warblers grace the summer woodland. No trip to the marsh is complete without a tour of the rehabilitation centre's interpretive displays. Hours are from 10 A.M. to 4 P.M. daily.

JASON ROGERS

Hanna–Chinook Area

Hanna and Chinook areas are good for prairie birds. Hanna lies northeast of Drumheller, west of the intersection of Highways 9 and 36. The 1:250,000 provincial map 72 M shows the back roads in the area (available from Map Town, 10344 105 Street NW, Edmonton, Alberta, T5J 1E6; phone [780] 429-2600). Motels are available in the town of Hanna. Several small hamlets in the area such as Cereal and Youngstown also have a motel or hotel. The Bale House ([403] 578-2519), northwest of Hanna, is a bed-and-breakfast located in an area of unbroken range land. Camping facilities occur at Little Fish Lake Provincial Park about 25 km south and 10 km west of Hanna. Piping Plovers breed on this lake.

Birding Features

Loggerhead Shrike and Ferruginous Hawk are common. Sprague's Pipit, Horned Lark and Baird's Sparrow contribute to the beautiful "prairie bell" symphony which greets you early in the morning in early June. The wet areas are teaming with shorebirds and waterfowl. There is even the possibility of spotting a Burrowing Owl standing by its hole in a ground squirrel colony. In the fields just south of Hanna you might find a Grasshopper Sparrow as well as many other prairie birds.

The ponds in the park at the Sheerness Power Plant yield a variety of waterfowl. To get there travel east of Hanna on Highway 9 to Highway 36. Drive south on Highway 36 about 20 km to the power plant. Travel the back roads east and west of Highway 36 in the area of the power plant looking for birds. Caragana hedges around the farmhouses and abandoned farmsteads often contain Loggerhead Shrike. Examine the small stands of stunted aspen for nesting raptors. Upland Sandpiper can be heard giving its long "wolf whistle" from the fields. Marbled Godwit, Long-billed Curlew and Willet are also present. Fields and range land yield a variety of sparrows, including such specials as Baird's, Lark Bunting and Chestnut-collared Longspur.

Another interesting drive is west of Hanna on Highway 9 to Secondary Highway 871. Bird this road to the tiny location of Spondin about 30 km north of the highway, turn west about 12 km on Secondary Highway 586, then south to Highway 9 (the Bale House is located about 6 km north of Highway 586 on Secondary Highway 872).

Sharp-tailed Grouse can be found in the area. If you travel from Hanna to Chinook down Highway 9, they can often be heard at dawn just off the highway on the road going south from Chinook. Birding the road that intersects Highway 9, 1.6 km west of Chinook, can yield many prairie birds, including McCown's Longspur. The longspurs are found in the rangeland 30 to 40 km south of Highway 9.

Waterbirds present are many such as Cinnamon Teal and Forster's Tern. Raptors include Ferruginous Hawk. Nesting shorebirds are Wilson's Phalarope and Spotted Sandpiper. Both Eastern and Western Kingbirds occur, as does Brown Thrasher.

BARB AND JIM BECK

Dinosaur Provincial Park

Dinosaur Provincial Park has the richest beds of dinosaur fossils in North America. Over 600 museum-quality specimens of these reptiles and other Late Cretaceous vertebrates have been collected from the park in the last 100 years. These fossils may be seen in major museums throughout the world, including the world-class Royal Tyrrell Museum in Drumheller, Alberta. The park also contains the largest area of classical Badlands terrain in Canada. About 160 species of birds have been reported to date and many of them nest regularly in the park. Look for a great variety of prairie and woodland birds, three species of cactus, sages, greasewood and in-situ dinosaur bones, which are protected. Commonly observed mammals include Mule Deer and Cottontail Rabbit.

The park, established in 1955, became a UNESCO World Heritage Site in 1979. Located 48 km north and east of Brooks, which in turn is 186 km southeast of Calgary on the Trans-Canada Highway, the park has a major visitor complex. A loop road and five self-guiding interpretive trails may be used to explore the core area of the park. Access to the large natural preserve is allowed only if visitors are accompanied by a park interpreter. Tours may be reserved in advance by calling (403) 378-4344 from May 1 to August 31, Monday to Friday, 9 A.M. to noon and 1 to 4 P.M. MST.

Visitor accommodation within the park consists of a partially serviced campground and a group camp area. Reservations may be made at (403) 378-3700. Motels, bed-and-breakfasts and hotels are available locally around Patricia, 16 km southwest of the park, Duchess and Brooks. Groceries and gasoline are available at Patricia or Brooks. Information on the park, including a bird checklist and a park newspaper, is available from Dinosaur Provincial Park, Box 60, Patricia, Alberta T0J 2K0; phone (403) 378-4342. Additional information on bird-finding in Dinosaur Provincial Park appears in *A*

Birdfinding Guide to the Calgary Region, by Joan F. McDonald (editor) (Calgary Field Naturalists' Society, 1993, pp. 143–148).

Birding Features

The first view of Dinosaur Provincial Park is dramatic, with gently rolling prairie suddenly dropping off into the Red Deer River valley, with badlands featuring hoodoos, gorges, mesas and coulees. At least 14 types of habitat for birds are within the park. About 10% of the 73 km² is prairie, 75% badlands and 15% riparian. The riparian habitat supports the greatest variety of birds. Breeding birds in the park are mainly those with an eastern and southern affinity. Relatively few northern and western species occur. The mean annual rainfall is 350 mm, most of which falls as rain from May to September; it is a semi-desert!

The variety of microhabitats provides the visitor, during the breeding season from May to early August, with opportunities to see Canada Geese nesting on cliffs or with young in the water and a few ducks, Great Blue Heron, American White Pelican and Spotted Sandpiper near the river. Raptors that nest in the park or come to feed include American Kestrel, Golden Eagle, Prairie Falcon and Great Horned Owl. Occasionally Red-tailed, Swainson's and Ferruginous Hawks are seen soaring over the badlands. In the badlands Mountain Bluebird, Say's Phoebe, Rock Wren and Common Nighthawk may be found nesting. Prairie birds include Sharp-tailed Grouse, Long-billed Curlew, Horned Lark, Chestnut-collared Longspur and Vesper Sparrow. In the cottonwood flats of the riparian habitat one may see Brown Thrasher, Spotted Towhee, Yellow-breasted Chat, Common Yellowthroat, Northern Flicker, sapsuckers and roosting Common Nighthawk. On sagebrush flats common sightings include Brewer's, Clay-colored and Lark Sparrows, Western Meadowlark, Common Grackle, Brown-headed Cowbird and Brewer's Blackbird.

During spring and early fall the riparian habitat is an excellent area in which to view migrating passerines and shorebirds. Look for Ruby-crowned Kinglet; American Pipit; Black-and-white, Orange-crowned and Black-throated Green Warblers; American Redstart; White-crowned, White-throated, Harris's and Lincoln's Sparrows.

NORBERT KONDLA
Revised by Hilary Tarrant

Lake Newell and Kinbrook Island Provincial Park

Lake Newell, the largest body of water in southeastern Alberta, was created in 1912. The lake, its shore sporadically lined with poplars and willows, numerous nearby irrigation ditches and occasional homesteads with planted trees, and the surrounding dry mixed-grass prairie provide a major stopover area for thousands of migrating waterfowl and are home to hundreds of upland birds. An added attraction is the excellent lake whitefish and Northern Pike fishing which can be done in spare moments away from birdwatching.

The lake was created as part of a major irrigation project by the Canadian Pacific Railway to attract settlers to the area. Settlers started to come to the area from 1915 to 1919. By the early 1930s, these pioneers were in financial difficulties. In 1935, the entire area was transferred to a board of trustees, composed of local farmers, and it is now the Eastern Irrigation District.

Kinbrook Island Provincial Park (501 ha) lies on the eastern shore of Lake Newell and is 16 km south of Brooks off Secondary Highway 873. Brooks is 186 km southeast of Calgary on Highway 1. Greyhound buses from points east and west stop daily at Brooks, where there are services needed by travellers.

Kinbrook Island Park campground is a first-come, first-served operation. For more information about the park, call (403) 362-2962. Tillebrook Provincial Park lies 11 km southeast of Brooks off Highway 1. For more information on Tillebrook call (403) 362-4525. Some reservations are accepted at both campgrounds.

Supplementary information on bird-finding in the area appears in *A Birdfinding Guide to the Calgary Region*, by Joan F. McDonald (editor) (Calgary Field Naturalists' Society, 1993, pp. 148–151). A bird checklist for Lake Newell is available from Fish and Wildlife District Office, Box 909, Provincial Building, Brooks, Alberta T1R 1B8; phone (403) 362-1232. Ducks Unlimited has a large office complex near the downtown core, and the Eastern Irrigation District has a wildlife officer who can help visitors with local natural history inquiries.

Birding Features

The many water bodies (many man-made) in the area provide habitat for a wide variety of birds not otherwise seen in the area. A 1999 May Species Count in the Brooks/Lake Newell area turned up 151 species of birds.

The more interesting birds include migrating Common Loon and breeding Red-necked, Horned, Eared and Western Grebes. Black-crowned Night-Herons can be plentiful. Double-crested Cormorants breed from mid-April until July in large numbers (close to 1000 nests in 1998) on Pelican Island at the south end of the lake. American White Pelicans nest on the island as well but in smaller numbers (about 20 nests in 1998). This island also contains a large colony of Caspian Terns (over 70 nests in 1998!) and California Gulls (about 100 nests); Ring-billed Gulls breed at the south end of the lake as well.

Tundra Swans often stop in large numbers during spring and fall, as do most geese species. White-fronted Geese stop in large flocks on fall migration, while the Canada Goose is a common summer resident. Most duck species can be found in fairly large numbers, and raptors are just as plentiful. Swainson's appear to outnumber Red-tailed Hawks. Northern Harrier, and the occasional Ferruginous Hawk and Prairie Falcon, can also be spotted. American Kestrel, Merlin and Golden Eagle are regularly observed in the area. Burrowing Owls can be found throughout the area in small colonies. Long-billed Curlews breed in the area, as do Willet and Marbled Godwits. Black-necked Stilts appeared on the May Count (67 in total!) as did Western Sandpipers, both species of dowitchers and a large number of Black-bellied Plovers; Whimbrels also migrate through here.

Marsh Wren can be heard in the bulrushes and the Sprague's Pipit song is given continuously in high flight. Horned Lark, Chestnut-colored Longspur, even McCown's Longspur, can be spotted in the local prairie grassland. The Western Meadowlark seems to sing from every fence post and sparrows include Spotted Towhee, Chipping, Clay-colored, Brewer's, Vesper, Lark, Baird's and Grasshopper.

The planting of trees around homesteads has attracted some warblers and Mourning Doves, as well as Baltimore Oriole, American Goldfinch and Gray Catbird, usually rare on the prairies; these trees are also used by innumerable migrants. Woodpeckers are not that plentiful because of a lack of suitable wood lots – but the occasional Northern Flicker can be seen.

NORBERT KONDLA
Revised by Bob Parsons and by John Findlay,
Kinbrook Island Provincial Park

Medicine Hat

The phrase "oasis on the prairies" is often applied to Medicine Hat. This is certainly true for birders! The city of 50,000 is heavily treed, with many parks of all sizes. The South Saskatchewan River winds through "the Hat" and surrounding area, as do three creeks (Ross, Bullshead and Seven Persons). Surrounding agriculture is a mix of ranching, dryland and irrigation farming.

Birdlife in Medicine Hat is further enhanced by Cypress Hills to the southeast, irrigation district lands of the Brooks region to the west, vast tracts of native prairie to the south and the huge military base – CFB Suffield – with much native prairie to the north.

As a result, bird diversity is exceptional, and the discovery of rarities is a common occurrence. Some, like Pinyon Jay and Scott's Oriole, have yet to be 100% confirmed. Others confirmed include Eastern Screech-Owl, Red-headed and Pileated Woodpeckers, Caspian Tern and Indigo Bunting. Every year, one or more new species are added to the local checklist: Glaucous Gull, Virginia Rail and Chestnut-sided Warbler are the latest.

Altogether, over 260 species have been recorded, with 120+ confirmed as breeding. Birding is good year-round. Summer birding is excellent. Spring and fall migration, with 20 species of warblers, plus Snow Geese and other waterfowl numbering in the hundreds of thousands, is truly exciting. Winter birding is far more interesting than might be expected, thanks to open water in the river and sewage lagoons almost all winter, residential feeders and plentiful trees and shrubbery. As of 1998, 93 species had been tallied during Christmas Bird Counts!

Up-to-date information and checklists, along with interpreter-led guided tours, are available from the Police Point Park Interpretive Centre (Box 2491, Medicine Hat, Alberta T1A 8G8).

Birding Features

The South Saskatchewan River valley provides the best birding. Violet-green Swallow, Rock Wren and Say's Phoebe are abundant in the Echo Dale Regional Park area. The cliffs and badlands along the entire stretch of the river could yield Prairie Falcon, Turkey Vulture – even a pair of Bald Eagles which have nested for several years. Pelicans and Double-crested Cormorants are common on the water.

However, it is the floodplains and their associated stands of plains cottonwoods that hold the greatest interest. Tops among these is city-owned 400-acre Police Point Park, a truly exceptional site with its blend of ancient (perhaps 300 years old) and younger cottonwoods, berry bushes, dryland grasses and cacti. Wood Duck and Common Goldeneye nest regularly; close by is a large Great Blue Heron colony. Kingbirds (Eastern and Western), Brown Thrasher, Tree Swallow and Baltimore Oriole are abundant. Birding in these treed floodplains is delightful all year.

Nearby creek valleys are scattered with tangles of shrubbery, yielding Gray Catbird, Loggerhead Shrike, Lazuli Bunting, Spotted Towhee and occasional Yellow-breasted Chat. On the open prairie, Long-billed Curlew, Marbled Godwit, Ferruginous Hawk and many of the prairie sparrows (Baird's, Brewer's, Clay-colored, Savannah, Vesper, Lark, Grasshopper) along with Lark Buntings can be easily found. The older residential areas of the city, especially Riverside, the Flats, and 1st and 2nd Street SW, host a wide variety of songbirds, which attract Merlins; House Finches have recently become established in a few of the newer areas.

Several small but lively marshes occur to the south of the city, their water sustained by irrigation systems. These marshes usually require a spotting scope for best viewing. The reward is a Who's Who of prairie waterfowl, plus Sora, American Bittern, Yellow-headed Blackbird, Marsh Wren and more. Several lakes lie within 20 minutes of the city. Murray Lake to the south is the best spot for the Snow Geese migratory spectacle and for White-winged Scoter; Rattlesnake Lake (especially the south and west ends) provides good migratory shorebird viewing, as does Cavan Lake to Medicine Hat's southeast. The salt lake, Chappice, to the north has breeding Piping Plover; however, permission is needed for access.

DENNIS BARESCO

Cypress Hills Provincial Park

The Cypress Hills stand 600 m above the surrounding prairie. This oasis of forest capped with grass-covered plateau contains a combination of climatic, geologic and biological systems found nowhere else in the grasslands of western Canada. Among the 200 species of birds spotted here (98 confirmed as nesting) are Wild Turkey; the Mearn's (pink-sided) race of Dark-eyed Junco, the only place it can regularly be found in Canada; and in the Saskatchewan portion of the hills, Trumpeter Swan. Cordilleran plants and butterflies, Moose, Elk, White-tailed and Mule Deer are also present.

The Blackfeet discouraged white traders and trappers until the late 1860s, leaving this area the last refuge in southern Alberta for wolf and Grizzly Bear. Fire destroyed most of the forest in 1886. Early European ranchers and farmers used the forest and grass resources from their first arrival in the area in 1883. The establishment of a Federal Forest Reserve in 1906 brought regulation to this resource extraction, which carried on until Cypress Hills Provincial Park was established on the Alberta side in 1951. Three major dams were built to provide water reservoirs for the herds of local cattlemen, and reforestation, regulated timber harvesting, fire protection and regulated grazing and haying were practised. In 1989, a Cypress Hills Interprovincial Park agreement was signed between the Alberta and Saskatchewan governments. This landmark agreement created Canada's first interprovincial park and gives the staff from the two provincial parks and Fort Walsh National Historic Site a mandate to cooperate in the protection of this "island" of montane forest and fescue grassland in a sea of dry mixed-grass prairie, ranch and farm land.

This 205 km² park lies 30 km east of Medicine Hat on the Trans-Canada Highway, and 34 km south on Highway 41. Greyhound bus services Medicine Hat. Hiking trails and paved and gravelled roads within the park are shown on a brochure available from the park office (see below).

There are several campgrounds, some completely serviced. Amenities are available at Medicine Hat and in the town of Elkwater, within the park. Year-round services include restaurant, grocery store, post office, gas station and motel. For information contact Visitor Services Officer, Cypress Hills Interprovincial Park, Box 12, Elkwater, Alberta T0J 1C0.

Birding Features

The hills are significantly cooler and moister than the surrounding plains. Consequently, plants and animals have both prairie and cordilleran affinities. Some species are found nowhere else in Alberta; others are to be found no closer than 300 km to the west. The best birding sites occur around Spruce Coulee, Reesor Lake and the town of Elkwater. The fire tower lookout west of Elkwater is another good spot. Descriptions below are based largely on an unpublished manuscript by C. A. Wallis and C. R. Wershler.

Fescue grasslands cover most of the upper plateau and much of the exposed slopes. Sharp-tailed Grouse are found in the low shrubbery coulees in the southern part and in the few remaining areas of lightly or ungrazed dense and tussocky grasslands. Watch for Upland Sandpipers in dense grass and shrub cover. Mountain Bluebirds are common throughout the hills in large part because of several nesting-box trails. Most years you can expect to record Eastern Bluebirds as well, though in low numbers. Sprague's Pipits prefer the dense ungrazed grasslands and isolated clumps of ungrazed grasses within shrub clusters. Western Meadowlarks are found throughout the grasslands. Lush grass on the lower slopes, and locally on the plateau, are favoured sites for Baird's Sparrows. Vesper Sparrows prefer grazed areas and are most abundant on drier, more heavily grazed slopes below the plateau and in shrubbery on the plateau. Chestnut-collared Longspurs occur in heavily grazed grasslands at the edges of the park.

Turkey Vultures can be expected to occur in the Cypress Hills every year. Look for Song Sparrows in open willow shrubbery adjacent to Elkwater Lake and along the broader stream valleys. Bobolinks and Le Conte's Sparrows have occurred with some regularity around the Elkwater beaver pond site. Redstarts occur in tall willows, often found in association with spruce and poplar. Mixed tangles of a variety of shrubs are favourite sites for Dusky Flycatchers and

White-crowned Sparrows. Gray Catbirds and Brown Thrashers are uncommon at lower altitudes near Elkwater Lake and in the Medicine Lodge Coulee area. Look for Yellow-breasted Chats in some of the surrounding coulees. Other birds found in shrubs at lower altitudes include Clay-colored Sparrow, Brewer's Blackbird and Spotted Towhee. Both wet and dry shrublands attract MacGillivray's Warbler and Common Yellowthroat. Both Black-headed and Rose-breasted Grosbeaks overlap in the hills but are uncommon. Lazuli Buntings are seen occasionally in tall shrubs and along woodland edges on semi-open south-facing slopes. Look for these birds in the southwest corner and along Battle Creek near the Alberta-Saskatchewan border.

The areas with deciduous trees attract Veery and Red-eyed Vireo. Mixed woodlands are favoured by Cooper's and Broad-winged Hawks. In mature woods, look for Northern Saw-whet Owl, Hairy Woodpecker, Ovenbird and Orange-crowned Warbler. Ruffed Grouse, introduced to the area, are found throughout the mature forests. The workings of Pileated Woodpeckers are sometimes seen here. Red-headed Woodpeckers have been reported and Winter Wrens are rarely seen. Common Poorwills appear sporadically in grassy forest openings along the edge of the plateau, but are more common in nearby Saskatchewan. Look for Audubon's race of the Yellow-rumped Warbler, pink-sided race of the Dark-eyed Junco, and White-winged and Red Crossbills in coniferous forests. Sight Western Tanagers around beaver ponds.

Townsend's Solitaire nests on exposed conglomerate cliffs at the northern edge of the escarpment.

Open water in the three main reservoirs attracts typical prairie waterfowl. There are plans to provide habitat for Trumpeter Swan, which once nested in the park. They still may be seen in the nearby Saskatchewan portion of the hills.

J. CAM FINLAY
Revised by Keith Bocking, Cypress Hills
Provincial Park, and Dennis Baresco

Pakowki Lake

One of the largest bodies of water in southern Alberta, Pakowki Lake contains a wide variety of birds. The lake was established as a federal Migratory Bird Sanctuary in 1920 and, to date, pressures to eliminate protection have failed to materialize. In drought years, much of the water dries up, except in the northwestern section. A weir built at this end in the mid-80s by Ducks Unlimited provides some control over the level of water there. This is the best birding spot. The site is approximately 30 km southwest of Medicine Hat on Highway 3, and 50 km south on Secondary Highway 885. The nearest town with visitor services and a provincial campground is Foremost, 10 km north and 28 km west of the lake. Here is where you can find White-faced Ibis. For information on occurrences of this bird up to 1992 in Canada, see "Distribution and Breeding Status of the White-faced Ibis, *Plegadis chihi*, in Canada," by J. P. Goossen, D. M. Ealey, H. Judge and D. C. Duncan in *Canadian Field-Naturalist*, 1995, 109: 391-402.

A bird checklist for Pakowki Lake can be obtained from the Fish and

White-faced Ibis

Wildlife Office, Sun Centre, 530 – 8 Street S., Lethbridge, Alberta T1J 2J8; phone (403) 381-5281.

Birding Features

Because of the lake's isolated location, little work has been done on the birds of the area. In years of less rain (about half of the time), small patches of water remain, particularly at the northwestern end, because of the weir, producing one of the best marsh birding sites in southern Alberta. The north-central part of the lake has numerous islands, ranging in size from a few hectares to several square kilometres. These islands make ideal nesting sites for colonial water birds. CAUTION: Stay away from these islands during the nesting season to avoid disturbance and possible loss of young.

Double-crested Cormorant and Black-crowned Night-Heron can easily be seen from the northern shore, along with Marsh Wren, Cinnamon Teal and American Bittern. In years of low water, American Avocets can be abundant, while in wet years waterfowl abound. The lake contains one of the few known nesting colonies of Forster's Tern in Alberta and one of the largest Black-crowned Night-Heron colonies in the province.

More significantly, the lake now appears to have a sizeable population of White-faced Ibises, unique in Canada – in the late 90s 10 to 20 pairs of this Canadian rarity have been reported on the impoundment above the weir.

A rare but regular visitor at the lake is the Black-necked Stilt. Also, Sage Grouse dancing grounds are found on the east side. However populations of this bird are dwindling.

J. CAM FINLAY
Revised by Jocelyn Hudon

Milk River Canyon and Vicinity

The Milk River Canyon and adjacent sites in extreme southeastern Alberta, and southwestern Saskatchewan, contain the only known breeding localities of Mountain Plover in Canada. Another bird of the American southwest, Black-headed Grosbeak, also nests here. Birds more usual to the north and west, such as Golden Eagle and Violet-green Swallow, have localized breeding outposts here too. Plants such as yucca, which normally don't reach north into Canada, are found. Fish and other aquatic animals of the Mississippi-Missouri river systems reach northwest into this country, as the Milk River is the only Alberta river to flow south to the Gulf of Mexico.

The area is accessible from the west at Milk River on secondary and tertiary roads east from Highway 4; from the northwest off Highway 61; and from the north, south on Highway 41 through the Cypress Hills. The nearest commercial accommodation, groceries and gasoline are at Foremost to the northwest, Milk River to the west, and Medicine Hat, far to the north. All of these communities are over 100 km away. It is advisable when travelling in this country from mid-June to mid-September to take drinking water, as the temperatures may reach very high levels.

Birding Features

Over 150 bird species have been reported from the area, with at least 90 nesting. From late April to mid-July, the normal complement of prairie waterfowl may be found on the sloughs and rivers. Turkey Vultures have been seen. Numerous nests of Ferruginous Hawk are observed along the coulees, but active eyries are few. At least four active nests of Golden Eagle are at this southeast outpost of their breeding range. Prairie Falcons are even more abundant with at least five active eyries located on ledges of sandstone outcrops or on cliffs. Sage Grouse are seen sporadically in the Lost River vicinity. They have a dancing ground north along Canal Creek.

This is the only area in Canada in which Mountain Plovers have been found nesting. The nesting habitat is within 15 or 20 km of the Canada-U.S. border, between Onefour and Wildhorse in the southeastern corner of Alberta. (See "Status and Breeding of Mountain Plovers [*Charadrius montanus*] in Canada," by C. A. Wallis and C. R. Wershler in *Canadian Field-Naturalist*, 1981, 95:2, pp. 133–136.) The best place to look for this plover is extensive unbroken grassland with very short native grasses. The birds arrive here about the second or third week of April and lay eggs about the second or third week of May.

Sage Grouse

Other summer nesters include Long-billed Curlews, which may be found in shorter grass, and Upland Sandpipers, found in thicker, taller grass. Willets and Marbled Godwits occur along slough edges and sometimes near the river. American Avocets are common along the edges of the larger sloughs, as are Wilson's Phalaropes. There are several pairs of Black-billed Cuckoos nesting along the lower Milk River. Burrowing Owls may be seen near the Milk River east of Comrey. Eastern and Western Kingbirds occur in wooded sites. Say's Phoebe nests commonly in badlands and coulees. Two different races of Horned Lark are present. The summer breeding race is the most common bird of the grassland. These birds move south for winter and are replaced by a northern race that overwinters in the area. The Violet-green Swallow breeds throughout the badlands and riparian woods, an eastern outpost of the breeding range. Other swallows that breed in the area include Bank along the Milk River; Northern Rough-winged along both the Milk River and Kennedy Creek; Barn around buildings; and Cliff with numerous colonies in coulees and the badlands. Interestingly coloured hybrids between the Bullock's and Baltimore Orioles occur in many larger cottonwood stands. These stands are also home to Black-headed Grosbeak, particularly along the lower Milk River. Lazuli Bunting nests in tall riparian shrubbery along the lower Milk River Valley. Gray-crowned Rosy-Finch has been observed going to roost in the evening within the urn-shaped mud nests of Cliff Swallows along the Milk River in February. The Spotted Towhee is common in woods along the river in summer. Lark Bunting is locally distributed in sagebrush country. Lark Sparrow is fairly common in the badlands and sagebrush flats and nearby woodlands. Both McCown's and Chestnut-collared Longspurs are fairly common in patches of shorter grass and near dried-up sloughs.

NORBERT KONDLA
Revised by Dennis Baresco

Waterton Lakes National Park

The Rocky Mountains abut the prairies at Waterton, creating sharply differing habitats within a very few kilometres. Over 120 years of records exist on this fine birding site, with over 250 confirmed species for the park. Plan a trip to include mountains, different types of forests, and the prairies, as many of these birds have narrow habitat preferences. An excellent bird list is available from the park office. This is one of the best places in Alberta to see Cassin's Vireo and Cassin's Finch. Vaux's Swifts have also nested in the park. The park contains Grizzly Bear, Moose, Elk, Mule Deer and, in a paddock, Plains Bison.

The area was virtually unknown to whites until 1858, when the Palliser expedition named the lakes after 18th-century English naturalist Charles Waterton. A local rancher, Fredrick William Godsal, pressed the government to protect the area, as originally recommended by William Pearce, Dominion Land Surveyor. Land for the park was set aside in 1895. Waterton and adjacent Glacier National Park in the United States were designated, in 1932, as the world's first international Peace Park.

The 525 km² park lies 276 km south of Calgary via Highways 2 and 5. Commercial buses run from Calgary throughout the summer. Special tour buses can be taken to both the Canadian and American portions of the park. Consult a travel agent for details.

Good paved roads, back-country hiking trails, amenities and major interpretive features are all illustrated on the park map-brochure. Boats travel from the marina at Waterton to the far end of the lake in Glacier National Park, Montana, providing spectacular scenery and an excellent array of birds.

Motel accommodations should be booked ahead of time. Sites at the three major campgrounds, which accommodate every type of recreational vehicle and provide winter camping, are available on a first-come basis. Through July and August they are often full by midday.

Contact the staff at the Park Warden Office for information on finding the rarer species. Several reports on the birds of Waterton are available at the park library. Further information may be obtained from The Superintendent, Waterton Lakes National Park, Waterton Park, Alberta TOK 2MO; phone (403) 859-2224.

Birding Features

Two major migration routes, Trans-mountain and Central, traverse the park. Several western species cross the adjacent low mountain pass to nest, or are blown over in severe storms. Other species reach their northern limit here.

Habitat types represented in the park (in order of decreasing species richness) are wetlands, deciduous forests, coniferous forests, prairie and prairie shrubland, mixed forests, slope and limber pine shrub land, krummholz, anthropogenic, conifer savannah, alpine and subalpine meadows, rock ledges and cliffs.

Seven birding areas include most of these habitats. The Maskinonge Lake marsh, with thick deciduous woods, contains ducks and upland birds. The area near the buffalo paddock and the hiking trail proceeding north from the elbow of the Blakiston Valley Road offer grassland species. The Chief Mountain Highway, southeast from the park gate, also offers grassland species; the first 1.6 km of this road contain deciduous woods and aspen parkland birds. The Crandell Lake area contains Lodgepole Pine forest. At Cameron Lake, dense, humid, spruce-fir forests, more typical of B.C., host western species such as the occasional Lewis's Woodpecker. Hike from here into the Carthew Lakes, where alpine habitat, Whitebark Pine, Subalpine Fir and Douglas-fir host their special birds.

Birds most commonly encountered in the park are Pine Siskin, White-winged Crossbill, Ruby-crowned Kinglet, MacGillivray's and Yellow-rumped Warblers, Swainson's Thrush, Yellow Warbler, Dark-eyed Junco, Fox Sparrow, Golden-crowned Kinglet, Red-breasted Nuthatch, Chipping Sparrow and Brown-headed Cowbird.

Formerly rare, American White Pelicans are now seen with some regularity. Great Blue Herons, while uncommon, are regularly observed. A few Trumpeter Swans nest in the park, part of a small regional breeding population in the foothills parkland of Alberta, as probably do Wood Ducks. Green-winged and Blue-winged Teals, Mallard, American Wigeon, Ring-necked Duck, Bufflehead and Common Merganser can be expected. A few Harlequin Ducks nest along the rivers. The common Barrow's Goldeneye nests here, where it may hybridize with the rare Common Goldeneyes. Golden Eagles nest and Bald Eagles migrate through. Ospreys nest near the lakes. A rare American Kestrel, Merlin, and Prairie or even Peregrine Falcon may be observed. All five grouse present are nesters: Sharp-tailed on the prairies, Ruffed in the parkland, Spruce and Blue in the forests, and White-tailed Ptarmigan in the mountain meadows. Sandhill Crane is a rare summer resident. Of the 15 or so species of shorebirds occurring, most are spring and fall migrants; Spotted Sandpiper nests along streams. A rare Black-billed Cuckoo may be observed, usually in the aspen along Waterton River. Of the eight owl species reported, the Great Horned, Long-eared (rare) and Northern Saw-whet Owls nest, as probably do Northern Pygmy-Owls. Since 1984, Vaux's Swift has been observed with some regularity in the park, though not every year. It bred in a chimney at the Prince of Wales Hotel in 1995; other breeding venues in the park are suspected. Of four hummingbirds recorded in the park, including the rare Black-chinned, the Calliope and Rufous are confirmed nesters. The nine species of woodpeckers include Pileated Woodpecker, Northern Flicker, Red-naped Sapsucker, Hairy, Downy, Three-toed and Black-backed, and all nest; rare Lewis's occasionally appear in the southwest corner of the park. Eleven species of flycatcher are found, mainly those of parkland habitat, but also Pacific-slope Flycatchers (maybe even the Cordilleran Flycatcher) on north-facing mountain cliffs. The pine and Douglas-fir forests of Waterton are probably the surest place to observe Cassin's Vireos in Alberta. Swallows include Violet-green (mountain), Tree (parkland), Bank, Northern Rough-winged, Barn and Cliff. American Pipit inhabits alpine meadows. Steller's Jay nests here, though is most commonly observed in the fall and winter. Black-billed Magpie (parkland) can be found, as can Clark's Nutcracker (mountains). Four species of chickadees occur here; while the Chestnut-backed Chickadee is still considered rare, it is encountered on a fairly regular basis. American Dippers are not unusual along streams. A variety of thrushes (including Townsend's Solitaire, Veery and Varied Thrush) and warblers (Yellow-rumped [mainly Audubon's], Townsend's and MacGillivray's) appear in the woodlands. The park plays host to a variety of sparrows (Chipping, Clay-colored [parkland], Vesper [parkland], Savannah [parkland], Fox [mountains, the slate-coloured subspecies *schistacea*], Song, Lincoln's and White-crowned), and Dark-eyed (Oregon) Junco. The prairies host Red-winged Blackbirds, Brown-headed Cowbirds and the occasional Western Meadowlark or Yellow-headed Blackbird. Adjacent woodlands produce Black-headed Grosbeak and, occasionally, Spotted Towhee. Lazuli Bunting often dot the open woodland, shrubbery and woodland edges on the park's slopes. Finally, a variety of finches occur (Gray-crowned Rosy-Finch, Pine Grosbeak, Cassin's Finch [relatively open coniferous and mixed-wood forests], White-winged Crossbill [numbers fluctuate from year to year], Pine Siskin, American Goldfinch [parkland], and Evening Grosbeak).

K. E. SEEL
Revised by Janice Smith and Jocelyn Hudon

Calgary

Calgary, with foothills and mountains to the west, prairies and irrigation lands to the east and south, and aspen parkland to the north and west, offers a variety of habitats for over 300 of the bird species that occur in Alberta, many of which nest within an 80 km radius of the city.

The city began with the arrival of the North West Mounted Police in the mid-1870s. Before that, the Blackfoot Confederacy, a strong Indian alliance, controlled an area from present-day Red Deer south into the state of Montana. The railroad came in the mid-1880s, bringing a flood of settlers. Today Calgary has become the Canadian headquarters for major oil- and gas-related companies – a white-collar city with a variety of cultural assets. In addition, with the heritage of ranching in the surrounding area, the "cowboy" element is still quite prominent.

The airport has direct links to many world cities. The east-west passenger rail and bus lines, and the Trans-Canada Highway, provide ready access. Campgrounds are widely available, particularly to the west and southwest, in Kananaskis Country.

Information on natural areas in and around the city is available from the 1975 book *Calgary's Natural Areas: A Popular Guide*, edited by Peter Sherrington and published by the Calgary Field Naturalists' Society. This guide is currently being revised, although no completion date has been fixed. *A Birdfinding Guide to the Calgary Region*, published in 1993 by the Calgary Field Naturalists' Society, is a must for anyone serious about birding the area. The bird-finding guide and other information is available from Calgary Field Naturalists' Society, P.O. Box 981, Calgary, Alberta T2P 2R4; phone (403) 285-8553. Another good source of information on birding is staff at the Inglewood Bird Sanctuary; phone (403) 269-6688. Calgary's rare-bird hotline is (403) 237-8824.

Birding Features

Inglewood Bird Sanctuary. This sanctuary, with more than 200 recorded species, is located in the east centre of the city along the Bow River. A checklist is available at the interpretive centre. Take 9th Avenue southeast from the city centre, staying west of the river as far as possible. The parking lot is south of 9th Ave. Over 4 km of trails connect the grasslands, shrub and riparian woods set on the banks of the Bow River. Washrooms, picnic tables, duck ponds and natural-history displays all add to an enjoyable visit. Inglewood Bird Sanctuary is a federal reserve long known for its migrants, spring and fall, and is part of the Canadian Migration Monitoring Network.

Shepard Sloughs. A drive through the prairie and agricultural landscape, southeast of Calgary, provides a good cross-section of local birdlife. In winter, Snowy Owls are usually present in several spots and raptors are common in spring and fall. A visit to the Shepard Sloughs at the height of migration can be accomplished in two to three hours. Proceed south from Calgary on Highway 2 and turn east on Highway 22X. Travel east across the Bow River beyond the subdivisions on the north side. Study the sloughs, all of which are good for water birds and shorebirds. At 11.3 km, explore three small sloughs. Turn north for about 0.8 km, where the road bends to the left, then straightens past another slough that has water during the spring. Farther along, beyond the next farmhouse, watch for Burrowing (although not seen recently) and Short-eared Owls in the pasture to the east. Turn right at the crossroads at 17.7 km, along the edge of Shepard, and proceed east. In spring scan the sloughs on the south. Turn north at 33.8 km. The paved road, Glenmore Trail, is at 37.0 km. Consult the bird-finding guide for Calgary, mentioned above, for additional detail.

Priddis and Radio Tower Sloughs. To see a cross-section of water birds and marsh species, drive south on Highway 2. Turn west onto 22X, just past the city limits, and proceed 0.8 km to Priddis Slough. Park on the available turnoffs, on either side. From mid-April to July, scan for a variety of water and shore-birds. A walk along the railroad track will sometimes produce warblers and sparrows. American Pipit often occurs here in fall. Proceed west 0.4 km and turn north on the short road to the Radio Tower Slough. This marshy water body contains a selection of ducks, coots, Sora, and Yellow-headed and Red-winged Blackbirds.

Frank Lake. This recently reclaimed and inundated lake lies 41 km south of Calgary on Highway 2, and 6 km east on Highway 23. Access is from the northwest and east ends. Lands surrounding the lake are private and permission should be obtained prior to any excursions. A hike of from four to seven hours should suffice to circumnavigate the lake. April to May and September to October are the best times to spot up to 500,000 water birds, with the odd rarity a good possibility. Consult the bird-finding guide for Calgary, mentioned above, for additional detail.

J. CAM FINLAY
Revised by Doug Collister

Bruce Lake and Irricana Sloughs

The area east of Highway 9 and southeast of the town of Irricana consists of prairie farmland with numerous sloughs and one good-sized lake. While there are no parks or designated sanctuaries, the wet areas provide good habitat for waterfowl and, to a somewhat lesser extent, resident and migrating shorebirds; the open farmland and pastures are home to a variety of prairie dryland species. A half-day drive during spring migration and nesting season (May to mid-July) can easily produce 50 or more species of birds, with smaller numbers earlier or later.

If you begin 40 km northeast of Calgary at Keoma, the trip is about 40 km long, for a total distance of 135 km round trip from the city limits. Twenty-five kilometres are on good gravel roads (dusty in dry weather); the other roads are hard-surfaced. Allow four to five hours for the loop, plus an hour round trip from Calgary, to give lots of time for stops. Gas, food and other supplies are available at Irricana.

The drive provides a good selection of sloughs. A few specific sites are mentioned, but it is best simply to stop at all likely-looking spots. It may help to remember that Range (Rge) Roads (Rd) run north-south and Township (Twp) Roads run east-west. More information is available in *A Birdfinding Guide to the Calgary Region*, by Joan F. McDonald (editor) (Calgary Field Naturalists' Society, 1993, pp. 54–59).

Birding Features

Start at the junction of Highways 9 and 566, 19 km north of Highway 1; mileages in parentheses are measured from this junction. Proceed east on Twp Road 262 for 8.5 km to Bruce Lake, passing the town of Keoma along the way. (Twp Rd 262 is the eastward extension of Secondary Highway 566.) Bruce Lake has two bays near the road. Black-crowned Night-Heron has nested in the cattails on either side of the road at the northwestern corner of the second bay, although a new house close by may have disturbed them; also scan the shrubs just above the water along the eastern shore of this bay, and along the south shoreline. From where the road leaves the second bay of Bruce Lake (9.3 km), continue east on Twp Rd 262 for 2.4 km to Rge Rd 261 (11.7 km) and turn left (north). Drive north for 6.6 km to a T intersection (18.4 km); sloughs on the right and left sides of the road shortly before the T intersection are the first of an extensive series of sloughs along this route. Turn left (west) at the T intersection onto Twp Rd 270 for 0.3 km, then turn right (north) onto Rge Rd 260 for 0.6 km to a small slough on the right (19.3 km), which can be good for migrating shorebirds. (The land here belongs to the Hutterite colony visible just to the north; please be respectful of private land, and bird only from the road.) Retrace your route south and then east for 0.9 km back to the T junction at Twp Rd 270 and Rge Rd 261 (20.2 km), then proceed 3.2 km east on Twp Rd 270 to Rge Rd 254 or 255 (23.4 km), marked by a small sign "Bull Test Station." (Somewhat confusingly, the Range Road is numbered 255 on the south side of this intersection, and 254 on the north side.) The second of the two large sloughs on the left side of the stretch of Twp Rd 270 leading up to this intersection can have Forster's or Common Terns, with Red-breasted Merganser in migration, but requires a spotting scope for best results. Turn left (north) onto Rge Rd 254 and proceed 5 km north to Twp Rd 273 (28.4 km). Turn left (west) onto Twp Rd 273 and drive west for 8.5 km, reaching Highway 9 (36.9 km) about 1 km south of the access to Irricana.

From April to October the sloughs are excellent for all resident prairie ducks including Mallard, three teals, Northern Pintail, Northern Shoveler, Gadwall, American Wigeon, Canvasback, Redhead, Lesser Scaup, Common Goldeneye, Bufflehead and Ruddy Duck, with smaller numbers of Ring-necked Duck, White-winged Scoter, and Common and Hooded Mergansers, with Red-breasted Merganser on migration, along with Eared, Horned and Red-necked Grebes, Double-crested Cormorant, and Great Blue Heron with Western and Pied-billed Grebes less frequent. Killdeer, American Avocet, Marbled Godwit, Willet, Spotted Sandpiper and Wilson's Phalarope are common summer residents, while migrating shorebirds pass through from the second week to the end of May, and from the end of July to mid-September, with smaller numbers somewhat earlier and later. Red-tailed and Swainson's Hawks, Northern Harrier and American Kestrel are common in summer, and Ferruginous Hawk can nest in the area but may be hard to find. Great Horned Owl is fairly common but usually well-hidden. Checking hawk nests from February to May often produces a few of these owls. Short-eared Owls are uncommon but worth keeping an eye out for. Savannahs are the abundant sparrow; stopping along the road can produce Vesper and Clay-colored in shrubbery along fences, Le Conte's in grassy pastures or ditches, Baird's uncommon but possible in unploughed pasture, and Lincoln's in shrubbery near water. Flocks of Tundra Swan, American Pipit, Lapland Longspur and Snow Bunting can be found on migration, as can American Tree Sparrow and the occasional Common Loon, Townsend's Solitaire, Say's Phoebe and Harris's Sparrow. Other common birds are Western Meadowlark, Brewer's Blackbird, Red-winged Blackbird in any wet area, Sora, Marsh Wren, Common Yellowthroat, and Yellow-headed Blackbird in cattails, Horned Lark in fields, and Common Snipe and Sprague's Pipit overhead.

WILLIAM J. F. WILSON

Kananaskis Country

Kananaskis Country is a major provincial multiple-use recreation area in the Rocky Mountains southwest of Calgary. Over 245 species of birds have been reported here. White-tailed Ptarmigan, Blue and Spruce Grouse and Calliope Hummingbird nest; Northern Pygmy- and Boreal Owls are heard or seen; and Three-toed Woodpecker can be found.

Long recognized for its scenic beauty, the area was part of Rocky Mountain National Park from 1902 to 1911 and Banff National Park from 1917 to 1931. The land was subsequently transferred to the province. In 1977, Kananaskis Country was established by the Alberta government under the premiership of Peter Lougheed, and the portion around the Kananaskis lakes designated Kananaskis Provincial Park. In 1986, the park was renamed Peter Lougheed Provincial Park. In 1996, the Alberta government designated nearly 80,000 ha at the heart of Kananaskis Country as the Elbow Sheep Wildland Provincial Park to protect critical foothills habitat for species such as Cougar, Black Bear, Bull Trout, Moose, Wolf and Bighorn Sheep. Bow Valley and Bragg Creek Provincial Parks are also part of Kananaskis Country.

The area covers 4160 km² and lies south of the Bow River and west of an irregular line that demarcates provincial forest lands through the foothills of the Rocky Mountains, west of the communities of Bragg Creek, Millarville, Turner Valley and Longview. It is bounded on the west by the eastern boundary of Banff National Park, the Continental Divide and British Columbia. Kananaskis Country comprises rugged mountains with extensive glaciers, alpine tundra and subalpine forests; beautiful lakes; several rivers (Kananaskis, Elbow, Sheep and Highwood) and their tributaries; and foothills.

For more information, check Kananaskis Country's official Web site at http://www.gov.ab.ca/env/parks/prov_parks/kananaskis/index.html or contact

Kananaskis Country, Suite 201, 800 Railway Avenue, Canmore, Alberta T1W 1P1; phone (403) 678-5508. Information is also available from the provincial government office in Calgary ([403] 297-6423), and from Map Town ([403] 266-2241) in Calgary. Note that government hours are 8 to 12 and 1 to 4:30 Monday to Friday. For additional detail on birding in the area, consult *A Birdfinding Guide to the Calgary Region*, by Joan F. McDonald (editor) (Calgary Field Naturalists' Society, 1993, pp. 86–90 and 94–119).

Birding Features

Most of the montane birds of Alberta as well as mountain specialties can be found on short hikes from the road. Birds to see in this region include Lazuli Buntings in open areas of scrub aspen and Mountain Bluebirds at bird boxes along fence lines. Along streams and rivers look for Harlequin Duck, American Dipper, Willow and Alder Flycatchers, Fox Sparrow and Northern Waterthrush. As you drive through the forests, stop and listen for thrushes, including Townsend's Solitaire on open ridges. Golden-crowned and Ruby-crowned Kinglets and Three-toed Woodpeckers are relatively common in these woods. Warblers, including Townsend's, Orange-crowned, Tennessee and Wilson's, abound in June. Open aspen slopes sometimes have Blue Grouse. At or near the Highwood Pass summit, get out and hike to see White-tailed Ptarmigan, Gray-crowned Rosy-Finch, Clark's Nutcracker and American Pipit. At the timberline be alert for Hammond's Flycatcher and Brewer's and Fox Sparrows.

At the University of Calgary research station near Barrier Lake, 9 km south of the Trans-Canada Highway 1, take the looped nature trail for a good variety of habitat and birds. Visitors are welcome to examine the property around the buildings. Watch for hummingbirds here and at the Barrier Lake Visitor Information Centre, 8 km south of Highway 1. The only Alberta record of a Green Violet-ear Hummingbird occurred here in 1996.

The Front Ranges of the Rocky Mountains are the site of a major migration of Golden Eagles in spring and fall. During the last half of March and early April, more than 4000 Golden Eagles move in a northwesterly direction across the Kananaskis valley along the Fisher Range. Counts of more than 200 eagles a day have been recorded. The Mount Lorette Ponds Day Use Area (about 20 km south of Highway 1 on Highway 40) is a good location from which to view this migration. The birds usually soar at mountain-top height, so a telescope is recommended. Fall migration peaks in early October. Up to 500 raptors a day have been recorded at this time, mainly Golden Eagle but also Bald Eagle, Sharp-shinned Hawk and Northern Goshawk.

Drive to the administration area near Lower King Creek. Check out the large shrub meadow to the south. In fall you may find a Calliope Hummingbird and several warbler and sparrow species. Ask the park naturalists about key spots.

At Upper Kananaskis Lake, scan for loons, grebes and ducks during migration, particularly fall. Hike the nearby trails for forest birds mentioned above. Look up – you may spot a Black Swift.

J. CAM FINLAY
Revised by Doug Collister and Jocelyn Hudon

Banff National Park

Banff, the oldest national park in Canada and second oldest in the world, lies within the Canadian Rocky Mountains. Over 260 bird species have been recorded in the park. Birds you have a good chance to spot, in season, include Harlequin Duck, White-tailed Ptarmigan, Black Swift, Three-toed Woodpecker, American Dipper, Varied Thrush, Townsend's Warbler and Gray-crowned Rosy-Finch. There are possibilities of sighting Northern Hawk, Northern Pygmy- and Boreal Owls and Cassin's Finch. Banff contains populations of Elk (Wapiti), White-tailed and Mule Deer, Moose, Bighorn Sheep and Mountain Goat. Some, like the elk, deer and sheep, may be seen very near or in town. Both Black and Grizzly Bears are common, so take appropriate precautions and don't leave food or garbage near your tent or picnic site.

The discovery of the hot springs in 1883 led to the establishment of the 26 km^2 Hot Springs Reserve in 1885. This was the birth of the Canadian National Parks system. Today the park has grown to 6641 km^2, composed of 65% alpine habitat and rock, 30% subalpine forests and only 3% montane lands.

The park lies 134 km west of Calgary. Highway 1 provides access to the Banff townsite and Lake Louise for several million visitors a year. Greyhound buses and VIA Rail run daily through the park between Calgary and Vancouver. Some of the Banff accommodation facilities provide regular pick-up service in Calgary. Several car rental agencies are located in Banff. There are few roads and more than 1100 km of trails for hikers and cross-country skiers. The park brochures, available from headquarters, show these, other amenities and special interpretive features. Commercial accommodation is in and around the town of Banff and at Lake Louise, 56 km north. Other cabins are available along Primary Highway 1A. Gasoline and related services, including a great variety of tourist shops, are found in Banff and Lake Louise. Minimum services, including gasoline, are also available at Saskatchewan Crossing, where the David Thompson Highway 11 meets the Jasper-Banff highway, 76 km north of Lake Louise. The David Thompson road links Banff with the Kootenay Plains (a prairie community occurring in the mountains) to Rocky Mountain House and Red Deer on Primary Highway 2 – an alternative and lovely route into the national park. Contiguous to the west of Banff, Yoho National Park lies along Highway 1, and Kootenay National Park along Highway 93. Both routes cross over mountain passes, bringing you into subalpine country and the birds occurring in these highlands. Ten serviced campgrounds are within Banff Park. Campsites are awarded on a first-come first-served basis, so plan on arriving early. Winter camping permits may be obtained from the park administration.

Information on the geological, natural and human history of the Canadian Rockies can be found in *Handbook of the Canadian Rockies,* 2nd edition by Ben Gadd (Jasper: Corax Press, 1995). Several popular books are available on the birds of the Rocky Mountains. One of these, by G. L. Holroyd and H. Coneybeare, *The Compact Guide to Birds of the Rockies* (Edmonton: Lone Pine Publishing, 1989), contains seasonal checklists for the different mountain national parks. A checklist of the birds of Banff National Park may also be obtained for $1 from Friends of Banff National Park, P.O. Box 1695, Banff, Alberta TOL OCO. Additional information on bird-finding in Banff National Park may be found in *A Birdfinding Guide to the Calgary Region*, by Joan F. McDonald (editor) (Calgary Field Naturalists' Society, 1993, pp. 121–138), or at http://www.worldweb.com/VertexCustomers/p/ParksCanada-Banff/ birding.html

There is also a special publication by the Bow Valley Naturalists: *Vermilion Lakes, Banff National Park: An Introductory Study*. This booklet may be obtained for $2 from Bow Valley Naturalists, P.O. Box 1693, Banff, Alberta TOL OCO.

Birding Features

Banff Park contains a wide variety of habitats from wooded valley, lowlands and hot springs to alpine glaciers. Birdlife is most abundant in the lower Bow Valley near Banff. To the west is the Continental Divide, and beyond, the wet, heavily forested mountains of British Columbia. To the east lie the dry prairies of Alberta. The low mountain passes allow bird stragglers from B.C. to appear regularly at Banff. Banff often reports species as first arrivals for Alberta in spring. Similarly, the Banff lowlands are often visited by prairie species. Birds may remain quite late into the fall before moving on.

Lake Minnewanka. The lake lies 6 km from Highway 1 northeast of the east exit for Banff. Continue on this road to check out Two Jack and Johnson Lakes. From early April to late May, scan the lakes for Common Loons and a variety of ducks, including Ring-necked Ducks and Barrow's Goldeneyes. Mountain Bluebirds gather insects along the roadside. From May to August, Violet-green and other swallows feed over the water. Migrating waterfowl again become common in September and October. Check the lakeshores for warblers and sparrows. Northern Pygmy-Owls and Western Tanagers may be found in the Douglas-fir stands along the road. Northern Saw-whet Owls nest in the deciduous woods near Bankhead. Pacific-slope Flycatchers may be heard on the north-facing cliff along the educational trail in lower Bankhead.

Banff Townsite. Here you'll find a variety of birds in early spring. Migrants, including American Robin, Red-winged Blackbird and Song Sparrow, appear in late March, particularly near the stables north off the Cave and Basin Road. In late April, look for the first Violet-green and Tree Swallows over the town. By mid-May the Cliff Swallow has arrived to nest under the Banff Avenue bridge. Check the woods in the old residential area at the foot of Tunnel Mountain for a variety of passerines. A hike on the Tunnel Mountain trail could produce Clark's Nutcracker, Northern Pygmy-Owl or Cassin's Finch. In winter, the town, with feeders behind many houses, has Clark's Nutcracker, three species of chickadee and the occasional White-breasted and Red-breasted Nuthatch. American Dipper winters at Bow Falls.

Cave and Basin Swamp. This swamp lies on the south side of the Bow River, along Cave Avenue, 2 km west of Banff. Park at the Cave and Basin lot and walk to the buildings, then take the path down through the trees to the marsh. This large wetland is fed by hot springs and remains partially open all winter. The tall willows growing in dense tangles around the marsh, together with the nearby spruce and pine forests, provide a variety of habitats well used by a mixture of birds. In late March to early May, look for such early species as a variety of ducks, Ruby-crowned Kinglet, Orange-crowned Warbler and Dark-eyed Junco. From late May to mid-July, look for ducks, including Barrow's Goldeneye and Cinnamon Teal; warblers such as Common Yellowthroat, Townsend's, Wilson's and American Redstart; and sparrows, including Savannah and Song. The swamp is a major staging area mid-August to November for several species of waterfowl, including Blue-winged and Green-winged Teal and Lesser Scaup. From October to April, the open water supports a large number of overwintering Mallards and Barrow's Goldeneyes, the odd Common Snipe, Killdeer, and passerine such as Winter Wren and Song Sparrow. Stop and look in the water at the marsh inlet for the introduced tropical fish. The shoreline has garter snakes, the only place in the park where these animals are found regularly.

Fenland Nature Trail. The trail, 0.5 km from town adjacent to the Mount Norquay Road, is the perfect spot for the early riser. The trail begins with mature White Spruce and leads into a maze of willows and sedge marshes with a clear stream flowing through. Reconnoitre in late March to early May for Mountain and Boreal Chickadees, Brown Creeper, early flocks of Golden-crowned and Ruby-crowned Kinglets, Orange-crowned and Yellow-rumped Warblers. From the end of February through to April, at moonrise, listen for such owls as Great Horned, Northern Pygmy- and Boreal. From mid-May to early July listen for a Varied Thrush and Townsend's Warbler. Other songs heard in June include those of Swainson's Thrush, Ruby-crowned Kinglet, Warbling Vireo, a variety of warblers (Orange-crowned, Yellow, Yellow-rumped, Common Yellowthroat and Wilson's), and sparrows such as Lincoln's and Song. From mid-August until early September, this is a good spot to locate mixed flocks of warblers and sparrows moving through the willows and spruce. In winter, you can almost always find the local common species.

Vermilion Lakes Drive. Begin just beyond the Fenland trail and drive west parallel to the Trans-Canada Highway 1 for 4 km. These large shallow lakes are connected by several small channels through sedge and willow flats. From April to late May, this is one of the most important areas in the park for migrating waterfowl. Open water appears in late April, and so do the water birds, including Tundra Swans and Cinnamon Teals, a variety of prairie ducks, and Hooded and Common Mergansers. Both Bald Eagles and Ospreys have nests beside the lakes. From late May to mid-July look for such rare park visitors as Red-necked and Pied-billed Grebes, and Cinnamon Teals. Willow Flycatchers may occasionally be heard in the willow flats along the roads. From late July on, the duck numbers increase to a peak in the last half of September. Winter brings Common Redpoll and Snow Bunting to the marshes. Check the small patches of open water at the warm springs on the third lake for American Dipper and a few ducks that stay all winter. In winter, Townsend's Solitaire can be seen on the slope above the road.

Muleshoe Picnic Area. This spot lies on Highway 1A, 5 km west of its origin from Highway 1. Park at the picnic area overlooking the Bow River. White Spruce, Balsam Poplar, willow and meadows are mixed with stands of Trembling Aspen and Lodgepole Pine, Douglas-fir and dry grassland. In April and May scan the adjacent oxbow lake and river for a variety of water birds, including Harlequin Duck and Common Merganser. Nearby woods contain Varied and Swainson's Thrushes and Townsend's Solitaire. Scrutinize the willows and open forest along the water for early migrants, including Ruby-crowned Kinglet, Orange-crowned Warbler and White-crowned Sparrow. Listen for Blue Grouse hooting in the open conifer woods on the slopes above the highway. In June to mid-July, go to the Douglas-fir and Lodgepole Pine forests on these slopes to locate Hammond's Flycatcher, Western Tanager, Townsend's Solitaire and other breeding birds. At this season, see if you can spot five species of swallow (Violet-green, Tree, Bank, Northern Rough-winged and Cliff) hawking insects over the water. Common Yellowthroat and White-crowned Sparrow have their nests nearby. The aspen forests contain a wide variety of birds, including Pileated Woodpecker, Olive-sided Flycatcher and Orange-crowned Warbler. To the north of Muleshoe, the road crosses a wetland. Stop and ferret out a great number of species, including Green-winged Teal, Willow Flycatcher, Brewer's Blackbird, a variety of warblers and Lincoln's Sparrow.

Sunshine alpine meadows. Access to the meadows requires a full-day, strenuous hike. Go prepared for inclement weather with lots of food and water. Take the road by this name, 10 km west of the Norquay interchange on Highway 1. Park the car at the end of the Sunshine road and hike up the ski-out trail. Pick up the topographic map sheet, Banff 82-O/4W, to keep from getting lost on these meadows. The rolling alpine heath, with herbs in the hollows and mats of Mountain Avens on the more exposed sites, is still mainly snow-covered in June. The trip is worthwhile at that time, or later after early July when the snow is gone, because of the abundance of White-tailed Ptarmigan, Mountain Bluebird, Townsend's Solitaire, Ruby-crowned Kinglet, American Pipit, Yellow-rumped Warbler, Gray-crowned Rosy-Finch, Dark-eyed Junco and Fox Sparrow. Skiers in the winter will be rewarded with the occasional White-tailed Ptarmigan, Common Raven, Clark's Nutcracker, and Mountain and Boreal Chickadees.

Johnston Canyon. This spot lies on Highway 1A, 23 km west of Banff and just east of the Eisenhower junction. Leave the car at the parking lot and hike along the trail up the creek 3 km to the lower falls or 5 km to the upper falls. The canyon is narrow, shady and cool and is surrounded by mixed stands of spruce and Lodgepole Pine. At dusk or dawn, come here to watch the Black Swifts arrive or leave. This is one of only two known sites (the other is Maligne Canyon at Jasper) where these birds regularly breed in Alberta. Their nests are difficult to spot. Look near the upper edges of the slimy canyon walls espe-cially just upstream and downstream of the lower falls. American Dippers may be seen passing in and out of the water, as they too nest here. The forests have Winter Wren, Townsend's and Yellow-rumped Warblers, and occasionally Pacific-slope Flycatcher.

The willow meadow. This site, 1.6 km north of Johnston Canyon, should have Common Yellowthroat, Brewer's Blackbird and Lincoln's Sparrow from late May through early July. A hike into the meadow will flush a Willow Flycatcher and three species of sparrow – Savannah, Clay-colored and White-crowned.

The Vermilion Pass burn. The spot is reached by taking Highway 93 southwest for 6 km from the junction with Highway 1. This 1968 fire site extends 9 km farther on to Marble Canyon. Park at Boom Creek, the Continental Divide, or at the Stanley Glacier Trail head. Year-round, scan treetops for Northern Hawk Owl which nests here. Blue Grouse are scarce, but also nest in the regen-erating lawn. Townsend's Solitaires and other more common species are found. The adjacent unburned woods are good sites to look for a Three-toed Woodpecker and Olive-sided Flycatcher. In winter watch for a White-tailed Ptarmigan, Clark's Nutcracker and chickadees.

Moraine Lake road. On the 9 km road 1.6 km east of the lake, stop at the ava-lanche slopes in June and listen for an Olive-sided Flycatcher ("quick-three-beers") and MacGillivray's Warbler songs, the flute-like notes of Hermit Thrush and call of Townsend's Solitaire. At Moraine Lake, park the car. In late May and June, the woods are echoing with the calls of Hermit, Swainson's and Varied Thrushes. From June to mid-July, look for a Harlequin Duck and American Dipper on the creek and lake. Check the meadows along the creek for Ruby-crowned Kinglets and White-crowned Sparrows. Take a walk in the forest above the road or towards Constellation Lake to find Winter Wren, Golden-crowned Kinglet and a variety of warblers, including Townsend's and Wilson's.

Bow River. May to early June is the best time to see Harlequin Ducks in Banff. Look for them in the Bow River between Castle Junction and Lake Louise. Stop at the pull-offs adjacent to the river on Highways 1 and 1A. Common Merganser and American Dipper may also be seen from these viewpoints.

Bow Summit. This site lies along Highway 93, 20 km north of the junction with Highway 1. Take the 1.5 km trail to Peyto Lake viewpoint; from here proceed on the 1 km looped trail around the upper edge of the timberline. This trail passes through a variety of habitats, including Subalpine Fir and Engelmann Spruce at the parking lot, to stunted fir with heath and meadow vegetation higher up. From June to mid-July, an early-morning stroll should produce Clark's Nutcracker, Varied and Hermit Thrushes and Fox Sparrow. There may be a chance to view a White-tailed Ptarmigan, American Pipit or Gray-crowned Rosy-Finch as they are all here above the treeline. Check the meadows south of the summit for Solitary Sandpiper, Mountain Bluebird, American Pipit, and Savannah and Fox Sparrows.

The avalanche slopes on the east side of the highway at Mount Wilson. This site lies 20 km north of the Service Centre at Saskatchewan River Crossing (junction of Highways 93 and 11). Park beside the highway at the old road. Hike along this trail to the base of the slope and bushwhack from here, looking for birds. The grassy meadows on the steep slope are separated by tangles of young aspen, alder, willow, rose and strips of more mature aspen forest. If Dusky Flycatcher is on your want list, here is the best spot in Banff Park to find this bird. You may also spot Golden Eagle, Rufous Hummingbird, Warbling Vireo and Orange-crowned and MacGillivray's Warblers.

Parker's Ridge. The ridge is accessed by a short but steep hike from the parking lot on Highway 93, 9 km south of the icefield's service centre and about 25 km north of Saskatchewan Crossing. As you climb the switchbacks in July listen for Fox and Golden-crowned Sparrows. Water Pipits, Horned Larks, White-tailed Ptarmigans and Gray-crowned Rosy-Finches may be seen in the alpine meadows on the ridge summit as you enjoy the spectacular view of the Saskatchewan Glacier.

Kootenay Plains. They lie just east of the park boundary and consist of flatlands from about 15 to 30 km east along the David Thompson Highway 11. On or near these plains you'll locate prairie birds, including several pairs of Western Meadowlarks. One year a pair of Black-headed Grosbeaks and another of Lark Buntings were spotted, the latter far west of their normal prairie range.

G. L. HOLROYD AND K. J. VAN TIGHEM OF CANADIAN WILDLIFE SERVICE,
R. SEALE OF BANFF INTERPRETIVE SERVICE, PARKS CANADA
Revised by G. L. Holroyd, Canadian Wildlife Service

Jasper National Park

Jasper, the largest of the Canadian mountain parks, lies along the eastern edge of the Continental Divide immediately north of Banff National Park. Over 250 species of birds have been reported. The park contains the southern breeding limits of the Willow Ptarmigan and one of only two known nesting sites of Black Swift in Alberta (other site in Banff Park, see elsewhere). There are large populations of Elk (Wapiti), some White-tailed and Mule Deer, Moose, Bighorn Sheep and Mountain Goats. A small herd of Mountain Caribou reside here at the southern limit of their range. Both Black and Grizzly Bears are present; Coyote and Timber Wolf are common.

Shortly after the transcontinental railroad went through the Yellowhead Pass to the West Coast, Jasper became a national park, in 1907. Today the Yellowhead Highway 16 bisects the park, providing access for the visitor to large tracts of wilderness, with over 1000 km of trails to explore. Highway 93 leaves the Yellowhead Highway at Jasper townsite and connects this park to Banff National Park to the south.

The 10,800 km² park, with 800 km² of valley bottom land, lies 310 km west of Edmonton on Highway 16. The town of Jasper, with the park headquarters, is another 48 km southwest from the entrance gate. Greyhound buses between Edmonton and the West Coast run through the park daily.

A small, grass-covered airstrip sits in the valley. There are a series of short roads and numerous hiking trails. The park brochures show these and other amenities. The main commercial accommodation is near to and in the town. Other cabins and amenities are available at Pocahontas and Miette Hotsprings near the east gate, at Sunwapta Falls, halfway to the Columbia Icefields and at the Icefields visitor centre at the south end of the park. Gasoline, other services, shopping and groceries are available in the town. There are 10 major campgrounds within the park. The main sites are south of town at Whistlers, Wapiti and Wabasso. Winter campers use special areas assigned by the park staff.

Information on natural and human history, and a seasonal bird checklist showing relative abundance and detailed descriptions, are included in *Birding Jasper National Park*, by K. Van Tighem (Jasper: Parks and People, 1988). The book, a bird checklist for the park ($1) and maps may be obtained from Friends of Jasper National Park, P.O. Box 992, Jasper, Alberta TOE 1E0 (e-mail: friends@incentre.net; Web site: http://www.visit-jasper.com/friendsofjasper. html). The interpretive service staff are found in the stone building on the main street in the centre of Jasper townsite. The park's Web site is at http://www. worldweb.com/ParksCanada-Jasper/

Birding Features

Habitats range from valley bottom wetlands to alpine tundra. To the west of the Continental Divide lie the wet forests of British Columbia; to the east, the Boreal mixed-wood, aspen parklands and prairies of Alberta. Rarities from both these areas are often found in the park. The Athabasca Valley is used as a migration route from the prairies to the West Coast.

Pocahontas Ponds. This area lies on the north side of Highway 16, 8.8 km west of the east park gate, and consists of willow-bordered sedge wetlands with nearby White Spruce. Osprey hunt here from early spring until fall. From mid-April to late May, look for Canada Geese, a variety of ducks, including Cinnamon Teals, and some migrating shorebirds. In June and July, passerines include Ovenbird, Magnolia and Orange-crowned Warblers, and Le Conte's Sparrow. From mid-July to September, the ponds are important staging areas for waterfowl and shorebirds. Up to 10 Great Blue Herons may hunt here.

Talbot Lake. The lake lies on the southeast side of Highway 16, 18 to 24 km from the east park gate and 25 to 31 km northeast from town. It is surrounded by a mixture of grasslands and spruce forest. The sedge bed complex at the north end is the most productive for the birdwatcher. From mid-April to late May, Bald Eagles are seen and waterfowl congregate on the lake. Species include Red-necked and Horned Grebes, Canada Goose, White-winged and Surf Scoters, Common and Barrow's Goldeneyes, Oldsquaw and Hooded Merganser. From mid-May to mid-July, listen for a Marsh Wren and Le

Conte's Sparrow at the north end of the lake. Common Loons and Canada Geese nest along the northern side, and Ospreys nest nearby. From mid-July to late September, watch for large concentrations of waterfowl, including White-winged and Surf Scoters and Hooded Mergansers.

The Celestine Fire Road. The road meets Highway 16, on the northwest side, 40 km from the east gate and 9.5 km north of the town. This one-way fire road parallels the Athabasca River on its northwest side for 33 km to the Celestine Lakes parking lot. Check with park staff or the sign for the times of the one-way access. The road winds through Lodgepole Pine, White Spruce and Douglas-fir forests and dry grassy slopes. Late April and early May are good times to come at moonrise to listen for Northern Saw-whet and Northern Pygmy-Owls near the Snaring district warden station. Blue Grouse and Townsend's Solitaires can be heard and seen at the forest edges near open slopes. In June and early July, Lewis's Woodpecker (rare), Say's Phoebe and Rock Wren occasionally are seen at the tight turn around the rock outcropping on the open slopes near Windy Point.

The Maligne Valley Road. This road stretches 48 km, from Highway 16, 1.5 km north of the town, to Maligne Lake. Maligne Canyon, with its several footbridges, is surrounded by pine forests. The water level of Medicine Lake is lowest during June but rises in July and August. Common Raven nests in Maligne Canyon from April to early May. Townsend's Solitaire nests on the open slopes above the canyon and at Medicine Lake. Pacific-slope Flycatchers may also be spotted along the canyon. Black Swifts are present in the canyon from late June to early September; this is one of their two known Alberta breeding sites (see Banff elsewhere for other site). Before dusk, go to the viewpoint 0.5 km south of the canyon to watch these birds return. Harlequin Ducks are best spotted at the outlet of Maligne Lake and on the upper Maligne River above Medicine Lake from mid-May to August. Cliff Swallows nest under the bridge at the outlet. In April and early May, listen for Boreal Owls after sunset along the lower end of Medicine Lake. Winter Wrens and Varied Thrushes can be heard in the deep spruce woods at the lower end of Medicine Lake across from the outlet. In winter, patches of open water remain on the Maligne River, especially at the outlet from Maligne Lake. American Dippers can be seen here throughout the year if you wait and watch. Pine Grosbeaks can be heard at the parking lot near the Maligne Lake concession.

Jasper Townsite. From late May through to early July, look for Rufous and Calliope Hummingbirds at feeders. In winter, feeders attract Steller's Jays, and Northern Pygmy-Owls occasionally prey on House Sparrows. The owls often sit on telephone wires.

Cottonwood Slough. Visit these wetlands 2 km from town, on the left of the road to Pyramid Lake. The complex of sedge-filled wetlands, beaver ponds, grassy slopes, pine and aspen forests is home to a variety of birds. It's one of the best places to bird in Jasper, especially if time is limited. At sunset, from March to early May, listen for Great Horned, Barred, Boreal and Northern Saw-whet Owls. Waterfowl, including Ring-necked Duck, are common from late April to late May, as are Pied-billed Grebe and Sora. In June and early July, watch for Rufous and sometimes Calliope Hummingbirds, Orange-crowned Warbler, Northern Waterthrush, Common Yellowthroat and Wilson's Warbler, and listen for the occasional Willow Flycatcher.

Athabasca River. American Dippers are seen on open river water throughout the winter.

The Whistlers' alpine meadows. Reach them by Sky Tram, which departs from near the parking lot 7 km southwest of Jasper off Highway 93. Before leaving town, check hours of tram operation. These upper meadows and rubble slopes are home for White-tailed Ptarmigan, Horned Lark, American Pipit, Gray-crowned Rosy-Finch and Fox Sparrow from June to late August. At the timberline transition look for Brewer's (Timberline race *Taverni*) and Golden-crowned Sparrows and the occasional Willow Ptarmigan. On the steep slopes at or below timberline, check for Townsend's Solitaire. In August, look for Sharp-shinned Hawk, Northern Harrier and Prairie Falcon.

The Valley of Five Lakes. These small, clear ponds lie about 6 km southeast along the hiking trail from Old Fort Point. This route passes through Lodgepole Pine and Douglas-fir forests, willow stands and open grassy slopes. A much shorter route is off Highway 93, 9 km south of its junction with Highway 16. This 2 km hike is an easy route. From mid-May to mid-July in the wetlands, look for Northern Waterthrush, Common Yellowthroat and MacGillivray's Warbler. In Douglas-fir stands, note Hammond's Flycatcher and Western Tanager. The lakes are home to Common Loon and Barrow's Goldeneye. Aspen forests house Ruffed Grouse and Hermit Thrush. In August Clark's Nutcrackers store Douglas-fir seeds on the slope near the lakes.

Amethyst Lake. The spot consists of a moist upper subalpine valley with large lakes, extensive sedge and willow meadows, flanked by open spruce and fir forests, and expanses of open alpine meadows. The lakes are reached either on foot or horseback on an overnight trip. Hike west from the Mount Edith Cavell road near its terminus, or west on the Portal Creek Trail from about three-quarters of the way up the Marmot ski road. The trip is about 15 km one way, or a 35 km loop. A primitive campsite at the lake and an outfitters' lodge both provide accommodation. Information on obtaining a booking for the lodge is available at the Jasper information office. This is a good area to look for Willow Ptarmigans at their southern breeding limit. Gray-cheeked Thrush has been noted singing here. Golden Eagles nest in the area. In the winter, this area is easily accessible on cross-country skis. Look for the tracks of flocks of Willow and White-tailed Ptarmigans that feed on the edges of the willow meadows. Once you find their tracks, follow them to the birds.

Throughout the park in winter, the hiker or cross-country skier should watch for roving bands of Black-capped, Mountain and Boreal Chickadees. Often they are accompanied by a few Red-breasted Nuthatches and Golden-crowned Kinglets. Ptarmigan watchers should take the cross-country ski trails along the open valley bottoms of Whistler's Creek near the Marmot ski area, Portal Creek, or the Maligne River upstream from Maligne Lake, to find these birds.

G. L. HOLROYD AND KEVIN VAN TIGHEM, CANADIAN WILDLIFE SERVICE AND J. PITCHER, INTERPRETIVE SERVICE, PARKS CANADA
Revised by G. L. Holroyd, Canadian Wildlife Service

Driving Loop: Edson/Cadomin/Hinton

The Edson loop includes foothill forests and mountain meadows. The trip provides an opportunity to explore Lodgepole Pine and Trembling Aspen-White Spruce forests, and Black Spruce-Tamarack bogs of the foothills. At higher elevations, you can find Engelmann Spruce forests and Subalpine Fir groves, together with two subalpine meadows higher yet.

Edson is 199 km west of Edmonton on paved Highway 16. The round trip through Edson-Hinton-Cadomin-Robb-Edson will take three days when paired with side trips to Silver Summit, north of Edson; to William A. Switzer Provincial Park, north of Hinton and south of Cadomin; to Prospect Mountain and Cardinal Divide. A quicker trip, to Cardinal Divide and Prospect Mountain only, can be undertaken from Edmonton in a two-day weekend. In one day, you can travel from Edmonton to Edson, up to Silver Summit and return to Edmonton.

Accommodation is found at several highway campgrounds around the loop, including one just south of Cadomin, often used as the midpoint. There are several motels and hotels in both Edson and Hinton. Those in Hinton fill up quickly from the Jasper Park overflow on busy weekends. Robb has one hotel. Restaurants and food stores are available in Hinton and Edson. Meals may be obtained in the Robb Hotel. Gas is available at all three places. Cadomin has a gas station and small grocery store, but both are closed on Sunday.

A bird checklist for the Cardinal Divide Natural Area is available from Edson Fish and Wildlife Office, Provincial Building, 111 – 54 Street, Postal Bag 9000, Edson, Alberta T7E 1T2; phone (780) 723-8244.

Birding Features

Begin at Edson. A variety of sideroads from here provide good birding. The best and most easily accessible route is north from town to the Silver Summit Ski Hill on Secondary Highway 748. The trip is good at any time of the year. Watch for Gray and Blue Jays, Black-capped and Boreal Chickadees, Ruffed and Spruce Grouse, Common Raven, Downy and Hairy Woodpeckers. If you're lucky, you may sight a Pileated, Three-toed or Black-backed Woodpecker. During the summer, Black Spruce bogs are likely to have Yellow-rumped Warbler, Hermit Thrush, Golden-crowned and Ruby-crowned Kinglets and possibly Yellow-bellied Flycatcher. In coniferous and mixed forests, look for a variety of warblers, including Magnolia, Northern Waterthrush and

Blackpoll. Watch and listen for Blue-headed Vireo, Swainson's Thrush, Western Tanager, Olive-sided Flycatcher, White-throated Sparrow and Winter Wren. Deciduous forests will have Red-eyed and Warbling Vireos, Tennessee and Yellow Warblers, Least Flycatcher, Western Wood-Pewee and Yellow-bellied Flycatcher. Birds of the wet willow-alder areas include Common Yellowthroat, Orange-crowned Warbler, Alder Flycatcher and Lincoln's Sparrow.

From October through April, look for Great Gray and Northern Hawk Owls. This is one of the best areas in Alberta to locate a Great Gray Owl. Winter finches, such as Common and Hoary Redpolls, Red and White-winged Crossbills, and Pine and Evening Grosbeaks are also seen regularly.

The next leg proceeds west from Edson to Hinton, where the country becomes more rolling. Birds to look for are similar to those on the Silver Summit leg.

To continue the circle, turn south off Highway 16 about 3 km west of Hinton, onto Highway 40 south to Cadomin. The country and birdlife are similar to those along the Silver Summit road. The streams, rivers and logged-over patches provide habitat in spring and summer for Spotted Sandpiper, Barn and Tree Swallows, and Mountain Bluebird. When you reach the turnoff to Cadomin (48 km south of Highway 16), turn south for 1 km to Cadomin. Another 3 km past Cadomin the road crosses Whitehorse Creek. The camp-ground is located at this crossing. Take a walk up and down the creek and look for an American Dipper. This bird usually nests under the waterfalls past the campground. The creek and adjacent woods often produce Harlequin Duck, Townsend's Solitaire, White-crowned and Chipping Sparrows, Dark-eyed Junco, and Boreal and Black-capped Chickadees. A stroll for a couple of kilometres up the trail along the side creek may produce Pacific-slope, Dusky and Olive-sided Flycatchers, Swainson's Thrush, Mountain Bluebird and Wilson's Warbler.

About 4 km past the campground, the road crosses Prospect Creek. Just before the crossing, a sideroad leads west to Prospect Mountain, 5 km from this point to the top and its alpine meadows. This road is now closed to motor-ized vehicles, but if you are prepared for a long hike it is well worth it as the birding at higher elevations is excellent. Along the way watch for clouds of butterflies, especially in wet spots on sunny days in June and July. Birds to look for include Pacific-slope and Dusky Flycatchers, Townsend's Solitaire and Mountain Bluebird. As you approach the treeline, watch and listen for White-crowned, Golden-crowned, Fox and Brewer's Sparrows. Above the trees in the alpine tundra, the most striking feature is the proliferation of flowers from mid-June and July to early August. Heathers and Mountain Avens form massive carpets. Dotted throughout are several species of saxifrage, Yellow Columbine, Moss Campion, louseworts and many others. Overhead in June, Horned Lark and American Pipit perform their aerial song displays. Small flocks of Rosy-Finches often drift by and can be seen foraging for food on the tundra. A careful search of these tussocks may turn up a family of White-tailed Ptarmigan. Occasionally a Prairie Falcon may fly over.

For those who are not prepared to make the long hike up Prospect Mountain, continuing along the road past Prospect Creek for another 20 km will take you to Cardinal Divide. The road climbs above the treeline at its highest point here, making it much easier to get to the alpine birding areas. Unfortunately, the road also makes access and thus use much greater and as a result the birding is generally not as good. Bird species are much the same as at Prospect Mountain; you will substantially increase your chances of seeing things by getting there early in the morning.

For the final leg of the trip, head northeast on Highway 40, then turn onto Highway 47 back to Edson. The vegetation and birdlife are much the same as on other legs of the loop.

TERRY THORMIN
Revised by Terry Thormin

Nojack – Carrot Creek

The site contains many warblers, thrushes and sparrows, nesting Sandhill Crane, and lots of owls including nesting Great Gray, Northern Hawk and Northern Pygmy-Owls, as well as the more common Great Horned and Northern Saw-whet Owls.

Evenings spent owling in this area are always rewarding. In the summer, listen carefully for the soft single hoot the Great Gray Owl gives to its young as you approach.

Nojack is 135 km west of downtown Edmonton on Highway 16 (Yellowhead). Ninton Junction has a small motel between Nojack and Carrot Creek on Highway 16. All services occur at Edson to the west. Camping is available at Minnow and Wolf Lake campgrounds described below.

Birding Features

Birding is best on the oil and gas development roads south of Highway 16 but a trip north to the bridge over the Lobstick River usually yields surprises. To reach it, take the road just east of Nojack, which runs north through the town of MacKay (Secondary Highway 751) for 5 km. Sandhill Cranes breed in the area. Listen for their calls from the road and watch for a pair with their young in the fields near the bridge. Marbled Godwits have occasionally been seen in these fields.

Travel back down to Nojack. Drive south of Nojack 1.6 km, then east 1.6 km. Turn right (south) for 3.2 km; at the T in the road, jog left (east) for a short distance, then turn right (south) at the start of the road to the Granada Gas Plant. Birding south on this road will yield many warblers, thrushes and possibly owls.

For the more adventurous, explore the oil and gas development roads farther in this area and in the area south of Carrot Creek, which is located about 18 km west of Nojack on Highway 16. Some well-gravelled gas and oil roads give access to muskegs and great nesting habitat for Great Gray and Northern Hawk Owls, and Palm and Blackpoll Warblers. It is a great way to explore the muskegs without getting your feet too wet. Because these roads frequently change, it is not advisable to travel far into this area without a recent 1:5,000 Resource Access Map (available from Map Town, 10344 105 Street NW, Edmonton,

Alberta T5J 1E6; phone [780] 429-2600). Map 83 G/12 covers the area adjacent to Highway 16. Map 83 G/5 is the area south of that and, for the really
adventurous, map 83 G/4 will take you to the Pembina River.

For more good birding, drive about 12 km past the town of Carrot Creek
on Highway 16 where a road goes south to both Wolf Lake and Minnow Lake
Campgrounds. Continuing south on this road leads you to the Pembina River
and connects to the gas and oil roads which run just north of the river.
Resource Access Map 83 F/1 has the connection to the gas roads on it.

In addition to the birds mentioned above, the lakes, streams and ponds in
the area have a large variety of common water birds, together with Common
and Forster's Terns, Osprey, Olive-sided Flycatcher, Swamp and Lincoln's
Sparrows, both Solitary and Spotted Sandpipers. Common Nighthawks feast
on the numerous flying insects. Woodpeckers are abundant, including both
Black-backed and Three-toed.

Other birds of the mixed-wood forest include Mountain Bluebird in more
open areas created by logging or fire. Cedar Waxwings nest here. Swainson's
and Hermit Thrushes can frequently be heard and occasionally a Veery appears.
This habitat is also home to the Blue-headed, Philadelphia, Red-eyed and
Warbling Vireos. Warblers are a specialty, including Tennessee, Orange-
crowned, Magnolia, Yellow-rumped, Black-and-white, Connecticut and
American Redstart. Other good birds to be expected include Western Tanager
and Rose-breasted Grosbeak. White-winged and Red Crossbills are numerous in some years.

BARB AND JIM BECK

Wabamun Lake

This large shallow lake 65 km west of downtown Edmonton and just south
of Highway 16 can produce some fine birding at any time of year. Local
birders know it as the hot spot for birding in late fall and winter because of
three power plants that keep part of the lake and a number of adjoining cooling
ponds open all year. More water birds have been recorded in the Wabamun
Lake Christmas Count than any other count in Alberta. The three plants
include the Wabamun Power Plant near the northeast corner of the lake,
Sundance just west of the southeast corner of the lake and the Keephills Plant,
not on the lake, but southeast of the southeast corner of the lake on Secondary
Highway 627.

Accommodation is available in the town of Wabamun, as are gas and
restaurants. Camping is available at the Wabamun Lake Provincial Park at the
northeast corner of the lake.

A checklist of the birds of Wabamun Lake Provincial Park can be obtained
at Box 30, Wabamun, Alberta T0E 2K0.

Birding Features

Summer birding at this lake is similar to birding at many other lakes in the
area, although this is a good area to look for Ospreys. Several of the large power
poles around the eastern end of the lake are used for nesting sites.

In late fall, as the colder weather sets in and as surrounding lakes freeze over, Wabamun becomes a magnet for any water birds already in the area or migrating through. Late fall and early winter is the time to look for unusual gulls and loons. Birds that have turned up include Glaucous and Iceland Gulls, Black-legged Kittiwakes and Red-throated and Pacific Loons. As more people bird the lake at this time of year, this list will undoubtedly grow.

Once winter truly sets in, the lake freezes over more and more, and the open water shrinks to an area concentrated around the east end of the lake. At this time the best place to view the lake is generally from the dock in the town of Wabamun. Here one can usually find a good variety of ducks and often one or two grebe species. Almost every regularly occurring species has been recorded at least once. Both Trumpeter and Tundra Swans have been seen. Another good place to look for these birds is Point Alison, just west of the town of Wabamun. Bald Eagle and Gyrfalcon often hang around in this area as well.

The Sundance Power Plant on the south side of the lake is not accessible without permission. It is best to phone TransAlta ahead of time to get permission. To get to the plant, take TransAlta Road south from Highway 16 (3 km east of the road to the Wabamun townsite). Make sure that you do not turn right into the Provincial Park about .25 km down this road. Follow the road about 13 km until you see a road going off to the right. This takes you right past the Sundance plant. About 3 or 4 km before you get to the plant office, there is a pull-off and trail going into the left. This goes to a cooling tower that often has Hooded Mergansers under it. The main cooling pond and the outflow canals often produce such unusual winter birds as Gyrfalcon, Bald Eagle, Great Blue Heron and Double-crested Cormorant. Other rarities have included American Black Ducks and Glaucous Gulls.

The Keephills Plant can be reached by continuing another 4 km down TransAlta Road to the T intersection of Secondary Highway 627. Turn left (east) here and you will quickly start encountering cooling ponds on either side of the road. As well as the usual ducks and geese, watch for Gyrfalcon, Rough-legged Hawk, Bald Eagle and perhaps even a Golden Eagle.

Woodland birding is also good here in winter. Wabamun Lake Provincial Park, accessed from the north end of TransAlta Road, sometimes has a Black-backed or Three-toed Woodpecker. The road that goes past the Sundance Road and along the south side of the lake passes through mixed and coniferous forests that can produce Boreal Chickadee, Gray Jay, Pine Grosbeak, redpolls of both species and, with a bit of luck, a Great Gray Owl or a Northern Hawk Owl. The small communities around the lake are good places for bird feeders and will often turn up an unusual species. Some of the more unusual winter birds include Rusty Blackbird, Yellow-headed Blackbird, Steller's Jay and Harris's Sparrow.

TERRY THORMIN

Blue Ridge – Goose Lake – Carson Lake

The triangle between Blue Ridge, Goose Lake, which is north of it, and the Carson Lake Campground, due west, is a very rich area for birds, including the much sought-after Connecticut Warbler, which can frequently be heard singing in the area between June 5 and 25. A large number of owls are present, including Barred, Great Gray, Northern Pygmy-Owl, Northern Saw-whet and Boreal. Woodpeckers are abundant, including many Black-backed and Three-toed. Exploring the logging roads is always rewarding.

There is a hotel in Blue Ridge, many hotels and motels in Whitecourt and public camping at Carson Lake Provincial Park.

From Edmonton drive west on Highway 16 (Yellowhead); turn north on Highway 33; northwest on Highway 43; about 80 km later turn north on Secondary Highway 658 to Blue Ridge town. Goose Lake is located approximately 22 km north of Blue Ridge on Secondary Highway 658.

To get to Carson Lake Provincial Park travel north through the town of Whitecourt on Highway 43; turn onto Highway 32 towards the town of Swan Hills. The access to the campground is about 11 km up Highway 32. Exploring the many logging roads in this area is always rewarding.

Birding Features

Bird the road that runs east and west of Blue Ridge. Six to 7.5 km west of Blue Ridge on the north side of the road looking down on the Athabaska River is a consistently good place to find Canada Warblers. Connecticut Warblers are common in the area but there are two particularly good places to find them. From the town of Blue Ridge, travel north across the Athabaska River. Shortly after crossing the river, Secondary Highway 658 is intersected by a big well-maintained gravel road (the main haul road for the mill) from the left (west). From this junction proceed north 3 km on Highway 658, then turn west (left) onto a gravel road. Bird this short road from Highway 658 to the main haul road, which it crosses again in a few kilometres; often Connecticut Warblers appear here. Return to Highway 658. An even better spot for Connecticut Warbler is farther up Highway 658 just before it reaches Goose Lake. As many as 21 singing male Connecticuts have been recorded in a 1.6 km stretch of road in this area. If you proceed up Highway 658, the road turns slowly to the east. Approximately 16 to 17 km from the first Connecticut Warbler site above, the road makes a right angle; turn north. Go another 3.2 km, then turn left (west) and you are at the start of the Connecticut Warbler area. Bird 3.2 km west on this road, then 3.2 km north and finally 6 km east. At this point you are near Goose Lake. Continue on the road taking the branches to the left and you reach Lone Pine.

The main haul road which is crossed by Highway 658 just north of Blue Ridge is a good place to bird, as are some of the well-maintained smaller logging roads which branch off it. An occasional Spruce Grouse crosses your path. A large number of owls are in the area, including Barred, Great Gray and Northern Pygmy-Owl, as well as the more common Great Horned and Northern Saw-whet. The muskegs and mixed woods in this area are good places to spend an evening owling. Woodpeckers are abundant in the mixed-wood forest, Black-backed and Three-toed. The lakes, small ponds and streams in the area have a large variety of water birds. If you are really lucky you may spot a cavity-nesting Hooded Merganser on a beaver pond near her nesting hole. Other special birds found near these wetter areas include Nelson's Sharp-tailed and Swamp Sparrows. You can hear and occasionally see some of the Sandhill Cranes which nest in the muskegs. Special shorebirds include Solitary and Spotted Sandpipers. Ospreys are near the lakes. Near beaver ponds listen for the "quick-three-beers" of Olive-sided Flycatchers. The mixed wood is home to Warbling, Blue-headed, Red-eyed and Philadelphia Vireos. Many warblers are present, including such specials as Black-throated Green, Black-and-white, Mourning and Wilson's Warblers. White-winged Crossbills and occasionally Red are found in considerable numbers in the conifer stands in good cone crop years.

BARB AND JIM BECK

Grande Prairie Region

The city of Grande Prairie is located at the southern end of a relatively flat island of prairie and parkland surrounded by boreal forest. This region, known as the Peace Parkland, is a primary breeding area for Trumpeter Swans. Swan numbers remained steady around 100 birds from 1946 to 1970, but have increased from about 250 birds in the mid-80s to about 350 at present. In addition to providing nesting habitat for swans, the numerous bodies of water to the west of Grande Prairie provide migration staging sites for other waterfowl and shorebirds. Whether travelling north to Alaska or the Yukon or circling through northwestern Alberta en route from points south, travellers should stop a day or two to explore the variety of habitats ranging from prairie to mountain. The city of Grande Prairie, with its 30,000 people, provides a good base.

Fur traders arrived in this country by the late 1700s, using the Peace River as the main water route. The first settlement of any size began at Lake Saskatoon, just west of Grande Prairie, in 1881. Reports of fertile land to the north led to homesteaders walking in from Edson (over 300 km to the south) in the late 1800s and early 1900s. The first school opened in Grande Prairie in 1913. From the arrival of the settlers, the economic base of the region has been agriculture. The establishment of a plywood mill in 1953 began a new chapter in resource development – forestry. The discovery of one of Alberta's largest gas-oil fields in 1978 has brought in more money and people.

Grande Prairie lies 460 km northwest of Edmonton. The main road, Highway 43, is paved all the way northwest, passing through spruce forests for most of the route. The city has a major airport, with three companies providing daily flights. Greyhound buses supply six daily runs to and from Edmonton. Cars can be rented at the airport or in town.

Good visitor services are offered here. Campgrounds are located at most of the provincial parks, at highway sites and within the city. Gasoline and repair service is limited to the city and the few larger towns in the vicinity. Travellers going southwest into the hills or away from the settled community should carry their own gasoline supplies and repair kits. Traffic on these roads is light.

The Peace Parkland Naturalists offer field trips in May and June and can also provide more detailed information about birding in the region. Write to them at Box 1451, Grande Prairie, Alberta T8V 4Z2 or call Muskoseepi Park at (780) 538-0451 for contact information.

Birding Features

City of Grande Prairie. A visitor coming to the area with very limited time should hike Muskoseepi Park in the centre of town. This corridor of natural vegetation in the Bear Creek valley encourages a variety of birdlife to come into the city. A paved walking and biking trail extends the length of the park and circles around Bear Creek Reservoir in the northwest. A spring walk in south Bear Creek (accessed at 68th Avenue and 100th Street) should turn up a variety of warblers plus Western Tanager, Rose-breasted Grosbeak and Swainson's Thrush. Crystal Lake, in the city's northeast, offers a boardwalk and observation blind from which one might spot Red-necked Grebe, diving and puddle ducks, Yellow-headed Blackbird, a number of sparrow species, and the occasional Trumpeter Swan. For more information on birding in the city, contact Muskoseepi Park Pavilion at (780) 538-0451.

Bear, Ferguson and Hermit Lakes. For anyone interested in waterfowl, a visit to these lakes just west of town is a must. County roads passing by all these sites, as well as along the north side of Clairmont Lake, offer good views of most species of diving and puddle ducks, as well as geese and often Trumpeter Swans (a pair of swans nests on Hermit Lake). Also watch wet fields for shorebirds such as Black-bellied Plover and American Golden-Plover, Sanderling and yellowlegs. The Clairmont sewage lagoon, immediately west of the hamlet of Clairmont, is also a good place to check for shorebirds and the occasional Peregrine Falcon.

Saskatoon Island Provincial Park. The island, bordered on both north and south by lakes but accessible by car, contains about 40 ha of developed land and 81 ha of natural woods with roads and trails. Aspen and willow, with scattered spruce, are interspersed with abundant Saskatoon bushes. Sedges and cattails spread along the shoreline. There is an excellent campground here. The village of Wembley, about 10 km south of the park, has groceries, a hotel and a service station.

The surrounding cleared farmlands make this park an island of native vegetation in a sea of crops. From late April to June, watch for five grebe species, Pied-billed, Horned, Eared, Western and Red-necked. Trumpeter Swans gather here before dispersing to their individual territories. Prairie slough ducks are found, including Canvasback and Redhead. Great Horned and occasionally Great Gray Owls may be present. Yellow-headed, Red-winged and Brewer's Blackbirds may all be seen at this site. In the nesting season from late May through to mid-July, look for Sharp-shinned and Cooper's Hawks; Merlin; American Kestrel; Sharp-tailed Grouse; Long-eared, Short-eared and Northern Saw-whet Owls; Rufous and Ruby-throated Hummingbirds; Hermit, Swainson's and Gray-cheeked Thrushes; and a variety of warblers and sparrows. From the last week in May to the end of June, a pair of Trumpeter Swans nests on a muskrat house on the extreme east or extreme west end of Little Saskatoon Lake (the southern smaller lake).

In the fall, late August through October, Saskatoon Lake acts as a staging area for huge flocks of Tundra Swan, Canada Goose and Mallard. Smaller numbers of Trumpeter Swan and an occasional Snow and Greater White-fronted Goose may be seen. Ducks are abundant. Bald and Golden Eagles hang around the water's edge and later on, in early November, they sit on ice around open patches of water to pick off the late-departing ducks. Large flocks of Lapland Longspur, Horned Lark, American Pipit and numerous Rough-legged Hawks pass through, as do Sandhill Cranes.

The winter observer can see Northern Goshawk; Ruffed and Sharp-tailed Grouse; Great Horned, Snowy, the occasional Great Gray and Northern Saw-whet Owls; and perhaps even a Gyrfalcon.

For further help at Saskatoon Provincial Park, telephone the park office at (780) 766-2636.

Saskatoon Mountain Natural Area. Rising out of the farmland west of Saskatoon Lake, Saskatoon Mountain is the highest point of land in the Grande Prairie area. Covered in mixed-wood forest, the site provides easy access to birds and plants typical of the northern boreal forest. Possible sightings include Ruby-crowned and Golden-crowned Kinglets; Western Tanager; Olive-sided Flycatcher; Blue-headed, Red-eyed, Philadelphia and Warbling Vireos; Mourning Warbler and Redstart. Access the natural area by turning north off Highway 43 at the Huallan corner and follow the paved secondary road as it climbs the mountain and curves to the west. Trails enter the forest in a number of spots on the east side of the large abandoned hayfield. Be sure to look south and west as you drive along the top – the view is fantastic. The hayfield once housed a federal radar station but now the area has been designated a provincial natural area. There is archaeological evidence on the mountain suggesting that early peoples travelling from the Bering land bridge used the site during the last ice age.

For the more adventurous interested in warblers and other boreal forest species, explore the logging roads south of the Wapiti River such as at the crossing of Iroquois Creek.

Kleskun Hills Natural Area. This 93 ha site protects one of the few remaining patches of native prairie vegetation beyond the breaks of the Peace River. You can reach the area by turning north off Highway 43, 20 km east of the city (follow the wildlife viewing signs). This unique site is home to a number of plant and animal species that are otherwise found much farther south. Watch and listen for Upland Sandpiper, Western Meadowlark, Eastern Kingbird, Vesper and Clay-colored Sparrows – and be careful not to step on cacti.

Finding Trumpeter Swans
These, the heaviest North American bird, nest on Hermit Lake (above), Little Saskatoon Lake (above) and on Flyingshot Lake just south of Grande Prairie.

Pairs of swans may also nest on each of Albright, Ponita and Preston Lakes, all of which are located northwest of Hythe, which is 58 km west of Grande Prairie on Highway 43. Swans may use other lakes in the vicinity, depending on the year. Local birds gather with flocks of non-breeding swans on Saskatoon and Bear Lakes prior to migrating to a warmer climate. The last swans leave in October.

For more information on Trumpeter Swans, contact the Grande Prairie Ducks Unlimited office at (780) 532-7960.

ELLEN AND GAVIN CRAIG
Revised by Margot Hervieux

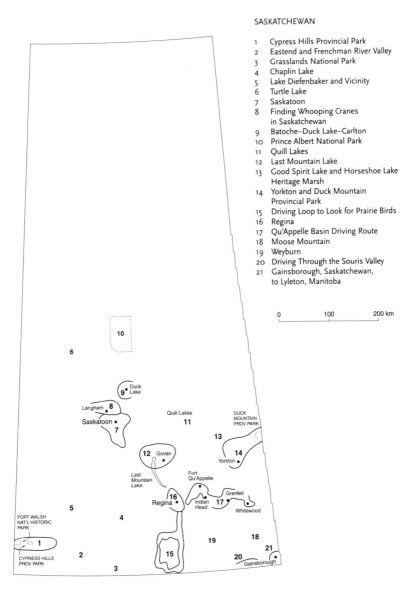

SASKATCHEWAN

0   100   200 km

10

6

9 • Duck
    Lake

Langham • 8
Saskatoon •   Quill Lakes   DUCK
        7   11   MOUNTAIN
                                      PROV PARK

                                        13

12 Govan •   14
                                    Yorkton •
Last
Mountain
Lake   Fort
            Qu'Appelle
        16   Grenfell
    Regina •   Indian   17 •
FORT WALSH   Head   Whitewood
NAT'L HISTORIC
PARK   5
                    4   18
                          19   20   21
    1   Gainsborough
CYPRESS HILLS   2   15
PROV PARK   3

SASKATCHEWAN

According to Euclidian geometry, the shortest distance between two points is a straight line. To many, Saskatchewan has been two points on the Trans-Canada Highway between Manitoba and Alberta. To the millions of birds that have been migrating from the warmer climes in the south to either Saskatchewan or farther north to the Arctic, Saskatchewan has always been a very popular place. Saskatchewan will afford those who are not used to the vast expanses of prairies, lakes and rivers, a variety of riparian, forest and prairie regions to enjoy as vacationers and birders.

Tourism Saskatchewan provides travel information and guide books and secures confirmed room reservations. They can be reached toll-free at 1-877-237-2273, at their Web site www.sasktourism.com, or by e-mail at travel.info@sasktourism for an official road map and free guide books on vacation, hunting and fishing sites as well as on accommodations (including camp-grounds, bed-and-breakfast locations) and events. For specific information on provincial parks, the Saskatchewan Department of Environment and Resource Management has a toll-free number (1-800-667-2757) as well as a Web site, www.gov.sk.ca/govt/environ/

Nature Saskatchewan and the Blue Jay Bookshop at 206–1860 Lorne Street, Regina, Saskatchewan, S4P 2L7, phone (306) 780-9273, has various brochures and booklets which are very useful for exploring the province. Their e-mail address is nature.sask@unibase.com

C. STUART HOUSTON
Revised by Martin Bailey

Cypress Hills Provincial Park

In Saskatchewan, as in Alberta, the Cypress Hills form islands of forest, with an upper tableland of fescue grass surrounded by bald prairie. Portions of the hills were not covered by ice during the last glaciation, the only place in Saskatchewan that remained ice-free. Consequently, they became a refuge for several species of plants not normally found in the province. Similarly, Trumpeter Swans and mountain species such as Townsend's Solitaire and Rosy-Finch (winter only) are still here. Turkey Vultures and introduced Wild Turkeys are also present.

The Cypress Hills have long served as retreats from the prairie for big game and man. The forested slopes offered shelter from winter blizzards and hot windy summers. Lodgepole Pines provided tepee poles for the nomadic plains people. The last major fire swept through in the late 1870s; consequently, the evergreen trees are almost all about a hundred years old.

In Saskatchewan, the park comprises two blocks of land of about 78 km². An additional 130 km² of neighbouring, privately held prairie are usually considered part of the birding trip, since these lands occur between the two park sections.

Access to both parts is by paved roads from Maple Creek: 52 km northeast of the West Block on Highway 271 and 27 km north of the Centre Block on Highway 21. Maple Creek is 8 km south of the Trans-Canada Highway, in the southwest corner of Saskatchewan. The Gap Road, a rough dirt trail passable only in dry weather, connects the two blocks. Fort Walsh National Historic Park sits immediately south of the West Block. A dirt road from Fort Walsh connects to the Alberta portion of the park.

Accommodation may be found in the park at the Cypress Hills Four Seasons Resort; phone (306) 662-4477. However, it is usually full; telephone for reservations one week in advance. Over 400 campsites in eight campgrounds fill up on the long weekends in spring and fall and during weekends in July and August. There is one primitive campsite in the West Block. Maple Creek has fine motel and hotel accommodation. Gasoline (only in summer) and a telephone are available in the Centre Block. The closest services are in Maple Creek, including a hospital and the RCMP.

Additional information is found in *Birds of the Cypress Hills and Flotten Lakes Regions, Saskatchewan,* by W. Earl Godfrey, Bulletin No. 120, National Museums of Canada, Ottawa; and *The Cypress Hills – A Natural History,* available from the Royal Saskatchewan Museum, Wascana Park, Regina, Saskatchewan S4P 3V7.

The park has a resident staff, and a park naturalist is available year-round. For further information, write The Superintendent, Cypress Hills Provincial Park, Box 850, Maple Creek, Saskatchewan S0N 1N0; phone (306) 662-5411;

or call Wayne Harris at (306) 746-4519 or leave a message at (306) 778-8218; e-mail him at wayne.harris.erm@govmail.gov.sk.ca; or write him at Box 500, Cheadle Street W., Swift Current, Saskatchewan S9H 4G3.

Birding Features

The hills, with their forested slopes of Lodgepole Pine (the only such forests in Saskatchewan) and White Spruce, are capped by a tableland of fescue prairie grasses. The habitat provides a unique opportunity to see several mountain bird species, including Dusky Flycatcher, Townsend's Solitaire, Audubon's race of the Yellow-rumped Warbler, MacGillivray's Warbler and Rosy Finch (winter only). Southern species may also be spotted, including the introduced Wild Turkey, Long-billed Curlew and Rock Wren. The best forest birding spot is along the Valley-of-the-Beavers Nature Trail.

From late May to late July is the best time for birding. Take Highway 21 south from Maple Creek and then the Park Road west to the administration area. The Valley-of-the-Beavers Nature Trail lies south of the administration building on the south side of Loch Lomond. On the trail, look for Dusky Flycatcher, Yellow-rumped (Audubon's) Warbler, MacGillivray's Warbler, Western Tanager and White-crowned Sparrow. On the northwest side of Loch Leven, adjacent to and west of the administration building, a short hiking trail leads to where Red Crossbills are often noted. Along the trail to Bald Butte, in the northwest corner of the Centre Block, look for Sprague's Pipits and Baird's Sparrows.

In dry weather, take the Gap Road towards the West Block. Watch for Long-billed Curlew, Upland Sandpiper, Sprague's Pipit, McCown's Longspur and Chestnut-collared Longspur. In the West Block, just before the ranger station, turn north and east to the Conglomerate Cliffs (nests of Townsend's Solitaire), Adams (White Pelican here) and Coulee Lakes (for Trumpeter Swan). In November and December, Townsend's Solitaire is found at springs along Adams Creek on the east side of the West Block or in ranch yards around the area. Around the cliff look for a MacGillivray's Warbler. Adams and Coulee Lakes are northeast of the cliffs. Nesting Trumpeter Swans occur on Coulee Lake and American Avocet can be found at both of these lakes. Drive back to the ranger station in the middle of the West Block. Proceed west beyond the station a short distance and then go north on the road. Look for Wild Turkeys on the Lodgepole Pine slopes. Farther along this road in the forests near the edge of the park, watch for a Red-breasted Nuthatch and Red Crossbill.

Return to the ranger station. Take a short drive west towards the west boundary, then get out and hike in the woods adjacent to Battle Creek. Look for a Dusky Flycatcher.

Proceed east, back past the ranger station, to the road to Fort Walsh. Go there to see the reconstructed fort and whisky trader's cabin. They are very well done and there is an excellent interpretive program. Return north to just south of the Gap Road, where a ranch road takes off to the south. Follow it past the first ranch, immediately south of Fort Walsh, and continue on to the second ranch. On the south side of this second ranch, take the road west towards another ranch. Look for Rock Wrens along this stretch. At the ranch and just to the west of it, check the brushy coulees and hillsides leading away from the hills for Lazuli Bunting and Lark Sparrow. Ranch stockyards are sometimes the place to spot a Rosy-Finch from December to February.

WAYNE HARRIS
Revised by Wayne Harris

Eastend and the Frenchman River Valley

Nestled in the Frenchman River Valley on Highway 13 is the town of Eastend. Coming west on Highway 1 from Regina go south at Gull Lake on Highway 37 to Shaunavon, then west on Highway 13 to Eastend. From Calgary proceed east on Highway 1 to Maple Creek; turn south on Highway 21 to the junction of Highway 21 and Highway 13 and drive east to Eastend.

Eastend is a major palaeontological site where finds from both Cretaceous and Tertiary periods are presently being unearthed. This unique area of short-grass prairie and steep river cut-banks provides habitat for over 250 bird species. A bird checklist is available from Joan Hodgins, Box 583 Eastend, Saskatchewan SON 0T0; phone (306) 295-4703, fax (306) 295-4702, e-mail jhodgins@sympatico.ca or Robert Gebhardt, Box 413, Eastend, Saskatchewan SON 0T0; phone (306) 295-3680, e-mail rg_negus_42@yahoo.com

Birding Features

In the wooded coulees dominated by spruce and pine are Red-tailed Hawk, Red-naped Sapsucker, Ruby-crowned Kinglet, Veery, American Robin, "Audubon's" Warbler, Ovenbird, Western Tanager, Spotted Towhee, Chipping and White-throated Sparrows, "Pink-sided" Junco, Red Crossbill and Pine Siskin. Both Eastern Screech- and Northern Saw-whet Owls may nest here.

The coulees dominated by Trembling Aspen and Green Ash hold Merlin, Great Horned Owl, Downy and Hairy Woodpeckers, "Red-shafted" Flicker, Western Wood-Pewee, Least and Dusky Flycatchers, Cedar Waxwing, Warbling Vireo and MacGillivray's Warbler.

In town watch for Common Nighthawk, Western and Eastern Kingbirds, Black-billed Magpie, Clay-colored Sparrow, Baltimore Oriole and House Finch. "Red-shafted" Flicker is common, with the occasional "Yellow-shafted" and hybrid birds to be seen.

Along the Frenchman River, which flows through town, are Yellow-breasted Chat, Northern Rough-winged Swallow and Bullock's Oriole. A drive out of town along a gravel road south of the Riverside Motel on the way to the Eastend Reservoir may be an opportunity to see Spotted Sandpiper; Ring-necked Pheasant; Belted Kingfisher; Red-naped Sapsucker; Mountain Bluebird; Gray Catbird; Brown Thrasher; Clay-colored, Vesper, Lark and Song Sparrows; as well as Brewer's Blackbird. At the reservoir you may see American White Pelican, Double-crested Cormorant and Great Blue Heron. Bank, Barn, Tree and Rough-winged Swallows are common sights.

The hillsides and cliffs of the Frenchman Valley are home to Say's Phoebe, Violet-green Swallow, Rock Wren and Mountain Bluebird. Thermals rising from the cliffs provide lift for Turkey Vulture and Swainson's, Red-tailed and

Ferruginous Hawks. Golden Eagle, American Kestrel, Merlin and Prairie Falcon are also in the area. Along the flats are Willow and Least Flycatchers; Ring-necked Pheasant; Eastern Kingbird; Clay-colored, Vesper and Savannah Sparrows.

The marshes and lakes of the valley provide habitat for American Bittern, Black-crowned Night-Heron, four or five grebe species and a likely place to attract vagrant egrets and White-faced Ibis. Nesting shorebirds include Killdeer, American Avocet, Willet, Spotted Sandpiper, Marbled Godwit, Common Snipe and Wilson's Phalarope. Other marsh birds are Sora Rail, American Coot, Sedge and Marsh Wrens, Common Yellowthroat, Le Conte's (and possibly Nelson's Sharp-tailed) Sparrow, Red-winged and Yellow-headed Blackbirds.

ROBERT KREBA AND JOAN HODGINS

Grasslands National Park

One of Canada's newest national parks, Grasslands is an excellent representation of native mixed-grass prairie little changed from 500 years ago. Park headquarters is located 125 km south of Swift Current, Saskatchewan, in the village of Val Marie. The park consists of two blocks covering three distinct landforms, Frenchman River Valley, Killdeer Badlands and Wood Mountain Uplands. Diversity of landforms, large extents of native prairie and rich habitat make this area excellent for birding. Beside birds watch for Antelope, Mule and Whitetail Deer, a variety of snakes, Short-horned Lizard and a profusion of wild flowers.

For more information contact the park office at (306) 298-2257 or by e-mail at grasslands_info@pch.gc.ca The park is open year-round.

Birding Features

Begin the visit with a stroll through Val Marie's oasis of wooded streets before exploring the park. In town, Purple Finches, American Goldfinches and Baltimore Orioles are common; Red-Headed Woodpeckers are a rare and special sight.

Head for the park by driving west from town along Highway 18, then turning south onto the "ecotour road" (marked with a Grassland National Park sign). Enter the park 15 km east of Val Marie. Watch for Loggerhead Shrike as you pass old farmsteads; they are often visible along fence lines or atop trees and shrubs. The ecotour road takes you into the Frenchman River Valley and the West Block. Black-tailed Prairie Dogs call this site home at the northern limit of their range. Look for Burrowing Owls, frequently seen sitting on or near mounds within the dog towns in the early morning and late evening. Mountain Plovers are a rare sight on the extensive colonies of Prairie Dogs.

April to June is a wonderful season to enjoy the birds of Grasslands. Long-Billed Curlew and Upland Plover make their way noisily across the prairie. High above the grass the song of Sprague's Pipits is heard throughout the park. Listen and look for the dancing grounds, or leks, of Sharp-tailed Grouse. Chestnut-collared and McCown's Longspurs can also be found in the uplands.

Ferruginous, Red-tailed and Swainson's Hawks are commonly seen, and Golden Eagles can be spotted circling high in the warm summer air.

You can circle through the west block and return to Val Marie to camp in the village campground or return to Highway 18 and continue east towards the town of Wood Mountain and the East Block of Grasslands National Park. Lark Buntings and Horned and Meadow Larks are common sights along the way.

Stop at Wood Mountain Regional Park for woodland birds in and around the park. The variety of warblers include Bay-breasted, Magnolia, Yellow, Yellow-rumped, Blackpoll, Tennessee and Ovenbird. Look for vireos and watch for Hermit and Swainson's Thrushes. Try the Wood Mountain Regional Park swimming pool after hiking in the heat and isolation of the East Block.

The East Block may be reached via Highway 18, south of Wood Mountain. Maps are available at the Rodeo Ranch Museum in the regional park. Park your vehicle near the park house at the end of the road; cross Rock Creek and explore the rugged lands of the East Block. Prairie Falcons are frequently found in the eroded hills and badlands. Sage Grouse may occasionally be seen in the coulees and draws, hidden in the shade of the bush from which they get their name. Sage Thrashers may be spotted in these raw, rough lands. More common are Chipping, Clay-Colored, Savannah, Baird's, Grasshopper, Brewer's and Lark Sparrows, all of which make good use of the extensive native prairie.

OLAF JENSEN

Chaplin Lake

Chaplin Lake is located adjacent to the Trans-Canada Highway, approximately 150 km west of Regina. Canada's second largest saline water body is approximately 51 km² in size. Surrounded by a complex of smaller fresh-water basins and mixed-grass prairie, this area attracts as many as 250 different bird species.

The lake was found by Lord Henry Chaplin during his trek across the prairies in pursuit of the large bison herds. In 1861, his party settled here and developed a small community near the two large salt-water lakes. In honour of the two founders, Chaplin and Johnstone, each had a lake named after him. In 1955 Lake Johnstone was changed back to its original name of Old Wives Lake to preserve the native culture of the area.

Information on natural and human history and a seasonal checklist are available at the Chaplin Interpretive Centre. The centre, located on the north side of the Trans-Canada at the entrance to the village, is open from the beginning of May until the end of August. For more information, contact the Projects Manager, Chaplin Tourism Inc., Box 30, Chaplin, Saskatchewan S0H 0V0; phone (306) 395-2223, or go to the Web site, www.sasktourism.sk.ca/chaplin

Birding Features

The Chaplin area has fresh and saline wetlands, surrounded by native prairie, cropland and coulees. The sodium sulphate mining operations at Chaplin Lake produce ideal conditions for shorebirds. The shallow water required for the solution mining operation produces expanses of mudflats resulting in large areas of feeding habitat. The highly saline water is ideal for the production of invertebrates such as midges, mosquito larvae and brine shrimp. Nearby small, fresh-water basins provide drinking and bathing facilities for birds actively feeding on the saline areas. The open expanses give good visibility to detect approaching aerial predators.

The site has a long tradition of use by arctic migrants. As many as 35 species of shorebirds have been observed using the lake. In spring and again in fall, birds coming from as far away as Tierra del Fuego will stop for a few days to rest and replenish energy reserves before continuing northwards or on their way back south.

Sanderling in excess of 60,000, almost half of the hemispheric population, annually use the lake, with the peak time being late May and early June. Baird's, Semipalmated and Stilt Sandpipers, along with a number of other species, can also be found in the thousands during this time. Due to the region's importance for migratory and breeding shorebirds, the complex of Chaplin Lake, Old Wives Lake and Reed Lake have been recognized as having hemispheric significance by the Western Hemisphere Shorebird Reserve Network.

The flats also provide a staging site for local nesting shorebirds. The diverse shoreline habitats, including the numerous dykes and small islands, are ideal for breeding Piping Plovers and American Avocets. Surrounding grasslands and grazing pastures give ample cover for upland nesters including Wilson's Phalarope, Marbled Godwit, Willet and Long-billed Curlew. Upwards of 7000 Wilson's Phalaropes and 2700 American Avocets have been observed in late July and early August at Chaplin Lake. The number of birds drops dramatically in late summer as shorebirds continue or begin their long journey to wintering grounds.

Chaplin Heritage Marsh. The Chaplin Heritage Marsh is located southeast of the main lake and village and is accessed from the southeast corner of the marsh. It was one of ten heritage marshes constructed in the province as a cooperative venture with the Government of Saskatchewan, Ducks Unlimited Canada, Saskatchewan Wildlife Federation and Nature Saskatchewan.

The marsh is a complex of wetlands comprising three main, deeper water bodies and several shallow, flooded lowlands. These wetlands are much less saline and support diving ducks, fresh-water wading birds and other marsh species. Some notable species that have been sighted include Glossy and White-faced Ibises, Virginia and Yellow Rails and Green Herons. In some of the larger basins, man-made nesting islands support breeding colonies of Ring-billed, California and Franklin's Gulls, American White Pelican and Double-crested Cormorant. In the surrounding reeds and rushes, look for large numbers of American Bittern, Sora, Marsh Wren and Black-crowned Night-Heron.

The uplands adjacent to the marsh are pristine native prairie. Many of the shorebirds and waterfowl that can be found in the marsh nest in this area. Other species recorded here are Baird's Sparrow, Lark Bunting, Burrowing and Short-eared Owls, Ferruginous Hawk, Loggerhead Shrike and Long-billed Curlew.

JOSH BILYK AND GERRY BEYERSBERGEN

Lake Diefenbaker and Vicinity

Lake Diefenbaker, 225 km long, originated in 1958 with the erection of two dams, the larger on the South Saskatchewan River near Cutbank, 175 km south of Saskatoon, and the other on the Qu'Appelle River near Bridgeford, 135 km northwest of Regina. The lake, within a day's drive of either city, and 12 other birding hot spots are fully described with maps in Frank Roy's *Birds of the Elbow*, a 325-page book published by Nature Saskatchewan in 1996 ($30). National Topographic Series maps (1:250,000) 72J, 72K and 72O cover the entire lake. (See Saskatoon writeup for prices and sources.) Contact Frank Roy for further advice on the area at (306) 374-8571.

Birding Features

The most spectacular birding experience in Saskatchewan occurs at the west end of the lake in late September and early October between Antelope Creek (north of Cabri) and Lancer Ferry (north of Lancer), a 55 km stretch of the South Saskatchewan River along Highway 738. The greatest concentration is around Galloway Bay (take dirt roads south and west from Highway 342 west of White Bear) and Miry Bay (reached by going north on a dirt road west of Cabri). In the 1990s more than half a million geese (mostly Greater White-fronted, but also Lesser Snow, Ross's and several subspecies of Canadas) and up to 160,000 Sandhill Cranes congregated here on their way south. The visual and aural experience of thousands of flocks of geese and cranes flying out to feed – as far as the eye can see – in grain fields through the pre- and post-sunrise period is awe-inspiring. Most birds return between 9 and 11 A.M., only to make the same trip again, for some as far as 25 km, flying out between 5:30 and 7 P.M., with the last birds returning after dark. The size of the concentrations is affected by the number of wetlands up to 160 km north of the lake. A few hunters are to be expected during the week (not on Sundays) but they do not seriously affect the spectacle.

The endangered Burrowing Owl can still be found around Kyle. On October 20, 1992, 123 Bald Eagles were seen on the dead trees and bars in Galloway Bay and westward.

Luck Lake. Once a periodically dry alkaline slough, oval in shape and 7.5 km across when full, Luck Lake has had permanent water since 1989, thanks mainly to Ducks Unlimited piping water in from an irrigation canal. They also constructed two dykes across the lake, totalling 8.6 km, and erected 10 nesting islands (subsequently occupied by colonies of California and Ring-billed Gulls). In the 1990s, the water-bird population reached 100,000, with September to early October counts as high as 9000 Tundra Swans, 60,000 geese, mainly Lesser Snows, 70,000 ducks and 15,000 Franklin's Gulls. Up to 15,000 shorebirds of 20 species have rested there between mid-July and mid-August. This mecca for birders is significantly enhanced by the drivable dykes. Luck Lake can be reached from several points between Birsay and Lucky Lake on Highway 45. National Topographic Series map 72O (1:250,000) covers the region.

Water birds are not the only attraction. In the last half of May and late

August, more than 100 species of birds have been found several times in one day in an area bounded by the roads closest to the lake. In total 230 species have occurred here, including 173 in a deserted farmstead on the northeast corner of the lake. As with all good birding areas, rarities have occasionally been noted, among them Green Heron, White-faced Ibis, Cinnamon and Tufted Ducks, Yellow Rail, Whooping Crane, Townsend's Warbler, Brewer's Sparrow and others.

Because of large numbers of Mallards, the north end of the west dyke is used as a bait station to deter the ducks from flying out to damage farmers' crops. Gates at both ends of the feeding site are locked for part of August and September. However, you can drive the dyke to that point and then turn around to return.

FRANK ROY AND BERNIE GOLLOP

Turtle Lake

The Turtle Lake drainage area is situated on a major flyway and at the contact point of Boreal Forest and Aspen Parkland in west-central Saskatchewan. Just south of the lake, the parkland gives way to valleys and ravines that descend from the Thickwood Hills to gently rolling plains that drain into the North Saskatchewan River. Knob and kettle topography provides many sloughs and saline basins.

Visitors from Edmonton and points west should take Highway 17 north from Lloydminster, then east on Highway 3 to near St. Walburg, where it joins Highway 26 to Turtleford; proceed east on 3 to either of two north-south resort access roads (Turtle Lake West and Turtle Lake East, 7 km farther). A Saskatchewan Grid Road map (available at Rural Municipal Offices) will help you during your travels.

If you come from the south via North Battleford, take Highway 4 north to Glaslyn, where you have two options: continuing north on 4 for 26 km into the forest just past Moose Country Service to the DNR road that winds west for 16 km to Turtle Lake Lodge and other resorts on the east side of the lake. The other choice takes you 18 km west on Highway 3 (past Fairholme) to the Turtle Lake East Road. Turn right (north) and enjoy some open range and sloughs before you reach the forest. Accommodation is available at Turtle Lake Lodge, Turtleford and St. Walburg.

Information about many birding hot spots and nature-viewing sites is available in a brochure, *A Birders Paradise*, available at local resorts, hotels, inns and bed-and-breakfasts, as well as from Nature Saskatchewan (call 1-800-667-4668 or 1-306-780-9273). It contains a checklist of 281 species identified within a triangle bordered by Highway 4 on the east, the North Saskatchewan River on the south and west, and the northern Continental Divide, which runs parallel and just beyond the northern perimeter of Turtle Lake. If you explore the many lakes, streams, drylands and marshes, you should have no trouble finding 100 species in one day from mid-May through June.

It is a good idea to carry food and water and keep your gas tank full. Keep a bottle of meat tenderizer handy to touch up mosquito or wasp or bee stings:

cell phones are operational at Turtle Lake now. And remember – this is bear country.

Contacts at Turtle Lake include Muriel Carlson (306) 845-3227 and E. M. Robinson (306) 845-2857.

Birding Features

The Turtle Lake Nature Sanctuary, owned by Nature Saskatchewan and located on the east side of the lake between Indian Point and Turtle Lake Lodge, is about 130 acres of lakefront property, with a shoreline trail that can delight both novice and expert. In peak migration, between May 20 and June 15, waves of warblers, thrushes and Rose-Breasted Grosbeak have been observed. Eight rare species of warbler nest on or near the sanctuary, along with Great Crested Flycatcher, Great Gray Owl, Pileated Woodpecker, Red-necked Grebe and Swamp Sparrow. Sabine's Gulls and Caspian Terns have been sighted here in June. Two viewpoints along the shoreline trail are more than 10 m above lake level so bring a spotting scope. Only foot traffic and bicycles are permitted. Pick up a self-guiding brochure about the sanctuary from the store at the lodge. If you have time, walk some trails on the Wildlife Lands immediately behind the sanctuary.

Indian Point, just south of the sanctuary, is a spruce-birch forest. Walk the loop. Check out trails behind the cottages; you may see Blackburnian, Black-throated Green and Cape May Warblers, Western Tanager, Baltimore Oriole and occasionally Rufous Hummingbird (believed to have nested here in 1997, as well as at St. Walburg, 30 miles, or 48 kilometres, west). Go south beyond Golden Sands Beach and walk the sandy shore to the Gran Swamp where you may call up Marsh Wrens and rails.

The north end of Turtle Lake is accessible only by boat (rent one at the lodge). See the Great Blue Heron colony on Spruce Island; watch for Common Loon, Bald Eagle, immature American White Pelican and Double-crested Cormorant, as well as the colonial nesting sites of Franklin's Gull, Western Grebe (occasionally Clark's), Forster's Tern and Eared Grebe. Local residents will point out the Osprey nest at the southern tip of Moonlight Bay.

To reach the forest north of the lake, go east on the DNR road to the junction with Highway 4, turn left for 28.7 km. At the stop sign on your left, look for an ungravelled fire-guard road known locally as the Bingo Highway, which circles well beyond the north end of the lake and eventually joins Grid Road 795 that goes west to St. Walburg. This back road provides access for logging trucks, so drive with care. The forest is home to 18 species of warblers and usually provides flyovers by raptors such as Broad-winged Hawks and Turkey Vultures.

Night "owling" is good on all of the above roads: expect Northern Saw-whet, Boreal, Great Gray, Barred and Great Horned Owls.

Grid Road 796, the Spruce Lake Road, originates part way up the west side of Turtle Lake. This road passes through some spectacular hills and crosses several streams and marshes before reaching the village of Spruce Lake on Highway 26. Look for American Bittern, Black-crowned Night-Heron,

Bonaparte's Gull, Sora, Yellow and Virginia Rails. Find White-winged Scoter, Common and occasionally Barrow's Goldeneye on Brightsand Lake.

Mudflats are rare in the area and are found mostly around Turtleford and Edam or spring-fed ponds near Paradise Hill. Farther west, the Monnery and Englishman Rivers are good birding sites as well. Piping Plover has nested at Russell Lake east of Edam and Marbled Godwit and Avocet are regular nesters there. Permission is needed from owners to view.

MURIEL CARLSON

Saskatoon

A city of 206,000 with the South Saskatchewan River flowing through it, Saskatoon is located near the southern edge of the Aspen Parkland, but much of the area west of the city is grassland. It is less than 150 km south of the boreal forest. Within 55 km of the city, 330 species of birds have been found, of which 125 breed regularly. During spring and fall migrations, a person can find more than 100 species in a day's search. A 1993 bird checklist for the area, showing relative abundance by season, is available from the Saskatoon Nature Society by phoning (306) 665-1915.

Several hotels and motels are along the river; some accept pets. There are public and private campgrounds in the city and nearby on major highways. Public campsites are provided at Pike Lake Provincial Park, 24 km southwest by way of Highways 7 and 60, at Blackstrap Provincial Park, 35 km south on Highway 11 beside a large reservoir of the same name, and at the Borden Bridge Campsite on the North Saskatchewan River, 50 km northwest on Highway 16. There are five vacation farms (bed-and-breakfast) in the area. Information on these and other sites, along with their facilities, is available from Tourism Saskatchewan as listed at the beginning of this section and from its Saskatoon branch, phone (306) 933-5900.

The best maps for the area are the National Topographic Series at a scale of 1:250,000 (1 cm = 2.5 km; 1 in. = 4 mi.): Saskatoon (73B) for the north part of the area and beyond and Rosetown (72O) for the south part. These are available for $11.25 each, from Saskatchewan Environment and Resource Management, toll free at 1-800-667-2757 in Regina or at their Saskatoon office on the University Campus (112 Research Drive, phone [306] 933-5766).

Weekly field trips are sponsored by the Saskatoon Nature Society in spring, summer and fall, less often in winter. For dates and meeting places, call (306) 665-1915 (Saskatchewan Environmental Society).

Habitats

Within 55 km of Saskatoon, about 65% of the land is sown to cereal crops and canola or remains in summerfallow; 25% is in pasture and 10% in woods, water or pavement. In years of heavy snow, literally thousands of sloughs (ponds) appear in spring. By fall they may have evaporated to fewer than 100. There are 18 named lakes (many of them alkaline and some seasonal) and 3 reservoirs: Blackstrap, 35 km south on Highway 11; Brightwater, 6 km west of

Hanley; and Bradwell, 3 km southeast of Bradwell. Just north of the airport is a large, typical prairie slough.

The original upland habitat consisted of prairie and aspen bluffs (groves). Today the most extensive natural areas are in five federal Prairie Farm Rehabilitation Act (PFRA) pastures, municipal and private pastures. Obtaining permission to enter these pastures has become more difficult in recent years. However, in the northeast part of the city (north of Konihowski Road.), a 12 ha reserve of native mixed prairie – the Saskatoon Natural Grassland – with a one-hour self-guided walking trail has been established. An interpretive centre for this site, from which there will be guided tours on various aspects of natural history, is expected to be opened in 2000. For details, phone the Saskatchewan Environmental Society at (306) 665-1915.

There are no forests near Saskatoon but Aspen Poplar bluffs liberally dot the landscape. The larger aspen stands are found southwest of Dundurn and Pike Lake, northeast of Asquith and near Borden. These areas appear in green on topographical maps. High densities of potholes (ponds) occur in wet years in the Strawberry Hills, north and south of Highway 5, 8 km east of Saskatoon; around St. Denis, 19 km east of town on Highway 5, and in the Allen Hills, 13 to 25 km east of Hanley. Extensive marshes may be found at Pike Lake, Indi Lake (3 km southwest of Blackstrap Reservoir), Rice Lake (24 km west of the junction of Highway 14 and Highway 7 and 5 km south), Brightwater Marsh (in spring) and Ducks Unlimited's Centennial Project, both within 5 km southwest of Dundurn.

Birding Features

The Saskatoon Nature Society has published an excellent 122-page guide to birding and other aspects of natural history within 55 km of the city – *A Guide to Nature Viewing Sites in and Around Saskatoon* – edited by Peter Jonker and Bernie Gollop. The guide has maps and seasonal lists of the birds found at each of 8 city and 11 country sites, with information on the other vertebrates, most common plants and butterflies. Published in 1992, it is out of print and being revised. A second guide to more than 20 other sites within a day's drive of the city (55 to 155 km) is expected to be published in 2000. It is edited by Jim Wedgwood.

The best birding sites within the city are the west bank of the South Saskatchewan River (225 species), the university campus (185), Forestry Farm Park and Zoo (a federal bird sanctuary; 175), Diefenbaker Park (175) and Cosmopolitan Park (170). The Meewasin Valley Authority has created a series of walking trails (paved and unpaved) on both sides of the river; most of these sites are along them.

Beyond the city, 245 species of birds have been found in Blackstrap Provincial Park; 225 in Pike Lake Provincial Park (which also has a park naturalist); 215 around Bradwell Reservoir; 175 at the Beaver Creek Conservation Area (which has an interpretation centre) on the South Saskatchewan River, 13 km south of the city on Highway 219; 152 at Radisson Lake, 70 km northwest; and 145 at Wanuskewin Heritage Park, 5 km north of the city on Warman

Road. Picturesque Eagle Creek 40 km west of town crosses Highway 14 and flows into the North Saskatchewan River.

Farther afield near Hafford is Redberry Lake, 80 km northwest of Saskatoon (take Highway 12 and then west on gravel Municipal Road 781). This federal bird sanctuary has hosted over 200 species of birds. While nesting islands for White Pelican (1500 birds), gulls and terns are protected, boat tours by the Pelican Project – phone (306) 549-2400 or 549-2558 – take passengers within sighting distance. A regional park at the lake's northwest corner has campsites, a concession and an interpretive centre (open by advance arrangements). The Quill Lakes, near Dafoe, 160 km east of Saskatoon on Highway 16, are a Ramsar site – a wetland of international importance – and a critical shorebird area for the western hemisphere. (Refer to this site elsewhere.)

The greatest diversity of birds occurs during the last two weeks of May and from the third week in August to mid-September. Shorebirds – up to 32 regular species – may be found in large numbers from July through September. In September and October, concentrations of White-fronted, Snow, Ross's and Canada Geese, Tundra Swan and Sandhill Crane appear on such areas as Goose, Radisson, Perdue and Rice Lakes (when they have water), Zelma Reservoir and along the South Saskatchewan River, north and south of the city. In May these arctic breeders are dispersed over many more wetlands and remain in the area for a much shorter period. Thirty-four species of waterfowl, 29 raptors, 28 warblers and 22 sparrows have also been found here.

The following species with ranges largely restricted to the prairie provinces breed in and around Saskatoon: Eared and Western Grebes, White-winged Scoter (on Redberry Lake), Swainson's Hawk, Marbled Godwit, American Avocet, Franklin's Gull, Western Kingbird, Black-billed Magpie, Yellow-headed and Brewer's Blackbirds, Spotted Towhee and Baird's Sparrow. There are more than 100 dancing grounds (leks) of Sharp-tailed Grouse – the provincial bird – occupied from March to early May. Summering, but not known to

Sharp-tailed Grouse

Whooping Crane

breed, are American White Pelicans (at the city weir), California Gulls and Forster's Terns. The nature viewing guide lists the sites where these birds can be found, but many breed on sloughs, on prairie and in aspen groves not specified in those lists. The Saskatoon birders listed as contacts may be able to tell you the best sites for individual species when you are here.

Ten species listed by the Committee on the Status of Endangered Wildlife in Canada are found here: the endangered Piping Plover (Buffer Lake and see nature guide); the threatened Peregrine Falcon (on the downtown Radisson Tower), Loggerhead Shrike and Sprague's Pipit (both widespread); vulnerable species: Ferruginous Hawk (occasionally), Yellow Rail (Pike and Porter Lakes), Long-billed Curlew (south of Proctor Lake, 15 km northwest of Hanley), Short-eared Owl and Caspian Tern (both rarely). Also found regularly in September and October within a day's drive of the city is the endangered Whooping Crane. Locations for this species can be obtained by contacting the Canadian Wildlife Service in Saskatoon (phone [306] 975-4087; fax: [306] 975-4089), which also has a hot line for reporting Whooping Cranes – (306) 975-5595.

Several Christmas Bird Counts are conducted in the area. Winter visitors include Bohemian Waxwings, redpolls, Snow Buntings and Snowy Owls.

J. BERNARD GOLLOP
Revised by J. Bernard Gollop

Finding Whooping Cranes in Saskatchewan

Western Saskatchewan is on the principal migratory path of the Whooping Crane. Fall is the best season to see these birds, which often linger near one spot, from several days to a week or more, on their leisurely movement southward. These cranes pass through the province from late September through October. The birds may travel singly, in family groups of both parents and an immature, or in flocks of several individuals.

In spring, the birds move quickly through the province on their way north. They may be seen from late April to mid-May, depending on the weather.

The Canadian Wildlife Service (CWS) coordinates spring and fall migrations of Whooping Crane. Updates of crane observations can be obtained from Brian Johns, Whooping Crane Co-ordinator, CWS, Saskatoon. Phone (306) 975-4109 or call the Whooping Crane Hotline at (306) 975-5595.

BRIAN JOHNS
Revised by Brian Johns

Batoche–Duck Lake–Carlton

Carlton has been renowned as a birder's paradise for 160 years and is a great attraction for anyone with an interest in the history of ornithology. The first naturalist to visit Fort Carlton, then the pemmican provisioning centre for all of the Hudson's Bay Company Territory (i.e., western Canada), was Dr. John Richardson, surgeon and naturalist with the first Franklin arctic expedition in 1820. Richardson spent from May 10 to 26 at Carlton. He was so impressed that he returned there for the spring migration at the end of the second Franklin expedition in 1827. To do so, he travelled a thousand miles on foot from Great Slave Lake to Carlton, between Christmas Day of 1826 and February 12, 1827.

The area lies about 75 km north from Saskatoon or south 55 km from Prince Albert. The visitor can breathe in the history by visiting the old fort, whose palisades and buildings have been rebuilt just as they were in Richardson's time. Guides at the Fort Carlton Historic Park will show you around in season, and one can still see the furrows made by the Red River carts going up the hill behind the fort.

Visitor accommodation, services and car rentals are readily available at either Saskatoon or Prince Albert. Both cities have campgrounds. Saskatoon is served by three airlines on a daily basis, and Prince Albert by two, in addition to bus service.

Since this is a major national historic site, much published tourist information is available from SaskTravel in Regina and Saskatoon. The National Historic Sites Information Service in Ottawa will, upon request, mail out an information package.

Birding Features

Carlton is on the scientific map as the type of locality where the Swainson's Thrush, Rosy Finch, Clay-colored Sparrow and Smith's Longspur were first described. Further, Dr. Richardson and his assistant, Thomas Drummond, described subspecies of the Hairy Woodpecker, Loggerhead Shrike and Rufous-sided Towhee. They noticed differences in the pale form of the Merlin, and in the Boreal Owl, for over a century known as Richardson's Owl.

Carlton was next visited by Captain Thomas Blakiston, the magnetic observer and meteorologist with the Palliser expedition. Blakiston was at Carlton from October 23, 1857, until about June 10, 1858.

The detailed reports of Richardson, Drummond and Blakiston allow an opportunity unrivalled on this continent to know the condition of birdlife prior to agricultural settlement. Today the summer visitor will, without difficulty, see and hear from the road Rufous-sided Towhee, in the coulee leading down to the fort, and hear on all sides the buzzing song of the Clay-colored Sparrow. Imagine the excitement Richardson must have felt in discovering these new birds!

On the other hand, some of the larger birds that were common in Richardson's time, especially the Trumpeter Swan, Bald Eagle, Whooping Crane and Sandhill Crane, no longer breed in the area. The Passenger Pigeon, seen in small flocks by Richardson, has been gone for 80 years. Trumpeter Swan skins are no longer a major article of trade with the Hudson's Bay Company.

Now that wetlands are less numerous, there are fewer bitterns, ducks, Sora, Willet and Marbled Godwit than Richardson described. The scavenging Common Raven was once more numerous than the American Crow. The latter has thrived and increased greatly with settlement. Similarly, Turkey Vultures are less likely to be seen, although with a little luck one may be spotted flying along the river. Hollow trees were more numerous in the wooded area, and Common Goldeneye, Bufflehead and Hooded Merganser more abundant. Today, at the little lakes between Carlton and MacDowall, particularly Roddick Lake, resident pairs of Common Goldeneye and Bufflehead may still be noted.

In the 1820s, Carlton marked a sharp boundary between treeless prairie, kept open by almost annual prairie fires from the south, and mixed forest of aspen and spruce of the north.

Much of the grassland has been ploughed and converted to grain fields. Swainson's and Ferruginous Hawks and the Upland Sandpiper are no longer common. The Ferruginous Hawk is gone; a few Swainson's Hawks and Upland Sandpipers remain on the pastures.

Carlton is still at the boundary between birds of the prairies and those of the mixed forest. Brown Thrasher and an occasional Say's Phoebe represent the more southern species; Gray Jay, Blue Jay, White-throated Sparrow and an occasional Pileated Woodpecker of the north still nest here. Some warblers of the mixed forest, including the Connecticut, are heard singing throughout June. In the aspen parkland, Gray Catbird, Veery, Red-eyed Vireo, Warbling Vireo, Rose-breasted Grosbeak and American Goldfinch are readily heard singing in the wooded coulees. Spotted Sandpiper and Belted Kingfisher occur along the river bank.

With settlement came new birds, including the Mourning Dove, as well as the introduced species, House Sparrow, European Starling, Ring-necked Pheasant, Gray Partridge and Rock Dove. The Black-billed Magpie, gone with the buffalo for about 30 years, returned in the 1930s and has become common since the late 1950s. The Mountain Bluebird, because of bird boxes, is now more common than ever before.

The visitor in late June and July will also encounter flowers in profusion, especially the Western Lily, Saskatchewan's floral emblem.

C. STUART HOUSTON

Prince Albert National Park

Prince Albert National Park preserves 2875 km^2 of Fescue Grasslands mixed with Aspen Parkland, which gives way to Boreal Forest in the northern half of the park. At least 227 bird species have been reported, including Great Gray and Boreal Owls, and a colony of 6000 to 7000 American White Pelicans. The park is home to numbers of Moose, Elk, Wolf, Lynx and Black Bear; it is, as well, the last home and resting place of Grey Owl, the author.

This block of wilderness lies 90 km north of Prince Albert, on Highway 2. The STC bus comes right to the town of Waskesiu, in the park, from June to September. At other times, the bus drops you off at the junction, about 15 km from the townsite. There are several hiking trails, with 100 km of cross-country ski trails through the rolling country. The park is a favourite of canoeists, who use the well-mapped-out routes, one of which leads to Grey Owl's cabin and grave.

Several motels and other privately operated accommodation units are available in the town. Reservations should be made well ahead for July and August. There are three major serviced campgrounds, plus primitive sites located on the canoe routes.

Information, including a park map showing trails and canoe routes, and a checklist, is available from The Superintendent, Prince Albert National Park, Box 100, Waskesiu, Saskatchewan S0J 2Y0; phone (306) 663-5322.

The naturalist-interpretive service operates all year. Drop them a note at the above address or contact them when you arrive.

Birding Features

The transition from mixed-wood forest to boreal forest makes this park a place to see a wide variety of bird species. Some, like the Veery and Sprague's Pipit, are near their northern limit, while others like the Wood Duck are at their western limit.

Perhaps the most frequently seen are boreal forest species. These include Great Gray and Boreal Owls, Black-backed Woodpecker, Gray Jay and Boreal Chickadee. Coniferous forest species easily spotted in the central and northern section of the park include Yellow-bellied and Olive-sided Flycatchers, and such warblers as Magnolia, Cape May, Black-throated Green, Blackburnian, Bay-breasted and Blackpoll. The northern bogs produce Nashville and Palm Warblers, Northern Waterthrush and Swamp Sparrow. Pine Siskin and White-winged Crossbill occur frequently. A great number of lakes, ponds and sloughs regularly provide habitat for most species of duck found in central Canada, as well as Common Loon and Red-necked, Western and Horned Grebes.

The fourth-largest pelican colony in Canada is on Lavallee Lake in the northwest corner of the park. The nesting island also hosts colonies of Double-crested Cormorant and Great Blue Heron. This is the only completely protected spot for American White Pelicans in Saskatchewan. This Special Protection Area, National Park Zone 1, is off limits to all visitors except by special permission.

Two of the many Prince Albert National Park's nature trails are excellent places to observe typical breeding birds of the park.

The Treebeard Trail, named for the hanging strands of *Usnea* (Old Man's Beard), is located near the end of Narrows Road close to Narrows Campground. The area is populated by large firs, White Spruce, Black Poplar and Aspen. Birds along the trail may include Blackburnian, Black-throated Green, Cape May, Bay-breasted, Connecticut, Mourning, Magnolia and Yellow-rumped Warblers, which are all summer residents here, as are Winter Wrens. Black-backed, Northern Three-toed, Hairy and Pileated Woodpeckers are permanent residents. Western Tanagers and Blue and Gray Jays are found along the trail. Breeding raptors include Northern Goshawk, Bald Eagle and Osprey.

While the Narrows Road is often closed during the winter, a small area of water remains open all year. Look for River Otter and, in early spring, Common Loon.

The Boundary Bog Trail is near the east entrance to the park. Yellow-rumped Warbler, Golden and Ruby-crowned Kinglets and Northern Three-toed Woodpeckers are found in the upland areas of the trail. Note the three species of vireos: Blue-headed, Red-eyed and Philadelphia. Particularly check for Philadelphia where White Spruce or Jack Pines have been topped by winds.

Spruce Grouse are permanent residents within the uplands. They are also found on some of the islands within the bogs of Boundary Bog Trail. The islands are accessible via floating boardwalks. Other summer residents of the bog are Palm Warbler, Olive-sided Flycatcher, Western Wood-Pewee and Swamp Sparrow.

Northern Goshawk and Great Gray Owl are permanent residents in this area, with Boreal Owl nesting along the East Entrance Road. Look for them in vacant Pileated Woodpecker holes in aspens along sandy ridges on hillsides.

MERV SYROTEUK
Revised by Bob Luterbach

Quill Lakes

The Quill Lakes area is an excellent place for migrant shorebirds, waterfowl and cranes in the fall. Few spots provide access to the massive salt-water lakes themselves, and fluctuating water levels greatly affect viewing possibilities. However, cultivated fields, isolated stands of Trembling Aspen, pastures, hayfields and wetlands surrounding the lakes can easily provide a competent birder with a respectable day list. The Quill Lakes area can be reached by travelling 150 km north of Regina on Highway 6 or 160 km east of Saskatoon on Highway 16.

Birding Features
East side of Little Quill Lake and Wadena Wetlands Trail System. Approximately 3.5 km south of Wadena on Highway 35, a gravel road leads west for 5.6 km to the Wadena Wildlife Wetlands viewing tower and trail. Trail maps are available on site. Looking west from the tower expect to see Eared and Pied-billed Grebes, American White Pelican, a variety of dabbling and diving ducks,

Northern Harrier, Franklin's and California Gulls and Bank, Cliff or Barn Swallows. Patient observers should be able to spot or hear American Bittern, Black-crowned Night-Heron, Common Snipe, Sora and Virginia Rails, especially around dusk. American Kestrel, Northern Flicker and Least Flycatcher are summer residents in the small woodland to the north of the tower. Common Yellowthroat and Marsh Wren are present in the marshes. Clay-colored and Le Conte's Sparrows occupy nearby meadows. Migrant Peregrine Falcons are occasionally seen here in spring and fall.

Road 640. This gravel road, which runs between Big and Little Quill Lakes from Wynyard to Quill Lake townsite, is a good route to view migrant (April and May) and breeding (May and June) water birds. Quill Creek crosses the road approximately 7 km south of Quill Lake townsite and is always worth a stop. Large numbers (often in the hundreds and maybe thousands) of Tundra Swans, Sandhill Cranes and Snow and Canada Geese use the cultivated fields along Road 640. Pied-billed Grebe, Ruddy Duck, Blue-winged Teal, Gadwall, Mallard, Northern Shoveler, Lesser Scaup, Redhead, Killdeer, Willet, Marbled Godwit, American Coot and both Red-winged and Yellow-headed Blackbirds use the local wetlands. Watch for American White Pelican, Double-crested Cormorant, Franklin's Gull and Northern Harrier overhead.

Mud – Little Quill Lakes control structure area. Ten kilometres south of Quill Lake townsite (or 22.5 km north of Wynyard) on Road 640, take the gravel road that leads east. Drive 4 km and then turn south until the road either ends at a small dam (about 5 km) or becomes too wet to travel. Once at the dam, a short walk to the east leads to the west side of Little Quill Lake. A short walk to the west leads to the east side of Mud Lake. Large colonies of American White Pelican and Double-crested Cormorant can be seen on the distant islands of Mud Lake. The waters of both lakes should be scanned for Eared and Western Grebes. The shores are probably the best (and most accessible) place to see migrant shorebirds at the Quill Lakes. However, viewing opportunities are strongly influenced by water levels. American Golden-Plover, Black-bellied and Semipalmated Plovers, Hudsonian Godwit, both yellowlegs, both dowitchers, Dunlin, Red-necked Phalarope, Ruddy Turnstone, Red Knot, Sanderling, and Baird's and Stilt Sandpipers are all possible. The beaches and surrounding uplands provide a summer home for American Avocet, Spotted Sandpiper, Marbled Godwit, Willet and the endangered Piping Plover. Marshy areas provide habitat for Black-crowned Night-Heron, Common Tern, Sora, Yellow Rail, Sedge Wren and Nelson's Sharp-tailed Sparrow. Large numbers of Canvasback, Franklin's Gull and Black Tern concentrate on the shores in midsummer. The local woodlands feature Red-tailed Hawk, Northern Flicker, Least Flycatcher, Western Kingbird, House Wren and Baltimore Oriole. Early spring and late fall migrants include Tundra Swan, Sharp-shinned Hawk, American Pipit, Snow Bunting and Lapland Longspur.

Mozart Area. The fair-weather roads to the north and east of the small town of Mozart provide access to several wetlands, willow thickets and aspen stands.

American Avocet, Black and Forster's Terns, Mourning Dove, Eastern Kingbird, Gray Catbird, Yellow Warbler, Song and Savannah Sparrows, Baltimore Oriole and Brown-headed Cowbird should be easily found in summer. Less common are American Bittern, Black-crowned Night-Heron and Hooded Merganser. Road crossings over Duck Hunting Creek should be checked for Eastern Phoebe and swallows. On fall-out days, migrant passerines such as American Redstart; Northern Waterthrush; Orange-crowned, Tennessee, Blackpoll and Cape May Warblers; and Harris's and White-crowned Sparrows are possible. One should find Bobolinks in moist meadows.

Access to Big Quill Lake. Fair-weather roads leading east from Highway 6 provide access to the west side of Big Quill Lake. Roads at 6.4, 9.6, 16.0 and 19.2 km north of the north junction of Highways 6 and 16 will take you east towards the lake. At the end of each of these roads, a walk will be required to access the lakeshore. Walk lengths depend on water levels but distances of up to 3 km can be expected. Rubber boots and insect repellent are recommended. Pastures along these roads should be checked for Swainson's Hawk, Upland Sandpiper, Sprague's Pipit, Chestnut-collared Longspur and Western Meadowlark. Big Quill Lake can also be viewed by travelling north on Big Quill Road (about 1.5 km), which is 2 km east of the town of Kandahar.

Windmill Point. On Highway 5, drive 13 km west of Wadena (just past the ghost town of Paswegin) and take the gravel road heading south. Go 3 km to a T junction and turn west for about 1 km. Take the fair-weather trail leading south, watching for raptors over the hayfields, and follow it as far as conditions permit. You should see an old windmill on the right. The woodlands and ponds near and to the south of this old yard offer a variety of habitats for several species of migrant and breeding birds. Trails heading east lead to the shore of Little Quill Lake. Continue south, exploring the area on foot until you reach the tip of Windmill Point. Heavy shrub cover and muddy areas will be encountered, but birding the point is well worth the effort. Rarities such as Barrow's Goldeneye and Oldsquaw have been found in this area. A network of fair-weather trails on the west side of Windmill Point can be reached by returning to the gravel road at the correction line and going approximately 2 km west.

BURKE KOROL

Last Mountain Lake

Large numbers of Sandhill Cranes and other water birds congregate each spring and fall on the wildlife management area north of Regina. The marsh and open water complex, surrounded by native grasslands, provides first-class habitat for nesting and migrating species. Whooping Cranes visit regularly, spring and fall. White-faced Ibis and all three white Egrets occur regularly.

The first Canadian federal and second North American bird sanctuary was established here in 1887. Created as the Last Mountain Lake Bird Sanctuary under the Migratory Birds Convention Act, lands set aside originally included

American White Pelican

the northern 17.6 km of lake. An additional 6100 ha of marginal farmland near the northern end of the lake was acquired in 1966 and 1967 to become the first federal-provincial wildlife area in Canada. In the following year, 1968, a further 3467 ha of provincial Crown land was added, and the Last Mountain Wildlife Management Unit was born.

Roughly 19 km by 8 km, the 15,600 ha management unit is reached from Regina by driving 76 km northeast on Highway 11, then taking Highway 2 north for 71 km to Simpson. Drive 13 km east and follow the signs to the head-quarters building and check in to find out about recent sightings. From Saskatoon, proceed south on Highway 11 for 80 km, then 56 km east on Highway 15 to Highway 2, south 7 km through Simpson, and east as above. A regional park on the east side lies about 14 km northwest of Govan off Highway 20. Here you'll find some modern trailer sites with electricity. Hotel accommodation is available in the nearby towns of Imperial, Simpson, Nokomis and Govan. Hospitals and medical facilities are available in Nokomis and Imperial. Gasoline outlets are found in all villages except Stalwart, with Nokomis and Simpson the best bet on Sundays. Retail outlets are closed on Monday. For a detailed checklist of the unit, contact the area manager at the headquarters building or write him: Manager, Wildlife Management Unit, Canadian Wildlife Service, Box 280, Simpson, Saskatchewan S0G 4M0; phone (306) 836-2022. A bird-banding station operates here from late May to early June and August through September. Contact Al Smith, Canadian Wildlife Service, 115 Perimeter Road, Saskatoon, Saskatchewan S7N 0X4; phone (306) 975-4091, for more information.

Birding Features
About 40% of the unit is lake and marsh; the remainder is grasslands with a small amount seeded as lure crops, which draw cranes and waterfowl off adjacent privately owned cropland. Obtain the excellent map from headquarters (see above) to allow easy location of roads around the complex.

Starting at headquarters, ask if there are any special species, such as Whooping Cranes (in the fall, September and October). Sandhill Cranes and Snow, White-fronted and Canada Geese come and go in great waves. They can best be observed from the road at headquarters as they go on their evening flight from fields to roost. Check the marshes beside the road just east of headquarters for Black-crowned Night-Herons. Swainson's Hawks are everywhere from May to September. Other raptors include eagles and Osprey, which are regulars from late April to mid-May and September to early November. Check the shelterbelts, particularly around headquarters and the regional park, for warblers during late August and early September. Le Conte's Sparrows are common in most grassy areas just east of headquarters.

Take the car and explore the rest of the unit. At every opportunity, scan the water for such species as Western Grebe, which occurs particularly in marshy bays. American White Pelicans fish in May and September. Good numbers of Tundra Swans occur in October and November. Shorebirds appear in huge waves in late May. Don't miss them! Loggerhead Shrikes are often present in shelterbelts along the west edge of the unit. At the northern end, Baird's Sparrows, Sprague's Pipits and Upland Sandpipers are common on native grasslands about 2 km west of the picnic site. At this spot, cross the north arm of the lake and take the trail south into grassy uplands between the water bodies. Listen for Sprague's Pipits, and Le Conte's and Savannah Sparrows. Forster's Terns may be ferreted out in the marshes east of here, on the easternmost arm of the lake.

If you are here in late fall, scan carefully for a Snowy Owl, common in late November.

On your way in or out, stop at Sailor's Bay on the southwest corner of the unit and inspect the grazed pastures southeast of the bog bay for a Chestnut-collared Longspur.

WAYNE HARRIS
Revised by Wayne Harris

Good Spirit Lake and Horseshoe Lake Heritage Marsh

Good Spirit Lake and marsh lie 50 km north-northwest of Yorkton and are accessible by Highway 9 or 16. The lake was originally called Kitchimanitou, later nicknamed Devil's Lake by early settlers, and eventually called Good Spirit, much more in keeping with the aboriginal name. The lake, 30 km² in size, has a depth of 4.5 to 6 m. It is flat, shallow and warm, resting on a bed of sand up to 5 m deep, and is ideal for all kinds of recreational use. Recent high water levels have greatly reduced the beach area.

The sand dune area, along the southeast side, stretches for 5 km with dunes rising up to 18 m high. These wind-formed structures were built when the lake level was lower. Now mostly stabilized by vegetation including Creeping Juniper, Bearberry, Water Birch, Red Osier Dogwood, Chokecherry and other shrubs, grasses and a proliferation of flowers, with some Trembling Aspen, the area is a haven for birds and other wildlife. Access to the dunes is by boat or canoe or on foot along the beach and well-marked internal trails.

Good Spirit Lake Provincial Park lies on the southwest side of the lake and has camping and picnic facilities. A park naturalist is on staff from mid-June to mid-August.

If you come for a visit, contact Joyce and Bill Anaka at (306) 792-4780.

Birding Features

Habitat around Good Spirit Lake, other than the dunes, is wooded, giving way to pasture, meadow and cultivated fields. A marsh adjoining the north end of the lake hosts Pied-bill, Horned, Eared, Red-necked and Western Grebes. During migration, the lake is a staging site for large numbers of geese and ducks.

Resident birds of prey include Northern Harrier, Cooper's Broad-winged and Red-tailed Hawks and Merlin.

Shorebird activity has decreased with higher lake levels but migration brings a good variety. Killdeer and Spotted Sandpiper are common on the beaches.

Other species found in the dunes and park include Great Blue Heron, Pileated Woodpecker, Western Wood-Pewee, Great Crested Flycatcher and Eastern Towhee. Common Ravens are year-round residents that nest locally. An active Mountain Bluebird nest box line along Highway 47 through the Good Spirit Community Pasture parallelling the west side of the park provides opportunities for viewing bluebirds in spring and summer. Regular warblers include Yellow, American Redstart, Ovenbird and Common Yellowthroat. Small numbers of Tennessee, Orange-crowned and Yellow-rumped are also present. Sparrows in abundance include Chipping, Savannah, Clay-colored and Vesper. Lark, Baird's, Le Conte's, Sharp-tailed and White-throated Sparrows are in smaller numbers. Rose-breasted Grosbeak and Baltimore Oriole are loud and common. Red-winged and Yellow-headed Blackbirds add colour and song to the marsh along a nature trail in the park. Listen for Sedge and Marsh Wrens in the same area.

Horseshoe Lake Heritage Marsh sits along the south side of Highway 229 and is 6 km southeast of Good Spirit Lake. For good viewing, park the car along the highway opposite the grid road that goes north to Tiny. A canoe is helpful. Canoe launching is through a nearby private livestock pasture, so keep gates closed at all times.

The marsh is a complex of shallow water ponds and upland habitat, managed by Ducks Unlimited, providing excellent places for a variety of wetland and upland species. Pied-billed, Horned, Eared and Red-necked Grebes are present. All the prairie ducks are here, including White-winged Scoter. Confirmed breeders include Common Goldeneye, Bufflehead, Ruddy Duck, American Coot and Sora.

In the uplands look for Sharp-tailed and Ruffed Grouse.

JOYCE AND BILL ANAKA

Yorkton and Duck Mountain Provincial Park

Yorkton provides a base from which to explore east-central Saskatchewan. From here you can sample waterfowl, shorebird and aspen parkland habitats north and south of the town. Move northeast to the Duck Mountains and experience the southernmost boreal forest in the province. Everything from Black-crowned Night-Heron and American Avocet, through Black-billed Cuckoo, to Common Loon and Boreal Chickadee is present.

The town has a variety of motels and other services. Campgrounds are nearby at York Lake, just south of town, and at Good Spirit Lake Provincial Park north 32 km and 17 km west. Yorkton is served by Greyhound and STC buses. Highway 10 from Regina intersects the Yellowhead Highway 16 at Yorkton.

Birding Features

The area is best visited from mid-May to early July when most breeding birds are on territory. The three best locations to see are York Lake Regional Park south of town; Good Spirit Lake Provincial Park north of Yorkton; and Duck Mountain Provincial Park to the northeast.

Begin at York Lake Regional Park. Take an evening stroll along the well-marked self-guiding nature trail that starts at the lake just west of the railroad track. Watch for a Black-crowned Night-Heron flying out to feed. A White-winged Scoter will be among the ducks on the lake. Listen for the Veery singing as though from the bottom of a rain barrel.

To the west 3.2 km is Rousay Lake, one of the best waterfowl marshes in western Canada, with numerous artificial nesting sites used by Canada Geese. South 6.4 km is Leech Lake, where the Sandhill Crane still nests successfully. These lakes are best explored by canoe, allowing a close look at Red-necked, Horned and Eared Grebes, Black-crowned Night-Heron and 10 resident species of duck. You will hear and often see Virginia Rail and Sora. Wilson's Phalarope and Black Tern are numerous.

American Avocets feed along the mudflats. Apart from the first two weeks of July, many species of sandpiper come through at different times. The "slough-pump" noise of American Bitterns can be heard. Adjacent grasslands boast the Upland Sandpiper in addition to Willet, Marbled Godwit, Baird's and Le Conte's Sparrows, and Chestnut-collared Longspur. Warbling Vireo and Least Flycatcher sing from every small aspen bluff nearby. The Black-billed Cuckoo is heard mainly in years when tent caterpillars are numerous. The ubiquitous Black-billed Magpie, after a lapse of 30 or 40 years from the buffalo's disappearance, came back in the 1930s and has been common since the 1950s.

If time permits, visit Good Spirit Lake Provincial Park. Follow Highway 9 north from Yorkton to Highway 229, then go west. At the park gate, ask for Joyce or Bill Anaka, keen local birders. Their residence phone is (306) 792-4780.

The lake was formed during a dry period centuries ago. Winds carved out an ever-deepening hole and deposited the sand as large dunes, especially near the southeast margin. Later, the hole became Good Spirit (or Kitchimanitou, as the Cree called it) Lake. The beach is wide and remarkably level. Bathers must wade for hundreds of metres into the water before reaching swimming depth; hence it is one of the safest beaches to be found anywhere for children. Away from the swimming areas, Spotted Sandpipers have regularly spaced territories along the beach. A colony of Bank Swallows occurs along the sand dunes. Depending on water levels, Common Terns sometimes nest.

The beach dunes are constantly shifting. Behind them is a second sand ridge, where plants have largely stabilized the sandy soil. On the level land beyond the ridge, you'll find House Wren, Gray Catbird, Cedar Waxwing and Clay-colored Sparrow.

Duck Mountain Provincial Park is 104 km northeast of Yorkton via Highways 10, 8 and 57. The park contains beautiful Madge Lake, with its many points and islands within boreal forest. The Common Loon and Common Goldeneye are the most obvious water birds. Many pairs of Ring-necked Duck occur on surrounding sloughs. In the mixed forest, look for ferns up to 1.5 m high and several species of orchids. Listen for Hermit and Swainson's Thrushes each evening, interspersed with the clear notes of the White-throated Sparrow. Search for the Pileated Woodpecker, Boreal Chickadee and Swamp Sparrow. Try to sort out the songs of 14 species of warblers, including the Nashville, Connecticut and Blackburnian. In suitable habitat with tall, thin aspen, Philadelphia Vireo may be found. These birds look like a yellow-tinged Warbling Vireo and sing like a Red-eyed Vireo, but higher and with a slower tempo. The world's first recorded nest of the Philadelphia Vireo was found on the edge of the Duck Mountains about 15 km south of the park gate. Ernest Thompson Seton located it while building a cabin on his homestead, 2 km southwest of the present Runnymede.

Blue-headed, Red-eyed and Warbling Vireos are also present. The Yellow-throated Vireo has been reported twice from Madge Lake.

C. STUART HOUSTON

Driving Loop to Look for Prairie Birds

This is a one-day trip; start early in the morning so as to have enough time to stop frequently. All the roads are paved but not all are in equally good condition. The route starts at Regina and returns to Regina. Services are minimal so take along your own food and water. Leave with a full tank of gas. It is essential to take a Saskatchewan road map.

An early morning in June is best to start this tour. Later in the day when the thermals begin to build, raptors will soar.

Proceed south from Regina on Highway 6 through cultivated farmland for the first half hour. Although in summer there is not much to be seen, in winter the road is a good place for Snowy Owls, sometimes by the dozen. In spring and fall, Rough-legged, Red-tailed, Swainson's and Broad-winged Hawks may be seen along this stretch of highway.

At the junctions with Highway 39 in the Corinne area, continue south on Highway 6. A small picnic ground on the east side of the highway gives a break and an opportunity to spot Loggerhead Shrike four or five feet above ground on an outside branch.

Stop along the highway and scan the pastures on the west side of the road. Baird's, Grasshopper, Savannah and Clay-colored Sparrows, Chestnut-collared Longspur, Horned Lark, Sprague's Pipit may all be seen and heard. Lark Bunting may be found in dry areas of short grass habitat. In wet years, Bobolink may turn up. Watch for Swainson's Hawk. Also look for Marbled Godwit, Avocet and Upland Sandpiper.

Some 32 km south of the junction of Highways 39 and 6 sits the abandoned Moreland grain elevator east of the road. At that point, a dirt road leads west. Park on the side of the dirt road and take a walk down it. Pastures are on both sides; a small creek and a bridge are a short walk away, allowing good looks at grassland songbirds and the birds associated with prairie creeks.

Continue south past the junction with Highway 13, past Ceylon, past Minton. South of Minton, Highways 18 and 6 join for a few miles. Keep heading south until Highway 18 turns west. Take Highway 18 and travel west to the Big Muddy Valley.

In the valley watch for Golden Eagle, Ferruginous Hawk, Prairie Falcon and Turkey Vulture, all of which breed here. A spotting scope will assist in finding these birds on the cliffs and hillsides or soaring in the wind. The road has little traffic, so you can stop as often as you like.

Just before ascending out of the valley again, stop at a little sideroad heading south; get out and walk up and down it, listening to the birds around you. Springs in this area provide habitat for Snipe, Sora, Yellow Rail, and Le Conte's and Sharp-tailed Sparrows. Mountain Bluebird and sometimes Eastern nest in the area. Rock Wrens can be heard from the rocks and cliffs. Say's Phoebe lives here, too.

Out of the valley, continue west along Highway 18 until the junction with Highway 34; turn north towards Bengough. Another descent into the Big Muddy Valley will take you to a (signed) road leading west along the valley edge to Castle Butte. Again, eagles, hawks and falcons will be seen, along with Rock Wrens. In this part of the valley, Vesper Sparrows sing from the sagebrush. Kestrels nest at Castle Butte. At the butte, leave the car and do some walking. Although all lands along this route are privately owned, many people come to enjoy the scenery around Castle Butte and some limited walking is acceptable.

Return to Highway 34 and continue north out of the valley. Bengough offers some services, depending upon day and time. Continue north. At the junction with Highway 13, keep north on Highway 34, skirting the edge of the Dirt Hills to come out at Avonlea. As before, keep watch for hawks overhead and by the roadside.

At Avonlea, turn east on Highway 334 and at Highway 6, turn north for the last half hour back into Regina.

CAROL BJORKLUND

Regina

Formerly the site where aboriginals piled discarded bones after major buffalo kills, Regina is located on the short-grass prairies. With the conversion of this area to cropland, few patches of native grass remain. As they have for millennia, large flocks of migrating Tundra Swan; Canada, Greater White-fronted and Snow Geese; and a variety of ducks all pass through, with various shorebirds and grassland birds resting on the low wetlands.

Regina has been the capital since the creation of the province in 1905; its physical geography underwent a major change in the 1930s when Wascana

Creek was dammed and Wascana Lake and Park were created. This man-made lake, adjacent marsh and parkland provide excellent habitat for waterfowl, shorebirds, warblers and sparrows. The Trans-Canada Highway runs through the city. Hotels and motels are numerous. Full-service campgrounds occur by the Trans-Canada at the eastern approach to Regina. Those travelling outside the city should be aware that many nearby centres have few services. Rural roads may be impassable in bad weather.

For exact directions and maps to the entire area, refer to *A Birdfinding Guide to the Regina Area* by Adam et. al., available from Nature Saskatchewan in Regina: 206-1860 Lorne Street, Regina, Saskatchewan S4P 2L7; phone 1-800-667-4668; e-mail: nature.sask@unibase.com

Also refer to *Birds of Regina* by Margaret Belcher, available from above.

Birding Features

In the winter there are few birds. Snowy Owls are found on flat farmland around the city, where Snow Buntings are erratic. Merlin overwinters, as do a few American Robins. Bohemian Waxwing feeds on Mountain Ash berries and White-winged and Red Crossbills are present. It is not uncommon for one or two Townsend's Solitaires to arrive during the winter and stay the season.

Regina is on the Central Flyway for migrating birds. Spring migration begins in March and lasts to early May. On Wascana Lake, Red-necked Grebe, Tundra Swan, Ringed-necked Duck, Greater Scaup, Hooded and Common Mergansers, Franklin's Gull and other waterfowl are found. In the trees surrounding Wascana Lake near the Legislative Building, all the following birds may be seen at the same time in the month of May: Cape May, Connecticut, Nashville, Mourning, Bay-breasted, Magnolia and Canada Warblers. As well, you'll find Harris's, Fox, White-crowned, White-throated, Lincoln's and Swamp Sparrows, plus Olive-sided and Great-crested Flycatchers.

The nesting season runs from late May into July and provides opportunities to observe a variety of behavioural characteristics of the large flock of Wascana Lake's resident Canada Geese. At this location, note the breeding Wilson's Phalarope, a few Common and Black Terns, some Marsh Wren and sizeable colonies of Yellow-headed and Red-winged Blackbirds.

In various city parks, among the bushes, both Spotted and Eastern Towhees may be seen. Similarly, Indigo and Lazuli Buntings, and Western and Scarlet Tanagers pass through the "Queen City." Indigo and Lazuli Buntings nest in the surrounding area.

In downtown Regina, Peregrines and Merlins nest. "Yellow-shafted" Flicker, Black-billed Magpie and House Finch breed in residential neighbourhoods, as well as the occasional Swainson's Hawk. Fall migrants include Hooded Merganser, Common Goldeneye and Rusty Blackbird. Large numbers of gulls roost overnight on Wascana Lake before it freezes over in November. In spring and fall look for migrating Veery and Gray-cheeked, Swainson's and Hermit Thrushes. Varied and Wood Thrushes are occasionally seen. In rural areas around the city in spring, great flocks of Lapland Longspurs with the occasional Smith's Longspur pass through. Sometimes McCown's Longspur can be found too. Look for American Golden-Plover and Buff-breasted Sandpiper in fields.

The dump sits on the northeast corner of Regina near the Cement Plant Slough. At the slough, Red-necked Grebe, Yellow-headed Blackbird, Forster's and Black Terns breed. Gulls, including California, roost on the slough after spending a day shopping in the nearby city dump.

During spring and fall migrations Cinema 6 slough, 3 km south of Regina, hosts Tundra Swan; Stilt; Baird's and White-rumped Sandpipers; and Long-billed and Short-billed Dowitchers. Breeding birds are Horned, Eared and Pied-billed Grebes, American Avocet, Willet and Yellow-headed Blackbird.

Monica Slough, southeast of Regina, hosts breeding Wilson's Phalarope, Marbled Godwit and Yellow-headed Blackbird.

East of Monica Slough is Lily Fields. Listen for Sprague's Pipit, Bobolink, Clay-colored, Baird's and Grasshopper Sparrows. Swainson's Hawk, Western Kingbird, Loggerhead Shrike, Marbled Godwit, Upland Sandpiper, Sharp-tailed Grouse and Chestnut-collared Longspur are seen and heard.

The village of Knoau lies 25 km southeast of Regina on Highway 33. West of the village nest some of the last Burrowing Owls on the Regina Plains. At Valeport Marsh, about 40 km north of Regina at the southern tip of Last Mountain Lake, Clark's Grebe breeds among Western Grebe. American White Pelican and Forster's Tern fish the waters.

In fall at Condie Reservoir, 10 km north of Regina on Highway 11, look for three species of scoters, Common Loon, Western and Clark's Grebes.

Also in the fall, Buck Lake, south of Regina, is visited by Snow, Ross's and Greater White-fronted Geese. Find Red-tailed and Rough-legged Hawks, Peregrine, Prairie Falcon and Gyrfalcon.

The fall hot spots are Regina Beach, Kinookimaw Beach, Little Arm, Lumsden Beach and Buena Vista on Last Mountain Lake. Use Highways 11 and 54 to reach Regina Beach. In November, when Last Mountain Lake is already partly frozen, it is easy to see Pacific and Common Loons. Hooded Merganser, Barrow's Goldeneye, Oldsquaw, Thayer's Gull, Red-throated and Yellow-billed Loons, Common Eider and all three scoters are here.

MARGARET BELCHER

Qu'Appelle Basin Driving Route

Visitors travelling through southern Saskatchewan often complain of the long tedious ride. They may not realize that the railroads and later the highways were laid along the most level strips of land, to save construction costs. To relieve the monotony, why not depart from Highway 1 and sample the beautiful Qu'Appelle Valley that parallels this road for more than halfway across the province? To assist in this exploratory trip, order a copy of the 168-page booklet *Birds of the Qu'Appelle, 1857–1969*, by E. Manley Callin, 1980, Special Publication 13, Nature Saskatchewan, from the Blue Jay Bookshop (see above). This is one of the finest local publications available anywhere.

Birding Features

The route begins at Whitewood, 68 km west of the Manitoba-Saskatchewan border on Highway 1. Turn north on Highway 9. The road soon crosses a now invisible and unmarked oxcart trail between Lower Fort Garry (Winnipeg) and Fort Edmonton. This route carried trading goods and later the early settlers. They saw this land as a treeless plain set afire almost every year by lightning, or by Indians to bring the buffalo north earlier in the spring. They observed Ferruginous and Swainson's Hawks as the common raptors. The Ferruginous has long ago disappeared and the Red-tailed Hawk is the most common raptor in the aspen bluffs. The once-common Upland Sandpiper, Long-billed Curlew, Baird's Sparrow and Sprague's Pipit are now found only on relict pastures.

Farther north, the Qu'Appelle Valley is breathtaking in its sudden appearance. The wide post-glacial valley, carved out by a river between 12,000 and 14,000 years ago, is completely out of proportion to the little river at its bottom. Stop at the parking area on the left, below the crest, and have a drink of cool, clear spring water. Climb the steep trail to the lookout spots above.

Across the valley, the north (south-facing) slope is covered mainly with short grass, brown in summer unless rainfall is above average, with only a few shrubs in the moister clefts of the hills. On the south side, below, note the dense tangle of Aspen, Birch, Saskatoon, Chokecherry and other shrubs; in places the bush is so impenetrable that Turkey Vultures can nest on the ground without fear of discovery. Look for one soaring high overhead. Listen in May for the drumming of the Ruffed Grouse – like an old tractor starting up. Try to "whistle up" a Northern Saw-whet Owl; listen for the "wheep" of a Great Crested Flycatcher; catch a fleeting glimpse of a Cooper's or Sharp-shinned Hawk or a Long-eared Owl. In June and early July, the Red-eyed Vireo is everywhere. Listen for the three most characteristic valley songs – those of the Veery, the Rose-breasted Grosbeak and the Spotted Towhee. Highway 9 is approximately the dividing line between Spotted and Eastern Towhee, the Western and Eastern Wood-Pewee, and the Lazuli and Indigo Bunting, as well as the western limit of the Bur Oak.

Note the buildings at the northeast corner of Round Lake. They mark the site of John MacDonald's XY Company fur-trading post from 1810 to 1814, and the site of Hugh McKay's Presbyterian mission and school, established in 1884. A cairn north of Camp McKay explains the geology of the area, including the flat terrace on the south side of the valley.

At bridges across the Qu'Appelle there are hundreds of nesting Cliff Swallows. These crossings provide good viewpoints from which to see a Great Blue Heron or Black-crowned Night-Heron. On the dry slopes on the north side of the valley, watch carefully for the Lark Sparrow.

Turn west along Highway 247, which follows the north edge of Round Lake and later of Crooked Lake. Along the margins of both lakes are the Belted Kingfisher and Common Tern. On the lake, on sandspits or points, you will usually see groups of nonbreeding one- and two-year-old American White Pelicans, and perhaps a Double-crested Cormorant or two, though their nearest breeding colony is on islands in the Quill Lakes, about 160 km to the northwest.

The marshes at the west end of each lake contain Virginia Rail and sometimes a colony of Western Grebe. At this point, in dry weather, there is a choice of continuing west along the valley to Lake Katepwa on a dirt valley road or returning to the Trans-Canada via Highway 47. At Indian Head, it is possible to tour the experimental farm founded in 1887 at the east edge of town, and the PFRA Tree Nursery Station south of town.

Turn north at Indian Head on Highway 56. The Skinner Marsh is in the valley southeast of Katepwa Lake. It has been restored and is controlled by Ducks Unlimited (Canada), with the cooperation of the Saskatchewan government, as a Canada Goose breeding project. Farther along Highway 56, you will see Katepwa Beach, a swimming beach and one of Canada's smallest provincial parks. At Lebret's Catholic mission, climb the stations of the cross. Farther along the road, stop and read the historic plaque that tells the tragic, romantic legend of how the valley got its name.

At Fort Qu'Appelle, contact Ron Hooper, phone (306) 332-6783, for up-to-date bird information. This spot, situated between Mission and Echo Lakes, was chosen as a North-West Mounted Police post in 1875 and later as a headquarters in 1880. At the end of Echo Lake, look for both Le Conte's and Sharp-tailed Sparrows, as well as the Marsh Wren and Common Yellow-throat.

At this point the rushed traveller can take Highway 10 as the quickest route to Regina and points west. Less-hurried visitors may wish to follow major grid road 727 west along the north shore of Pasqua Lake and then out of the valley west for 20 km, jogging north 3.2 km on major grid 240, and then west on an unnumbered grid road with sheaf signs, another 22 km to Highway 6, which leads directly south into Regina. You now have an option of turning southwest on Highway 99, a final valley road that leads into Craven, past Kennell Church in its picturesque location on the south side of the river. Continue on Highway 20 to Lumsden, then take Highway 11 southeast to Regina, or northwest to Saskatoon. Large flocks of geese and waders are seen in the valley, especially in spring and fall migration.

For more information on what is happening in the central part of the Qu'Appelle Valley, from Lumsden to Katepwa Lake, contact Trevor Herriot at (306) 585-1674. In the eastern region from Whitewood to Round and Crooked Lakes, John Pollock at (306) 735-2921 will help you.

C. STUART HOUSTON
Revised by Trevor Herriot

Moose Mountain

The Moose Mountains are an island in a sea of prairie. These highlands consist of an aspen forest with numerous lakes, the White Bear Indian Reserve and Moose Mountain Provincial Park. The site is a biological niche similar to the Aspen Parkland of the northern plains and the Boreal Forests even farther north. A Saskatchewan Natural History Society special publication, *Birds of Moose Mountain* by Nero and Lein (1971), now out of print, is an excellent introduction to the birds of the area.

The mountains lie 40 km west of the Manitoba border and 80 km north of the American border. From Brandon drive south on Highway 10 to Highway 2. Proceed through Souris to the Saskatchewan border. Here Manitoba Highway 2 changes to Saskatchewan Highway 13. At Carlyle go north on Highway 9 to Kenosee Lake in Moose Mountain Provincial Park.

From Regina travel east on Highway 1 to White City. Head south on Highway 48 until it ends at Highway 9. Go south to Kenosee Lake.

Birding Features

The Moose Mountains contain White-Breasted Nuthatch and Great Crested Flycatcher, the latter near its western limits for Canada. This is the only place in Saskatchewan where White-throated Vireo, long considered hypothetical, may be located.

Here in southeast Saskatchewan, species common to the parkland and Boreal Forest, including Common Loon, Red-necked Grebe, Common Goldeneye, Bufflehead, Turkey Vulture, Broad-winged Hawk, Ruffed Grouse, Yellow-breasted Sapsucker, Ovenbird, and Yellow-rumped, Mourning and Black-and-white Warblers are found.

In winter Pileated Woodpecker takes up residence. A June sighting has raised the possibility that this bird may breed here.

GREG BOBBITT

Weyburn

Weyburn lies in the southeast corner of Saskatchewan, 110 km southeast of Regina on Highway 39, or 120 km north of the American border on the same road. Motels can be found in town; campers can use the River Park campground. The area around Weyburn consists of gently rolling farm land interspersed with unbroken ranch land. Over 280 species of birds have been spotted here. Numerous grassland and upland species are found from mid-April until the end of October. During dry years the shoulders of the gravel roads are host to Lark Bunting.

The best resource for a birder is *A Guide to the Flora and Fauna of Tatagwa-Souris Valley* by Ray Belanger. It lists other birding hot spots, complete with maps and expected species plus a complete checklist for the Weyburn area with a list of contacts. Pick up the book at Weyburn City Hall. For more information see the article "Weyburn Shorebird Study" in the March 1994 issue of the *Blue Jay* published by Nature Saskatchewan.

Birding Features

From mid-April to the end of May there are several spots to search. The best place for sparrows, warblers and other passerines is the hospital grounds. Here at the Souris Valley Regional Care Centre in the northwest corner of the city just off Highway 13 there are walking trails and scattered benches. The concentration of small birds provides food for a large number of migrating raptors. Cooper's, Sharp-Shinned and Broad-winged Hawks regularly pause on their north and south movements. Both Willow and Alder Flycatchers have bred in the park grounds. Bring rubber boots to walk along the tiny creek that flows through the grounds, where you may find migrating birds that are not readily found elsewhere.

The other area of special interest is the Secondary Sewage lagoons. Travel southeast of Weyburn on Highway 39, 1.6 km past the Nickel Lake turnoff.

Turn south until you cross the Souris River. Take the first right and travel about 0.8 km. The lagoons are on the south side of the road. The gate is locked, but you may cross the wire fence and walk up to the cells. Over 40 different species of shorebirds have been noted here, including Piping Plover, Red Knot and Ruddy Turnstone. The fields around the lagoon host Vesper and Savannah Sparrows. The sloughs and fields have been home to Ferruginous Hawks, Burrowing Owls and Bobolinks.

In fall look for the odd Whooping Crane and many species of migrating waterfowl. All three species of scoters have been spotted on the Nickel Lake reservoir during fall migration.

Winter is usually fairly quiet. Birding in town is concentrated at feeders where there is usually an overwintering White-throated or Harris's Sparrow. The fields around Weyburn play host to numerous Snowy Owls and flocks of Snow Buntings interspersed with Lapland Longspurs. There is usually a Golden Eagle on territory here too.

KEITH SAKATCH

Driving Through the Souris Valley

Begin at Roche Percée, southeast of Estevan, along Highway 39. It is essential to take a Saskatchewan road map.

There are two sections to this route. One is a short (1 km) segment travelling west from Roche Percée and returning to it. The longer section follows a road eastward along the Souris River valley and ends at Highway 9.

The Souris is a small, meandering river system with riparian woods. Trees grow along the bank where farms have cut to the river's edge. Birding is best in June, particularly the last half of the month, for Lazuli Bunting.

Birding Features

West (shorter) segment. From a small monument at the edge of town, take the grid road that leads west to connect with Boundary Dam. The river winds close by the road and Wood Ducks may be seen in some of the oxbows. A short distance away, a large wagon wheel and a sign to the Wengen ranch will mark the entrance to a private road. Just past the site, Field Sparrows sing from the hillsides. Park at the edge of the road and walk up the hill to get a better look. Check for Rose-breasted Grosbeak, Eastern Bluebird, Lazuli Bunting, Catbird and Spotted Towhee. Two crescents of vegetation have Black-headed Grosbeaks on either side of the road. A bit farther on find the buffalo compound. Above it, among mine spoil piles, are Rock Wrens.

Once you begin to come out of the valley, turn around and head back to Roche Percée. In town, House Finches sing and Eastern Phoebe nests under the bridge.

East (longer) segment. At the townsite, again use the small monument as a guidepost. Drive east past the remnants of the pierced rock, from which Roche Percée gets its name. Initially you will travel on the south side of the valley, south of the river.

At the picnic site, a short distance east of town, look for Eastern Bluebird, Eastern Wood-Pewee, Great Crested Flycatcher, Rose-breasted Grosbeak, Spotted Towhee and Lark Sparrow. The picnic site is good for Eastern Screech Owl, American Redstart, and Warbling and Red-eyed Vireos. Black-and-white Warblers are everywhere here and all along the valley.

At a concrete ford crossing over the river, expect Hooded Mergansers and Wood Ducks. Look north of the river to the hillsides. To the west Field Sparrows are found; on the east hill, where old Taylorton cemetery is located, are Rock Wrens and Mountain Bluebirds.

After leaving the cemetery, go back to the road and turn east. Willow Flycatchers may be spotted near the intersection. In oxbows along the road, watch for Wood Ducks and Hooded Mergansers. Continue east to Longney's Crossing. Cross over the Souris and carry on eastward on the north side of the valley.

At first you will travel a distance away from the river. Two large rocks up on the hillside host Rock Wren. Crossing this prairie section, Grasshopper Sparrow may be seen on either side of the road. You will then enter the area set aside as Critical Wildlife Habitat. A small coulee begins south of the road on the hillside, running parallel to the road and then swings south to join the Souris; here may be found Yellow-breasted Chats and lots of Willow Flycatchers. A Texas gate marks the end of the wildlife lands.

About 0.8 km east of the Texas gate, the river comes sweeping towards the road. Both Eastern and Western Wood-Pewees can be found, as well as Black-billed Cuckoo, Yellow-breasted Chat, Black-headed Grosbeak and many Willow Flycatchers.

Continue eastward, as the river swings back and forth. At a swinging bridge and another concrete crossing near the headquarters to Coaldale PFRA pasture, expect Great Blue Heron and pelican.

At the junction with the North Portal Grid, on an all-weather road, you may spot an Eastern Bluebird and Common Nighthawk north on the hillside in the PFRA pasture. From the bridge south of the intersection look for Wood Ducks. At the nearby farmstead there are Say's Phoebes.

Continue east. The river meanders back and forth and the vegetation is shorter here. Seven kilometres farther east, the river comes right up to the road. The weir is frequented by Great Blue Heron and Rough-winged Swallow. Nearby are Black-headed Grosbeak, Orchard Oriole and even Yellow-throated Vireo.

Continuing east, expect lots of White-breasted Nuthatches, Blue Jay, Spotted Towhee, both species of kingbirds, Great Crested Flycatcher and Black-billed Cuckoo.

At Highway 9, turn south. Almost immediately, an entrance to a campground appears on the east side of the highway. The entrance drive will run parallel to the highway and then curl in to the picnic site. Willow Flycatcher, Black-billed Cuckoo, Yellow-throated Vireo and Eastern Wood-Pewee have all been found here. An added bonus are the numbers of very large painted turtles to be found at this site.

The route ends here. Use your road map to return to home base.

BOB LUTERBACH AND CAROL BJORKLUND

Gainsborough, Saskatchewan, to Lyleton, Manitoba

This section of mixed-grass prairies and scattered woodlands lies in the extreme southeast corner of Saskatchewan and the southwest corner of Manitoba. More than 250 species of birds have been recorded in the area. Most pasture land and prairie is found in the vicinity of PR 256 south of Pierson and PR 251 west of Lyleton, including backroads in the area.

Prior to settlement, the area was treeless grasslands with wooded river bottoms. Settlement began in the 1880s, and today only a few isolated pockets of original prairie remain. Over 70% of the land is under intense cultivation, mainly for cash crops. With the planting of trees and shrubs around homesites and in towns, combined with trees and shrubs spreading to roadsides, railroad embankments and in upland pastures, strips and islands of woodland now attract a wide variety of birds.

The area lies about 130 km southwest of Brandon, Manitoba, or about 250 km southeast of Regina. Buses service the major nearby towns of Melita and Pipestone in Manitoba and Carnduff in Saskatchewan. For bus information on Manitoba and nearby routes phone the bus depot at Grey Goose Bus Lines (204) 784-4500; Greyhound (204) 982-8747; the bus depot is at 487 Portage Avenue, Winnipeg. The railroad spur lines have been terminated. Hotels, gasoline and services are available in several communities.

Information on the area is well documented in an excellent report, *Birds of the Gainsborough-Lyleton Region*, by Richard W. Knapton, 1979, Saskatchewan Natural History Publication No. 10. It is available for $3 from the Blue Jay Bookshop (see above).

Material for this section was taken from this report, which includes a detailed description of all birds recently seen in the region.

Birding Features

The gently rolling country contains two small rivers, each running eastward: Gainsborough Creek in the north and Antler River to the south. Temporary and semipermanent sloughs are found in numerous small depressions. These are generally not saline, with the larger and deeper ones supporting stands of cattails, reed grass and bulrush. The shallow temporary sloughs are often overgrown with sedges and grasses. The recent practice of increasing the amount of productive land by draining wetlands has reduced marshes and sloughs to less than 1% of the total area in this corner of Manitoba. Shelterbelts around farmsites and windbreaks on the edges of fields, combined with woodlands along roadsides, railroads and some pastureland, provide a break in the never-ending grain fields. This was a good region in which to find Burrowing Owl in pastures. Today Burrowing Owls are virtually extirpated; for Say's Phoebe check abandoned farms and barns anywhere in the area; Dickcissel is sporadic, absent most years; Lark Bunting is present in good numbers (sometimes hundreds) in dry years, absent or nearly so in wetter years. Upland Sandpiper, Sprague's Pipit, Baird's and Grasshopper Sparrows are still fairly common and widespread. Since the 1980s Ferruginous Hawk has re-established itself in the area; although not as common as Red-tailed or Swainson's Hawks, a day in the field should turn up one or two. The best season is from late May to mid-July.

Key spots to bird include the Gainsborough Dam on the creek of the same name, 9 km south of Gainsborough. Horned, Eared and Western Grebes breed here. The Black-crowned Night-Herons have a small colony at the dam and others on the creek. Other water birds use this water body for nesting and as a staging area on migration.

The Pierson Wildlife Management Area of bluffs, potholes and irregularly shaped fields lies 8 km southwest of Pierson. Several potholes have been blasted out, wildlife food plots cleared, and 10,000 trees and shrubs planted on this 194.3 ha block. A second unit within the same management area lies 14.5 km east of Pierson. This 64.8 ha of river bottom woodland, with grass-covered slopes, provides another birding spot worth visiting.

There are two larger bodies of water in the region: the dam on Ralph Wang's farm contains 1.5 ha of water surface and lies 10 km southwest of Pierson. This is private property, so ask for permission before entering. Mr. Wang came to this area as a boy in the 1940s and has carefully observed and recorded the wildlife for over 20 years. The other spot is the Ducks Unlimited (Canada) dam about 7 km west of Lyleton; it rarely has any open water and is a small marsh.

John Murray, a very keen birder from Lyleton, has kept almost daily records since 1968. He may know of other good spots worth visiting. He is retired and lives in Lyleton.

The scattered sloughs in the area, together with the above-mentioned dams, attract the normal complement of water birds from late April to early October. The Northern Harrier is the most numerous and widespread nesting raptor and begins arriving in late March. Shorebirds are common migrants from mid-May to early June and in September. Watch for American Golden and Black-bellied Plovers. The Gainsborough Dam is a particularly good spot for these species. In winter look for Golden Eagle.

The invasion of Orchard Orioles in this area 25 years ago now makes it possible to spot easily both this species and the Baltimore Oriole, sometimes in the same bluff. Other birds to watch for include Wild Turkey, Ring-necked Pheasant and Gray Partridge. Willow Flycatchers occur regularly in coulees and along creeks where shrubbery, such as hawthorn and willow, provides nesting sites. Particularly reliable have been the coulees along the east side of Highway 83, south of nearby Melita.

RUDOLF F. KOES
Revised by Rudolf F. Koes

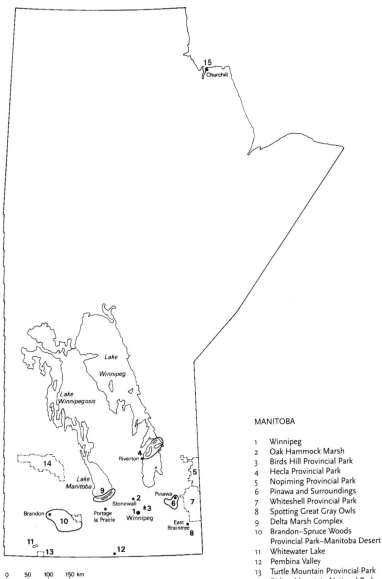

MANITOBA

1   Winnipeg
2   Oak Hammock Marsh
3   Birds Hill Provincial Park
4   Hecla Provincial Park
5   Nopiming Provincial Park
6   Pinawa and Surroundings
7   Whiteshell Provincial Park
8   Spotting Great Gray Owls
9   Delta Marsh Complex
10 Brandon–Spruce Woods
    Provincial Park–Manitoba Desert
11 Whitewater Lake
12 Pembina Valley
13 Turtle Mountain Provincial Park
14 Riding Mountain National Park
15 Churchill

MANITOBA

Manitoba's habitats range from prairie and parkland to hardwood and boreal forest to low arctic tundra. Most of these lie within a couple of hours' drive from Winnipeg (the tundra at Churchill is a short, albeit expensive, airplane flight away). Such variety hosts a truly phenomenal number of bird species. They come from the east, west, north and south of North America. Manitoba's birders hold the North American "Big Day" records for June and July, and Canadian records for all months from May through September. Southern Ontario is the only other place in Canada where you can approach this number of species.

The southern and western portions of Manitoba are part of the prairie pothole, or slough, basin of North America, most of which lies in Canada. An aerial survey of western Canada in 1955 found 1,335,000 potholes. By 1961 there were barely 49,000 left! Drought, combined with drainage for agriculture, took a heavy toll. These prairie sloughs are 10 times more productive in waterfowl food than similar water bodies in the east; 50 to 80% of all migratory ducks in North America breed on them. No wonder this region is sometimes called a "duck factory."

The province contains substantial populations of some of the "most wanted" species in North America, including Spruce Grouse, Yellow Rail, Ross's Gull at Churchill, Northern Hawk Owl, Great Gray Owl, Three-toed Woodpecker, Sprague's Pipit, Connecticut Warbler, and Baird's and Le Conte's Sparrows. All except the gull are readily accessible in the southern section of the province along a good road system. Ross's Gull is not as reliable as it once was. Although there are still annual sightings (through 1999), its continued occurrence in Churchill is in doubt.

The population is spread in a thin strip along the far southern agricultural belt. Southern woodlands occur in a thin band north of that strip. Boreal forest covers the northern half of the province and on the eastern edge penetrates far south. The arctic-subarctic region lies in a band on the north, with low arctic tundra at the far northeast, adjacent to Hudson Bay.

Early June is the best time to come. There are still a few migrants going north, but from late May to early July all local breeders are on territory. Waterfowl and birds of prey pass through in April and early May. Shorebirds and land birds come through in May in peak abundance. In August and early September, shorebirds return, as do the northern land birds. Waterfowl stop here before the long flight south in September and October. November through March, search for the Northern Hawk, Great Gray and Boreal Owls.

Selection of a few hot spots is always difficult. However, a few areas stand out in order of preference: Churchill for the arctic tundra and ocean birds, the least remote, least expensive place to view them in North America. The only other fairly accessible comparable spot is the Dempster Highway in the Yukon; Oak Hammock Marsh for water birds; the Brandon area for Yellow Rail and prairie-slough water birds; Pinawa for boreal and hardwood forest birds, including Great Gray and Boreal Owls. The above four spots are musts for the serious birder. The Delta Marsh complex offers prairie marsh birds in abundance; Riding Mountain National Park has boreal and hardwood forest and numerous parkland and prairie birds, including all prairie pothole ducks, five Canadian grebes, Northern Saw-whet and Barred Owls, Spruce Grouse, both "three-toed" woodpeckers, and a large number of warblers, including Golden-winged. A bonus is the resident naturalist, who can help you find that elusive, hard-to-spot species. There are many large mammals in the park, such as Moose, White-tailed Deer, Black Bear, Wapiti and Beaver which add to the overall visit.

A visitor with a half day to spare in Winnipeg and no car should go to Assiniboine Park; using a car, you can easily spend this time at Oak Hammock Marsh. A full day could begin early in the morning within the boreal forest at Pinawa and include an afternoon at Oak Hammock. A second day would allow a visit to the Brandon area. To see most species at Churchill requires at least three full days if you fly in, or a week if you travel by train.

Manitoba has an extremely active and friendly group, the Manitoba Rare Bird Alert. They have all offered to help and can refer you to other members if there is a need. Contact Norm Cleveland, phone (204) 253-9622; Rudolf F. Koes, 135 Rossmere Crescent, Winnipeg, Manitoba R2K 0G1, phone (204) 661-0763; Gordon Grieef, 31 Cara Cove, Winnipeg, Manitoba, R2N 3C2, phone (204) 253-4425; e-mail grieefg@mb.sympatico.ca; Robert Parsons, 68 Thatcher Drive, Winnipeg, Manitoba R3T 2L3, phone (204) 269-6388; e-mail rparsons@icenter.net The four active clubs in the province may be contacted through the Manitoba Naturalists' Society, 401–63 Albert Street, Winnipeg, Manitoba R3B 1G4, phone (204) 943-9029; Web address www.wilds.mb.ca/mns

There are two bird-finding guides available for southern Manitoba: *Birder's Guide to Southeastern Manitoba*, by N. J. Cleveland, S. Edie, G. D. Grieef, G. E. Holland, R. F. Koes, J. W. Maynard, W. P. Neily, P. Taylor and R. Tkachuk, second revised and enlarged edition, 1988, 91 pp.; and *Birder's Guide to*

Southwestern Manitoba, by C. W. Cuthbert, J. I. Horton, M. W. McCowan, B. G. Robinson and N. G. Short, 1990, 99 pp. Also available are *Field Checklist of the Birds of Manitoba* (1986) and *Field Checklist of the Birds of Southeastern Manitoba* (revised 1995). All are available from the MNS; contact them for prices.

Other material is available from the Manitoba Museum of Man and Nature, 190 Rupert Avenue, Winnipeg, Manitoba, R3B 0N2 with a Web site at www.chin.gc.ca/MMMN/English/

Finally, for Churchill, a must is *A Birder's Guide to Churchill*, by Bonnie Chartier, published in 1994 by the American Birding Association. It can be ordered at 1-800-634-7736 (ABA Sales) or may be available at various stores in Churchill.

The Official Highway Map and a Manitoba Vacation Guide are available free from Explore Manitoba Centre, 21 Forks Market Road, Winnipeg, Manitoba R3C 2T7; phone (204) 945-3777.

Maps and brochures for all provincial parks are available at the Department of Natural Resources, 200 Saulteaux Crescent, Winnipeg, Manitoba, R3J 3W3; phone (204) 945-6784.

Birdwatchers wishing to consult additional literature on the birds of the province will find sources in *Manitoba Bird Studies, 1744–1983*, by M. K. McNicholl, Manitoba Natural Resources and Manitoba Museum of Man and Nature, Winnipeg, 1985.

The compilation of this chapter was greatly assisted by notes, suggestions and other types of help from Gord Grieef, Wayne Neily, Robert Nero, Martin Siepman, Peter Taylor and Ian Ward.

RUDOLF F. KOES

Winnipeg

The oldest settlement in western Canada can boast that it is near the geographic centre of North America. Winnipeg began as a settlement in 1812. For almost half a century it was the headquarters of the mighty Hudson's Bay Company, which owned and dominated most of western Canada and part of the north-western United States. Today, Winnipeg has a population of over 600,000.

Birding Features
Assiniboine Park. The park, set along the banks of the Assiniboine River, is noted for its passerine migration. Almost all warbler species found in Manitoba can be seen in the park during the latter half of May. This is also an excellent site to study the differences between Hermit, Swainson's and Gray-cheeked Thrushes during spring migration.

The 160 ha park is the largest and most popular outdoor facility in Winnipeg. It lies 6 km west of downtown, on the south bank of the Assiniboine River. By car, it is reached via Wellington Crescent or Corydon Avenue; or west via Portage Avenue to Overdale Street and a hike across the footbridge. The Portage or Charleswood city buses will bring you there.

The diverse habitat, including lawns, gardens, Bur Oak and river bottom forests, together with the adjacent river, attracts a great variety of species, especially during migration. Birding is best done along the south bank of the river, east and west of the footbridge on the trails, and in the English Garden immediately west of the bridge.

In the early spring, from April to early May, watch for over a dozen species of sparrow. In the second half of May, the warblers come in waves, with almost all species to be found in Manitoba passing through here. Breeding birds include Wood Duck, Red-headed Woodpecker and Yellow-throated Vireo. In the fall, beginning in early August and peaking in late August to mid-September, look for up to 5 species of vireo and over 20 different warblers. August also brings the Ruby-throated Hummingbirds into the English Garden. In winter check for waxwings and finches.

La Barrière Park. Straddling the La Salle River, this park contains river bottom woods surrounded by open grassy spots. The area offers a good concentration of migrating smaller birds in both spring and fall.

The park is located 5.6 km south of Highway 100 (Perimeter Highway), at the south end of Winnipeg. Drive south from the city on Highway 75 to Highway 100 and then go west for 1 km, turn south at the first intersection (Waverley Street). There are several good walking trails in the park on both sides of the river. Beware of Poison Ivy in season! For more information, contact the Manitoba Naturalists' Society at the above address.

During the nesting season, from late May to mid-July, check for Broad-winged Hawks and Great Horned Owls in the dense woods. In addition, Red-headed Woodpecker, Yellow-throated Vireo, Orchard Oriole, Rose-breasted Grosbeak and Lark Sparrow are present.

St. Adolphe Bridge. This is a spot to watch for raptors in the spring. Proceed south from Winnipeg on Highway 75; 11 km south of Highway 100 you will hit PR 429; proceed east on 429 about 1.6 km to the bridge, cross it and park on the wide shoulders off the road to watch migration.

The Red River Valley is a major funnel for migrating raptors. In late March and early April, look for the Red-tailed Hawk, which is the most common, Rough-legged Hawk, Golden and Bald Eagles, Northern Harrier, Merlin and American Kestrel. The river and adjacent farmlands provide habitat for Canada Geese, ducks and other birds passing through.

BIRDER'S GUIDE TO SOUTHEASTERN MANITOBA
Revised by Rudolf F. Koes

St. Vital Park. Nestled in a bend of the Red River about 6 km south of the city centre is small, but productive, St. Vital Park. Access to the park is off River Road, which can be reached via Routes 52 or 62 and St. Vital Road from downtown Winnipeg. The park features a loop road, several walking trails, deciduous woodlands and grassy fields. The best areas are located in the eastern half of the park and along the river. During migration it can rival Assiniboine Park for variety of passerines. The open woods along the river bank allow good looks at flycatchers, vireos, thrushes, warblers and sparrows, and check for Bank Swallows and Northern Rough-winged Swallows over the river. In recent years the park has been the most reliable spot in the city to see Indigo Bunting; in the last few years even Lazuli Bunting and hybrids between the two species have been noted. Check particularly the woods to the east and southeast of the parking lot at the Duck Pond for these species. (This pond may at times harbour Wood Ducks and Solitary Sandpipers, but is usually not productive.) Also be on the lookout for Yellow-throated Vireos, which may be heard along the river.

Although the river itself rarely has good birds, during spring break-up and fall freeze-up gulls may concentrate at open patches of water; both Great Black-backed and Glaucous Gulls have been seen here at these times.

Kildonan Park. Like Assiniboine Park, this spot is well worth a visit, especially if your transportation is restricted to Metro Transit. The location on Main Street makes it readily accessible from downtown Winnipeg on the North Main bus.

Most of the warblers of southern Manitoba have been seen here at one time or another, although numbers do not usually reach those of Assiniboine Park. The open lawns with stately oaks constitute one of the most reliable spots in the Winnipeg area for Red-headed Woodpecker in the summer. Cooper's Hawk nests regularly in tall oaks near Rainbow Stage.

MARTIN K. McNICHOLL
Revised by Rudolf F. Koes

Oak Hammock Marsh

This major man-made development illustrates how a private organization and different levels of government can unite to develop a top birding area. Lying within a half-hour drive of Winnipeg, its diversity of habitats has attracted over 250 species since 1935.

This marsh and lake sit in a broad lowland known as St. Andrews Bog. For years the remnant marsh attracted a variety of water birds. Restoration began in 1967 as a cooperative venture with Ducks Unlimited (Canada) and the federal and provincial governments. By the spring of 1974, they had produced 1418 ha of wetlands, including one large pond in the shape of a duck.

The present 3645 ha Oak Hammock Marsh Wildlife Management Area is about 24 km north of Winnipeg. Access is by either Highway 7 or 8. On Highway 7, proceed north to Highway 67, east 8 km to PR 220 and then north on PR 220 for 4 km to the main parking lot. The Highway 8 access route is north from Winnipeg to Highway 67, west 6.5 km to PR 220, and then north to the parking spot.

A sightings board at the east side of the parking lot should be consulted and a checklist is available in the interpretive centre. The centre also houses various displays, a gift shop and a restaurant and is well worth a visit.

Birding Features

Agricultural lands surround the marsh. However, the management authority has included 1904 ha of upland habitat, providing sufficient variety of habitat to attract 105 species to breed. Dykes control the water levels and also provide access to several separate areas by foot. Five observation mounds give views of the whole complex.

The birds begin arriving at the start of the spring thaw in April. Waterfowl, including over 100,000 Snow Geese, come in until mid-May. Shorebirds arrive a little later. They come in May and early June, with 36 species found in North America having been recorded here. At times, one species such as Hudsonian Godwit or Red-necked Phalarope will dominate for a few days. Check the clumps of alders and willows near the main parking lot for the waves of warblers that pass through in May and late August. The birds that stay begin breeding in late May and continue into July. Watch for them as you hike along the dykes. The fall migration begins with shorebirds in mid-July and continues until late September. Waterfowl numbers reach a peak in late September to early October. At that time, look for Sandhill Cranes by the hundreds and Ross's Geese among the thousands of Snow Geese returning south.

This spot has become noted for sightings of such southern herons as Green, Little Blue, Tricolored and Yellow-crowned Night-Heron. Rare egrets such as Cattle, Great and Snowy are also seen.

The large concentrations of birds attract falcons, especially Prairie and Peregrine, and other raptors, including Bald Eagles in late fall (late October-November) and Snowy Owls from late fall to early spring. Along the west side of the marsh you can frequently find Sharp-tailed Grouse, Short-eared Owl and Le Conte's Sparrow.

BIRDER'S GUIDE TO SOUTHEASTERN MANITOBA
Revised by Rudolf F. Koes

Birds Hill Provincial Park

Birds Hill, with its Bur Oak, aspen, variety of conifers and deciduous shrubs, is a near-urban park with over 185 species of prairie, parkland and boreal forest birds reported. The park hosts a good-sized herd of White-tailed Deer, some Coyote, Red Fox and other small mammals.

Named after the Bird family, the first landowners in 1824, the area changed hands many times. The park was established in 1962, with the northern section formally declared a provincial park in 1964, and the remainder added later.

The highlands were built by a stream carrying sands and gravels to a delta in former Lake Agassiz. This all took place eight to ten thousand years ago.

The 3350 ha park is split: lands on the south for high-density recreation and the remainder left in a natural state. The lands lie adjacent to Highway 59, about 24 km northeast of Winnipeg. Bus service to the park from downtown Winnipeg runs a few times a day only in summer. One main driving loop circles the southern, active recreation area. A sideroad leads to park headquarters. A major horse-riding trail lies on the north side, as do several nature and hiking trails. Roads and trails are illustrated in the park material.

Visitor accommodation includes that at Winnipeg and nearby communities. Campers and trailer users have a major campground in the park, located off the South Drive loop road.

Information on the park, including an excellent brochure and a comprehensive bird checklist, is available from The Chief Ranger, Birds Hill Provincial Park, Department of Natural Resources, R.R. 2, Dugald, Manitoba ROE OKO; phone (204) 222-9151.

Birding Features

The main forests are aspen and Bur Oak communities separated by grasslands. There are further stands of White Spruce, plus Black Spruce bogs. A White Cedar bog and a man-made lake and lagoon add diversity. This variety of habitat provides opportunities to sight Pied-billed Grebe, Great Blue Heron and a variety of waterfowl. Northern Goshawk is most often seen in the fall. American Woodcock is found in low areas at dusk in the south end from mid-April to late May. Listen for a Northern Saw-whet Owl in the mixed and coniferous woods along the eastern and southern sections through April and May. Sprague's Pipit is rare but has been seen in meadows in the spring. Northern Shrike comes in late fall and winter. The mixed and coniferous woods provide a variety of warblers in June. Indigo Bunting is present in the open, drier sections in June and July. In winter, a variety of finches appear.

A drive around the loop road of the south should bring an Indigo Bunting and Eastern Towhee. Look east of the west gate on the north side of the road, and also just east of the traffic circle. At the circle, turn right and proceed south and east. At the turn in the road, where it swings from south to east, check on the west side for an American Woodcock or Northern Saw-whet Owl. Continue to the north leg of the loop. Just before meeting the road from the east gate, scan the east side for another Northern Saw-whet Owl, warblers and (in season) winter finches. Check the area around the east gate (off PR 206) for Eastern Bluebird and Lark Sparrow. Return to the loop. Just beyond, as the road heads northeast, there is a sideroad heading north to the headquarters and the ranger station. Take this side trip to spot the occasional crossbill and warbler, west of the headquarters buildings. Return to the loop and continue west.

For further specific locations, check with park staff and the interpretive service at headquarters from early May to September.

RUDOLF F. KOES
Revised by Rudolf F. Koes

Hecla Provincial Park

Superb boreal forest birding is available at and near Hecla Island. Spruce Grouse, Black-backed Woodpecker and Boreal Chickadee can usually be found in late fall or winter, with Northern Hawk Owl and Three-toed Woodpecker a possibility. Numerous passerines are here from late May to early July. Nearby Lake Winnipeg offers opportunities to view water birds. The big-game enthusiast can see Moose on the island, and some deer, Timber Wolves and a few Red Foxes.

Settlers arrived in the area from Iceland in 1875–76 after the eruption of Mt. Hekla in their homeland destroyed their farms. In 1878 they formed the self-governing republic of New Iceland, with their own constitution and a provisional government that levied taxes and organized schools. In 1881 the boundaries of Manitoba were extended to include the republic. Today much of the cleared land has regrown and attracts a variety of birds and mammals.

The island, located about 145 km north of Winnipeg, may be reached by following Highway 8. The trip can be extended north to Matheson Island on PR 234. Greyhound bus travels part way up the road, but the best access is by car. The trip may be made in one long day; a more leisurely two-day trip will cover the return. There are a series of hiking, cross-country ski and snowshoe trails in the park. A park map and brochure are available at the entrance gate during summer.

Commercial accommodation may be obtained in a luxury resort hotel at Gull Harbour, with more moderately priced cabins nearby at the north end of the island. Camping facilities occur at Gull Harbour and near Beaver Creek along PR 234, halfway to Matheson Island. There is a nice bed-and-breakfast in the village of Hecla.

Birding Features
A visit can be made at any time of the year. Go in spring from mid-May to early July. A fall trip would be best in August and early September. November still has a good number of birds, especially lingering Bald Eagles, Pine Grosbeak and waterfowl. After that it can be very cold and stormy, even into March.

The spring trip would begin on PTH 8 north to the Winnipeg Beach turnoff; take PR 229 east to PTH 9 and proceed north. Between Winnipeg and Winnipeg Beach, common roadside species include Horned Lark, Western Meadowlark, Brewer's Blackbird and Vesper Sparrow.

Proceed north to Gimli on 9; take PR 222 to Camp Morton, about 8 km north of Gimli, and enter Camp Morton Park. Scout out the area for migrant land and water birds as this site is a good birding area.

Yellow-headed Blackbird

Continue north on PR 222, then move to PTH 8 and on to Riverton. Travel east on PR 329 to the shores of Lake Winnipeg. The Riverton Marsh is known for its many water birds. Scan the water and marsh vegetation for a variety of waterfowl, rails, Marsh and Sedge Wrens, Yellow-headed Blackbird, and Le Conte's and Nelson's Sharp-tailed Sparrows.

Reach Hecla Island via Highway 8 east. Just over the causeway to the park, but before the entrance, scan the marshes on both sides of the road or visit the boardwalk indicated by signs, on the south side of the road. Reconnoitre for waterfowl, rails, Alder Flycatchers and others.

Return to Highway 8 and enter the park. About 200 m beyond the entrance there is a gravel road leading south. Park on the shoulder of the main road. Proceed beyond the barrier for a 1 km stroll, looking for a variety of passerines, including Lincoln's Sparrow.

Continue the drive east on Highway 8 for about 20 km, to the end. Birding is excellent along this stretch, with several stops a must. Sample both the coniferous and mixed woods for a variety of birds, including Pileated Woodpecker, Gray Jay, Black-capped and Boreal Chickadees, Winter Wren, Swainson's Thrush, both kinglet species, numerous warblers and sometimes crossbills. An alternative route through the picturesque village of Hecla branches off to the east (right) just over 10 km past the park entrance. This scenic stretch takes little extra time and is well worth it. At Gull Harbour take a spotting scope and scan the water for American White Pelican, Double-crested Cormorant, diving ducks, gulls and terns. Check the sky for an occasional Osprey. The end of the road has some good walking trails on which to find warblers, etc.

To extend the visit, return to the junction of Highway 8 and PR 234. Take 234 north to the end of Matheson Island. This is an 85 km road with no services. Fill up with gasoline before departing. The first stretch of road is generally open, but soon coniferous forests take over. Boreal species are common, with a Northern Hawk Owl more often seen on this stretch than in most other places. On the return to Winnipeg, you can either retrace your path or proceed straight south all the way on 8.

A fall visit may produce waves of migrating passerines, particularly at the far end of the island on PR 233. Hike the trails at this location and watch for these and the accompanying Sharp-shinned Hawk, Merlin and the occasional Peregrine Falcon.

In winter, the fields between Winnipeg and Winnipeg Beach often contain Sharp-tailed Grouse and flocks of Snow Bunting. At the north end of Hecla Island, at the termination of the road, look for Bald Eagle, "three-toed" woodpeckers, Boreal Chickadee, Red-breasted Nuthatch, Northern Shrike, Evening Grosbeak, both redpoll species, both species of crossbill and Pine Grosbeak. An occasional Northern Hawk Owl or Spruce Grouse may show up. Going farther up to Matheson Island will possibly, as in summer, result in a view of a Northern Hawk Owl.

RUDOLF F. KOES
Revised by Rudolf F. Koes

Nopiming Provincial Park

Some of the finest upland boreal forest birding in eastern Manitoba is found in the south end of Nopiming Provincial Park, along the Bird River Road. This route is particularly good for spring warblers.

The area has always been known for its fishing and trapping potential, but it came alive after gold was found in 1911. Claims were staked, and a major mine operated from 1926 to 1937 at the north end of the park.

Nopiming is located along the Manitoba-Ontario boundary, immediately north of Whiteshell Provincial Park, about 160 km by road northeast of Winnipeg. To reach the park, drive to Lac du Bonnet, the last source of gasoline and other services, and then take PR 313 and 315. An alternative route would be a driving loop of about 350 km (two or more days) north and east from Pine Falls on PR 304 and back south on 314 and 315. All these roads may be rough, especially during or after rain. When taking the loop, fill up your gas tanks at Lac du Bonnet, Pine Falls, Manigotagan and Bissett, the only services in the area.

The closest commercial accommodation is at Lac du Bonnet, with several motels and lodges. Campsites occur at Bird Lake in the south and others to the north.

Most of the birding information in this area has been taken from *Wings along the Winnipeg* by Peter Taylor. This book, available from the Manitoba Naturalists Society, gives detailed descriptions of the birding opportunities in the area (including Pinawa and surroundings and Whiteshell Provincial Park). If you require more information or help, contact him at P.O. Box 597, Pinawa, Manitoba ROE 1LO; phone (204) 753-2977.

Birding Features

The Bird River Road (PR 315) from PR 313 to Bird Lake is excellent for boreal forest warblers from late May to early July. It is one of the few spots in Manitoba where the Northern Parula can be expected. In late March or early April, come here to listen for owls, including Great Horned, Barred, Boreal and Northern Saw-whet. Later, in the peak breeding season, explore for Great Crested Flycatcher, Yellow-bellied Flycatcher (at the edge of dense stands of young spruce), Eastern Wood-Pewee, Red-breasted Nuthatch, Brown Creeper and Winter Wren. There are small numbers of Hermit Thrushes, numerous Swainson's Thrushes, Veeries and an abundance of warblers. These include Black-and-white, Nashville, Magnolia and a small number of Black-throated Green, especially in the mature coniferous forest near Bird Lake. In addition, there are Blackburnian and Chestnut-sided Warblers, Ovenbird and Northern Waterthrush at several spots near the Bird River. Mourning Warblers are present, and Canada Warblers lurk where the understory is especially dense. Scarlet Tanagers and Pine Siskins may be heard or seen. In some winters both PR 313 and 315 provide good prospects for sighting Northern Hawk Owls and Great Gray Owls.

RUDOLF F. KOES AND PETER TAYLOR
Revised by Rudolf F. Koes

Pinawa and Surroundings

The Pinawa area contains a mixture of forest and spruce bogs with some cleared farmland. Over 150 species of birds may be seen here in a day during late May. This was part of the area in which 205 species were recorded in a single day on May 23, 1987. In winter, Northern Hawk Owl, Great Gray Owl and both species of "three-toed" woodpeckers may be seen.

The Winnipeg River was an important fur-trading route in the 18th century. Major settlement began in the late 1880s, with cutting and burning of the forest, as there was no native prairie. Clearing continues to this day. The forests have been almost completely logged over, with present growth mainly secondary. An extensive series of dams, with six hydroelectric plants, was built to harness the power of the Winnipeg River. The largest, at Seven Sisters Falls, offers tours.

The town of Pinawa, founded in 1963 in conjunction with the Whiteshell Nuclear Research Establishment, lies 112 km east and north of Winnipeg. Numerous secondary roads can keep a birder busy for two days in the late spring.

Accommodation in the town of Pinawa consists of one small motel, open year-round. There are two campgrounds 10 km west of town, one privately operated and serviced, the other a wayside primitive facility. The region is an active summer resort, with gasoline and other services available from at least May through September.

Come for birding in late spring from mid-May to early July. Bring insect repellent along! In winter, dress warmly and be prepared with emergency clothing and footwear, sleeping bag, candle, etc., as temperatures are known to fall very low.

A book by Peter Taylor has been published on the surrounding area. (See previous site for title and address to obtain a copy.)

Birding Features

Most of the country within 3 km of the Whitemouth River, and some land along the Lee and Winnipeg Rivers, is cultivated. Marginal pastureland lies along the edges. The remainder of the country is forested with Trembling Aspen, the most abundant species, growing on well-drained sites. White Spruce, Balsam Fir, birch and Balsam Poplar are also present. Black Spruce and Tamarack are found in the wet areas, and Jack Pine grows on rock outcrops and sandy ridges. This diversity of habitat attracts a great variety of birdlife that breeds from late April to July.

The townsite of Pinawa is a small, recently created island of parklike habitat set in second-growth boreal forest. Consequently, the birdlife within the town is unique for the area. Begin the exploration within the community by looking for Red-headed Woodpecker, Least Flycatcher, large numbers of Cliff Swallow and Purple Martin, House Wren, Brown Thrasher, Warbling Vireo and Baltimore Oriole. Now move to the forests at the edge of town to search for a variety of warblers.

Expand the range to the trails radiating out from the north end of the diversion dam at the head of the Pinawa Channel, located at the very end of PR

211. These hiking trails sometimes have ankle-high water in many places. Some are even impassable during wet weather. Before leaving the car, make sure you have a compass; stay on the well-defined trails. The bush trails are excellent for boreal birds from mid-May to early July. Begin the search for a Great Crested Flycatcher, Eastern Wood-Pewee, the odd Yellow-bellied Flycatcher, Brown Creeper, Winter Wren, Hermit Thrush and myriad warblers. They should include Nashville, Chestnut-sided and Ovenbird, all of which are common. The Northern Waterthrush will be near the channel. Listen for the Connecticut Warbler near clearings in the Black Spruce, together with abundant Mourning Warblers. A Scarlet Tanager should be seen.

Return to town, drive about 2 km west, then take Cemetery Road north of PR 211. This north road is passable for about 3 km in dry weather, but stay off in wet seasons or when it looks like rain. A round trip of hiking and birding should take about five hours. Many warblers occur here in late spring. Search for Red-eyed Vireo, Great Crested Flycatcher, Veery, and Chestnut-sided and Mourning Warblers, all common to very common. The American Redstart has an unusually high concentration. Proceed for about 3 km, to where the road takes a sharp turn west and soon becomes impassable. At the west bend, take the 100 m trail north to where the Pinawa Channel widens into a large marsh. Stop and scan the water, or launch a canoe for a more detailed look. Least and American Bitterns, Mallard, Blue-winged Teal, Common Goldeneye, Sora, Virginia Rail and Marsh Wren all occur and recently a pair of Trumpeter Swans investigated the marsh. Retrace your steps the 100 m and continue west and north on the trail. Inspect the mature conifers for a Winter Wren and a possible Black-throated Green Warbler. This road or trail ends in a Black Spruce bog, which should produce Boreal Chickadee, Golden-crowned and Ruby-crowned Kinglets, Yellow-rumped Warbler and Connecticut Warbler.

Two other spots to check are the Winnipeg River in and near town, and the sewage lagoon, for a variety of waterfowl including Wood Ducks and Hooded Mergansers. The latter site is reached from a road that takes off south from PR 211, about 1 km west of the cemetery road. Leave your vehicle off to the side of the road at the gate, even if it is open, and walk in. At the lagoon, moulting male Wood Ducks gather in summer; Virginia Rail and Sora are seen, and migrating flocks of various species pass through. Look for small numbers of Black Scoters, a rare Peregrine Falcon or a Yellow Rail. Return to PR 211 and continue west, looking for Indigo Bunting along the side of the road in June. At the Pinawa Fish and Game Association Waterfowl Sanctuary, check for the many male Wood Ducks moulting in July.

The Seven Sisters Falls forebay, Natalie Lake, is located south of Pinawa and east of Highway 11, on PR 307. This body of water is often a good place to watch migrating waterfowl in early May. The top of the dam is the best vantage point. Scan for Common Loon, often large numbers of Red-necked and Horned Grebes, and smaller numbers of the other grebe species. American White Pelican, Double-crested Cormorant and Tundra Swan come in mid-May. Greater Scaup often occur in large concentrations with other ducks.

White-winged Scoter appears most springs. Caspian Terns regularly pass through in late May, early June and September. Late fall, from late October to early December, offers excellent chances for "Northern" species, such as scoters, Harlequin Duck, Oldsquaw and Glaucous Gull, or even rarer strays. Other dams downstream (McArthur Falls, Great Falls and Pine Falls) should also be checked at this time. The vicinity of Pine Falls is especially productive in late fall. All these places can be reached by following Highway 11 north and west from Seven Sisters Falls.

From Seven Sisters Falls south to Whitemouth there is a network of farm roads from which to look for birds living in open country and forest. This strip is particularly good for raptors in spring and fall, including Red-tailed and Rough-legged Hawks, Northern Harrier, Northern Goshawk, Merlin and Short-eared Owl. In winter Gyrfalcon is sometimes noted. Sharp-tailed Grouse are present all year and use several dancing grounds from March to May. Sandhill Cranes are seen from April to September and are most common during migration. A few Marbled Godwits probably breed south of River Hills. Passerines include Western Kingbird, Horned Lark, Black-billed Magpie and Brown Thrasher; the Eastern Meadowlark has been found, together with Vesper and Clay-colored Sparrows. The area is good from April to September, but the best time is during spring migration in April and May. For a detailed sideroad description of a four- to six-hour trip through this strip, refer to Taylor's *Wings along the Winnipeg*, mentioned previously.

The Bog River extensive marsh complex lies east and north of Whitemouth, north of Highway 44. The marsh is largely impenetrable, but is accessible from a gravel road that zigzags north and east from the junction of Highways 44 and 11, just east of Whitemouth. Along this road look for Eastern and Mountain Bluebirds. At the end of the road a powerline right-of-way runs northeast to cross the south end of the marsh. Try a canoe trip upstream from this right-of-way to PTH 44. This marsh and river complex harbours Green Heron and Least Bittern on occasion and is a good place to view Sandhill Crane, Virginia Rail, Sora, Yellow Rail and Nelson's Sharp-tailed Sparrow.

Return to Highway 44 and proceed northwest. Reconnoitre for American Woodcocks along the way. Listen at dusk for them from mid-April to early June. Pine Warblers occur regularly in some mature Jack Pine stands along 44. In mixed stands of aspen, birch and Jack Pine, stop and hunt for Scarlet Tanagers. Listen for Indigo Buntings along the highway.

This whole region contains many Black Spruce bogs, but the finest accessible one is alongside PR 435 near Milner Ridge, about 3 km east of the junction with 214. The spot lies west of Pinawa, north from Highway 44. This is the locality to come to in June for Spruce Grouse; both Three-toed and Black-backed Woodpeckers nest in this bog; Boreal Chickadee, Gray Jay, Hermit and Swainson's Thrushes, Solitary Vireo, Nashville and Yellow-rumped Warblers are all here; the Connecticut Warbler breeds in the more open stands, with up to four being heard at once; Golden-crowned and Ruby-crowned Kinglets, Yellow-bellied Flycatcher (rare), Alder and Olive-sided Flycatchers, and Lincoln's Sparrow are noted on any visit. If you enjoy flowers, a late June trip could produce a variety, including seven species of orchid. In winter this is the place to observe Spruce Grouse, Northern Goshawk, perhaps Three-toed and Black-backed Woodpeckers, Gray Jay and White-winged Crossbill.

PETER TAYLOR
Revised by Rudolf F. Koes

Whiteshell Provincial Park

Whiteshell contains numerous lakes, trails, canoe routes and recreation spots. A wild goose sanctuary and game bird refuge provides other attractions.

The first recorded visit to the area was made by the La Verendrye expedition in the spring of 1733. The Winnipeg River, which flows through the north end of the park, then became an important fur-trade route from Montreal. The last major use was in 1870, when Colonel Wolseley's troops used it on the way to Red River to fight the Metis. With the push to have a railroad linking Canada, construction began here in 1877, with the line opening in 1883. At the turn of the 20th century, there was an unsuccessful attempt to farm the area. The soils were too poor. The first of many summer cottages that now dot the area was built in about 1920. The Manitoba government established the Whiteshell Forest Reserve in 1931. In 1939, Alfred Hole founded the goose sanctuary, beside the community of Rennie. In 1961 the whole area became a provincial park.

The park lies about 145 km east of Winnipeg via either Highway 1 or Highways 15 and 44. Greyhound bus services the park via the Trans-Canada Highway at least once a day on the way through. There is an extensive system of hiking and interpretive trails and canoe routes throughout the park. The routes are illustrated on the park map-brochure, which also shows the available campsites, interpretive features and interesting spots. The lengthy Mantario Hiking Trail, which passes through the area, has an excellent brochure.

Commercial visitor accommodation may be obtained at several places, including Falcon Lake and Rennie, plus lodges scattered throughout. Check the park brochure for these and the locations of 17 campgrounds, some of which are serviced. Information and brochures on the park and other features are available from Travel Manitoba (see above).

Birding Features

The roads through the park, particularly PR 307, which loops through the north and west side, skirt several lakes. From April to September, a survey of these water bodies should produce Common Loon, Common Goldeneye, Ring-necked Duck, Common and Hooded Mergansers, Spotted Sandpiper, Bald Eagle and likely an Osprey. Raptors flying across the road include Broad-winged, Sharp-shinned and Cooper's Hawks. Watch for a Turkey Vulture, particularly in the Rennie River area. You may also spot Ruffed and Spruce Grouse; Barred and Great Gray Owls; Pileated, Hairy and Three-toed and Black-backed Woodpeckers; Yellow-bellied and Olive-sided Flycatchers; and several species of vireos, warblers and sparrows.

A visit to the Alf Hole Wild Goose Sanctuary at Rennie will prove reward-ing. Here you'll see Canada Goose, Wood Duck, Ring-necked Duck, scaup, Great Blue Heron and American Bittern. Go into the interpretive centre to see the displays on geese. Ask the staff about other local places to explore.

RUDOLF F. KOES
Revised by Rudolf F. Koes

Spotting Great Gray Owls

Southeastern Manitoba is probably the best, easiest and most accessible area in North America to look for a Great Gray Owl. The birds live in remote north-ern coniferous forests. In recent years they have been found nesting in extreme southeastern Manitoba, in inaccessible boglands, on provincial forest land and adjacent areas. They may be spotted from Pine Falls, east of Lake Winnipeg, to near the U.S. border at Sprague.

The owls may be ferreted out from November to April, with the best times being January and February. These are the months when severe cold, deep snow and often low rodent populations force the birds out of the woods. Expect to sight them at all times during the day, but more likely just after dawn or near dusk. Drive slowly; look for telltale plunge spots where they have been hunting; examine the deciduous trees near spruce-tamarack forests for the characteristic dark, round-headed shape. If the grader gets through and ploughs out the sideroads and forestry roads, try these trails as they usually are more productive.

Before departing make sure you have a full tank of gasoline, warm parka, mitts, tuque, warm boots, sleeping bag, candle and a shovel. Don't take any chances, as cars break down in cold weather.

There are several good spots to search, with the best roads as follows: Proceed north from Winnipeg on Highway 59 to PR 317; take it slowly east-ward to Lac du Bonnet, and then carefully search PR 313 and 315, both good sideroads, to find the birds. Turn south onto PR 520 and follow it to PR 211, then head west and return to Highway 11; travel south again on Highway 11 to the junction with PR 506; take 506, another key road, slowly down to Highway 1; swing east on 1 to PR 308 and follow it south to Sprague, near the border; take Highway 12 west to the junction with PR 210; follow 210, another good possibility, slowly to Marchand; move straight north on the sideroad to meet Highway 1; go east on 1 for 6 km to just across Brokenhead River and then take the sideroad, if it is open, north to Highway 15. Return west to Winnipeg on 15; or else continue searching and go east to Elma; then north to Highway 44 and follow it generally east to meet 1 near West Hawk Lake. Return west on Highway 1 to Winnipeg. To find out more about this large owl, read the award-winning book *The Great Gray Owl (Phantom of the Northern Forest)*, by R. W. Nero (Washington: Smithsonian Institute Press, 1980).

ROBERT W. NERO
Revised by Rudolf F. Koes

Delta Marsh Complex

One of the largest and most famous (for birding) fresh-water marshes in the world, the Delta Marsh, lies on the south shore of Lake Manitoba. The diverse habitat has produced about 300 species of birds.

The Delta Waterfowl and Wetlands Research Station, a privately funded centre for research, was founded in 1938. With the success of the centre, the University of Manitoba also established a field station in 1970. Neither centre is public, and hence special permission is required before entering. Write Delta Waterfowl and Wetlands Research Station, R.R. 1, Portage la Prairie, Manitoba R1N 3A1; and University Field Station (Delta Marsh), 230 Mackray Hall, University of Manitoba, Winnipeg, Manitoba R3T 2N2.

The Delta Marsh complex spans some 22,000 ha and lies 20 km north of Portage la Prairie. A car is essential to get to the marsh (see below for access). Accommodation is at a variety of motels and hotels in Portage la Prairie. Campgrounds are located at St. Ambroise and Lynch's Point, on the east and west sides of the marsh, respectively.

A checklist is available from the Department of Natural Resources, 200 Saulteaux Crescent, Winnipeg R3J 3W3; phone (204) 945-6784.

Birding Features

The marsh complex consists of a treed beach ridge adjacent to the lake, behind which lie some of the largest stands of *Phragmites* in North America. There are open and closed marshes, some of which are linked to long narrow channels from the lake. A relict stand of hackberry trees, shrubs, sand beaches and sloughs add to the diversity, including 121 species of birds that have bred, or now breed, and an additional 111 that migrate through regularly. Four search spots are recommended.

Lynch's Point on the west side is accessible by proceeding north on PR 242 from Highway 16. The stand of trees in and near the unserviced campground on

Canvasback

the point is good for migrating passerines in May and August. Large concentrations of Snow Geese, with a few Greater White-fronted and Ross's among them, occur here from late April through early May and from late September through early October. The minimal beach area is not attractive to shorebirds.

Delta, in the middle, is reached via PR 240 north from Portage la Prairie. The nearby area is alive with birds from mid-April to early October. In the spring, look for grebes and ducks, including mergansers. American White Pelican and Double-crested Cormorant occur from spring to fall. Mid- and late May are best for flycatchers, vireos, thrushes and warblers. Swallows, mainly Tree and Bank, cluster by the thousands on telephone wires and trees in late July and early August.

If you have permission to enter the Delta Waterfowl and Wetlands Research Station, it is reached by travelling to the end of PR 240 and turning east at the stop sign. Check for herons and shorebirds along the way.

The east Delta beach is reached via the road going north immediately east of the Delta channel. This beach usually has a variety of terns, including Forster's and Caspian. In spring scan for several ducks, including Greater Scaup, and shorebirds, including Red Knot (rarely) and Hudsonian Godwit.

The west Delta beach is reached by driving west 3 km from the end of PR 240 to the Assiniboine River diversion outlet. The nearby vegetation contains some of the highest nesting densities of Gray Catbird, Yellow Warbler and Baltimore Oriole in North America. Look for Orchard Orioles too. Check the diversion outlet into the lake for other species. Do not enter the University Field Station grounds without prior permission, as you may disrupt research.

St. Ambroise sits at the northeast side of the complex and can be reached via PR 430 north from Highway 1. The land around the unserviced campground provides opportunities for excellent birding, particularly in late May and early September. Scan the two small islands offshore for American White Pelican, Double-crested Cormorant and Caspian Tern. Use the observation tower at the end of the nature trail that leaves the parking lot. The beach is good for Piping Plover, with Nelson's Sharp-tailed Sparrow nearby. See what else you can find.

Sideroads PR 227, PR 411 and PR 430 are roads just south and east of the marsh that are worth a visit. Along PR 227, 5.2 km west of PR 430, lies the Portage la Prairie garbage dump. Accessible most of the time, it is most productive in spring when thousands of Herring, Ring-billed and Franklin's Gulls are present. This is a reliable location for California Gulls (late April to early June), and Glaucous and Lesser Black-backed Gulls have also been seen.

PR 411 and PR 430 south and east of St. Ambroise are bordered by woodland and pasture land and are usually reliable for Upland Sandpiper, Black-billed Magpie, Eastern Bluebird, and occasionally Sharp-tailed Grouse and Sprague's Pipit.

BIRDER'S GUIDE TO SOUTHEASTERN MANITOBA
Revised by Rudolf F. Koes

Brandon–Spruce Woods Provincial Park–Manitoba Desert

A circular trip east and south of Brandon could turn up some of those "most wanted" birds on your list, such as Sharp-tailed Grouse, Yellow Rail and Baird's Sparrow. In this area, the late Jack Lane of Brandon began the first Bluebird Trail in western Canada. Because of him and his helpers, Mountain and Eastern Bluebirds are fairly common here.

The route passes through country ranging from completely cultivated fields to forests to sand hills and a sand "desert." The approximately 160 km trip should take a leisurely day or a very full morning.

The city of Brandon and town of Carberry contain a variety of motels, hotels and other services. Camping is available just west of Brandon and in Spruce Woods Provincial Park. VIA Rail stops at Brandon and Greyhound buses service the major communities. Winnipeg has the nearest major airlines stopover.

If you plan a visit to the sand dunes, obtain a copy of the booklet *The Sandhills of Carberry*, by Jack E. Dubois. Write to the Manitoba Museum of Man and Nature (see above) for a copy.

Birding Features

Late May to early July is the best time to come. Begin the tour in Brandon. Follow PR 457 east through Chater to the junction with PR 340. Between Chater and the junction, reconnoitre the pastures for Sprague's Pipit, Grasshopper Sparrow (it is best to explore section roads to the south), Chestnut-collared Longspur and other grassland birds.

To cut time and still see Yellow Rail, turn north on PR 340 and drive towards Douglas. Just south of town, the road runs straight through one of the best Yellow Rail marshes in Manitoba. Observers have reported over 15 here. In wet years rubber boots are needed. In dry times the rails are very scarce and hard to find. Bring a flashlight to spot them after dark. Check for other water birds, Sharp-tailed Grouse, and Le Conte's and Nelson's Sharp-tailed Sparrows nearby. To return to Brandon, go north through Douglas and west on the Trans-Canada Highway.

To continue the trip, return to the junction of PR 457 and 340; take 340 southeast. Check fields on both sides of the road for several kilometres for Swainson's Hawk, Upland Sandpiper, Sprague's Pipit and Grasshopper Sparrow. Although formerly more common, the odd Baird's Sparrow may be encountered. Roadside wires should be checked for Eastern and Mountain Bluebirds, particularly in the vicinity of nest boxes.

At Shilo the pavement turns to gravel and the road swings straight south through the National Armed Forces Gunnery Range. On this stretch, watch for Mountain Bluebird, Sprague's Pipit and Grasshopper Sparrow. Explore the woods in the Assiniboine River bottom and around Treesbank to the south, looking for Yellow-throated Vireo and Indigo Bunting. Continue on PR 340 and turn east on PTH 2; at Glenboro, go north on PTH 5. Immediately before the Assiniboine River, a gravelled sideroad leads east into Spruce Woods Provincial Park. The woods along this road may provide good birding.

Return to PTH 5; drive north across the river. About 300 m beyond the bridge, turn west into the parking lot for the Spirit Hills Interpretive Trail. This is the trail for a unique walk into a "desert." The 3 km footpath covers deciduous and mixed woods, shifting and stabilized sand dunes, and the edge of the Assiniboine River Valley. This Manitoba desert contains dunes over 30 m high and sometimes 60 m wide. They are the deposits of a massive river that produced a major delta where it entered the former Lake Agassiz at the end of glaciation, 12,000 years ago. Although the sand dunes give the impression of a desert, rainfall here exceeds the limits of a true desert. Birds found here include Indigo Bunting and both species of crossbill.

As you continue north on PTH 5, inspect wires and fences along the roadside for Mountain and Eastern Bluebirds. At Carberry, either go east to the Delta Marsh (see above) or return west via PR 351. Along this short route to Highway 1, more bluebirds, Eastern Towhee and Lark Sparrow may be seen.

RUDOLF F. KOES
Revised by Rudolf F. Koes

Whitewater Lake

Whitewater Lake is a large, shallow body of water in the southwest corner of the province, situated between the towns of Boissevain and Deloraine, about 70 km south-southwest of Brandon. Accommodations and services are available in these communities. In addition, camping is possible in Turtle Mountain Provincial Park, about 20 km south of the lake. The lake is best known for its large numbers of migrant waterfowl and shorebirds, with attendant raptors. Since the early 1980s water levels have dropped due to prolonged drought, to the extent that the lake had virtually disappeared in the early 1990s. Restoration efforts by Ducks Unlimited, coupled with wetter weather, have helped to return the area to some of its former glory. As an added bonus, a recently constructed system of dykes and an observation mound now improve access and visibility.

To reach the most productive area, follow Highway 10 south through Boissevain, turn right (west) at the Ford dealership at the south edge of town, go 1.6 km west, 1.6 km south, then drive 11 km west to a road called Road 123 W. Turn north here and follow the road to the lake a few kilometres ahead. From the parking area at the observation mound, dykes run north and east. Access to the remainder of the lake is complicated and roads may not be in service from one year to the next due to fluctuating water levels. For the adventurous birders, it is probably best to try any gravel road that seems to lead in the direction of the water.

Birding Features

From early April on, thousands of swans, geese and ducks start returning. While many ducks remain to breed in the area, the majority will be migrants. Among the abundant Canada and Snow Geese, smaller numbers of Ross's and Greater White-fronted Geese can be found. Somewhat later grebes and shorebirds appear, and flocks of longspurs in the surrounding fields should be checked for Smith's Longspur. Late summer can be particularly productive: during August 1999, visitors turned up as many as 10 Great Egrets, 47 Cattle Egrets and 5 White-faced Ibises near the observation mound! Shorebirds were also well represented at that time, with dozens of American Avocets, Willets and Long-billed Dowitchers visible at close range.

From September to November, waterfowl return. This is also a good time to find Bald Eagle. During late summer and early fall there is always a chance for a Ferruginous Hawk or Prairie Falcon. Check each raptor carefully. The whole area is visited rather infrequently, so there are all sorts of discoveries to be made by the intrepid birder!

RUDOLF F. KOES
Revised by Rudolf F. Koes

Pembina Valley

The Pembina River meanders through a deep valley, cut in the Manitoba Escarpment long ago, and connects a number of superb birding locations, two of which are mentioned here.

Pelican Lake at the town of Ninette is the most reliable place in Manitoba to see Clark's Grebe. To reach it from Winnipeg, follow Highway 2 west to Highway 18, then follow Highway 18 south to Ninette. From Brandon take Highway 10 south, then Highway 23 east. From the junction of Highways 18 and 23 in Ninette, drive about 1 km east on 23. Pull off next to a small bridge just before the road starts its climb out of the valley. Scan the numerous Western Grebes on the lake for the odd Clark's Grebe. Hybrids may also be present. Grassy Lake, across the highway to the north, may contain other grebes and waterfowl, plus a variety of marsh birds along its edges. This area is best viewed from Highway 18 immediately north of Ninette. A spotting scope is recommended. Late May to early July is the most productive time, but most species will be present well into fall.

Near the hamlet of Windygates, just north of the Manitoba–North Dakota border, the valley is much deeper and narrower than at Ninette. This is the area that has become a favourite among Manitoban hawk-watchers. In early and mid-March, the first Bald Eagles and Canada Geese pass through. One or two wintering Golden Eagles may circle overhead or the first migrant may appear. From late March to mid-April the bulk of migrants come through. On good days a thousand or more Red-tailed Hawks fly over (the top count is about 3700!), while Bald Eagle and Sharp-shinned Hawk numbers may reach triple digits. Smaller numbers of all other regularly occurring Manitoban diurnal raptors are seen, including Ferruginous Hawks and Prairie Falcons. Besides the spectacle of hawk migration, huge flocks of Snow Geese may fill the skies, with up to 150,000 having been reported; a steady stream of other waterfowl, pelicans, cormorants, Sandhill Cranes, shorebirds and gulls provides additional entertainment.

Best conditions for optimum numbers are during clear days, with southerly or easterly winds, particularly just prior to major air pressure depressions moving through. Even on days with northerly or westerly winds, some birds will still be on the move, although then primarily in the morning. On peak days, birds may continue migrating nearly until sunset.

This bottleneck site – about one and a half hours southwest of Winnipeg by car – can be reached by following Highway 3 from Winnipeg to Morden, then PR 432 south from Morden and finally PR 201 west to the valley. The most popular observation location is along the road about halfway up the north slope, but wind conditions may make other spots more desirable. Pull off to the side, sit down in your lawn chair and scan the eastern horizon, where the birds will be popping up. During a lull in the activity, check the valley floor for Wild Turkey, Mountain Bluebird or, particularly early in the season, Northern Shrike.

There are no services in the immediate vicinity, so make sure to gas up and get food in Winnipeg or Morden.

RUDOLF F. KOES

Turtle Mountain Provincial Park

The Turtle Mountains are made up of an island of deciduous forest rising out of the prairies in southwestern Manitoba. These hills are home to a variety of birdlife ranging from Common Loon, colonies of Great Blue Heron and Black-crowned Night-Heron, to such eastern species as Northern Cardinal and Northern Parula. Those interested in cultivated flower gardens can enjoy the International Peace Garden, sponsored and maintained by people from both sides of the border. Painted Turtles are common in the park, as are Beavers.

Since the end of glaciation 10,000 years ago, native people used the hills as shelter. Later the Metis hunters from Red River (Winnipeg) would sometimes overwinter in these hills to allow an early spring start to the buffalo hunt on the southern plains. During the 1860s and 1870s, the Sioux Wars in the U.S. drove "renegade" Indians north to seek safety from the U.S. Cavalry, which halted at the 49th parallel. The border came to be called the "Medicine Line" for this reason. Settlers flooded the plains in the late 1800s. Increased human activity finally resulted in two major fires, in 1897 and 1903. Only a few remnant stands of mature deciduous forest were left. The park became a timber reserve with a ranger headquarters built in 1911. These forest rangers cut fireguards and roadways, and encouraged grazing to get rid of the dry grasses and low bush. Even with these precautions, a fire swept in from North Dakota in 1921 and consumed a large section of the reserve. No more fires have occurred since then. The central part of the reserve became a park in 1961.

The park lies 100 km straight south of Brandon on PTH 10, or about 280 km southwest of Winnipeg via PTH 2 and 10. Greyhound buses service Boissevain, the nearest town, 21 km north of the park gate. VIA Rail service and car rentals are available in Brandon. Trails and roads, which are not all-weather, are liberally sprinkled throughout the very hilly country. These routes are well illustrated in the park brochure (see below).

Two campgrounds provide some services for the visitor. Commercial places to stay are found in surrounding towns or at Brandon. Gasoline, groceries and other necessities may be obtained at these communities.

Information on summer and winter opportunities, plus a park map and brochure, may be obtained from Department of Natural Resources, 200 Saulteaux Crescent, Winnipeg, Manitoba R3J 3W3; phone (204) 945-6784.

Naturalists are stationed at the park in summer to assist you in your visit. Contact them at the park office for recent sightings.

Birding Features

The rolling hills of the Turtle Mountains are covered with about two-thirds deciduous forest and one-third lakes and sloughs. Trembling Aspen is the main tree species, with Black Poplar, White Birch, ash, Manitoba Maple, elm and Bur Oak interspersed throughout. The understory is rather dense in places. A visit from mid-May to mid-July will provide opportunities to spot a wide variety of water and land birds.

A number of species have been found breeding here, far to the west of their usual range. These include the Northern Cardinal, which has nested near the park office, and the Northern Parula, which is more than 300 km west of its nearest usual breeding spot in Manitoba.

Other birds in the area include Common Loon, a good population of Red-necked Grebe, Double-crested Cormorant, a variety of dabbling and diving ducks, Willow Flycatcher (a suspected breeder), Marsh and Sedge Wrens, Eastern Bluebird, Yellow-throated Vireo, several warblers, Yellow-headed Blackbird and a possible Scarlet Tanager.

RUDOLF F. KOES
Revised by Rudolf F. Koes

Riding Mountain National Park

Set on the Manitoba Escarpment, the sharply defined northern and eastern boundaries of Riding Mountain National Park are some 450 m above surrounding farmland. The park sits at the crossroads of three major vegetation zones: eastern deciduous forest, northern boreal forest and western grasslands. This mixed habitat results in almost 500 species of plants and attracts over 250 species of birds. Of these birds, 154 species are regular (fairly common to abundant) breeders, another 18 are rare breeders within the park but more abundant just outside, and 6 occur as summer visitors. The park is home to numerous Elk (Wapiti), Moose, deer, Beaver, Timber Wolf, Black Bear, Lynx, plus about 30 Plains Bison in an enclosure. It also sits on the line that seems to divide the range of the Satyrid Butterfly. These insects are observed east of the park only on even-numbered years and west in the odd-numbered.

In 1906 control of this area passed to the Forestry Branch of the federal government. Roads were poor and visitation was limited. Riding Mountain was declared a national park in 1930. This 2978 km² area lies north of Brandon on PTH 10. Greyhound buses service the park in the summer. There are over 160 km of hiking and horse trails through the forest and meadows and by the many lakes. These trails, amenities and major interpretive features are shown on the park brochure.

Accommodation includes over 300 units of motels, hotels and cottages in the village of Wasagaming. These are heavily booked in July and August. However, the abundant campsites range from fully serviced trailer units to primitive camp spots. Two group camping locations are also available. Winter campers have a choice of two spots. The village contains all services needed for a comfortable stay in the summer. In winter, nearby towns have the required services.

Information on the park, including a comprehensive checklist of birds, is available from The Superintendent, Riding Mountain National Park, Wasagaming, Manitoba ROJ 2HO. Year-round interpreters are stationed at Wasagaming. Call them at (204) 848-2811.

Birding Features

Riding Mountain, with its prairie, meadows, aspen groves, eastern and boreal forests, and numerous lakes, attracts a wide variety of birds. During the nesting season, from about the first of June to mid-July, the park is one of the most productive areas in North America for locating different species.

The several lakes and contiguous boreal forests are home to Common Loon, five of six species of grebe found in Canada, American White Pelican, Double-crested Cormorant, and about 10 colonies of Great Blue Heron; all the prairie ducks, and even Forster's Tern, are found nesting here; a Turkey Vulture, Northern Goshawk or Cooper's Hawk may be spotted. There are several nest locations of Bald Eagle in the park. These kings of the air are most readily seen at several lakes, including Whirlpool, Audy and Moon. Osprey, Merlin and Spruce Grouse are regularly noted. Northern Saw-whet Owls are especially common around Clear Lake and can be heard late at night from late March to the latter part of May, together with Barred Owls. Three-toed and

Western Grebe

Black-backed Woodpeckers, Gray Jays and Boreal Chickadees are regular in this northern forest.

The deciduous forests are noted for the Great Crested Flycatcher, Eastern Wood-Pewee and Yellow-throated Vireo. The Golden-winged Warbler, a true eastern species, is common on the eastern and northern sides of the park. The Connecticut Warbler nests in aspen groves. These birds are most often found along Highway 19 and vicinity. Scarlet Tanager, Indigo Bunting and Eastern Towhee can also be found in these deciduous forests. The park lies within the overlap zone of the Eastern and Western Kingbirds, Eastern and Western Wood-Pewees, Eastern and Mountain Bluebirds, and Indigo and (occasionally) Lazuli Buntings.

The grasslands are good sites for Sprague's Pipit, especially at the Audy Prairie in the bison enclosure, northwest of Clear Lake. Sharp-tailed Grouse and Western Meadowlark can be located in fields immediately adjacent to the park on the south and southwest sides.

Some of the special spots to visit are noted below. Contact the interpreters for others.

Wasagaming, the village, is a good spot to look for a variety of warblers and other boreal species. They can be spotted in the tall spruce.

Evergreen Trail begins at the north shore of Lake Katherine, 9.6 km east of Wasagaming via Highway 19 and the Lake Katherine access road. A stroll along this 1.6 km path could produce Connecticut and Mourning Warblers as well as Le Conte's Sparrow, particularly along the first section.

Ma-ee-gun Trail provides access to boreal species. It is reached via Highway 10, 6.9 km northwest of the junction with Highway 19.

Highway 19 leads east from Wasagaming through boreal forest and is recommended as a particularly good route. Stop several times and check the woods for boreal species, particularly Spruce Grouse and Gray Jay. A large area along the road, burned in 1980, is the most reliable location for Great Gray Owl and Western Wood-Pewee.

Burls and Bittersweet Trail, on the east end of Highway 19, is good for most species during migration. You'll also spot several of the eastern deciduous-nesting species, many of which are rare to uncommon in Manitoba.

Highway 361, farther north on the east side, runs west from Highway 5 at McCreary and takes you to the park's Mount Agassiz Ski Hill. This is a good area for eastern species, particularly about 4.8 km within the park boundary. Watch for Golden-winged Warbler, Indigo Bunting and Eastern Towhee, all of which are common here.

A winter trip to the park could produce a Northern Goshawk, both Black-backed and Three-toed Woodpeckers, and winter finches, including crossbills.

In the spring and early summer, check the sloughs around Minnedosa, south of the park on Highway 10, for a wide variety of waterfowl. Check the area also for Eared Grebe and Canvasback, Swainson's Hawk and Wilson's Phalarope.

A. ANGUS MacLEAN AND RUDOLF F. KOES
Revised by Rudolf F. Koes

Churchill

Churchill sits on the shore of Hudson Bay, in the taiga, the transition zone between the tundra and boreal forest. It is a paradise for birders wishing to see arctic flora and fauna within a short time and at a reasonable cost. To date, about 275 bird species have been reported, including that rarity from the Arctic ice floes and Siberia, Ross's Gull. The only other comparable and reasonably accessible arctic site is the Dempster Highway in the Yukon.

The area has been inhabited since at least 950 B.C. A trading post was built in 1717. The first astronomical observations taken in Canada were done here in 1769. Samuel Hearne made his epic overland trip to the Arctic coast from here. Later, when western Canada needed a prairie port, one was built here and linked to the outside by rail in 1929. Naturalists now flock to the spot every year, swelling the resident winter population of 800 to around 1500 in summer.

The port lies at the mouth of the Churchill River. It is accessible by rail and air from Thompson or Winnipeg. There are several hotels and bed-and-breakfasts, but accommodation may be hard to find from late May to the end of July. Arrangements should be made well in advance.

The best time to come is between late May and mid-July, with mid- to late June offering the greatest number of birds. At this time, however, there are hordes of insects – a mosquito head net and insect repellent are essential. Weather in this season is very unpredictable: it may rain, be very windy, cold, warm, foggy, all in one day. Bring rain gear, a down jacket or parka, a warm hat and mitts.

The services of commercial tour operators are available. One of the best is Bonnie Chartier, Churchill Wilderness Encounter, Box 9, Churchill, Manitoba ROB OEO; phone (204) 675-2248, fax (204) 675-2045; she is an experienced birder who is excellent in the field and can often provide useful information. To cover the area well, a car should be rented, if one is not willing to take a commercial tour. Rental cars are few in number, so book well in advance.

An absolute must is the book *Birds of the Churchill Region, Manitoba*, by Joseph R. Jehl, Jr., and Blanche A. Smith. This 87-page book is considered *the* standard reference for the area. It is being updated and should appear within a year or two. Birders should enquire locally as to its availability. It is available from the Manitoba Museum of Man and Nature (see above). Another indispensable reference, *A Birder's Guide to Churchill*, by Bonnie Chartier, published by the American Birding Association (ABA) in 1994, is available at several local stores or through the ABA. The booklet describes all the hot spots in detail, has a complete species list, and even lists mammals, amphibians, butterflies, moths and plants. It also provides information on transportation, lodging, local tours and restaurants. For those interested in more than birds, obtain *Wildflowers of Churchill*, by Karen Johnson, published by the Manitoba Museum of Man and Nature in 1987. A fully illustrated guide to the flowers of the area, it is carried by local stores. There is other material locally, but some of it is outdated and none is crucial.

Don't forget to take a boat trip to observe Beluga Whales – an unforgettable experience! Information as to when and where the trips depart is available locally.

Birding Features

To cover the area thoroughly, a week between early June and mid-July should be set aside. However, a long-weekend visit could be enough time for a keen person to observe at least the majority of the species. A birding day can begin at 3 A.M., at daylight, and last to 11 P.M., with some light past midnight in June.

"Churchill specialties" include Pacific Loon, Oldsquaw, Common and King Eiders, Willow Ptarmigan, Yellow Rail, American Golden Plover and many other shorebirds, Parasitic Jaeger, gulls including Thayer's, Sabine's, Ross's and Little, and Arctic Tern. The Ross's Gull has been seen since 1978 and has bred infrequently since 1980. Sightings of this species have become less predictable in the 1990s; in the last four years of the 1990s often not more than one or two birds had shown up. Other species include Common and Hoary Redpolls and Smith's Longspur. This is one of the few readily accessible places in North America where Harris's Sparrow can be found nesting.

Reference to the maps in *A Birder's Guide to Churchill*, mentioned above, will show the best observation areas are:

Cape Merry, at the mouth of the Churchill River near the port facility. Scan for Pacific and Red-throated Loons, Common and King Eiders, Parasitic Jaeger, gulls mentioned above, and others, including terns.

Akudlik, just west of the airport, where ducks, Yellow Rail and others can be ferreted out in the marshes and lakes.

Launch Road and Old Road to Fort Churchill. Scan the bay for both species of eiders and scoters. The west-end beach near the point has shorebirds. Don't forget the garbage dump for gulls. East of the dump look for American Golden Plover, Whimbrel, Stilt Sandpiper, Short-billed Dowitcher and Hudsonian Godwit. Particularly survey Bird Cove on the bay for shorebirds. Take a short drive southwest of Bird Cove to explore for warblers and redpolls. West and south of the National Research Council launch site, at the east end of the road, check out the lakes for loons and Oldsquaw. Watch along Launch Road for Willow Ptarmigan, with Rock Ptarmigan seen here only in winter. Smith's Longspur also is noted on this road.

Landing or Farnworth Lake Road. This road south from the west side of the airport could produce Yellow Rail and numerous shorebirds as mentioned above.

Goose Creek Road south along the Churchill River provides easy access to geese, Tundra Swan, scoters and upland birds. Watch for a Bohemian Waxwing, and Common and Hoary Redpolls along here. About 4 km south on the road, watch for hawks and owls. Farther south, about 8 km from the start of the road, turn right just past the cottage development and proceed to the weir across the river. Scan the rocks below the weir for shorebirds and check the gulls at the rapids for Little and Ross's Gulls. Return to Goose Creek Road and continue south. From here on the road is known as Hydro Road. The marsh and willows in the next stretch are particularly good for American Bittern, Yellow Rail, Alder Flycatcher and a host of warblers and sparrows. At the bridge over Goose Creek, scan upstream for an Osprey nest. The first 1 to 2 km past the creek often harbour Yellow Rail and Nelson's Sharp-tailed Sparrow. At the end of Hydro Road, from the river's edge, check for Common Loon, Tundra Swan, Bald Eagle and Little Gull. Shorebirds are present along various sections of Goose Creek and Hydro Roads. This is but a sampling of the richness of the avifauna. The ground and air appear alive with birdlife.

Twin Lakes. This area can be reached by continuing past the Rocket Range on Launch Road. The road is quite bumpy, so drive carefully. Twin Lakes Road is very good for Willow Ptarmigan and the large "meadow" (= tundra) just north of the lakes is probably the best location to find shorebirds and Smith's Longspur on territory. The woods around Twin Lakes often produce Spruce Grouse, Bohemian Waxwing, Boreal Chickadee and Pine Grosbeak. A large burn south of West Twin Lake has been productive for Three-toed and Black-backed Woodpeckers in recent years.

RUDOLF F. KOES, BONNIE CHARTIER
Revised by Rudolf F. Koes

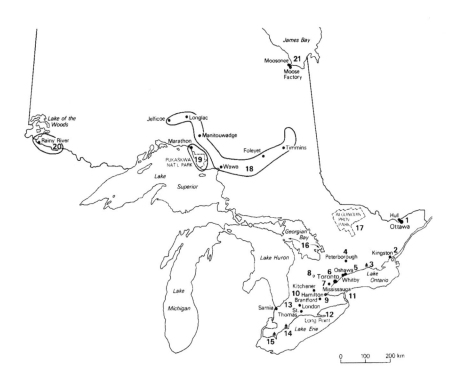

ONTARIO

ONTARIO

Ontario is a huge province, second in size only to Quebec. The distance from north to south is 1690 km at its maximum extent, and from east to west 1609 km, with an area of 891,198 km². It borders four of the five Great Lakes in the south and James Bay and Hudson Bay to the north. Its habitats are numerous and varied, from the Carolinian forests around Point Pelee, the most southerly point in Canada, through the farmlands and cities of the south and central areas, to the lake-studded Precambrian Shield and the boreal forests of the north.

Most birders have heard of Point Pelee, with its spectacular spring migration of warblers and other land birds peaking in the second week of May, but increasingly visitors are adding in other destinations to a spring trip, often including Algonquin Provincial Park for its Spruce Grouse, Gray Jay, Boreal Chickadee and other northern species. In the northwest corner, Rainy River near the Manitoba border offers a western flavour, with American White Pelican, Black-billed Magpie, Western Meadowlark and Brewer's Blackbird. Summer breeding birds range from Hooded Warbler at Long Point on Lake Erie, Prothonotary Warbler and Acadian Flycatcher at Rondeau, American Bittern and Sedge Wren on the Carden Plain, and Yellow Rail and Connecticut Warbler at Rainy River. Fall migration lasts longer and is less concentrated than spring, but often offers amazing numbers and variety at migration hot spots such as Pelee, Thunder Cape, the Toronto Islands and Prince Edward Point from August to the end of October. Watching the amazing fall hawk migration along the north shores of Lake Ontario and Lake Erie is increasingly popular at spots such as Holiday Beach near Windsor, Grimsby on the Niagara Escarpment, High Park in Toronto and Cranberry Marsh east of the city. The Niagara River in late November and early December plays host to one of the greatest gull spectacles in the world, with up to 14 species possible in one day.

Winter birding is often excellent too, with the more accessible southern parts of the province treated to visitors from the north, including Gyrfalcon, Snowy Owl, Northern Hawk Owl, Bohemian Waxwing and Snow Bunting, as well as crossbills and other "winter finches."

If you have just one or two weeks to visit Ontario and can pick your dates, probably the best time would be the second and third weeks of May, to enjoy the southern overshoots at Pelee, perhaps including Mississippi Kite, Worm-eating and Kentucky Warblers, Summer Tanagers and Blue Grosbeaks, and add on a quick dash to Algonquin. If you are visiting Toronto with half a day to bird watch, visit the Leslie Street Spit at the eastern end of the harbour, good at almost any season of the year, but only readily accessible at weekends; with a day or more, explore the lakeshore marshes east of the city from Pickering to Oshawa.

There are several Rare Bird Alerts across the province. The Toronto RBA is currently at (416) 350-3000 (ext. 2293). For names and addresses of clubs across the province, contact The Federation of Ontario Naturalists, 355 Lesmill Road, Don Mills, Ontario M3B 2W8; phone (416) 444-8419. If you have access to the Internet, the Ontario Field Ornithologists have an excellent Web site at www.interlog.com/~ofo or e-mail ofo@interlog.com for information on outings, meetings and site guides; their mailing address is Box 455, Station R, Toronto, Ontario M4G 4E1.

An excellent resource for visiting birders is Clive Goodwin's revised edition of *A Bird-Finding Guide to Ontario* (1995) published by the University of Toronto Press and widely available at bookstores. The second edition of the *Annotated Checklist of the Birds of Ontario* by Ross D. James (1991) is obtainable from the bookshop of the Royal Ontario Museum in Toronto and elsewhere. Pocket-sized field checklists of Ontario birds are regularly updated and obtainable from the Federation of Ontario Naturalists and from the Ontario Field Ornithologists. Rare bird report forms can be obtained from the O.F.O. Web site.

Information on where to stay, general tourism material and maps may be obtained from Ontario Tourism, 1-800-ONTARIO, www.ontario-canada.com or www.travelinx.com or by writing to Bell Global Solutions-TraveLinx, BCE Place, 181 Bay Street, Suite 350, Toronto, Ontario M5J 2T3.

LINDA AND CHIP WESELOH
Revised by Margaret Bain

Ottawa–Hull

Ottawa, Canada's capital city, is visited by birders from across the continent and other places around the world. In excess of 320 species of birds have been recorded within a 50 km radius from the Peace Tower on Parliament Hill. From mid-May through September it is possible to see in excess of 100 species a day and, in May, almost 200 species are possible.

Ottawa has a population of 750,000 people; the Ottawa-Hull area, approximately 1 million. Montreal is a two-hour drive to the east, and Toronto five hours to the southwest. The Ottawa River runs east and west across the city and separates Hull in Quebec from Ottawa in Ontario. There are many hotels and motels in the region and most large city services are available.

The Ottawa Field Naturalists Club is very active and can be contacted for basic information at (613) 722-3050. A bird status line provides a recorded message with recent bird sightings at (613) 825-7444. To report sightings in the Ottawa area, call (613) 825-1231.

The National Museum of Nature, containing many nature-oriented displays including birds and a substantial bird specimen collection, is worth a visit. Find it at the corner of Metcalfe and McLeod Streets in downtown Ottawa.

A map of the city and surroundings, produced by Pathfinder, is available in most convenience stores and gas stations. The Federal Department of Energy, Mines and Resources produces topographic sheets on a scale of 1:50,000.

Other than the sites listed below, there are numerous additional good birding places within the National Capital area. Visitors to Ottawa who are unfamiliar with the region are encouraged to call the Ottawa Field Naturalists Club (number listed above).

Weather
Winter in the Ottawa area lasts from November through March with temperatures often in the -10°C to -20°C range and occasionally dropping as low as -35°C. Warm spells or thaws do occur. Snow usually arrives, to stay, in December and often accumulates to thigh-depth in natural areas.

Spring usually arrives in April, and often by May temperatures are in the mid- to high 20s.

Summer is often hot and humid, with temperatures in the high 20s to low 30s. Biting insects can be a problem.

Fall usually starts in September, with the leaves changing into brilliant golds and yellows at the end of the month. Temperatures can vary dramatically in this season from hot to very cold and windy.

Birding Features
Ottawa is at the southern range of a number of the more northerly species of birds and, consequently, is visited in winter by those seen much more infrequently in southern Ontario. These may include Black-backed Woodpecker; Three-toed Woodpecker; Snowy, Great Gray and Boreal Owls; Northern Hawk Owl; Bohemian Waxwing; Gray Jay; and Gyrfalcon. Since open water

is at a premium in winter, waterfowl is scarce and limited to a few unfrozen areas such as Deschennes Rapids at Britannia, the Champlain Bridge, the Rideau River at Carleton University, Billings Bridge and at Black Rapids off Highway 16, north of Fallowfield Road.

Feeders are always a good source of winter birds, and Varied Thrush have become annual or bi-annual in the area.

May, June and July are the peak nesting periods. September is always a good month for south-bound warblers. October and November are usually good for waterfowl.

The Ottawa River is the single largest natural feature that affects birding in the Ottawa area. Birders with limited time to spend are encouraged to "follow the river corridor."

Shirley's Bay. This is a Crown Game Preserve and Department of National Defence firing range (a definite contradiction in terms). The site is one of the best birding spots in the entire Ottawa area. The Ottawa Field Naturalists Club has an access agreement providing birders with permission to enter to the base of the dyke. However, to walk beyond the gate, seek specific approval by contacting the club at (613) 825-1231 for further information. Shirley's Bay can be reached by taking Carling Avenue west to Range Road going north to the end of the road at a parking lot on the Ottawa River. Park and follow a trail along the shoreline to the base of the dyke which stretches 1 km out into the Ottawa River. The dyke, enclosing an open bay of the Ottawa River, connects two islands. The bay is home to numerous puddle ducks from April to November. Up to 20 species of waterfowl can be found here in the fall. The mudflats, which appear in midsummer through fall, are often active with migrating shorebirds. Warblers use the dyke as a highway, especially in fall. The wet woodland located between the base of the dyke and the road into the firing range is an excellent place in May and September for migrant vireos, warblers and songbirds. The river side of the dyke is good in both spring and fall for loons, grebes, scoters and other diving ducks. The dyke is also a good place to view raptors migrating overhead in both spring and fall.

Andrew Haydon Park East. This area is still known as Ottawa Beach by the local birding community, but members of the public would not be aware of this name. Lying on Carling Avenue in the City of Nepean, just east of Acres Road, this is one of the best birding spots in the region. The park, on the south side of the Ottawa River, presents excellent views of the river at one of its widest points. Ottawa Beach, with sandy mudflats, hosts shorebirds and gulls in summer and fall; diving ducks can be seen farther out on the river. The trees and limited woodlands around here can also be good for warblers in migration. The Ottawa River acts as a highway for a number of migrating birds including Arctic Tern, Brant and Purple Sandpiper. All three species of jaeger have been seen in this stretch of the river.

Brittania. This large area actually stretches from Andrew Haydon Park east along the Ottawa River to Lakeside Gardens and Brittania Pier, then east again to the Brittania filtration plant. A bike path and walkway exists from Andrew Haydon Park to Brittania Road, north to Cassels Road, and turns right towards the filtration plant and Mud Lake. You can cover the entire area on foot. By car from Andrew Haydon Park, go east on Carling Avenue to Richmond Road, turn left (a 45-degree turn) a short distance to a traffic light at Poulin Street, again turn left and continue down Poulin around a left-hand bend to Brittania Road, right on Brittania Road to the end and right again on Cassels Road.

The bicycle path from Andrew Haydon Park to Lakeside Gardens follows the Ottawa River, with views of the river and sightings of a variety of shorebirds in the fall (Spotted Redshank was seen here in 1998). Gulls, terns, ducks and geese can also be found here. The wooded area along this path can be good for warblers and landbirds.

Lakeside Gardens is a park and beach area with a large rock pier or jetty protruding out into the Ottawa River. It's a good spot to view birds which use the Ottawa River as a migration corridor. Look for Arctic Tern, Red-throated Loon, Purple Sandpiper, Glaucous and Iceland Gulls, as well as a large variety of diving ducks, including all three species of scoter. The pier has served as an overnight refuge for a Northern Wheatear in the mid-1990s.

Brittania Filtration Plant may be the premier birding location in the Ottawa area. A variety of habitats exist close together, resulting in outstanding bird diversity. The filtration plant itself sits at the end of a point of land jutting out into the Ottawa River. A narrow channel runs between the plant and an island in the main part of the river. This area and the rapids on the river west of here remain open in the winter. Barrow's Goldeneye and Thick-billed Murre (1995) have been seen. A ridge, running between Mud Lake and the Ottawa River just west of the filtration plant, is an excellent place for warblers and sparrows during spring and fall migration.

Mud Lake, a relatively small, shallow pond in the centre of the Brittania birding area, attracts a wide variety of ducks in fall. Black-crowned Night-Herons congregate here in August and September. A mixed wood lot surrounding Mud Lake gives good birding all year, with spring and fall the best times. A large percentage of birds recorded in the Ottawa 50 km circle have been recorded at the Brittania birding site. From May through September, you should find Belted Kingfisher, Common Flicker, Brown Creeper, Red-eyed Vireo, Yellow Warbler, Rose-breasted Grosbeak and Scarlet Tanager. Up to 30 species of warblers have been reported from here over the years. The Deschennes Rapids, which can be viewed from the ridge or from the end of Vanier Road in Aylmer, P.Q., is a roosting and feeding site for gulls and terns. Franklin's and Laughing Gulls, Arctic and Common Terns, as well as Glaucous, Iceland, Lesser Black-backed and Thayer's Gulls have been seen.

Nepean Dump. To reach the site, in the City of Nepean, drive south on Moodie Drive and turn left onto Trail Road to the well-marked location. This regional dump is best from October through February when the "white-winged gulls" can be present in substantial numbers. Lesser Black-backed Gull is occasional, and California Gull has been seen.

Richmond Fen. Located approximately 15 km south of Nepean Dump, these wetlands lie southeast of the Village of Richmond. Drive to the train tracks at the southeast edge of town and park. Walk south along the railroad line for about 4 km, to enter the Richmond Fen. The sedge fen is best birded after dark, or pre-dawn, in late May and early June. Yellow and Virginia Rails, Sora, Common Moorhen, Whip-poor-will, Sedge Wren, Black-billed Cuckoo and Least Bittern are all possible.

Champlain Bridge. This bridge, connecting Ottawa and Aylmer, P.Q., is found at the intersection of Island Park Drive and the Ottawa River Parkway. Scan the river from the Ontario side of the bridge, or go halfway across and turn right onto Bate Island. Warblers may be found on the island in migration. The water here remains open all year, with loons, grebes, waterfowl and gulls seen at the appropriate time of year. Barrow's Goldeneye is present each winter, but is often best seen from Parc Brébeuf in Hull. To reach Parc Brébeuf, cross the Champlain Bridge to the first traffic light, turn right (east) until you come to Begin Street, turn right again (south) until you come to a park with a large statue at the entrance – Parc Brébeuf.

Clyde Woods. Take the Queensway (Main East/West Highway 417) exit at Maitland Avenue and drive south about .75 km. Turn east onto Glenmount, and then left onto Castlehill Crescent. Follow it to Clyde Avenue, turn left and park at the dead end. These woods have a well-worn system of trails throughout. In May and June, and again in August through October, migrating songbirds use the forest as a resting and feeding place. However, Clyde Woods is best known to Ottawa birders as a place for owls. In April listen and look for Long-eared and Northern Saw-whet Owls. Great Horned Owls may be present all year; Boreal Owls have overwintered here; Great Gray Owls may come in irruption years. A rock quarry north of the parking area has Rock Doves, which attract birds of prey in winter. Thus it has become a principal feeding area for Gyrfalcons in those years when they come to the Ottawa region. Residential construction has recently modified the open fields south of Clyde Woods. The impact of this development on the woods as a haven for owls remains unknown at this time.

Central Experimental Farm and Arboretum. This large area extends from Carling Avenue to Baseline Road, east of Fisher Avenue and has a number of good bird habitats. Look for Bohemian Waxwings feeding on crabapples in the arboretum in winter. Gray Partridges can be found in the fields, and American Golden and Black-bellied Plovers may be seen during migration.

Vincent Massey and Hog's Back Parks. These two adjoining parks are located on the east bank of the Rideau River, about 5 km north of the airport. Enter Vincent Massey parking lot off Heron Road, and Hog's Park parking lot off Hog's Back Road, between Riverside Drive and Prince of Wales Drive. These parks attract substantial pedestrian traffic, but still contain good bird habitat.

Both parks act as migrant traps in spring and fall, particularly for warblers and vireos. Explore them on foot using the various footpaths and trails.

Ottawa International Airport. The best birding areas lie south of the airport perimeter off Leitrim Road. Grasshopper and Clay-colored Sparrows breed in open fields off Leitrim Road in spring and summer. From December through March, look for Rough-legged Hawk, American Kestrel, Snowy Owl and Northern Shrike. Owls may be found occasionally in the wooded lot below the hill on Leitrim Road opposite the airport runway.

Jack Pine Trail. This path sits off Moodie Drive, south of Robertson Road in Bells Corners and is well signed. The winter feeder, maintained by the Ottawa Field Naturalists Club on a well-signed and well-maintained trail, usually attracts most winter species, including the occasional Black-backed or Three-toed Woodpecker.

Anderson Road/Mer Bleu/Ramsayville Marsh. Take the Anderson Road exit off the Queensway (Highway 417). Ridge Road runs to the east and provides access to the Mer Bleu Peat Bog. The Ramsayville Marsh lies about 2 km north of Highway 417 on Anderson Road. In summer, this cattail marsh may contain Pied-billed Grebe, American Bittern, Least Bittern, Virginia Rail, Sora, Marsh Wren and Swamp Sparrow. In 1999, a Henslow's Sparrow was singing on territory off Ridge Road.

Common Loon

Gatineau Park (Province of Quebec). The park, located on the north side of the Ottawa River, has numerous access points. The Parkway is entered opposite Begin Street in Hull and runs up the middle of the park. The property is owned and operated by the National Capital Commission, which has available a checklist and park map. Many species breed here, several of which are uncommon or absent elsewhere in the local region. Breeding birds may include Common Loon, Yellow-bellied Sapsucker, Olive-sided and Alder Flycatchers, both kinglets and a variety of vireos and warblers. A winter trip can produce woodpeckers, winter finches and possibly Bald and Golden Eagles.

Low to Poltimore (Province of Quebec). This site lies at the limit of the 50 km birding circle utilized by the Ottawa Field Naturalists Club. Take Highway 550 in Hull across the Gatineau River, turn immediately onto Highway 307 heading north to Poltimore. Take the signed road west to Low. Alternatively, take Highway 5 and then Highway 105 north to Low, and then the gravel road east to Poltimore. The area is fairly remote with no services, so a full tank of gas, coffee, snack and warm clothing in winter are required. A detailed map of the area is a necessity, since some of the birding may be on sideroads. Regular winter birds such as Common Raven, White and Red-breasted Nuthatches, Evening Grosbeak, Pine Siskin and American Tree Sparrow can be found. Species that may require an extra effort to locate include Gray Jay, Boreal Chickadee, White-winged and Red Crossbills, and other northern finches.

STEPHEN GAWN
Revised by Michael Tate

Kingston

Situated on the northeast corner of Lake Ontario, at the start of the St. Lawrence River, Kingston is host to at least 350 bird species. Greater Scaup, Oldsquaw and White-winged Scoter come in large numbers, and the Ruddy Duck is now a regular visitor; the Wild Turkey is also a regular; the Snowy Owl is often common in winter.

Founded in 1673 as a fur-trading post and strategic military stronghold, this city, which was the capital of Canada in the 1840s, contains many ancient fortifications and early Canadian landmarks. Old Fort Henry, originally built in 1812 and later rebuilt in 1832–36, has been completely restored as a museum of military history. Kingston is about 210 km east of Toronto via Highway 401. The city is serviced by Voyageur and Greyhound bus lines, VIA Rail and Air Canada, and has campgrounds, motels and hotels.

Birdwatchers intending to visit the area frequently should obtain a copy of the 608-page book *Birds of the Kingston Region*, by H. R. Quilliam (Kingston: Kingston Field Naturalists, 1989). Information on this area has been drawn from Helen R. Quilliam's article "The Kingston Region: The Birds," in *Seasons* Vol. 22, No. 1, 1982.

Birding Features

Kingston sits at the northern limits of some bird species and the southern ranges of others. In spring, birds coming north across Lake Ontario often stop in great numbers to rest after a night flight, particularly if they meet a cold front. Under these conditions check city gardens, islands in the lake, or Prince Edward Point, 88 km west of the city by road or 43 km as the crow flies. In the fall, migrating birds often wait out bad weather on the north shore of the lake.

Kingston has gained some fame for the great influx of owls that feed on the hordes of meadow voles on Wolfe and Amherst Islands. Their Christmas

Bird Count has had more Snowy Owls than any place on the continent. In addition often large numbers of wintering Rough-legged Hawks feed on these voles. Ten species of owl have been spotted in the area, including both Barn and Barred. In 1978–79 over 30 Great Gray Owls also feasted on these voles. Amherst Island contains a variety of habitats, ranging through open fields, wood lots, marshes and sandy beaches, most of which is private land. At the east end, the Kingston Field Naturalists (KFN) owns a large area that encompasses shoreline, fields, marsh and gravel bar extending into Lake Ontario where shorebirds are usually quite numerous, particularly in migration. The Whimbrel can generally be counted on to stop around May 24. The Upland Sandpiper and Wilson's Phalarope are fairly common nesters. Check out the wood lots for late-migrating and nesting passerines. Short-eared Owls are regular, as are Northern Harriers and Red-tailed Hawks.

Moving northeast from the city about 40 km on 401, watch for the signs to the Ivy Lea Bridge. This is a good spot to look for enormous rafts of Greater Scaups in both spring and fall. Other ducks gather in huge flocks too. In winter, diving ducks appear in rafts where the current keeps the St. Lawrence open between the islands. Use the bridge to scan for a Bald Eagle attracted by the large supply of food. In spring, one can count 19 or 20 species of duck from the bridge. Look for Wild Turkeys around the Canadian Customs office.

Spots within the Canadian Shield to search out include Canoe Lake Road, Otter Lake Sanctuary, the Rideau Trail near Gould Lake and Frontenac Park. Check these sites for Golden-winged, Cerulean and Prairie Warblers, and the occasional Blue-winged Warbler. They have all become more numerous in recent years. Regular singers in June include Eastern Wood-Pewee, Yellow-throated Vireo, Red-eyed Vireo, Ovenbird, Rose-breasted Grosbeak and Indigo Bunting.

Prince Edward Point, projecting out from Quinte Peninsula, contains a national wildlife area. The point is well studied, with a regular bird-banding station in operation and many years of daily bird surveys to draw from. In late May, the trees are filled with flycatchers, vireos, warblers and grosbeaks, with the nearby ground full of thrushes and sparrows. Look for the Green Heron that nests near the harbour. You can often spot a Double-crested Cormorant as you stand on the shore by the lighthouse. At this site, check for Bonaparte's Gull and Caspian Tern loafing on shore. Nearby, listen for Eastern Towhee. In autumn, large numbers of Northern Saw-whet Owls pass through and are banded.

Revised by Ron Wier

Presqu'ile Provincial Park

Located on the north shore of Lake Ontario, near the midway point between Toronto and Kingston, Presqu'ile's peninsula is host to a diverse flora and fauna, especially birds. Over 300 species have been recorded, including several vagrants. Over 130 have bred, and the park's Breeding Bird Atlas square was the third highest in the province. A bird sightings board is located at the camp office.

Presqu'ile operates two interpretive centres as well as guided walks and other programs during the summer. Several special events are geared to birding, such as the waterfowl-viewing weekends and spring and fall migration weekends. The park has nearly 400 campsites, as well as a group campground, a long beach for swimming, picnic areas, store, interpretive trails, including a marsh boardwalk, and ski and walking trails. Several motels are nearby, as well as numerous bed-and-breakfasts, campgrounds and restaurants in and around Brighton.

Birding Features

Despite being a small park, Presqu'ile has tremendous habitat diversity, allowing for a disproportionately rich avifauna. Virtually any part of the peninsula can have birds but several areas stand out as being especially interesting and should be given priority.

On Presqu'ile's two offshore islands, High Bluff and Gull, one of the largest bird populations on the Great Lakes is established with nesting Ring-billed, Herring and Great Black-backed Gulls, Common and Caspian Terns, Black-crowned Night-Heron and just recently Great Blue Heron and Great Egret. Gull Island was also host to Canada's first nesting Cattle Egret in 1962. Both islands are closed to visitors during the nesting season from mid-March to mid-September to protect the birds; report any violations to the park wardens. Using hip waders, it is usually possible to cross the typically knee-deep channel to Gull Island (never try wading to High Bluff – there is a strong current between the islands), which can be excellent for shorebirds, including Purple Sandpiper in November-December, waterfowl, falcons, sparrows (especially Nelson's Sharp-tailed in late September/early October), pipits and Snow Bunting in season. In most winters, a Snowy Owl or two frequents the island.

Presqu'ile is best known for shorebirds and the beach from the gate to Owen Point is the key area. Spring movements occur during a fairly restrictive period (mid-May to early June) and can involve huge groundings of over 10,000 birds, whereas fall migration is drawn out over a longer period (late June to early December) but rarely involves more than 750 birds at any one time. However, species diversity is large, especially in late August when up to 20 species at a time is possible. Thirty-nine species have been recorded to date, including Mongolian Plover – a first for Canada – American Oystercatcher, Curlew Sandpiper, American Avocet, Marbled Godwit, Buff-breasted and Western Sandpipers. A trail has been established along the natural beach from Beach 4 to Owen Sound to allow close viewing without disturbing these nervous birds. This area is also excellent for other water birds and migrant hawks and passerines. Merlin and other raptors are a regular feature when shorebirds are present in numbers.

Extensive marshes make up the northeastern section of the park and can be most easily accessed via the Marsh Boardwalk Trail. While in decline, these marshes still offer habitat to some much sought-after species. Marsh Wren, Swamp Sparrow and Common Yellowthroat are abundant; less common are Common Moorhen, Pied-billed Grebe, American and Least Bittern, Virginia Rail and Sora. Black Tern formerly nested here but has recently died out, and the endangered King Rail has nested in some years (please avoid using tape playbacks).

Nearby are "the Fingers" – forested spits of land which bisect the marsh.

They are most easily accessed from the old pumphouse road between Beaches 2 and 3 exits on the east side. Walking into the woods you are immediately struck by the northern character of this habitat, and the bird life reinforces this observation. Nesting birds include Purple Finch; Yellow-rumped, Pine, Canada and Nashville Warblers; Red-breasted Nuthatch; and Golden-crowned Kinglet. It's also good for Great Horned Owl and Ruffed Grouse. During migration, two sites stand out for songbirds – the Calf Pasture and the Lighthouse area. Both seem to attract and hold birds, sometimes by the thousands during heavy flights.

Calf Pasture is an old field region with a small marsh and small stands of trees. The field itself has been home to Eastern Meadowlark, Bobolink, Savannah Sparrow and formerly Henslow's, but planted conifers have diminished its attractiveness to open-country birds. Clay-colored Sparrows recently colonized the area but were absent in 1999. The isolated patches of trees around the boat launch area can be fantastic for warblers, flycatchers, thrushes and other songbirds on big days. Over the years many rarities have been seen here but none can compare to the Sulphur-bellied Flycatcher discovered here in the autumn of 1986. On good flight days, during fall, large numbers of hawks, especially Sharp-shinned, soar over the fields.

The Lighthouse and Paxton Drive is the other major songbird concentration point. Several small trails wind their way around the lighthouse area, and all along Paxton Drive can be terrific places to look in spring and fall. Most of the songbirds ever recorded in the park have been seen along this stretch, including many of the southern warblers such as Hooded, Kentucky, Worm-eating and Prothonotary. The lighthouse is probably the best place to look for Orchard Orioles and Red-headed Woodpeckers in May. Waterbirds can be impressive offshore, especially in winter, and have included such rarities as Harlequin Duck and King Eider. Please note that numerous private landowners live on the peninsula's north shore along Bayshore Road, so respect their property boundaries when birding nearby. If watching waterfowl along Bayshore, please pull the car well over so as to not impede traffic from the residences on the point.

It can be worthwhile to take a drive along Lighthouse Lane (formerly Lakeshore Drive) and watch the lake for water birds. Grebes, loons and ducks can sometimes be found in numbers. As noted earlier, there are many other good sites in the park to visit, so exploration is always worthwhile.

R. D. McRae
Revised by R. D. McRae

Peterborough

The County of Peterborough straddles the Canadian Shield, separating the Carolinian forests, agricultural lands and extensive cattail marshes to the south from the mixed and boreal forests to the north, in a line that roughly divides the county in half. Scattered throughout are many hundreds of lakes, swales, creeks and rivers. The birding potential is very high, based primarily on the diversity of habitats. Both "southern" and "northern" species breed within its confines during the summer, and many irruptive species visit there most winters, including Black-backed and Three-toed Woodpeckers, Great Gray Owl, Boreal Chickadee, Bohemian Waxwing and all the winter finches.

Steeped in history that dates back to the early 1800s, the county has recognized its heritage, and many opportunities to "visit" the past exist. Water sports, skiing, camping and hiking provide ample opportunities for the traveller who chooses Peterborough as a destination.

The birding history of the area is documented in *Our Heritage of Birds – Peterborough County in the Kawarthas* (1983; 190 pp.) by Doug Sadler; the status of mammals is recorded in *The Mammals of Peterborough County* (1987; 125 pp.) by Geoff Carpentier, both published by the Peterborough Field Naturalists' Orchid Press. Bus service is available and many highways wind their way towards the county – Highway 28 from the north, Highway 7 from the east and west, and Highway 115 from the south. Ample accommodation and camping exist in and near the City of Peterborough.

Birding Features

The Cavan Swamp is a large remnant bog that once covered much of the area west and south of the city. The habitat that once typified this area has been preserved in a relatively pristine state. To reach it, travel west along Highway 28, skirting the edge of the city and turn left on County Road 9. Within about a kilometre you will see the bog on both sides of the road, and travelling westerly you will notice the edge of the bog near the Village of Mount Pleasant on County Road 10. Exploring the roads immediately to the east and west will delineate the boundaries of the site. Visitors to the bog may find many mid-northern breeding species, such as Northern Saw-whet Owl, Winter Wren, various warblers, Alder Flycatcher, as well as many marsh and wetland nesting species. A visit in mid-July should result in finding many rare orchids, pitcher plants, sundew and Labrador tea. In the winter look for owls and northern woodpeckers and finches.

Miller Creek, once again, represents a habitat that is fast declining in southern Ontario. The extensive cattail marshes are cut by numerous channels and ponds that allow excellent views of many marsh nesting species. Viewing opportunities are enhanced by the erection of a viewing tower and meandering trails that follow the edge of the marsh. Typical nesting species include Virginia Rail, Sora, American Bittern, Green Heron, Osprey, Northern Harrier, Marsh Wren, Common Moorhen and American Coot. To reach the marsh, travel north along County Road 24 from the Riverview Zoo in Peterborough or along County Road 18 from the Village of Bridgenorth, which intersects County Road 24. Turn west off County Road 24 on Township Road 7 for about 3 km and you will see the signed entrance on your left.

Lakefield Marshes lie within the Town of Lakefield. As you enter the town, from the south on County Road 29 (formerly Highway 28), turn west at the first traffic light, just before the Otonabee River, and drive to the end of the road. Park your vehicle here and proceed to canoe about 0.4 km to the extensive marshes, where you will be rewarded with nesting rails, Osprey,

Common Loon, Black Tern, American and Least Bitterns, Marsh Wren and Common Moorhen.

Proceeding north from Lakefield on Highway 28, you will soon enter Precambrian Shield country and notice that the urban side of Peterborough is mostly behind you. North of Burleigh Falls and Woodview, Petroglyphs Provincial Park is signed. Turn east on Northey's Bay Road and travel through extensive mixed boreal forest for about 11 km to the park entrance. Many trails crisscross the area. This is a popular destination in all seasons, whether you choose to hike, bicycle or cross-country ski. You may take the 5 km self-guided trail to High Falls (27 m) or choose the approximately 5 km long road, both of which lead to the petroglyphs site. The park holds the largest locally known collection of Indian rock carvings, dating back almost a thousand years, with over 900 found to date. The site is protected by a building with many glass windows, so that the carvings may be viewed at any season, but are most accessible in summer. The local native community still uses the site for various ceremonial purposes. The park is an excellent place to view northern nesting species, such as Olive-sided Flycatcher, Gray Jay, Blue-headed Vireo, Winter Wren and sometimes Black-backed Woodpecker. Adjacent areas will produce Golden-winged Warbler, sapsuckers, Yellow-throated Vireo and Red-shouldered and Broad-winged Hawks. Winter birding may turn up both crossbills, northern woodpeckers, finches and of course eagles. The area is most famous locally for its wintering eagles. Every year between 10 and 15 Bald Eagles and one to three Golden Eagles winter in the area. Patience while walking the trails or driving the roads should lead to spectacular views of these majestic birds. Among their favourite spots that are accessible to the public is the Haultain dump, north of the turnoff you took from Highway 28 to reach the park and the Kashabog dump. To reach the dump, leave the park parking area and travel east to County Road 6, about 1.5 km and turn north. Follow this to the first road on the right and follow that to the first road on the left. About 2 km from the latter junction, you will see the dump on your right. Both sites are best visited early or late in the day, when the local populace has left them to the animals. Beware of bears at these sites.

There are a series of sewage lagoons throughout the county, which used to be very productive, but current management practices have reduced their attractiveness to many birds – but you never know! The Omemee lagoons, west of Peterborough on Highway 7, are located north of the town on County Road 7 (Sturgeon Road). Turn west on Beaver Road, near the Gliderport. The Town of Lindsay lagoons are much more extensive and still produce many good bird sightings. To reach them, travel west from Omemee on Highway 7 and then go north on County Road 36 (formerly Highway 36), where you will find these water bodies just behind the municipal landfill site. The berms are well maintained and viewing is relatively easy. The Havelock lagoons are located east of Peterborough, off Highway 7, in the Village of Havelock. Success here will vary from year to year, depending on the water levels, but as these are essentially not managed by the town, the potential is quite high to find good birds. The lagoons are east of Highway 30, immediately south of town, along the Old Norwood Road, where you will turn right at the first small gravel road you see which will lead you to the lagoons. The road may be fenced at times, so you may have to walk in about a kilometre. Finally, the Lakefield lagoons may be productive, but they are more managed than Havelock's, so the potential may be lower. In the past they have produced Spotted Redshank, Little and Franklin's Gulls, Blue Grosbeak, Yellow-headed Blackbird, Red-necked Phalarope, Western Sandpiper and Ruff. To reach these lagoons, travel east from Peterborough on Highway 7, and turn north on Highway 134. Turn left on County Road 33 and you will shortly see the lagoons on your left. Once you have explored these lagoons, a scenic drive back to Peterborough may be had if you simply keep going in the same direction along this small road until you hit the Otonabee River, where you will turn left. The road follows very close to the river all the way to Peterborough.

A. GEOFFREY CARPENTIER
Revised by A. Geoffrey Carpentier

Durham Region

Durham Region is the municipality lying immediately east of the city of Toronto. Although it is undergoing rapid industrialization and subdivision development, it still affords a series of very productive marshes along Lake Ontario, several excellent wooded areas for migrants and breeding birds, and the more upland Oak Ridges Moraine for local specialties such as Clay-colored and Grasshopper Sparrows. These diverse habitats in a relatively small space have resulted in some record-breaking "Big Days" for the province.

Highway 401 east from Toronto provides the main access by car and bus, and there is also a frequent commuter train service from the city. Accommodation and services are readily available throughout. A birding hotline is updated twice weekly at (905) 576-2738.

Birding Features
Pickering. The first community east of Toronto along Highway 401 is on the east side of the Rouge River Valley, now preserved as the largest urban park in the country. This 32 km strip of heavily wooded valley lands ends in marshes at the river mouth and affords excellent birding, especially in migration. The valley can be entered at several spots. To explore the south end, leave Highway 401 at Whites Road (Exit 394), go north to the first intersection and turn west on Highway 2, Kingston Road, for 2 km, then south on Rougemount Drive, which can be followed to the lake and also gives access to the west entrance to Petticoat Creek Conservation Area, itself an excellent birding area. Harlequin Duck occurs almost annually off the stony beach in winter, and the cliffs at the entrance to Petticoat Creek give excellent views of loons, grebes and diving ducks; egrets and rare herons have been seen at the mouth of the river and there is a colony of Cliff Swallows under the railway bridge. To sample upper sections of the Rouge Valley, return to Highway 2 and go west to the next intersection with Altona Road, then north on Altona Road to Twyn Rivers Drive and west to two river bridges where there are footpaths to the north and south.

Frenchman's Bay, east of Petticoat Creek, has marshes and a good shore-bird area at its north end. In the winter this spot often attracts unusual gulls. From the White's Road exit go south to Bayly Street, then east on Bayly. Go south off Bayly on West Shore Boulevard to explore the western side or, farther east, down Liverpool Road for the eastern side; a little farther east still, again off Bayly, Sandy Beach Road gives access to Hydro Marsh, excellent for shore-birds, marsh birds, Black-crowned Night-Heron and ducks, as well as many warblers in migration in the small wood lot.

Claremont Conservation Area. Take Highway 401 to Brock Road (Exit 399) and proceed north for about 13 km to the village of Brougham. Head east to Greenwood and turn north along Westney Road for about 1.6 km to the park gate. The area has large sections of land covered in mature forest. Common resident species include Ruffed Grouse, Eastern Screech-Owl, Pileated Woodpecker, large numbers of Red-breasted and White-breasted Nuthatches and Purple Finch. Summer breeders include Cooper's, Red-shouldered and Broad-winged Hawks, Whip-poor-will, seven species of flycatcher, Cedar Waxwing and a large and diverse collection of wood warblers. Winter brings Golden-crowned Kinglet, Bohemian Waxwing, Pine Siskin and a variety of "winter finches."

Ajax. Ajax lies immediately east of Pickering, on the shore of Lake Ontario and still has a good cattail marsh at Corner Marsh. Leave Highway 401 at Brock Road (Exit 399) and proceed east on Bayly Street to Squires Beach Road, go south to McKay Road, then keep going east to the corner of Montgomery Park Road and Frisco Road. Development has unfortunately reduced Corner Marsh to a shadow of its former self, but it is still a good spot for shorebirds, gulls and ducks with some rarities such as American White Pelican and an American Avocet from time to time. The end of Frisco Road is another good lake-watching spot, especially for concentrations of Red-necked Grebes in spring and fall. This also brings you to a pleasant section of the Waterfront Trail, which gives continuous good views of the lake. Walk west to the outlook at the foot of Montgomery Park Road, known locally as Moore Point, where Northern Gannet, King Eider and Ivory Gull have been some of the many rarities spotted in recent years, or east to Rotary Park and the cliffs beyond overlooking the stony beaches where Dunlin and Purple Sandpiper may linger in late fall.

Whitby. The town of Whitby, east of Ajax and west of Oshawa, is accessible off Highway 401 on Exit 410, Brock Street. The region contains two conser-vation areas, several lakeshore wood lots, and extensive tracts of mature forest in local creek valleys and nearby tablelands. Lynde Shores Conservation Area, usually considered the best birding spot, can be reached by going south on Brock Street to Victoria Street and taking Victoria west for about 3 km. Look for the Lynde Shores Conservation Area entrance sign on the south side of the road. Parking is available in the adjacent lot. The site boasts a variety of habi-tats, including both cattail and Carr type marshes, wooded creek valley, mudflats on the floodplain, sand and gravel beach, and abandoned orchards and fields. No other spot in the entire region has produced such a variety of bird species. Visitors should expect anything, including such rarities as Red-throated Loon, Glossy Ibis, Yellow Rail, Black-legged Kittiwake and Sharp-tailed Sparrow. The lakeshore provides ideal viewing for migrant waterfowl, while nearby fields and wood lots host a diverse number of passerines that move through. Regular breeding species include Mute Swan, Gadwall, Northern Harrier, Virginia Rail, Sora, Black-billed Cuckoo, six species of flycatcher, Chestnut-sided Warbler, Common Yellowthroat, Rose-breasted Grosbeak, Indigo Bunting, and Swamp and Song Sparrows.

To get to Thickson's Woods, widely thought to be one of the best birding spots in southern Ontario, return to Victoria Street, drive east to Thickson Road (for some reason, the road does not have the apostrophe "s" !), and south to the lake. Alternatively, from Highway 401 take Exit 412, Thickson Road, straight southward. The road stops at the lake at the entrance to a private cottage community; park on Thickson Road and walk in to this area, either along the clifftop road or east along the Waterfront Trail north of the woods to the entrance gate. This mature stand of pine, maple and oak, and the adjoining marsh, are owned by a non-profit conservation group, the Thickson's Woods Heritage Foundation, which provides well-marked trails for public use. Spring migration is often spectacular, with sightings of many southern overshoots such as Worm-eating, Kentucky and Hooded Warblers, Summer Tanager and Orchard Oriole. Carolina Wren has nested here for several years, as have Blue-gray Gnatcatcher, Wood Thrush and occasionally Pine Warbler. Great Horned Owl nests, and Long-eared and Northern Saw-whet Owls can sometimes be found; the open clifftop areas to the west of the woods are often good for wintering Short-eared Owl and Rough-legged Hawk. Least Bitterns have been seen in the adjoining Corbett Creek marsh; Marsh Wrens nest there; Sedge Wrens and sparrows can sometimes be found in the nearby grassy areas. The clifftop itself gives excellent views of Brant and scoter flocks in spring, and the bay often holds impressive concentrations of loons, grebes and diving ducks.

Whitby Harbour. Lying between Lynde Shores and Thickson's Woods, this site is also worth a visit for its shorebirds, waterfowl, gulls and terns. Take Brock Street South from Victoria Street to the harbour, which can be viewed from the small bridge over the creek on Brock Street or from the parking lot beside the harbour mouth, reached by continuing east on Water Street at the foot of Brock.

Heber Down Conservation Area. To reach this inland area, leave Highway 401 at Exit 410 on Brock Street and drive north through the town of Whitby for about 3 km to Taunton Road. Drive west for 1.6 km and north on Country Lane to the park. The site occupies an ancient lakeshore and glacial embayment, providing an interesting blend of biogeographical features. Much of the valley is covered by a mature growth of White Cedar, maple, hemlock, pine and oak. Numerous nature trails provide access to nearly all the unique spots. The site is particularly alive in May and September. Resident species include

Hooded Warbler

Ruffed Grouse, Great Horned Owl, Pileated Woodpecker, White and Red-breasted Nuthatches and Purple Finch. Summer breeders from May to early July include Red-shouldered Hawk, American Kestrel, Black-billed Cuckoo, Eastern Screech-Owl, Whip-poor-will, several species of flycatcher, Wood Thrush, Veery, Ovenbird, Mourning Warbler, Rose-breasted Grosbeak, Eastern Towhee and White-throated Sparrow. A winter visit could provide the above-mentioned resident birds together with Evening and Pine Grosbeaks, Common Redpoll, Pine Siskin and both species of crossbill.

Oshawa. Oshawa's main claim to fame is the Oshawa Second Marsh which is now being managed as a nature reserve with the help of General Motors of Canada, the City of Oshawa and the Oshawa Harbour Commission. This 150 ha cattail marsh holds hundreds of ducks in migration and is also a prime shorebird site when water levels are low in fall. It was the site of the first known nesting of Little Gull in North America and remains a good spot to see these gulls, especially as they move through in spring. The marsh has produced many rarities, including Little Blue Heron, Snowy Egret, Glossy Ibis, Eurasian Wigeon and Ruff. Public access is now excellent, with a good system of walking trails starting from the parking lot of the General Motors head office at the northwest corner of the marsh. There are two good viewing platforms on the north edge of the marsh: one close to the southwest corner of the parking lot and the other, a double-decker, farther west along the trail following the north edge of the cattails.

To reach this splendid birding area, leave Highway 401 at Harmony Road (Exit 419) and go south on Farewell Street to Colonel Sam Drive, which then runs east to the General Motors corporate building. As well as the marsh, there are grassy areas good for sparrows and even Short-eared Owls. Plantings of native fruiting trees attract migrants and overwintering birds. Also the site gives access to the pebble beach with good views of Lake Ontario.

Darlington Provincial Park lies directly to the east of Oshawa Second Marsh. You can walk eastward into the park from the General Motors parking lot, or take your car back to Highway 401 and travel east to the next intersection, Courtice Road, Exit 425, then follow signs to the park. An entrance fee is charged in summer. There are both camping and picnic facilities and a good series of walking trails. The wooded ravine and small tree-lined roads through the camping area are often full of warblers, Scarlet Tanager and Rose-breasted Grosbeak in migration, especially in windy or rainy weather; the ravine also shelters winter strays such as the occasional Hermit Thrush. The sandy spit running west along the edge of the lake often turns up interesting shorebirds, gulls and sparrows; Piping Plover and Nelson's Sharp-tailed Sparrow have been seen here. The lake itself should also be carefully checked for unusual waterfowl, which have included Harlequin Duck, scoters, and both Common and King Eiders; the best lakewatching spot is the clifftop at the eastern boundary of the park, preferably in the early morning.

The Oak Ridges Moraine. This site is the low, rolling, hilly area north of the lakeshore. It supports grassland and woodland species such as Upland Sandpiper, Whip-poor-will, Black-billed Cuckoo, Eastern Bluebird and Grasshopper and Vesper Sparrows. Christmas-tree plantations in the sandy soil host Eastern Towhee and Chipping, Field and Clay-colored Sparrows. This beautiful upland area can be accessed by several routes north from Highway 401, including County Road 57 north through Bowmanville (Exit 431) to Burketon and the Long Sault Conservation Area.

J. ROBERT NISBET
Revised by Margaret Bain

Toronto

Toronto is Canada's largest city, yet birding opportunities are very good without leaving the urban area. Three hundred and seventy-six species have been accepted by the Rarities Committee of the Toronto Ornithological Club within a 48 km radius of the Royal Ontario Museum to date and new ones are being added almost annually. This total exceeds that of any other region in Ontario, including well-known birding areas like Point Pelee and Long Point.

For tourist information, call (416) 203-2500 (Toronto) or (416) 314-0944 (Ontario). For public transportation information, dial (416) 393-4636.

The best local publication is *A Birdfinding Guide to the Toronto Region* (1988) published by Clive E. Goodwin but now unfortunately out of print and somewhat out of date. Copies are next to impossible to obtain from regular bookstores and no reprinting is planned.

The Toronto Rare Bird Sightings Hotline phone number is (416) 350-3000, ext. 2293. It is updated every Friday at suppertime, Sunday evening and at other times when there are birds of exceptional interest. It would be wise to check messages for a week or two before coming to Toronto as information is often not repeated due to time limitation. The Toronto Rare Bird Alert is currently headed by Harry Kerr at (416) 481-7948, Jerry Guild at (905) 823-1973 and Ron Scovell at (416) 745-9111, all of whom will be glad to help.

Birding Features

The Toronto waterfront has much to offer at all seasons but especially in winter when huge flocks of diving ducks, including Oldsquaw and Greater Scaup are readily seen. Each year in midwinter 25 to 30 waterfowl species are counted in the Toronto region. Migration of passerines in spring or fall is usually best observed at Tommy Thompson Park and on the Toronto Islands. Both trips require the best part of a day. Fall hawk migration is best observed from the hill beside the Grenadier Restaurant in High Park. Get off the subway at the High Park stop and walk south about 500 m.

By March, the earliest spring migrants appear. Northbound birds peak in numbers in the third week of May. The woodlands offer superb birding at this time with some species already nesting, while others such as warblers are moving through in large numbers.

At this time, shorebirds may include Ruddy Turnstone, Red Knot, Whimbrel and occasionally a flock of Brant or scoters. June and July can be hot, though it is always cooler near the lake. Birds are often discovered at this time by song. In recent years, many Toronto birders have turned to butterflying in summer and the hotline may contain current information on this subject.

Shorebirds begin moving south by the end of June and reach their peak numbers by August. Fall passerine migration reaches its peak from the end of August to the end of September. In August flocks of Common Nighthawk can often be seen in the evenings flying over the city. In mid-September, after passage of a cold front, up to 10,000 Broad-winged Hawks in a day can be seen following the north shore of Lake Ontario. Up to 100 hawk-watchers throng the hill next to the parking lot of the Grenadier Restaurant at these times to witness the spectacle. Another drawing card has been the Golden and Bald Eagle migration at the end of October.

By the end of November, most birds have gone south and the winter influx has begun. From 85 to 95 species are usually found on the Toronto Christmas Count conducted on the Sunday closest to Christmas.

Toronto Island Park. This is perhaps the best single bird watching area in the city and is made up of 13 islands located in the harbour. Ferry service departs from the foot of Bay Street at the waterfront (there's a streetcar from Union Station subway stop). Ferries go to Ward's Island, Centre Island and Hanlan's Point. In winter service is less frequent. The best area is the Island Nature Sanctuary (not signed as such) just north of the Island Nature School. Here you can escape the huge crowds of picnickers in the warm days of summer. Another very good place is just south of the village on Ward's Island. In winter, species such as Red-bellied Woodpecker and Carolina Wren are sometimes found attending the feeders behind the houses on Ward's and Algonquin Islands. Hanlan's Point draws more than its share of migrants; the beach on the west side should be checked for shorebirds and ducks. Cliff Swallows nest at the pier on the south side of Centre Island. You should obtain a map and ferry schedule before setting out in order to optimize your time spent on the island.

Toronto's rarest bird ever, a Variegated Flycatcher, was present for a month in the fall of 1993. It was discovered at the lighthouse by two birders visiting the island for the first time.

Tommy Thompson Park (aka Leslie Street Spit or Eastern Headland). This peninsula was constructed from truckloads of rubble from dump trucks beginning in the 1960s and can now boast of some fairly mature woodlands. Marshes and shorebird habitat are being introduced. More than 300 species have been recorded here. A free shuttle bus goes out every half hour and will also bring you back if you wish. This service is offered from May 24 weekend until Thanksgiving. Check the Leslie Spit Hotline at (416) 661-6600, ext. 233, for current wildlife information.

Local birders usually ignore the bus going out, preferring first to check the cattail marsh on the east side of the base and the meadows and aspen woods on the west side of the base. As you walk south, the peninsula narrows and ducks, loons and grebes are more easily seen on the water. The first bay on the right is often the best place for shorebirds in season and for roosting gulls. The first peninsula on the right, unimaginatively named "D," is good for migrating warblers; Long-eared Owls are often found in the wooded areas beyond the yacht club.

The enclosed ponds on the left are good for a variety of ducks, including Redhead and Canvasback, while Common Tern nests on the rafts supplied by the Canadian Wildlife Service. The second peninsula on the right, which is "C," has a large Black-crowned Night-Heron colony, so access is not permitted in breeding season. At other times it seems to be a favourite haunt of the large owls such as Great Horned. "B" peninsula may hold Northern Saw-whet Owl or even, in the right winter, Boreal. The base of the dyke connecting to "C" peninsula often has shorebirds, and the open overgrown area of "B" is excellent for sparrows.

Some time should be spent at the lighthouse at the tip. Jaegers have been spotted from this elevated location in fall and many flocks of waterfowl fly by in winter.

Another good lakewatching spot is at the end of the newer peninsula to the east. Harlequin Duck often winters here. Between these two tip locations are extensive open areas with, depending on the season, Short-eared Owl, shorebirds, Snow Bunting and other birds of the open countryside.

It is 4.8 km to the tip and there is no protection from the wind, so dress accordingly.

Lambton Woods. This is an extensive area of hardwood forest on the west side of the Humber River. To reach the site, go east on Edenbridge Drive from Royal York Road. James Gardens, on Edenbridge, is at the entrance. There was a Hermit Warbler here in 1984. Lambton Woods is excellent for land birds and can even have some waterfowl on the river. During migration in spring and fall, warblers, vireos, sparrows and flycatchers are common, while Eastern Screech-Owls are always present. A feeder is maintained in winter about 200 m south of the Lambton Woods sign and many of the houses at the top of the hill have bird feeders as well. This is a good area to find Pileated and Red-bellied Woodpeckers in winter and Olive-sided Flycatchers in late May.

Sunnybrook Park. Toronto has many fine ravines, and Sunnybrook is one of the biggest and best. It is adjacent to the west branch of the Don River. Pileated Woodpecker and Eastern Screech-Owl can be found year-round, and the conifers often attract winter finches. Other good ravines, not described here, include Cedarvale, Etobicoke Valley in the west and the Rouge in the east.

High Park. The vegetation of this west-central park has undergone an extensive restoration program in recent years. The oak-savannah habitat is coming back due to selective planting and annual burns. Grenadier Pond is fast returning to its former pristine beauty. It holds dozens of Northern Shovelers in winter. Migrating passerines are best seen from the bank above Grenadier Pond or along Spring Road in the east half of the park. Migrants that have remained in the park a few days tend to drift to the south in the Colborne Lodge area. The hawk watch is conducted from the hill just north of the restaurant parking lot from August 28 to November 30 each year. Raptor numbers typically exceed those of Hawk Mountain, Pennsylvania.

Colonel Sam Smith Park. Located at the foot of Kipling Avenue in west Toronto, it holds shorebirds and ducks in season, and the many mature spruce trees at the base can be excellent for migrating warblers.

Humber Bay East and West. These parks can be reached at the foot of Park Lawn Road on the Queen Street streetcars. Humber Bay East permits close views of overwintering ducks, because they are often fed by the locals. More-distant views can be obtained by looking northwest from the tip of Humber Bay West, and a good variety of gulls can often be found roosting on the piers of the yacht club. A few shorebirds are usually present in the mouth of Mimico Creek between the two parks in migration.

LINDA AND CHIP WESELOH
Revised by Hugh Currie

Mississauga and Oakville

The region immediately west and northwest of Toronto, including Mississauga, Oakville and the counties of Peel and Halton, has always been a high-quality birdwatching locale. Unfortunately, over the last 15 or 20 years urban sprawl has left but small pockets of refuge behind. GO Transit lines and related bus service provide access to some sites. Check with their office for schedules.

Birding Features

The Lake Ontario waterfront still retains highlight spots. To discover them, drive Lakeshore Road from east to west, stopping periodically at roads terminating at the water to scan the shoreline. Ducks and geese are most numerous from September to March. Favourite locations include Marie Curtis Park, opposite the Long Branch GO Transit station on Lakeshore Road at Etobicoke Creek; Albert E. Crookes Memorial Park, found along Goodwin Road south of Lakeshore Road; the St. Lawrence Starch Plant, at Port Credit Harbour via Stevebank Road south of Lakeshore or via Port Street; Jack Darling Memorial Park and Rattray's Marsh, located 1.6 km east of Meadowwood Road, west of the Lorne Park traffic light; Lakeside Park, reached via Winston Churchill Boulevard, or south on Southdown Road; Oakville Harbour, via Mary Street; and Bronte Harbour, found by driving south on Bronte Road or by the Queen Elizabeth Way and Lakeshore Road.

A trip to the shoreline is always worthwhile, even to watch the big ships; you may spot a variety of ducks such as Redhead, Greater and Lesser Scaups, Common Goldeneye, Common Eider, Common and White-winged Scoters, and maybe even a Barrow's Goldeneye or Harlequin Duck. Shorebirds arrive in April and May and again in September and October. They include Ruddy Turnstone, Red Knot, Dunlin, Sanderling and even Purple Sandpiper. Watch for the occasional Great Black-backed Gull.

The river valleys are, as in most Canadian cities, among the last refuges for wildlife. Take a walk in any of the four leading to Lake Ontario: the Port Credit River and Etobicoke, Sixteen Mile and Bronte Creeks. A wide mix of plants, birds and mammals can be spotted in summer and winter. These valleys can be entered at the numerous east-west road crossings except for the Queen Elizabeth Way and Highway 401.

The Niagara Escarpment stands out as a ridge from the Niagara Peninsula in the south to Tobermory, northwest of Toronto at the tip of the Bruce Peninsula. Much of its length is rocky and inaccessible, with extensive wooded tracts. Often these are the only native woods left and hence are considered some of the finest accessible birding areas in Ontario. To gain access to some of the spots, drive north to Campbellville, at interchange 38 west of Toronto on Highway 401, and take the first road to the right, or east (the fourth line). Within the first 3.2 km, the Mahon, Turner and Robertson tracts are indicated by signs. Two others, the Britton and Cox tracts, may be reached from the sixth line. These sites, with rocks and trees providing shelter and secluded nesting locations, are great for birding from April to July. However, look out for the hordes of mosquitoes! Common bird species include Turkey Vulture, Northern Goshawk, Cooper's Hawk, both species of cuckoo, Yellow-bellied Sapsucker, Brown Thrasher, Wood Thrush and Blue-gray Gnatcatcher. Vireos and warblers abound, particularly in late May and June. A sampling of warblers includes Golden-winged, Blue-winged, Yellow, Cerulean, Chestnut-sided, Mourning, Hooded and American Redstart, to name a few. Look for a Rose-breasted Grosbeak.

During the harsh winter months, the few birds that do occur on the escarpment include Ruffed Grouse, Hairy and Downy Woodpeckers, the occasional Three-toed Woodpecker, White-breasted and Red-breasted Nuthatches, Northern Shrike and the "winter finches."

There are several conservation areas in the region. Mountsberg, with its nature interpretation centre, nature trails and observation tower, is worth a visit

Northern Cardinal

for fall and spring migrating water birds. Also check the Palgrave and Clairville conservation areas (refer to a Metro Toronto map for directions).

BARRY RANFORD AND LINDA CRAIG

Luther Lake

Luther Lake, about 38 km straight north of Guelph or about 75 km west-northwest of Toronto, has three attractions: the lake, with its large variety of water birds, including 15 species of ducks which have nested, many of them every year; the northern woods, with both southern Ontario species and northern birds such as Ruby-crowned Kinglet; and Wylde Lake, an unusual raised boreal bog in which Lincoln's Sparrows nest, one of the southernmost points for this species.

The complex comprises some 6500 ha, with about 2025 in open water. The marsh was established when the headwaters of the Grand River were dammed in 1952. A permit is required to put any boat, including a canoe, on the main lake prior to July 31. Permits may be obtained from the superintendent's house at the dam. Outboard motors are not allowed.

Access to the area is best gained by car. Nearby Arthur (about 10 km south-west) and Orangeville (about 24 km east) are served by Gray Coach (bus); taxis may be hired at either place. Commercial accommodation is available at both towns. Camping is not permitted in the Luther complex, but there are several public campgrounds within a few kilometres. There is a small entrance fee, payable at the dam entrance.

The eastern end of the lake and dam. From the intersection of Highways 9 and 10, just east of Orangeville, take Highway 9 west for 22.9 km, or 3.7 km past the turnoff to Grand Valley. Turn north onto an unmarked dirt road (the next north turnoff, 1.6 km farther west, has a microwave tower about 200 m west of it). Drive 8.2 km north; turn west onto an unmarked dirt road; proceed 3.7 km to a sharp right-angle bend in the road and proceed north 3.2 km to the dam and parking lot on the west side of the road. Hike the road that parallels the north shore for about 2.4 km to a lookout tower, which provides excellent viewing of the lake. If you are coming from Arthur, the unmarked dirt road turnoff north from Highway 9 lies 14.7 km east of the intersection of Highways 9 and 6.

Wylde Lake. This raised bog may be reached from Orangeville by driving west 26.2 km on Highway 9 to an unmarked dirt road. This is the boundary between Wellington and Dufferin Counties. Look for the sign. Drive north for 5.3 km to the point where the road takes a sharp left turn. Park on the shoulder and walk eastward for about 1.5 km to the lake. Carry a compass when hiking in this area. On a dull day it is very easy to get lost in the Wylde Lake region of several square kilometres. From Arthur, the unmarked dirt road lies 11 km east on Highway 9.

Northern woods. These woods are reached from the dam site parking lot. From the dam, an internal road not open to vehicles curves through the northern part of the area, roughly parallelling the shore for 6.4 to 8 km. This road provides access to the large block of woodland on the north shore of the lake. The far end of this road can also be reached via Concession 8/9 off West Luther Township. From the dam about 2.4 km along the trail, a lookout tower provides a good overview of the lake. Continue to hike for 5.6 km from the dam, to a trail signposted "Esker Trail," which leads, in 0.8 km, to a second observation tower. This trail provides good views of a willow swamp.

Further information, together with details on permits mentioned above, may be obtained from Grand River Conservation Authority, 400 Clyde Road, Cambridge, Ontario N1R 5S7; phone (519) 621-2761.

Birding Features
Main or Luther lake. Good overviews of the main lake may be had from the dam and especially the observation tower 1.6 km south of the dam. The latter tower is reached from an internal road, open to private vehicles, that leaves the parking lot at the dam. To best see the marsh and its birds, a canoe is very useful. The safest launch site is at the eastern end of Concession Road 617 (the road which leads out of Damascus to the east from the village store). Unfortunately and regrettably, at the time of writing, the GRCA has closed off this access, and currently canoes may be launched only from the dam access point. Canoeists should be aware that this launch site can become more hazardous in the frequent event of a strong west wind springing up during the course of the day; they would be wise to listen to the weather forecasts before putting out.

Waterfowl that breed, in approximate order of abundance, are Mallard, Gadwall, American Wigeon, Blue-winged Teal, Lesser Scaup, Redhead, Ring-necked Duck, American Black Duck, Green-winged Teal, Northern Pintail,

Wood Duck, Hooded Merganser, Canvasback and Northern Shoveler. Not all of these species breed every year. Several pairs of Common Loons nest on the lake; also Pied-billed Grebe, Great Blue and Green Herons, Black-crowned Night-Heron, Least Bittern (sparsely), American Bittern, Virginia Rail, Sora, Common Moorhen, American Coot, Northern Harrier, up to seven pairs of Ospreys, Wilson's Phalarope on the islands, Black Tern, Marsh Wren and Swamp Sparrow. In recent years Sandhill Cranes have been seen throughout the summer, although breeding has not been proven. Very recently several White Pelicans have summered without nesting. Double-crested Cormorants are now present in large numbers, and Caspian Terns are usually to be found on the islands in summer; so far neither species has been shown to nest.

In the fall, as the lake is drawn down, large areas of mudflats are exposed on the semi-floating bogs scattered through the lake and around the edges. These floating bogs are essentially bottomless; avoid walking on them.

Wylde Lake. This lake contains one of the southernmost breeding locations of Lincoln's Sparrow. Search and listen for them at the sharp bend in the road where you leave the car.

Northern woods. Look here for the usual woodland species of southern Ontario. A bonus includes a number of rather boreal species, such as Winter Wren, Ruby-crowned Kinglet and Nashville Warbler. At the dam parking lot, a Purple Martin colony is active in season.

DAVID BREWER
Revised by David Brewer

Hamilton and Burlington

Hamilton, locked between Lake Ontario and the Niagara Escarpment, offers a wealth of cosmopolitan attractions combined with some fine birdwatching spots. The city, with a population of 306,500, is home to Canada's two major steel-producing firms and contains the largest open-air food market in our country. Nearby Burlington, to the north, houses the Joseph Brant Museum of Indian relics.

The two cities lie southwest of, and adjacent to, Metropolitan Toronto, on the southwest end of Lake Ontario. Access and accommodation are both easy to find.

Birding Features
Dundas Marsh. This site, often called Cootes Paradise, lies within the grounds of the Royal Botanical Gardens, west of the harbour and Highway 403. The marsh is considered to be the best all-round bird-finding spot in the district. To find the area, take King Street west onto Marion Crescent Park in the lot adjacent to the Children's Garden House. Spencer Creek flows into the western end of the marsh at the Dundas Hydro Pond and the Old Dejardins Canal. The creek may be reached on King Street by proceeding west past

McMaster University and turning right on Cootes Drive. Cross the creek and park on the shoulder. Walk north to both the pond and canal; a path follows the canal east to the centre of the marsh. At the end of the "willows" in the marsh, if the water is low, a mudflat appears, attracting shorebirds, gulls and terns. Westdale Ravine, on the south shore of the marsh, is a prime spot for viewing spring migration.

Hamilton Harbour. The east end of the harbour contains a landfill site. Here, in water kept open by the actions of the steel mills, you'll spot 10 to 15 species of overwintering waterfowl. Specialties such as Barrow's Goldeneye and Tufted Duck have been recorded in recent years.

Grimsby Peak. This is the best place for hawk watching. The area lies 19.2 km east of Hamilton, off the Queen Elizabeth Way. Exit at Christie Road; follow it south through town and up the very steep hill. Turn right (west) at the top of the hill and continue for about 1.6 km to signs for the Beamer Conservation Area.

Beverly Swamp. The swamp plays host to a horde of nesting land birds. From the junction of Highways 5 and 6 (Clappisons Corners), drive north on Highway 6 to West Flamboro Concession No. 8. Turn left and proceed 6.4 km to the swamp. Several kilometres of poorly drained woodlands attract a variety of nesting birds. From May to July, survey for Yellow-bellied Sapsucker, Acadian and Willow Flycatchers, Winter Wren and White-throated Sparrow.

50 Point Conservation Area. This area lies 15 km east of Hamilton. Take 50 Road off the Queen Elizabeth Way. Drive east from 50 Road for 1.5 km to the entrance to the conservation area and drive through to the lake. Lakewatching here is especially good in the fall, when Northern Gannet, scoters, jaegers and kittiwakes have all been seen almost annually.

JOHN OLMSTED
Revised by John Olmsted

Kitchener, Waterloo, Brantford and Cambridge

These communities occur at the boundary between the Great Lakes–St. Lawrence forests of Sugar Maple and American Beech to the north, and Carolinean forests of oaks and hickories to the south. Birds of both forest types regularly breed here.

Kitchener was founded in 1799 by Mennonites from Pennsylvania. German settlers came in 1833 and called the village Berlin. The name was changed at the height of World War I.

These cities lie about 60 km southwest of Toronto, with Highway 401 the main route for vehicular traffic, including regular bus service. A variety of accommodation services and recreational opportunities are available. Before you visit, order the 1:50,000 topographic map 40 P/8 Cambridge from the Map Distribution Office in Ottawa.

Birding Features

The Grand River Valley, running south through Kitchener and Brantford to Lake Erie, represents the southern forest type of the area. Portions of the valley bottom contain virtually unbroken forest for long distances. Parks Canada has recognized the entire area between Cambridge and Paris as a National Site of Canadian Significance.

An auto tour of the western portion of the valley begins in Cambridge (an amalgamation of the former towns of Galt, Preston and Hespeler). Drive south along West River Road. This road begins just east of the intersection of Highways 97 and 24A on the west side of the Grand River, in the old town of Galt. Proceed south and note the forested ridge to the west. The Galt Ridge, a terminal moraine, was left when the last glacier from the east was stalled for a time before melting back. The road lies between the river (on the east) and the forested ridge (on the west), providing access to an excellent natural area. These lands extend from the river west over the ridge along a small river valley to Beake Pond, locally called Taylor's Lake, near Highway 24A. All of the land is privately held, but permission to enter is usually allowed if you ask. Habitats include upland deciduous forest, mixed and coniferous swamp, and old fields. Birds to look for in May to mid-July include Green Heron, Blue-winged Teal, Turkey Vulture, Ruffed Grouse, Eastern Screech-Owl, Ruby-throated Hummingbird, Downy Woodpecker, Eastern Kingbird, Brown Thrasher, Cedar Waxwing, Common Yellowthroat, Bobolink, Eastern Meadowlark and Eastern Towhee. A pair of Red-shouldered Hawks has bred in these woods for many years – the last pair remaining in local counties.

Both Golden-winged and Blue-winged Warblers breed in the forests surrounding Taylor's Lake. Nashville and Chestnut-sided Warblers are found in the swamps and upland forests, respectively. American Bittern and Sora have been heard frequently in the marsh at Taylor's Lake. White-throated and Swamp Sparrows, as well as Least Flycatcher, breed in the excellent bog 1 km south of Taylor's Lake. Both Upland Sandpiper and Clay-colored Sparrow have been found in the central fields north of the powerline.

As you continue to travel south on West River Road, notice the bridge crossing the Grand on your left. A large colony of Cliff Swallows nests on the concrete bridge supports. This is also an excellent spot to view waterfowl on the river in the winter. Continue south and you soon start to travel upwards as the road leaves the valley floor. Turn right onto the first road and head west. Cottrell Lake, on the right, causes the road to make a curving detour. Continue west, straight through the next intersection, and you soon enter the large Sudden Tract Forest. Park at the small parking lot provided on your right.

Sudden Tract is owned by the Region of Waterloo and is open for recreation, with several well-developed trails. The woods contain nesting Red-bellied Woodpecker. In 1981, Acadian Flycatcher moved into the woods beside a small pond north of the parking lot. Look for Louisiana Waterthrush, which has been reported at times.

When you leave the Sudden Tract, head east, back the way you came. This time turn right, south, at the first road 1 km from the parking lot. Drive south to the next road and turn left. You are now travelling east on the Brant/

Waterloo County Line. Turn south, at the first road, and head down the hill into the valley again. The forest along these slopes is northern in character, with Alder Flycatcher, Brown Creeper, Winter Wren, Black-and-white Warbler, Chestnut-sided Warbler, Northern Waterthrush and White-throated Sparrow all breeding west of the road. To the east, the drier forested slopes contain Yellow-throated Vireo and Blue-winged Warbler. The vireo is usually found in the drier mature forests of the valley. Both Red-eyed and Warbling Vireos are quite common, while Philadelphia and Blue-headed Vireos come as migrants only.

Travel south until you meet the pavement of the Glen Morris Road. Turn west and proceed away from Glen Morris for 2 km or until a gravel road appears on your left. Take it and head for the forested ridge in the distance. Go through the turns and stop just as the road crests and leaves the forest. You will find a gravel trail to hike on the east, heading down into the valley. You are now in the Pinehurst Lake–Spottiswood forest complex. It is an area full of rare southern plants and birds. After walking for 100 m down the trail, you will see a small path heading off to the left. Follow it to the Indian Lookout to obtain a view of the Grand River Valley. When you resume your walk down the gravel road, towards the skeet club in the valley, listen carefully. These forests contain breeding Acadian Flycatcher, Blue-gray Gnatcatcher, Yellow-throated Vireo, Cerulean Warbler, Chestnut-sided Warbler and American Redstart. Yellow-billed Cuckoo and Yellow-breasted Chat have also been found along the continuation of this forest west of the township road. Pied-billed Grebe and Wood Duck are on the lakes along the ridge west of the road. Northern Bobwhites and Gray Partridges are sometimes found in nearby fields.

To return to Cambridge, either retrace your route or take a longer circle route. The directions for the latter are as follows: Continue south on the road you are now on until it stops at Highway 24A on the edge of Paris. Turn left onto 24A; travel down into the town centre. Turn left at the main intersection and cross the bridge over the Grand River. Turn left again at the first

Scarlet Tanager

street and follow this road along the east side of the river all the way back into Cambridge.

The Crieff Bog–Puslinch Wetland is a rich and diverse swamp complex with a decidedly northern flavour. The coniferous swamp and other wetland types, marsh sedge meadow, spring and river, serve as the headwaters of the Fletcher Creek.

Drive south from 401 along Highway 6, 2 km from Morriston to the first road to the west. Take it and drive west to the first road; turn left onto this gravel road and head down towards the swamp. Turn left again into the conservation area parking lot at the edge of the forest. In 1981, 70 species of breeding birds were found in the immediate vicinity. North of the parking site, an old gravel pit has been set up as a long-term natural regeneration research project. North and east of the pit, many sparsely vegetated old fields contain large numbers of Grasshopper Sparrow. In addition, Savannah, Vesper, Chipping, Field and Song Sparrows are all commonly found. Upland Sandpiper occurs here and in the fields south of the railroad tracks. Watch for several pairs of Indigo Buntings that live along the hedgerows.

Immediately south of the parking lot, in various portions of the swamp, breeding birds to be found include Sharp-shinned and Broad-winged Hawks; Long-eared Owl; Brown Creeper; Alder Flycatcher; Black-and-white, Nashville and Mourning Warblers; Northern Waterthrush; White-throated Sparrow; and Swamp Sparrow. In the deep swamp south of the YMCA camp, south of the county line on the next road south, Swainson's Thrush and Canada Warbler have been seen.

The wetlands are best known for their rare plants, including Showy Lady Slipper (hundreds), Yellow Lady Slipper, Bog Candle Orchid, Calopogon, Loesel's Twayblade, Round-leaved Sundew and Pink Pyrola.

East of the parking lot, a fine upland wood is easily reached by a well-marked walking trail. Birds of mature forest occur, such as Great Horned Owl, Hairy Woodpecker, Great Crested Flycatcher, Eastern Wood-Pewee, Blue Jay, Red-eyed Vireo, Wood Thrush, Ovenbird, Scarlet Tanager and Rose-breasted Grosbeak. In some years, Pine Warbler has been heard singing in the tallest White Pines.

In 1976 Ontario Hydro constructed the large powerline through the swamp, west of the road. Both Blue-winged and Golden-winged Warblers breed in the shrubbery under the powerline south of the railroad tracks. Veeries also sing in this area.

Walk the railroad tracks immediately south of the swamp to find the sedge meadow and marsh complex. This is a nesting area of Virginia Rail, American Woodcock and Common Snipe. In some years Sedge Wrens have appeared in late June and stayed to breed. It is also the best area to see and hear Swamp Sparrow. Black-billed Cuckoos are frequent in the drier spots. Purple Finches have occurred in the swamp forest south of the tracks and Eastern Phoebes have nested in the culvert under the tracks.

PAUL F. J. EAGLES

Niagara River

The Niagara River is 56 km long and is the international boundary between Canada (Ontario) and the United States (New York). The river connects Lake Erie to Lake Ontario and has an elevation difference of 99 m. This elevation is most prominent at Niagara Falls, where the fall of water at the Canadian Horseshoe Falls is 54 m and 56 m at the American Falls.

The Indian names of "Onguiaahra" and "Ongiara" appear on early maps and mean "The Strait" or "Thunder Falls." By the time the first white man arrived, the name Niagara was in general use, no doubt derived from these Indian names.

The river, which can be covered in one long day from Toronto, is a must for fall birdwatchers. The principal attraction is water birds which congregate from mid-October until late December. It is possible to observe almost all of the waterfowl species of eastern North America along with late-migrating shorebirds, loons and grebes. The chief item, however, is the gulls – up to 14 species have been recorded in a single day. To date, 19 gull species have been observed on the river. Bonaparte's, Ring-billed, Herring and Great Black-backed are abundant, while Little, Iceland, Glaucous, Thayer's and Lesser Black-backed are found on most days. Black-legged Kittiwake and Franklin's, Black-headed and Sabine Gulls make brief annual visits. Laughing, Mew and California are occasional and there are three records of Ivory Gull. The first Ontario Slaty-backed Gull was spotted here in 1992 as was a Ross's Gull in 1995.

The river provides a good source of fish for the birds with numerous small species, as well as larger fish sucked into the hydro turbines to be chopped up into small morsels, ideal gull food.

Birding Features

Begin the trip at Niagara-on-the-Lake, reached via Highway 55 leaving the Queen Elizabeth Way east of St. Catharines. As you enter Niagara-on-the-Lake, Highway 55 turns into Mississauga Street and ends at Queen Street. Turn left here and continue along the lakeshore (Queen Street turns into Niagara Boulevard) until you reach Wilberforce Drive. The feeders along this street (especially at 8 Wilberforce) are excellent sites for Tufted Titmouse, Carolina Wren and the usual nuthatches, siskins, redpolls, goldfinches and woodpeckers. Return to Niagara-on-the-Lake via Niagara Boulevard and Queen Street. On the way, go towards the lakeshore at every opportunity; you will eventually reach Front Street. Front becomes Ricardo Street. South of the marina off Ricardo, several laneways lead to the river. It is best to come here near sunset from November to February when the gulls head out to roost on Lake Ontario. On peak days thousands of Bonaparte's Gulls pass by. In the same community, Shakespeare Avenue and its crossroads are good year-round for Tufted Titmouse, Red-bellied Woodpecker, Carolina Wren and in winter Pine Siskin and others. During spring and fall migration this area can be very rewarding. Also the 16.6 ha Niagara Shores Conservation Area along Lakeshore Road lies less than a kilometre west of Shakespeare Avenue. Here look for Red-bellied and Red-headed Woodpeckers and Tufted Titmouse, with a possibility of Hoary Redpoll with the Common Redpolls.

Queenston. The Boat Launching Ramp is accessed off Princess Street Park in the upper lot; walk down the path to the lower lot at water level to watch gulls feeding on the river. This is the best place to find Little Gull among thousands of Bonaparte's. Both Franklin's and Sabine's Gulls are possible. Return to the upper lot and walk the path heading south along the river. About halfway to the visible Queenston-Lewiston Bridge ahead, you will arrive at a clearing between the path and the river. This is the best spot on the river to look for Black-headed Gull.

Sir Adam Beck Hydro Overlook. On the Niagara River Parkway directly above the generating stations, look straight down into the gorge to note the wing and tail patterns of the gulls foraging below. This is the place to find white-winged gulls including Glaucous, Thayer's and Iceland. The Lesser Black-backed is regular and Franklin's is seen occasionally. Mew, California and twice Ross's Gulls have been seen from here.

Whirlpool Rapids Overlook. Continuing up the Niagara Parkway, it is worth stopping at this overlook for the view alone. Mingling with the many feeding Bonaparte's Gulls may be an occasional loon, scoter or a Ross's Gull seen in 1995.

Niagara Falls/Gorge. Many water birds gather under the falls to feed on material deposited in quiet eddies. Among the common gulls look for Glaucous, Iceland, Thayer's, Lesser Black-backed and Little, as well as many species of ducks. Sabine's and Franklin's Gulls and Black-legged Kittiwake are almost annual, with two or three records of Ivory Gull seen from here. Double-crested Cormorant and Common Loon are frequent, and a Pacific Loon made a brief visit in 1995.

The Old Toronto Hydro Building. Overlooks to the north and south of the Hydro building, which sits above the falls opposite the Horticultural Greenhouse (free parking in winter and rest rooms), provide a wide variety of birds. Glaucous, Iceland, Little and Lesser Black-backed Gulls can often be found feeding or resting in the rapids. Rarities have included Purple Sandpiper, Harlequin Duck, Eurasian Wigeon, Barrow's Goldeneye, and Red-necked and Red Phalaropes.

The Old Pump House Building. The overlook behind this building, just south of the Old Hydro Building, provides a broader view of the rapids and a further opportunity to look for gulls and Purple Sandpipers (up to a dozen, with a few every winter). Several duck species may be here, including Gadwalls in the quieter waters close to shore.

Opposite the Pump House lies the 16.2 ha Dufferin Island Park. In late fall, milder conditions created by the proximity of the river and falls make it an excellent spot for lingering migrants and a fruitful place for vagrants.

The Control Structure. A short distance upstream from the Pump House are a series of gates used to control the amount of water flowing over the falls.

Almost any gull may be here. On the north (downriver) side, Little, Lesser Black-backed, Sabine and white-winged Gulls may be mixed in with large numbers of Bonaparte's. A Slaty-backed was on the breakwater here in 1992. Large numbers of diving ducks feed in the rapids, and a female King Eider spent a month in 1989. Purple Sandpipers may be spotted on the small islands.

On the south side of the control structure, large numbers of gulls rest on the breakwater. Beyond the breakwater, look for scaup and Canvasbacks that rest and feed with a few Redheads and Ring-necked Ducks. Less common sightings have included Eared Grebe, Parasitic Jaeger, Red-necked Phalarope and Snowy Owl.

Fort Erie. The drive upstream to Fort Erie along the parkway allows close views of many duck species. Canvasback, Redhead, Bufflehead, Common Merganser, Common Goldeneye, American Black Duck, American Wigeon, Greater Scaup and others are evident. In Fort Erie and west to Jaeger Rocks, just south of Old Fort Erie, the open waters, shorelines and even the grassy lawns collect birds blown down the lake. Most years Franklin's and Sabine's Gulls appear in September and October. Little Gulls and sometimes a Black-legged Kittiwake may appear in December and January with special vagrants.

MARTIN PARKER AND CHIP WESELOH
Revised by Kayo J. Roy

Long Point Region

Internationally recognized as a Globally Important Bird Area, a Ramsar wet-lands site and a UNESCO Biosphere Reserve, the Long Point region offers some of the very best birding in Canada. The Point is noted for its massive "fall-outs" of migrating songbirds, its huge numbers of staging waterfowl (includ-ing thousands of Tundra Swans), an impressive list of vagrants, and its many Carolinian breeding species. About 370 species have been recorded in the Long Point checklist area.

Because migration is a largely a weather-controlled, hit-and-miss phe-nomenon, you'll want to spend several days birding here. There are many very good local bed-and-breakfasts, while most of the motel accommodations are available in Simcoe and Tillsonburg, each about 40 km away. Excellent camping is available at Turkey Point and Long Point Provincial Park, and in some of the local conservation areas. But the best possible way to experience the birds of Long Point is to volunteer with Bird Studies Canada's Long Point Bird Observatory migration monitoring program.

Bird Studies Canada (formerly Long Point Bird Observatory) (BSC) is a nonprofit organization dedicated to research directed at the conservation of birds and their habitats across Canada. Its migration monitoring program at Long Point has been operating since 1960 and, with over 650,000 birds banded, is North America's most productive songbird banding operation. This program collects daily information on the numbers of all migrant birds at three field stations – at the tip of the point (the Tip), at another station about halfway out (Breakwater), and at one at the base of the point (Old Cut Field Station and Visitor Centre). From the banding and count data, population indices and trends are produced on an annual basis.

At the very least, you should drop by the Old Cut station to see the banding, chat with other birders to find out what's around, record your observations on the sightings board, and check out the Visitor Centre. The migration monitoring program is run largely by volunteers who come from all over the world to assist in the observatory's programs and experience Long Point firsthand. If you are interested in volunteering or learning more about volunteer opportunities and the program, contact the Landbird Program Coordinator at Bird Studies Canada/Long Point Bird Observatory, P.O. Box 160, Port Rowan, Ontario NOE IMO; phone (519) 586-3531, e-mail: lpbo@bsc-eoc.org or visit the Bird Studies Canada Web site at www.bsc-eoc.org, which supports an online weekly summary of bird activity as well as a complete review of BSC's programs. Also available is an annotated checklist of the birds of the Long Point region and a detailed bird-finding guide (complete with maps) for 44 of the region's hot spots.

Birding Features

LPBO's Remote Field Stations. Long Point is a natural lure for vagrants and rarities: American White Pelican; Tricolored Heron; Brant; Mississippi Kite; Gyrfalcon; Purple Gallinule; Willet; Franklin's and Sabine's Gulls; Say's Phoebe; Scissor-tailed Flycatcher; Carolina Chickadee; Bewick's Wren; Black-capped Vireo; Kentucky Warbler; Dickcissel; Varied Bunting; Gray-crowned Rosy-Finch; Cassin's, Le Conte's and Nelson's Sharp-tailed Sparrows; and Smith's Longspur. And then there's Snowy Egret, American Avocet, Curlew Sandpiper, Ruff, Black-headed and Franklin's Gulls, Band-tailed Pigeon, Chuck-will's-widow, Worm-eating and Kentucky Warblers, Blue Grosbeak, Hooded Oriole and Henslow's Sparrow. The list is seemingly endless and grows every year.

Long Point, extending 32 km into Lake Erie. The core area of the Long Point Biosphere Reserve is strictly managed as a nature reserve, so much of the point is off-limits to the general public. Access to the observatory's Tip and Breakwater field stations is by boat only, and even then, observatory participants must be content with a certain amount of confinement. Owing to the extreme fragility of the sand-dune ecosystem, nobody is permitted to walk onto the remote sections of Long Point without express permission from the management authorities. Trespassers will be prosecuted!

So the best way to experience the remote areas of Long Point and the true essence of bird migration is by participating in LPBO's migration program as a volunteer. Accommodations at the remote stations are available to those who can commit at least a week of their time. The program is very popular, so be prepared to book your visit several months in advance. There is a very small fee for those staying for periods less than a month, while long-term volunteers are provided with free food and accommodation. Even if you're not interested in banding but can help out in other ways, the observatory is happy to accommodate you. Data recorders, birders who can handle daily censuses and other observations, handy persons, artists and photographers are always welcome.

Big Creek Marshes. From the intersection of Highway 59 and Regional Road 42 just east of Port Rowan, drive 0.7 km south on Highway 59 to a pull-off on the west side, at the north end of the causeway. There are ponds on both sides of the road; the west pond is shallow and often has exposed mudflats, which attract a good variety of shorebirds, gulls and terns in late summer and fall. This is also a favourite area for Tundra Swans in the spring. The traffic on the Highway 59 Causeway is often heavy, so make sure you and your car are well off the road. Drive another 1.8 km south and park in the parking lot on the west side for a hike along the dykes of the Big Creek National Wildlife Area. Early in the morning or a little before sunset, there are apt to be large movements of herons, ducks and shorebirds over the marsh. You should see Black-crowned Night-Herons, but watch for some of the more unusual herons too. Great Egrets and Sandhill Cranes are increasingly regular. You might also find assorted bitterns, rails (perhaps a King Rail), Black Terns, harriers and all the marsh passerines. Across the highway from the marsh parking lot, be sure to scan the shoreline and bay for waterfowl, gulls, terns and shorebirds.

Old Cut Field Station. Old Cut Boulevard is 3.5 km east of where Highway 59 Causeway takes an abrupt bend towards the east, or two blocks west of the Long Point Provincial Park boundary in case you overshoot. The two-storey, grey board-and-batten building on the east side of Old Cut Boulevard is LPBO's third field station, and the only one that is easily accessible. There is a sign on the lawn, and parking is available in a lot across the street. Stop by to observe the banding operation and to find out what birds are around. Please do not disturb the mist nets or the birds in them. These nets are checked on a very regular basis by trained observatory personnel.

The Old Cut station area is a superb hot spot for passerines. This tiny area often turns up more than 100 species of birds in a single day. Rarities here have included Mississippi Kite; American Swallow-tailed Kite; Barn Owl; Acadian Flycatcher; "Lawrence's," Yellow-throated, Worm-eating, Swainson's, Kentucky and Connecticut Warblers; Summer Tanager; Lark Bunting; Clay-colored and Le Conte's Sparrows; and Yellow-headed Blackbird. The area is also good for Northern Saw-whet Owl in the fall.

Once you have explored the tiny woods here, walk up Lighthouse Crescent to Highway 59 and turn left towards the provincial park, checking the trees and lawns on either side, but please respect the privacy of the local residents and stay on the roadside.

Long Point Provincial Park. Located at the east end of Highway 59 on Long Point, the park is a great migrant trap for passerines. Northern Mockingbird, Ash-throated Flycatcher, White-eyed Vireo, Kentucky and Hooded Warblers, Yellow-breasted Chat, Summer Tanager, Lark Bunting and Henslow's Sparrow are among the rarities seen recently in the park. Sedge Wren can sometimes be found near the observation stand opposite the campground. In fall, Northern Saw-whet Owl can be found in the pine plantations, and there is often a good passage of accipiters overhead. While the lakeshore here is seldom interesting, it's worth a quick look (Snowy Plover has turned up here once).

Port Rowan. From Highway 59, take Regional Road 42 east to Mill Road. Drive north for 0.7 km, park in a pull-off on the right, and walk up into the fenced-in viewing area for the Port Rowan sewage lagoons. The lagoons can be excellent for ducks in the spring, especially Ruddy Duck, Northern Shoveler, Ring-necked Duck and Hooded Merganser. Because water levels are often high, numbers of shorebirds are usually low, but anything is possible. Ruff and American Avocet have been found here. From the lagoons, retrace your steps to Regional Road 42, turn left and drive into Port Rowan. The road bends sharply to the left at the marina. Stop and park in the large parking area overlooking the bay on your right and look for shorebirds and water birds down below. Drive one more block into "downtown" Port Rowan and turn east at Wolven Street, which later becomes Lakeshore Road (aka the Talbot Trail). There is another overlook of the bay about 0.5 km to the east. Again, it's worth stopping for waterfowl and gulls, but you'll find a scope handy.

Turkey Point. From Port Rowan, continue east on Lakeshore Road until you come to St. Williams. Turn left at Regional Road 16, and then immediately right, back again onto Lakeshore Road. There is a vehicle pull-off for a great overlook of the Turkey Point marshes 4.7 km east of Regional Road 16. A scope is an absolute necessity here, as there are often large flocks of distant waterfowl, shorebirds, herons, gulls and terns. Continue east for several kilometres to Regional Road 10 and you'll arrive at Turkey Point. This whole area, including Turkey Point Provincial Park, makes for excellent birding in every season. There is a large diversity of breeding species in the park and surrounding plantation forests. Check the bay and the Turkey Point shoreline at any time of year for water birds and shorebirds, but be prepared for masses of tourists along the beach in summer. The most productive shoreline area is along Ordnance Avenue. Follow Regional Road 10 south and turn right at the bottom of the hill. Drive 1.2 km and turn left at Ferris Street, then right at Ordnance Avenue. Explore the entire length of the beach up to the end of the road, where there is a restaurant and large parking lot. Bald Eagles can often be seen in trees west of the restaurant. Little Gulls are quite regular and often occur in impressive numbers in both spring and fall. This is also the best place to see Whimbrel in spring (between May 18 and 26).

Lee Brown Waterfowl Management Area. From Port Rowan, drive 4 km west of Highway 59 on Regional Road 42. On the south side is a large observation tower – it's not necessarily worth the climb, but it *is* worth checking out the small pond here, especially in spring for Eurasian Wigeons, and perhaps Snow Geese and Sandhill Cranes. A few kilometres farther west along Regional Road 42, look for the blue and white sign marking the Big Creek-Hahn Marsh Unit. Turn south and drive to the parking lot. A dyke affords a good view of the marsh. This spot can be good for Virginia Rails, Soras and sometimes a King Rail. Scan the distant dead trees for Bald Eagles.

Surrounding forests. No visit to the Long Point region is complete without visiting some of the area's outstanding forests. Among the most interesting is the

South Walsingham Forest (aka Wilson's Tract and Coppen's Tract), a large part of which is owned by the Long Point Region Conservation Authority and accessible to birders. North of Port Rowan, turn west from Highway 59 onto Regional Road 60, travel 3.5 km and turn south on the West Quarter Line. With over 100 breeding species, this is one of the region's best birding spots from mid-May through July. Along with the typical forest species, you should have no problem finding both cuckoos, Blue-winged and Golden-winged Warblers and their hybrids, Cerulean Warblers, Louisiana Waterthrushes and Hooded Warblers. With some luck you might come across Wild Turkey, Broad-winged Hawk, Pileated Woodpecker and Acadian Flycatcher.

Noted mostly for its spectacular Carolinian forest and rich diversity of breeding birds, Backus Woods (also owned by the Long Point Conservation Authority) can be accessed from Highway 24 via a well-hidden woodland parking area located 1.7 km east of Highway 59, or from the sand road (Concession IV) south of Highway 24. Highlights among the more usual breeding birds include Red-shouldered Hawk; Barred Owl; Cerulean, Blue-winged, Golden-winged and Hooded Warblers; and Louisiana Waterthrush. Prothonotary Warblers occur in wet years when the sloughs are full. Acadian Flycatchers are fairly regular and Pileated Woodpeckers are common.

Travelling 2 km east from Backus Woods on Highway 24, turn north at the East Quarter Line Road for 1.4 km, then east onto the sand road concession. Here is the St. Williams Forest, managed by the Ontario Ministry of Natural Resources. Like the others in the region, this forest has an exciting array of breeding birds. Much of it is a conifer plantation, which gives the site a distinct northern element to its avifauna. At the same time, it is also home to several Carolinian species. Drive the sand road and walk the network of forest trails and firebreaks (a compass may come in handy). A host of interesting birds can be found breeding here. Where else in Canada can you find Wild Turkey; Golden-crowned Kinglet; Blue-headed Vireo; Hooded and Pine Warblers; Red-breasted Nuthatch; Hermit Thrush; Yellow-rumped, Blackburnian and Cerulean Warblers; and Dark-eyed Junco nesting in the same contiguous forest? Look for Prairie Warbler at the northwestern end of the sand road, and for Louisiana Waterthrush in the swampy northeastern sections of the forest.

JON D. McCRACKEN
Revised by Jon D. McCracken

London and Area

London, lying 150 km southwest of Toronto, is the centre of a rich farming area at the more northerly limit of the Carolina forest. The Thames River and deciduous forests attract a wide variety of birdlife. South, on Lake Erie, Hawk Cliff witnesses the passage of thousands of raptors every year. An extensive series of walking trails leads through the parklands along the river.

Birding Features

London. Enjoy a variety of birds while in the city itself. Peregrine Falcon nests in the core. In migration, many species follow the river. Woodlands and parks in the Thames River Valley host typical nesting species. Invest in a city map to follow the directions below. The Thames Valley Trail Association maintains trails all along the river. Access points include many bridges and parks. Of particular note are Springbank Park and Greenway Park, along Springbank Drive West, and Fanshawe Conservation Park, which is at the east end of the city accessed from Clarke Road. Gibbons Park is located just west of St. Joseph's Hospital on Grosvenor Street. The north branch of the river from Adelaide Street on the north side of the river out to Highbury can be good for birds, especially migrants. Access is from bridges at either end. Meadowlily Woods is a good woods for seeing birds, especially during migration. Park along Meadowlily Road, which runs south of Commissioner's Road east of Highbury Road.

Two spots worth a visit are Westminster Ponds and Sifton Bog. The former is located behind the London Information Booth on Wellington Road South. Use the many trails in this conservation area to look for nesting and migrant birds. The bog is located on Oxford Street West, just west of Hyde Park Road. Park across at the Oakridge Mall parking area and walk over Oxford down into the trail and out on the boardwalk to enjoy the bog and its nesting birds. In season, migrants from the bogs in the north seem to like using this unique habitat in London.

Komoka Park Reserve. Located just west of London, the reserve stretches along the Thames River from Kilworth to Komoka. There are several entrances. Take Commissioner's Road west out of London (Byron) and it becomes Glendon Drive (previously County Road 14). The second road to the west from Byron is Gideon Road (formerly County Road 3), which goes to the south and then curves west. Take Gideon for about 3 km to a lane across from the Versa Care Nursing Home at Brigham Road. Park in the lot at the end of the lane. There are other access points farther down Gideon Road as well, including the Komoka Bridge at Komoka Road (formerly County Road 16), the first actual road on the right past those other spots. Another access is from Glendon Drive at Kilworth. You continue west on Glendon past Gideon for about 1 km to Kilworth and park in the parking lot beside a small old white house (which could be torn down by now) just off the south side of the road on the high ground before the river. The lakes at the intersection of Komoka Road and Glendon Drive provide waterfowl views during migration. If you're on Gideon, turn north on Komoka Drive and go to the intersection, but if you're on Glendon, continue west past Kilworth for about 5 km and you will see the lakes on the south side of the road as you get to the intersection with Komoka Road in Komoka. These lakes were made naturally by groundwater in old gravel pits.

About 100 species have been found nesting in the reserve. Specialties include Blue-winged, Louisiana and several other warblers, Pileated and Red-bellied Woodpeckers, and many others. It is also an important migration route. Follow the trails through a variety of habitats such as mature woodlands, riparian woods, overgrown pasture, open fields, wooded swamps and ravines. Ducks and other waterfowl stage at the old gravel-pit lakes. You will need a scope to help, as the lake is fairly large. Good hiking boots are essential.

Strathroy Sewage Lagoons. Go west from London taking Fanshawe Road, which becomes Egremont Drive (formerly Highway 22) to Hickory Road (formerly County Road 39) and go west on Hickory into Strathroy, where it is called Metcalfe Street. As you get past Caradoc Street, the road forks and you take the right fork. It is called Albert Street for a while, but it becomes Napperton Drive (formerly County Road 39) outside of Strathroy. Continue west until just past the Strathmere Lodge complex. Turn left on Pike Road and head south over the tracks to the second gate, where there is a small parking area. Although admittance is restricted, birders, but not their cars, are permitted. Use a scope to scan for waterfowl during migration periods; if the water is low, shorebirds are commonly seen, including phalarope, Stilt Sandpiper and yellowlegs when the water is low.

Sarnia Lighthouse. The site occurs in Sarnia, west about 85 km from London. On Highway 402 drive to the last turnoff at Bridge Street. Follow it to St. Clare and continue north across Michigan Avenue to Victoria Street. Turn left onto Victoria, then turn right at Fort Street. Proceed north to the water's edge. This spot is good for observing loons, geese, gulls and jaegers during the fall, especially in October and November with north winds.

Hawk Cliff. This special site is located at the end of Elgin Road 22 (Fairview Avenue from St. Thomas), on the Lake Erie shoreline. Coming from London, take Highway 4 south, turn east on Elgin Road 27 (Union Road) and then go south on County Road 22. After the stop at County Road 24, follow the "Hawk Cliff" signs straight to the lake. Public access is on the roadside only. Other public roads that go down to the lake can also be investigated. Bring a lawn chair as well as your binoculars.

In southern Ontario, hawks tend to follow the coast of Lake Erie during fall migration. At different times from September through November, most raptors, including some rare ones, will wing along the lake, particularly after a cold front has come through, when the wind is from the northwest. On the lake just east of Port Stanley, at one particular spot, called Hawk Cliff, you can watch as the birds fly right past, sometimes large "kettles" of a few thousand Broadwinged Hawks, sometimes steady streams of accipiters and some daytime migrating passerines. The Ministry of Natural Resources and Hawk Cliff Banders operate viewing weekends in September.

Starting in early September and continuing for at least the month, you can usually see Kestrel, Sharp-shinned Hawks and harriers flying by. By the second week in September, Broad-winged Hawk mass migration can occur. Watch at the end of September for Peregrine Falcon; in early October for Red-shouldered Hawk; Northern Goshawk and Golden Eagle in mid-month; and Red-tailed Hawk towards the end of the month. Migration can finish sometime in November.

Skunk's Misery. Located west of London, by about 40 minutes, this public land is worth the trip. Hooded, Cerulean and six other species of warbler, Pileated and four other woodpeckers, Acadian Flycatcher, and many other Carolinian species are found here. Every trip yields something. Follow Highway 2, Longwoods Road, west of London (Lambeth) to Wardsville, and turn north on Hagerty Road (formerly County Road 1), to Newbury. Go west on Concession Drive (formerly County Road 14), which is the first intersection in Newbury. The first road west on Concession Drive is Dogwood. The next is Sassafras. Between these roads, except for a small farm on the south side of Concession Drive, all the forest, approximately 220 ha of sand plain and swamp forest, is public land and can be accessed by any of the fire and logging roads that enter from that whole block of land, to Centreville Road, which is the next road south from Concession Drive. Other forested areas nearby are public and private property, all accessed by the same type of path or lane. Obey signs for posted areas and ask permission where possible. There will be a need for waterproof boots and insect repellent, depending on the season.

PETE READ
Revised by Pete Read

Rondeau Provincial Park and Nearby Spots

Rondeau, a sand spit projecting approximately 8 km into Lake Erie, contains the largest stand of southern hardwood left in Ontario. Some 337 species of birds have been recorded here, with 136 found breeding. Come here to find Prothonotary Warbler and Red-bellied Woodpecker, as well as numerous land and water birds. Look for thousands of Broad-winged Hawks on migration and other birds of prey, plus an excellent potpourri of warblers, including Worm-eating, Northern Parula, Cerulean, Kentucky and Hooded. The rich forest and other habitats harbour a diverse plant life, with more than 850 species recorded, including some 68 that are quite rare to Ontario.

The 3254 ha park lies southeast of Windsor-Detroit, 22 km south of Highway 401 at Interchange 101. There are opportunities to boat, canoe, fish, camp, hike and cycle; there are also 8 km of bathing beach. Commercial accommodation may be found in nearby Chatham, Blenheim and other summer resorts.

The park has a major interpretation program and a variety of natural-history displays. Write Park Naturalist, Rondeau Provincial Park, R.R. 1, Morpeth, Ontario NOP 1X0; phone (519) 674-1768 or (519) 674-1750.

Birding Features

The southern hardwood forest, extensive marsh and shallow harbour make Rondeau a must for active birders, both during migration in April-May, September-October and in the nesting season of late May and June.

Bates Marsh, with water and marsh on both sides of the road, lies 4 km south of Chatham-Kent Road 3, on Chatham-Kent Road 15. Stop and scan the wet areas for water birds, especially Mallard, teal and herons. At low water levels, shorebirds use the mudflats on migration. Look for Killdeer, yellowlegs, Dunlin and dowitcher. Continue another kilometre to the park.

About 1 km inside the park, look for the picnic ground. The Marsh Trail entrance sits just off the main road on the right. This 7 km biking and hiking trail begins by winding through the edge of an oak forest bordering on the marsh. During migration, numerous warbler species are spotted. The marsh, at this point, is usually not frozen in early spring and thus attracts various species of waterfowl and shorebirds. The southern half of the trail provides excellent chances to spot Great Blue and Green Herons; Black-crowned Night-Herons; Least and American Bitterns; the park's resident Bald Eagle; Virginia Rail; Sora; Forster's, Common and Black Tern; and Marsh Wren.

To reach the spicebush walking trail, go back to the main road and south for another 1.4 km. This trail takes you through a beech-maple forest, with spicebush understory. Warblers and other woodland birds are common in spring. Reconnoitre for nesting Wood Duck, Black-billed Cuckoo, Red-headed Woodpecker nesting along the western side of the trail, Red-eyed and Yellow-throated Vireos, Common Yellowthroat and Northern Cardinal.

The Tulip Tree Trail begins beside the Visitor Centre. To reach it, continue south from Spicebush Trail along the main road for 2.3 km to Gardiner Avenue, and follow it to the Visitor Centre. The trail penetrates a pine-oak forest and then a beech-maple stand. In addition, there are several sloughs that are crossed via boardwalks. Check out the trees for Tulip, Sassafras, Shagbark, Hickory and Black Walnut. Nesting birds include Wood Duck, Hooded Merganser, Yellow-billed and Black-billed Cuckoos, and Great Crested Flycatcher; Winter Wrens have nested; Prothonotary Warblers nest in the adjacent sloughs. A Pileated Woodpecker is often seen or heard.

Around the Visitor Centre, look and listen for American Woodcock and Whip-poor-will. The feeders are usually stocked throughout the year, so check for various woodpeckers, including Red-bellied, and for nuthatches, orioles, sparrows and finches.

Take the Lakeshore Road from the Visitor Centre south to the entrance of the South Point Trail. This trail leads through an open Black Oak forest to the shore of Lake Erie and then north through a beech-maple forest. Many of Rondeau's rarest bird records have been seen from this trail, including Sage Thrasher; Yellow-crowned Night-Heron; Yellow-throated, Swainson's, Kirtland's and Townsend's Warblers; Harris's and Henslow's Sparrows; and Bewick's Wren. In May watch for rare southern warblers, including Worm-eating, Northern Parula, Yellow-breasted Chat, Cerulean, Hooded and Kentucky. Birds that nest include permanent residents such as Carolina Wren, and Great Horned Owls and Eastern Screech-Owls. Acadian Flycatcher can be found and Brown Creeper, Blue-gray Gnatcatcher, Indigo Bunting, Yellow-throated Vireo and Wood Thrush are typical along the trail. The most common warblers are Yellow, Common Yellowthroat and American Redstart. Open grassy areas and edges often have sparrows passing through, including Lincoln's and Clay-colored, while Song and Swamp Sparrows are long-term residents and will nest.

The South Point Trail serves as access to the South Beach, a narrow sand barrier beach separating the south end of the park's forest, marsh and bay from Lake Erie. Here you may find thousands of migrating waterfowl. Shorebirds, marsh birds, gulls and terns are also numerous. Look for Herring, Ring-billed and Bonaparte's Gulls. Rare species such as Black-headed, Franklin's, Laughing and Little Gulls periodically appear, and southern herons such as Little Blue and Tricolored are most frequently observed from this vantage point.

The Morpeth Cliffs are great for viewing waterfowl spring and fall, and migrating hawks can be abundant in the fall. To reach these cliffs, leave the park and continue northeast along the road that follows the Lake Erie shoreline (Chatham-Kent Road 17) for about 5.5 km. Park safely off the road at the point where it turns away from the lake towards Morpeth, and enjoy the view looking down on the waterfowl and up to the hawks.

P. ALLEN WOODCLIFFE
Revised by P. Allen Woodcliffe

Point Pelee National Park

Point Pelee is widely regarded as one of the best places to experience bird migration in all of North America. This distinction can be largely attributed to its geographic position. It is situated on the north shore of Lake Erie, near its western end. Each spring, this triangular-shaped peninsula is one of the first landfalls that weary wings strive for after crossing the lake. Later, in the fall, its shape also functions by concentrating southward migrants before they depart for warmer destinations. In all, the Pelee birding area boasts almost 370 species of birds. In fact, it is not unusual to see between 25 and 30 species of wood warblers on a good day during peak migration in spring. However, of the approximately 90 species that actually stay to nest, only 7 or 8 are warblers. In late August and September look for the multitudes of Monarch Butterflies as they put on a show en route to their wintering grounds in Mexico.

Not only is Point Pelee the southernmost place in mainland Canada, it also recently (1999) acquired, with the generous help of the Nature Conservancy of Canada, the southernmost location in all of Canada, Middle Island. This tiny 19 ha piece of land sits almost exactly on the international border, south of Pelee Island. Even though both pieces of land rest as far south as the northern boundary of California, they boast an array of flora and fauna typically found farther south. Highlights include Canada's only Wild Hibiscus, the Pink-flowered Swamp Rose Mallow, Prickly Pear Cactus and shrubs such as Hoptree and Spicebush. Point Pelee is also one of the only places in Canada to see Eastern Moles, or at least evidence of their underground burrows. A flash across your car headlights at night may very well indicate the presence of the recently reintroduced (1993/94) nocturnal Southern Flying Squirrel. No venomous snakes are present in the park.

Major transportation links to the park can be found in Windsor or Detroit, located about 50 km to the northwest along Highway 3. Those wishing to visit in May should look for accommodations well in advance, preferably six months or more. Motels are found in Leamington and other nearby communities. Campsites in the park are restricted to educational groups only, but several commercial campgrounds are located in the immediate area.

A variety of park activities are offered throughout the year, but without exception the largest and most popular is the Festival of Birds, held during the month of May. In collaboration with the Friends of Point Pelee (FOPP), daily birding walks, workshops and evening presentations are offered. For more information on the Festival of Birds, contact FOPP at (519) 326-6173, fopp@wincom.net, or try their Web site at http://www.wincom.net/~fopp For other park-related information contact Point Pelee National Park, 1118 Point Pelee Drive, R.R. 1, Leamington, Ontario N8H 3V4; phone (519) 322-2365, or check out their Web site at http://parkscanada.pch.gc.ca/pelee

Birding Features
Pelee offers the visiting birdwatcher a variety of habitats to explore, from the beach at the tip to Hackberry-dominated woods and maple swamps, Red Cedar savannahs and overgrown meadows. However, the largest habitat found in the park is the marshlands and wet meadows. They account for close to two-thirds of the 1566 ha peninsula. Because the park is so small, helping preserve the health and integrity of the entire ecosystem is an important goal. With this in mind, access to these habitats is restricted to the extensive network of trails. This not only provides migrating birds with added space to seek food and shelter, but also helps reduce any trampling on rare plants.

For many, the visitor centre is where the birdwatcher's day begins. Not only does it provide access to a variety of trails, it is usually a hub of activity, featuring high-class displays and dioramas as well as an up-to-date sightings book. The parking lot is an excellent location to look for raptors. In spring, Mississippi Kite, Black Vulture and Swainson's Hawk have all been recorded among more common species. In the fall, northeast winds help to funnel large numbers of Broad-winged Hawks into the park.

From the visitor centre, you can also take the "train" to the tip. This is the best place to see the spectacle of migration. Come early in the morning in spring and watch tiny dots on the horizon grow larger and make landfall. Many a rare bird has been discovered this way. Willet is a rare but regular spring visitor. Later in fall, thousands of migrating Blue Jays and Monarchs compete for attention. A close scan of the loafing gulls and terns can be rewarding, and shorebirds also favour the very tip. Moving north, the area between the tip and Loop Woods can be especially productive for passerines during migration. Waves of warblers, vireos, kinglets, flycatchers and thrushes all move through. Blue-gray Gnatcatcher and Indigo Bunting are abundant. Located nearby, the famous Sparrow Field does attract its namesake, but it is becoming increasingly shrubby. More productive places for the difficult-to-see sparrows are the west beach area near the train stop at the tip, the various beach parking lots, or the grassy fields south of the DeLaurier House. In addition to Grasshopper, Clay-colored, Le Conte's and Nelson's Sharp-tailed Sparrows, Pelee remains the most reliable place in Canada to find the endangered Henslow's Sparrow. During migration, beachside habitats can also produce other rarities such as Western Kingbird, Blue Grosbeak and, if you're really lucky, Kirtland's Warbler!

One of the most popular trails is the Woodland Nature Trail, located immediately south of the visitor centre. It passes through Hackberry woods, maple swamps and regenerating Red Cedar savannah. Watch for both Red-bellied and Red-headed Woodpeckers, Orchard and Baltimore Orioles, Carolina Wren, Scarlet Tanager, Rose-breasted Grosbeak, and a wide variety of warblers including Hooded, Prairie, Cerulean, Kentucky and Worm-eating. In both spring and fall, the woods can be alive with the sounds of scratching feet as hundreds of migrating White-throated Sparrows actively forage in the leaf litter. Even in winter, the Red Cedars provide shelter for hardy Yellow-rumped Warbler and Hermit Thrush.

Immediately north of the visitor centre, Tilden's Woods also offers excellent birding. In spring, the wooded sloughs attract Louisiana Waterthrush and Prothonotary Warbler, as well as Solitary Sandpiper. Sadly, Prothonotary Warbler has not nested here since the mid-80s. Green Herons are summer residents. Also watch for nesting White-eyed Vireos. The seasonal birding trail leading north to DeLaurier takes you through shrubby thickets and overgrown meadows. This is one of the best places to search for the Yellow-breasted Chat. On occasion, it even sings at night! If visiting during spring, stop at the DeLaurier parking lot at dusk to witness the impressive display flight of the American Woodcock. During the day, the DeLaurier area attracts Field Sparrow, Willow Flycatcher and Eastern Bluebird.

The observation tower at the marsh boardwalk provides excellent views of the Pelee Marsh. The best times to visit are at dawn and dusk when the retiring Least and American Bitterns are more apt to fly low across the reeds. Also look and listen for Virginia Rail, Sora, Common Moorhen, Marsh Wren and Black Tern. Swamp Sparrow and Common Yellowthroat are abundant.

Check picnic areas along west beach in spring, especially those south of the park gate. Because the woods here are narrow, they create a bottleneck for northbound migrants, thereby concentrating their numbers. Summer Tanager, Yellow-throated Warbler and Scissor-tailed Flycatcher have all been spotted moving past.

Immediately north and east of the park gate, extensive agricultural fields attract open country birds such as Horned Larks, American Pipits and in winter Snow Buntings. They also support migrating flocks of Black-bellied and American Golden-Plovers, Ruddy Turnstone, Whimbrel and, in late August and early September, Buff-breasted Sandpiper. Roosting gulls are not uncommon during the day.

Hillman Marsh Conservation Area, located approximately 5 km northeast of the gate, is an excellent place to observe spring waterfowl and herons. Most noteworthy are the nesting King Rails and Least Bitterns. Forster's Terns and Great Egrets are regular summer residents. Although unreliable of late, shorebirding can be exceptional when water levels in the marsh are low.

Wheatley Harbour is located about 3 km northeast of Hillman Marsh. The harbour offers the visitor a chance to observe gulls up close as they roost along the docks or fly back and forth following the fishing boats. Every few years a Laughing Gull is found among the noisy aggregations of Bonaparte's Gulls. Along the north shore, the long sandy beach can occasionally be productive for shorebirds during migration. Across the road from the harbour, the small wood lot bordering Muddy Creek is a good place to look for Great Egret,

Bobolink

Great Blue Heron and, less frequently, Black-crowned Night-Heron. Yellow-crowned Night-Heron has also been found here.

The drive from Wheatley to Leamington along Essex Road 34 passes Kopegaron Woods Conservation Area on the south side. This 19 ha mature swamp forest features a lovely loop trail that crosses over sections of boardwalk. In addition to seeing foraging groups of songbirds, look for Northern Waterthrush and Red-headed Woodpecker in May. Louisiana Waterthrush is a definite possibility. Late lingering Rusty Blackbird may also be found. Aside from the birds, this is probably the best place to see spring wildflowers in the area. Enjoy!

WILLIAM J. CRINS
Revised by Karl Konze

Georgian Bay Islands National Park

The islands in Georgian Bay, with temperatures buffered by surrounding waters of Lake Huron, lie in the transition between northern Canadian Shield and southern deciduous forest. Over 200 species of birds have been recorded, of which 75 to 100 are nesting.

Georgian Bay Islands National Park is one of the more recently established havens in our country. Thirty-five species of amphibians and reptiles provide the natural-history highlight for the islands. Otter, an occasional Fisher, Marten, Black Bear and Moose add to the experience.

The 67 islands making up the park are split into two segments. The east group lies over 100 km north of Toronto off Highways 400 and 69 and Muskoka County Road 5. The western group of islands is situated off the north end of the Bruce Peninsula, with access from Tobermory at the end of Highway 6. In summer, a water taxi or private boat is the only means of entry. In winter, cross-country skis, snowshoes or snowmobiles are used to cross the frozen bay. Sixteen different campsites are provided on the islands. Commercial accommodation may be obtained on the mainland. An interpretive program is offered. Write The Interpretive Service, Georgian Bay Islands National Park, Box 28, Honey Harbour, Ontario POE 1E0; phone (705) 756-2415.

Wye Marsh. On your way to the park, stop in at the nearby Canadian Wildlife Service interpretive centre at Wye Marsh near Midland. Naturalists are there to help you.

Bruce Peninsula. Straight west from Midland across Nottawasaga Bay, the Bruce Peninsula should be visited as part of your trip to the western group of islands in the national park. The "Bruce," with its rugged northern cliffs on the east side and coniferous forests adjacent to a gently sloping west shoreline, provides habitat for a wide selection of birds. It contains one of North America's finest displays of rare wildflowers, ferns and orchids.

Birding Features

Beausoleil Island, the largest of the group and the centre for interpretive activities, lies just off Honey Harbour. The island's west side contains a very complex mixed forest of ash, aspen, hemlock, cedar and fir. The most common nesting birds include Barred Owl, Red-breasted Nuthatch and Winter Wren. Twelve species of warbler have been recorded as nesting, including Magnolia, Black-throated Green and Canada.

The central southern section of Beausoleil Island includes a dense, closed-canopy hardwood forest. At least five species of woodpecker nest, including Pileated, Red-bellied and Red-headed. Six species of flycatcher are found regularly, including the Acadian Flycatcher, which has extended its range considerably north to this spot. Over 12 species of warbler are present, including the Cerulean. Three vireos are here too, including the Yellow-throated.

The north end of the island consists of rugged Canadian Shield habitat with scrubby vegetation such as White Pine, White Oak and ground juniper. In spring and early summer, common sounds of a Brown Thrasher, Yellow-rumped and Prairie Warblers, and White-throated and Song Sparrows are everywhere. Thermal air currents along the bay area are used by Red-tailed, Red-shouldered and Broad-winged Hawks, as well as by Turkey Vultures.

The waters and shoreline around and between the islands regularly host Great Blue Heron; Mallard; mergansers; Osprey; Spotted Sandpiper; Herring and Ring-billed Gulls; Common and Caspian Terns; and Belted Kingfisher. The occasional Double-crested Cormorant, Green Heron and Black-crowned Night-Heron are also noted.

LESLIE JOYNT

Algonquin Provincial Park

One of the largest (763,310 ha) provincial parks in Canada, Algonquin lies in the transition zone between coniferous forests of the north, and broad-leaved trees of south-central Ontario. Spruce Grouse, Gray Jay and Boreal Chickadee cohabit with Brown Thrasher, Wood Thrush, Baltimore Oriole, Scarlet Tanager and Indigo Bunting. Indeed, there are 266 species on the park's check-list, with 138 known to have bred and 90 species considered common. In some sites, more than 100 species nest within a 10 km block. Moose, White-tailed Deer, Black Bear, Wolf, Beaver and Otter are common.

The park lies 193 km north of Toronto via Highway 11 to Huntsville, and then Highway 60 east for 43 km to the West Gate. The East Gate lies 5 km from Whitney and is reached by travelling north on Highway 127 from Bancroft, or west along Highway 60 from Barry's Bay.

Eight campgrounds and three private lodges occur within the Highway 60 Corridor. Obtain park information brochures and a variety of publications on natural and human history themes at the gates or the museum bookstore. Publications, including *Checklists and Seasonal Status of the Birds of Algonquin Provincial Park* (not free) with abundance and seasonal-occurrence bar graphs, may be obtained by writing Algonquin Provincial Park, Box 219, Whitney, Ontario KOJ 2MO, or via the Algonquin Web Site (www.algonquinpark.on.ca). Phone (705) 633-5572.

Birding Features
Most birds recorded for Algonquin can be found along the 56 km Highway 60 Corridor between the West and East Gates. There are 13 nature trails along the route.

Begin at the West Gate. Proceed for 3 km to the Oxtongue River Picnic Ground. Check along the river for Black-backed Woodpecker, Gray Jay, Boreal Chickadee and Northern Parula. Listen at night for Northern Saw-whet Owl. The Whiskey Rapids Trail at Kilometre 7.2 may produce Belted Kingfisher, Spruce Grouse, Black-backed Woodpecker, Least and Yellow-bellied Flycatchers, Boreal Chickadee, Brown Creeper, Ruby-crowned Kinglet and several warbler species. On the Hardwood Lookout Trail at Kilometre 13.8 listen for Yellow-bellied Sapsucker, Pileated Woodpecker, Eastern Wood-Pewee, Wood Thrush, Black-throated Blue Warbler, Ovenbird and Scarlet Tanager.

The Mizzy Lake Trail begins at the junction of Highway 60 and the Arowhon Road, at Kilometre 15.4, and visits nine small lakes and ponds along an 11 km loop. The Wolf Howl Pond and West Rose sections are particularly good for American Bittern; Wood and Ring-necked Ducks; Hooded Merganser; Spruce Grouse; Common Snipe; Black-backed Woodpecker; Olive-sided, Yellow-bellied and Alder Flycatchers; Boreal Chickadee; Winter Wren; Rusty Blackbird; and Lincoln's Sparrow. This area can also be reached by driving up the Arowhon Road to the old abandoned railbed, turning right there and driving along the railbed to a locked chain gate; proceed on foot from there to Wolf Howl Pond.

Check the old airfield, accessible by following the Mew Lake Campground Road at Kilometre 30.6 past the campground office and woodyard to a parking lot (on the left). The old field habitat is good for breeding Merlin, Savannah and Vesper Sparrows and Bobolink, with Horned Lark, American Pipit, Le Conte's Sparrow, Lapland Longspur, Snow Bunting and Eastern Meadowlark present in migration.

The Trailer Sanitation Station at Kilometre 35.6 may produce American Bittern; Great Blue Heron; Wood Duck; Hooded Merganser; Olive-sided and Alder Flycatchers; and Chestnut-sided, Mourning and Canada Warblers. Try the Lookout Trail at Kilometre 39.7 for Broad-winged Hawk, Common Raven, Wood and Hermit Thrushes, and Dark-eyed Junco.

The Spruce Bog Boardwalk at Kilometre 42.5 is one of the most reliable sites for Spruce Grouse, particularly in April and May. Also look for Olive-sided and Yellow-bellied Flycatchers, Black-backed Woodpecker, Gray Jay, Boreal Chickadee, Hermit Thrush, Ruby-crowned Kinglet, and Nashville and Magnolia Warblers. The adjacent Sunday Creek Bog could produce American Bittern, American Black and Ring-necked Ducks, Common Merganser, Northern Harrier, Belted Kingfisher, and Swamp and Lincoln's Sparrows.

Stop at the Visitor Centre (Park Museum) at Kilometre 43 to see the magnificent habitat dioramas, and talk to a naturalist about current sightings. Gray Jays frequent the bare feeder here (visible from the viewing deck) from fall through spring.

At Kilometre 46.3, take the Opeongo Lake Road through spruce bogs and marshes. It can be excellent for Spruce Grouse; Black-backed Woodpecker; Olive-sided, Alder and Yellow-bellied Flycatchers; Boreal Chickadee; Swainson's Thrush; Lincoln's Sparrow; and Rusty Blackbird.

The same trip during winter in heavy seed years can produce large numbers of Evening and Pine Grosbeaks, Common Redpoll, Pine Siskin, and both Red and White-winged Crossbills. Be sure to check the feeders at the gates, Missesing Ski Trail and Visitor Centre.

RICHARD KNAPTON AND RON TOZER
Revised by Ron Tozer

Timmins to Jellicoe

Northern Ontario is famous for its mining communities, friendly people and good representation of northern birds, such as Great Gray Owl, Three-toed and Black-backed Woodpeckers and numerous warblers. With two main highways looping through the country, a visitor can spend an enjoyable week in late June viewing birds, spectacular floral displays and Moose.

These lands were roamed by Indians for thousands of years. The rivers and lakes were the routes for them and the fur traders travelling west. The railway was built after the discovery of minerals in the very early 1900s. Roads followed in the 1960s.

Timmins is an easy two-day drive north of Toronto by Highways 11 and 101, through North Bay. The good birding season of June also is the time for mosquitoes and blackflies. Commercial accommodation is available in various communities. Camping sites are fairly numerous at provincial parks and several private resorts. Stock up on food and other supplies at Timmins. Gas stations are few, located only at the major communities. Carry a spare gas can, extra supplies and a warm sleeping bag.

There is very little literature available on the area. Write Timmins District Office, Ministry of Natural Resources, 896 Riverside Drive, Timmins, Ontario P4N 3W2. Ask them to refer your letter to other district offices if the information you request is not in their jurisdiction.

Birding Features

The Riverside Inn at Timmins makes a good base from which to survey the surroundings. Northern Harriers, Common Snipe and Alder Flycatchers fly over the fields behind the parking lot; Lincoln's Sparrows sing nearby. To explore, begin at or before dawn at Kamiskotia Lake, on the west side of Timmins, about 15 km northwest of the inn on Highway 576. The dump, 1 km north of the lake, should have a serenading Hermit Thrush, Mourning Warbler and Dark-eyed Junco. A Common Loon may call. While Yellow-bellied Sapsucker drums, Winter Wren sings its silvery cascade and Northern Waterthrush calls from the burn at the turn in the road. South of the lake, a few Hermit Thrushes, numerous Swainson's Thrushes and a Veery will sing. A dozen different warbler species twitter along the route, with Tennessee, Nashville, Magnolia, Ovenbird and Mourning being the most common.

Slip up to Cochrane, north about 80 km on Highway 11. Ask the local people for directions to Lillabelle Lake, which lies 5 km north and east of town. In 1957 the following birds were reported: Common Loon, Red-necked Grebe, American Bittern, Mallard, American Black Duck, Blue-winged Teal, Ring-necked Duck, Lesser Scaup, Ruddy Duck, Osprey and Solitary Sandpiper.

Highway 101 will take you west to Foleyet. About halfway along this road from Timmins watch for Half-way Restaurant. A short distance farther west, look for the bog where dead trees stand across the road from a big sand bank. A Black-backed Woodpecker nested here. About 16 km east of Foleyet you'll see the Mooseland Resort, with a few rooms and meal service. Accommodation is limited, so book ahead.

Continue west and stop regularly to listen for from 15 to 17 warbler species. Rarities include Northern Parula and Wilson's Warbler. Listen for Olive-sided Flycatcher, Red-breasted Nuthatch, Ruby-crowned Kinglet, Evening Grosbeak and Lincoln's Sparrow.

Continue west on Highway 101 beyond Foleyet for about 10 km, watching for Merlin. At the large burn area with skeletons of tall birch reaching above the new growth of cherries and birch, locate the bridge across the narrows of Burntwood Lake. You should be able to spot Common Loon families; listen to the Hermit Thrush; list the different warblers and Lincoln's Sparrow. Farther west, you'll pass The Shoals Provincial Park and cross the Prairie Bee River, where the variety of marsh life is unequalled in this part of Ontario.

Approaching Wawa, watch for the spectacular canyon that contains an outlier population of Indigo Buntings, together with Winter Wren, Ruby-crowned Kinglet and Northern Waterthrush. Stop at the Husky gas station and restaurant about 10 km north of Wawa on Highway 17; listen and scan for birds.

At White River there are several motels along Highway 17. Those on the south side of the road have marshes with Blue-winged Teal; perhaps Ring-necked Duck; Common Snipe displaying; and Lincoln's Sparrow singing. The Shell restaurant overlooks a small lake with a variety of waterfowl and Cliff Swallows for you to watch while breakfasting. A small colony of Bobolink adds to the effect.

Between White Lake Provincial Park and Highway 614 you will find Gloria's Motel, a bit quieter than those at White River. The forest around Gloria's and the lake across the highway south of the motel make for good birding. Turn north onto 614 and continue towards Manitouwadge.

Manitouwadge contains one motel of the same name. Reserve in advance. A Barred Owl has been spotted across the lake north of town; about 10 km north of town by the side of the Industrial Road, check for a Great Gray Owl, usually in young growth following a burn or clear cut.

This is the road for woodpeckers. Watch for Common Flicker, Pileated Woodpecker, Yellow-bellied Sapsucker, or Hairy Woodpecker, all drumming and nesting. A nesting pair of Black-backed Woodpeckers has been noted at the marsh with dead firs, about 20 km north of the town along the Industrial Road. At this spot also search for Ring-necked Duck, Hooded Merganser, Rusty Blackbird and Olive-sided Flycatcher.

Turn west onto Highway 11 to Longlac. There are several good motels both here and farther on at Geraldton. Longlac, at the north end of the very long Long Lake, sits by an extensive marsh on the north side of the highway. At this point a bridge spans a narrow neck of water. Stop for American Bittern, Black Tern and other marsh birds. Late May is the time for shorebirds on the beach on the south side of the highway. Try driving north on the sideroad about 3 km east of Longlac off Highway 11. You may spot a Great Gray Owl from 5 to 10 km north on this road. Hermit and Swainson's Thrushes are common along this road.

Go back to Highway 11 and drive east to Klotz Lake Provincial Park, about 20 km east of Longlac. There are good camping facilities here. This is about the wildest section along Highway 11, a "hot" area with good chances for Spruce Grouse, a scolding Solitary Sandpiper, Bonaparte's Gull, Black-backed Woodpecker, Yellow-bellied Flycatcher, Bohemian Waxwing, Bay-breasted

Warbler, Wilson's Warbler, Rusty Blackbird, Evening Grosbeak, Purple Finch and Pine Siskin.

Now proceed west towards Geraldton. Beyond Suckle Lake, a few kilometres west of Longlac, look along the north side of the road for the small clearing and longhouse by the lake and an extensive alder swamp. Cliff Swallows nest under the eaves of the house; listen for a Yellow-bellied Flycatcher and Connecticut Warbler near the alders.

The Park Bay View Motel, a few kilometres east of Geraldton, lies across a small lake from a good camping area. Nearby lakes boast a good variety of waterfowl, and the wet spots approaching Geraldton are good for shorebirds in season.

Farther on at Jellicoe, stay at the Cedar Shores Motel, which is quiet between arrival and departure of aircraft. The nearby lakes contain a variety of waterfowl, including Common Goldeneye. Mourning Warblers are common along the highway. There are northern outliers of populations of Scarlet Tanager and Rose-breasted Grosbeak.

DR. J. MURRAY SPEIRS
Revised by Dr. J. Murray Speirs

Marathon: North Shore Lake Superior

Lake Superior's north shore, at Marathon, offers opportunities to spot both species of Three-toed Woodpecker as well as large numbers of Rough-legged Hawks and a wide diversity of shorebirds on migration. In June a vast collection of orchids is waiting to be found.

Marathon lies 302 km east of Thunder Bay on the Trans-Canada Highway 17. Pukaskwa National Park sits to the southeast and Neys Provincial Park to the west. Both parks harbour remnant herds of Woodland Caribou. Several campgrounds are available along the highway. A variety of motels occur in town and along the highway. All services are available, as many hunters and fishermen use the area regularly. Topographic maps are available in Marathon. Ask for map 42 D/gw Marathon and 42 D/15 Coldwell.

Birding Features

The most productive area in town lies on either side of the CPR line, southward for about 3.2 km to Escort Ridge. These grassy meadows, birch, willow and poplar stands are bounded on the west by the lake shore and on the east by a high glacial ridge. Survey carefully in fall for a mix of passerine species and such rarities as Townsend's Solitaire, Blue-winged Warbler and Cassin's Sparrow. The Peninsula Golf Course and high school playing fields are particularly good for shorebirds such as Buff-breasted Sandpiper.

The 60 m high Escort Ridge is a good place to spot migrating birds in fall. Access to the top lies along the trail just west of the scree slope in an adjacent forest area. The commanding view provides an excellent opportunity to watch tens of thousands of winter finches on their way west and numbers of hawks, including hundreds of Rough-legged.

Day tripping from Marathon is suggested. The two largest stretches of continuous sand beach on the Canadian north shore of Lake Superior are accessible from here: the Pic River mouth and Neys Provincial Park. Both areas also provide habitat for resident Spruce Grouse, Northern Goshawk, both Three-toed and Black-backed Woodpeckers, Gray Jay and Boreal Chickadee. The beaches host migrating shorebirds.

To reach the mouth of the Pic River, go 6.4 km south of Marathon to Highway 627 (Heron Bay Road); continue south 10.4 km through part of the Heron Bay Indian Reserve to the mouth of the river. The bridge over the Pic River, connecting Heron Bay Road to the north end of Pukaskwa National Park, lies 1.6 km north of the mouth of the river. The actual river mouth is partly owned by the American Can Company but access is not restricted. However, remember to respect private property.

Neys Provincial Park lies about 24 km west from Marathon on Highway 17. Here you should search for resident Spruce Grouse, Northern Goshawk, both species of three-toed woodpecker, Gray Jay and Boreal Chickadee. In late May and June the woods are full of thrushes, vireos and warblers. Fall migration may bring such rarities as Summer Tanager and Western Kingbird.

The two abandoned fishing communities of Jackfish and Coldwell act as bird oases, with unique habitats foreign to most of the typical Superior shore-line. These include sand beach with adjacent long-grass meadows and open scrub deciduous growth. These sites provide excellent foraging and staging opportunities for migrating sparrows. Many stray species, including Northern Wheatear, have also stopped here on their travels.

To reach Coldwell, drive on Highway 17 about 4 km east of the Neys Provincial Park gate, to the east side of the Coldwell peninsula. To reach Jackfish, drive west along 17, watching for the Prairie and Steel Rivers. About 3 km west of the Steel River bridge, look for a road leading southwest to the CPR line and the timber loading yard. Leave the car in the yard and walk about 1.2 km west along the tracks to the site of Jackfish.

J. ROBERT NESBIT

Rainy River–Lake of the Woods

The Rainy River–Lake of the Woods region is an area unique to birding in Ontario. This small parcel of cultivated land, sandwiched between the boreal forests of Manitoba, Minnesota and Ontario, attracts western birds in numbers and variety found nowhere else in the province. Black-billed Magpie, Sharp-tailed Grouse, Marbled Godwit, Western Meadowlark and Brewer's Blackbird can be found in the scrubby pastures and hayfields. Le Conte's Sparrow, Sedge Wren, Sandhill Crane and Yellow Rail frequent the large wet meadows and marshes. American White Pelicans and Double-crested Cormorants nest on isolated islands on Lake of the Woods, as have Piping Plovers and even American Avocets.

To reach the area, drive west from Fort Frances on Highway 11 or south from Kenora on Highway 71, which meets 11 east of Rainy River. Topographic maps Rainy River 52D/15 and 52D/10 Scale 1:50,000 will help. Gas stations are few and far between, and most of the roads are gravel.

Accommodations are available at the Roadrunner Motel in Rainy River. Other motels are found in Baudette, Minnesota, across the river. Light-housekeeping cabins may be rented at Oak Grove Camp and Windy Bay Lodge. Lake of the Woods Provincial Park on Highway 621 has campsites, as do Camp of the Woods and Oak Grove Camp, both near Rainy River.

Birding Features
Begin at the Rainy River sewage lagoons. Turn north off Highway 11 on the sideroad just east of the railway station. After crossing the railway tracks, you'll see a dirt road to the left. The lagoons are a few hundred metres down this road. Shorebirds and ducks are present in migration, and in late May up to 1000 Wilson's Phalaropes have been counted.

Return to the sideroad and turn left (north); drive to the first crossroads (1.3 km); turn left again and travel 1.5 km, to where there is an aspen wood lot on your left and open fields to your right. These fields produced singing Sprague's Pipits in June of 1980 and 1998. The wood lot holds Connecticut Warblers and Eastern Bluebirds in breeding season.

Another 0.5 km to the west, you'll come to Highway 600, the main north-south road of the region. Turn north and drive slowly, watching the fields and fence rows for open-country species such as Western Kingbird and Western Meadowlark. In breeding season it is a good idea to stop often and listen. Upland Sandpipers are heard more often than seen; Sprague's Pipits were dis-covered in this fashion.

Drive north on Highway 600 for 3.2 km, to River Road; turn west, and after 1.6 km you'll pass an ill-defined crossroad. The grassy track to the north leads into willow and alder thickets which yield a Golden-winged Warbler in late May and June.

Approximately 6 km to the west of Highway 600, you'll reach the Rainy River. River Road follows the river north from here for a short distance.

Going north from the river, you'll pass through extensively cultivated fields which hold large flocks of longspurs in early spring. These should be scanned carefully for rare species. Check the area around the Microwave Tower for Black-billed Magpie, Sharp-tailed Grouse and Western Kingbird.

Approximately 4 km after leaving the river, turn left to cross Wilson Creek, then almost immediately turn north again. You can also turn right and follow the Wilson Creek Road to Highway 600. This road is excellent for Sandhill Crane, Le Conte's Sparrow, Sharp-tailed Grouse, Sedge Wren and sometimes Short-eared Owl. Turn around and retrace your route to Wilson Creek. North of Wilson Creek 1.8 km, a road runs west to Oak Grove Camp, which lies on the bank of the Rainy River. Look for Hill's Oak, a species rare in Ontario.

Back on the River Road, go north 2.5 km until it turns east for 2 km, then north for 0.8 km and then finally east again. At this second right turn, the fields on either side of the road usually contain feeding flocks of blackbirds, includ-ing Brewer's and Yellow-headed. Sandhill Cranes are often heard or seen flying to the north at this point.

Drive east 6 km; you'll rejoin Highway 600 at the point where the highway makes a 1.6 km jog to the east before the road turns north again. Two kilometres north of this left turn in the highway, you'll see a grassy clearing on the left (west) which often contains Sharp-tailed Grouse. A further 6 km north, you'll come to a sideroad leading to the west. Watch for the old white schoolhouse at the intersection. This dirt road runs 5 km to the lake, where you'll have an excellent view of Sable Island just across the inside channel. The extensive sedge marshes to the south have had Yellow Rail, Le Conte's Sparrow and Sandhill Crane.

Returning to Highway 600, continue north for 1.6 km. The highway turns east here but you'll want to continue north on the road which leads to the lake and the government wharves. Scan the lake for American White Pelican.

Back at the stop sign at Highway 600 where it goes east, turn right on the gravel road heading west. Travel as far west (2.6 km) as you can before turning north to the lake (another 1 km). The road eventually ends at a rocky hill. Park and walk over the hill to a windswept view of the Lake of the Woods. The forest here is known as Budreau's Woods and produces a variety of migrants in the spring and fall. In the spring when conditions are right, hawks migrate overhead as they follow the shore of the lake north. A path through the woods leads to Budreau's Beach, which runs off in a crescent to the southwest. The beach is often good for shorebirds in migration. Around a rocky point, visible at the far end of the beach, you'll have a fine view of the north end of Sable Island. The land here is privately held. Please obtain permission before crossing. This is another spot for waterfowl concentrations in the spring.

In May and June, scan the beaches of the island for shorebirds, gulls and rare species such as American Avocet and even Black-necked Stilt. Later in July thousands of Franklin's Gulls loaf on the beaches of the island. It's best to allow a good deal of time to cover this spot as it's one of the best sites in the region.

Return to Highway 600 and take it east for 11.6 km to Highway 621. Lake of the Woods Provincial Park is located 5 km to the north on Highway 621. Campsites are available there. Highway 621, to the south of its junction with Highway 600, runs through several kilometres of boreal forest offering such northern species as Common Raven, Gray Jay, Boreal Chickadee and occasionally three-toed woodpeckers.

You'll eventually return to Highway 11 by travelling straight down Highway 621. Here you turn west (right) to return to Rainy River. All the sideroads between Highways 621 and 600 can prove fruitful. Continually scan the wood lots and fields for Black-billed Magpies. They have nested along Worthington Road 3, which is three sideroads east of Rainy River.

Another important spot worth checking is the Highway 600 marsh, which borders Highway 600 for 2 or 3 km. The best access point is 13.5 km north of Highway 11. The marsh has been dry for several years due to effective drainage ditches but still produces Sharp-tailed Grouse, Le Conte's Sparrow and Sedge Wren in late May and June. To the east lies a large tamarack bog. Sandhill Cranes have been heard calling from the bog and may nest here. As well, in April of 1982, two Great Gray Owls were heard calling at this spot.

RON RIDOUT
Revised by Dave Elder

South James Bay: Moosonee–Moose Factory–Shipsands Island

The "true north" for the Ontario birder, Moosonee lies about 18 km upstream from the mouth of the Moose River on James Bay. Northern birds abound in the tidal marshes of lower James Bay and the adjacent complex of fen-bog muskeg.

Indians have been here for centuries, utilizing the game. The Hudson's Bay Company in 1673 established a post on Moose Factory Island, which became a major fur rendezvous centre. There was a succession of intense struggles between rival fur companies at this site. Nothing remains of the original structures today except a blacksmith shop and powder magazine of the early 1800s.

No roads lead into the area. Access in summer is by train, a four-and-a-half-hour excursion from Cochrane. The train leaves Cochrane at 8:30 A.M. Saturday to Thursday and departs Moosonee at 5:15 P.M. June 27 to September 7. Telephone (705) 472-4500 for reservations. Cochrane sits on Highway 11, north of North Bay and Timmins. Air flights from Timmins are daily, except Sunday.

Visitors will find accommodation at three lodges in Moosonee. Contact the Ministry of Industry and Tourism (see above) for names and addresses. Camp at Tidewater Provincial Park. Water taxis or freighter canoes will take you to both Moose Factory Island and the park.

Information and bird checklists are available from Moosonee District Office, Ontario Ministry of Natural Resources, Box 190, Moosonee, Ontario POL 1Y0.

Birding Features

The two villages, the tracts of boreal forest and the variety of extensive fen habitats provide fine northern birding opportunities. During migration in late April and May and again in August and September, the townsite contains hordes of Horned Larks, White-crowned Sparrows, Lapland Longspurs and Snow Buntings; an occasional Northern Wheatear is often seen. From May through October, regularly encountered birds include Merlin; Osprey; Spruce, Ruffed and Sharp-tailed Grouse; Black-backed and Three-toed Woodpeckers; Gray Jay; Common Raven; Boreal Chickadee; Winter Wren; Swainson's Thrush; Ruby-crowned Kinglet; Philadelphia Vireo; Black-and-white, Tennessee, Orange-crowned, Yellow, Magnolia, Yellow-rumped, Palm and Wilson's Warblers; Northern Waterthrush; American Redstart; Evening and Pine Grosbeaks; Purple Finch; White-winged Crossbill; and White-throated, Fox and Lincoln's Sparrows.

In winter look for the three grouse species, Black-backed and Three-toed Woodpeckers, Northern Hawk Owl, Great Gray and Boreal Owls, Common Raven, Northern Shrike, Pine Grosbeak, both redpolls and White-winged Crossbill. Willow Ptarmigan are present along the coast and at some inland locations in variable numbers.

During spring migration, water birds include Common Loon, Brant (Atlantic race), Snow Goose (including blue phase), Canada Goose, Oldsquaw, all three scoters, several species of ducks, jaegers, Bonaparte's Gull, and Common and Arctic Terns. In the fall, the area hosts one of the world's most extraordinary goose hunts. Along the tidal flats of James Bay, hundreds of thousands of geese stop to feed on the way from the far northern breeding grounds. Hunters fly in (in numbers nearly as great as the geese) to harvest their quotas.

A trip to the river mouth, 19 km away, and the Shipsands Island migratory bird sanctuary can be made via motorized canoe. You can also see the adjacent coastal marsh areas of the James Bay shoreline by canoe. In summer this marsh and adjacent willow-alder complex will produce a variety of ducks, Merlin, Sandhill Crane, Yellow Rail, Common Snipe, Greater and Lesser Yellowlegs, Marbled Godwit, Wilson's Phalarope, Bonaparte's Gull, Philadelphia Vireo and Le Conte's, Nelson's Sharp-tailed and Savannah Sparrows.

The coastal marshes host vast flocks of Snow Geese and an occasional Ross's Goose during migration. Several species of duck are common, including Mallard, American Black, Green-winged and Blue-winged Teals, Northern Pintail, Northern Shoveler, American Wigeon and Lesser Scaup. Spectacular shorebird concentrations occur during spring and fall passage. Common species include Semipalmated and Black-bellied Plovers; American Golden-Plover; Ruddy Turnstone; Whimbrel; both yellowlegs; Red Knot; White-rumped, Least and Semipalmated Sandpipers; Dunlin; Short-billed Dowitcher; Sanderling; Marbled and Hudsonian Godwits; and Wilson's Phalarope. Never common, but fairly regular during migration, are Red-necked Grebe, Northern Goshawk, Golden and Bald Eagles, Gyrfalcon, Peregrine Falcon, Stilt and Buff-breasted (fall) Sandpipers, Red-necked and Red Phalaropes, all three jaegers, Little Gull and Black Guillemot.

PAUL PREVETT

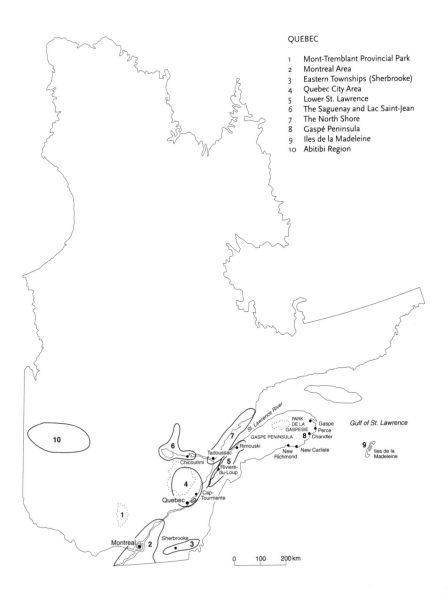

QUEBEC

1 Mont-Tremblant Provincial Park
2 Montreal Area
3 Eastern Townships (Sherbrooke)
4 Quebec City Area
5 Lower St. Lawrence
6 The Saguenay and Lac Saint-Jean
7 The North Shore
8 Gaspé Peninsula
9 Iles de la Madeleine
10 Abitibi Region

QUEBEC

Quebec, with major international air, sea and land connections, is among the most easily reached places where marine and boreal hard-to-locate species can be found. Those of particular interest that can be ferreted out quickly include Northern Gannet, Razorbill, Common Murre, Black Guillemot and Atlantic Puffin, all at Bonaventure Island. Both three-toed woodpeckers, the Boreal Chickadee and Bicknell's Thrush may be spotted frequently in several places near major centres.

The province has three distinct regions. The farmlands of the St. Lawrence Lowlands lie adjacent to the St. Lawrence River, which cuts southwest-northeast through the province. The Appalachian Uplands are part of a chain that extends from the Gaspé Peninsula into the eastern United States as far as Alabama. These uplands include the Eastern Townships (east of and adjacent to Montreal), with peaks as high as 1268 m at Mont Jacques-Cartier in the Chic-Chocs in the Gaspé. This high country hosts mountain birds and even caribou. The third area, the Laurentian Plateau, covers four-fifths of the province and lies north of the St. Lawrence and Ottawa Rivers. Characterized by rounded rocky elevations and many lakes, these lands are covered with boreal forests in the south, grading to tundra in the north.

Quebec has a multitude of islands, including an archipelago, Iles de la Madeleine, in the Gulf of St. Lawrence. This group of islands offers a unique opportunity to observe sea and land birds in a beautiful setting.

Quebec is Canada's largest province, covering 1,356,797 km². The north boundary is Hudson Strait and Ungava Bay; James and Hudson Bays are on the west; the Gulf of St. Lawrence lies on the southeast. The offshore waters make seabird watching very attractive. Inland, the lowlands of the St. Lawrence Valley grade upward into the Appalachians of the Gaspé, and the rolling boreal hills and flatlands north of the St. Lawrence provide a wide selection of habitats in which birds may be sought.

May is the month of migration. Coming to visit at that time, you can see birds moving towards the Arctic, while local species are setting up breeding territories. Make your visit for marine species from June 24 through July.

Winter birds move south into the settled country, so come then for the boreal hard-to-find species.

One of the top birding areas in the province is the Gaspé Peninsula, where both boreal and seabirds are found easily. The many ferries that ply the St. Lawrence River provide a visitor with both fresh-water and marine species. If you come from May through mid-July, stop at Westmount Summit in Montreal to look for easily accessible and abundant species. Mont-Tremblant Park, north of Montreal, is an excellent spot to look for the many eastern warblers during the nesting season. The largest concentration in the world of the greater subspecies of Snow Goose is found at Cap Tourmente, east of Quebec City, in spring and fall.

In a half day in Montreal you can easily get up to Westmount. If you have a full day, go north to Mont-Tremblant Park for those warblers. You can do Cap Tourmente in a half day out of Quebec City. The Gaspé needs at least three full days once you arrive there, since the best birding is at the far eastern end. You may have to wait in Percé a few days before you can get over to Bonaventure because of bad weather and/or rough seas. Similarly, it takes three days for Iles de la Madeleine, plus two days' travel time each way from Montreal.

You can e-mail or telephone the following birders, who offer assistance to visitors:

Pierre Bannon (Montreal): pbannon@total.net (514) 766-8767
Richard Yank (Montreal): rfyank@ibm.net (514) 457-1116
Guy Zenaitis (Montreal): gzenaitis@videotron.ca (514) 256-8118
Mabel McIntosh: (514) 695-5576
Dona Gail Gaudet (Iles de la Madeleine): donagail@cancom.net
Felix H. Hilton (Montreal): hiltonfh@total.net
Michel Bertrand (Montreal): bertrmi@colba.net (450) 649-2364
Nelson Roy (Saint-Hyacinthe): nellus@ntic.qc.ca
Normand David (Montreal): ndavid@netrover.com
Pierre Poulin (Gaspé): oiseaux@globetrotter.qc.ca

The following are Web sites containing information about birds in Quebec:

Rare Birds of Quebec maintained by Nelson Roy. Rare birds seen recently in the province: http://www.ntic.qc.ca/~nellus/hotbirds.html
Birds of Quebec by Denis Lepage. An information page about birding in Quebec: Numerous links. http://www.ntic.qc.ca/~nellus/quebangl.html
Quebec Checklist with status (partly bilingual): http://www.ntic.qc.ca/~nellus/listann.html
The Province of Quebec Society for the Protection of Birds maintained by Eve Marshall: http://www.minet.ca/~pqspb/

Maps of the province and any tourism information may be obtained from the Quebec Tourist Office, 1001 Dorchester Square (between Peel and Metcalfe) in Montreal. Telephone: 1-800-363-7777 (toll free). They also have a Web site at http://www.tourisme.gouv.qc.ca/

Very serious birders will want to buy the *Quebec Road Atlas* (255 pages) published by La Cartothèque and available in most bookstores for $26.95. The Canadian Automobile Association (CAA) may also provide information. Their Web site is at http://www.caa-quebec.qc.ca/

MABEL McINTOSH
Revised by Pierre Bannon

Mont-Tremblant Provincial Park

Set in the Laurentian Mountains, Mont-Tremblant is an excellent place to locate many of the eastern warblers and such boreal species as Black-backed Woodpecker, Gray Jay and Boreal Chickadee.

The 3200 km² park lies about 145 km north of Montreal. Take the Laurentian Autoroute No. 15 to St-Faustin and watch for signs to the park as you drive north through the community of Lac Superieur. There are several campgrounds in the park, with motel accommodation in adjacent communities. Massive hills, deep valleys, waterfalls and lakes and streams make this a popular vacation site. A variety of hiking, skiing and snowmobile trails provide easy access to the woods.

Birding Features

In summer, when the woods of Montreal are quiet, come up here to look for many eastern warblers. Once inside the park, drive north along the main road for a few kilometres before stopping to listen and search. About 27 km north of the gate, look for the path to Lac Tador to locate Spruce Grouse, Yellow-bellied Flycatcher and Rusty Blackbird. If you don't find Spruce Grouse, continue on to Lac Savane, where they are best found in August. At various spots, stop and ferret out Black-backed Woodpecker, Gray Jay, Boreal Chickadee, Olive-sided Flycatcher and various nesting warblers. Red and White-winged Crossbills have been infrequent visitors in summer.

MABEL McINTOSH
Revised by Pierre Bannon

Montreal Area

Montreal lies on the St. Lawrence River, along which a great variety of birds pass on migration. Ducks and geese are plentiful from late March to early May and again from late September to November. Waves of passerines also come through. Summer visitors would be advised to spend a day or two in the Laurentian Mountains, to the north, for boreal species and eastern warblers.

The Montreal area was first explored by Jacques Cartier in 1535; a fur-trading post was established by Samuel de Champlain in 1611; a settlement was founded in 1642. It remained under France's rule until 1760, when the British took possession.

Montreal is second in size only to Paris among French-speaking cities of the world. It lies immediately east of the northeast corner of Ontario. The Trans-Canada Highway runs right through the city, connecting it to both ends of the country. From the United States, Interstate 87 runs due north from New York to link up with Quebec's Autoroute 15 at the border.

Montreal is served by two major airports, Dorval and Mirabel. Dorval airport is located on the Island of Montreal, in Dorval municipality. The Mirabel airport lies farther north, some 30 minutes away from Montreal. Since September 1997, Mirabel has handled cargo and charter flights only; Dorval handles domestic, North American and international flights. The two main domestic airlines are Air Canada and Canadian Airlines. Both offer regularly scheduled flights between Montreal and most major cities.

VIA Rail Canada provides transcontinental rail service within Canada. VIA Rail's Montreal terminus will leave you at the downtown central station, situated at 935 de la Gauchetière Street West. Consult VIA Rail Canada at their Web site: http://www.viarail.ca/ or phone (514) 989-2626.

The Montreal Bus Central Station is at 505 de Maisonneuve Street East (corner of Berri). The Voyageur bus company has a Web site at http://voyageur.com/infoe.htm For access to places outside the Island of Montreal, call (514) 842-2281 for bus schedules and fares. For help and directions to access any of the Montreal Island sites by public transport, call the STCUM (Société de transport de la communauté urbaine de Montréal) at 514-AUTOBUS (288-6287) or consult their Web site at http://stcum.qc.ca/

For any other information, see the Montreal Official Tourist Information Web site at http://www.tourism-montreal/org/ The Montreal hotline telephone numbers are (514) 648-2400 for French and (514) 989-5076 for English.

We also suggest the site guide *Birdfinding in the Montreal Area*, by Pierre Bannon, published in 1991 by the Province of Quebec Society for the Protection of Birds (PQSPB) and the Centre de conservation de la faune ailée de Montréal.

Birding Features

Spring and fall are the best birding seasons for Montreal. Migrants begin arriving around the end of March and finish about early June. They return around mid-July and terminate in December. People from western Canada looking for eastern warblers, or those from south of the border interested in such boreal species as Spruce Grouse, Gray Jay and Boreal Chickadee, should go north to the Laurentians in summer.

Mount Royal Park. Mount Royal Park, located near downtown Montreal, was created in 1874 and today represents one of the largest remaining green spaces on the island of Montreal. It's best in spring, but the park and adjacent cemeteries provide ready access to a good variety of spring and fall migrants, as well as wintering birds.

By car, Mount Royal parking lots can be reached from the east via Camillien Houde Parkway at the corner of Mont Royal and Park Avenues, or from the west from Côte-des-Neiges Road. Check out the cemeteries as well.

By bus, take bus 11 from the Mont-Royal Metro station.

Westmount Summit Park. To the west of Mount Royal Park is a tiny wooded area owned and maintained by the City of Westmount. During the month of May, birders from across the province flock to this heavily used urban oasis to witness impressive concentrations of passerines that often pause here during migration. No fewer than 33 species of warblers have been sighted over the years.

By car, from Côte-des-Neiges Road, take Belvedere Road up Westmount Mountain (across from Remembrance Road). Turn right onto Summit Road and drive to Summit Circle, which goes all the way around the park.

By public transport, from Guy-Concordia Metro station take bus 66, 165 or 166 to Côte-des-Neiges and Belvedere.

Nuns' Island (Ile des Soeurs). Despite rapid loss of habitat to urbanization in recent years, the west end of the island still offers varied habitat. Pied-billed Grebes nest on the pond, Rusty Blackbirds and Northern Waterthrushes visit the moist woods in spring, owls and woodpeckers appear frequently in winter and Gray Partridges and an occasional Short-eared Owl inhabit the fields. Offshore, Red-throated Loons and Ring-necked Grebes are spotted annually. An impressive 283 species have been reported on the island over the years, including 34 species of warblers.

By car, go south on Decarie Boulevard (Highway 15) or the Bonaventure Autoroute. Just before the Champlain Bridge, take the Nuns' Island exit. Park at the end of Ile des Soeurs Boulevard.

By public transport, from LaSalle Metro Station take bus 12 to the end of Ile des Soeurs Boulevard.

Montreal Botanical Gardens. While most visitors are attracted to this 73 ha site by the exquisite floral displays, local birdwatchers have also found the Montreal Botanical Gardens of great interest. Spring offers a nice variety of migrating passerines, while feeding stations attract winter birds, and therefore raptors, in good numbers.

By car, from downtown Montreal, take Autoroute 40 east and Pie IX south, or Notre Dame Street East and Pie IX north.

By public transport, take the Metro to Pie IX station.

Morgan Arboretum. The arboretum is a sanctuary of 245 ha forming part of Macdonald College in Sainte-Anne-de-Bellevue at the western tip of the island of Montreal. It has the largest remaining wooded stands on the island, and a tremendous variety of trees, shrubs and plants, both native and exotic. Good birding is found in all seasons. Nesting species include Scarlet Tanager, Ovenbird and Pileated Woodpecker. During the fall, the arboretum offers one of the best sites in southern Quebec from which to observe raptor migration. The nearby Ecomuseum is also worth a visit.

Take Autoroute 40 west to Exit 41 towards Chemin Sainte-Marie. At the first intersection, turn left to the entrance.

Bois de l'Ile Bizard. The Bois de l'Ile Bizard Nature Park, one of the Montreal Urban Community's regional parks, occupies 178 ha on Ile Bizard. Varied habitat includes an extensive system of boardwalks and overlooks in the swamp, abandoned fields, mature Sugar Maple-beech forest and stands of White Cedar. A wide variety of birds is found here; Great Horned Owl and Red-shouldered Hawk regularly nest in the woods while Sora, Virginia Rail and Least Bittern are found in the marsh. In summer the park is heavily used by cyclists.

Take Highway 40 to Boulevard St-Jean North; continue to Gouin Boulevard and turn left (west). Follow signs to Ile Bizard Bridge. Cross to the north side of the island on Rue Centrale, turn right on Chemin du Bord du Lac. Watch for park signs.

Ile de la Visitation. This small regional park located along Rivière des Prairies at the north end of the island of Montreal is especially interesting to birders for its concentrations of large gulls in winter. In late afternoon, thousands of Greater Black-backed and Herring Gulls, accompanied by Iceland and Glaucous Gulls, congregate above the hydro dam to spend the night. The occasional Lesser Black-backed Gull has also been seen.

By car, take Highway 40 to Christophe Colomb-Papineau Avenue; turn north on Papineau Avenue; turn right onto Henri-Bourassa Boulevard, left onto Rue de Lille, right onto Gouin Boulevard and left into the parking area.

By public transport, from the Henri Bourassa Metro station, take bus 69 to Rue d'Iberville, and walk north for one block.

The LaSalle waterfront. The Lachine Rapids is one of the finest natural sites along the St. Lawrence River. Herons, ducks, gulls and terns abound at the bottom of the rapids. Eurasian Wigeon, Arctic Tern and Caspian Tern can be spotted in season. Wintering ducks are present in large number.

By car, this site is reached using LaSalle Boulevard. There is a municipal parking lot at the corner of 6th Avenue. Also check the bottom of the rapids at the corner of Fayolle Street to the north.

By public transportation, from the Angrignon Metro station, take bus 110 to the corner of Central and Bishop Power Streets. Walk to LaSalle Boulevard.

The Sainte-Catherine Locks. The St. Lawrence Seaway locks at Sainte-Catherine provide a splendid view of concentrations of waterfowl and gulls, as well as ships. Even in mid-winter a variety of ducks and gulls (including Iceland and Glaucous Gulls) frequent the fast-moving current, sometimes attracting a Snowy Owl or a Bald Eagle. Double-crested Cormorants are plentiful in season. Great Blue Heron, Black-crowned Night-Heron and Great Egret nests are visible among the taller trees on Heron Island, situated in mid-river across from the locks. Herons are known to have nested on this island for over 400 years!

By car (30 minutes from Montreal), take the Champlain Bridge, and then the first exit after the bridge towards New York State (No. 15 south / No. 132 west); take Exit 46 (LaPrairie/Salaberry) and turn right on to Marie-Victorin Boulevard. Drive 5.2 km and turn right at the Sainte-Catherine Locks. Or take the Mercier Bridge. At the south end of the bridge, take the left exit (LaPrairie-132 east), drive 6.5 km, turn left onto rue Centrale and go to Marie-Victorin Boulevard. The locks are a little farther on.

By public transport, call Les autobus Ménard (1-800-363-4543). They provide transportation from the Voyageur bus terminal (Berry/UQAM Metro station).

Longueuil Shoreline. Marie-Victorin Park is located 5 km east of Montreal in Longueuil, between Highway 132 and the south shore of the St. Lawrence River. The park offers bicycle paths and lookouts along the river. During spring, summer and fall, a walk along the shoreline can produce a variety of ducks, shorebirds and gulls.

By car (30 minutes from Montreal), take the Champlain, Victoria or Jacques Cartier Bridge south and Highway 132 east, or L.-H. Lafontaine Tunnel and Highway 132 west. The best spot for viewing is reached by a pedestrian over-pass off Marie-Victorin Boulevard, east of Roland-Therrien Boulevard.

By public transport, take bus 17 from Longueuil Metro station to Marie-Victorin Park.

Hudson and Saint-Lazare. With its 120 nesting species, Hudson is one of the most attractive summer birding sites near Montreal. Among the several points of interest, Aird's Pond, west of the village on Main Road, is highly recommended. Look for Finnegan's Market. Turn in and park near the road. This private property is available to birders, but be respectful. Check the pond, then turn right, walking along the railroad track. Check the marshy area on both sides of the track and the fields farther west. Green Heron and Sedge Wren have nested there in recent years.

Nearby Saint-Lazare has large stands of eastern White Pine and spruce hosting nesting Golden-crowned Kinglet, Hermit Thrush, Solitary Vireo, Cape May Warbler and Dark-eyed Junco. The pinery along Chemin Poirier is recommended.

By car (45 minutes from Montreal), take Highway 40 west and Exit 22 to Chemin Côte Saint-Charles. Drive north to Main Road and turn left for Finnegan's Market. To reach Chemin Poirier from Finnegan's Market, back-track to Chemin Côte Saint-Charles and drive south past Highway 40. Turn right on Chemin Sainte-Angélique and then left on Chemin Poirier. Parking could be a problem there.

Paul Sauvé Park, Oka. This provincial park is located northwest of Montreal along Lake of Two Mountains, just east of the village of Oka. Bordered by sandy beaches, marshes and the lake to the south, and by the Oka hills to the north, the 1800 ha park offers a wide diversity of habitat that has attracted 210 bird species. White Pine forest within the park is home to nesting Pine Warbler, while stands of Sugar Maple harbour Yellow-throated Vireo.

By car (45 minutes from Montreal), take Autoroute 13 north and Autoroute 640 west to the end. Turn right on Highway 344 to Oka village, where signs will direct you to the park.

Mount Saint-Bruno. Mount Saint-Bruno is one of the 10 Monteregian Hills that rise above the St. Lawrence Lowlands. It is recognized as one of the most beautiful and ornithologically productive sites in the Montreal area. Among the more unusual resident species are Turkey Vulture, Red-shouldered Hawk, Barred Owl and Pine Warbler.

By car (30 minutes from Montreal), take Jacques-Cartier Bridge, Taschereau Boulevard and Highway 116 to Autoroute 30; or Champlain Bridge and Highway 10 to Autoroute 30. Exit by Chemin des 25, and follow signs to the park.

Mount Saint-Hilaire. Mount Saint-Hilaire is also one of the Monteregian Hills and is easily reached by car. The mountain has been designated as a Biosphere Reserve by the United Nations, and much of the area is owned and managed by McGill University. A nature centre and interpretative programs are offered to the public. In recent years, nesting Peregrine Falcons and Common Ravens have been of special interest to local birders.

By car (45 minutes from Montreal), from downtown, take the Jacques-Cartier Bridge and Taschereau Boulevard to Highway 116 to Mont St. Hilaire village. From the west end, take Champlain Bridge and Highway 10 east to Exit 29. Follow Highway 133 north to the village. Once there, follow signs to the nature conservation centre: from Highway 116, take rue Fortier, then Chemin Ozias Leduc to Chemin de la Montagne. Turn left at Chemin des Moulins and then left to the Gault Estate.

Chambly Basin. This is an excellent site for grebes, waterfowl and gulls. Horned Grebe and Red-Necked Grebe are easy to find, especially in spring but also in fall. Small gulls are usually abundant in November and early December. Most are Bonaparte's but check for Black-headed, Little and Ross's Gulls as well as Black-legged Kittiwake, which have appeared in the last few years. Osprey is common in spring. An Ancient Murrelet caused great excitement in October 1998.

By car (45 minutes from Montreal), take Highway 10 east from Champlain Bridge and Exit 22. Drive north on Fréchette Boulevard, then turn right on Bourgogne Street at the basin. Park at Fort Chambly and walk behind the old fort to scan the basin.

Saint-Jean-sur-Richelieu. Like Chambly, Saint-Jean-sur-Richelieu lies along the Richelieu River to the south. This site is interesting mostly in late fall when migrating waterfowl stop upstream at the bridge over the river. Barrow's Goldeneye are seen annually, while an occasional Harlequin Duck shows up. Flocks of Bonaparte's Gulls could include an occasional Little Gull or a Black-legged Kittiwake.

By car (45 minutes from Montreal), take Highway 10 east from Champlain Bridge and Exit 22 towards Saint-Jean-sur-Richelieu. Drive south on Highway 35, then take the exit to Boulevard du Séminaire-Sud. At the traffic lights, go straight to the river and turn right on Champlain Boulevard. Soon you will see a parking area along the river on the left. Scan the river from there.

Saint-Paul-de-l'Ile-aux-Noix. The fields on the west side of the Richelieu River between Saint-Jean-sur-Richelieu and Saint-Paul-de-l'Ile-aux-Noix are flooded almost annually in spring, except after a very dry winter. Check the flooded fields from the many side streets between Highway 223 and the river. In early spring, look for waterfowl. Later in spring (May), check for shorebirds. Ruff and Marbled Godwit have been seen almost annually in recent years.

By car (60 minutes from Montreal), the directions are the same as for Saint-Jean-sur-Richelieu, but at the exit, turn right on Boulevard du Séminaire-Sud. This will lead you to Highway 223.

George H. Montgomery Bird Sanctuary at Philipsburg. This bird sanctuary is the PQSPB's pride and joy. It covers about 480 ha lying on both sides of Highway 133, between the village of Philipsburg and the U.S. border. Situated on the shore of Missisquoi Bay at a point where the foothills of the Green Mountains meet the plain of the St. Lawrence Valley, it includes samples of most ecosystems found in the region. Most species of birds occurring in southern Quebec and northern New England have been seen here. Among species generally uncommon in Quebec but regularly breeding here are Northern Rough-winged Swallow, Yellow-throated Vireo, Eastern Towhee and Field Sparrow. The beaver pond supports Wood Duck, Least Bittern, Sora and Virginia Rail. Golden-winged Warblers have nested in the sanctuary, and Cerulean Warblers have been found regularly. Recently, Tufted Titmice have been found nesting in the sanctuary. In late fall, stop at the Philipsburg wharf and scan the bay for rare gulls and jaegers.

By car (60 minutes from Montreal), take the Champlain Bridge from Montreal and Autoroute 10 east to Highway 35 south and Highway 133 south. At the flashing amber light in Philipsburg, turn left and drive 0.8 km on Chemin Saint-Armand. Turn right onto a gravel road that leads to a parking area. A $2 contribution is requested.

Hemmingford. This rural area, located near the U.S. border, is favoured by birders looking for Wild Turkeys. Nesting hawks and Clay-colored Sparrows also attract birders there. Wild Turkeys can be found almost anywhere along the secondary roads between Highways 15 and 219. Fisher Road is particularly good in this respect. Use the Cartothèque Road Atlas to find your way through all the secondary roads.

By car (45 minutes from Montreal), take the Champlain Bridge and Autoroute 15 south. Exit at Murray Road (Exit 13).

Beauharnois Dam. The area surrounding the Beauharnois hydroelectric station is one of the best anywhere in the region for observing gulls and terns. From September to January, concentrations have reached 20,000 birds, with all the common species (Ring-billed, Herring and Great Black-backed and others) and an astounding number of vagrants (including such rarities as Little, Mew, Ivory, Sabine's, California, Franklin's, Laughing, Black-headed and Lesser Black-backed Gulls) have been encountered. There are also ducks (including large rafts of scaup and mergansers) and shorebirds to be found.

By car (45 minutes from Montreal), from Montreal, take the Jacques-Cartier, Champlain or Mercier Bridge to Highway 132 west. The dam is just west of Beauharnois on Highway 132.

The next five sites are located within 10 to 15 minutes of the Beauharnois dam.

Maple Grove. This is the most reliable site in southern Quebec to see Caspian Tern. August is the best month. The Ile de la Paix Wildlife Sanctuary located offshore hosts nesting ducks, herons and a Double-crested Cormorant colony. The site is only 10 minutes from the Beauharnois dam.

From the Beauharnois dam, backtrack on Highway 132. After the sign for Maple Grove, turn left on Saint-Laurent Street and left on McDonald Street. Drive to the end and park near the playground on the right. Walk along the fence towards the shoreline. Look offshore for Caspian Terns.

Sainte-Martine Dam. This site located along the Châteauguay River is excellent for shorebirds from mid-July to late October. About 25 different species of shorebirds have been reported there, including Baird's and Stilt Sandpipers, Long-billed Dowitcher and Wilson's Phalarope, which are seen annually. Peregrine Falcons, Merlins and Ospreys are also fairly regular during this period. A good variety of southern herons have also been reported. This site is 15 minutes from the Beauharnois dam.

From the dam, backtrack east on Highway 132, turn right on Highway 205 and right again on Highway 138 until you reach Restaurant Grégoire on the right. Park behind the restaurant and walk to the shore. If coming directly from Montreal, take Mercier Bridge and Highway 138.

Saint-Étienne Marshes. Numerous ponds are maintained by Ducks Unlimited on the south side of the Beauharnois Canal. These ponds are interesting from early April till November for waterfowl, herons and shorebirds. Least Bitterns nest here. Huge concentrations of blackbirds roost here in the fall. The site is located within 10 to 15 minutes from the Beauharnois dam.

From the dam, backtrack east on Highway 132, turn right on Highway 236 and then right on Montée Saint-Joseph. After crossing the bridge, go straight on Rang Sainte-Anne to the end of the road. To get to the ponds, you have to go behind some farm buildings to the left of the road.

Saint-Timothée Marsh. This marsh, located 10 minutes from the Beauharnois dam, hosts a small heronry, nesting Common Moorhen and numerous ducks. In late summer, this is an excellent site to see Great Egrets, especially in the evening when they come to roost overnight. In recent years, Bald Eagles have also been regular in late summer. Willow Flycatchers nest in the willow clumps bordering the marsh.

From the Beauharnois dam, drive into the tunnel under the seaway, turn left at the garage on Rang Sainte-Marie. Drive 5 km to a small parking area on the left. Walk across the bridge to the marsh.

Saint-Louis-de-Gonzague Pond. This pond attracts thousands of Greater Snow Geese in late fall (mid-October to mid-November). Ross's Geese, Greater White-fronted Geese and Eurasian Wigeons can also be found. A Pink-footed Goose has caused excitement in recent years. This site is 15 minutes from the Beauharnois dam.

From the Saint-Timothée Marsh, drive south and turn left on Boulevard Pie XII. Park before the seaway near the bridge and walk on the gravel road going west along the canal. Scan the pond for waterfowl.

Dundee. Although rather distant and isolated, this spot is regularly visited by Montreal birders. The Lake Saint-François National Wildlife Area, a territory of 12 km² represented mostly by marsh lands, is one of the most remarkable birding sites in southern Quebec. Herons, ducks and rails are the main groups of birds to be found. Specifically, Great Egret, Yellow Rail, Willow Flycatcher and Sedge Wren should be looked for. Among the many points of interest, we recommend the Great Egret Trail, which takes you on a 3.7 km dyke surrounding a pond. This site is accessible from Highway 132, 0.8 km before reaching Point Fraser Road. This last road is also worth a visit. Finally, you will be delighted by Point Hopkins Road, but be careful, as it is private. This road has to be taken from the other side of the Salmon River in the United States. It winds through a vast marsh where Yellow Rails can be heard at night and, as expected, are very difficult to see.

By car (90 minutes from Montreal), from the south shore of Montreal, take Highway 132 West. From Ontario, this site is easily reached by crossing the river at Cornwall and taking U.S. Highway 37 East.

Baie-du-Febvre. This site, located on the south side of Lake Saint-Pierre, is one of the major staging areas for the Greater Snow Goose in spring. In recent years, counts have exceeded well over 200,000 birds in April. Ross's Geese and Greater White-fronted Geese have also been found annually in small numbers. Rough-legged Hawks are abundant in April and Ruddy Ducks nest in summer. After the departure of the geese in May, the wet fields attract shorebirds into the area. There is hunting in the fall.

By car (90 minutes from Montreal), take Autoroute 20 east to get onto Autoroute 30 east to Sorel. Once at Sorel, continue on Highway 132 east to Baie-du-Febvre. Do not forget to visit the interpretation centre in the village.

Saint-Barthélemy. Located on the north side of Lake Saint-Pierre, the site has flooded fields in spring, which are the main attraction. Large concentrations of waterfowl including Snow Geese are present in April. Shorebirds stop over in May. In late summer, check the Route du Fleuve along Lake Saint-Pierre for Great Egret.

By car (90 minutes from Montreal), from Montreal, take Autoroute 40 east. Take Exit 155 at Saint-Barthélemy and make your way to the sideroad that runs parallel to Autoroute 40 on the south side.

MABEL McINTOSH AND BOB BARNHURST
Revised by Pierre Bannon

Eastern Townships (Sherbrooke)

The region lies east of Montreal and south of Quebec City, near the U.S. border. Its mountains, lakes, forests and agricultural lands are home to 312 species of birds, of which 178 nest here. In addition to those found in the Montreal area, you may find some boreal nesters such as Black-backed Woodpecker, Gray Jay, Boreal Chickadee, Bicknell's Thrush and Blackpoll Warbler on the highest mountain tops.

Hotels, motels and campsites occur at Sherbrooke, the major centre. Mount Orford Provincial Park, 25 km west of Sherbrooke, offers good camping facilities in beautiful surroundings. For information on birding in this region, contact the Société du Loisir Ornithologique de l'Estrie, CP 1263, Sherbrooke, P.Q. J1H 5L7. We also suggest the following site guide (in French): *L'observation des oiseaux en Estrie*, by Denis Lepage, published in 1993 by the Société du Loisir Ornithologique de L'Estrie.

Birding Features

Lake Boivin Nature Centre. Located at Granby, west of Sherbrooke, the site consists of an extensive marsh covering the north end of the lake. An observation tower and several trails provide an overview of the lake and site. Waterfowl is

Red-shouldered Hawk

most abundant in spring and fall, while summer nesting birds include Least Bittern, Virginia Rail, Black Tern and Willow Flycatcher. A long list of rarities brings birders here.

Take Exit 74 from Autoroute 10 and drive north on Boulevard Pierre-Laporte. Turn left on Highway 112 and follow signs to the Nature Centre.

The Katevale Marsh. This site is located at the south end of Lake Magog. Nesting species include Green Heron, Marsh Wren, Least Bittern and many more water birds. A trail gives access to the marsh and a small island called Ile du Marais. An astonishing total of 226 species have been reported for this relatively small site.

Take Exit 121 from Autoroute 10 and drive south on Autoroute 55 to Exit 29. Follow Highway 108 east for about 1 km, then turn left on Chemin du Ruisseau. Follow the signs to the parking area.

Mount Orford Provincial Park. The park offers good opportunities to birdwatch while camping on the site. The woodlands host nesting species such as Yellow-throated Vireo, Pileated Woodpecker, Barred Owl, Common Raven and Turkey Vulture. A total of 65 km of trails offer opportunities to explore a diversity of habitats. Water birds occur on the ponds and lakes. Excellent sites lie at the north end of Etang aux Cerises and Etang Huppé.

From Autoroute 10, take Exit 118 and follow Highway 141 north to the park entrance.

Mount Mégantic. At an altitude of 1100 m, this mountain located 60 km east of Sherbrooke is one of the highest summits in southern Quebec. A road gives access to the top to explore a boreal forest and find Black-backed Woodpecker, Gray Jay, Boreal Chickadee and Blackpoll Warbler all nesting. This is probably the best place in southern Quebec to find Bicknell's Thrush. Visit here between mid-May and mid-July and preferably during the last two weeks of June for this thrush.

From Lennoxville just south of Sherbrooke, take Highway 108 east. At Cookshire, turn right on Highway 212 east. At Notre-Dame-des-Bois, turn left on Chesham Road. After 3 km, turn left and follow the signs to the observatory. The summit is 9 km from there.

PAUL BOILY
Revised by Pierre Bannon

Quebec City Area

Quebec City was founded in 1608 by the famous French explorer Samuel de Champlain. Four hundreds years later, Quebec City, with its obvious links to history, remains unique in North America. The cradle of French civilization in America, it is the only fortified city north of Mexico. Considered for a long time as a strategic post of prime importance, Quebec City overlooks the majestic St. Lawrence River, the route taken by discoverers, colonists, traders and armies heading for the heart of the continent. From Cap Diamant, a look to the east towards Ile d'Orléans and Cap Tourmente takes the imagination farther than the eye can see, to the river's end and the Atlantic Ocean.

Because the area is closer than Montreal to the St. Lawrence estuary and to the Canadian Shield, the birds found in the region reflect this diverse habitat. The region lies at the centre of the best birding spots in the province. By car, it is only 2 to 3 hours to the Lower St. Lawrence, the Saguenay–Lake Saint-Jean region and the Montreal area. Cap Tourmente, one of the top birding spots in the province, is where numerous species of birds converge from all other regions of the province.

Information about lodging and travelling is available from the Web site of the Greater Quebec City region at http://www.quebec-region.cuq.cq.ca/eng/otcle.html For bird information, write to Club des ornithologues de Québec, Domaine Maizerets, 2000 Montmorency, Quebec, P.Q. G1J 5E7. The hotline telephone number (French) is (418) 660-9089. We also suggest the following site guide (in French) *Guide des sites ornithologiques de la grande région de Québec*, by Pierre Otis, Louis Messely and Denis Talbot, published in 1993 by the Club des ornithologues de Québec.

Birding Features

Cap Tourmente National Wildlife Area. Located on the north shore of the St. Lawrence River 50 km east of Quebec City, this 2230 ha site was created in 1969 to protect staging habitat for Greater Snow Geese during migration.

The Cap Tourmente National Wildlife Area was recognized as a wetland of international importance (Ramsar site) in 1981, and is famous for the tens of thousands of Snow Geese flying in and out in spring and especially in fall. The area is home to 288 bird species, of which 125 nest.

The juxtaposition of the river, great coastal marshes, flatlands and mountains make Cap Tourmente a site of remarkable beauty, and opportunities for

Snow Goose

discovering and observing nature are endless at any time of year.

A visit to the interpretation centre is a good way to begin. From there a network of nearly 18 km of hiking trails of varying length and difficulty leads to the secrets of Cap Tourmente's birdlife. Some of the most interesting nesting species include Least Bittern, Peregrine Falcon, Yellow Rail, Sedge Wren and Nelson's Sharp-tailed Sparrow. The long list of rarities seen include Pink-footed Goose, Bean Goose, Ruff, Northern Wheatear and many others.

From Quebec City, take Highway 138. East of Sainte-Anne-de-Beaupré, turn south on Prévost Street and follow the signs. For information, write Cap-Tourmente National Wildlife Area, Saint-Joachim-de-Montmorency, Quebec, P.Q. GOA 3X0; phone April to October (418) 827-4591, November to March (418) 827-3776.

Parc des Grands Jardins. This park, situated about midway between Quebec City and Chicoutimi, is covered in boreal forest. Come here to spot both species of three-toed woodpeckers, Gray Jay, Spruce Grouse, Bicknell's Thrush, Blackpoll Warbler and other boreal forest specialties.

A driving loop is suggested to explore this park by car. A full day is needed. From Quebec City, take Highway 175 north. At the north end of Lake Jacques-Cartier, look for a small road to the right. Take it, and after about 25 km you come to Lake Malbaie. Scan the lake for ducks. White-winged Scoters nest here. From there, continue northeast, soon reaching Parc des Grands Jardins. Stop frequently. Spruce Grouse may be seen on the side of the road, especially in August. Scan the sky for a possible Golden Eagle. After 35 km, you reach Highway 381, which takes you to Baie-Saint-Paul. From there, proceed to Quebec City on Highway 138 west.

Ile d'Orléans. The site sits just east of Quebec City. Mudflats and surrounding waters at the western tip of the island are excellent for diving ducks, grebes and loons. Spring is the best time for Greater Snow Geese and Eurasian Wigeons.

From Quebec City, take Autoroute 440 or 40 to the bridge to Ile d'Orléans. Look for a small parking area near the south end of the bridge. At the western tip of the island, it is best to park on Horatio-Walker Street to check out the river.

Montmagny. Montmagny is situated on the south shore of the St. Lawrence, about 80 km east of Quebec City. Several thousand Greater Snow Geese gather each spring and fall near the wharf of this small municipality. A ferry takes the visitors to Ile aux Grues, off Montmagny, one of the best sites in the province to look for Yellow Rail, and also a good spot to locate Nelson's Sharp-tailed Sparrow and shorebirds.

From Quebec City, take one of the bridges to the south shore of the river and drive east on Autoroute 20, take Exit 378 and follow the sign to the wharf. The ferry crosses to Ile aux Grues only at high tide.

PIERRE BANNON

Lower St. Lawrence

This region extends from l'Islet-sur-mer to Matane along the south shore of the St. Lawrence River. Spartina marshes are typical along the coastline. Representative species include Nelson's Sharp-tailed Sparrow, Black Duck and Black-crowned Night-Heron. In spring, fields are crowded with Greater Snow Geese, Canada Geese, Brant and dabbling ducks. Common Eiders are omnipresent offshore, and it is not uncommon to find a King Eider. Red-throated Loons are also common in May, and shorebirds are abundant in late summer.

For the traveller heading to the Gaspé Peninsula, a number of sites are easily reached from Highway 132. Numerous birds, including shorebirds, are more easily found at half tide. Consult local newspapers for tide tables or consult these Web sites: http://www.pleinair-quebec.com/tables.html and http://www.chs-shc.dfo-mpo.gc.ca/chs_hq/nautpubl/PREDF.html

You can obtain information on birding in the lower St. Lawrence by contacting the Club des ornithologues du Bas-Saint-Laurent, P.O. Box 118, Pointe-au-Père, P.Q. G5M 1R1; Hotline phone number (French) is (418) 725-5118.

Birding Features

Rivière-Ouelle. This small village is located about 10 km east of La Pocatière. The wharf offers an excellent observation point to scan the river. In May, look for scoters, King Eider, Northern Gannet, Red-throated Loon, Parasitic Jaeger and Razorbill. The bay just west of the wharf is good for shorebirds and gulls.

About 3 km past Rivière-Ouelle, turn left from Highway 132 onto a small road leading to Pointe-aux-Orignaux, where you will easily find the wharf.

Cacouna. This small town sits about 10 km east of Rivière-du-Loup along Highway 132. This is probably the best place in the province for water birds. The number of rarities found there is very impressive and include Little Egret, European Golden-Plover and Garganey. Nelson's Sharp-tailed Sparrows and Yellow Rails nest.

From Highway 132, east of the town, two roads give access to the site. The first one leads to the Gros-Cacouna Harbour. From this road, scan the mudflat on the left-end side when the tide is low and inspect the basin on the right end side as well as the pond and the marshes beyond. The second road, which is about 2 km farther east, crosses wet prairies. At the intersection, the left arm goes to a pond and the right arm to the coastline.

L'Isle-Verte. This small village is about 15 km east of Cacouna. Standing at the wharf at low tide, note the extensive mudflat, which hosts a good mixture of geese, ducks and shorebirds in season. The mouth of the river on the left-end side is excellent for rare gulls.

From Cacouna, drive east on Highway 132. First stop at the bridge over the river just west of the village. In the village, turn left on the road leading to the wharf to scan the mudflat.

Trois-Pistoles. The mouth of the Trois-Pistoles River east of the town is excellent for shorebirds, but the main attraction here is the ferry crossing the St. Lawrence River to Les Escoumins on the north shore. In season, the probability of seeing birds such as the Northern Gannet, Black-legged Kittiwake, Razorbill, Arctic Tern, Parasitic Jaeger and Red-necked Phalarope is excellent. Northern Fulmar, Sabine's Gull, Greater Shearwater and Manx Shearwater are also possible but very rare. The crossing takes 65 minutes and the best time is from August through October. Take the return trip to increase your chance to see rarities. Consult the following Web site for information on schedule and fares: http://icrdl.net/basques/traverse/index.htm For reservations, phone Trois-Pistoles at (418) 851-4676 or Les Escoumins at (418) 233-4676.

From Isle-Verte, drive east on Highway 132 and follow the signs for the ferry.

Saint-Fabien. This site is well known for its excellent hawkwatching in spring. On a good day in April, Golden and Bald Eagles are often seen.

Saint-Fabien is about halfway between Trois-Pistoles and Rimouski. At Saint-Fabien, turn left on the road to Saint-Fabien-sur-Mer and stop at the rest area on the right to look for hawks migrating from the southwest to the northeast.

Rimouski. Ducks, geese, herons, shorebirds and passerines can be found at this site, which includes a 3 km long marsh just west of Rimouski. From Highway 132, take Rue des Vétérans to a small parking area after the railroad track. A 3 km long trail crosses the marsh between the observation tower and the mouth of the Rimouski River.

Pointe-au-Père. In late summer, this is one of the best sites in the province for shorebirds. The list is impressive and includes such rarities as Bar-tailed Godwit and Curlew Sandpiper. Seabirds are sometimes seen from the shore after a strong gale in fall.

Pointe-au-Père is 7 km east of Rimouski. Inspect the marsh from Highway 132 and along Chemin du Quai. Check from the tip of the wharf for seabirds.

PIERRE BANNON

The Saguenay and Lac Saint-Jean

This land of boreal forest is bisected by southern deciduous stands that follow along the Saguenay River. Such habitat variation results in a mix of southern and northern birds, with over 300 recorded. It is the northern limit for at least 20 species, including Black-crowned Night-Heron, Virginia Rail, Mourning Dove and Indigo Bunting. Several northern species come this far south, including Willow Ptarmigan in winter.

Lac Saint-Jean, over 30 km in diameter, sits about 400 km northeast of Montreal or approximately 200 km north of Quebec City. The almost circular lake was once a glacial trough and an arm of the sea. Missionaries, the first white men to come north, arrived here in 1647. A fur-trade post was built in 1676. Settlers finally arrived in the late 1840s. Many of their homes and churches remain today, the result of true craftsmanship.

Highways 40 and 155 will bring you in from Montreal; Route 175 takes you up from Quebec City. Several flights leave daily from both Montreal and Quebec City into Bagotville Airport, a 10- to 15-minute drive from Chicoutimi, the main city in the region. Bus and rail services are also available. A good number of hotels, motels, campgrounds, restaurants, service stations and other tourist amenities are present. Reservations are recommended for the peak season in July and August.

For information on birding in the Saguenay–Lac Saint-Jean region, write to the Club des ornithologues amateurs du Saguenay–Lac Saint-Jean, CP 1265, Jonquière, P.Q. G7S 4K8, or phone Germain Savard at (418) 543-1906. The local hotline (in French) is (418) 696-1868.

Birding Features

Peak times to visit the region include April 15 to May 20 and September 1 to November 1 for waterfowl; May 1 to June 1 and August 5 to October 20 for shorebirds; May 20 to June 10 and August 5 to September 20 for land birds.

Willow Ptarmigan generally reach the northern extremities of Lac Saint-Jean in small numbers each winter. In peak years they are abundant as far as the lake itself. To find this bird in winter, take the logging road north from Sainte-Monique, near Pointe Taillon on the north shore of the lake, north through Saint-Ludger-de-Milot for 150 km to Chutes-des-Passes. There are no services beyond Milot, so be sure you have spare car parts, warm clothing, emergency rations and lots of gasoline.

The Saguenay Valley is part of the migration corridor between James Bay, to the northwest, and the St. Lawrence River. Several western stragglers regularly get caught up on this route. Here Connecticut Warbler and Le Conte's Sparrow reach the eastern limit of their range.

The two following sites are highly recommended.

Saint-Gédéon. This small municipality is located off Highway 170 on the eastern shore of Lac Saint-Jean. The main attraction there is a highly productive marsh that hosts nesting Black Terns. The marsh has produced an impressive list of rarities over the years.

From Chicoutimi, take Highway 170. Once at Saint-Gédéon, take Chemin de la Plage towards the lake.

Saint-Fulgence. Saint-Fulgence is located 16 km east of Chicoutimi along Highway 172. Just south of town, a 3 km long, 0.5 km wide strip of shoreline provides one of the few suitable stopovers for waterfowl, and particularly shorebirds, passing through the valley. The area has produced over 200 species, including Yellow Rail and Nelson Sharp-tailed Sparrows. A nature interpretation centre has been built here.

To get there from Chicoutimi, take Highway 172 east.

RICHARD YANK

The North Shore

The north shore of the St. Lawrence River near the mouth of the Saguenay River is known worldwide for its whale watching. Shallow waters at the junction of these two rivers produce abundant shrimp and capelin, attracting scores of whales. A boat trip in August should provide Beluga, Minke, Fin, and possibly Humpback and Blue Whales. The area is part of the new Saguenay–St. Lawrence Marine Park. For information on the area, contact Parks Canada, 182 rue de l'Église, P.O. Box 220, Tadoussac, P.Q. GOT 2AO; phone (418) 235-4703.

Jacques Cartier visited in 1535 during his exploration of the St. Lawrence. Pierre Chauvin built Canada's first trading post here in 1600 as the headquarters for his fur-trading monopoly. The oldest wooden chapel left standing in North America, built in 1747, contains the bell from a Jesuit church that sat on this site in 1641. This north shore remained a quiet area of fishing villages for 300 years, until exploitation of vast forest and water-power resources began in 1930.

From Quebec City, reach the area along Highway 138 east, or along Highway 20 on the south shore of the St. Lawrence to Rivière-du-Loup, then cross the river by ferry (crosses four to six times a day in summer and less frequently in winter) to Highway 138 at Saint-Siméon. Reservations are needed for the ferry, as the trip is very popular in summer. A good variety of inns, motels and hotels are available. Reservations are recommended during the summer.

Birding Features
A driving loop is the way to explore the North Shore. Come in the spring (late April to early June) or fall (August to early September) for abundant

Snowy Owl

shorebirds. Begin by taking the ferry from Rivière-du-Loup across to Saint-Siméon. As you cross, scan for water birds. Upon landing, drive to Les Palissades, a park 27 km northwest on Highway 170. Check out the good birding habitat here. Return southeast to Highway 138 and proceed north on it to Baie-Sainte-Catherine. At half to high tide, check the water's edge for shorebirds that feed and roost regularly. Continue over the Saguenay River on a free five-minute ferry ride to Tadoussac. This is a good overnight spot. Take a cruise to whale-watch in season. In fall (September-October), Tadoussac is one of the best hawk-watching sites in the province. There is also a banding station operating there.

Continue on Highway 138 to Grandes-Bergeronnes. The wharf and mouth of the river, which empties into the St. Lawrence, should produce a variety of waterfowl including Brant, eiders, herons and shorebirds. Just beyond the community, watch for Parc Bon-Désir; look here for a variety of species, including water birds, raptors, shorebirds, warblers and finches.

Continuing north, stop at the harbour at Les Escoumins to see Ospreys that often fish here at half tide, and the gulls. Check for Little Gull among the numerous Black-legged Kittiwakes and Bonaparte's Gulls.

Proceed to Pointe Romaine, about 10 km farther. Scrutinize the birds on the mudflats at half and full tide for something you've missed. At the next three communities, Sault-au-Mouton, Saint-Paul-du-Nord and Sainte-Anne-de-Portneuf, take time to reconnoitre the salt marshes, mudflats, sandy areas and flats during half and high tides. At the latter town, a 4 km sand spit provides some of the best shorebirding on the north shore and a close view of Parasitic Jaeger. To access this site, look for a path behind two old buildings in front of 368 Principal Street (Highway 138).

Now return to Les Escoumins, take the ferry across to Trois-Pistoles and continue your trip. An alternative is to take the Matane-Godbout ferry to return on the south shore. This ferry ride provides chances from early November to early December to spot Dovekie, Thick-billed Murre and Northern Fulmar. In August and September, jaegers are common and Sabine's Gull fairly regular.

MARGARET ELLIOT
Revised by Richard Yank

Gaspé Peninsula

Set at the northeastern end of the Appalachian Mountains, which extend down into the southeastern United States, the Gaspé is surrounded by water on three sides. This thumb of land into the Atlantic Ocean provides opportunities to ferret out everything from Woodland Caribou on and near the tundra in the highlands, to warblers and finches in the boreal forests. At the east end, hundreds of thousands of seabirds nest in huge colonies. More than 150 species of birds nest on the Gaspé Peninsula, with more than 300 species having been recorded.

Off the mainland, near Percé Rock on the eastern tip, Jacques Cartier arrived with his three ships on July 24, 1534, to claim the region for France, and so began Canada. Long before Cartier landed, fishermen had been harvesting the abundance of fish found in the nearby sea. They later established clusters of homes around the perimeter of the Gaspé. Shipwrecked sailors and United Empire Loyalists in the 1700s added to the mix of peoples. Communities remained isolated, with the sea the only access, until the highway (now 132) was completed in 1929. Today many of the people, whose families have been here for up to 300 years, still split cod, salt it and dry it on wooden racks along the beach.

Accommodation, including hotels, motels and campgrounds, is plentiful, particularly at the east end. July is a busy month, so contact your local travel agent for reservations.

There is one main birdwatchers' club for the whole of Gaspé, Club des ornithologues de la Gaspésie. Contact them at Box 334, Pabos, P.Q. GOC 2H0. There are several parks, with visitor and interpretive centres. For information, contact Percé Wildlife Interpretation Centre at (418) 782-2721, Percé and Parc de l'Ile-Bonaventure-et-Du-Rocher-Percé, Box 310, Percé, P.Q. GOC 2L0; phone (418) 782-2240.

Birding Features
The one road around the perimeter, Highway 132, allows a visitor to make a leisurely or quick trip, sampling different habitats along the way. A five-day trip is the minimum time recommended for birders touring the Gaspé.

Gaspé Provincial Park (Parc de la Gaspésie). This rugged region lies in the Chic-Choc Mountains. One of the few herds of Woodland Caribou in the east resides on the slopes of 1268 m Mount Jacques Cartier, the highest peak in these mountains. Moose, White-tailed Deer and Black Bear are also plentiful. As many as 150 species of alpine flowers abound on the 30 km² summit of Mount Albert. The fisherman may angle for salmon and trout in the rivers. There are more than 240 km of hiking trails to explore. Naturalists provide information and guided walks to the top of Mount Albert and Mount Jacques Cartier. The boreal forest and alpine tundra attract over 240 species of birds, including Water Pipit and Common Redpoll. To reach the park, take Highway 132 along the south shore of the St. Lawrence River to Ste-Anne-des-Monts, then drive south on Route 299 into the park. There are campgrounds and other amenities for the visitor.

Forillon National Park. At the eastern tip of the Gaspé, on Highway 132, the park appears as a massive, tilted block emerging from the sea. Nearly 230 species of birds have been reported, with 94 nesters. The 200 m high cliffs of Ordovician and Devonian rocks abut the gulf waters; pebbled beaches and small coves of the Bay of Gaspé indent the southern side. Telescopes mounted on headlands assist the visitor in spotting Pilot Whales, seals in good numbers, and hosts of seabirds on the cliffs. White-tailed Deer and Moose abound. The cliffs also contain species of alpine plants that inexplicably occur here. Naturalists are available to provide guided walks and programs. Three regular campgrounds plus a winterized one await the visitor. Nearby villages offer a variety of accommodation outlets.

This 240 km² park is home to large colonies of Double-crested Cormorants, Herring Gulls and Black-legged Kittiwakes. Ducks, birds of prey, warblers and finches are numerous during spring and fall migration. They are best observed in the valley of L'Anse-au-Griffon and the salt marsh of Penouille at this time.

The address of the park is Forillon National Park, 122 De Gaspé Boulevard, Gaspé, P.Q. G4X 1A9; phone (418) 368-5505; e-mail: parcscanada-que@pch.qc.ca; Web site: http://parcscanada.risq.qc.ca/forillon

Barachois Salt Marsh and Pointe-St. Pierre. Continuing along Route 132, stop at Gaspé and see the fish hatchery, which annually produces a million salmon and trout fry for Quebec's lakes and rivers. A visit to the Gaspé Regional Museum is essential to learn of the history of the peninsula. They have a variety of temporary displays that change through the year. Admission is $3.50. Telephone (418) 368-1534.

Drive on south to Pointe-St-Pierre, just beyond St-Georges-de-la-Malbaie. The exposed cape provides excellent viewing of seabirds. Watch for all species of falcons too. In front of the cape, scan the small rocky island used by Common Eiders for nesting and Great Cormorants, to rest. These birds, as well as Oldsquaw and mergansers, are recorded regularly in spring and fall. Carefully study any gathering for Harlequin Duck, Purple Sandpiper and Dovekie, at times reported. In winter thousands of Oldsquaws remain.

The Barachois of Malbaie, 5 km farther west, contains the mouths of four rivers emptying into the sea. The resultant huge salt marsh is sheltered from heavy seas by an 8 km sandbar. Birds are everywhere. The new Highway 132 and the old road provide access to wet meadows, marsh and the open sea. The marsh provides food and a resting stop for migrating geese, ducks and sandpipers each spring and fall. From mid-April to mid-June, water birds are plentiful. Such rarities as Little Blue Heron, Glossy Ibis, Greater White-fronted Goose, Eurasian Wigeon, Redhead, Ruddy Duck, Sandhill Crane, Willet and Wilson's Phalarope have been spotted in spring and early summer. Just offshore and in bays, scan for rafts of Brant, scoters and mergansers. In summer, cormorants and gulls rest on dry land. Many waterfowl nest, including a variety of ducks, and sometimes such rarities as Yellow Rails and Nelson's Sharp-tailed Sparrows. The surrounding fields and forests shelter a variety of land birds. By mid-July, the shorebirds begin arriving and some are seen as late as November. The hunting season opens the third week of September. Stay away for at least the first weekend.

Behind Barachois the roads go inland. Take Vauquelin Road. From early June to early July, the morning hiker can spot 15 species of warbler as well as numerous other land birds.

Percé and Percé Wildlife Interpretation Centre. The great shiplike block of limestone rising 86 m from the sea is the landmark of Percé. The community was once the largest fishing port on the Gaspé. Today it is a resort town. The centre contains exhibits and films on the natural history of the wildlife of the Atlantic coast. The Northern Gannet film is worth the trip. Discover seaweed, shellfish and other creatures in tide pools. The self-guiding nature trail, walking trails

Northern Gannet

and naturalist-led walks add to the visit. The centre and scheduled activities are available to the public from June 24 to September 1; the rest of the year, reservations are required. At low tide you can walk across to Percé Rock, sculpted by the Atlantic for millions of years. Watch for nesting Great and Double-crested Cormorants, Herring Gull, Common Murre and Black Guillemot on the rock. Don't forget to arrange for your trip to Ile Bonaventure.

Behind the town, Mont Ste.-Anne and Mont Blanc provide excellent views. Take one of the trails, such as the Crevasse or the Grotto, and check out the plants as you climb. On the way up, ferret out Common Raven, Boreal Chickadee, Bicknell's Thrush, Pine Grosbeak, White-winged Crossbill and Fox Sparrow.

Ile Bonaventure. The provincially operated island park, just off Gaspé, is also a migratory bird sanctuary under the auspices of the Canadian Wildlife Service. Today some 100,000 birds, including the world's second-largest Northern Gannet colony, provide a spectacular sight in June, July and early August. More than 150 species of birds have been recorded in the immediate area. The naturalists at Percé Wildlife Interpretation Centre lead free guided walks along the main trail. None of the four trails crossing the island is more than 3 km long. No admission is charged to enter the park, but a fee of $10 to $16 per person (1999) is levied as a ferry charge.

The boat circles the island, then deposits its visitors. The last boat departs from the island at 5 P.M. Overnight stops are not allowed.

The 4.16 km² island, 3.5 km offshore, was used by French fishermen as a summer base, probably before Jacques Cartier arrived in 1534. In 1690 the English drove some French settlers off the island. By 1831, 35 families were located here. As fishing declined, most people left, with a few staying to till the land. By 1963 all permanent residents had gone. A few buildings still stand

Red-headed Woodpecker   TWTHORNIN/82

as a monument to their courage to live on such a barren land. For a glimpse into the past, step into some of the buildings and talk with the historical interpreters. The eastern and northern cliffs were declared a sanctuary in 1919. Since 1971 the island has been owned by Quebec Tourism, Fish and Game Department, and in 1974 the whole island was declared a migratory bird sanctuary. Whales and seals are a common sight off the island and more than 450 species of plants have been identified, not including the mushrooms, mosses and lichens, yet to be studied.

The seabirds draw the visitor. Nesting species include Leach's Storm-Petrel, Northern Gannet, Herring Gull, Black-legged Kittiwake, Razorbill, Common Murre, Black Guillemot and a few Atlantic Puffins. Other interesting species include the odd Greater Shearwater in summer, Harlequin Duck year-round, the odd Purple Sandpiper in spring, Red-necked Phalarope in fall, a few jaegers also in fall, and an occasional Thick-billed Murre in summer. The surrounding shallow, rich seas provide food. Come in late June or July since the kittiwakes, murres and Razorbills begin departing near the first week in August. Numerous land birds nest on Bonaventure. Warblers are common. It is quite easy to spot a Pine Grosbeak or Fox Sparrow. At the end of August or early September, come for erratic species passing through, including Red-headed Woodpecker, Great Crested Flycatcher, Yellow-breasted Chat, Dickcissel and Lark Sparrow.

Cap-d'Espoir. This spot, 16 km west of Percé on Highway 132, overlooks Double-crested Cormorant colonies. Other seabirds are regular too, including Black-legged Kittiwake and Great Cormorant.

Other spots. Excellent birding is found at several sites along the Gaspé south coast adjacent to the Baie des Chaleurs. Stop at the mouths of rivers and marshes. Most locations are along Highway 132. Recommended spots include Chandler, 30 km southwest of Cap-d'Espoir; Port Daniel, another 35 km, where you should not only check the coastline, but drive north into the deep forests of Reserve Port Daniel for warblers and other upland birds; Paspébiac, a further 37 km; Bonaventure, around the bend another 22 km, contains a museum housed in a 200-year-old building, among the first built by the Acadian settlers. Saint-Siméon, 7 km farther, is another site to check out. Move on to New Richmond, 32 km up the bay. North of New Richmond 15 km, near Saint-Edgar, a forest interpretive centre is open in summer. Nature trails occur along the Petite Cascapédia River. Guided walks are provided for visitors. The centre and programs are free. Then proceed to Carleton. Here you can birdwatch and drive to the top of the 580 m Mount Saint Joseph to obtain an exceptional view of the Gaspé coast and the north shore of New Brunswick. Proceed south, off the highway, to the end of the point at Miguasha. The Miguasha Fossiliferous Site lies 6 km southwest of Nouvelle on the road leading to the Miguasha-Dalhousie ferry. The site contains a museum and laboratory open to the public in summer. Tours are given around the property. You can learn more about fish and watch an Osprey.

RÉAL BISSON
Revised by Pierre Poulin

Iles de la Madeleine

Lying 250 km southeast off the Gaspé Peninsula, the archipelago of Iles de la Madeleine is a unique spot for birders. With nearly 300 species reported, including thousands of water birds, masses of shorebirds on migration, and northern species in the upland Black Spruce forests, a visitor can spend a minimum of two full days exploring lagoons, mudflats, high cliffs and forests.

The islands were first visited by Jacques Cartier in 1534, but not settled until 1755 when the Acadians were expelled from Nova Scotia. Today the 14,000 people who live here earn a living from tourism and fishing. French is the predominant language; English is spoken by the approximately 2000 people inhabiting Grosse Ile to the north and the 50 families on Ile de la Grande Entrée beside Grosse Ile. Ile Brion, 19 km north of Grosse Ile, is uninhabited.

The archipelago consists of nine islands and a few islets. The six larger islands are linked by 51 km of sand dunes. The islands can be reached in a five-hour ferry ride from Souris, P.E.I.; there are two runs per day. Fifty vehicles can be carried, with food trucks given priority. The CTMA group has been operating a ferry service between Prince Edward Island and Ile de la Madeleine for more than 25 years. The islands are also linked to Montreal 10 months out of 12 by a two-day cruise. For information, phone 1-418-986-3278 or 1-888-986-3278 or fax 1-418-986-5101. They also have a Web site at http://ilesdela Madeleine.com/ctma/madeleine2.htm Eastern Provincial Airways and QuebecAir both service the islands from Montreal, Quebec, Mont-Joli, Sept-Iles, Gaspé, Charlottetown and Halifax. Avis and Budget have cars for rent at the airport on Havre aux Maisons. Excellent roads provide easy access to all birding sites.

Over a dozen motels and hotels offer a range of accommodation on the islands. Six campgrounds are available, including ones at the south side of Havre-Aubert, at Gros Cap on the south end of Cap-aux-Meules, near Fatima on the north side of the same island, and one in the middle of Grande Entrée. The one hospital is at Cap-aux-Meules.

For additional assistance, or to forward a list of birds you noted on a visit, contact Club d'ornithologie des Iles de la Madeleine, CP 1239, Cap-aux-Meules, P.Q. GOB 1BO.

Birding Features

The red sandstone islands contain two large and several small tidal lagoons. Elevations range up to 168 m on the highest hills of Havre-Aubert and Cap-aux-Meules. The dunes are covered by Beachgrass, with the uplands containing stunted Black Spruce and Jack Pine. Extensive forests are separated by pastures and abandoned land invaded by alders.

The outstanding nearby birding sites of Great and Little Bird Rocks are accessible only during totally windless days (maximum of 10 days per year). The water surrounding these rocks is so shallow, especially at low tide, that an approaching boat may strike the rocky bottom if there is even a minimum swell. On perfect days, a fisherman from Grosse Ile can be hired to take you out. On the oval rock, thousands of Northern Gannets, Black-legged Kittiwakes and hundreds of Common and Thick-billed Murres, Razorbills and Atlantic Puffins nest. The Little Rocks, about 1 km away, are entirely occupied by Northern Gannets.

On the ferry out to the Iles de la Madeleine, look for pelagic birds. If you leave from Souris, P.E.I., the last three hours of the five-hour trip are usually quite rewarding. Greater Shearwater and Leach's Storm-Petrel are common. Sooty and Manx Shearwaters, Wilson's Storm-Petrel, Sabine's Gull, and Red and Red-necked Phalaropes are only occasional. If luck is with you, you may spot a Northern Fulmar. Northern Gannets are numerous as you approach the archipelago, and alcids are commonly observed.

The best time to come to the archipelago is from mid-May to early July. Migrants include Canada Geese, which come in from mid-May to mid-June. Common Goldeneyes pass through in spring and reside here in winter. The Oldsquaws outnumber every other duck in spring, fall and winter. Common and Red-breasted Mergansers are common migrants. Glaucous and Iceland Gulls are numerous spring migrants; some winter here.

Breeding birds are numerous. A small local population of Horned Grebes nests on the relatively inaccessible ponds of Pointe de l'Est Sanctuary (see below) and on the northern part of Havre-aux-Basques. American Black Duck, Northern Pintail and Green-winged Teal are the most common nesting ducks. Mallard, Blue-winged Teal, American Wigeon and Ring-necked Duck are less numerous breeders. A small population of Greater Scaup nests at the same sites as the Horned Grebe mentioned above. Common Eiders nest regularly on Brion Island and Red-breasted Mergansers nest in fair numbers on Pointe de l'Est ponds. Great Blue Herons feed all over the archipelago but nest only on Grosse Ile. American Bitterns are common on every pond. Virginia Rail is rare, but Sora is very common on every wet field and marshy spot. Semipalmated Plover and Least Sandpiper nest in Havre-aux-Basques and around Grosse Ile. Piping Plovers are scattered on all beaches but are difficult to locate. Every alcid found in the east, except the Dovekie, nests on the archipelago. A good spot to find alcids is the Bird Rocks. Alternatively, look for these species on Brion Island.

Brion Island can be reached from Grosse Ile using a local fisherman as a guide. These men can be hired for a reasonable fee to go directly to the island, or even circle it, before landing you. A walking trail circles the island. Atlantic Puffins are common on the northwestern and southern (below the lighthouse) sides on the southeast end, where you will also spot numerous Great Cormorants. At the far eastern end, check the seals basking on the cliffs. A few murres occur in the summer. A colony of more than 2000 Black-legged Kittiwakes is located on the northeastern side, along with numerous Razorbills, Great Cormorants and Atlantic Puffins.

Black Guillemot is a common nester in the red sandstone cliffs all around the archipelago. A good spot is under the Etang-du-Nord lighthouse. Great Black-backed and Herring Gulls are the most common gulls and are year-round residents. They nest on Seal and Range Islands inside the lagoon on Grosse Ile, and on Brion Island. Black-legged Kittiwakes are abundant breeders, with colonies on the north and northeast sides of Entrée Island, Brion Island and the northeast side of Bird Rocks. Terns nest in large colonies in Havre-aux-Basques; on the three small islands at Havre-aux-Maisons; near the harbour between Pointe-aux-Loups and Detroit Bridge; on the ponds at Pointe de l'Est; and on Brion Island. The Arctic Tern makes up 5 to 10% of the population, while Roseate Tern is represented by just a few pairs. The Northern Harrier is the most abundant bird of prey and is well distributed over the islands. The Osprey is a rare nester. Merlin is a common breeder in the stunted Black Spruce woods. The Mourning Dove is a scarce breeder found in small numbers. The Boreal Owl nests around Solitary Lake on Havre-Aubert, near the Gros Cap trailer park on Cap-aux-Meules, and at the Pointe-de-Fort face of Cap de l'Est on Grosse Ile.

Northern Flicker is the only common woodpecker; others are scarce to rare. The Yellow-bellied Flycatcher is the only common member of its group. It is found breeding in the Black Spruce forest. The Horned Lark, an abundant breeder, remains all year but is rare in winter. The Bank Swallow is probably the most common breeding land bird on the archipelago and occurs on all the sandstone cliffs. Tree and Barn Swallows are regular breeders too. The Common Raven is a common nester on the cliffs. Many pairs may be found on Cap de l'Est on Grosse Ile in May and June. American Crows are numerous year-round and flocks can be observed congregating at dusk to roost.

The Black Spruce forest draws several species to breed, including Boreal Chickadee; American Robin; Hermit and Swainson's Thrushes; Veery; Golden-crowned and Ruby-crowned Kinglets; Tennessee, Yellow-rumped and Blackpoll Warblers; and White-throated and Fox Sparrows. Bicknell's Thrush may be spotted at the top of the highest wooded summits on Havre-Aubert and Cap-aux-Meules Islands. In the alder groves watch for Yellow, Chestnut-sided and Mourning Warblers, Common Yellowthroat and a few Song Sparrows. When you locate an area of woods and swamps, survey for Red-winged and Rusty Blackbirds, Palm and Wilson's Warblers, Lincoln and Swamp Sparrows.

The spectacular fall migration of thousands of shorebirds (mid-July to October) is worth coming to see. They feed intensely on mudflats and fields before heading south. Almost every shorebird from the east has been reported. American Golden-Plover and Black-bellied Plover are numerous, with the latter more common. Ruddy Turnstone; Greater and Lesser Yellowlegs; Red Knot; White-rumped, Least and Semipalmated Sandpipers; Dunlin; dowitchers; and Sanderling are common and can be found everywhere in season. Look for Whimbrel in small flocks on beaches, marshes, wet fields, and fields with wild berries in July and August. Common Snipe and Pectoral Sandpiper are common in marshes and wet fields. Hudsonian Godwits may be spotted in flocks, with up to 400 birds in Havre-aux-Basques, where they gather before their departure south. Red and Red-necked Phalaropes are rare but may be encountered out at sea.

Other fall migrants include occasional Red-necked and Horned Grebes. The three scoter species are common in the fall and are often seen in summer. Oldsquaws outnumber every other duck in fall and winter and are regular in November, with flocks of 500 or more. Harlequin Ducks are scarce and unpredictable, but regular around Old Harry Head on Ile de l'Est late in the fall. Flocks of a few hundred Common Eiders are around in late fall. The Dovekie is a late fall visitor. Some years it is more abundant than others. Glaucous, Iceland and Ring-billed Gulls are common fall migrants, with Glaucous and Iceland being common winter residents too. The Bonaparte Gull is a common migrant. The Black-headed Gull is a regular from August to December, with flocks of up to 30 birds. Check at Havre-aux-Basques and just west of the Gros Camp trailer park on Cap-aux-Meules, where they have been spotted in recent years. Caspian Terns are reported every year from various spots in August and September. Northern Goshawk, and Rough-legged and Sharp-shinned

Hawks are regular fall migrants. The Peregrine Falcon has been recorded in the fall at Havre-aux-Basques, feeding on the numerous shorebirds and ducks. The Snowy Owl is a regular winter resident. Regularly one or two will remain over summer near Pointe-aux-Loups on the sand dunes and at Brion Island, feeding on the introduced rabbits.

The good road system allows a visitor to explore the island thoroughly. Two driving loops have been set up, each requiring a leisurely day.

South Driving Loop. Begin at sunrise at tiny Lake Solitaire, just south of the junction of Lapriere and Alpide Roads on Havre-Aubert. This is one of the few fresh-water bodies on the islands. By starting here before dawn, you may even hear a Boreal Owl. At dawn you could hear a Bicknell's Thrush in a walk around the lake. Also look for warblers. Take Lapriere Road south to the main road and turn west towards Etang-des-Caps. Stop at several viewing spots, including the small sideroad on the left, Etang-des-Caps. Continue on the main road and swing east on Montagne Road. Turn south on Pointe-des-Canots Road if it is dry and drive to the end. As you walk down to the water at the southern end of Havre-aux-Basques, listen for songbirds. Here, gulls and terns often rest. Check them out for Black-headed Gulls and other rarities. Piping Plovers occur here with other shorebirds. A hike of less than a kilometre to the west at the end of this road brings you to Etang-des-Caps Lake to spot ducks and listen for American Bittern and rails.

Return to Montagne Road and continue east to Highway 199, where you will swing north towards Cap-aux-Meules. Stop a few times along Havre-aux-Basques to scan the water. At one or two sites, hike through the wet grass on the west side of the road. Carefully scrutinize the shorebirds that are feeding heavily. You may locate a Willet, Stilt or Buff-breasted Sandpiper, Marbled Godwit or a Ruff, or maybe even a phalarope. At the northern end of this arm, just before Cap-aux-Meules, look for the tern colonies and study the birds for a good comparison between Common and Arctic. You may also see Horned Grebe and a variety of other water birds with young, in season.

Turn west at the first road, Chiasson, and drive to Etang-du-Nord. On the beaches around the little lake, south of the harbour, explore for shorebirds and gulls. South of this lake, on Goelands Island, Great and Double-crested Cormorants are spotted sunbathing and preening. Scan the sea for birdlife. Continue northeast beyond Fatima and turn north off the main road, onto Poirier Road. Stop near Cap Vert Lake on the west side. You should observe grebes, ducks and American Coots. Take a stroll on the nearby marshy fields on the north side of the lake and listen for Sora and Nelson's Sharp-tailed Sparrow. Carefully check for shorebirds, particularly American Golden-Plover, Buff-breasted Sandpiper and Godwit. At the far end of Poirier Road, scan to the north to the long dune where gulls are numerous. At low tide the mudflats are used by shorebirds and gulls. This should complete the day. If you have energy left, go owling at night. Try every wooded lot, open field or marsh for Great Horned, Long-eared or Boreal. The latter were recently reported near the Gros-Cap Provincial Trailer Park on the south end of Cap-aux-Meules and at Solitaire Lake.

North Driving Loop. Begin at sunrise on the highest summit of Cap-aux-Meules Island, near the junction of Patton and de l'Eglise. Climb the hill to the radio antenna and listen carefully. You may hear Yellow-bellied Flycatcher; Hermit, Bicknell's and Swainson's Thrushes; warblers; and sparrows. Proceed to Highway 199 going north towards the community of Havre-aux-Maisons. Stop before the iron bridge; inspect the point to the west and the lagoon for ducks, shorebirds and gulls, with Caspian Tern a good possibility. Beyond the bridge survey the mudflats for shorebirds.

Continue on 199 to the windmills near the north end of Havre-aux-Maisons and take the gravel road, de la Cormorandiere, to its end. This puts you on Dune de Sud. Piping Plover should be running along the dunes. Take your telescope and look out east about 2 km to Shag Island, aptly named for the colony of Great Cormorants that nest on it. Take a walk in early summer along the dunes, and you'll spot these birds flying overhead with their white flank patches clearly visible.

Return to 199; near the Detroit Bridge, three small islands in the lagoon host a mixed colony of Common and Arctic Terns. A few pauses as you drive along the beaches and lagoon shore, from the bridge to the salt mine on Grosse Ile, provide opportunities to scan for shorebirds. Particularly check the small ponds between Pointe-aux-Loups and Grosse Ile. The Grosse Ile bay seems to draw rare shorebirds, including Willet, Stilt Sandpiper, Ruff and Hudsonian Godwit. Nelson's Sharp-tailed Sparrow is said to nest on the north side of the bay across the road from the wharf. Continue on 199 to Pointe de l'Est National Refuge. In summer, staff provide guided tours. The schedule is displayed in all post offices.

Turn east on Old Harry Head Road. Drive to the end and climb to the cliff top to scan for seabirds. In fall, this is one of the best sites for alcids. Following a summer windstorm, alcids, shearwaters, petrels, jaegers and fulmars may be expected.

At Grande Entrée Harbour, the final stop, check both inside and outside the lagoon. On the inside, at low tide scan for possible rarities among the shorebirds and gulls. Near the end of summer, on the outside, thousands of cormorants, gulls and kittiwakes congregate to feed on the small fish that utilize this area. Late in the fall, from the end of October onward, the Dovekie is fairly abundant in the lagoon and at Old Harry Head.

If there is still light, return on 199 to Gros Cap on Cap-aux-Meules. The small pond just west of the campground and south of the road often has rare species.

YVES AUBRY

Abitibi Region

Abitibi is in far western Quebec. The birdlife reflects this western location, with nesting species such as the Sharp-tailed Grouse, Sandhill Crane, Connecticut Warbler and Le Conte's Sparrow. The study of the avifauna of Abitibi is still in its infancy, but the foundation of a bird club there in 1981 is responsible for a recent interest by local people in birdwatching. Every year, new discoveries are made, showing the potential of the region.

From southern Quebec, reach the region on Highway 117, which crosses the LaVérendrye Wildlife Reserve. This is a five- to six-hour drive from Montreal. The area may also be accessed from northern Ontario on Highway 66. Motels and hotels are easily found in Val d'Or, Amos and Rouyn-Noranda, the main cities of the region.

For information on birding the region, write to Société du Loisir ornithologique de l'Abitibi, CP 91, Rouyn-Noranda, P.Q. J9X 5C1.

Birding Features

Some of the best birding spots of the region are found around Lake Abitibi in the extreme western part. South of the lake, take the road west of Roquemaure and explore Ruisseau Antoine. Fields around Roquemaure and Palmarolle host Le Conte's Sparrow. In September and early October, hundreds of Sandhill Cranes stop in the fields near the lake.

Another interesting area is the region north of Val d'Or. Stop in Rang 1 and 2 west of Barraute to find Sharp-tailed Grouse and Sandhill Crane.

Finally, Highway 109 north of Matagami opens opportunities to spot Willow Ptarmigans in winter, especially during invasion years.

PIERRE BANNON

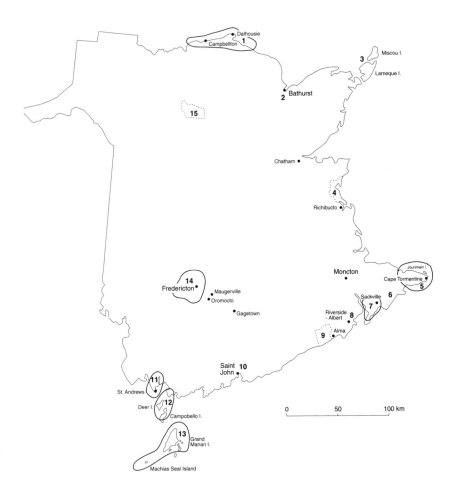

NEW BRUNSWICK

NEW BRUNSWICK

Most people interested in avifauna come to this province for marine species, including pelagic birds in the outer Bay of Fundy. The variety of warblers and other species that nest in the Acadian forests are an additional pleasure. Birds of boreal distribution, especially in the highland areas of the province, are of particular interest to birders from warmer climates.

Land birds frequently sought by visitors include Spruce Grouse and Black-backed Woodpecker. Finding the grouse often takes a lot of effort or some luck. Breeding Common Eider and Black Guillemot, shorebird concentrations on the upper Bay of Fundy, and gulls from the ferries south of St. Andrews are all spectacular at certain seasons. This variety of birds, combined with the colony of Atlantic Puffins and Razorbills at Machias Seal Island, could make your stay in New Brunswick a visit to remember!

The province stretches about 400 km in length and width and is 90% forested (or regenerating following cutting). Much of the present forest originated following fire, lumbering or other disturbance during the past 200 years. Deciduous woods of Sugar Maple, beech and Yellow Birch are found on well-drained hilltops and slopes; Balsam Poplar or Silver Maple grow with some surviving White Elm on river floodplains. Widespread breeding species include Yellow-bellied Sapsucker, Red-eyed Vireo, Ovenbird, Black-throated Blue Warbler and Rose-breasted Grosbeak. Characteristic of floodplains are Veery, Warbling Vireo, Yellow Warbler, Northern Waterthrush and Baltimore Oriole.

Mixed forests prominent in much of the province include Red and White Spruce, Balsam Fir, White and Yellow Birch, Red Maple, White Pine, hemlock, Tamarack and aspens. This mixed vegetation attracts a large variety of birds. Ruffed Grouse, Hermit Thrush, and Nashville, Northern Parula, and Blackburnian Warblers are usually conspicuous breeding species.

Spruce-fir coniferous forest occurs mainly in the northern areas and close to the foggy Fundy coast. Red, Black or White Spruce and Balsam Fir are the principal trees. Breeding birds include Spruce Grouse in unsettled areas, Black-backed Woodpecker, especially where there are dying or recently dead trees; Yellow-bellied Flycatcher; Boreal Chickadee; Winter Wren; a wide variety of warblers, including Magnolia, Cape May and Bay-breasted; and Pine Siskin. Confined mainly to the northern highland areas are Three-toed Woodpecker, Bicknell's Thrush, Blackpoll Warbler, Pine Grosbeak and Fox Sparrow.

Black Spruce-Jack Pine coniferous forests occur on poor soils such as glacial sand plains. This habitat has a relatively small variety of birds but may be the best place in which to find Spruce Grouse. By contrast, rich wet sites, often dominated by White Cedar, usually are nesting habitat for numerous species, including Canada Warbler and Brown Creeper.

Nonforested habitats are less common but often are interesting. Fields attract Northern Harrier, American Kestrel, Bobolink and Savannah Sparrow, among others.

Open bogs have few nesting birds, mainly Common Yellowthroat and Savannah Sparrow, with Lincoln's Sparrow and Palm Warbler in the scrub around the edges.

Fresh-water marshes occur mainly along the lower Saint John Valley and in lowlands near the coast.

Impoundment areas attract a wide diversity of water birds, including American Bittern, Pied-billed Grebe, American Black Duck, Blue-winged Teal, Sora and Common Snipe.

The numerous ponds, lakes and rivers have a variety of birds, including Common Loon, Common Goldeneye, Common Merganser, Spotted Sandpiper and Belted Kingfisher.

Tidal marshes are scattered, mainly near river mouths, especially at the head of the Bay of Fundy and along the eastern coast. Nelson's Sharp-tailed Sparrow is the characteristic nesting species, but a variety of herons, ducks and other birds frequent these areas.

Salt-water lagoons and sandy beaches are found mainly along the eastern coast. There you should find Piping Plovers nesting, and numerous Great Blue Herons, Red-breasted Mergansers, Ospreys and Common Terns. The lagoons host an abundance of shorebirds and water birds during fall migration.

Island seabird colonies are most numerous in the western Bay of Fundy, with a few in Miramichi Bay and Baie des Chaleurs. You'll commonly find Double-crested Cormorant, Common Eider, Great Black-backed and Herring Gulls, Common Tern and Black Guillemot. Leach's Storm-Petrel, Razorbill, Atlantic Puffin and most of the Arctic Terns are confined to the area near Grand Manan.

In deeper waters offshore, local breeders are joined in summer by southern hemisphere seabirds, including Greater and Sooty Shearwaters and Wilson's Storm-Petrels spending their winters in the north. Small numbers of Northern Gannets and Manx Shearwaters may also be seen in summer near the mouth of the Bay of Fundy. Gannets are numerous off the Acadian Peninsula in the northeast.

The best time to come is from late May to mid-July for breeding species, the last week in July to mid-September for shorebird migration, and late August to mid-October for land bird movement. In December and January look for wintering ducks and seabirds in the outer Bay of Fundy. Most of the northern and eastern coast is frozen by early January. Late winter is often of little interest unless there is an incursion of northern finches or birds of prey. In late April and throughout May you can encounter the best of spring migration.

Key spots to visit include Grand Manan, for everything; the Passamaquoddy Passages, for inshore marine birds and gull concentrations; the Fundy National Park and Mary's Point areas, for birds of shore, forest and marsh; the Tantramar Marshes; Miscou Island, for breeding Piping Plover and Nelson's Sharp-tailed Sparrow, and for fall migration; the wetlands of the Jemseg area, for ducks and marsh birds.

Any of these sites can be visited in a half day, except Grand Manan and neighbouring Machias Seal Island, which require a minimum of three days to cover both islands. Fundy and Kouchibouguac National Parks can also be sampled in half a day.

Atlas of Breeding Birds of the Maritime Provinces, by Anthony J. Erskine (Nimbus Publishing and Nova Scotia Museum, 1992) contains a wealth of information about the distribution, habitats and abundance of breeding species. *New Brunswick Birds: An Annotated List*, prepared by the New Brunswick Bird Records Committee, provides a year-round overview (available in 2000). The New Brunswick Federation of Naturalists publishes a provincial checklist.

A number of local guide booklets and checklists are mentioned at appropriate places in the text. Additional ones are available for the Moncton and Edmundston areas. Up-to-date information on all these publications is maintained on the Nature NB Web pages at http://www3.nbnet.nb.ca/maryspt/Books.html

The New Brunswick Bird Information Line ([506] 382-3825), the Moncton Naturalists' Club Nature Information Line ([506] 384-6397), and the French language La Ligne Buse ([506] 532-2873) are all located in the southeastern corner of the province. For quickly passing news of rarities, there is a telephone grapevine system and extensive use of the NatureNB mailing list. (See http://www3.nbnet.nb.ca/maryspt/InfoLines.html)

The following offices may also be able to provide advice or news: Natural Science Dept., New Brunswick Museum, Saint John ([506] 643-2300) and Canadian Wildlife Service, Sackville ([506] 364-5044).

For assistance and the names of clubs in various localities, contact the main organization: New Brunswick Federation of Naturalists, 277 Douglas Avenue, Saint John, N.B. E2K 1E5, or consult the federation's Web page at http://www3.nbnet.nb.ca/maryspt/NBFN.html

People who have offered to help you include, by area:

Alma/Albert: David Christie or Mary Majka, 435 Mary's Point Road, Harvey, Albert County, N.B. E4H 2M9; phone (506) 882-2100, e-mail: MarysPt@nbnet.nb.ca

Blacks Harbour: Ken MacIntosh, e-mail: coopers@nbnet.nb.ca
Campbellton/Dalhousie: Mike Lushington, P.O. Box 5501, Dalhousie, N.B.
E8C 3C2; phone (506) 684-5688; e-mail: mhlca@nbnet.nb.ca
Fredericton: Don Gibson, 50 Golf Club Road, Fredericton, N.B. E3B 5M4;
phone (506) 454-3261; e-mail: gibsondg@nbnet.nb.ca
Grand Manan: Brian Dalzell, 62 Bancroft Point Road, Grand Manan, N.B.
E5G 3C9; phone (506) 662-8650; e-mail: dalzell@nbnet.nb.ca
Lamèque: Hilaire Chiasson, 242 ch. Pte-Alexandre, Lamèque, N.B. E8T 2K2;
phone (506) 344-2286.
Sackville: Kathy Popma, 40 Weldon Street, Sackville, N.B. E4L 4N4; phone
(506) 536-3052; e-mail: popma@nbnet.nb.ca; Colin MacKinnon, phone (506)
364-5039.
Saint John: Jim Wilson, 2 Neck Road, Quispamsis, N.B. E2G 1L3; phone (506)
847-4506, fax (506) 849-0234; e-mail: jgw@nbnet.nb.ca
St. Andrews: Tracey Dean, phone at work: (506) 529-1220, home (506) 529-4794.
    To obtain a good road map and other material useful to a visitor, contact
Tourism New Brunswick, P.O. Box 12345, Woodstock, N.B. E7M 5C3; phone
toll free in North America 1-800-561-0123; e-mail address: nbtourism@
gov.nb.ca or check their Web site http://www.tourismnbcanada.com

DAVID CHRISTIE

Campbellton to Dalhousie

The western end of Baie des Chaleurs attracts well over 200 species, with more
than 100 known as nesting. Habitat diversity and a waterfowl staging area make
the area quite productive. Access by car is via Highway 17 from the west and
Highway 11 from the east, by VIA Rail or by air, landing at the Charlo Airport.

Birding Features
Tidal flats and fresh-water marsh, hardwood, softwood and mixed woods,
meadows with hedgerows and rocky coastline are all represented. Route 11
serves the area as the main highway, but better birding is mostly along Route
134. From west to east, beginning at Tide Head, the following are interesting sites:

Atholville-Tide Head Boom. Turn north off Highway 134 onto Boom Road at
the Tide Head-Atholville boundary. Proceed 300 m to view the marsh from
the Margaret Doyle Lookout. Continue 1 km, stopping at several spots. In
spring the marsh is often flooded and covered by high tides. Waterfowl are best
seen from mid- to late May and mid-August to October; waders, from late
July to October. To the right of the road, a non-odorous sewage lagoon often
hosts waterfowl.
    Sugarloaf Provincial Park, which has a nice campground, lies at the western
edge of Campbellton on Route 11. From the extensive trail system, ferret out
flycatchers, warblers and other forest species from mid-May to mid-September.
    Restigouche Estuary has several thousand scoters, predominantly Black,

between Campbellton and Dalhousie in late April and May, and five common species of gulls: Great Black-backed, Ring-billed, Herring, Iceland and Bonaparte's. Glaucous Gull is uncommon.

Bon Ami Point and Rocks. In Dalhousie, proceed east on Victoria Street to its end at Bon Ami Point. This is a spring and fall stopover area for waterfowl and a breeding site for Double-crested Cormorant, Black Guillemot and gulls. In late April and early May, you'll see Surf and Black Scoters; November and December are good for both species of goldeneye. Over 200 Barrow's Goldeneyes have been observed here. Gyrfalcon has been observed fairly regularly in winter.

Eel River Lagoon and Head Pond. Take Route 134 about 5 km southeast from Dalhousie to where it crosses the sand bar at the mouth of the Eel River. Park by the road on the south side of the lagoon. The mudflats and water of the tidal lagoon are interesting for herons, ducks, shorebirds and gulls. Rarities have been discovered here during migration. Upstream, above the dam, the cattail marsh and headpond are of exceptional interest for northern New Brunswick. Here you may spot Pied-billed Grebe and Hooded Merganser and several other duck species. Walk to the marsh along the lagoon. A canoe gives best access, but a trail along the southern shoreline connects Route 11 and the village of Eel River Crossing. Water birds are most numerous during May and September. Shorebirds are best in May and late July to October.

Charlo River Estuary. Take Riverview Drive, off Route 134 (about 9 km east of Eel River, or east of Exit 375 from Route 11) to an estuary that provides excellent birding, particularly as a gathering area for waterfowl and shorebirds in both spring and fall. Concentrations of Bonaparte Gulls occur in July and August. Female Harlequin Ducks with broods of young have been seen here in midsummer of several years.

ALAN MADDEN
Revised by Mike Lushington, Irene Doyle,
Margaret Gallant Doyle and Alan Madden

Bathurst

Along the way from the Restigouche to the islands at the tip of the Acadian Peninsula lies the small city of Bathurst. Interesting birding locations are scattered around Bathurst Harbour, which is particularly attractive to migrant waterfowl, gulls and terns. Two of the best sites lie on the east side of the harbour. From Route 11, exit onto Miramichi Avenue north towards the city centre, turn east at Bridge Street, then after about 2 km go left on Carron Point Drive.

Daly Point Reserve. A parking area on the left, 1 km from Bridge Street, provides access to 2 km of trails through field, woodland and salt marsh, and an observation tower overlooking the marsh and harbour.

Carron Point. At the end of Carron Point Drive, turn left on Bayshore and drive to Carron Point, which gives an excellent view of the harbour, its entrance channel and Baie des Chaleurs. Gulls, terns and Red-breasted Mergansers nest on the small islands in the harbour. Great Blue Heron and Osprey pass over from nearby nests. Small numbers of shorebirds may be present.

DAVID CHRISTIE

Miscou Island and Lamèque Island

Set at the "Land's End" of New Brunswick, these two islands, particularly Miscou, have changed little since they were settled over two centuries ago. They are good spots in spring, summer and fall for resident and migrating land and water birds. The historical richness of the area is best portrayed at the nearby Acadian Historical Village, about 40 km west of the islands on Route 11, just west of Caraquet. The two islands lie in the northeastern corner of the province, off Highway 11, on Route 113. Some commercial accommodation and camping is available on the islands and at the town of Lamèque. Stop at an ecological centre on Route 313 in Lamèque for more information on birds. For additional help, contact Hilaire Chiasson (see above).

Birding Features
The area offers bogs, long beaches and windswept low forests. For migrants, come in April and May, and again from August to mid-October. In June and July, check the woodland for songbirds and watch for breeding Piping Plovers on the beaches.

On your way out to the islands, stop at Shippagan to check the harbour on both sides of the bridge for gulls and shorebirds. Shippagan and Lamèque are important fishing centres. The spring passage of water birds, mainly eiders and scoters, is readily visible from the eastern shore of both islands. In seasons other than spring, hurry on to Miscou Island.

On arrival at Miscou Harbour, at the southern end of the island, look for a gull and tern roost near the bridge, and in late summer for shorebirds such as Hudsonian Godwit and yellowlegs. Proceeding north on Route 113, turn east on the Wilson Point (Pte. Noire) Road, which runs first through woods where there are numerous passerines in summer.

Moving on to the peatlands, you can expect to see Northern Harrier, Savannah Sparrow and, in late summer and early fall, Whimbrel. At the T junction, turn north, drive to the end of the road and park. You are now at the southern end of Mal Bay South, a shallow lagoon that is good for herons, ducks, geese and shorebirds. Walk north along the marshy shore about 1.5 km to the lagoon outlet, then return along the beach. Check Mal Bay for shore and water birds, the beach for shorebirds and the sea for Northern Gannet, cormorants, ducks and gulls. Now head back to Route 113 and turn north.

A sideroad marked Plage de l'Ouest (West Beach) leads to the beach and dunes on the Baie des Chaleurs. Route 113 crosses a fair amount of bog on the way to the northern end of the island, where Lac Frye frequently attracts gulls, terns and shorebirds. At the end of the road, at Miscou Lighthouse, you will often find a small number, but good variety, of migrant shorebirds on the beach. Offshore there are likely to be loons, Northern Gannets, cormorants and sea ducks. You can walk southeast along the beach to reach Mal Bay North, an area similar to Mal Bay South. It's about 3 km to the northern part of the lagoon, 5 km to the outlet. Several rare species of shorebirds have been found there.

HILAIRE CHIASSON
Revised by Hilaire Chiasson

Kouchibouguac National Park

The diversity of easily accessible habitat enables birders to visit sites ranging from a barrier island system to bogs, and to see numerous bird species in a short time. At Kouchibouguac (pronounced koo-she-boo-GWAK), birders have reported 217 species, with 90 confirmed nesters. Waterfowl are particularly abundant on migration. Don't miss the herd of Gray and Harbour Seals at the mouth of the St. Louis River.

The park, a 238 km² segment of maritime coastal plain, is located on the shore of Northumberland Strait about 100 km north of Moncton and 45 km south of Miramichi City along Highway 11. The SMT bus service passes the park every day. The nearest VIA Rail station is at Rogersville, 35 km west of the park entrance. An extensive system of hiking and bicycle trails and 50 km of roads are open for your use.

Accommodation is available along Route 11 in nearby communities such as St-Louis-de-Kent. The park has a major campground, group tenting and wilderness camp areas. Commercial camping is available along the highway.

The park has a detailed bird checklist and brochure showing the roads and trails. For more information check with the park library; they have a major unpublished avifaunal survey of the park. Write or telephone Interpretive Service, Kouchibouguac National Park, Kouchibouguac, N.B. E0A 2A0; phone (506) 876-2443.

Birding Features

Forests, constituting 52% of the park, are dominated by conifers and mixed stands. Bogs cover 21% of the land area. Estuaries and lagoons make up 18%; open fields, 4%; salt marshes cover 3%. The barrier island system is only 2%, and ponds and brooks less than 1% of the area. The seacoast is the major feature on the east side.

Spring migration from mid-April to mid-May brings in water birds, birds of prey, blackbirds and sparrows. From late May to early June, waves of shorebirds, flycatchers, warblers and swallows arrive. Nesting occurs from late May to July. Fall migration begins in late July; the best time is August for shorebirds and some water birds such as Northern Gannets and cormorants. September brings masses of songbirds and waterfowl. In October and November, Canada Geese pass through. The best times for the largest number of species are late May and mid-September.

Each nature trail covers a different habitat type and offers good birding. Kelly's Beach and Callander's Beach are fine vantage points from which to overlook large areas of the lagoon systems. A good telescope is useful. The barrier island system is another good area. From late spring to early fall, a walk from Kelly's Beach, on the boardwalk across the dunes to the ocean, should prove very satisfying. You should see Northern Gannet, cormorant, waterfowl and Osprey, shorebirds (notably nesting Piping Plover), gulls, terns and Nelson's Sharp-tailed Sparrow. During breeding season, Tern Island supports a colony of several thousand Common Terns.

To best observe the eider and scoter migration along the shore in spring, go to the community of Point Sapin, just north of the park. From there you can continue north on Route 117 to Escuminac, explore along the shore of Miramichi Bay towards Miramichi City, and return to the park on Route 11. The shallow inshore waters of Miramichi Bay are bordered by sandy beaches, salt marshes and small, sheltered estuaries, worth checking from April through October.

About 30 km south of Kouchibouguac, the Irving Eco-centre, La Dune de Buctouche (phone [506] 743-2600), on Route 475, off Route 11, 10 km from Buctouche, is an interesting seashore site. An interpretive centre sits at the base of a sand spit that extends 10 km across Buctouche Bay. Its sandy beaches, dunes and salt marsh support species similar to those found at Kouchibouguac.

THE LATE ROBERT LEBLANC AND HARRY WALKER

Cape Jourimain National Wildlife Area and Cape Tormentine

These marshes on the southeast tip of New Brunswick have produced over 200 species of birds. The average person should easily locate 40 to 50 during a four-hour visit in spring or fall.

The land was farmed for over 150 years. The settlers dyked it for hayland and later abandoned it when the seas broke down their dykes. Prominent road and railway beds were built across the marshes in the 1960s as part of a proposed causeway to Prince Edward Island. Brackish ponds formed on one side of the road and salt marshes remained on the other. The area was set aside as a national wildlife area (NWA) in 1979. Now, the approach road for the Confederation Bridge to P.E.I. follows the old causeway's right-of-way. In response to a large influx of traffic, a sensitive nature-based tourism project is being developed.

The Cape Jourimain Nature Centre is an evolving effort to bring environmental education initiatives together with pro-active conservation at this centrally located stopover for both human and avian travellers. The effort brings together a community-based nonprofit corporation and the Canadian Wildlife Service in a unique effort to protect the National Wildlife Area by controlling visitor use. The Nature Centre, with completion anticipated in 2000, and a network of four walking trails averaging 3 km in length will let visitors discover the natural and cultural history of the property. Exhibits, interpretive staff and trail signage will help point out the importance of this diverse wildlife habitat. Visitors can expect to pay a user fee on the opening of the facilities.

To reach the 640 ha site, drive east on Route 16 to the Cape Jourimain exit, the last interchange before the bridge, and follow signs to the centre's parking areas.

There are three small motels, inns and bed-and-breakfasts nearby in the villages of Bayfield, Murray Corner, Cape Tormentine and Little Shemogue. Campgrounds are available at Murray Corner and Cape Tormentine. Other services are available nearby. Two helpful brochures, a map with a description of the area, and a checklist of the birds giving abundance and season of occurrence are available from the Canadian Wildlife Service (CWS) in Sackville. Contact Colin MacKinnon (in Sackville, see above) for more information.

Birding Features

Cape Jourimain National Wildlife Area (NWA) is made up of a complex association of salt and brackish marshes, barrier beach, sand dunes and uplands, with the old roadbed down the middle. Most of the upland is covered with grasses, shrubs and stands of young evergreen and deciduous trees. To explore its varied habitats, proceed on foot from the parking area as directed by staff or the site brochure.

The best times to visit are mid-March to mid-May for migrant water birds; mid-May to early June and August through September for migrant passerines; June and July for nesting Ospreys, Common Terns, Willets, warblers and Nelson's Sharp-tailed Sparrows; in early July plan on spending a minimum of four hours to cover the wetlands, higher areas and seacoast adequately.

Waterfowl and shorebirds are the most abundant and conspicuous birds on the cape. Waterfowl are present year-round, except when the marshes are frozen in mid-winter. Dabbling ducks occur in the marsh, and sea ducks in the coastal waters.

Some 20 species of shorebirds are regulars and 30 species have been observed in recent years. Some stop over in the spring, but July to September is the best time to watch for waders. You can spot Semipalmated and Black-bellied Plovers, Willet, both yellowlegs, Red Knot, Hudsonian Godwit, Least and Semipalmated Sandpipers, and others.

Look for common Great Blue Heron and occasionally other heron species such as Little Blue Heron, Great and Snowy Egrets and Glossy Ibis. The lighthouse is used by a large colony of Cliff Swallows. Ospreys cruise the marshes, with Northern Harrier on the uplands all summer and fall. Winter brings Rough-legged Hawks and an occasional Snowy Owl.

The now closed ferry terminal site at Cape Tormentine is best for observing migrating loons, grebes, cormorants and sea ducks from late summer through to November. Come here from late October to mid-May for Glaucous and Iceland Gulls.

STUART TINGLEY, AL SMITH AND PETER BARKHOUSE
Revised by Steve Ridlington

Sackville and Tantramar Marshes

These formerly tidal marshes derive their name from the French term *tinta-marre*, applied to the *grand bruit, accompagné de désordre* of the many waterfowl that inhabited the wetlands. The Canadian Wildlife Service (CWS) reports over 250 species. Several birds are probably more numerous here than anywhere else in the Maritimes, including American Bittern, Northern Harrier, Virginia Rail, Short-eared Owl and Marsh Wren.

The marshlands were protected from the sea with dykes built by Acadians and other settlers, creating 207 km² of agricultural lands. Parts of the upper reaches have been impounded as waterfowl management areas by the CWS and Ducks Unlimited (Canada), but the highlight of the area is Sackville Waterfowl Park. The Trans-Canada Highway, Route 2, crosses the lower Tantramar. Regular services and accommodation are available in Sackville, home of Mount Allison University.

From Route 2, take exit 541, turn southwest onto Main Street and go 0.3 km to visit the Canadian Wildlife Service building, which is located on the left, down Waterfowl Lane. Here you'll find a permanent wildlife exhibit and a board updated with daily observations in the Sackville Waterfowl Park. The CWS has a bird list giving status and dates of occurrence. Write for a copy to Environment Canada, CWS, P.O. Box 6227, Sackville, N.B. E4L 1G6.

Birding Features

Sackville Waterfowl Park. From the CWS building go back to Main Street and turn left. Go 0.4 km (or 0.7 km from Route 2) to the main park entrance, located just past a nursing home on the left. Park on the right in front of the octagonal tourist information building where information about the park and bird checklists are available.

In a very compact area, the waterfowl park offers a good diversity of birds, although wetland species predominate. The best birding periods are late May and mid-August. Groomed gravel trails and boardwalks with handrails make it a family walk. Children can get a close look at birds that otherwise can be just dots in the distance. July is when various duck broods are being paraded around. Do not feed them.

Binoculars and scopes are necessary in the park for detailed observations, but the birds have become accustomed to people and are often closer than normal. An observation tower allows perusal of the larger lagoon and some shoreline. The park is wheelchair accessible but is a bit of a rough ride or push. You can spend three hours doing a careful bird trek or 30 minutes on a quick inspection.

Although the official total of birds observed in the park is about 150 species over 10 years, a tally of 50 species is attainable on a good day during spring and fall peak periods. The park waters freeze from about mid-November to early April.

A typical mid-August bird list will include, on a "seen daily" basis, Pied-billed Grebe, Mallard, Black Duck, Gadwall, American Wigeon, Northern Shoveler, Ring-necked Duck, Green-winged and Blue-winged Teals, Least Sandpiper, Short-billed Dowitcher, Lesser and Greater Yellowlegs, Wilson's Snipe, Killdeer, Ring-billed Gull, Belted Kingfisher, Red-winged Blackbird, Swamp Sparrow, and a variety of common land birds. Seen on the same August day on a regular basis are Sora and Virginia Rail and American Bittern. Various other water birds, as well as hawks and falcons, occur.

Fort Beauséjour Marsh. Both dyked and tidal marshland can be visited near Fort Beauséjour National Historic Park, not far off the Trans-Canada Highway at Aulac, about 7 km east of Sackville. From Route 2, take exit 550 to Aulac and follow signs towards the fort. On Route 16 from P.E.I., continue straight under the overpass and follow signs to the fort.

The old fort site offers a good view of the upper part of Cumberland Basin and the surrounding marsh and upland. In early spring and in fall, migrating flocks of scoters, eiders and Canada Geese pass overhead. At the far end of the fort parking lot, a rather rough track leads to the right. In summer this is usually dry but can be muddy. Along this track, on the left, are two large impoundments across the railroad tracks. They can be observed from a distance with a scope. To access the impoundments, drive along the track about 0.7 km, park and walk left down a rough track just past the Ducks Unlimited sign on the left. Listen and look carefully before crossing the railway tracks, the main CNR line. The impoundment dyke can be muddy, and cows and bulls can be about. Waterfowl, shorebirds and raptors are common. The best months are May to October. Return to the Trans-Canada Highway the same way you came.

The tidal marsh along the bay can be reached by continuing downhill from the Fort Beauséjour parking lot, keeping to the left of some sheds. Pass a gate, cross the railway track with caution and continue to the sea dyke at the absolute end of the Bay of Fundy. Walk west along the dyke towards the mouth of the Tantramar River. Nelson's Sharp-tailed Sparrows are in taller wild grasses here and are often seen perched on fence lines. In late summer and early fall, Whimbrel, sandpipers, American Golden-Plover, Bald Eagle, Short-eared Owl, Northern Harrier and waterfowl can be seen. It is not a good idea to take a short cut across fields where cattle are pastured. Retrace your path to the start.

High Marsh Road. This route crosses the middle of the Tantramar for about 12 km through hay and pasture land, an area full of grassland and open-country birds, with a chance to sight water birds flying up from the creeks and ditches. In the twilight hours after sundown, watch for Short-eared Owls. The powerline towers and barn roofs are good places to scan for Snowy Owls and Rough-legged Hawks in the winter. During spring, the road may be muddy. From Sackville, take Route 940 and 1.6 km north from Route 2 turn right onto Harper Lane. A sewage lagoon on your right is visited annually in early May by Wilson's Phalarope and is always worth a look. Continue over the bridge to the stop sign, turn left and at 0.7 km veer right at the Y onto Church Street, then right again 1 km later onto the High Marsh Road. Alternatively, take Route 16 towards P.E.I. for 9 km from Aulac and turn left on Parson Road to Jolicure. At the Jolicure crossroads, turn left on High Marsh Road and follow it to Middle Sackville.

White Birch Road. On Route 940, about 4 km north of Middle Sackville, turn left on White Birch Road. Two impoundments, 0.8 km and 1.2 km in, are very productive for waterfowl. In summer also watch for Black Terns, which often nest in the area. Songbirds are abundant in the roadside bushes and trees.

Revised by Katherine Popma

Driving Loop: Dorchester to Sackville

To see 50,000 Semipalmated Sandpipers in one flock is a thrill never to be forgotten. This is the area to do it, on a 45 km round trip. From Dorchester, on Route 6, halfway between Moncton and Sackville, turn southwest on Route 935 to Johnsons Mills and Upper Rockport, where you turn east to Sackville. You can go the reverse way around the loop, but this puts you on the opposite side of the road from the shore, and it is more difficult to spot the birds. The town of Sackville contains all services and an office of the Canadian Wildlife Service, off Main Street.

Birding Features

The Rockport–Dorchester Cape area is unique for its road access near extensive intertidal areas with shorebird roosting sites. The pebble beaches and intertidal mudflats provide habitat for large numbers of shorebirds to roost during high tide and to feed during low tide. Roosts of Semipalmated Sandpipers reaching upwards of 50,000 can be approached to within 15 m by car.

The best time to come is from mid-July to mid-September. The truly peak numbers occur within a very short period of time (the first week of August) and can easily be missed. White-rumped Sandpiper, Dunlin and Sanderling are generally seen later in late September and October. Time your visit to the Dorchester Cape to Johnsons Mills leg for between two hours before and two hours after high tide. At that time the birds roost near or on the road. To avoid flushing these gatherings, approach them by vehicle rather than on foot, since a human figure flushes them more easily than a vehicle.

About 8 km south of Dorchester on Route 935, you will reach the shore of Shepody Bay at a broad cove known as Grande Anse. This is the site of the first large shorebird roost. A parking lot and viewing stand are located at the major roosting site on that beach. At peak season, interpreters are on site to answer questions. The second roost lies about 2.5 km south. The third spot is about another kilometre.

Other birds to watch for at this season include a few hundred Semipalmated Plovers and Black-bellied Plovers, a few Ruddy Turnstones, several Red Knots, a couple of hundred White-rumped and Least Sandpipers, Dunlins, Sanderlings and Short-billed Dowitchers. A few Hudsonian Godwits may be there too. Watch for Great Black-backed, Herring and Ring-billed Gulls. Black Scoters typically swim offshore.

After another 3 km, the road crosses the peninsula to Upper Rockport on Cumberland Basin. Turn left and drive towards Sackville until you reach an area of Black Spruce with some Jack Pine on the left. Stop here to look for Palm Warblers and Spruce Grouse. Pine Grosbeaks may also be spotted. You'll have to hike around to find the grouse.

PETER W. HICKLIN, REID MCMANUS AND STUART TINGLEY
Revised by Peter W. Hicklin

Albert County Coast–Shepody National Wildlife Area

Visit one of the major staging areas for migrant shorebirds on the Atlantic coast. During the second and third weeks of August, you could spot 50,000 or more Semipalmated Sandpipers at Marys Point.

This area lies along Routes 114 and 915 just east of Fundy National Park. There is no public transportation. Accommodations are available in the park and from Alma eastward to Hopewell Cape.

For more information, refer to contacts in Albert/Alma (see above), the Interpretive Centre at Marys Point (phone [506] 882-2544, during shorebird season) and the booklet mentioned in the Fundy Park section.

Birding Features

The area encompasses a great variety of habitat, including spruce-fir forests, turbid coastal waters, brushy upland fields, dykelands used for pasture and hay, mixed forest, tidal marsh, intertidal mudflats, rocky shore, impounded fresh-water marshes, streams, lakes and villages.

In addition to the shorebird migration from the end of July to mid-September, look for marsh birds in summer; geese from mid-March to mid-April; eiders and scoters from late March to early May; hawks and eagles in late March and April; and passerines coming through in April and May. Rarities occur mainly in the fall.

Take the driving loop from Alma east to Riverside-Albert and return (about 75 km). Heading east out of Alma on Route 114, bear right onto Route 915 towards Waterside. Some of the steep grades and curves are unsuitable if one is towing a large trailer.

Waterside Marsh, 11.5 km from Alma, is a tidal marsh with numerous ponds, fronted by a long gravel beach. It attracts herons, geese, ducks, shorebirds (mainly at high tide) and gulls. In spring watch for rafts of sea ducks on the bay offshore. Nelson's Sharp-tailed Sparrow nests in the taller marsh grasses.

Past Waterside, scenic Cape Enrage, a 6.5 km side trip on Cape Enrage Road, is a good location to observe seabird migration in March, April and May.

Back on 915, 11.7 km east of Cape Enrage Road, turn right onto Marys Point Road and drive 3.1 km to the Marys Point section of Shepody National Wildlife Area (NWA). Park at the Interpretive Centre and walk down the 200 m trail to the beach. During August, up to 100,000 Semipalmated Sandpipers rest here at peak season. Hundreds to a few thousands of Semipalmated Plovers; White-rumped and Least Sandpipers; Dunlins; and Sanderlings may be seen at the peaks of their migration. The birds rest on the beach between periods of intense feeding on the mudflats. Birding is usually good from about two hours before high tide to two hours after high tide. Do not approach the roost closely or otherwise frighten the birds. Patient observers have ample opportunity to see the birds in flight as the flocks adjust their position on the beach or manoeuvre to avoid a hunting Peregrine Falcon or Merlin.

About 2.5 km farther along Marys Point Road, a "tidal dam" and dyke system at Harvey prevents the sea from flooding the Shepody River and adjacent former marshland now used for agriculture. Short-eared Owls usually occupy the pastures and hayfields during summer and may be seen at dusk, by driving the agricultural road that crosses the dam from Harvey to Hopewell Hill, a distance of about 4.7 km.

Beyond the dam, Marys Point Road rejoins Route 915. Turn right towards Riverside-Albert, 3.7 km away, then left towards Alma. On the left, 3.3 km along Route 114, the Calhoun Marsh, a Ducks Unlimited impoundment, is a great spot for waterfowl. It can be easily observed from the boat-launch area. A half kilometre farther, turn left on the Marsh Road and stop just past the creek, 0.9 km from the 114. To the west is the 560 ha Germantown section of Shepody NWA. Seven large impoundments have good numbers of breeding marsh birds. These are observed by walking west along the dykes. Early morning and evening are the best times. To return to Fundy Park, go back to 114 and turn left towards Alma (21.5 km).

DAVID CHRISTIE, MARY MAJKA AND MIECZYSLAW MAJKA
Revised by David Christie and Rob Walker

Fundy National Park

Facing the sea along a line of cliffs, the rolling plateau lands of Fundy National Park average about 300 m above the sea. Over 250 species of birds have been recorded, with at least 96 as fairly regular nesters, including Black-backed Woodpecker.

Settled about 1820, the land was used for agriculture and lumbering. Since the park was established in 1948, the remaining fields have been reverting to forest.

The 207 km² park lies 80 km west from Moncton and 60 km east of Sussex, on Route 114. The park contains 70 km of roads and 100 km of trails. At the park and in adjacent Alma, there is a variety of accommodation and campgrounds, including a winter campsite.

A handy guidebook, *Moosebirds and Sandpeeps – Birds in and around Fundy National Park*, is available from the Fundy Guild book shop in the park. For local help, contact The Superintendent, Fundy National Park, P.O. Box 101, Alma, N.B. E4H 1B4; phone (506) 887-6000.

Birding Features

Mixed forest dominates the park, followed by spruce-fir and deciduous forest; turbid coastal waters lie along a 22.5 km coastline; the remainder (5%) of the land is old fields and human-dominated sites, wetland thickets, meadows and bog, intertidal rock, gravel and mud, lakes, and swift, rocky rivers.

During spring and fall migration, birding can be interesting all along the coast, particularly near park headquarters and at Herring Cove, Matthews Head and Point Wolfe. Watch for small birds in the bushes and at the edge of the woods. At and just after dawn, large flocks may pass low overhead.

In April and early May, loons and sea ducks can be watched from Matthews Head and at the far end of the Coppermine Trail. Take your spotting scope.

Winter is a quiet time for birding. During a good cone crop year, winter finches will come in numbers. Check the bird feeders in Alma for rarities.

Probably the most sought-after bird is the Black-backed Woodpecker. Its foraging area shifts as conditions change. Concentrate on sites where spruce and fir are dying or very recently dead, with bark still tight. The bird is perhaps most regular along the Caribou Plain Trail.

During the breeding season from mid-May to early July, woodland species are of most interest. Rise before dawn and take the trails to spot them. Favourite summer spots include Wolfe Lake, Caribou Plain Trail, the park headquarters area including the Upper Salmon River Trail, the mouth of the Upper Salmon River, Maple Grove Road and Coppermine Trail. Yellow-bellied Flycatchers are easily observed from the Kinnie Brook Trail where it descends into the valley bottom.

DAVID CHRISTIE
Revised by David Christie and Rob Walker

Saint John

Clinging to the shores of the Bay of Fundy, Saint John is one of the oldest cities in Canada. Nesting gulls and cormorants, combined with coastal marshes and a ferry trip across the bay, result in a checklist of 212 regular species, of which 110 are nesters.

Champlain anchored in the bay and named the river in 1604. A small trading post built in 1631 mushroomed into an instant city with the influx of a few thousand Loyalists in 1783. The city was in its heyday during the wooden-ship-building era of the 19th century. Today a visitor can explore those earlier days with a stroll along the Loyalist Trail through downtown Saint John.

Lying on Highway 1, Saint John is served by air and bus. A visitor has a large selection of accommodations, including campsites. One of these sites lies in Rockwood Park, a pleasant birding location with an extensive trail system.

Finding Birds Around Saint John, a booklet published by the Saint John Naturalists' Club, briefly covers the sites listed below, plus others within 50 km of the city. It should be available through the New Brunswick Museum, where the Natural Science Department has an extensive collection of birds and information on their distribution in New Brunswick. Refer above for contacts in Saint John.

Birding Features

The habitats range from deep and shallow sea, sandy sea beach, salt- and fresh-water marshes, to coniferous and deciduous woods and open fields.

Irving Nature Park and Saints' Rest Marsh. They lie on the western outskirts of the city south of Highway 1. Stop on the shoulder of the eastbound lane for a quick scan over the marsh for herons, ducks, shorebirds and gulls. An elevated travel information centre (where a local checklist is available) provides safer parking and a good view of the central portion of the marsh. About 0.6 km east of the centre, pull over at the entrance to the Lancaster sewage facility; scan for waterfowl.

To visit the Irving Nature Park and south side of the marsh, take Catherwood south, Exit 107A (westbound) or 107B (eastbound) from Route 1. Catherwood becomes Bleury. Turn right on Sand Cove Road, 0.5 km off the highway. The sewage lagoon can be reached by walking down a lane on the right from a small parking area 2 km along Sand Cove Road. Farther along, park at the end of Sand Cove Road to explore the sand beach and edges of the marsh on foot. Scan seaward to Manawagonish Island where Double-crested Cormorant, Great Blue Heron, and Great Black-backed and Herring Gulls nest. High tide brings migrating shorebirds to the upper beach and marsh in late summer and early fall. Taylors Island is a wooded peninsula at the far end of the beach. That portion of the nature park offers a boardwalk into the marsh and a driving loop and extensive system of foot trails to explore the woodland and overlook the bay and a large mudflat (where fall migrant shorebirds feed at low tide).

Reversing Falls. Take the Reversing Falls exit (107A or 107B) off Highway 1 to Route 100. Cross the Reversing Falls Bridge to the east, turn left on Douglas Avenue and take the next left onto Falls View Avenue to Falls View Park.

In summer, many Double-crested Cormorants feed in the rapids and fly up and down the river. Study the small islands in the rapids for eggs and chicks of Great Black-backed Gulls and cormorants that nest here.

In winter, scrutinize for Common Goldeneye and Common Merganser. Walk to the right along the shore for other ducks and gulls resting on the upper island or in Marble Cove, a shallow cove above the rapids. The cove is also viewable with a scope from behind the New Brunswick Museum building at 277 Douglas Avenue.

Great Black-backed Gull

Courtenay Bay. This shallow bay, just east of the city centre, is full of water at high tide and is mostly mudflat at low tide. Crown Street provides access to viewing points for observation of gulls and ducks from fall through spring. The end of Hanover Street, three blocks north of the Courtenay Causeway that crosses the bay, is the best vantage spot in the area to examine Iceland Gulls at close range.

Red Head Marsh. This cattail marsh, on the eastern side of Saint John Harbour, is 3.3 km south of the Courtenay Causeway. Drive south on Bayside Drive and turn right onto Red Head Road. Park by the sea wall at the marsh. Observe from the road or hike the sometimes rough trail along the south edge of the marshes. Stay on shore to avoid falling through treacherous mats of floating vegetation. The marsh interior can be explored by canoe along creek channels.

This is a nesting site for several species at the northern edge of their range: Green Heron, Common Moorhen and Marsh Wren. Pied-billed Grebe and a variety of ducks are common. The site is best visited from early May to late June and mid-August to mid-October. Come in early morning to hear rails call. Check the sea side of the road for water birds.

Princess of Acadia ferry ride: Saint John to Digby, Nova Scotia. To reach the Bay of Fundy ferry terminal, take Exit 109 off Route 1 in west Saint John. This is not a consistently good pelagic trip, but from July through October you should see shearwaters and other deep-sea species. From November through January, look for Black-legged Kittiwakes and other gulls, Razorbills and other alcids. For schedules and fares, phone Bay Ferries at 1-888-249-7245.

DAVID CHRISTIE, CECIL JOHNSTON AND JAMES WILSON
Revised by David Christie

St. Andrews

Visitors to St. Andrews can expect to enjoy late 1700s architecture as well as a good variety of shorebirds on migration. Overwintering waterfowl include eiders, scoters, Bufflehead, grebes, loons and scaups.

After the American Revolution, many Loyalists fled from Maine to settle here. Several brought houses by barge, section by section, and rebuilt these "prefabricated units." Check at the tourist office for examples of late 18th-century and early 19th-century buildings. Don't miss the Greenock Presbyterian Church, built in 1824, the best of them all.

St. Andrews lies about 17 km south of Highway 1, in southwestern New Brunswick. It is a tourist area with lots of accommodation, including a campground at Indian Point.

A checklist, *Birds of St. Andrews*, is available at Sunbury Shores Arts and Nature Centre, 139 Water Street; phone (506) 529-3386. Refer above for contact in St. Andrews.

Birding Features
Pottery Cove. This flat muddy beach beside the historic Block House on Joes Point Road attracts shorebirds and gulls (Bonaparte's), which move through in

late May and return from late July to mid-September. It is also a good location to observe diving ducks in winter. Nearby is a public nature trail, Two Meadows, with potential for songbirds.

Indian Point. The site is about 1.5 km from downtown, at the end of the peninsula, south along Water Street. The beach and water attract a variety of species. Shorebirds and gulls gather on the intertidal zone of bedrock, sand and mud. Purple Sandpipers are here in winter. The inshore salt water attracts a diversity of water birds, including loons, eiders and scoters from fall through spring. Look for King Eiders among the huge rafts of Common Eiders in winter. Ospreys and Bald Eagles are frequently spotted. Check the bushes and woods, at the end of the point and around the sewage lagoon for songbirds during migration.

The Bar Road. This road to Ministers Island lies just over 2 km from St. Andrews on Route 127 east (Mowat Drive). Turn east on the Bar Road to the intertidal gravel bar. The bar is submerged at high tide, so park your car above high-tide mark and remember about the tide when walking. This is an attractive area for loons, grebes, cormorants and ducks, with a few shorebirds. The protected salt-water and gravelly tidal flats, with trees and shrubs along the road, make a visit from October to late May worthwhile.

DARYL LINTON
Revised by Tracey Dean

Deer Island and Campobello Island

The rich marine resources at the entrance to Passamaquoddy Bay attract large numbers of gulls and an interesting array of other seabirds. Bonaparte's Gull gatherings reach 30,000, the largest on the Atlantic coast of Canada.

A free ferry service to Deer Island operates hourly during daylight from Letete, on Route 772, off Highway 1 at St. George. In summer only, you can reach Campobello Island from Deer Island, on a commercially operated ferry. Campobello is also accessible by bridge from Lubec, Maine (on State Route 189, off U.S. 1).

Birding Features

The most attractive elements of this spot are the turbulent deep passages between islands, the sheltered coves and harbours, rocky intertidal sites, and coniferous and mixed woods.

Come from August to November to see Bonaparte's Gull; mid-October to early January for kittiwakes. Common Eider, large gulls and Black Guillemot are present all year. The concentration of gulls attracts such scarce or vagrant species as Black-headed, Little, Franklin's and Sabine's Gulls in the fall. Masses of Red-necked Phalaropes used to concentrate in the passages during late summer, but have been rare since the mid-1980s.

The ferry from Letete to Deer Island crosses Letete Passage, where there are several small islands. Black Guillemot is often seen very near the boat.

Common Eider, Surf and White-winged Scoters and Red-breasted Merganser are present from fall through spring. Bald Eagles are frequently observed.

Once on Deer Island, go south to the park at Deer Island Point, an excellent viewing area (usually best around high tide) for the gulls, which congregate in Head Harbour Passage. If the birds are too far away, check to see if the commercial ferry will take you over to Campobello and back as a foot passenger without the loss of too much time. These birds shift back and forth with the currents that bring food supplies to the surface. A winter trip should include the sheltered harbours at each village for Bufflehead and other ducks.

Campobello Island also gives good views of the birds in Head Harbour Passage. The best spots are at the northeastern end, between Wilsons Beach and East Quoddy Head (Head Harbour Light). At the latter exposed site, the deep water attracts many species at any time of the year. The beaches within Roosevelt Campobello International Park sometimes are rewarding for shorebirds.

DAVID CHRISTIE
Revised by David Christie and Ken Macintosh

Grand Manan Archipelago

New Brunswick's preeminent birding destination, Grand Manan and its 16 outlying islands, sprang to prominence among naturalists following a chance

Great Cormorant

visit from John James Audubon in 1833. He was fascinated with the Herring Gulls on White Head Island that had taken to nesting in wind-stunted conifer trees in order to protect their nests from egg collectors. The small offshore islands still offer protection to thousands of nesting gulls, common eiders and alcids, as well as hundreds of pairs of guillemots and cormorants. Pelagic species, such as shearwaters, storm-petrels, phalaropes and gannets, often abound in nearshore waters from July through October. At least 350 species of birds have been recorded in the archipelago, including many first records for the province.

First settled in 1784 by United Empire Loyalists, the island has been logged over several times. The island is a complex of young woodlands dominated by White and Red Spruce, Tamarack, White Birch, ash and Red Maple. Grand Mananers make their living from the sea, searching out herring (sardines), lobster, scallops, sea urchins, groundfish, dulse, rockweed, periwinkles and clams. Salmon aquaculture has burgeoned in the 1990s and may soon be the number one industry.

The main island is 25 km long by about 10 km and is reached by car ferry from Blacks Harbour, off Route 1, on Route 776. The ferry runs three times per day most of the year, but summer service is augmented by a second smaller ferry, and up to six trips per day take place from late June to early September. Call Coastal Transport at (506) 662-3724 for information on sailing times. Fares are reasonable. Arrive 60 to 90 minutes before sailing time. There are several hotels, bed-and-breakfasts and housekeeping units, but they should be booked months in advance, particularly for visits during July and August. Camp at Hole-in-the-Wall Campground in North Head, and Anchorage Provincial Park Campground near Seal Cove. Charter air service, by small plane, is available from the Saint John Airport. Car, bicycle and kayak rentals are available. The Grand Manan Tourism Association maintains an excellent Web site, containing a wealth of information about the island at http://personal.nbnet.nb.ca/gmtouris/

One keen birder resides on Grand Manan; Brian Dalzell can offer assistance by phone or e-mail (see above) most of the year, but may be unavailable in summer.

A visit to the Grand Manan Museum to see the more than 300 species of local mounted birds contained in the Moses Memorial Collection of Birds is highly recommended. A pocket birding guide, *Grand Manan Birds*, is available for about $5 from the museum and various other island outlets.

Birding Features
The habitat is extremely diverse, including coniferous and mixed woodlands, brushy fields and exposed headlands, precipitous cliffs and rocky intertidal areas, salt marsh, mud and sand flats, and shallow inshore waters along the eastern shore. Marine waters to 100 m deep are found immediately to the west and north of the island, and up to 200 m offshore to the east and south. April and May, and August through October, are best for small migrant land birds and shorebirds. Breeding seabirds are present from mid-May through early August, with pelagics most common from July through October. Wintering alcids are best found from late November to late January.

Laughing Gull

The archipelago abounds with many fine birding areas, but the following locations have consistently proven to be the most rewarding, and worth an hour or two of exploring in any season:

Grand Manan Channel. The channel is crossed by ferry from Blacks Harbour. The 35 km passage of about 90 minutes offers possibilities of seeing a variety of pelagic species. The last 30 minutes of the crossing are often the most productive. The tidal upwellings off the northern tip of Grand Manan can attract thousands of Black-legged Kittiwakes, shearwaters, Razorbills and Common Murres in season. Kittiwakes are best seen from September through January; jaegers and shearwaters from August through October; murres and Razorbills from November through January. Crossing during the middle or later stages of a rising tide is most productive. Several whale-watching tours operating from Grand Manan offer good opportunities for pelagic birding in late summer and early fall.

Long Eddy Point (The Whistle). The point lies at the extreme northern tip of Grand Manan, about 4 km from the village of North Head. This location can be good for migrant passerines, especially in the fall following a night with northerly winds. Activity is usually greatest in the first two hours after dawn, along the edges of woods and lawns around the lighthouse and the former keeper's home. From the lighthouse, scan the sea for shearwaters, gulls, cormorants, guillemots and terns feeding in the Long Eddy, a pronounced tidal rip. A rising tide is usually the best time to spot them. From March through May, hundreds of loons, thousands of scoters and eiders, and many other waterfowl migrate up the Grand Manan Channel. In December and January, large numbers of kittiwakes, murres, Razorbills and perhaps Dovekie can be seen milling about in the tidal rips.

Swallowtail Light/Lighthouse Road. This is one of the most productive areas on the island for migrant passerines. The rocky point lies within easy walking distance of the ferry landing. It and adjacent areas are popular with day trippers who leave their vehicles in Blacks Harbour and those with an hour or two to kill while waiting for the ferry. On the way to Swallowtail, don't forget to check Poodle Alley, Pettes Cove, the trail to Net Point, Durant Drive and Old Airport Road. The bushy areas and low coniferous growth provide good habitat for migrant songbirds in both spring and fall. The parking area at the top of the concrete stairway down to the lighthouse often produces interesting vagrants. A walk out to the end of the point affords good views of kittiwakes, eiders, Razorbills, gulls and shearwaters in season.

Castalia Marsh. The tidal salt marsh at Castalia is one of the best spots on the island for herons, ducks, shorebirds, gulls and a variety of small land birds. The marsh lies east of the main road, 8 km south of the ferry terminal. The entrance is on the left via the Marsh Road, marked with a street sign and a picnic table sign that reads "Castalia." The road out to the picnic area often washes over during winter storms, so it may be impassable until a grader arrives in late spring.

Proceed along the sea-wall road by car or foot to the picnic area. Check the beach grass and upper edges of the marsh for sparrows; scan the sea for ducks and grebes, the inner marsh for shorebirds and gulls. Past the picnic area is a large wild rose thicket in and around which several rare birds have been found over the years. It is unwise to drive any farther. Nelson's Sharp-tailed Sparrows can often be heard singing out in the marsh from this point. The gravel spit at the end of the road often has pipits, larks, buntings and longspurs in season and is a good vantage point to scan the salt marsh for herons, ducks and shorebirds. Walking back along the beach at or near high tide will often produce some good shorebirds.

White Head Island. This fishing community of about 200 souls has only a general store and post office. With only about 5 km of paved road, it can be easily birded in half a day. The free ferry leaves from Ingalls Head and takes about 30 minutes to cross. On the crossing look for sea ducks, cormorants and Black Guillemots. At the ferry landing, first turn right and bird on foot along the road, paying particular attention to the area behind the Post Office and as far as the causeway for migrant passerines. Other good spots include Battle Beach, Long Point, Sandy Cove Pond, Marsh Point, Northern Pond, Prangle Point, Gull Cove and Langmaid Cove. Arrive back at the ferry at least 45 minutes before departure to ensure getting on.

Anchorage Park/Long Pond Beach. To find the site, turn left off the main road about 3 km south of Grand Harbour. The park comprises a provincial campground and the adjacent Grand Manan Migratory Bird Sanctuary, consisting of Long and Great Ponds, the prime example of a barrier beach and barachois system on the island. The alders on the east side of the campground are often alive with warblers and sparrows after migratory fallouts. Also check the roadside adjacent to the sewage lagoon at the west end of Long Pond. Long Pond Bay is by far the best area on Grand Manan to find Red-necked and Horned Grebes; White-winged, Black and Surf Scoters; and Bufflehead. The extensive sand beach is good for Sanderling and Semipalmated Plover. During October and November, the two ponds often hold good numbers of Pied-billed Grebe, Ruddy and Ring-necked Ducks, Green-winged Teal, American Black Duck, and Greater and Lesser Scaups. Planned trails around the fringes of Long and Great Ponds make it easier to find some of the uncommon boreal species that breed on Grand Manan, such as Lincoln's Sparrow, Wilson's Warbler, Blackpoll Warbler, Yellow-bellied Flycatcher, Palm Warbler, Boreal Chickadee, Northern Waterthrush and Ruby-crowned Kinglet.

Southwest Head. The southernmost tip of the island is a sight to behold, with vertical basalt cliffs rising almost 100 m directly out of the sea. It is also the best example of a "Krummholz" forest on Grand Manan, with gnarled spruce, fir and alder along the headlands providing ample evidence of the severe pruning effects of winter wind and ice. A small colony of Black Guillemots nests in rock crevices below the lighthouse, and you can often watch them swimming underwater from the lofty heights. The trail along the cliff leading north goes to Bradford Cove Pond, worth a walk at any season, but especially from August through October when migrating passerines often make first landfall here. During periods of southerly winds in September and October, small flights of Sharp-shinned Hawks, Merlins and other raptors often take place. In late fall and early winter, alcids can often be seen by the hundreds feeding within a kilometre or two of shore, both at Southwest Head and nearby Southern Head Beach. Exercise extreme caution when approaching the edge of the cliffs.

Machias Seal Island. The 11 ha treeless island has been a federal migratory bird sanctuary since 1944 and is home to some 1500 pairs of Atlantic Puffin. Other resident birds include at least 2500 pairs of Arctic Tern, 150 of Razorbill, 100 of Common Tern, 100 of Leach's Storm-Petrel, small numbers of more widespread species and the occasional nesting pair of Common Murre, Roseate Tern, and Laughing Gull. More than 255 species of birds have been recorded on and around the island.

Machias (pronounced ma-CHY-iss) Seal Island is 18 km south of Grand Manan and 16 km off the coast of Maine. Although the island is also claimed as American territory, Canada has "squatter's rights" by virtue of having built a lighthouse here in 1832 and maintaining a manned presence ever since. Access is by chartered or private boat, with an imposed limit of 26 landed visitors per day, which is split between Canadian and American tour boat captains. Charters are available from Seawatch Tours, Seal Cove, N.B.; phone (506) 662-8556; Norton Puffin Tours, Jonesport, Maine; phone (207) 497-5933; and Bold Coast Charter Company, Cutler, Maine; phone (207) 259-4484. All have informative Web sites. Reservations should be made months in advance if you hope to actually land on the island. The Canadian tour boat runs only until early August; the Americans often run until early September.

Don't expect to see Leach's Storm-Petrels as they remain in their burrows during daylight hours. The puffins come ashore in early April and remain until late August. Peak hatching occurs in mid-June, and the young are abandoned starting in late July. Within two weeks, the fledglings make their way down to the sea – almost always at night. The terns are back by mid-May, with nesting well under way by early June. A pair or two of Roseate Terns nest on the island, but they can be difficult to find.

A summer warden is present on the island from late May through early August to guide visitors. Bring plenty of film to photograph obliging puffins (almost within reach!) and other seabirds from one of several blinds along the perimeter of the island. During May, June and August, be on the lookout for vagrant land birds. On the way out watch for shearwaters, storm-petrels, phalaropes, gannets, loons and jaegers. Be sure to look over nearby Gull Rock for first-year Great Cormorants, and of course, gulls. Overnight visitors are not allowed. Contact CWS in Sackville, N.B., for a copy of their pamphlet and bird checklist.

Revised by Brian Dalzell

Fredericton

The provincial capital is nestled in the St. John River valley, set in a forest mosaic approximately 100 km from the Bay of Fundy. Although well inland, Fredericton can boast a number of bird sightings that may be considered coastal. The river plays a major role in the natural history of this city of 50,000. Abandoned railway lines, closely parallelling the river, have been converted into a 50 km linear trail system that permits easy access to many good birding sites.

Fredericton experiences four distinct seasons; summer may be hot and winter extremely cold, causing rivers and lakes to freeze over, whereas spring invariably features a freshet that floods the lowlands, and autumn frost paints the hillsides with vivid colour.

Seasonal and habitat contrasts and marked spring and autumn migrations provide good year-round birding.

More information on the sites listed below and others of particular interest to the naturalist is given in *A Nature Guide to Fredericton and Vicinity*, available at the City of Fredericton Tourist Information Centre.

Birding Features

Odell Park. The park is essentially a forest of 120 ha surrounded by residential homes. A network of trails radiates out from the Odell Park Centre on the north side. Forest habitat ranges from old-growth hemlock, tolerant hardwoods and spruce-fir stands. The site is a good place to observe songbirds in migration and nesting seasons. Great Crested Flycatchers, Red-eyed Vireos and many species of warblers and thrushes reflect the variety of woodland habitats. Year-round residents include Barred Owls, Pileated Woodpeckers and Golden-crowned Kinglets.

Enter Odell Park at the intersection of Rookwood Avenue and Waggoners Lane.

Fredericton Wildlife Refuge. Established along the St. John River to protect young waterfowl from muskrat trapping, the refuge is bounded by a pedestrian (former railway) bridge and the Princess Margaret Bridge, the river shore on the north side and Waterloo Row to the south. The great variety of aquatic, edge and floodplain habitats, and the St. John River acting as a migration corridor, render the area especially attractive to birders.

During migration, watch for dabbling, bay and sea ducks plus an occasional loon and grebe. During hunting season this area becomes a safe haven and waterfowl numbers increase significantly. Black Duck and Common Goldeneye flocks may exceed 300 birds. Many other birds funnel through the refuge on migration.

Over the years, 211 species have been tallied at this location. Rarities include Leach's Storm-Petrel, Sabine's Gull, Western Kingbird and Kentucky Warbler.

The refuge is transected by the Salamanca Trail and is easily accessed off Waterloo Row (Route 102). Parking is available near the ballpark.

University of New Brunswick Forest. The UNB Woodlot is a mainly coniferous forest and lies on the southern edge of the city. Among a variety of other habitats, the conifers attract some boreal species, such as Spruce Grouse, Black-backed Woodpecker, Olive-sided Flycatcher, Gray Jay and Boreal Chickadee. White-winged Crossbill may be present when the cone crop is abundant. It is also one of the better local places for Whip-poor-will and Northern Saw-whet Owl.

The Corbett Marsh, a Ducks Unlimited impoundment, provides habitat for Red-winged Blackbird, dabbling ducks and more elusive marsh birds, such as American Bittern, Virginia Rail and Sora.

The main entrance to the woodlot is near the Hugh John Flemming Forestry Centre, located off Route 101 (Regent Street). A map of the road system within the woodlot is available at the centre.

Mactaquac Dam. The open water below the hydro-electric dam at Mactaquac is an excellent spot for winter birding. It serves as a gathering place for Common Goldeneye and Common Merganser, Herring and Great Black-backed Gulls, and Bald Eagle. Unusual sightings have embraced Great Cormorant, Laughing Gull and Purple Sandpiper.

The dam is reached via Route 105 on the north side of the river and is about 20 km upriver from Fredericton. En route, other interesting sites are passed. At Douglas, Currie Mountain's mantle of White Pine attracts nesting Pine Warblers, many other songbirds and Great Horned Owls. At Mouth of Keswick, just west of the intersection of Routes 104 and 105, flooded fields in spring attract a variety of waterfowl and shorebirds, including occasional rarities.

Jemseg. Downriver from Fredericton, excellent birdwatching opportunities occur along the north side of the river from McGowans Corner to Jemseg, and on to the Gagetown ferry and the village of Gagetown. The highway follows the St. John River, which is on the Atlantic Flyway, and the flooding of the intervale land coincides with spring migration.

Use care; traffic is currently heavy along the McGowans Corner to Jemseg highway (Route 2). When a new Trans-Canada route opens late in 2001, this section will become Route 105, traffic will be much lighter and observation conditions more pleasant. From Jemseg follow the signs towards Gagetown ferry.

Black-backed Woodpecker

Twenty-eight species of waterfowl have been tallied over the years. An added attraction is the fact that birds can often be viewed closely in roadside sloughs or on the river. Canada Goose, Black Duck, Green-winged and Blue-winged Teals, American Wigeon and Ring-necked Duck are the main species.

Glossy Ibis and Wilson's Phalarope may be seen most springs. Black Tern is observed on its way to nearby nesting sites. Rarities have included Purple Gallinule, Ruff, California Gull and White-winged Tern.

In winter, the intervale between McGowans Corner and Jemseg attracts Rough-legged and Red-tailed Hawks and occasionally Snowy Owls and Northern Hawk Owls.

Revised by Don Gibson and Peter Pearce

Mount Carleton Provincial Park

Set in the northern forested and unpopulated section of New Brunswick, Mount Carleton Provincial Park includes relatively high country with several hard-to-find species, such as Black-backed and Three-toed Woodpeckers, Bicknell's Thrush and Fox Sparrow, all nesting here. About 150 species of birds have been reported, with 105 as confirmed nesters.

The 181 km² wilderness park includes Mount Carleton, at 820 m the highest point in the Maritimes. Headquarters is at Nictau Lake, just off Route 385, 115 km northeast of Plaster Rock, or 52.5 km east of Saint-Quentin via Routes 180 and 385. The park is also located on the Canadian extension of the Appalachian Trail. The nearest gas, food and other services are at Riley Brook, 75 km south, and Saint-Quentin to the west. Camping space and limited cabin space are available at Nictau Lake. There is no commercial transportation into the park.

In summer, most of the park is accessible by canoe on the lakes, or by hiking the numerous trails. Roads are usable by car. In winter, park headquarters is reached by car and access to the remainder is by snowmobile, cross-country skis and snowshoes. The park is staffed year-round. For detailed information, including a checklist, contact Tourism New Brunswick (see above). For help, refer to contacts in Plaster Rock (see above).

The Tobique River, which drains Nictau Lake, is noted for its scenic beauty and canoeing. The water level is usually too low in mid to late summer near the park, but pleasant canoeing and birding are easily combined farther south, in the area of Nictau and Riley Brook.

Birding Features

A 1923 fire burned much of the park. Today it is dominated by birch and aspen. Unburned portions are covered in spruce, fir, pine and birch. Come from the last week of May to mid-July. Blackpoll Warbler, Pine Grosbeak and Fox Sparrow are found near the lake at park headquarters. The trail to the top of Mount Carleton penetrates scrubby forest at high elevations. These upper forests on Mount Carleton, Sagamook Mountain and other high points are likely places to see a Bicknell's Thrush. The bird may also occur at lower

NOVA SCOTIA

C anada's most southeasterly province contains several habitats, ranging from high and coastal "barrens" lands to lowland valleys. The high country is inhabited by such boreal birds as Spruce Grouse, Gray Jay and Pine Grosbeak. In the lowlands, look for Gray Catbird, Bobolink and Rose-breasted Grosbeak. A selective but undefined barrier for the dispersal of certain birds, other animals and plants exists in the New Brunswick–Nova Scotia boundary area. Hence many birds found nesting in eastern Canada west of Nova Scotia have not been recorded breeding in this province. These include (as of 1999) Red-shouldered Hawk, Eastern Screech-Owl, Three-toed Woodpecker, House Wren and Rufous-sided Towhee. Still others have just recently entered the province to breed. Being so far south and east, Nova Scotia tends to be visited by many species rare to Canada. People on Sable Island, part of the province but 150 km to the east, consistently report new birds for the province, Canada, and even North America. Small islands (some are sanctuaries) adjacent to Cape Breton and the southern and eastern shores are used as nesting havens for seabirds.

The 34,280 km^2 province has a population of 943,000, mostly concentrated along the coasts and in the fertile Annapolis Valley. Early settlers, particularly in the north near New Brunswick, dyked up the long inland bays. These marshlands were "reclaimed" and converted to hay crop production. With the demise of the horse as a major factor in our society, some dyked lands became vacant and converted to marshes, either naturally or under current multi-jurisdictional management. These new fresh-water wetlands are major sites for production of waterfowl and other birds. In some areas (e.g., Grand Pré) dykelands of mixed agriculture provide interesting habitats all year for open-country wildlife.

The southern half of Nova Scotia rises gently from the sea on the south side to between 30 and 150 m near the north highlands. Topography of the south area is of slight relief and contains innumerable lakes, streams, bogs and

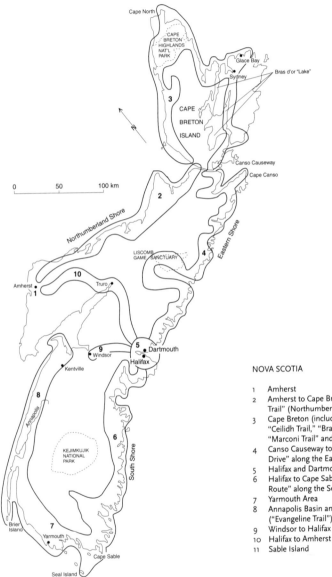

NOVA SCOTIA

1 Amherst
2 Amherst to Cape Breton: "Sunrise Trail" (Northumberland Shore)
3 Cape Breton (includes "Cabot Trail," "Ceilidh Trail," "Bras d'Or Lake Drive," "Marconi Trail" and "Fleur-de-lis Trail")
4 Canso Causeway to Halifax ("Marine Drive" along the Eastern Shore)
5 Halifax and Dartmouth
6 Halifax to Cape Sable ("Lighthouse Route" along the South Shore)
7 Yarmouth Area
8 Annapolis Basin and Valley ("Evangeline Trail")
9 Windsor to Halifax
10 Halifax to Amherst
11 Sable Island

barrens. The northern half of the province, including Cape Breton, consists of true uplands. Ranges of hills, mountains and plateaus reach elevations of over 300 m, and in Cape Breton, heights of over 425 m are attained. Most of Nova Scotia is covered by second-growth coniferous (spruce and fir) or mixed forest, with stunted conifers, as well as bogs and heathy "barrens" along exposed coasts. The main area for hardwoods occurs generally north of Truro in a wide, east-to-west belt.

A visitor to Nova Scotia should avoid the freeways and use the secondary roads, to experience the local atmosphere and to see many more birds. Ducks begin incubating in April. There are 22 warbler species found nesting here. Come in June to find them. However, this month tends to be cool, with high water in creeks and swamps. Use rubber boots and bring insect repellent. July is hot during the day and cool in the evening. Plan a trip to the Bird Islands off the northeast coast of Cape Breton, and perhaps islands on the Eastern Shore, for mid-May to late July. Note that nesting petrels can be seen only at night; during the day they're nowhere near the nesting islands (except, of course, those in their burrows); also the young of alcids are hardly ever seen on or near the nesting islands; they leave the colonies at night and go out to sea.

By mid-July, shorebirds begin returning. August weather becomes more settled and remains so through October. In late August and through mid-October you should have good birding, particularly on the islands off the south-western tip, including Bon Portage, Seal and Brier. This season and later are the times to set up your telescope on the beaches and headlands to scan for gulls. Black-headed Gulls may appear in September and will stay all winter, particularly at Glace Bay, Halifax Harbour and Cole Harbour. Bonaparte's Gulls gather coastally from late August through November and perhaps longer. Glaucous and especially Iceland Gulls are around from November through March.

A late-summer or fall offshore boat trip, easiest from Brier or Long Islands or Digby Neck for whale watching, should produce a good mix of pelagic seabirds, such as Greater, Sooty, and Manx Shearwaters; Kittiwake; Puffin and other possible alcids; phalaropes; Gannet; Leach's and/or Wilson's Storm-Petrels; and possible jaegers or skuas. A boat tour of Cape Breton's Bird Islands in summer will get you some seabirds (Puffin, Razorbill, Kittiwake), and others may be got from ferry trips across the Gulf of Maine, Bay of Fundy, or to and from Newfoundland. Whale watching and other kinds of boat tours are offered in most coastal locations in N.S.

At the north end, Amherst, with its dyked lands, probably contains the widest diversity of breeding species in the province. Around Halifax, be certain to spend at least half a day on a short loop from Dartmouth to Chezzetcook Inlet on Highway 207 looking for marsh and seabirds. Boreal species are seen easily along the short stretch north of Halifax to Windsor. The seeker of rarities should perhaps contemplate getting to either Seal Island in the southwest or, much more difficult and expensive, to Sable Island.

A visitor to Halifax should go to the harbour, then east on the Highway 207 loop, and finally north towards Windsor. This can all be done in a day. The Amherst marshes, Cape Breton or the southwest each take two to three days. In a week of long days, you can cover the province. However, there will be little time to see such places as the Fortress of Louisbourg (one of the best historical parks in the world), the Miners' Museum at Glace Bay, the Alexander Graham Bell National Historic Park at Baddeck, Grand Pré Natural History Park at Grand Pré, or many other historic parks and museums. All of these places should be visited, since they represent key chapters in Canadian history.

The main birders' group in the province is the Nova Scotia Bird Society, c/o The Nova Scotia Provincial Museum, 1747 Summer Street, Halifax, N.S. B3H 3A6, (e-mail at ip-bird@chebucto.ns.ca). The Web site at http://www.chebucto.ns.ca/Recreation/NS-BirdSoc/ contains information on how to join and order books and checklists; lists upcoming field trips and meetings; provides a telephone information line ([902] 852-CHAT [2428]) and information for visitors; reproduces the latest issue of *Nova Scotia Birds* (quarterly journal); and has links to other Web birding sites, etc. Order their excellent, detailed provincial guide called *Birding Nova Scotia*, 1991 edition, ed. J. S. Cohrs, $12. It has been a major source of the information for this chapter. The museum also has displays of mounted birds.

To get regional information, contact the person listed below for the area you're interested in.

Province-wide: Ian McLaren (902) 429-7024; e-mail, iamclar@is.dal.ca or Blake Maybank (902) 852-2077; e-mail, maybank@ns.sympatico.ca

Annapolis Valley: Richard Stern (902) 678-1975; e-mail, rbstern@ns.sympatico.ca

Antigonish County: Randy Lauff (902) 867-2471; e-mail, rlauff@juliet.stfx.ca

Brier Island: Carl Haycock (902) 839-2960; e-mail, bioscarl@TartanNET.ns.ca

Cape Breton Island: Cathy Murrant (902) 737-2684; e-mail, cmurrant@highlander.cbnet.ns.ca or Dave McCorquodale (902) 794-2172; e-mail, dmccorqu@sparc.uccb.ns.ca

Shelburne and Yarmouth Counties, including Cape Sable Island: Murray Newell (902) 745-3340; e-mail, murcar@klis.com

Amherst area: Tony Erskine (506) 536-2333

Halifax region: Blake Maybank (902) 852-2077; e-mail, maybank@ns.sympatico.ca

Pictou County: Ken McKenna (902) 752-7644; e-mail, kenmcken@north.nsis.com

Kejimkujik National Park and Seaside Adjunct: phone (902) 682-2772 or fax (902) 682-3367; or check Parks Canada Web site at http://parkscanada.pch.gc.ca; or write to P.O. Box 236, Maitland Bridge, N.S. B0T 1B0.

For excellent references check the following:

Birds of Nova Scotia, 3rd edition, 1986, by Robie W. Tufts, with revisions by members of the N.S. Bird Society under the coordination of Ian A. McLaren, co-published by Nimbus Publishing Ltd. and the N.S. Museum of Natural History, Halifax. This book is on-line at http://www.ednet.ns.ca/educ/museum/mnh/nature/nsbirds/bons.htm

Atlas of Breeding Birds of the Maritime Provinces (N.S., N.B., P.E.I.) (1986–1990 atlassing years) by Anthony J. Erskine, 1992, co-published by Nimbus Publishing Ltd. and N.S. Museum of Natural History, Halifax.

Birding in Metro Halifax, by Clarence Stevens, 1996, Nimbus Publishing Ltd., Halifax.

The Atlantic Canada Nature Guide, by Harry Thurston (with photographs by Wayne Barrett) (covers Nfld., N.B., P.E.I., N.S.), 1998, Key Porter Books, Toronto.

To obtain a highway map and the Doers and Dreamers Travel Guide, phone 1-800-565-0000 (from Canada or the U.S.A.) or (902) 425-5781 (from outside North America); visit the provincial government's Web site at http://explore.gov.ns.ca; or write to N.S. Department of Tourism, P.O. Box 130, Halifax, N.S. B3J 2M7 (e-mail, nsvisit@fox.nstn.ca). Another valuable resource to purchase is *A Map of the Province of Nova Scotia*, 1992 Edition, with index of geographical names (a book of 45 map-sheets, each 50 km square, scale 1:250,000 [1 cm = 2.5 km]), available at most bookstores in Nova Scotia.

Many visitors to Nova Scotia arrive by car at Amherst, heading for Cape Breton and the Cabot Trail. This chapter has been arranged to suit such an itinerary: along the Northumberland Shore, a full circle through Cape Breton, then down the mainland shore from Canso around to Truro.

J. WOLFORD
Revised by J. Wolford

Amherst

The impoundments managed by Ducks Unlimited and the Canadian Wildlife Service near Amherst are full of various marsh birds. With over 200 species reported from these sites, there is more diversity here than at any other location in Nova Scotia. The Tantramar Marshes of the New Brunswick–Nova Scotia border region also support very dense populations of breeding Northern Harriers and Pied-billed Grebes. The underlying gypsum deposits here have provided a soil base which results in an interesting assortment of uncommon ferns and other plants.

European settlers arrived in the 17th century and began dyking the salt marshes. For centuries these converted lands were used for hay and pasture, at least until the 1940s, when the use of the horse declined and the market for hay faded. The area became a sanctuary in 1947, and the Chignecto NWA resulted from federal government acquisition of lands in the 1970s. Ducks Unlimited (Canada) constructed impoundments in the Amherst Marshes (just north of Amherst) in the mid 1970s. Amherst contains all regular amenities, with bus and rail service too.

Information for this region was gathered from a variety of sources. The Canadian Wildlife Service produced a comprehensive brochure, map and checklist for the Chignecto NWA. For more information contact them at Chignecto National Wildlife Area, P.O. Box 1590, Sackville, N.B. E0A 3C0.

Birding Features

The woodlands of the area are dominated by conifers, including spruce, Balsam Fir and Larch. Eastern Hemlock occurs on the slopes and ridges. A few

Sugar Maple and Yellow Birch are all that remain of the once-dense hardwood stands. The old farmsteads range from open fields covered by goldenrod to growths of rose, alder and young conifers. The wetlands are managed carefully to provide maximum production of water birds. The dykes have impounded water to create shallow fresh-water marshes. Water draw-down, mechanical removal of dense vegetation, periodic mowing of old farm fields, and selective cutting of trees are all undertaken to further enhance wildlife production.

Amherst Marsh is located just off the Trans-Canada Highway, 1.8 km south of the New Brunswick border. To view the area, leave the highway at LaPlanche Street, or take the first exit into Amherst, and loop around to rejoin the Trans-Canada heading back to New Brunswick. This will allow you to park on the gravel shoulder on the marsh side of the road, nearest the impoundment ponds. Scan the area for breeding Pied-billed Grebe, Northern Pintail, Blue-winged and Green-winged Teals, American Wigeon, Northern Shoveler, Wood Duck, Redhead, Ruddy Duck, Sora, American Coot, Black Tern and Marsh Wren. Walk along the dykes for a better look.

Chignecto NWA. This wildlife area consists of the Amherst Point Migratory Bird Sanctuary on the south side of the road and the John Lusby Marsh on the north side. Leave the Trans-Canada Highway at the Victoria Street exit in Amherst and head southwest for about 2 km; find the parking lot on the left. Take time to walk around in both the sanctuary and the salt marsh. The birds here are similar to those of the Amherst Marsh. Note American Coot and Common Moorhen, both of which have nested, and listen for Virginia Rail. The variety of habitat caused by eroding gypsum sinkholes brings all sorts of different birds, particularly during migration in May and September.

Nova Scotia's only colonies of nesting Purple Martins are located at Oxford, Collingwood Corner area, and Amherst (see *Birding Nova Scotia* for details).

J. WOLFORD
Revised by J. Wolford

Amherst to Cape Breton: "Sunrise Trail" (Northumberland Shore)

On leaving Amherst, the traveller should take Highway 6 to Pictou. The birding is usually excellent along the Northumberland Strait in all seasons. The shore is easily accessible in several spots, or may be reached using sideroads, which are usually gravelled. There are several campsites and a variety of motels, hotels and restaurants from which to choose. The area retains a strong Scottish flavour. A visitor should try to take in one or more local fairs or gatherings that each community sponsors in the summer.

Birding Features

On the drive east, take one or more of the sideroads to the sea, as they often traverse salt marshes or skirt brackish lagoons. East of Pugwash 8 km along Highway 6, don't miss Wallace Bay National Wildlife Area. From Wallace, drive 8 km west, and a big sign will direct you onto a paved but neglected road north.

Go 1 km. Look for the water-control gate, where signs show a road leading to a parking lot; from there a circular nature trail allows the exploration of a mosaic of many habitats for marsh, water and land birds. It follows a dyke between the river/salt marsh and a large impounded marsh, turns onto another dyke across the marsh, then loops back through a few different types of forest. Allow 1 to 2 hours for the 4 km. This is one of many areas that attract a variety of shorebirds from mid-July through September.

Scan the sea at any likely viewpoint in the fall for Canada Geese, Greater Scaups and both goldeneyes. In late summer look for Bonaparte's Gulls. In spring, transient Brants often rest along the shore.

At Pictou, along the causeway across the harbour on Highway 2, you will see some old wharf pilings that support a very visible and thriving nesting colony of Double-crested Cormorants. East of New Glasgow, instead of taking the main highway east, take the more interesting Highway 245 at Exit 27 just east of Sutherland River. The drive around the tip of Cape George, is worth the time. About 15 km east of the turnoff from the freeway, beyond Merigomish and about 1.8 km from Barneys River Bridge, watch for the turn towards the sea and Merigomish Island (alias Big Island). Drive to the end of the road. Migrating geese and ducks rest in the shallow water, and shorebirds can be found on the beach south of the sand spit leading to the island. Particularly check for Whimbrel, which come regularly in August. Beware of soft sand on the shoulder of the road.

Continue around Cape George Point and head south. Beyond Morristown about 3.5 km, watch for the sideroad down to the water at Jimtown. Cormorants, mostly Great, have a big colony at Crystal Cliffs, near the community. Avoid a visit to the colony in May or June, since gulls and ravens will take eggs and chicks if the parents are disturbed.

Continue on towards Antigonish. There you will find St. Francis Xavier University, established in 1853; the oldest continuing newspaper in the Maritimes, *The Casket*; and Canada's oldest Highland Games. Go down to Antigonish Harbour to check the tidal marsh; the best access points are back along Highway 337, northeast of town. During spring and fall migration many waterfowl rest here. Several species also breed in this secluded area. Bald Eagles, which are common, may have caused the current rarity of formerly abundant local Ospreys (Nova Scotia's provincial bird).

Still in the Antigonish area, some very nice sandy beaches are Mahoney's Beach, just south of Jimtown; Monk's Head; and especially Pomquet Beach Provincial Park, northeast of Pomquet. Poison ivy is extremely common above these beaches.

J. WOLFORD
Revised by J. Wolford

Cape Breton (includes "Cabot Trail," "Ceilidh Trail," "Bras d'Or Lake Drive," "Marconi Trail" and "Fleur-de-lis Trail")

Bras d'Or Lake, an inland body of salt water, and its surrounding shores contain one of the largest concentrations of nesting Bald Eagles in northeastern North

America. The adjacent Bird Islands, with colonies of Atlantic Puffin, Razorbill and other seabirds, add to the experience. The area abounds in history, particularly because of the Fortress of Louisbourg, one of the largest and most realistic restoration sites in the world. At Baddeck, the Alexander Graham Bell National Historic Park displays inventions from the telephone to aviation technology developed by this genius. Many local activities are more Scottish than in the Highlands of Scotland.

History began here with Portuguese settlers, about 25 years after the landing of John Cabot in 1497, followed by colonists from France and Scotland over the next three centuries. Today, numerous museums, especially the coal miners' story told at Glace Bay, add to an in-depth look at the region's past.

The one land entrance to Cape Breton is the 1.4 km long Canso Causeway, opened in 1955. In the ice-free harbour on the east side, watch for giant supertankers, some larger than three football fields, discharging oil at Point Tupper, south of Port Hawkesbury. A bus from Sydney services the area. Accommodation and services are available at any of the larger centres.

Birding Features

Once across the causeway, start to head east on Highway 104, towards Sydney and the Fortress of Louisbourg. Turn south immediately after the causeway, turn south and drive about 5 km to Point Tupper. Turn east and then south onto 104 and continue for about 40 km to St. Peter's. To the south, at Cape Auguet and Petit-de-Grat on Isle Madame, and southeast at Point Michaud via Highway 247, are excellent heathy headlands loaded with berries to attract migrant shorebirds from mid-July to September.

Take a sideroad, 247, south to Point Michaud. Return by Highway 247 to Highway 4 and continue east towards Sydney, where you can take the ferry from North Sydney to Newfoundland. If you stay, continue on to Glace Bay and the Miners' Museum. Black-headed Gulls are usually found at Glace Bay from September through the winter. Go south and east on 255 towards Donkin and Port Morien, to the sanctuary (ask locally for exact location). Here from November to April you can spot Black-headed Gulls in fair numbers, together with Canada Geese and many ducks. From mid-July into fall, watch for a variety of shorebirds, including Willet and Common and Arctic Terns. Continue south and west on 255 and 22 to Louisbourg. On the way, stop and scan for gulls and shorebirds.

Head towards Sydney on 22; loop around it via North Sydney, on 125 and 105. Farther west, take appropriate roads to either Big Bras d'Or or Englishtown, the two departure points for boat tours to the Bird Islands. On these islands you'll find thousands of seabirds from mid-May to mid-August. The operators are Bird Islands Tours, Ltd. (at Big Bras d'Or, e-mail birdisld@ fox.nstn.ca; phone 1-800-661-6680) and Puffin Boat Tours (at Englishtown, e-mail puffin@auracom.com; phone 1-877-2-PUFFIN). Expect a 2.5-to-3-hour trip in a safe, roofed boat; it cannot land on the sanctuary islands but will skirt them closely, to afford good views of Puffin, probably Razorbill, Kittiwake, Black Guillemot, both Great and Double-crested Cormorants, gulls, Bald Eagle and Gray Seal. Leach's Storm-Petrels nest here, too, but are not visible during the day. The trip costs about $30 per adult, $13 per child. Accommodation is available at campgrounds or motels not far from Big Bras d'Or.

Return to Highway 105, continue west to Exit 12, and turn right to Englishtown. At this community, barring the mouth of St. Ann's Bay, is a spit, which provides a good resting spot for Bald Eagles, shorebirds, gulls and terns.

Back on 105, continue to Exit 11. You now have the choice of going north along the Cabot Trail or taking a jaunt southwest to Baddeck, the former summer home of Alexander Graham Bell and now site of a museum of his inventions. There is also a birding spot at nearby Nyanza, 14 km to the west. Scan the water here for Great Blue Heron, nine species of ducks, Bald Eagle, Osprey and Common Tern.

Now retrace your route northeast on Highway 105 to Exit 11 and turn left onto the Cabot Trail, around the north end of Cape Breton. Stop at park head-quarters to consult with a naturalist. Try the nature trail at the southeast end of the park, behind Keltic Lodge (Middle Head). You may find several boreal species, including Spruce Grouse, warblers and Evening Grosbeak in summer.

Established in 1936, Cape Breton Highlands National Park covers 950 km² and forms part of the upper tableland of Cape Breton. The highest point in Nova Scotia, 532 m, occurs here. The western coast has spectacular cliffs that rise nearly 300 m above the sea. Tree cover includes Hemlock, White Pine and Balsam Fir on the higher elevations. Large areas of the central plateau are devoid of trees. Over 180 species of birds have been recorded. Information, including a bird checklist, is obtainable from The Superintendent, Cape Breton Highlands National Park, Ingonish Beach, N.S. B0C 1L0; phone (902) 285-2270.

Watch for Northern Gannets diving off the coast. Great and Double-crested Cormorants, Great Black-backed and Herring Gulls, Common and Arctic Terns, Black Guillemot and Common Raven all nest along here. American Black and Ring-necked Ducks, Common and Red-breasted Mergansers and Common Goldeneye breed on the inland ponds. Northern Goshawk, Bald Eagle, and Spruce and Ruffed Grouse are common. A variety of shorebirds migrate through from late July to November, including Black-bellied Plover, Ruddy Turnstone, Whimbrel and White-rumped Sandpiper. Listen for the rel-atively common Barred Owl in May and June. Possible sightings of Moose, Lynx, Black Bear, Beaver and other mammals would be bonuses.

There are over 20 hiking trails from Warren Lake and Black Brook on the park's eastern side to the Cheticamp area at the southwest corner. Camping is available at seven campgrounds from mid-May to late October.

North of the park, leave the Cabot Trail just west of Cape North and head north to Bay St. Lawrence. Park the car and walk east to Money Point in late September or October. Birds rest on the point on their way south. You could spot Northern Shrike; American Tree, White-crowned and Fox Sparrows; and others. Return to the car and the Cabot Trail; work your way through the park and then along the west shore to Cheticamp River, the southwest entrance to the park. Take the trail behind the campsite and follow it along the river. In May and June, watch for Yellow-bellied Flycatcher, Blackburnian and Blackpoll Warblers and Northern Waterthrush. Ask the park naturalists where to try for the Bicknell's Thrush (recently split from the Gray-cheeked).

The steep cliffs on the southern tip of nearby Cheticamp Island have nesting colonies of Great and Double-crested Cormorants plus Black-legged Kittiwakes.

Follow the Cabot Trail south through Margaree Forks, then east to North East Margaree. From here, proceed north through Margaree Valley; drive about 1.5 km north and turn right off the paved road; follow this gravel road about 12 km north through Rivulet to Kingross and Big Intervale, 1 km west. You may wish to return on the much more primitive "wagon trail" south of Big Intervale to the pavement at Portree, thence to North East Margaree and Margaree Forks, and onto Route 19. The road up the river valley to Kingross and Big Intervale goes around Sugarloaf Mountain, with these hills rising 487 m. Above you will be spectacular though remote scenery and good woodland birding.

Continue south on Highway 19 to Harbourview, 3 km south of Port Hood. At this point, leave 19 for the road that runs along the beach through Maryville then back to Highway 19, about 8 km south of where you left it. This sideroad takes you by the Judique, Catharine and McKay's Ponds. These barrier beach ponds provide havens for ducks and shorebirds. Watch for Bald Eagles.

J. WOLFORD

Revised by J. Wolford

Canso Causeway to Halifax ("Marine Drive" along the Eastern Shore)

The drive from the Canso Causeway to Halifax combines natural history, history and magnificent scenery. Nova Scotians call this stretch the "Eastern Shore." You will find a region of sheltered coves, friendly villages and quiet woodlands. The boreal habitat is mixed with seaside marshes. Look for a good variety of warblers, including Blackpoll, and shorebirds in mid to late summer. You can also take a launch across to the Eastern Shore Bird Sanctuary to look for nesting Common Eiders, etc. Leach's Storm-Petrels nest here too, but are only visible and especially audible at night when they approach or leave their burrows.

Canso, founded in 1518, survived Indian raids, capture by the French and attacks by pirates. The other communities in the area were established much later.

The Marine Drive, skirting the shore from the Canso Causeway to Dartmouth-Halifax, covers nearly 370 km of twisting roads. There are many communities and services along the way.

Birding Features

Once off the Canso Causeway, turn left, or southeast, onto Highway 344 and follow it around to Boylston. You might wish to explore the roads on both sides of the lower Milford Haven River and Guysborough Harbour. Birds of the water, marsh and upland are usually quite abundant here.

Follow Highway 16 south and east out to Canso. The "barren" headlands around this area are covered with Crowberry. Flocks of Whimbrel stop and feed on their way south from mid-July to September. Retrace your route to the junction with Highway 316 and take this road southwest along the shore to New Harbour. The estuary provides easy observation of migrating water and shore birds. Scan for Baird's and Buff-breasted Sandpipers and godwits in late summer.

The area around Country Island, at the mouth of Country Harbour, has recently been found to support nesting Roseate Terns, a threatened species in Canada. This area is also a site of feverish developmental activities, because of the pipeline for natural gas from Sable Island landing at Goldboro, the site of a new gas-processing plant.

Continue on to Isaac's Harbour North and across on the ferry; swing west to join Highway 7 just beyond Jordanville; turn south on 7 to Sherbrooke. The town's oldest section, Sherbrooke Village, has been restored to its condition of about a hundred years ago, when it was a boom community. Go in and observe carding and spinning, weaving on antique looms, and blacksmithing.

Follow 7 south to the rugged coast adjacent to boreal forest. These woods have a variety of northern bird species, including Blackpoll Warbler on the outer wooded headlands and islands and Lincoln's Sparrow in the Black Spruce bogs. The Common Eider is often seen in June and July with young. The numerous inlets may contain flocks of all three scoters on their way south in the fall.

Continue about 4 km beyond Ecum Secum to the sideroad heading north. Check the marshes along the Ecum Secum River at Fleet Settlement on the east side of the river (1 km north and then branch to the right for another kilometre), and at New Chester (go back south to the Y junction, take the northwest road on the west side of the river and drive about 5 km north). You should spot a variety of water birds, including Great Blue Heron, American Bittern and Common Snipe.

Return to the highway and continue west. At the next community, Necum Teuch, and at Harrigan Cove, 12 km farther, you could charter a boat for exploring the offshore islands. However, within the Eastern Shore Islands Wildlife Management Area, from Round Island (east) to Little White Island (west), landing on the islands is prohibited during the breeding season. Some of these islands are owned by the N.S. Bird Society, and many of them are managed by the N.S. Department of Natural Resources.

Breeding birds on the islands include Common Eider, Double-crested Cormorant, Common and Arctic Terns, Herring and Great Black-backed Gulls, Black Guillemot, and (audible and visible only at night) Leach's Storm-Petrel. Fox Sparrows may be among the breeding songbirds.

To sample some excellent back-country woodland birding, take the loop north (374) through Liscomb Game Sanctuary, west to Highway 224, then back south to Highway 7 near Sheet Harbour. The circle begins just over 20 km west of Harrigan Cove and immediately east of Sheet Harbour. When you drive north into the sanctuary, take note of which way you go, as there are many side trails. Keep heading north along the lake, then follow the river. Angle a bit northwest to Trafalgar. The numerous lakes, streams and forest in this 453 km² game sanctuary have abundant wildlife and good fishing. Nesting boreal species of birds are everywhere from mid-May through June. At Trafalgar, drive southwest to join Highway 336 at Dean.

From Sheet Harbour, continue along the shore drive for another 41 km to Ship Harbour. Just beyond this community, take the loop road southeast along the bay down to the point at Little Harbour. Retrace your route about 3 km north, then proceed west to Clam Harbour. Continue for 2 km and take the left fork through Clam Bay, then north to regain Highway 7 just east of Lake Charlotte. During late April and May, and again from mid-July through September, shorebirds rest and feed along these beaches. The nearby forested areas contain Spruce Grouse.

At Musquodoboit Harbour, about 18 km beyond Lake Charlotte, take the road south to Martinique Beach and the game sanctuary. The trip of approximately 12 km is worthwhile for the numerous Great Blue Herons, various ducks, geese in the fall through spring, nesting Osprey and large numbers of shorebirds.

Return to Highway 7, where you may continue to Dartmouth-Halifax or take a side trip north for woodland birds. For the side trip, head north from Musquodoboit Harbour on Highway 357. You'll follow the Musquodoboit River for about 40 km to Middle Musquodoboit and the junction with Highway 224. Take 224 west to Highway 102, then south to Halifax. From mid-May through June, you should add several woodland species to your list.

If you decide to continue west on Highway 7, turn south onto Highway 207; it lies about 13 km west of Musquodoboit Harbour (just prior to meeting Highway 107). This section of road provides a comprehensive look at a wide variety of Nova Scotia birds. If time is limited, this is one area not to miss (refer to Halifax area: Chezzetcook to Dartmouth, below). You'll see Bald Eagle, nesting Osprey, a variety of shorebirds (including Purple Sandpiper from late fall to spring), plus many others.

J. WOLFORD
Revised by J. Wolford

Halifax and Dartmouth

Near this centre of Canadian history, a birdwatcher can find over 60 species during an easy day in June. Take a trip out to sea; find boreal species like kinglets just north of the city, and locate 15 breeding species of warbler plus the "Ipswich Sparrow" (a race of Savannah Sparrow from Sable Island) during migration. A short distance north of these twin cities, the Waverley Game Sanctuary hosts Black Bear, Moose and Deer.

Halifax was founded in 1749. It and Dartmouth are full of echoes of our past, from press gangs who walked the street, through privateers who auctioned off their goods from a warehouse, to the home of one of the Fathers of Confederation. The modern city of high-rises still retains streets where Wolfe and Captain James Cook walked. The latter supervised the construction of the oldest naval dockyard in North America, begun in 1759.

In 1752, the first salt-water ferry system in Canada was established between Halifax and Dartmouth. Canada's first responsible government met in the sandstone Province House on February 2, 1848. Between the two cities, Bedford Basin and Halifax Harbour are large enough to hold the combined world navies. Dartmouth Park was built by New England Quakers who revised the first town plan to include a common (grassy opening) in 1785. The many parks in both cities, and the 26 lakes in Dartmouth, provide havens for birdlife.

Accommodation is readily available in Halifax. The international airport lies northeast of the city complex, just east of Highway 102.

Birding Features

Halifax. If you come here from late fall to early spring, go down to the docks and sewer outfalls along the waterfront. You will spot a variety of gulls, including Glaucous, Iceland, Great Black-backed, Herring, Ring-billed, Black-headed, Bonaparte's and very possibly others. Lesser Black-backed, Mew (Common) and possibly Thayer's Gulls have been seen in recent winters. Also there for winter viewing, perhaps on one of the N.S. Bird Society's popular "Sewer Stroll" field trips, are a variety of ducks, loons, grebes, cormorants, and often alcids.

Check with the Bird Society about any planned boat trips out of the Halifax area for pelagic birds. You might find shearwaters, storm-petrels, gannets, kittiwakes, alcids, phalaropes, jaegers, etc., and perhaps whales, dolphins, or porpoises, as well as various near-shore birds.

Dartmouth. The immediate Dartmouth area has several sites to examine: Sullivan's Pond, about six blocks north of Dartmouth Cove, lies at the south end of Lake Banook, along Prince Albert Road. The pond is excellent for waterfowl in winter. To reach Russell Lake, on the southeast side of Dartmouth, go east from the Circumferential Highway (111) on Portland Street (207) for a long block and then turn right onto Baker Drive, which gets you close. Scan for waterfowl. Bell Lake lies farther east along Portland Street to Bayswater Road (west side of the lake), or Ayr Avenue (east side). Follow either of these streets around the lake to Dorothea Drive on the north side of the marshy end to find a variety of waterfowl.

Dartmouth to Hartlen Point and on to Chezzetcook. South of Dartmouth, and then east to Head of Chezzetcook, you'll find practically every kind of habitat in Nova Scotia, plus good vantage points.

Hartlen Point, south of Dartmouth on Highway 322 beyond Eastern Passage, has become one of the premier spots for birding, and for finding many rarities as well as regular species of birds of the land, marshes, shorelines, and even open ocean. You'll find lots of details and maps in *Birding Nova Scotia*, and the same can be said for Dartmouth to Chezzetcook.

Drive back to Eastern Passage, then turn right and make a coastal tour of Cow Bay and Rainbow Haven and then to Cole Harbour. Get on Highway 207 and do the "Lawrencetown Loop" – exploring coastal side trails and abandoned railway rights-of-way – through West Lawrencetown, Conrad's Beach/Fox Point, Lawrencetown Beach, the loop to Three Fathom Harbour, Seaforth, Grand Desert, West Chezzetcook, and beyond. Phone (902) 852-CHAT (2428) for up-to-date information on any upcoming field trips in these areas, as well as current provincial sightings.

From May through early July, look for American Bittern nesting in the marshes, with American Black Duck, Green-winged and Blue-winged Teals, and Ring-necked Duck. Ospreys and Bald Eagles both nest in this area; the latter may be seen throughout the year. Short-eared Owls are sometimes found in the open dune areas at Conrad's and Lawrencetown Beaches. Stop at the White and Black Spruce forests for boreal species. Listen and look for Yellow-bellied and other flycatchers; Gray Jays are quite numerous; four species of swallow can be spotted; Black-capped and Boreal Chickadees and kinglets are abundant; about 15 species of warbler may be seen, the most common being Black-and-white, Nashville, Northern Parula, Magnolia, Yellow-rumped, Chestnut-sided, Blackpoll and Common Yellowthroat. Look for the Ipswich Sparrow during spring and fall migration in the dunes close to shore; this area is the closest to their breeding ground on Sable Island. The Sharp-tailed Sparrow nests in salt marshes, whereas the Savannah Sparrow is more likely along the drier margins.

In the fall and winter, look for Common and Red-throated Loons and Red-necked and Horned Grebes feeding close to shore. You may spot up to 100 Great Blue Herons feeding in shallow inlets at low tide during migration in the fall. Large flocks of Canada Geese and Black Ducks appear in the fall and remain all winter. Common Goldeneye, Bufflehead, Oldsquaw, Common Eider, all three species of scoters and Common and Red-breasted Mergansers are winter residents. Look for Black-headed Gulls in Cole Harbour and elsewhere in fall and winter. Purple Sandpipers are regular in winter on Fox Island off Conrad's Beach.

Snowy Owls are sometimes found on Devil's Island off Hartlen Point, or in the open dunes at Conrad's or Lawrencetown beaches. At Lawrencetown Beach, check the fresh-water and salt-water marshes. Farther east about 5 km, at Three Fathom Harbour, scan for more waterfowl. This stretch of coast is also a good site to watch large movements of Horned Lark, Water Pipit, Lapland Longspur and Snow Bunting during fall and winter.

Halifax to Sambro. Birding in the Halifax area would not be complete without a tour south along the west shore of Halifax Harbour, especially from fall through winter to spring. On the west side of the Northwest Arm (a long bay off Halifax Harbour), take either the Herring Cove Road or the Purcell's Cove Road – the latter is initially more coastal, but they join up later, at Herring Cove. Continue south through Bear Cove and Portuguese Cove, and don't miss the high lookout at Chebucto Head, from which seabirds and whales can often be spotted. Explore Ketch Harbour and the Sambro area. (The N.S. Bird Society's "Sewer Strolls" in winter usually start at Hartlen Point in the early morning and finish at dusk somewhere north of Sambro.)

Halifax West. Take Route 333 southwest of the city to Peggy's Cove and then north along the shore to Highway 3 west. This half-circle will bring you in contact with mainly boreal species. A visit to the inshore waters should provide Herring and Great Black-backed Gulls, and Common and Arctic Terns. In late summer and fall, scan the ocean for numbers of loons, grebes, cormorants, alcids and sea ducks.

J. WOLFORD
Revised by J. Wolford

Halifax to Cape Sable ("Lighthouse Route" along the South Shore)

The South Shore, as Nova Scotians call the strip from Halifax to Cape Sable, was home to the mariners who dominated the region in the 1800s to early 1900s. The people of Lunenburg once owned the largest deep-sea fleet fishing the Grand Banks off Newfoundland. The pride of their fleet, *Bluenose*, was the fastest sailing ship afloat in the 1920s and 1930s.

Settled by Germans, Swiss and United Empire Loyalists, the area today retains some fine examples of small fishing communities, including Peggy's Cove at the southeast corner of St. Margaret's Bay. Birding is fair along this stretch of coast, but the atmosphere to be had in the communities is worth the trip. In Liverpool, you can imagine you are back in the late 1700s fighting to save your home from French, Spanish and Yankee privateers, or getting ready to sail to the Caribbean in retaliation for a raid on your ships down there.

This approximately 250 km stretch of road is a major highway, 103, but you'll be rewarded with scenery and other diversions, including birds, if you take the time to explore shoreline loops on the Lighthouse Route. And don't miss the many white sand beaches, with endangered Piping Plovers trying to survive on them, in Lunenburg and Shelburne Counties. Accommodation abounds together with other amenities.

Birding Features

Proceed west from Halifax on Highway 103 to avoid the suburban area adjacent to the city. Take Highway 3 from Interchange 4, west along the northern shore of St. Margaret's Bay to Hubbards (north of Fox Point). The best time to visit the bay is from late fall through winter, to look for Red-throated Loon, Red-necked and Horned Grebes, Great Cormorant, goldeneyes, Oldsquaw, mergansers, Thick-billed Murre and occasional Common Murre, and Dovekie. In the colder months, head south of Hubbards on Highway 329, loop around the Aspotogan Peninsula and back north to Highway 3 at East River. Scan the waters for seabirds.

In recent years, the islands southwest of the Aspotogan or Blandford Peninsula have been found to support nesting colonies of threatened Roseate Terns. Also, well offshore to the south, Pearl Island has nesting seabirds, including puffins.

At East River, watch for the highway sign, "East River Point." At 3.4 km west of this sign, look for the abandoned road on the north side of Highway 3. This old road, which leads to an abandoned power dam, should be hiked for a kilometre or more upstream along the East River to spot a good collection of warblers from late May to early July.

Proceed west on Highway 3 and follow it south to Lunenburg. Take coastal Route 332 to Kingsburg, on the tip of the peninsula, for ducks and shorebirds in early spring and late fall. Loop back on 332 northwest to Bridgewater. This community is the centre of a network of roads good for spotting flycatchers, warblers and finches in the varied woodland habitat. If you arrive here in late July or August, you may be lucky enough to experience the often spectacular Common Nighthawk migration along the La Have River.

At Bridgewater, turn southeast onto Highway 331, which follows the west bank of La Have River. Go past La Have for about 8 km to Crescent Beach. This is one of the best sites along the South Shore for migrating ducks and shorebirds. The road behind the beach affords excellent views on foot or from the car of wading birds in the salt marsh and mudflats when the tide is out a bit. The woodlands along this route also abound in birds. West of Crescent Beach, in and around the estuary of Petite Rivière (including Risser's Beach Provincial Park), look for nesting Spotted Sandpiper, Willet, Osprey, kingfishers, Bank Swallows, etc.

Southwest along Route 331, find the beach at Cherry Hill by looking for an access road, poorly marked, just north of the fire hall. As with many beaches in N.S., the dunes shelter an extensive tidal or salt marsh, which can be very productive for wading and other birds. Then continue on 331 to rejoin 103 and on to Liverpool where Highway 8 heads north to Kejimkujik National Park (see below).

From Liverpool, take either 103 or Route 3. Two very nice white sand beaches can be explored at Summerville Centre (Summerville Beach) or at the end of the road southeast of South West Port Mouton (Carter's Beach) – confused? And Mouton is pronounced Ma-toon!

Farther along 103, probably the province's most spectacular white sand beach is accessible from Port Joli. Follow the road along the east shore of Port Joli Bay, which incidentally is full of water birds, especially geese and ducks, during spring and fall migrations and through the winter. The same can be said of the next two bays to the southwest. Some viewing of Port Joli and Port l'Hebert Bays can be done from the car, carefully, along Highway 103. In all three bays, you should be able to spot Canada Goose, Brant, cormorants, loons, grebes, American Black Duck, Greater Scaup, and goldeneyes, often in large flocks, as well as Northern Pintail, Green-winged and Blue-winged Teals, mergansers, and other possible diving and dabbling ducks (and terns, herons, kingfishers, Osprey, etc., in summer).

Back along the edge of Port Joli Bay, watch for signs for the Seaside Adjunct of Kejimkujik National Park. From a new parking area and signage, a nice path passes through mixed forest and shrubs and boggy open areas (with bog plants like orchids and pitcher plants). It's about a 40-minute walk to the idyllic St. Catherine's River Beach, dunes and salt marsh. One caveat: from April through July most of the beach may be roped off and inaccessible, in order to protect nesting Piping Plovers. Inquire ahead of time by contacting Kejimkujik via the Parks Canada Web site: http://parkscanada.pch.gc.ca – or write to P.O. Box 236, Maitland Bridge, N.S. BOT 1BO; phone (902) 682-2772, fax (902) 682-3367.

The inland part of Kejimkujik National Park is accessible via Highway 8 either north from Liverpool or south from Annapolis Royal. This is a very large area of mostly wilderness, soon to be much larger with the addition of the new Tobeatic Wilderness Area (formerly Wildlife Management Area). It is mostly mixed forest with many hiking trails, but is perhaps best known for its many lakes that make it a premier canoeing area. Contact the park (see above) to get natural history information, a bird checklist and other information.

Farther along Route 103, turn off to the south at Sable River. This road begins as pavement but soon becomes gravel. Follow the east bank of Sable River to the far south. In the area of the Jones Harbour wharf, bird the nearby beach and shore. The road ends to the northeast at Johnston's Pond (at Little Port l'Hebert). Park here and walk southeast or northwest. This area hosts most local shorebirds in addition to woodland birds. Look for Harlequin Ducks in winter, as well as all those bay birds mentioned above.

Return to Highway 103. Immediately west of Sable River, turn south along Highway 3 for about 3 km; branch off to the southeast on the road to West Middle Sable; follow it south along the west side of Sable River. Stop several times, particularly at Louis Head Beach, to explore habitats and paths. The nearby forest edges are wintering areas for the Yellow-rumped (Myrtle) Warbler.

Continue southeast just over 2 km to Little Harbour; swing straight south towards Arnold. This dirt road terminates in a large open field on Hemeon's Head, with the sea in sight to the east, south and west. Park the car and walk along the clearly marked path heading west along the beach. Look for Whimbrels on headlands with low-growing berry-bearing shrubs. The other shorebirds concentrate in a large area of tidal marsh flats behind the barrier beach, starting about 2.4 km from your car. To reach these, walk to the west end of the beach; then, with amphibious footwear, at low tide, walk north towards the middle of Matthew's (= Little Harbour) Lake along the flats. Up to 27 species of shorebirds pass through here, including Hudsonian Godwit. Along the upper beach is one of many places in N.S. where Northern Wheatear might appear in September or October.

This is a good time to mention an excellent new pamphlet called *Birding on the Lighthouse Route in Shelburne County*; to get it, contact either the Shelburne County Tourism Coordinator, (902) 875-3634, buspark@atcon.com, Web site http://www.shelburne.nscc.ns.ca/tourism/mainpage.htm; or South Shore Tourism Association, (902) 624-6466, ssta@fox.nstn.ca. This pamphlet provides a checklist and maps and details for 13 sites in the county.

From Little Harbour, north of Hemeon's Head, drive northwest to Highway 3, then south to Lockeport. Check out the small Crescent Beach there, but continue south to West Head. Access is via a private pasture with cows. This rocky promontory is a popular area for hunting sea ducks in October and November. Watch your step, and the waves, on the rocks.

Return to Highway 3 and follow it north to Jordan Falls, then take 103 west to Exit 26 at Shelburne. Take Route 203 north towards the Ohios for the most accessible inland birding locations in this area. This drive meanders for about 40 km along the scenic Roseway River, crossing it many times. The hardwood and conifer hills, fields and many wetlands provide numerous opportunities for watching a wide variety of bird life. Many logging and fire roads become walking areas for birders in search of grouse, hawks, owls, freshwater ducks, Black-backed and other woodpeckers, 23 species of warblers, and many others.

Continue west from Shelburne to Clyde River; swing south through Port Clyde, then southeast through Port Saxon, North West and North East Harbours to Ingomar, where the pavement ends. Take the dirt road south to

East Point, a good spot for watching migrants of both land and water birds, particularly during bad weather. To the north, Round Bay beach and Red Head are also worth exploring.

Return to Port Clyde and head south again, first on the road that leads to Blanche (park and then walk), and then to Baccaro Point. Both headlands are good places for a variety of birds (Baccaro) and seabirds (south of Blanche). North of Baccaro Point, Crow Neck Beach is another lovely spot for Piping Plover, etc.

At Port La Tour, swing west and north to Barrington. Follow Highway 3 south and then take Route 330 across the causeway onto Cape Sable Island (not to be confused with far-offshore Sable Island! – see below). This is certainly one of the best birding areas in eastern Canada. Continue south through Clark's Harbour, south of which is a fork where you can go straight to The Hawk or left to Daniel's Head (= Donald Head on map).

Along the road out to Daniel's Head, to the south are dunes and a long beach of white sand (extends from the Head all the way past The Hawk). To your north look for vantage points for viewing the mudflats for wading birds when the tide is partly out. Also check around the fish plant and the railway cars and parked trucks etc. for migrant land birds. The long beach harbours nesting Piping Plovers, and recently American Oystercatchers have occurred and nested nearby. A walk in the area of The Hawk can be very productive for migrants, including raptors, shorebirds (in numbers and diversity), and just about any songbirds that you can imagine, and then some! This area is renowned for rarities. Slightly north of The Hawk area is a wharf and fish plant, which is a great viewing spot for the mudflats when the tide is ebbing or coming in.

Not far offshore from The Hawk is a long, sandy island accessible only by boat – ask at the post office in Clark's Harbour or elsewhere. A long walk on this island can be very fruitful – don't neglect to look around the lighthouse. Over 30 species of warblers have been seen hawking insects around the buildings. Breeding birds on or near the island include the oystercatchers mentioned above, Common and Arctic and perhaps Roseate Terns and Bank Swallow. Black-crowned Night-Heron are regular in this area, since they nest on both Cape Sable Island and Bon Portage Island (see below).

If you come in winter, look for loons, grebes, diving ducks (including Common Goldeneye, Bufflehead, Oldsquaw, all three scoters and mergansers), gulls, murres, Dovekie, Black Guillemot, Horned Lark, Lapland Longspur and Snow Bunting.

For any questions about Cape Sable Island, including boat trips, contact Murray Newell, one of several very keen birders there ([902] 745-3340 or murcar@klis.com).

West from Cape Sable Island, two offshore islands, Bon Portage and Seal, have long histories of bird observations. Bon Portage (or "Outer Island" on some maps), now owned by Acadia University and managed by Acadia's Biology Department, is quite close (a few kilometres) and easy to reach, via a fishing boat from Shag Harbour or by arrangement with Acadia Biology (phone [902] 680-1444 [cell phone on the island]). This island offers lighthouse buildings in which to stay (for a charge) and lots of migrant birds, especially from August through October. There's a nesting colony of Black-crowned Night-Herons, but perhaps Bon Portage's biggest claim to fame is the more than 50,000 pairs of Leach's Storm-Petrels in nesting burrows. The fairy-like atmosphere created by the petrels' calls in the air and underground after dark has to be experienced!

In contrast, Seal Island, which is perhaps better for rarities, is much harder to access, since it's 32 km from Clark's Harbour. There is no regular boat service to the island. Lobster fishermen will occasionally take passengers during the spring and autumn. You should make inquiries via the N.S. Bird Society Bird Information Line, (902) 852-CHAT (2428) or e-mail, ip-bird@cfn.cs.dal.ca, to find out about any upcoming field trips (spring, fall holiday weekends) to either Bon Portage or Seal. This would be the easiest and cheapest way to access either island, especially Seal. You need to be totally self-sufficient for any visit, especially to Seal, with food, sleeping bag, lantern, stove and fuel, and good boots; inquire about water. Accommodation on Seal Island can be obtained either via the Bird Society or by contacting Mrs. Mary Nickerson, P.O. Box 336, Clark's Harbour, N.S. B0W 1P0, well ahead of time, to reserve a cabin. Despite the difficulty with access, Seal Island is a delight to visit, a perfect size for exploring on foot, with walking made easy by grazing of lots of sheep. A visit of three or four days (or longer if you get stranded by weather!) will increase your odds of being there for a wave of migrants. *Birding Nova Scotia* contains a map and lots of details about Seal Island.

A bonus awaits you in spring and fall on both Bon Portage and Seal Islands. Banding teams from Acadia University monitor annual numbers of songbirds and raptors by trapping and banding them.

J. WOLFORD
Revised by J. Wolford

Yarmouth Area

Long points of land extend into that area between the Bay of Fundy and the Atlantic Ocean. Here, at the extremity of Nova Scotia, are ideal landing and departure sites for birds. Shallow bays between these points offer sanctuary to overwintering loons, grebes, geese and ducks, and feeding sites for migrating herons and stray egrets. The wooded back country attracts a wide variety of nesting land birds, including at least 15 species of warblers.

Acadians settled here in 1768, after they had been expelled elsewhere by the English. In the late 19th century, ship-building flourished in Yarmouth; Nova Scotia's 3000 sailing ships made up one of the largest merchant fleets in the world and made Yarmouth the richest port on the Atlantic coast. Today many of the farms are abandoned, but Yarmouth thrives on an active tourist trade, now augmented by the fast ferry from Bar Harbour, Maine.

Birding Features

In winter, a visitor should spot the usual finches, as well as House Finches and Northern Cardinals, and Yellow-rumped Warblers, Horned Larks, American

Goldfinches, American Tree Sparrows, Snow Buntings and occasional Lapland Longspurs.

Yarmouth. From mid-July to early September, a drive around town should produce a number of species. The flats and beaches on both sides of Yarmouth Harbour are resting and feeding sites for Semipalmated and Black-bellied Plovers, Ruddy Turnstone, Willet, both species of yellowlegs, Short-billed Dowitcher and others. After the peak of migrant shorebird numbers in mid-August, look for Dunlin and Pectoral Sandpiper and many other species.

Ferry Crossings from Portland, Maine, and from Bar Harbor, Maine. These crossings, to and from Yarmouth, are particularly good for seabirds if the day is free of fog. From spring to fall, look for Greater and Sooty Shearwaters, Leach's and Wilson's Storm-Petrels and Northern Gannet.

Shorebird Route. Proceed south from Yarmouth on Main Street. At the head of Kelly Cove (or Kelley's), about 2.5 km south of the railway level crossing at the edge of town, take the narrow track to the right, southwest over a low hill and down to a small sand beach and tidal marsh. At low tide, look for a variety of water birds. This is also a good spot for the late-arriving Nelson's Sharp-tailed Sparrow (after June 1). Parking can be difficult. You may want to leave the car on the paved road and hike down the several hundred metres to the beach.

Continue south on the paved road, then turn sharp south to reach Chebogue Point. Park at the end of the road and hike along the pebbled ridge to the drumlins, about 1 km east. Expect a wide collection of ducks and shorebirds in spring and fall. In late fall, look for Horned Lark, Snow Bunting and Lapland Longspur. If you come at high tide, check the gravel spits fringing the salt marsh near the end of the road for large numbers of Black-bellied Plovers, Greater and Lesser Yellowlegs, Red Knots and smaller shorebirds, too. Nearby pastures host American Golden Plover in August and September, possibly with other upland "shorebirds" like Buff-breasted Sandpiper.

Return north, then swing northeast through Central Chebogue to Highway 3. Proceed east on it for about 2 km, then turn south on 334; leave 334 and take the road south to Pinkney's Point. About 2 km south from the fork off 334, you will find the Melbourne Bird Sanctuary (tidal Melbourne Lake).

The large shallow inlet is used as a staging and wintering area for thousands of Canada Geese, American Black Ducks and a wide variety of other water birds. This is a favourite fall and winter spot for Ring-billed and Black-headed Gulls. Continue south to Cook's Beach; it serves as a fine roosting site for sandpipers at high tide. South towards the village of Pinkney's Point, the extensive marshes and shallow pools provide excellent habitat for Great Blue Herons, Black-bellied Plovers, yellowlegs and other species, including large flocks of Willets in the fall.

Return to Highway 334, and then go south on it through Wedgeport and Lower Wedgeport to Wedge Point. You are now on the extreme tip of Tusket Wedge, where migrants congregate while waiting for good weather.

This is a good time to mention the Tusket Islands and the summer boat cruises that are available, either from Wedgeport or from Yarmouth. These three-and-a-half-to-four-hour trips should encounter seals and seabirds, and the latter might include Roseates among the other terns. For Wedgeport Cruises, phone 1-800-566-TUNA or check out the Web site, http://www.grass-routes.ns.ca/tourism/Tours/argyle.htm; for Tusket Island Tours Ltd. in Yarmouth, call (902) 742-1236 for information.

With regard to the threatened Roseate Terns, a good place to see them in summer is farther south, along Route 335 off either 103 or 3. Drive to Middle West Pubnico, southwest of which lie two small islands called The Brothers. Ted D'Eon, a pharmacist, has been the volunteer guardian of a mixed colony of terns, including up to 60 pairs of Roseates. Phone Ted ahead of your visit – (902) 762-2097 – for information about possibly seeing any Roseates.

Inland Exploration. This trip is best from late May to very early July to spot or hear land birds on territory. A wide diversity of species is possible here, including Common Loon, American Bittern and other water birds. Take Highway 1 from Yarmouth about 4 km to Hebron. Turn northeast onto 340, where the sign says Carleton-Deerfield. From here it is about 10.5 km to Ellenwood Lake Provincial Park. Past Deerfield, turn right at the park and Braemar Lodge signs; follow these signs in.

After checking out the park, take the shortest road back south to Highway 103. To get there, follow Pleasant Lake Trunk 3 from the sign at the park entrance. At Pleasant Lake on 3, turn right and head back to Yarmouth.

Another inland site worth exploring is along Highway 340, south from Weymouth or north from Yarmouth. At Corberrie is a Mini-Wilderness Park, an excellent place to have a short walk. Among the mature hard- and softwood trees you may see a variety of warblers and other woodland birds, including Pileated Woodpecker. Also look for water birds in Wentworth Lake, where the path skirts the shore.

About 24 km north of Yarmouth, and 1 km south of Beaver River, is Bartlett's Beach, a good habitat for shore and water birds. Also check out the marsh at Salmon River, and the marsh and lighthouse at Cape St. Mary's. Other marshes and beaches that might be productive can be found farther north along Highway 1, e.g., between Meteghan River and Saulnierville, south of Church Point, across the bridge at Weymouth North. Time your visit near high tide.

J. WOLFORD
Revised by J. Wolford

Annapolis Basin and Valley ("Evangeline Trail")

This fertile valley produces apples that are famous across Canada. Forested long ridges ("mountains") lie adjacent. Varied habitats provide havens for everything from seabirds to the Bald Eagle.

Nova Scotia's first permanent European settlers arrived from France with Champlain in 1605 at Port Royal (now re-created in an historic park that is worth a visit). The valley was settled by French-speaking Acadians, who were later expelled by the British and replaced by New Englanders and then United Empire Loyalists. The area breathes history at such sites as Port Royal, just west of Annapolis, and a "living museum" of Nova Scotia's agricultural history at the New Ross Farm, 40 km south of Kentville. Fort Anne and Grand Pré Historic Parks are also very important sites.

Highways 1 and 101 run through the region, with numerous sideroads providing access to the Bay of Fundy and the nearby hills. Tourism is a major industry, with widespread services of all types.

A visitor to Wolfville, at the east end of The Valley, should contact the Blomidon Naturalists Society (P.O. Box 127, Wolfville, N.S. BOP 1X0) for information and/or guides for local birdwatching.

Birding Features

Digby Neck. If you're heading for Brier Island – and you should be, since Brier has so many birding perks, both land and sea – there are some good spots along Digby Neck and Long Island, off Route 217. Also be aware that getting to Brier Island requires two short, cheap ferry rides. There are only two important things about the ferry times: heading southwest, the ferry leaves East Ferry hourly on the half-hour; and, heading northeast, at Westport the ferry departs at 25 minutes past every hour – the other ferry times are based on the timings of those just mentioned.

At the northeastern edge of St. Mary's Bay, a dirt road skirts the shore between Highways 101 and 217. From the dykes, check out the tidal flats or water, depending upon the stage of the tide, for shorebirds and water birds. Along Route 217, there are sometimes-productive ponds at Rossway.

All of Digby Neck and Long Island are extensions of the basalt ridge called the "North Mountain" of the Annapolis Valley. This long ridge is a migratory highway, especially in fall, for small birds and raptors, so watch especially for vultures, accipiters, buteos and falcons, etc. These all accumulate on Brier Island and can be spectacular in September and October.

Still on Digby Neck, at Tiddville Route 217 climbs and provides an elevated lookout over a marsh on your left (east). This wetland often holds ducks, Pied-billed Grebe, herons, etc. Weather permitting, both ferry rides provide possible viewing opportunities.

At the southwest end of Long Island, Freeport Harbour can be very productive for various wading birds at any stage of the tide, but especially when it's partly out. Shorebirds, best in late May or August to October, travel back and forth between here and Pond Cove on Brier Island.

Check the Doers and Dreamers Tourism Guide for both accommodations and boat tours, which can be found from Digby to Westport. Now there are at least 11 different operators that offer boat trips for whales and seabirds, from Little River, East Ferry, Tiverton, Freeport and Westport.

Brier Island. This is the westernmost point in N.S., and its entire natural history is interesting, from its picturesque columnar basalt of Triassic-Jurassic age to rare plants (a large part of the west end is now owned by the Nature

Conservancy of Canada) to migrant birds of land and sea, as well as the whales, plankton, etc.

Birding Nova Scotia contains a map and detailed descriptions of areas to explore.

The area has a long history of commercial boat tours, originally from Brier Island but now available elsewhere nearby, for whales and seabirds. The area north of Brier out to Grand Manan Island especially is a hot spot, mainly because of strong tidal currents and underwater ledges that combine to bring krill, copepods, etc., to the surface in the daytime. South of Brier can also be very productive. The whale-watching season is from late June through October, with August being the best month not only for wildlife but also for good weather. Since the weather is chancy, try to have more than one or two days in the area. (Also see New Brunswick about doing this from Grand Manan.)

The boat trips average about four hours for $35 (1999 prices) per adult. Besides the porpoises, dolphins and whales (Right, Humpback, Finback and Minke are most likely), what are the summertime seabirds? Shearwaters (Greater, Sooty, Manx), gannets, alcids (puffins, possibly razorbills and murres), kittiwakes, storm-petrels (Leach's, Wilson's), phalaropes in fall (Red, Red-necked), possibly jaegers (Parasitic, Pomarine) and skuas (South Polar, Great).

On the island, the best lookout spots for seabirds are at the Northern and Western Lighthouses. During some winters lots of various seabirds can be visible from all shores and even in Westport Harbour. Besides usually pelagic birds (gannets, kittiwakes, alcids Razorbills, both kinds of murres, dovekies, possibly fulmars), other winter water birds include Common Eider, Oldsquaw, Common Goldeneye, Red-breasted Merganser, possibly Harlequin Duck (try off Whipple Point), Brant, Common and possibly Red-throated Loons, Red-necked and Horned Grebes, Great Cormorant, Purple Sandpiper (especially on Gull Rock) and various gulls. (Halifax Harbour is best for winter gulls.)

A special spot for nesting Common, Arctic and sometimes a few Roseate Terns is Peter's Island, at the southern end of Westport Harbour. Best viewing of terns is probably from the old and new ferry wharfs at Westport.

Brier Island can be hopping with songbirds in spring, especially May to early June, but it's much more justly famous for its songbirds, raptors and shore-birds in autumn (late August through October). The best places are Pond Cove for shorebirds (especially when the tide is partly out), Westport to Western Light for raptors, and just south of Northern Light for songbirds. The latter area has some Acadia University land containing a banding station that operates only briefly now, usually in late August or early September. The clearings and the lanes cut for mist-netting can be superb or very boring. All migration periods are iffy in that sense, and for this reason, as well as the iffy weather for pelagic trips, we suggest a stay longer than one to two days. Be sure to keep scanning skyward for those kettles of migrant Broad-wings, Sharp-shins, Turkey Vultures, harriers, Merlins, American Kestrels, goshawks, Red-tails, eagles, Ospreys, early Rough-legs and possibly Cooper's Hawk.

Probably the most productive walks on Brier Island are (1) to Pond Cove, either from the Gull Rock Road (best access) or the Pond Cove Road, (2) from Western Light along the shore past Whipple Point to Pond Cove, and (3) from

Westport north along the road to Northern Light. For shorebirds in both spring and fall, tidal flats at the south edge of Westport and in Freeport Harbour are other places to check, besides Pond Cove.

Digby and Annapolis Royal. The western part of the Annapolis Basin is an excellent place to look for water birds in winter. In Digby itself, try viewing first off the large fishing wharf in town, then in the bay just northwest of town, and then northward along the road to the Digby-to-St. John ferry. This latter road is perfect for birders, since it's along the shore and is wide enough to park on the shoulders. Winter aquatic birds will include loons, grebes, Black Guillemot and a variety of diving ducks, including Oldsquaw, Bufflehead, goldeneyes (possibly two kinds), Greater Scaup and Red-breasted Merganser. (The ferry trip, especially in July through October, may give views of pelagic birds and whales.)

Another good spot for winter diving birds, especially Greater Scaup and Common Goldeneye, and often Barrow's Goldeneye, is the inland side of the Annapolis Causeway just south of the Tidal Power Plant at Annapolis Royal.

Also at Annapolis Royal, from late spring through fall a nice stroll can be had at the Historic Gardens, from which you can access the salt marsh and dykes to the south. Just north of there the bridge over Allains River has nesting Cliff Swallows.

The Annapolis Valley and North and South Mountains. To Nova Scotians the Annapolis Valley means more than the watershed of the Annapolis River and tributaries. It's an east-west trough, between two long ridges or "mountains" up to 260 m high, extending eastward from Annapolis Royal at least to Wolfville and, in this book, to Windsor. The ridges shelter the richly agricultural Valley, with its small farms, fields, orchards, ponds and wood lots. At the Valley's east end, Wolfville to Windsor, the huge tides of the Minas Basin expose wide expanses of biologically very rich mudflats and salt marshes. Most of the latter have been "reclaimed" for agricultural purposes, and these dykelands also have their own suite of birds. The mudflats attract a spectacular migration of shorebirds from mid-July to October.

The North Mountain, from Cape Split and Cape Blomidon, extends to the southwest all the way to Digby Neck and to Brier Island. This ridge along the Bay of Fundy is a natural "highway" for migratory raptors, especially Broad-wings and Sharp-shins, from August to October. All along the foot of the mountain, north from Highway 221, the wooded slopes have an interesting mix of species like Pileated Woodpecker, Ruffed Grouse and Barred Owl. The shores of the Bay of Fundy, at Parker's Cove, Port George, Margaretsville and other points, are birded primarily in winter, for sea ducks, alcids, etc.

On the South Mountain there's a huge area of mixed forests, woods roads (tracks), and both lakes and hydro-electric reservoirs. South from Kentville, follow Highway 12, or New Ross Road, 16 km to Butler Road, then turn left and drive it and walk it at your own speed in May or early June, looking and listening for a wide variety of warblers, vireos, flycatchers and thrushes.

Now let's consider the Valley itself, from west to east. For a combination of marsh, meadow and agricultural birds, don't miss Belleisle Marsh. At Belleisle along Highway 1, look for a tall-steepled white church on the south edge of the road. Just west of that, turn south and drive to a parking area, which has a map of the project, a recent multi-jurisdictional wetland reclamation combined with dykeland agricultural pursuits. The impoundments here are full of interesting marsh birds from April through November. This is an area for walking, canoeing and kayaking.

Middleton has a very good "show" of Chimney Swifts, every dusk from mid-May to early August. After sunset up to 650 swifts circle and then acrobatically dive into a large chimney on the Middleton Regional High School, where they spend the night. The school is one block north of the Tim Horton's coffee-doughnut shop on Highway 1, just west of town. Best dates are late May or late July to early August. Other shows of roosting swifts in Nova Scotia occur at Bear River (Oakdene School), Wolfville (Front Street nature centre), New Glasgow (Temperance Street School) and elsewhere.

Eastern King's County is justly renowned for overwintering Bald Eagles (December to March). As many as 525 form concentrations around poultry farms for the feedings of normal daily chicken mortalities. The area is north from Avonport and Grand Pré to Kingsport and Medford, west to Woodside and Sheffield Mills, and south to White Rock.

Eastern King's County also has ponds which are regularly checked from spring to early winter for waterfowl, shorebirds, etc. Details are in *Birding Nova Scotia*. Some of these areas are the Port Williams sewage ponds (southwest of Port Williams); Canard Pond (west of the flashing light on Highway 358, southwest of Canning); Harris's Pond in Canning (just north of the T junction as you get to Canning from the south on Highway 358); riverside park at the east end of Canning; Canning Aboiteau (water-control structure on Habitant River), east of Canning; Van Nostrand's Pond at Starr's Point (northwest of Prescott House Museum); White Rock Pond (just south of White Rock).

A really nice site north of Canning is Blomidon Provincial Park. Drive through Canning heading east, then follow the signs to the park (10 to 15 minutes north of Canning). From the lower park gate, either drive or walk up to the top of Cape Blomidon (lots of nice trails, or use the road) in late May to early June or September-October. These mixed woods can be jumping with migrant warblers, vireos, sparrows and others.

From Wolfville to Avonport, but especially north of Grand Pré, is a complex of dykes, agricultural dykelands (fields of hay, turf, corn, wheat, barley, oats, etc.), salt marshes, mudflats and beaches. The dykes and dykeland roads are public, *but* be very careful not to get in the way of agricultural operations – local Marsh Bodies (farmers' associations) pay for the maintenance of these roads. In summer look for Bobolink, Savannah Sparrow, harriers, etc. In winter, birders can usually find Rough-legged and other hawks, as well as Horned Larks, Snow Buntings and Lapland Longspur.

Shorebirds in the southern Minas Basin provide spectacular aerobatic shows from Kingsport to Wolfville to Grand Pré to Windsor, from mid-July to late August. After that a goodly diversity of plovers and sandpipers passes through until mid-October or later.

Grand Pré's Evangeline Beach is one area for viewing these flocks, and the best times are from two hours before to two hours after high tide. Incoming tides push the birds off the tidal flats – look for big flocks in flight (up to tens of thousands!). Roosts at high tide are either on the upper beaches or in ploughed dykeland fields. Therefore driving the dykeland roads at high tide can be very interesting.

Note that some "shorebirds" such as American Golden-Plover and Buff-breasted Sandpiper don't often go to the shore. They can be found in appropriate ploughed fields, or fields with short vegetation, at any stage in the tide cycle.

To get to Evangeline Beach, drive north from Grand Pré (off Route 1). At the T junction, you can turn left and then right to get to the campground and motel where there is a sign about this being a Western Hemisphere Shorebird Reserve. The most predictable aerobatic shows and roosts are to your east from here. So either walk along the beach as the tide is rising or falling (but be careful not to get stranded), or drive back to that T junction and drive east. Now you have two options. At Pheasant Road drive north, park at the north end of that road, and nicely ask permission from cottage owners there for viewing access to the beach. Or, back at that T junction, drive east to the end of the dirt road, park your car, and walk along the main dyke west to where the trees end. From the beach there, you can walk west to find shorebird flocks roosting, beginning to feed, or arriving from the dykeland fields. The "peeps" are dominated by Semipalmated Sandpiper, but look for various other species with them. Also watch for hunting Merlin and Peregrine Falcon.

Just east of where you parked above, off the east end of Long Island (a pre-dyking island), is Boot Island, a federal sanctuary which in summer is the only local site for nesting Great Blue Heron, Double-crested Cormorant and Great Black-backed and Herring Gulls.

Another terrific spot for shorebirds in recent years is the causeway mudflat at Windsor. The mudflat dates back to 1970 when the causeway was completed, and now it's rapidly becoming a new salt marsh. Look for many thousands of "peeps," hundreds of Short-billed Dowitchers and, later in fall, lots of Black-bellied Plovers. Often a good viewing area is at the Windsor Tourist Bureau at the east end of the causeway.

J. WOLFORD
Revised by J. Wolford

Windsor to Halifax

Birding Features

Highways 1 and 101 cross the province to Halifax. Highway 1 is slower but much more interesting for seeing the countryside and access to side trips. Here we'll mention only one spot along the way. Halfway between Windsor and Halifax along Route 1 at Mount Uniacke, is Uniacke Estate Museum Park. This historic colonial-style mansion and surrounding grounds are part of the Nova Scotia Museum complex, and recently a pleasant set of trails, partly along the old mail road, has been and is being developed. This spot is popular with the Bird Society and other naturalists groups for outings, and its mixed and coniferous forests and wetlands can be quite productive in spring or fall.

J. WOLFORD

Halifax to Amherst

Birding Features

Highways 2 or 102/104 will take you from Halifax north to Truro and beyond to New Brunswick. A side trip would be to turn left onto 214 at Exit 8, about 35 km north of Halifax near Elmsdale. Follow 214 north for 5 km to Route 14. Take 14 northwest for about 15 km to Highway 354, then go north on 354 to Noel and Route 215.

Check out the small lighthouse park at Burntcoat Head, site of the biggest tides of the world at over 16 m! Then follow 215 east along the coast and south back to Highway 102, or turn on Highway 236 to get to Truro. West of here, in the lower Shubenacadie River Valley, is an important site for overwintering Bald Eagle, as is eastern King's County near Wolfville (see above). This area is almost certain to produce Red-tailed Hawks. Ruffed Grouse and Ring-necked Pheasants are abundant along this looped trip. In wet areas, watch for American Bittern, American Black Duck, Green-winged and Blue-winged Teals and Sora. Check the few lakes for nesting Pied-billed Grebe and Ring-necked Duck. American Woodcock breed in the alder thickets, and the Common Snipe can be heard displaying on spring evenings. Open fields hold Bobolink. At the salt marshes, listen carefully for Nelson's Sharp-tailed Sparrow.

In fall and winter, the trip almost certainly will produce large flocks of Horned Larks and Snow Buntings. Watch for scattered Lapland Longspur in these flocks. In some years, Common Redpolls may also be abundant.

Another interesting looped trip takes you east of Highway 102 in a circle. Leave 102 at Exit 9 and proceed northeast to meet Route 224 about 1 km north of Shubenacadie. Follow 224 about 50 km to Upper Musquodoboit; proceed north on Route 336 to meet 289 at Upper Stewiacke. Follow 289 back west to Highway 102 at Exit 12, just west of Brookfield. The drive passes through a mixture of farm and woodland. In the forests, keep alert for Pileated and Black-backed Woodpeckers. From Route 224 check out Lake Egmont, 2 km straight south of Cooks Brook on a sideroad; look for the Wood Ducks that use the houses set out for them. Search in hardwood forests in June for the Black-throated Blue Warbler and Ovenbird. If you find a stand of mature conifers, stop and listen for Bay-breasted Warblers.

At Truro, you have a choice of travelling straight northwest to New Brunswick on 104 or the much longer route on 2. Highway 4 proceeds through the Wentworth Valley between hardwood-covered hills. Watch for Red-tailed Hawk, Great Horned Owl and Pileated Woodpecker.

J. WOLFORD
Revised by J. Wolford

Sable Island

Sable Island is difficult and expensive to visit. Perhaps the rarity-seeker should first consider Seal Island, then Brier Island, then Cape Sable Island. Many of the very unusual birds that turn up on Sable Island are spotted by people who are on the island often and/or for long periods of time.

It lies nearly 300 km southeast of Halifax, the major departure site for a visit by air, and it's 150 km from N.S.'s closest point. You must obtain permission from the Canadian government in order to get on the island. Quoting from the "Conservation Strategy for Sable Island" (1998), "At present, access ... is regulated under the ... Canada Shipping Act ... mandated to the Canadian Coast Guard, Department of Fisheries and Oceans.... People who require no assistance in getting to the island and who are essentially self-supporting are often given permission to land.... At present there is no organised tourism to Sable." Questions related to possible low levels of sustainable tourism there are currently under consideration by a new group called the Sable Island Preservation Trust.

Contact the Coast Guard at (902) 426-3907. Also inquire there about possible accommodations in government buildings, as well as the possible use of all-terrain vehicles that are on the island.

Sable has a long and interesting history of human occupation going back to life-saving stations established in 1801. Currently, at the West Lighthouse, an upper-air weather station is operated by Environment Canada's Atmospheric Environment's Branch. Systematic weather records began in 1891 and are a very important component of the global monitoring network. Weather-station personnel act as wardens, enforcing both Shipping and Migratory Birds regulations, since Sable is a federal Migratory Bird Sanctuary. Surrounding Sable Island is an offshore field of natural gas that is just now being developed and tapped.

For birding information, including a detailed description of the island's habitats, history, etc., we recommend the following: "The Birds of Sable Island, Nova Scotia" by Ian A. McLaren, 1981, in *Proceedings of the N.S. Institute of Science*, Vol. 31(1); and *Sable Island – Nova Scotia's Mysterious Island of Sand*, by Bruce Armstrong, 1981, Formac Publishing Co. Ltd., Halifax.

The island, a curving strip of sand with beaches, dunes, vegetation, ponds and marshes, is 41 km long and up to 1.5 km wide. By 1981, 325 species of birds had been recorded here, including more than 85 vagrant species, some of which were new records for North America or Canada, and at least 25 of which were new for Nova Scotia. Perhaps the most exciting recent species was a Black-tailed Gull.

Sable has a diverse fauna and flora and is stabilized primarily by its vegetation cover and ocean currents. The best known component of its fauna is a population of 150 to 400 feral horses, introduced in the 18th century. A resident population of Harbour Seals bears pups from mid-May to mid-June, and a much larger herd of Gray Seals has pups from late December to early February. There are 170 kinds of plants, most diverse around the fresh-water ponds and within heathy communities.

Birding Features

This information is taken from McLaren's 1981 paper (see above). The tree-less, long sandy bar offers a stopover for migrating waterfowl and shorebirds and an unexpected landfall for migrant land birds. Rarities have included Little Shearwater, British Storm-Petrel, Roseate Spoonbill, Black-tailed Gull, Cave Swallow, Worm-eating and Hermit Warblers. Come from early to mid-May and mid-August to mid-September for migrants; nesters are best in June.

Pelagic species can be spotted from your boat, helicopter or plane, as you arrive or depart, and at the island's tips. The Northern Fulmar is regular in May and June and in September; Cory's Shearwater is most common in July; watch for Greater Shearwater at the tips in summer, especially when winds are easterly; Sooty and Manx Shearwaters are most numerous in early summer; Northern Gannet is regular too. At the tips, these species may be watched rounding the ends or feeding in the turbulent shallow waters. Also look for Black-legged Kittiwake and rare gulls and terns.

Water birds, herons, rallids and shorebirds are to be sought around the island's numerous and widespread brackish and fresh-water ponds. Wallace Lake is now reduced to a few often-flooded remnants, with the westernmost part most attractive for shorebirds. The complex of fresh-water ponds between West Lighthouse and the Meteorological Station is the best place for nesting ducks and shorebirds and for many visiting species. Also check out the dyked area southwest of West Lighthouse, and the generally brackish ponds at the Old No. 3 Life-saving Station for shorebirds. The relatively deeper pond 1.3 km west of No. 3 Station is good for waterfowl.

Search for land birds in the more densely vegetated areas. Look around the above-mentioned ponds and in the higher shrubs. By late summer Marram Grass, Beach Pea and Seaside Goldenrod cover the tops of the dunes. These insect-rich "thickets" attract the migrants, including hordes of recently fledged young Ipswich Sparrows from late August to November.

Be sure to inspect all human-made structures, even if derelict and almost gone or buried, including buildings, towers, lighthouses, rose gardens and dykes. Many of the most interesting rarities have occurred around the house nearest the West Lighthouse.

Northern Parula

Among the 16 species now nesting regularly on Sable Island, probably the most interesting are the nearly endemic Ipswich (Savannah) Sparrow, Roseate Terns (fewer than 10 pairs among the 1100 to 1400 pairs of Arctics [65%] and Commons [35%] combined), two kinds of shorebirds at the southern edge of their breeding ranges (30 to 40 pairs of Least Sandpipers and 5 to 10 pairs of Semipalmated Plovers), and up to 30 pairs of Red-breasted Mergansers. Also nesting gulls are abundant, with up to 1500 pairs of Great Black-backs and 2700 pairs of Herrings. The gulls, of course, are hard on the nesting terns.

J. WOLFORD
Revised by J. Wolford

PRINCE EDWARD ISLAND

O ur smallest province draws visitors to experience its quiet, beautiful, long sand beaches and pleasant pastoral landscapes. The Great Blue Heron is one of the most commonly sighted birds; Great and Double-crested Cormorants fly from their nesting cliffs within close view; Piping Plovers nest in fair number on some of the beaches.

Mi'kmaq Indians named it Abegweit – Cradled on the Waves. Jacques Cartier renamed it Ile Saint-Jean when he landed in 1534. The British later christened it in honour of Prince Edward, Duke of Kent, in 1798. Covering 5656 km², with a population of 135,000, the lands rise as high as 142 m from the sea. The underlying bedrock is red sandstone, resulting in red soil. About half of P.E.I. is covered in woodland; the remainder is cleared, much of it in agriculture. A variety of crops is produced, including potatoes, grain and hay. Woodlands are held in many small parcels, but there are extensive areas of contiguous forest. Many woodlands are owned by non-farmers. A band of low hills traverses the central part of the island in a north-south direction. A second hilly area is found around Caledonia. The rest of the province is quite level to gently rolling. Shorelines consist of red sandstone cliffs, barrier sand dune systems sheltering salt-water bays, and salt marshes with estuaries. Most of the bays are shallow, with many sand bars. Most of the larger rivers are tidal for a considerable length. There are several bodies of water called lakes, but they are small by mainland standards.

Water birds are common because of the nearness to the sea. Warblers move through in late May, shorebirds come south in late July and August. Piping Plover may be found on territory from May to July. Gannets can be seen during most ice-free months. The Island is largely surrounded by ice in winter. Wintering ducks are most numerous from December to March.

Prince Edward Island National Park is considered one of the best birding sites in the province. Different species are found at all seasons in this area of wood lots, sand beaches and marshes. The park and the cormorant colony at Cape Tryon, west of the park, can be visited in a half to a full day. Most of the spots in this province can be covered in two days to a week, depending upon how fast you move.

No rare bird alert telephone number exists. Visiting birders should write ahead to the main natural history society for help: Natural History Society of P.E.I., Box 2346, Charlottetown, P.E.I. CIA 8CI. Tourism P.E.I. provides a

PRINCE EDWARD ISLAND

1 Confederation Bridge, the Ferries
  and Arrival in P.E.I.
2 Blue Heron Drive (Central P.E.I.)
3 Lady Slipper Drive (West P.E.I.)
4 Prince Edward Island National Park
5 Charlottetown
6 Kings Byway Drive (East P.E.I.)

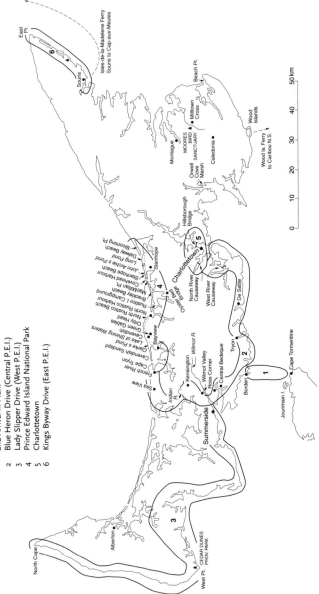

detailed map of the province, showing the different drives and loops mentioned below. For a copy, write Prince Edward Island Tourist Information Centre, P.O. Box 940, Charlottetown, P.E.I. C1A 7M5; phone (902) 892-2457; e-mail, tourpei@gov.pe.ca

Tourism Information Service, visitor guide and map ordering is available at 1-888-PEI-PLAY (1-888-734-7529), (902) 963-2391, or outside North America (902) 629-2400 or (902) 368-4444; fax (902) 629-2428. There's a Web site with interactive maps, visitor's guide, information on some walking trails, and more at http://www.gov.pe.ca/ or www.peiplay.com

The latest "official" P.E.I. bird checklist is now on the Web at the above address.

WINIFRED CAIRNS
Revised by Dan McAskill

Confederation Bridge, the Ferries and Arrival in P.E.I.

Links to the mainland include the recently opened 13 km Confederation Bridge from P.E.I. to New Brunswick and car ferries to Nova Scotia and Iles de la Madeleine in Quebec. Note that the Confederation Bridge closes to high-sided vehicles during high wind periods. Warning lights on approach advise of this event. These closures are usually of short duration. If travelling to either N.S. or N.B., you pay tolls only when leaving P.E.I. The Nova Scotia link, operated by Northumberland Ferries, is 22 km off Highway 106, at Caribou. The trip to Wood Islands, P.E.I., lasts 90 minutes; there is regular service from spring through fall. If vigilant in late autumn, you sometimes see Storm-petrels. Ferry information is available from 1-888-249-7245. The second ferry carries visitors from the Iles de la Madeleine to Souris, on the southeastern shore of P.E.I., a 134 km ride. Iles de la Madeleine ferry information is available at 1-418-986-3278. Schedules and rates are available from the P.E.I. Tourist Information Centre (see above).

There is bus service from Moncton, N.B., where there are VIA Rail and Amtrak (via Montreal) stops, to Charlottetown. Air service is provided to and from Charlottetown to Toronto and Halifax. Within P.E.I., there is no public transit system. However, during the summer, a double-decker bus takes guided tours from Charlottetown to the north shore. If you talk to the driver, it is sometimes possible to be dropped off at the far end and picked up a few hours later on the return ride to town.

To do any serious exploring, a car is necessary. There are numerous car rental agencies on the island, as well as a variety of accommodation. About 288 km of improved hiking and biking trail called the Confederation Trail has been established on the old rail bed. For updates on extensions phone (902) 894-7535.

Birding Features

The ferries provide opportunities to spot sea ducks and Northern Gannet, especially in the fall. Ferries don't run in winter.

WINIFRED CAIRNS
Revised by Dan McAskill

Blue Heron Drive (Central P.E.I.)

Upon arrival at Borden, drive the 3 km to Carleton and turn left onto Blue Heron Drive (Route 10). This loop around the perimeter of central P.E.I. provides a scenic drive along the coast. Great Blue Herons are quite abundant, with up to a dozen often spotted in one area. Canada Geese feed in the grain and potato fields and rest on bays and estuaries. Caspian Terns and Ospreys are occasionally spotted.

Birding Features

All of P.E.I.'s eight Great Blue Heron colonies are found on offshore islands. The birds come to the estuaries, river mouths, ponds and marshes to feed. These heronries are believed to have some of the largest populations in eastern Canada. In spring and fall migration, watch for Canada Geese at Central Bedeque, near the junction with 1A, about 13 km along Route 10 from Carleton. You may see geese at Ross's Corners, 2 km farther on, or at Wilmot Valley, 3 km farther; then turn right on 107 for 2 km. The Wilmot River, with bordering farmland, is a favourite stopover for migrating Canada Geese in March and April. Later in the season look here for Caspian Tern. After continuing another 6 km along Blue Heron Drive, turn left off Route 2 and drive 5 km to the Indian River Wildlife Management Area and the adjacent salt marshes along the river proper. Walk east along the trail on the north side of Indian River to lookouts. You should be able to spot more waterfowl species here than in most ponds on P.E.I. Scan for numerous Canada Geese, American Black Ducks, some Gadwalls, Blue-winged Teals, Northern Shovelers, Greater Scaups and occasionally Ruddy Ducks. In late summer watch for flocks of

Great Blue Heron

Whimbrel and American Golden-Plover in the hayfields between Hamilton and French River.

Once on the north shore, you can't miss the high and stable red sandstone cliffs. At Cape Tryon these cliffs support a large colony of cormorants, the best and most easily accessible in the Maritimes. The upper sites are primarily home to Great Cormorant; those lower and nearer the sea house mostly Double-crested. To reach the cape and colony, proceed through French River and turn left off Blue Heron Drive, towards the sea; proceed on the paved road for about 1.5 km to the T intersection; turn left onto the unpaved road and drive about 0.5 km; turn right down a farm lane to the sea. You'll spot No Trespassing signs on the fields on either side. They do not apply to the lane you are on, only to the adjacent land. Continue past the house to the lighthouse at the end. The colony occupies beautiful sandstone cliffs on both sides of the lighthouse.

Return to Blue Heron Drive and continue south to New London. Take time to visit the green-trimmed white cottage, the birthplace of L. M. Montgomery, author of *Anne of Green Gables*.

During summer and fall, the drive along this north shore should produce Caspian Tern, particularly around the mouths of bays. Many pairs of Ospreys nest in the province. Watch them fishing in the coastal bays, estuaries and rivers.

If you are in this area in winter, look for sea ducks on open water under bridges, such as at Bayview, 2 km north of Stanley Bridge. At Stanley Bridge, drop into the P.E.I. Marine Aquarium which features over 750 mounted birds from around the world, butterflies, and mammals, in addition to live seals and other marine life. Continuing northeast, you arrive at Cavendish, where Green Gables, the old farmhouse, was immortalized in *Anne of Green Gables* and other novels. Visit the restored Green Gables House at Prince Edward Island National Park. This is also the first of several entrances into the park, one of the best birding areas in the province (see below). There is an entrance fee into the park in peak season.

After continuing along Blue Heron Drive another 18 km, you will arrive at Oyster Bed Bridge, where sea ducks gather on the open water in winter. After another 3 km, turn straight south towards Charlottetown, 20 km away.

To complete the loop, leave Charlottetown on Highway 1 west, also called Blue Heron Road, which proceeds north, west, then south for a short distance. The North River Causeway lies 5 km from central Charlottetown along this route. Watch for wintering sea ducks on the open water beside the bridge. You should be able to spot American Black Duck, Common and Barrow's Goldeneyes and Common Merganser. Ten kilometres farther on Blue Heron Drive (don't forget to leave Highway 1 at Cornwall), you will pass over the West River Causeway. Look for the largest concentration of wintering sea ducks in the province. These include American Black Duck, Common and Barrow's Goldeneyes and Common Merganser. Also watch for wintering Bald Eagles. The eagle population has increased and they can be seen often at any of the overwintering sites. If ducks suddenly flush, look for an eagle.

Continue along this shoreline route another 38 km to DeSable, where Canada Geese are usually spotted. DeSable is also a fairly good site for shorebirds in July and August if you have a scope. Together with the geese, puddle ducks are present in spring and fall. At Tryon, another 11 km, Brant are present in April and May if you turn off the highway and go down to Tryon Point. Drive a further 11 km to reach Carleton and the Confederation Bridge.

WINIFRED CAIRNS
Revised by Dan McAskill

Lady Slipper Drive (West P.E.I.)

To explore the west end of P.E.I., where half the province's potatoes are grown, proceed west from Summerside. Follow Highway 11 around the shore or cut across country on 2; transfer onto 14 and drive west down to West Point and Cedar Dunes Provincial Park. Eastern White Cedar and White Spruce grow over low rolling dunes in the area. Good woodland trails are found in the park, but watch for poison ivy along trail edges. Warblers are abundant in the forests; sea ducks, gulls and terns are found near the sea. Check out the wooden lighthouse that is over a century old and has been converted into a restaurant and inn and now offers food and lodging.

Continue up the west side along 14, then turn off near the tip, on Highway 12, to North Cape. You can drive right to the point where a restaurant and gift shop sit. The land here consists of open exposed cliffs. This is a good spot to observe sea ducks, especially in spring for some species, late summer and fall. Look for Common Eider, scoters and gulls. If you are lucky, you may spot a Northern Gannet too. In late summer watch the local people who come here to gather Irish Moss from the shores. This practice of pulling metal baskets through the water to harvest the moss dates back to World War II when supplies of agar from Japan were cut off and rakers could make $20 per day. The industry has declined in recent years.

WINIFRED CAIRNS
Revised by Dan McAskill

Prince Edward Island National Park

The park is a favourite birding spot on the island, with over 257 species recorded. Twenty or more Great Blue Herons may often be spotted simultaneously as they forage in the marshes and on beaches along park roads. Piping Plovers nest at several places along the sand beaches.

The long sand beaches on the north shore of P.E.I. have been a popular playground for over a hundred years. Dalvay-by-the-Sea, an elegant historic summer hotel, was constructed in 1895 as a summer home. Today visitors can enjoy its beauty during an overnight stay.

The approximately 26 km² strip of land making up the park stretches 40 km along the north central coastline. Charlottetown lies 24 km south on Highways 6 or 15. There are several access points to enter the park, with Highway 6 the main trunk corridor, lying parallel to, and south of, the shore. A park brochure shows the different access points, beaches and hiking areas. Four park campgrounds are provided with one for pre-arranged group bookings.

For reservations phone 1-800-213-7275. Commercial accommodation may be obtained both within and outside the boundaries. There is an entrance fee into the park during the peak season. An adjunct park, Greenwich, lies east near St. Peters.

The CWS has a 231-page report, *Avifaunal Survey of P.E.I. National Park*, by K. Martin and W. Cairns, published in 1979. For more information, contact The Superintendent, Prince Edward Island National Park, 2 Partners Lane, Charlottetown, P.E.I. CIA 5V6; phone (902) 672-6350.

Birding Features
The park consists of red sandstone cliffs, barrier beach and dune systems; shallow salt-water bays bordered by salt marshes; cranberry bogs, ponds, mixed shrubs, coniferous and deciduous woodlands; and old fields now largely grown up into White Spruce. The outstanding features are the great dune lands. Each dune looks like a strip from the Sahara Desert. The dunes are held stable by Marram Grass, with roots penetrating down 3 m in search of water. However, heavy human traffic spells doom to these grass patches, so take care and avoid walking on them.

Spring brings Great and Double-crested Cormorants back to the area and their nesting cliff west of the park at Cape Tryon (see above) and at Cape Turner. These birds feed in the gulf and bays near the park all summer. The nesting area of Piping Plovers and sometimes a few Arctic Terns may usually be seen at Covehead Harbour entrance using a scope and sometimes binoculars. The plovers usually nest on shore below or adjacent to the bridge. After moving east of the west end of the spit for about 2 km along the beach road, you will arrive at Clarke's Pond. This is a favourite area for nesting and summering ducks. Look for Mallard, American Black Duck, Northern Pintail, Green-winged and Blue-winged Teals, American Wigeon, Ring-necked Duck and Red-breasted Merganser. The Lake of Shining Waters, on the west side of the road immediately north of Cavendish, is good for summering ducks. Check out the wood lots for warblers and other woodland species, as this is one of the better spots for land birds. Take a walk along the Homestead Trail, which starts from the Cavendish campground. Here you'll find excellent habitat variety and spectacular views of small estuaries, bays and fields with scattered coniferous and deciduous woodlands.

After moving east about 3 km along the beach road to Orby Head, you arrive at a small colony of Black Guillemots in the cliffs. Continue east to North Rustico Beach at the point where the road jogs south to North Rustico. Check North Rustico Beach for Caspian Terns; they regularly occur here during late summer and fall. Follow Highway 6, Blue Heron Drive, down and around to the intersection with Highway 15; take the latter road north to the beach road and then straight west by Rustico Island Campground to the end of the road on Robinson's Island. Look for a possible Osprey nest. Piping Plover nest north of this causeway, so keep a careful watch. The wood lot around the campground should produce warblers and other land birds in fair numbers from late May to July. A paved road to the point stops at the campground and you can walk to the tip on an old roadbed. There are often some really good birds here up to

September and sometimes October. Watch for shorebirds, mergansers and sometimes Short-eared Owls along the causeway. The large number of buoys support a small segment of the Island's Blue Mussel industry.

Now proceed east along the beach road to Brackley Beach, which lies at the T junction with Highway 15. This is a good area for migrating waterfowl. Scan the sea for Common Eider and the three scoter species. After continuing along the beach east another 4 km or more from the T junction, you come upon Covehead Bay to the south of the road and Covehead Harbour. There is an extensive salt marsh here, and open water in winter. The best time to come is mid- or high tide. In spring, look in the harbour for Canada Goose, Brant and a variety of ducks. Later in summer, check this marsh beside the road between Brackley Beach and Covehead Harbour for migrating shorebirds. The site is the best one known in the area to find these birds on migration. Scan the sea again for the same species as found off Brackley Beach. Look along the edges of the marsh for nesting Spotted Sandpiper, Willet and Sharp-tailed Sparrow. Piping Plovers also nest at Covehead Harbour. At the bridge across the harbour, check the tern colony, where there are abundant Common and sometimes a few Arctic. Caspian Terns are also often observed in the harbour. Watch for Bald Eagles and Ospreys.

Now proceed to John Archie's Pond on the sea side of the beach road, about 1 km east of the harbour bridge. Look for the variety of summering ducks mentioned previously, as well as Pied-billed Grebe and sometimes other grebes in late summer and autumn. Stanhope Beach is a good spot to look for the Bank Swallows that nest in the adjacent cliffs. Continue along the beach road about 5 km from the Covehead Harbour bridge to search for Long Pond, a fairly large pond on the landward side. Waters here hold a variety of the same summering ducks mentioned previously.

A walk along the Bubbling Springs Trail offers birding blinds overlooking the pond. In late summer and autumn, Bufflehead, Hooded Merganser and scaups might be seen here.

The final spot to explore from mid summer through to winter is Blooming

Piping Plover

Point, the finger of land farthest east. You can reach this point by boat or by following Highway 6 east, 8 km from Stanhope to Mill Cove, and then on 219 for 6 km to 218; follow 218 north through Blooming Point, approximately 3 km to the end of the pavement. Turn left on the "Y" at the end of the pavement and drive down to the beach (about 2 km). Then walk west along the long spit of land, about 6 km one way to the far west end. Watch for waterfowl, marsh birds and Osprey while crossing Deroche Pond on the way to the beach. This is a beautiful, peaceful walk, but hot in the summer. Take plenty of drinking water and make sure you have sun protection to avoid sunburn. Watch for the numerous animal tracks in the dunes. Avoid colonies of Piping Plover and terns. The latter are the same as mentioned above. You should see swallows roosting along this beach in late summer. Watch for the occasional pelagic bird floating the air currents above the waves or plunging into the water in search of fish.

The Osprey nests in the general vicinity of these beaches and sometimes is spotted hunting over the ponds and salt-water bays. Watch for Northern Harrier, the commonest raptor, cruising over the dunes and marshes.

Come in August to watch large flocks of migrating swallows roosting all along the beaches. The shorebirds begin appearing in mid-July and decline as autumn progresses. Scrutinize each flock for Semipalmated Plover, Black-bellied Plover, Ruddy Turnstone, Whimbrel, Spotted Sandpiper, Greater and Lesser Yellowlegs, Red Knot, Pectoral Sandpiper, White-rumped Sandpiper, Least Sandpiper, Dunlin, Short-billed Dowitcher, Semipalmated Sandpiper, Hudsonian Godwit and Sanderling. The best spot to see these shorebirds lies in the marsh between Covehead Harbour and Brackley Beach (see above). Inspect the small marshy ponds and sandy shores throughout the park for these birds. Gulls are regularly seen along the sand bars and bays. Study them for Great Black-backed, Herring, Ring-billed and Bonaparte's. In spring and autumn watch for Iceland or Glaucous Gulls.

If you are a winter visitor, check for open water at Covehead Harbour. Look just south of the park at the Oyster Bed Bridge causeway south of Rustico Bay. Examine MacMillan Point, reached by driving along Route 6 from Stanhope, southwest through Covehead to West Covehead (about 5 km from Stanhope). Take the narrow road north from West Covehead to near the point. These three spots should produce a complete collection of wintering ducks, including American Black Duck, Common and Barrow's Goldeneyes, Oldsquaw and Common Merganser.

WINIFRED CAIRNS
Revised by Dan McAskill

Charlottetown

Charlottetown, the smallest provincial capital and largest city in Prince Edward Island, is the birthplace of Canada. Here, in September 1864, the Fathers of Confederation met and signed articles that led to our nation forming in 1867.

Prince Edward Island was first settled by 300 Acadians in 1720; Port la Joie, at Rocky Point, is now the site of Fort Amherst National Historic Park. The

French colony was captured in 1758 by the British, who then moved across the harbour and established Charlottetown in 1764. Several downtown buildings date from the mid-1800s, giving a special character to the community. A visit to Beaconsfield Historic House located on Kent Street at the base of the boardwalk extending along Victoria Park's harbour edge will provide insights into the Island's past.

Birding Features

In the southwest corner, Victoria Park, consisting of about 200 ha, overlooks the harbour. The park is a mixture of hardwoods and open spaces with a variety of woodland birds. At the east end of the city, close to Hillsborough Bridge spanning the Hillsborough River, open water in the winter attracts sea ducks and large numbers of American Black Ducks. Check the stone pilings on this bridge from May to July for Common Tern nests. Cormorants also regularly roost along this bridge.

A visit to Ellen's Creek in northwest Charlottetown, off North River Road, will often produce many shorebirds and waterfowl in either spring or late summer. The Routes for Nature and Health walking trails off the west end of Beach Grove Road offer deciduous forest birding with lookouts on the estuary.

WINIFRED CAIRNS
Revised by Dan McAskill

Kings Byway Drive (East P.E.I.)

This loop on the eastern end of P.E.I. begins on the wharf at Wood Islands. This is the docking site for the ferries to Nova Scotia. The sand islands and shallow marshes constitute a good place to look for birds while waiting for the ferry. Scan for the Common Tern colony, Great Blue Heron, American Black Duck, a variety of gulls and, in the fall, migrating shorebirds. Leave your car in the parking area and take the ferry round trip as a passenger in late summer and early autumn for sightings of scoter, mergansers, loons and sometimes storm-petrels.

If you are heading to Charlottetown, stop at the salt marshes of Orwell Cove Wildlife Management Area. This site, 32 km north of Wood Islands, can be seen readily from the road running off the highway into Orwell Cove and out to the point (about 3 km from the highway). Stop here, especially during spring and fall migration, for geese and ducks. While you're in this area, the Macphail Woods Ecological Forestry Project trails offer excellent woodland birding opportunities. Turn northeast off Route 1 near the Orwell Corner Historic Village. If not visiting the museum, continue past the entrance to a T intersection and turn right. Proceed a few hundred metres past the end of pavement and park at Macphail Homestead. The trails start from here. Macphail House features a seasonal restaurant, and work is under way on a natural history education centre.

Now return through Wood Islands and continue east on Routes 4 and 18 to near the cliffs of Cape Bear and Murray Head and out to Beach Point, about

25 km east. From the cliffs, watch for Northern Gannet and other pelagic birds. Check the harbour at Beach Point for cormorants, Red-breasted Merganser, and Great Black-backed, Herring and Ring-billed Gulls, all of which nest in this area. Continue around the point to Murray River. A visit to the base of MacLure's Pond in winter will often yield large numbers of Common Goldeneye, Common Merganser, American Black Duck, and sometimes a Bald Eagle or Belted Kingfisher. The cattail edge of the pond and adjacent woodland trails sometimes make the area a good site for morning birding. Then take Highway 4 across to Milltown Cross, 10 km north of Murray River. At Milltown Cross, you will find the Sturgeon River and the Harvey Moore Migratory Bird Sanctuary. This spot, 5 km south of Montague, is a haven for Canada Geese and ducks that frequent the ponds. A variety of upland birds may be spotted along the hiking trails. The rivers and bays around Montague are home to the Bald Eagle. Eagles were able to survive the pesticide-induced decline in this area. These birds served as a base to start rebuilding the Island's Bald Eagle population.

From Montague take Routes 4, 5, 2 and 16 out to East Point, the eastern limit of the province. Come to the point in late May, late September and early October to watch the variety of migrating raptors. During migration, watch the woodlands at the point for Island rarities such as Blue-gray Gnatcatchers or the cliffs for Peregrine Falcons. During spells of open water, scan the sea for Northern Gannet, cormorants, Common Eider and scoters. The waters adjacent to the causeway entering Souris are worth scanning for Brant and other waterfowl in spring and autumn, as well as shorebirds during their migration. The New Harmony Demonstration Woodlot located about 4 km north of Route 16 on Route 303 is great for woodland birds. A stop at Black Pond located about 10 km east of Souris on Route 16 will usually yield a variety of puddle ducks and occasionally some of the rarer waterfowl on the Island.

WINIFRED CAIRNS
Revised by Dan McAskill

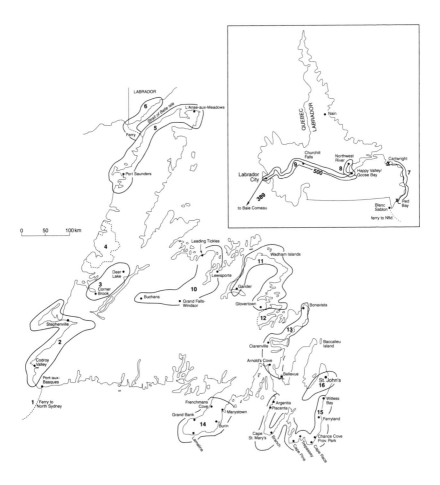

NEWFOUNDLAND

NEWFOUNDLAND

The Province of Newfoundland and Labrador ("Newfoundland") is closer to Europe than any other part of North America. It is a large province, stretching from Cape Chidley in the far north of Labrador to Cape Race on the southeastern tip of the island of Newfoundland. The habitats are largely those to be expected in a boreal coastal environment, although tundra conditions exist in the north. The topography of the province is varied. The majority of the island is hilly and rolling but fairly low-lying, the highest points being generally less than 500 m. Western Newfoundland is dominated by the ancient Long Range and Anguille Mountains, which are a part of the Appalachian Mountain chain. The highest peaks reach 800 m. In Labrador, dense conifer forests and expansive bogs in the south give way to spectacular barrens and mountains to the north.

The entire province is well-endowed with ponds, rivers and lakes. The marine coastlines are awe-inspiring. Thousands of islands and precipitous sea cliffs provide excellent nesting habitat for marine birds. These sites are made more attractive by their close proximity to feeding grounds.

The avifauna of Newfoundland is relatively modest if measured by the number of nesting species. However, many exotic vagrants have been recorded, notably from Europe. Newfoundland is also one of the best locations in Canada to seek out seldom-seen pelagic and northern species. Birdwatchers visiting the province will often be in search of such species as Dovekie, Thick-billed Murre, Atlantic Puffin, Ivory Gull, the east coast shearwaters, Rock and Willow Ptarmigan, Boreal Chickadee and Gray-cheeked

Thrush. Birders from the United States are often interested in finding the nesting wood warblers, many of which they see only in migration.

Gull-watching, a growing subspecialty in the birding world, can be pursued to advantage in Newfoundland. The St. John's area has recorded up to 13 species in a single winter, with 11 species on a single day. Many species are present in a variety of age classes, making comparison between species (and inevitable resulting identification headaches!) possible. Large concentrations of gulls also winter at Corner Brook and in other coastal locations.

Newfoundland's large size (it is almost 1000 km from Port aux Basques to St. John's, without any side trips) makes it daunting to plan a birding trip. Several days, and preferably weeks, would be needed to give the island a proper examination. Seasons are also critical, since a winter trip will involve an entirely different itinerary from other times of the year. However, there are many hot spot destinations in the province.

Spring:
Western Newfoundland – Codroy Valley (waterfowl, Piping Plover, flycatchers, wood warblers, sparrows), Stephenville Crossing (waterfowl, gulls and terns, raptors)
Central Newfoundland – Terra Nova National Park (waterfowl, Spruce Grouse, Black-backed Woodpecker, Boreal Owl, flycatchers, wood warblers), Bonavista (vagrant European species, especially in March and April)
Eastern Newfoundland – St. John's (waterfowl, gulls, seabirds, vagrants)
Labrador – Goose River (wood warblers), Churchill Falls Road (Spruce Grouse, Three-toed Woodpecker)

Summer:
Western Newfoundland – Cheeseman Provincial Park (Piping Plover), Gros Morne National Park (returning shorebirds in late August, Rock Ptarmigan)
Central Newfoundland – Terra Nova National Park (Black-backed Woodpecker)
Eastern Newfoundland – Cape St. Francis, Cape Spear, Cape Race, Cape Pine, St. Shott's, St. Vincent's, Pt. La Haye, Cape St. Mary's (shearwaters, Northern Gannet, jaegers, gulls, terns, alcids, Great Cormorant [Cape St. Mary's especially]), Renews, Pt. Verde (Arctic Tern)

Fall:
Western Newfoundland – Codroy Valley, Stephenville Crossing (waterfowl, shorebirds, raptors), Picadilly, St. Paul's (shorebirds)
Central Newfoundland – Terra Nova National Park (waterfowl, shorebirds)
Eastern Newfoundland – Burin Peninsula, Garnish to Burin via Lawn (shorebirds, vagrants), Bellevue Beach (shorebirds, Bald Eagle), St. John's, Renews, Cape Race (migrant shorebirds, raptors, thrushes, warblers and sparrows, vagrants)

Winter:
Northwestern Newfoundland – St. Anthony, L'Anse aux Meadows (Ivory Gull, Gyrfalcon, Snowy Owl, Dovekie, Thick-billed Murre)

Central Newfoundland – Terra Nova National Park (waterfowl, vagrants)
Eastern Newfoundland – St. John's (Northern Goshawk, Peregrine Falcon,
gulls, vagrants), Cape Spear, Cape Race, Biscay Bay, Pt. La Haye, Cape St.
Mary's (Red-throated Loon, Red-necked Grebe, Common Eider, King Eider,
Harlequin Duck [Cape St. Mary's especially], scoters, Bald Eagle, Purple
Sandpiper, gulls, Dovekie, Thick-billed Murre, vagrants)

There is currently no birding hotline in Newfoundland. Bird information
is best taken from the Internet or by contacting local birders by e-mail or phone.
Rare bird information is posted regularly on "Birding in Canada" (try www.
web-nat.com/bic/index.html) and on the newsgroup "nf.birds." "Birding in
Canada" includes a list of private e-mail addresses for Newfoundland birders.
A weekly birding column by John Pratt called "Winging It" appears in *The
Telegram*, a provincial daily newspaper, on Saturdays. The article, including back
issues, can also be read on the Internet at www.thetelegram.com. The Natural
History Society of Newfoundland and Labrador publishes the official provin-
cial checklist and has many birding members. The society can be contacted at
Box 1013, St. John's, Newfoundland A1C 5M3, or by visiting its Web site at
www.nhs.nf.ca

Birders travelling to Newfoundland will require warm clothing in most
months. Coastal birding can be very chilly, even in July and August. Rain gear
and protection for optics are highly recommended, especially if boat trips are
part of your itinerary. Sturdy, waterproof footwear is a general requirement.
Black flies and mosquitoes can be bad in any month from May to September,
but tend to be worst from May to early July. In Labrador, biting insects are a
very serious consideration, and bug jackets are at times essential. Any of the
field guides covering eastern North America will be satisfactory as a reference,
and you may want to consider bringing a European guide, as well. Birding supplies are available locally, although the selection may be modest in many
centres. Check the Yellow Pages under "Bird Feeders and Houses" for phone
listings. Repair services for optics are hard to find. Check with local birders if
this becomes a consideration. Accommodations can be found at, or near, most
important birding sites. Often these are bed-and-breakfast operations. The
Newfoundland Department of Tourism can provide further information on

Rock Ptarmigan

accommodations ([709] 729-2830). Advance bookings for rental cars are strongly recommended. Rental vans for tour groups can be difficult to obtain and should be arranged well in advance. If you are planning to use the ferry service and will want a sleeping cabin, this should also be booked well before your travel dates.

Anyone using this guide to find birds in Newfoundland should obtain a good highway map for the province, a provincial checklist, and of course a field guide to the birds of eastern North America. The information in this chapter is based on highway routes current for 1998−99. Extensive highway reconstruction in Newfoundland, especially in the area of St. John's, will undoubtedly modify some of the routes in the near future. Labrador is also experiencing major highway development, which will make various areas accessible by road for the first time. As this book goes to press, there are plans to link Cartwright to Red Bay by road, and further plans to link the coastal part of Labrador to Goose Bay by highway. Two more national parks – one in the Torngat Mountains to the north, and a second in the Mealy Mountains just south of Lake Melleville – are also anticipated. Further information is provided in the "Building Resources" section at the end of this chapter.

JOHN PRATT

The Ferries

Newfoundland is served by large ferries departing from North Sydney, Nova Scotia. A year-round service runs to Port aux Basques on the southwest corner of Newfoundland, while a summer service adds an extra run from North Sydney to Argentia, Placentia Bay. The Port aux Basques run takes less than 10 hours, while the Argentia run takes roughly 16 hours to complete. Schedules and fees are adjusted yearly, so it is best to check with Marine Atlantic, the service provider, well in advance. Ferry cabins are at a premium in the tourist season and should be booked months before your intended sailing dates. Call Marine Atlantic at 1-800-341-7981 for current information.

Birding Features

The Argentia ferry, which runs only in the summer, is a better "birding" ferry. It passes through rich feeding grounds off the south coast of Newfoundland and runs fairly close to major seabird colonies, including Cape St. Mary's (see section on Cape St. Mary's later in this chapter). The Port aux Basques ferry produces more modest numbers of species, but offers the possibility of a "walk-on" trip originating and ending at either terminus. Intrepid walk-on passengers for the Argentia ferry will have to spend a full day on Newfoundland (or Cape Breton) before returning. On the Newfoundland side, a day trip to Cape St. Mary's would be a good way to spend the time if transportation can be arranged. See information on Cape Breton in the chapter on Nova Scotia as well.

In winter, large numbers of Iceland and Glaucous Gulls are likely to be encountered, along with Black-legged Kittiwakes. Look for various species of alcids, including Thick-billed Murre, Dovekie and Black Guillemot. Atlantic

Puffin, Common Murre and Razorbill are also possible. Northern Fulmar is quite common in winter. Ivory Gulls are rare visitors from the Arctic and are more likely to be seen in years when arctic ice has moved into the strait.

Spring crossings will produce decreasing numbers of arctic gulls, Dovekies and Thick-billed Murres, and increasing numbers of Common Murres, Northern Gannets, Storm-petrels and, in late spring, the first shearwaters. Wilson's Storm-petrels seem more frequent on the Nova Scotia side of the straits. Leach's Storm-petrels can be seen on the Newfoundland side, often in huge numbers. The Argentia ferry is generally far more productive for Leach's Storm-petrels than is the Port aux Basques ferry.

Three species of shearwaters are likely to be seen in summer. Manx Shearwater breeds in Newfoundland, while Sooty and Greater Shearwaters travel north from the southern hemisphere to winter on the Grand Banks. All three species can be seen from the ferries, although Manx Shearwater is far less common than the other two. A rare fourth species – Cory's Shearwater – may be encountered less than annually, on average. Great care must be taken to be sure the bird you see is indeed a Cory's Shearwater and not an imma-ture Greater Shearwater, few of which are illustrated in field guides. Shearwater movements are tied to the movements of caplin, a tiny fish that appears on the Grand Banks in huge numbers every summer. Great Cormorant may be seen at the North Sydney end of both runs, and in the vicinity of Cape St. Mary's on the Port aux Basques run.

Other seabird species that can be seen from the ferries in summer include South Polar Skua and the less common Great Skua. Again, care must be used to distinguish these species. Pomarine and Parasitic Jaegers also occur. Long-tailed Jaegers are rare but may be seen on occasion. Close to land, Atlantic Puffins, Razorbills, Common Murres and Black Guillemots become more common, especially on the Newfoundland side of the Argentia run. Northern Gannets can be seen on either run, but are very numerous as the Argentia ferry enters Placentia Bay.

Late summer passages on the ferries will continue to produce high numbers of shearwaters. Alcids will also be present, but their numbers will decline. Whimbrels begin to migrate through in late July and will continue to be seen through August. Black-legged Kittiwakes and storm-petrels will continue to be common into the fall. Common Loons and Red-throated Loons will be in evidence later. By this time, the Argentia ferry will probably be discontinued for the season.

Fall trips on the Port aux Basques ferry may produce migrating raptors as well as gulls, alcids, gannets, loons, shearwaters and storm-petrels. By late November, the species list will be restricted to a few gulls and alcids. This is probably the least attractive time to take the ferry, due to weather and a general lack of birds.

The most productive areas of the two runs are close to land on each side. On the Nova Scotia end both runs follow similar paths. Birders are strongly advised to be on deck for the first two or three hours of the crossing after departing North Sydney. On the Port aux Basques run, birding can be fairly good all the way across. On the Argentia run, the part of the trip that is within eight hours of Argentia is generally the most productive.

Birders are advised to prepare for cold and wet weather on ferry crossings. The boats offer full amenities, so a hot cup of coffee and a warm, dry spot are never far away, but shelter from the elements while on deck can be tricky to find. Although the boats are very large, the seas can be quite rough. Telescopes are generally useless. Remember that many of the birds will be seen from above, while passing below the level of the boat's bow. When the birds are plentiful, the action can be mesmerizing, with birds appearing apparently out of nowhere and disappearing just as quickly. Anyone not familiar with pelagic birding is strongly encouraged to study their field guide before setting out. Peter Harrison's excellent guide, *Seabirds: An Identification Guide,* is highly recommended. Remember to consider the winter and immature plumages for southern hemisphere species.

JOHN PRATT

Southwest Newfoundland: Port aux Basques to Port au Port

The west coast of Newfoundland from Port aux Basques to Stephenville has been a major birding destination of Newfoundland birders for many years. Recently, more has been learned about the Port au Port Peninsula, adding further destinations to an already packed west coast itinerary. This part of Newfoundland is essential territory for any serious "lister."

Port aux Basques. The town of Port aux Basques does not offer much of importance to the birder, apart from an opportunity to fuel up, get provisions on board, and get used to Newfoundland's rather astronomical gas prices. However, the lovely sand beach at Grand Bay West (only a kilometre or so north of Port aux Basques) gives spring and summer visitors their first chance to look for Piping Plover, which has been nesting on this beach in small numbers for several years. Watch the lagoons behind the sand dunes for vagrant herons, coots, dabbling ducks and shorebirds. Caspian Terns have been seen here.

Cheeseman Provincial Park. Cheeseman Park is about 10 km outside Port aux Basques. It is noted for Piping Plover nesting on its sandy beaches. Its campgrounds and picnic areas offer the arriving birder an excellent opportunity to begin looking for Newfoundland passerines. Least, Yellow-bellied and Alder Flycatcher have been recorded here. Eastern Kingbird shows up in spring, especially in coastal areas along the old rail bed. Blue-headed Vireos have been seen regularly in the campground. Warblers recorded in the park include Mourning, Magnolia, Cape May, Blackburnian and Canada, as well as the more common northeastern warblers. Sharp-shinned Hawks have nested in the park. Laughing Gulls have been recorded at the beach, and Snowy Egrets have also been seen there. Extreme rarities include Orchard Oriole, Say's Phoebe and Great Crested Flycatcher. Park staff are interested and knowledgeable, and should be told of any unusual sightings.

Cape Ray. This coastal community can be reached either by turning off Route 1 about 15 km out of Port aux Basques, or by following the old road to the town from Cheeseman Provincial Park. Cape Ray is an excellent vagrant hunting location. The coastal areas often harbour exhausted strays, while the dense alder beds along the roads through the town should be searched for breeding warblers, sparrows, vireos and other species. Route 408 between Route 1 and the town should be searched on a warm spring morning for singing Winter Wren, Blue-headed Vireo, Tennessee Warbler, Mourning Warbler, Black-throated Green Warbler, Swainson's Thrush and Yellow-bellied Flycatcher, among other species. Alder Flycatcher may be found closer to the town, particularly in the large alder beds to the south of Route 408.

The Starlight Trail. This easy trail leads up into the Long Range Mountains from the side of Route 1. To find the trail head, you must look for a large parking lot on your right as you travel east (towards Stephenville). This is located near Tompkins and is about 15 km from the intersection of Route 408 and Route 1. The trail itself begins at the back right corner of the lot. Follow the trail up into the enchantingly stunted forest of White and Yellow Birch, where you can listen for Ovenbird and Veery, as well as many species of warblers. The view of the Little Codroy Valley is stunning, even if you don't find the birds, but hearing a Veery call on this hill slope, as the sun pierces the fairytale green canopy, is a wonderful experience. If you can't find the trail head, it is worth checking with local residents who will no doubt be able to direct you.

Tompkins. The little town of Tompkins is split by Route 1. Watch for a local road going east towards the mountains just as Route 1 veers west. A hydro substation on the east side of Route 1 is a good mark. This little road is an excellent location for Cape May Warbler and has produced Chipping Sparrow, Woodcock (in May), Rose-breasted Grosbeak and Ruby-throated Hummingbird.

Doyles. Doyles is the entry point to the Grand Codroy Valley, but it is also a good birding spot. There are a couple of gas stations and a well-stocked general store at Doyle's. Birding highlights are likely to be found on the quiet local road running east from Route 1. Park at the service station and walk this road, which goes in a loop and winds up back at Route 1. Look for Ruby-throated Hummingbird, Rose-breasted Grosbeak, warblers and sparrows. A large pasture can be reached via a farm road about halfway along the local road. This is a good place to look for farmland birds. The alder thickets along the river will produce a variety of songbirds in season. At the northerly corner of the local road there is an unpaved extension leading to a gravel pit. Follow the road into the pit and look for a marsh pond to your right. This pond is a good location for swallows, Ring-necked Duck, Common Grackle and other icterids. Alder Flycatcher has been found here.

Within the Grand Codroy region are several main birding locations, although a birder with some time to play with will delight in the many farm roads and trails, far too numerous to detail here.

Grand Codroy. Actually a large area running from Doyle's to Upper Ferry, this region has excellent wetlands where dabbling ducks can be found. Look for Northern Shoveler, other waterfowl and swallows at Widgeon Pond. To locate this pond, look for an antique store on the right (river) side of the road. A farm road behind the store leads towards the river. Walk down the road to a hayfield, then study the pond between the field and the road for ducks. A short distance later, the road reaches an intersection. By continuing straight you will eventually wind up at the mouth of the Grand Codroy River. A turn will take you across the river to O'Reagan's. Study the backwater at the intersection for ducks and Great Blue Heron. Ruby-throated Hummingbirds have been seen at feeders in the neatly kept yards in this area. The entire region bears careful study and can easily support a full day or more of birding. If you decide to stay a night, cottage accommodations are found at O'Reagans. Gillis's Cabins have been a traditional spring favourite with Newfoundland birders for years, and Martin's Cabins offer a very commendable alternative. Grand Codroy Park is a privately operated park with many amenities.

Broom's Brook. This spot is a favourite spring walk for local birders. To find it, follow Route 406 towards Millville. Just as the road crosses Broom's Brook, it makes a very sharp turn to the west (downstream). A dirt road leads upstream along the northwest bank of Broom's Brook. Follow this road until common sense says you should stop. Park your vehicle and follow the road, which soon becomes a trail, down to the valley floor where you will find cleared land and possibly some active farming. A trail leads northeast along the bank of Broom's Brook for several kilometres until it fords the brook. This trail is an excellent place to listen for Olive-sided Flycatcher, Blue-headed Vireo, Bay-breasted Warbler and Blackburnian Warbler. Other rare warblers seen here include Northern Parula and Chestnut-sided. Some local inquiries about the exact location and route of the trail may be called for. The meadows at the intersection of Broom's Brook and Route 406 have produced Bobolink in the past.

Grand Codroy estuary. This area begins at Grand Codroy Park and widens rapidly towards the river mouth, 10 km away. The entire estuary is excellent birding habitat from spring to late fall. In spring, look for returning waterfowl and songbirds. Great Blue Heron, rare elsewhere in the province, should be seen daily from early June on through the summer. Listen for American Bittern and possible Sora or very rare Virginia Rail on calm evenings. Shorebirds make use of the extensive mudflats at the mouth of the river, where Piping Plover has nested and where Willet, also rare in Newfoundland, is often seen. Bay ducks, including Common Eider, Red-breasted Merganser and scoters, congregate offshore. Large numbers of Common Loons and a few Red-throated Loons may be encountered in early June. Songbirds arrive and either continue northward or settle in to nest. Newfoundland rarities have included Parula Warbler, Least Flycatcher and Scarlet Tanager. Nesting species include Swamp, White-throated, Lincoln's, Fox and Song Sparrows, Yellow-bellied and Alder Flycatchers, and about 10 species of wood warbler, including Blackpoll.

In summer, nesting waterfowl are in evidence throughout the estuary. Nesting passerines include Savannah and Swamp Sparrows, American Goldfinch and Common Grackle. Terns, including occasional Caspian, dive for fish at the river mouth. By mid-August the first of the returning shorebirds should appear on the mudflats. Species diversity is greater during southward migration. Watch for Dunlin; Sanderling; Semipalmated, White-rumped, Baird's and Least Sandpipers; Greater and Lesser Yellowlegs; Black-bellied and American Golden Plovers.

Fall birding brings raptor migration with the possibility of dozens of Ospreys concentrated over the estuary, along with passing Rough-legged and Sharp-shinned Hawks, Peregrine Falcon, Merlin and Kestrel. Waterfowl are still very much in evidence. This area has produced Hooded Mergansers on a few occasions. Songbirds migrate through up to October, although fall songbird opportunities do not rival those of the spring.

Loch Lomond. Not quite the picturesque gem that its name suggests, this small pond on the road from Upper Ferry to St. Andrew's can be a good place for ducks, swallows and flycatchers, including Eastern Kingbird. Listen for Cape May Warbler and Chipping Sparrow. The pond is roughly circular and about 750 m across. It sits below a broad, sloping farm field.

Cape Anguille. This is the most westerly point on the island of Newfoundland. From the low land near the lighthouse you can sea-watch for Great Cormorant and passing gannets, a few alcids, sea ducks and loons. The marsh behind the fish plant in the community of Cape Anguille regularly produces Sora.

Outside the Codroy Valley area, the next good birding spots are north towards Stephenville.

Codroy Pond Resource Road. This dirt road leading up to the top of Bald Mountain is located about 40 km north of the intersection of Route 1 and Route 406. You should park off the road and walk, but remember there may be unexpected traffic. There is a very good assortment of spring songbirds on this road, including many species of warblers, sparrows and thrushes. Winter Wren, Veery, Blue-headed and Philadelphia Vireo, and Parula Warbler have all been recorded along with many others.

Flat Island. Take the road to St. George's about 4.5 km north of the intersection of Route 1 and Route 403. Flat Island can be scanned with a good telescope from the public wharf, or you may find a local resident who you can hire to take you across to the island. This long sandy spit hosts nesting Piping Plover and Willet in summer. Common Black-headed Gulls have nested on this island.

Stephenville Crossing. With its long sandy beaches and the large tidal estuary at the confluence of several large rivers, Stephenville Crossing is a superb birding location.

In spring, watch for congregations of waterfowl heading north. Canada Goose, American Wigeon, Black Duck, Red-breasted Merganser and Greater Scaup are often found in fairly large numbers. Shorebirds will also be present.

In summer, waterfowl linger while swallows hunt over the water with Spotted and Least Sandpipers nesting along the shoreline. Caspian Terns are seen often, along with Common Terns. Common Black-headed Gulls are seen annually in good numbers. The estuary is an excellent place to watch for Ospreys and Bald Eagles. Vagrant herons, including Snowy Egret and Great Egret, have been reported. After strong onshore storms you may find a Leach's Storm-petrel or two, resting in the estuary. The small ponds on either side of Route 490 often produce both dabbling and diving ducks.

Fall brings the return of waterfowl and shorebirds, along with very high numbers of Ospreys and modest numbers of other raptors in migration, including Bald Eagle, Northern Harrier, Merlin, Sharp-shinned Hawk and occasionally a Goshawk. Scoters may be seen offshore.

Stephenville. Follow Route 490 to Stephenville. The seaside drive along Kin Court from the airport to the port area can produce vagrants. The rarest known so far was a Fork-tailed Flycatcher that showed up at Stephenville Golf Course – Newfoundland's only record! More mundane species may include American Bittern and Rusty Blackbird in the marshy ditches. The Stephenville sewage outfall is near the mouth of Warm Brook and can be a good birding location. Follow Route 490 (Main Street) to the intersection with Queen Street; turn left. Follow Queen Street until it turns sharply to the right (west). Just past the turn you will see Kin Court to your left. Stay on the paved road with the airfield to your left, and proceed along until the ocean is close at hand on your right. Park and walk out over the beach. A quick scan will locate birds hovering near the sewer out-fall. Drive farther along Kin Court to locate the golf course. The port area is at the end of Kin Court.

This route has other birding opportunities As you drive down Queen Street from Main Street, you will see the brook running beside the road towards the ocean. You can take a sharp right-hand turn into a gravel parking area immediately after turning onto Kin Court, and follow the dirt road along between the high bank on the east, and a scrubby area between the road and the beach to the west. The gravelly banks of the brook often produce Killdeer, and Caspian Terns are found on the sand bar in the brook itself. The small marsh may support a few Red-winged Blackbirds. The barrier beach should also be scanned, especially in winter, for gulls. You can overlook the marsh from the top of the hillside. Either climb the hill, or drive along Queen Street until you see a trailer court to your left (on the sea side). The trailer court is on an unnamed crescent. Drive towards the water; there is room to park your car overlooking the marsh. The beach can be reached by driving farther along Queen Street to Gallant Street, and turning left. The road leads down to the beach.

Port au Port Peninsula. This is the heart of French Newfoundland. In fall, the beach at Picadilly is an excellent shorebird location by Newfoundland standards, with many species including Semipalmated Plover; Black-bellied and

American Golden-Plover; Greater and Lesser Yellowlegs; Semipalmated, White-rumped and Least Sandpipers; Sanderling; Dunlin; Pectoral Sandpiper; and Hudsonian Godwit all possible. It is also one of the best locations in Newfoundland for Caspian Tern. To reach Picadilly, take Route 490 west to Route 463, then head north.

The road to Long Point is reached by going to Lourdes at the end of Route 463 and turning right, or northeast. The road is wooded on both sides for almost the entire length. You can't drive to the tip. You have to park and walk the last kilometre along the beach. In late summer, notable fall-outs of warblers and sparrows have been recorded at Long Point.

As a birding destination the Port au Port Peninsula is still something of an unknown quantity, but initial reports are encouraging. If you are adventurous, this may be your chance to discover something really big!

JOHN PRATT

Corner Brook to Deer Lake

Corner Brook. Corner Brook, sometimes called Newfoundland's second city, is the main service centre in western Newfoundland, and the best place in this region for you to pick up necessities you may have forgotten. If you need topographic maps of the region, try Barnes Sporting Goods Store, 16 Humber Road. Corner Brook is served by two airports, one at Stephenville and the second at Deer Lake. The city is located in a bowl surrounded by mountains, at the upper end of a fiord. Birding potential is great, but reliable records date back only to the 1980s.

Large flocks of gulls, including Greater Black-backed, Herring, with Glaucous and Iceland in winter and Ring-billed in summer and fall, congregate in Humber Arm, close to the city. Drive along Marine Drive, which parallels the upper, northeastern, end of the Arm from the intersection of the Trans-Canada Highway and Route 440, past the paper mill and the city's sewage outflow to the Curling, southwestern, end of the city. Kingfishers have been seen summer and winter at the bridge near the intersection. The most convenient places to pull over, so that you can scan the waters, are near one of the industrial buildings. Greater Scaup, with the possibility of Lesser, and Common Merganser should be present. Bald Eagles are regularly seen flying over the Arm. Immediately south of the mill, where there is a pull-off near the sewage outflow, look for a large flock of Common Goldeneyes, with the possibility of a Barrow's. Black-headed Gulls have also been seen here. Ospreys often patrol the Humber Arm in summer, and Double-crested Cormorants have become regular fall visitors. A 2 km drive along Route 440 brings you to a small cove of the Arm, with a small beaver pond on the right of the roadway. Black Duck, Green-winged Teal and the occasional Wood Duck frequent the pond in spring and summer. The cove is another place to check for gulls, as is the municipal dump on a nearby side road.

In spring and early summer, visit the trail system running along Corner Brook Stream. A brochure for the trail is available from the Tourist Bureau, at the junction of the Trans-Canada and Confederation Drive. You can find the trail by going to the municipal park (Margaret Bowater Park) on O'Connell Drive, or by going to the Glynmill Inn, a major Corner Brook landmark. A stairwell leads down to the trail from the inn's parking lot. A small wetland lies below West Valley Road and can be reached by going to the end of Brook Street. This wetland occasionally supports dabblers. Along the trail, listen for warblers, sparrows and finches. A branch of the trail from Bowater Park leads to the Participark trail on University Drive (also accessible from the parking lot behind Sir Wilfred Grenfell College). Black-throated Green, Yellow-rumped and Mourning Warblers; Ovenbird; Boreal and Black-capped Chickadees; Red-breasted Nuthatch; and Ruffed Grouse are usually present on the upper part of the trail system. Tennessee and Yellow Warblers can often be found in the small fen next to the parking lot. Northern Waterthrush is common wherever alder thickets are present.

East of Corner Brook, the Trans-Canada Highway runs beside the Humber River, bypassing three rural villages on the way to the town of Pasadena (25 km east). Exits 8, 9 and 10 will take you onto service roads for Steady Brook, Humber Village and Little Rapids. These are worth exploring in winter, spring and early summer. There are several feeders in each of the communities. Stop the car and walk along the service roads or through the villages to obtain views of the Humber River, mixed boreal forest and farmland. Red-breasted Merganser, Common Goldeneye and Belted Kingfisher are common on the river through the summer. The wooded areas have Boreal and Black-capped Chickadees, Pine Siskin, Pine Grosbeak, Purple Finch and Blue Jay, as well as some of the boreal warblers. The western loop roadway in Humber Village is a good place to look for White-winged Crossbill in summer or winter. American Goldfinches and Ruby-throated Hummingbirds are becoming more common. There is a service road for the Marble Mountain downhill ski facility in Steady Brook which offers a viewpoint for the impressive Steady Brook Falls before turning into a pleasant unused logging road through mixed boreal forest. Ask locally for instructions to find the start of the road. As well as many of the common boreal forest birds mentioned earlier, Winter Wren, Bay-breasted Warbler, Swainson's Thrush and Gray Jay have been seen here.

Deer Lake. The area lies 50 km east of Corner Brook. Check the tail-race from the power plant for diving ducks including Common Goldeneye, Greater Scaup and Red-breasted Merganser. The sandy shores of Deer Lake are attractive to terns and gulls in spring, summer and fall. Deer Lake is also the jumping-off point for travel to Gros Morne National Park and the Great Northern Peninsula on Highway 430 (the Viking Trail).

You may wish to make a side trip to Cormack, a farming community with plenty of cultivated land. In fall, check farm ponds for migrating dabblers. In spring, check for nesting Killdeer.

Network of boreal forest roads. An extensive network of roads leading through the boreal forest exists both west of Corner Brook and north of Deer Lake. These roads, used by loggers, anglers and hunters, traverse a variety of habitats, including everything from fresh cut-overs to multi-generation forests. Finches including Pine Grosbeak, White-winged and Red Crossbills, Purple Finch and Pine Siskin may be present, especially in good cone years. Boreal forest warblers and sparrows nest throughout. Northern Hawk Owls have been seen west of Corner Brook, where several of these roads can be accessed directly from the Trans-Canada Highway within 10 to 15 km of Corner Brook.

North of Deer Lake, a network of these roads can be accessed from Nicholsville on Highway 430.

Note: Many of these woodland roads are unmarked and can be confusing. Make sure you obtain a map or go in the company of a local person if you are unfamiliar with back-road travel.

LOIS BATEMAN AND JOHN PRATT

Gros Morne National Park

The largest of Atlantic Canada's national parks, Gros Morne is located on the west coast of the island portion of Newfoundland. This 1805 km² protected area is representative of the Western Newfoundland Highlands Natural Region, comprising coastal lowlands, frontal slopes and upland barrens. Renowned for its geological history and features, fiord lakes like Western Brook Pond and the unique "lunar landscape" of the Tablelands, the area attracts visitors from around the world.

The entrance to the park lies approximately 40 km north of the town of Deer Lake, on Highway 430, the Viking Trail. Here at Wiltondale a side trip on Highway 431 takes you to the enclave communities of Bonne Bay and Trout River. Travelling north on Highway 430 from Wiltondale, you will arrive at the park headquarters at Rocky Harbour, and farther on, at the northern boundary of the park at Cow Head.

An excellent trail map provides information on hiking and interpretive trails. *The Tuckamore*, the main park publication, provides visitor information on park programs and facilities. Both are available at the Visitor Centre.

The park has five campgrounds as well as back-country camping areas. Commercial accommodation is readily available throughout the park area.

For full information, write to the Park Superintendent, Gros Morne National Park, P.O. Box 130, Rocky Harbour, Newfoundland A0K 4N0; phone (709) 458-2066 or visit the Web site at http://www.grosmorne.nf.ca

In 1999 236 species of birds were listed for Gros Morne with approximately 100 confirmed as breeding. A high number are migrants or vagrants with sightings somewhat happenstance. The prime birding season is May through September, which corresponds with the peak tourist season resulting in most facilities and services being readily available. The system of trails and facilities is coastally oriented and provides adequate access to the majority of the better bird habitats. Access to the upland plateau region is more difficult when searching for species more typical of the sub-arctic.

Park roads generally parallel the western coastline. Much of the park is free of development except for hiking and interpretive trails.

Here at Gros Morne you will likely encounter krummholz, known locally as tuckamore, for the first time. The bane of hikers, but a haven for birds, tuckamore is stunted, gnarled Balsam Fir or White Spruce, shaped by the wind into a distinctive profile and easier to go around than to go through.

Birding Highlights (Mainly Spring/Summer)

Lomond – Trout River area. At Wiltondale, take Highway 431 to Lomond, Woody Point and Trout River, to experience the Lomond River Valley, the South Arm of Bonne Bay and the unique geology of the Tablelands.

The area from Lomond to Woody Point is hilly and relatively well drained, although sections of fen and bog occur. Forest cover is predominantly softwood interspersed with deciduous species, including White Birch and Red Maple. Some of the more common birds here include Yellow-bellied Flycatcher; Ruby-crowned Kinglet; Swainson's Thrush; Northern Waterthrush; Mourning, Yellow, Magnolia and Black-throated Green Warblers; Ovenbird; Fox Sparrow; White-throated Sparrow; and Pine Siskin.

Ospreys and Bald Eagles are likely seen at the Lomond River estuary. Stop at the Glenburnie salt marsh for migrating waterfowl, shorebirds or the ever-present gulls. Near the fish plant at Winterhouse Brook, Herring, Ring-billed and Greater Black-backed Gulls are usually numerous. In spring keep a watch for Iceland Gulls and returning Common Terns.

From Woody Point to Trout River you will drive through a geological feature known as the Tablelands. This serpentinized barren landscape has few plants and fewer trees. Greater Yellowlegs nest on the summit and Rock Ptarmigan may be seen along the way. On the nearby Lookout Hills Trail, Willow Ptarmigan have been known to nest. At Trout River Pond follow the trail along the shore and watch for Spotted Sandpiper on the beaches. Alder Flycatcher is a possibility for those with a keen ear.

Southeast Hills to Rocky Harbour. Following Highway 430 north from Wiltondale takes you from the Southeast Hills along the East Arm of Bonne Bay past Deer Arm estuary and on to the enclave community of Rocky Harbour. Be alert along this stretch of highway for Ospreys and Bald Eagles which nest near the hydro lines and the high cliffs overlooking East Arm. Ospreys are also a common sight over the harbour in Rocky Harbour. The outlets of the many streams entering East Arm should be scanned for migrating waterfowl, especially Common Goldeneye, Common and Red-breasted Merganser, and Black Duck. During fall Common Loons are more likely seen in salt water near the shore.

Deer Arm Brook provides further opportunities for sighting waterfowl. Bald Eagles often sit on snagged logs in the river. Belted Kingfishers rest on downed trees hanging out over the river bank.

The trail head for the James Callahan Trail leading to Gros Morne Mountain and the highest point in the park at 806 m elevation is located here at Deer Arm. Travel through mature fir and mixed forest stands, heath and rock barrens, for incredible views and a variety of bird life.

The hike to the base of Gros Morne is moderately easy while the trip up Gros Morne and return is strenuous and challenging. The full round trip takes six to seven hours to complete. The diversity of habitats, including insect-damaged Balsam Fir stands, attract a variety of birds, such as Boreal and Black-capped Chickadees, and Hairy, Downy and Black-backed Woodpeckers. Ruby-crowned Kinglets are more often heard than seen as are a number of warblers and thrushes. The ponds at the base of the mountain attract Common Merganser, Common Goldeneye and Common Loon. Common Snipe can be heard winnowing during the breeding season. Search the short scrub treetops for American Tree, White-crowned and Fox Sparrows. Common Redpoll may also be present.

On the mountain summit, scan the ground carefully for Water Pipit and Horned Lark, as well as Rock Ptarmigan. Look closely as both Rock and Willow Ptarmigan are found on Gros Morne. Whimbrel and American Golden-Plover may be present on the rocky ledges overlooking Ten Mile Pond.

Rocky Harbour. The community of Rocky Harbour is a good birding location if you are energetic enough to search the shoreline, open fields, alder swales and wooded edges. Many vagrant species have been sighted. Of most interest to birders are the gull species, which arrive in winter near the community wharf. Iceland, Glaucous and Common Black-headed appear regularly during the ice-free period. Ring-billed Gulls are common throughout the summer.

Lobster Cove Head. A point of land at the northern entrance to Rocky Harbour is the site of the Lobster Cove Head Lighthouse and a bird banding station. The most common species found in the area, in decreasing order, are Northern Waterthrush, Blackpoll Warbler, Ruby-crowned Kinglet, Yellow-rumped Warbler, Yellow-bellied Flycatcher, White-throated Sparrow, Lincoln's Sparrow, Yellow Warbler, Black-and-white Warbler, American Robin, Boreal Chickadee, Black-capped Chickadee, Fox Sparrow and Mourning Warbler. Sharp-shinned Hawk and Merlin commonly prey on these small birds. Walk the trails on the Head, particularly in spring and fall, and you may be rewarded with a storm-driven vagrant not currently listed for the park.

Green Point–Bakers Brook. This is a coastal location with a connecting trail, accessed either from the bridge at Baker's Brook or the campground at Green Point. Shallow ponds attract migratory waterfowl and shorebirds as well as their share of vagrants. American Black Duck, Northern Pintail, Green-winged Teal and Canada Goose are regular visitors. Spotted Sandpipers are known to nest. In the tuckamore and taller trees, spot Magnolia, Blackpoll and Mourning Warblers. Savannah Sparrows are common on the open bogs.

Western Brook Pond and Snug Harbour Trails. The trail to Western Brook Pond is a pleasant walk across open bog, over wooded limestone ridges and through stunted mixed softwood forest. Common Yellowthroat, Winter Wren, Hermit Thrush, Savannah Sparrow and Hairy and Downy Woodpeckers are present.

A side trip to Snug Harbour may flush the introduced, and expanding, Ruffed Grouse and Spruce Grouse.

St. Paul's Inlet. This area of tidal flats and salt marshes is one of the prime water-fowl and shorebird resting and staging areas in the province. Surrounding grasslands are important habitat for land birds and shorebirds. Migrating waterfowl include American Black Duck, Northern Pintail, Green-winged Teal, Red-breasted Merganser and Canada Goose. Species expanding their range include Northern Shoveler, American Wigeon and Ring-necked Duck. Migratory shorebirds include Semipalmated Plover, White-rumped and Semipalmated Sandpiper, Ruddy Turnstone, Sanderling, Short-billed Dowitcher and both Lesser and Greater Yellowlegs. American Golden-Plover and Black-bellied Plover frequent the open grassland and salt marsh. Three species of terns have been sighted. Common and Arctic Terns nest nearby and Caspian Tern, an uncommon visitor, makes an appearance in late summer. Double-crested Cormorant are increasing in numbers. In the nearby tuckamore, Song Sparrows have bred while Tree Swallows swoop overhead. Horned Lark, Water Pipit and Snow Bunting are regular fall visitors. This is an area to expect the unexpected. Large rafts of Red-breasted Merganser form in October.

Cow Head and Shallow Bay. This area at the north end of the park includes the Cow Head peninsula with its unique limestone melange, and the white sand beaches of Shallow Bay. Several near-shore islands with names like Stearin Island, support nesting Common and Arctic Terns, which are under stress from nesting Greater Black-backed and Herring Gulls. Spring and fall are the best times to scan the ocean for sea ducks like Common Eider and White-winged Scoter. The endangered Harlequin Duck has been sighted in the area.

If you are returning south towards Rocky Harbour, scan the open bogs along the highway for low-flying Northern Harriers. The Short-eared Owl, or lopper, as it is known locally, may make a brief appearance.

JOHN PRATT AND BRUCE BRADBURY

Northern Peninsula and L'Anse aux Meadows

On the tip of this peninsula, Vikings landed at L'Anse aux Meadows about a thousand years ago. Today, at this world heritage site, you can visit the remains of their seven buildings, as well as a smithy and two cook pits. Displays at the interpretive centre show a variety of articles found, including a soapstone wheel used for spinning wool. This flywheel, the earliest European household implement found in North America, is identical to items found at Viking sites in Greenland, Iceland, Sweden and Norway.

Highway 430 north to the tip is approximately 360 km one way from Gros Morne National Park. There is air service to St. Anthony on a year-round basis. However, bad weather often interrupts the service, so if you use it, be prepared to stay a few days longer than expected. If you drive, there are a couple of campgrounds along the way, at River of Ponds and Pistolet Bay. Commercial accommodation is available at scattered communities along the route. Starting just north of Gros Morne National Park, they include Daniel's Harbour, Hawkes Bay, Port au Choix, Roddicton, Main Brook, Plum Point, St. Barbe, Pistolet Bay and St. Anthony.

Birding Features

On the way look at the good stands of Balsam Fir on the west-facing slopes, together with White Spruce. White Birch groves are scattered among these evergreens. At the northern tip, the forests grade into open woodland with traces of tundra. The soil is minimal, with extensive peatlands prevailing. Watch for ponds that host Northern Pintail and Green-winged Teal.

At River of Ponds, about 80 km north of Gros Morne National Park, stop and look at the displays of early artifacts. Farther north about 40 km, stop at Port au Choix National Historic Park to see artifacts from the Indian people of 2400 B.C. The visitor centre has excellent displays.

If you come in the spring or fall migration period, go out to the Ferolle Peninsula, about 60 km north of Port au Choix. This point is a landfall for land birds. Look for warblers and sparrows, as well as shorebirds. The shore-line north of here to Flower's Cove has numerous bays and coves that attract shorebirds and gulls. You'll see huge ships passing offshore in the Strait of Belle Isle from here. North of Flowers Cove, you can stop at Shoal Cove East to check for concentrations of shorebirds migrating in late summer. A small head-land to the west of the community is the best destination, and from there you can view both the cove itself and the waters of the Straits of Belle Isle.

Near the north end, stop in at Eddies Cove, the last community on the shore before Route 430 turns inland. The cove is about 120 km north of Port au Choix. The Strait of Belle Isle between Labrador and Newfoundland pro-vides access to pelagic birds, which come in close during storms. Sea winds from north and south should drop birds on this landfall. From late July, August and into September you should see a variety of shorebirds. Another nearby site to check out is Green Island Cove, about 12 km west of Eddies Cove along 430. The Short-eared Owl has been seen near Green Island, as have a variety of shorebirds.

Cape Norman, at the end of Route 435, just north of Cooks Harbour, is a natural landfall. It catches ocean wanderers and wind-blown migrant land birds. Come here on a windy or foggy day for Greater, Sooty and a few Manx Shearwaters, Leach's Storm-Petrel and Northern Gannet, which are all regular. Scrutinize the gulls for Iceland, Ring-billed and Common Black-headed Gulls. Watch for Black-legged Kittiwake. All three jaegers have been spotted in the fall. Shorebirds are usually noted at this rocky point, with Ruddy Turnstone and Whimbrel common in July and August. Don't forget the nearby marshes for ducks on migration and a possible Northern Harrier or Short-eared Owl.

Drive back down and across to Route 437. Then proceed north on it towards Pistolet Bay Provincial Park. Drive down to the end of the road at Cape Onion and Ship Cove to spot pelagic species in late summer. Hope that a northeast gale will blow good numbers of shearwaters and jaegers into the inner bay. Shorebirds include the regular numerous White-rumped Sandpipers in the fall. You may spot Red and Red-necked Phalaropes at this time too. Land birds are usually few.

Reached from Route 436, by the shore, L'Anse aux Meadows is a major landfall, attracting a variety of migrants. The site has become one of the province's birding hot spots. Birdwatching is most productive in early winter, but there is a wealth of birdlife year-round. In April to early May, European Golden-Plovers have occurred. The Ivory Gull also comes through off the point after northeast storms from December through March. May winds have brought in a Black-tailed Godwit and Eurasian Wigeon. A few pairs of Common Loons nest inland, as do American Bittern, Canada Goose, American Black Duck, Green-winged Teal, Greater Scaup, Common Eider on offshore islands and Red-breasted Merganser. The Rough-legged Hawk breeds in the offshore islands and may come in, as may Northern Harrier. In the uplands you should locate Willow Ptarmigan. Common Snipe and Spotted and Least Sandpipers breed here. Common and Arctic Terns have nesting colonies along this area. Other breeders to search for include Horned Lark, Gray-cheeked Thrush, Ruby-crowned Kinglet, Water Pipit, northern warblers mentioned in other areas (see above), Rusty Blackbird, large numbers of Common Redpolls, some Savannah Sparrows, numerous White-crowned Sparrows and scattered Swamp Sparrows. Razorbill, Common Murre and Atlantic Puffin sometimes come inshore from mid-June to early August. Black Guillemots breed on the nearby islands.

Greater and Sooty Shearwaters come in because of fog. You are almost certain to find Northern Fulmar and Northern Gannet in summer. In late summer, Manx Shearwater and Wilson's Storm-Petrel often appear. Fall is the time to see large numbers of jaegers and gulls. Up to 10,000 Black-legged Kittiwakes have appeared offshore in late August to early September. Jaegers

Greater Shearwater

also appear in numbers, with all three species possible, together with a few Great Skua. Ring-billed Gulls may come in from more western colonies. Migrant shorebirds stop, with the best site to observe them located along the beach among the kelp near the historic site. Whimbrel is the most common shorebird in August to early September. Survey shorebird flocks for Red Knot, Pectoral and Baird's Sandpipers, Dunlin, Short-billed Dowitcher, White-rumped and Buff-breasted Sandpiper.

Winter is the best season for your visit. You could be rewarded with species seldom seen in Atlantic Canada. Thick-billed Murre and Dovekie regularly occur. King Eider is irregular, along with Common Eider. In the harbour you'll find Glaucous and Iceland Gulls.

Go to Round Head from mid-October to early May for Gyrfalcon. Round Head is the high, rounded promontory immediately northeast of the community. It can be reached by walking along a trail that follows the shoreline for a distance of about 1 km. The dark phase Gyrfalcon is common from late October on, and the white phase in March and April. Snowy Owls are best seen in half and fading light or on dull days as they sit on the barrens. The Short-eared Owl is also present. There are rare but regular records of Northern Wheatears.

A continuation of the trip could be a drive to St. Anthony. If you use the air service in or out of this community, check the weather and airline offices before making final plans. The coastal lands around St. Anthony are mainly barrens and tuckamore. Willow Ptarmigan, Horned Lark and Water Pipit are common and widespread breeders, as are Common Redpoll and White-crowned Sparrow. They all breed on the barrens or in the scrub growth. The mature forest holds Mourning Warbler, Common Yellowthroat and year-round Gray Jay and Boreal Chickadee. Look for Lincoln's and Fox Sparrows in the open areas. European wanderers often show up.

A few Northern Wheatears appear regularly. European vagrants have occurred on occasion. Fall migration at St. Anthony is not as good as at L'Anse aux Meadows.

Fishing Point Lighthouse, Saint Anthony Bight and Goose Cove are the good spots to observe from, particularly in winter, when the Ivory Gull may come in close to shore. Large flocks of Common and King Eiders, Glaucous Gull and Black Guillemot appear in mid-winter. The Dovekie often appears in large numbers. The Gyrfalcon is a regular visitor. A Snowy Owl may show up too.

If you have an extra week, you may want to take the ferry between St. Anthony and Goose Bay, Labrador, across the Strait of Belle Isle. Another similar ride is from St. Barbe across to Blanc-Sablon, Quebec. There is a chance to spot whales too. Summer birds include Northern Fulmar, Greater and Sooty Shearwaters, and Leach's Storm-Petrel; look for large flocks of Black-legged Kittiwake, scoters, Razorbill, Thick-billed and Common Murres, Black Guillemot and Atlantic Puffin (fairly common). In the fall, watch for all three jaegers, a possible Ivory Gull, Dovekie, the odd Gyrfalcon and Snowy Owl, and a few Lapland Longspurs within flocks of Snow Bunting.

BRUCE MACTAVISH

Strait of Belle Isle and South Labrador Coast

The narrow Strait of Belle Isle is crossed on an 18 km ferry trip from St. Barbe on Newfoundland to Blanc-Sablon in Labrador. You will see a variety of pelagics on this little-over-an-hour trip. If you are short of time, stay on for a return ride, a total of four hours. The ferry runs from June to freeze-up in November or December. The road on the Labrador side is about 70 km long from the ferry landing at Blanc-Sablon north to Red Bay. The rest of this eastern shore region is connected by boat and ferry.

You will find commercial accommodation at L'Anse-au-Clair, Forteau and L'Anse-au-Loup.

Birding Features

On the trip over, scan for Northern Fulmars, which are fairly common; Greater and Sooty Shearwaters, numerous from June to late September; Manx Shearwater, a regular late summer to early fall bird. You should see Leach's Storm-Petrel; Oldsquaw and Common Eider are regularly seen in spring and fall; look for several hundred Red and Red-necked Phalaropes from August through October. Pomarine and Parasitic Jaegers often are spotted from mid-May to October. Long-tailed Jaeger is occasionally present in August and early September. Look for the large flocks of immature Black-legged Kittiwakes that

Atlantic Puffins

gather in late summer. Very rarely a Sabine's Gull turns up from late July to September. You should spot a few Razorbills, and Common and Thick-billed Murres; Atlantic Puffins are usually seen off Blanc-Sablon with young birds close to the boat in August.

Blanc-Sablon. Although in Quebec, this community serves as the link between Newfoundland and Labrador. On the ferry run, look for the following birds. Red-throated Loon is noted in numbers up to 100 in mid- to late August. Greater and Sooty Shearwaters move inshore in early summer during the capelin run. Manx Shearwater can be seen in small numbers in summer. A few water birds, including Blue-winged Teal and American Bittern, are noted. In late July, look for large numbers of Northern Phalarope. Small flocks of other shorebirds appear, including Least Sandpiper and Short-billed Dowitcher. Check out the gulls for a few Pomarine and Long-tailed Jaegers in the harbour at this time. In late summer Black-legged Kittiwakes are the most numerous. A few Common Black-headed Gulls are present in mid- to late summer. Shorebirds in early fall include White-rumped and Semipalmated Sandpipers.

Red Bay. This community is the site of the discovery of the Basque whaling galleon. This discovery, and detailed archival checking, has proven that these sailors lived here 50 years before Champlain. The galleon sank in 1565, with insurance paid the following year to the owners in Spain. Whale oil recovered from the wreck in 1978 was still in good condition. The ship is the earliest European vessel yet found in Canadian waters. Look for Red-throated Loon in summer and fall and also Harlequin Duck, Oldsquaw and Common Eider in large numbers in fall.

Spot all three scoters in summer. Other birds seen are similar to those mentioned above. However, also search for Northern Hawk Owl and Boreal Owl, and Great Horned and Short-eared Owls from farther south, all nesters at times. Black-backed and Three-toed Woodpeckers may be found. The Gray-cheeked Thrush is found in the forests, with the Horned Lark and Savannah Sparrow in open country. American Tree and White-crowned Sparrows are common.

Henley Harbour to Cartwright. This eastern coast of Labrador is served by the coastal boat. The ride to the several communities on the way offers a good glimpse into fishing lifestyles before the modern world came along. The shore is very barren and windswept, with steep cliffs. Water birds are the main attraction. You should find flocks of Greater and Sooty Shearwaters. Scan for Red-throated Loon. Flocks of ducks, including Oldsquaw, Common Eider, scoters and Red-breasted Merganser are regulars. Scan the sky for a Rough-legged Hawk. Razorbills nest in nearby colonies and should be present from spring to late summer. Search the bays for Red Phalarope; the shores should be examined for sandpipers and plovers. The Northern Wheatear is a very local breeder on the Labrador coast from Cartwright north.

BRUCE MACTAVISH

Labrador

Labrador is a vast land, difficult to access for birders, but rewarding for its great beauty. For all its size, Labrador has few roads. A short strip of paved highway runs along the Strait of Belle Isle from the ferry terminal in Blanc-Sablon (actually in Quebec) to the town of Red Bay, where visitors can see the partially restored remains of an ancient Basque whaling station. A gravel road of uneven quality connects Happy Valley/Goose Bay with Churchill Falls and Labrador City/Wabush, which are in turn connected to the "outside world" by Route 389 to Baie Comeau in Quebec. Many coastal communities have airstrips, and a coastal boat service operates from the island of Newfoundland in the summer months and runs north as far as Nain, providing access to many tiny towns and villages scattered along the length of Labrador's rugged marine coast.

Since this book first appeared in 1984, much has been learned about Labrador birdlife, and it is now possible to give some basic bird-finding information for the more accessible areas.

BRUCE MACTAVISH, PAUL LINEGAR AND JOHN PRATT

Seabirds Seen from the Coastal Boat

The coastal boat, running from Red Bay to Cartwright, stops in many small communities. It stays inshore, making it possible for travellers to watch for nesting seabirds as they pass close to colonies and feeding grounds. Razorbills, Common Murres, Thick-billed Murres, Black Guillemots and Black-legged Kittiwakes will all be present in the breeding season. Shearwaters and petrels will also occur. In spring and fall, small flocks of Red or Red-necked Phalaropes may be seen. The Gannet Islands Ecological Reserve just off Cartwright supports a major Razorbill colony (but ironically, no gannets!).

BRUCE MACTAVISH, PAUL LINEGAR AND JOHN PRATT

Happy Valley/Goose Bay to Northwest River and Sheshatshiu

This is the most densely populated part of Labrador, due in large part to the existence of a large airport that was once part of a major American air force base. Air forces from several NATO countries continue to use this base for low-level flight training each summer.

Birding Features

Being so far inland, this is not a particularly good area for seabirds, but it may be worth checking at Northwest River for gulls and terns. Shorebirds occur in migration, and several species are present in summer.

In summer, the dense alder, poplar and birch-covered roadsides are home to many songbirds, including Least Flycatcher, Hermit Thrush, Ruby-crowned Kinglet, Red-eyed Vireo, Yellow, Tennessee and Orange-crowned Warblers. Conifer woods harbour Hairy, Black-backed and Three-toed Woodpeckers and Spruce Grouse. Scrubby areas are likely to produce White-crowned Sparrows. Red-tailed Hawks and Ospreys are common raptors.

Dabbling ducks are common. Northern Shoveler has nested at Otter Creek, where the seaplane base is located. Other species to be expected in the area include American Black Duck and Green-winged Teal.

Among birds most likely to be seen in flight, look for Bank Swallow, Tree Swallow and Common Nighthawk.

Most birds leave in winter, but Hoary Redpoll, Common Redpoll and other winter finches may be seen. Bohemian Waxwings may also be spotted. Snow Buntings are regular feeder birds in various parts of Happy Valley/ Goose Bay.

BRUCE MACTAVISH, PAUL LINEGAR AND JOHN PRATT

Trans-Labrador Highway: Goose Bay to Labrador City–Wabush

This road used to be very difficult to travel across, but recent upgrading has made it much more civilized, although it is still unpaved. The road passes through a variety of habitats, most common being Black Spruce forest. Many of Labrador's boreal species may be seen from the road. Look for Spruce Grouse in any season and Willow Ptarmigan in winter. Northern Hawk Owls occur fairly regularly, while Northern Goshawk is more rare. Both may be found year-round. Black-backed and Three-toed Woodpeckers and Gray Jays are also resident. Bald Eagles may be seen along the rivers in summer. The Labrador City/Wabush area will produce most of these species, as well.

BRUCE MACTAVISH, PAUL LINEGAR AND JOHN PRATT

Central Newfoundland – The Exploits Region

Central Newfoundland is slowly emerging from anonymity as an area of considerable birding potential. A recent study entitled "Birdwatching in the Exploits" (1999, Exploits Valley Economic Development Corporation) demonstrates the many opportunities for birders throughout this large and ecologically diverse area. Birders visiting the Exploits area should check with the corporation, or visit the Tourist Information Chalet in Grand Falls–Windsor, where a copy of this report, and a companion report entitled "Trails of the Exploits," may be obtained at nominal cost.

The Exploits region, named for the Exploits River, has long been associated with timber harvesting. Generations of logging activity, combined with warmer than average temperatures in summer, have produced a great diversity of habitat types and plant communities. Edge environments abound, and bird diversity appears to benefit as a consequence. The north part of the region is typified by a protected marine environment, with hundreds of small islands, inlets, estuaries and intertidal areas. Some of the more sought-after species likely to be encountered in the region include Spruce Grouse, Gray Jay, Boreal Chickadee, Rusty Blackbird and White-winged Crossbill. This is truly an area to be explored.

Birding Features
Grand Falls – Windsor. Located on the Trans-Canada Highway, this is the economic centre of the Exploits region. Several trails of note can be visited,

including the Corduroy Brook Trail, a 6 km walk that traverses a variety of natural and urban habitats. The Exploits River flows through town, and the Environmental Resources Management Association has established a trail along a short section of the river, starting near the Salmonid Interpretation Centre. Although the trail is only 500 m long, it has produced such species as Palm Warbler and Spruce Grouse. Grand Falls–Windsor is the logical starting point for birding forays into the surrounding area. Beothuk Provincial Park just west of the town can be a good birding location, where Spruce Grouse, woodpeckers and flycatchers are "target" species.

Buchans. Buchans is one of the few truly "inland" communities in Newfoundland. It was a major mining centre in its heyday, and a stop on the now-defunct Newfoundland Railway. To reach Buchans, take the Trans-Canada Highway 27 km west to Badger from Grand Falls–Windsor; turn south on Route 370. Buchans is a further 73 km from Badger, but the drive is worth it. Check along the way for Black-backed Woodpecker and Spruce Grouse. Yellow-bellied Sapsucker, uncommon in Newfoundland, may be encountered in this area. The Buchans avifauna is typically boreal. Watch for Northern Harrier in open barren areas, and listen for Rusty Blackbird and Palm Warbler in the same habitat. Boreal sparrows including Lincoln's, White-throated, Swamp, Fox, Savannah and Dark-eyed Junco should be present in season. White-winged and Red Crossbills may be encountered in conifer forests.

Bay of Exploits. Take the Trans-Canada Highway east from Grand Falls–Windsor to Bishop's Falls and the intersection of Route 350; proceed north about 25 km to Northern Arm. Look for the trail head of Pendragon Trail. This 1.2 km trail takes about 25 minutes to walk, and leads south to Evans Point. A variety of habitats will offer an opportunity to spot many breeding warbler species, including Blackpoll, Palm Warbler, Northern Waterthrush and Wilson's Warbler, as well as several others typical of the region. Other boreal specialties that may be seen include Boreal Chickadee and Rusty Blackbird. At the end of the trail, check the estuary and mudflats for waders in fall. The bay will probably produce Common Loon in most months when water is open.

Continue north along Route 350 to Leading Tickles. The drive is about 60 km, so you may want to stop at Point Leamington and Glovers Harbour on the way.

Point Leamington. Here check out Rowsell's Hill Nature Trail, located at the entrance to the town. The species mix is typically boreal, including Pine Grosbeak, Boreal Chickadee and Rusty Blackbird. Birders should be alert for Spruce Grouse throughout this area. Otter Pond Trail, encircling Otter Pond, is a much less challenging walk through low brush and marsh. Watch for a variety of warblers including Palm. Gray Jay has been recorded here.

Glovers Harbour. This site is about 25 km north of Point Leamington, on a short sideroad leading west from Route 350. Look for the Bayview Nature Trail, a challenging uphill hike with a chance to see a variety of warbler species, Boreal

Chickadee, Spruce Grouse, Gray Jay and Bald Eagle, among others. The end of the hike affords a great view of the surrounding countryside.

Leading Tickles. Here find East Tickle Trail. This 3 km walk through largely coastal habitat offers great scenery and good birding opportunities. Species to watch for include Boreal Chickadee, Yellow-bellied Flycatcher, Spruce Grouse, White-winged Crossbill and Gray Jay. The waters of Leading Tickles should be scanned for seabirds and ducks in season.

Lewisporte. From Grand Falls–Windsor, proceed east along the Trans-Canada Highway to Notre Dame Junction and the intersection of Route 340. Take Route 340 north about 12 km to Lewisporte, located on the shores of Burnt Bay. This area can be excellent for waterfowl, including Common and Red-throated Loons, in fall and winter. Shorebirds frequent the muddy flats, and Ospreys are seen here in high numbers on occasion. Bald Eagle is likely to be found.

JOHN PRATT, c/o EXPLOITS VALLEY ECONOMIC DEVELOPMENT
CORPORATION, LARRY ANDREWS AND GEOFF BEATON

Gander, "The Loop," and Glovertown

Several villages and communities along the northeast coast of the province provide interesting locations to explore. Highway 1 cuts inland through Gander, away from the coast. Time permitting, go north and east from Gander on 330 and back south on 320 to join the Trans-Canada at Gambo. The loop takes you through a mix of communities that depend on the sea for existence. Islands in Bonavista Bay to the south and east support a relatively large population of Bald Eagles and Ospreys. Watch for them as you skirt the coast. At Gambo, the Trans-Canada Highway is built on a huge glacial deposit, skirting Freshwater Bay.

Highway 310 goes east from 1 at Glovertown. Take it to visit Salvage. It was isolated for nearly 300 years until a road was built in the late 1940s. Local artifacts can be viewed in the museum.

Glovertown has become the main service area for visitors to Terra Nova National Park to the immediate south. The community has several good craft shops, in addition to an active group of birders. Birding information for the Glovertown and Terra Nova region is best obtained from the Interpretation Service at Terra Nova National Park.

Birding Features
Gander. Gander is an airport town and a major service centre for this part of Newfoundland. Before the dawn of long-distance jets, Gander was a major Trans-Oceanic Plane Stop ("TOPS") facility. It has seen extensive military use, as well. Gander is located in an area that has been alternately logged and burned over many times. The typical forest cover is a mix of conifers and small hardwoods, and the many roads and clearings have created superb "edge" environments where a mix of resident and migrant songbirds can be found. The

Thomas Howe Demonstration Forest just east of Gander offers good trails for birdwatchers. A trail with bird feeding stations has been developed around Cobb's Pond. Go north towards Gander Bay on Highway 330. Look for the Cobb's Pond Rotary Park on the west side of the highway. This is a good place to look for woodpeckers, Spruce Grouse, Ruffed Grouse, Brown Creeper and a variety of breeding songbirds, including finches, warblers and sparrows. The pond itself may produce a variety of dabbling ducks.

Jonathon's Pond Park. This park is located on Highway 330, about 10 km north of Gander. It is typified by large stands of aspen and birch, and supports some interesting birds, including Ovenbird and Hermit Thrush. It is also a good place to camp if you are planning to spend some time in the area.

Gander Bay to Gambo – the "Loop." Highway 330 leads north to Carmanville and then east to Lumsden, Cape Freels and Wesleyville. The loop is completed by taking Highway 320 from Wesleyville to Gambo. This route is a bit off the beaten track, but it does give birders access to a variety of habitats within a fairly short distance. Check Gander Bay for Common and Red-throated Loons in fall and early winter. In fall, the muddy shorelines should be scanned for migrating shorebirds. An alternative route along Highway 332 from Gander Bay to Carmanville will allow you to stay close to the coast, while the shorter route along Highway 330 will take you through mixed forest and cut-overs. Where the road descends into stream valleys with tall conifers and birches on either route, listen for Black-throated Green Warblers singing in June. At Carmanville you will find services, including accommodations. This area has been extensively logged, resulting in a lot of deciduous scrub. There are also extensive tracts of re-planted conifer forest. Listen for Magnolia Warbler, Alder Flycatcher and Common Yellowthroat where the habitat is especially scrubby. Veery is rare in Newfoundland but has been recorded in the Carmanville area.

Gander Bay. The road north from Gander, Highway 330, takes you through varying habitat to the sea. Stop at a couple of sites and explore for a wide variety of species. When you reach the bay, scan out to sea for seabirds, then continue following the coast to Musgrave Harbour.

Musgrave Harbour. At Musgrave Harbour you will begin a drive of several kilometres that runs close to the coast. Offshore you will just be able to make out the Penguin Islands. These little islands support a surprisingly rich avifauna. Check at Musgrave Harbour for boat trips. Species found on the islands include Leach's Storm-Petrel, Great Black-backed Gull, Caspian Tern, Common Tern, Arctic Tern, Atlantic Puffin and Common Eider. A lighthouse is located on North Penguin Island.

Wadham Islands. Set out in the Atlantic, southeast of Fogo Island, these islands are good spots for seabirds. Boats are available from Musgrave Harbour. The islands contain Leach's Storm-Petrel, Arctic Tern and Atlantic Puffin in summer.

Lumsden. The Lumsden/Cape Freels area is known for its expanses of fine, sandy beaches. A visit in the fall can produce migrating shorebirds, including Hudsonian Godwit, Short-eared Owl, Northern Harrier, Horned Lark, Lapland Longspur and Water Pipit. Windmill Bight Park is a good place to camp. More elaborate accommodations can be found at Wesleyville, a few kilometres down the road.

Gambo. At Gambo, you will re-join the Trans-Canada Highway. There is a very large and rocky estuary here – look for loons, Canada Geese, dabbling ducks and mergansers in late summer and early fall.

Glovertown area. Fire has raged over this area at times during the past 30 years. A few stands of spruce, fir and birch are still left, together with pockets of Tamarack, which are good places to look for Palm Warbler. Begin your visit along Station Road, the best birding site. The birch, cherry and alder thickets attract a wide and numerous collection of land birds in late summer. Move to the boggy spot behind the school where the scattered Tamarack and shrubs host Wilson's Warbler and Swamp Sparrow in summer. Explore the shrubs and low growth by the Shore Road in South Glovertown. Look for warblers and sparrows, with a possible Chipping Sparrow. Where Route 1 crosses the Terra Nova River there is a small dirt parking lot where you can pull off the highway. Survey the meadows for American Kestrel. A Rough-legged Hawk is possible in spring and winter. A walk along the road leading down the river should produce a variety of nesting warblers and sparrows. You may also find a Red-winged Blackbird, although the Rusty Blackbird is more common. Check the adjacent spruce forest for Red Crossbill and Pine Grosbeak.

The waters at the mouth of the Terra Nova River are good for Double-crested Cormorants in spring, before they move over to Traytown. In late summer and fall, watch for flocks of Common Goldeneye, with the possibility of one or more Barrow's among them in late fall and winter. White-winged and Black Scoters also appear here at South Glovertown, near the river. Look for a Red-winged Blackbird and waxwings. Both Cedar and Bohemian have been spotted here.

A winter visitor should check the feeders for Blue Jays, Hairy Woodpeckers and a stray Dickcissel among wintering sparrows. Northern Shrikes come in November and are found in the spruce along the river.

Traytown and Cull's Harbour are connected by a single-lane causeway. The fast current keeps an expanse of bay open all year. Look for Double-crested Cormorants from late spring on. Shorebirds appear in spring and should be checked on the mudflats near the causeway. Several species of vagrant European shorebirds have been recorded in this area in spring. Gulls also use these mudflats. The midsummer flocks of Greater Yellowlegs are augmented by Semipalmated Plover and White-rumped Sandpiper in mid- to late fall. Scan for hunting Bald Eagles and Ospreys and a possible Northern Goshawk.

Now move on to the Shore Road and woods for Tennessee Warblers and kinglets in the alders and spruce-fir complex. You should see the Belted

Kingfisher, which nests here and is conspicuous along the shoreline from May to September. The adjacent highlands contain a few resident Willow Ptarmigan.

GREGG STROUD AND JOHN PRATT

Terra Nova National Park

Terra Nova, on the east coast of Newfoundland, hosts an excellent mix of birds. Look for nesting Common Loon, summering Leach's Storm-Petrel, Northern Gannet, wintering Barrow's Goldeneye, numerous breeding Bald Eagles and Ospreys, and up to a dozen species of shorebirds, including occasional strays. Other birds to be seen are several gulls and terns, with a few Arctic that breed at a Common Tern colony; Black Guillemot; resident Great Horned and Boreal Owls; a good chance for Black-backed Woodpecker; Yellow-bellied Alder Flycatchers; Gray-cheeked Thrush; and several warblers, including Tennessee, American Redstart, Black-throated Green, Ovenbird, Northern Waterthrush, Magnolia, Palm and Blackpoll. Crossbill numbers have declined notably in recent years, but both Red and White-winged Crossbills may be seen infrequently in many areas of the park, especially in years when there is a good cone crop. Then to top it off you can whale-watch for up to five species in the peak period from late June to early August. Shore hikes almost certainly will bring you numerous tracks of River Otter and Mink. Moose, Black Bear and Lynx are often spotted in the uplands.

The 402 km² park lies at the head of Bonavista Bay. Buses operate twice a day from the ferry at Port-aux-Basques and St. John's. Rental car and road cruiser services are available in St. John's. There are several wharves for docking and numerous trails and interpretive loops, all shown on park brochures. A new Marine Interpretation Centre has been opened at the Salton's Brook Wharf area. This is also a good place to access the trail leading back to Newman Sound Campground, from which the intertidal flats of Inner Newman Sound may be observed. Accommodation is plentiful within the park, with a large campground of over 400 serviced sites on Newman Sound near headquarters; another one with 100 serviced sites is 3 km from the north gate. Of the five smaller spots, two are winterized, one fully, and the other is a primitive one. Supplies and commercial accommodation are available in Musgravetown, Bunyan's Cove, Port Blandford, Terra Nova, Charlottetown, Glovertown, Traytown and other nearby communities.

The park features an information centre with interpreters stationed in headquarters at the head of Newman Sound. Write The Superintendent, Terra Nova National Park, Glovertown, Newfoundland A0G 2L0; phone (709) 533-2801.

A comprehensive checklist of park birds is available at the interpretive centre, where you can also check for the latest in local bird information.

Birding Features

The landforms are gently rolling, with a good collection of ponds and streams. The forests are Black Spruce and Balsam Fir with groves of Tamarack and White Birch. Open bog and fen communities are scattered with some local

Cladonia parkland. Rock barrens and bogs tend to dominate the highlands. The major water features, the sounds, are former deep glaciated valleys with narrow restrictions at their mouths. The reduced salt-water flow caused by these restrictions tends to produce conditions with unique marine life.

Malady Head. Take the hiking trail from Site 62 in the campground up to a lookout point near the top of Malady Head. On the way, you should find Gray-cheeked Thrush. If you go in early morning or evening, listen to the flute-like songs of Hermit, Swainson's and Gray-cheeked Thrushes. On top, on the barrens, inspect for Blackpoll Warbler and Fox Sparrow. You should see at least one Bald Eagle and an Osprey from the lookout point.

Louis Hills and Burnt Point. Located in the northwest section of the park, the hills have been burned over and now the lower slopes are covered with heath and blueberries. Near the shore look for Belted Kingfisher and Swamp Sparrow. Shorebirds can be found in mid- to late summer on the beach. Common Loons and Double-crested Cormorants occur on the water in summer and fall. Warblers found in these woodlands are more abundant than elsewhere in the park and include Yellow, Ovenbird, Mourning, Wilson's and American Redstart. West of the turnoff to Burnt Point, look for the Yellow-bellied Flycatcher; east of this turnoff you may find an Alder Flycatcher in the dense roadside cover. You could see a Purple Finch or a Common Redpoll on the road. Look for both crossbills on the Louis Hills trail.

Blue Hill Trailhead. Come here to find that elusive Black-backed Woodpecker, all year. You will probably spot Northern Goshawk, Merlin, Ruffed Grouse and maybe a Great Horned Owl. Sightings of Red Fox and Lynx are possible.

Salton's Brook and Buckley's Cove. Beyond Highway 1, a bog and fen system is used by breeding Canada Geese and Greater Yellowlegs. Check Salton's Beach or the wharf and bridge area for River Otter and Mink. At the wharf in winter, search the flocks of ducks for Greater Scaup, Barrow's Goldeneye, Common Murre and Black Guillemot. Make sure you follow the trail east towards Buckley's Cove to find warblers and Red and White-winged Crossbills. Take the hike in early fall for shorebirds and a possible Bald Eagle.

Headquarters Wharf to Newman Sound Day Area. This 2 km coastal trail is one of the better year-round birding hikes in the region. Vegetation includes a forest of Balsam Fir, clumps of Red Maple, elderberry and alders. Several sand spits and rocky shores add to the habitat. August and early September are the best times for Northern Goshawk and Bald Eagle. Look for Semipalmated Plover and Semipalmated Sandpiper on the sandy shoreline. Least Sandpiper may be found near the tiny salt marsh just below the Headquarters Wharf parking lot. White-rumped Sandpipers are found on the rocky and pebbly beaches in early October. They move to the lower margins near Big Brook Flats later on. Gulls of several species are on Rocky Point at high tide and on the boulders in midchannel at other times. Wintering waterfowl are numerous and varied and include American Black Duck, Common Goldeneye, and possibly Barrow's Goldeneye. Watch for the River Otter in winter.

Big Brook Flats. This area has recently gained status as a bird sanctuary and International Biological Preserve. Waterfowl are very common. Shorebirds are not as numerous here as in western Newfoundland, but the diversity of species makes up for modest numbers. Gulls appear in large flocks. Nearby woods have Yellow-bellied Flycatchers and Ruby-crowned Kinglets. Go to the Newman Sound campground to listen for Great-Horned and Boreal Owl in late winter and early spring. Riverside bushes and marshes host Alder and Olive-sided Flycatchers, a few Palm Warblers, American Redstart, and Swamp and Lincoln's Sparrows.

Puzzle Pond Trail. Take this trail from Big Brook to Ochre Hill. Spot breeding Ring-necked Duck, Northern Goshawk, Boreal Owl, Black-backed Woodpecker, Palm and Mourning Warblers, and Lincoln's and Swamp Sparrows. Explore the large bog close to the Ochre Hill Trail intersection for a Three-toed Woodpecker. The nearby woods hold several Ruby-crowned Kinglets, Northern Waterthrush and Dark-eyed Junco. You may see a Moose as you stroll.

Bread Cove Trails. To reach the bogs and softwood forests north and east of Ochre Hill, take the trail beyond the Puzzle Pond turnoff and proceed east. You should find Yellow-bellied Flycatcher, Hermit Thrush, Golden-crowned and Ruby-crowned Kinglets, and several warblers including Magnolia, Yellow-rumped, Blackpoll and Palm. There is a possibility of a Winter Wren on this or adjoining trails. The bogs and fens that dot the area house Swamp and Lincoln's Sparrows.

Sandy Pond Trail. Begin beyond the last parking lot and look at the variety of plants. Note the Spruce Budworm and Birch Casebearer damage to the trees. This abundant insect life attracts Yellow-bellied Flycatcher, Tree Swallow, and Blackpoll, Black-and-white and Palm Warblers. The wet areas are favourites for American Bittern, a few ducks including nesting Ring-necked, and Swamp and Lincoln's Sparrows.

Outer Newman Sound. If whale-watching appeals to you, take a boat tour. A Bald Eagle is likely to be around. Copper Island has a large gull colony. You should see a few seabirds, such as Northern Gannet and Black Guillemot. Dovekies are abundant in winter. It also has a growing Black-legged Kittiwake colony.

Clode Sound Beaches. Try Tidewater (marked on park maps as Platter's Cove) first; it lies south of Charlottetown at the spot where the road drops sharply towards the shore, past a huge rockface. Take the trail through fir and alder between two streams. Bald Eagles and Ospreys are usually here close at hand. Flocks of American Black Duck, Common Goldeneye and Red-breasted Merganser are close to shore. Try nearby woods for warblers.

Proceed a little farther south to Cobbler's Beach and the parking lot and picnic area. Common Loons are especially plentiful in September and may be joined by Leach's Storm-Petrel. Bald Eagle, Osprey and a migrant Sharp-shinned Hawk and Merlin are almost a certainty here and at Northwest River, a little farther along.

GREG STROUD

Bonavista to Bellevue Beach

This part of Newfoundland is relatively new territory for birdwatchers, but it has been very productive, especially in spring. The Bonavista area, in particular, has become associated with European vagrant species that occur after spring storms. The Arnold's Cove and Bellevue Beach area attracts gulls, waterfowl and shorebirds.

Bonavista. This spot, generally acknowledged as the landing site of John Cabot in 1497, continues to host the occasional European visitor. Eurasian Blackbird, Common Redshank, Pink-footed Goose, European Golden-Plover and Little Egret are some of the rarities sighted in this area over the past few years. Other European species known to occur include Lesser Black-backed Gull and Eurasian Wigeon. Of course, there are no guarantees concerning any of these species, but a visit during an onshore storm in spring could prove worthwhile. Local species include breeding Atlantic Puffin, Common and Thick-billed Murres, Razorbill, Dovekie (in winter) and Black Guillemot year-round.

Clarenville. Clarenville has hosted a growing flock of Common Black-headed Gulls in recent years. Check Shoal Harbour as well. A waterfowl sanctuary attracts Canada Geese, American Black Ducks, Mallards, a few Pintails and Green-winged Teals. No doubt other ducks visit occasionally, as well. Ospreys and Bald Eagles can be quite common in intertidal areas. The lush deciduous woods around Shoal Harbour can provide good songbird opportunities. The old rail bed runs through alder thickets that support thrushes, flycatchers, warblers and sparrows.

Arnold's Cove. Check the waterfowl sanctuary from the small parking area for small gulls including Common Black-headed and Bonaparte's, diving ducks including Greater Scaup, plus Canada Goose, Black Duck, Mallard and Pintail. Red-breasted Mergansers may also be present in winter. Common Black-headed Gulls and dabbling ducks also show up at Arnold's Cove Harbour. Continue down into the community and you will find the harbour on your right.

Bellevue Beach. If you want a long but pleasant walk, visit Bellevue Beach Park. From the park you can walk the length of the barrier beach – about 4 km each way. This will bring you to the mudflats at the entrance to the lagoon. You will also find thick stands of stunted spruce and fir where songbirds nest and may shelter during migration. Storm-driven seabirds are often found from this beach after strong northerly gales in summer and fall. In winter, look for Red-necked

Grebe, Greater Scaup, Red-breasted Merganser, Common and Red-throated Loons, Dovekie, Thick-billed Murre and Black Guillemot. In late summer and early fall, check both sides of the beach for shorebirds, especially at low tide. This walk can be a half-day excursion if the weather is nice and you have a picnic lunch with you!

By driving around the large lagoon to the town of Bellevue itself, you can view the gut where the lagoon empties into Trinity Bay. A telescope is advisable, since the gut is fairly wide. You may be able to hire someone in Bellevue with a boat to take you across to the tip of the beach. Turn right at the bottom of the access road from the Trans-Canada Highway (use the Route 203 intersection), then keep the lagoon in sight as you drive counter-clockwise. The far side of the gut is an excellent location for shorebirds at low tide in fall. Black-headed Gulls are seen here regularly. The mudflats, where most of the birds congregate at low tide, can be viewed from a grassy point (ask for directions to the cemetery). An offshore island with gulls and Common Terns can also be seen from this location. The lagoon is extremely popular with Ospreys and Bald Eagles.

JOHN PRATT

The Burin Peninsula

"The Boot," as it is known in Newfoundland, is a trip in itself, but the birding can be rewarding. Jutting into the Atlantic Ocean, this long peninsula is often a landfall for storm-driven birds. Many coastal beaches support a variety of shorebirds each fall. Accommodations are available throughout the region, with many hotels, motels, camping and bed-and-breakfast operations.

Birding Features

Almost all of the harbours and bays around the lower part of the peninsula are good for shorebirds in fall. The beaches at Garnish, Fortune, Point au Gaul, Taylor's Bay, Lord's Cove, Lawn and Little St. Lawrence should all be checked by serious birders. However, the following are the "highlight" destinations.

Frenchman's Cove. This is a good place to base your birding operations. Camping and rental cottages are available, and the birding around the community can be excellent. Check the large brackish lagoon for diving ducks, flocks of Canada Geese, and vagrant herons in fall. A short walk out to Frenchman's Cove Head, to the north of the community, will give you a good chance to find terns, including Caspian, which is rare in eastern Newfoundland. When storms blow onshore, especially in summer and fall, look for alcids and pelagics, including Atlantic Puffin; all three jaeger species; Sooty, Greater and Manx Shearwaters; Leach's Storm-Petrel; and Northern Fulmar. Several rarely recorded species of gull have been seen from this vantage point over the years.

Grand Beach. This long sand and shingle beach shelters a large lagoon. The access road, which is somewhat north of the town of Grand Beach, is not well marked and can be badly rutted, but if you ask locally, directions will be provided. Look for all manner of eastern shorebirds in fall, including Pectoral Sandpiper. Buff-breasted Sandpipers have been seen on the grassy top of this beach. The lagoon and barrier beach are also good places to look for gulls and terns.

St. Pierre Ferry. The ferry to the French island of St. Pierre departs from Fortune. St. Pierre is an exciting birding destination, but outside the scope of this book. There are several excellent sources of information on St. Pierre, including bird reports published in *The Osprey*, and Roger Etcheberry's monograph, *Les Oiseaux de St. Pierre et Miquelon*. From the ferry you can see many pelagic and locally nesting species including Atlantic Puffin and Manx Shearwater. If you are compiling a "Newfoundland" list, remember to ask the crew to tell you when you cross into French territory!

L'anse à Loup Beach. Again, access to this beach is not well marked, and local inquiries will save a lot of time. The effort to find it is worth making, however. This beach can support some of the less common shorebirds, including Dunlin, Short-billed Dowitcher, Buff-breasted Sandpiper and Hudsonian Godwit. It is also a good place to find gulls and terns, and to watch for migrating raptors in fall.

Grand Bank. The town of Grand Bank has many charming gardens and thickets, which are likely to harbour songbirds in migration. One of the best records for this town was a Prothonotary Warbler seen in late summer – but don't go there expecting to find that rare bird! More likely will be local breeding songbirds. Grand Bank is a major service centre for the southern Burin.

Pieduck Point. A "Pieduck" is a goldeneye, and these tough little birds might be seen at this exposed location, but it is most notable for aerialists like swallows and Chimney Swifts. With a large, sweeping expanse of open barrens, these acrobats of the air are easy to spot (if they are around) during migration. Merlin, Peregrine Falcon, Short-eared Owl and Northern Harrier have been seen here, too. To get to this spot, watch for a wharf and a large boat shed well below highway level about 25 km south of Grand Bank. A narrow dirt road leads down over the barrens.

Point May. This can be one of the better locations for smaller shorebirds, including Semi-palmated and Least Sandpipers, Semipalmated Plover and Ruddy Turnstone. The grassy beach top and nearby meadows may produce both local and vagrant songbirds. To get to the beach, leave the main highway and follow town roads towards the ocean, which will always be visible. The barrier beach runs east from Point May towards Calmer, but a wide opening in the beach means that you cannot walk all the way around the lagoon. Seals are often seen sunning on the rocks on the Calmer side of the opening. Horned Larks and Savannah Sparrows are common in the weeds along the beach top.

Lamaline. Turn away from the ocean at Lamaline, and look inland. The wet meadows and the banks of The Barasway (a large brackish pond to the north of the highway) produce many shorebirds. This seems to be a good place to look for Red Knot, although the reason for that isn't too clear. Newfoundland's first Stilt Sandpiper record came from here, too. All of Lamaline Bay, which is dotted with rocks and kelp-covered shoals, is good for shorebirds. Hundreds of Greater Yellowlegs, along with a few Lesser Yellowlegs, sometimes congregate here at low tide.

Allan's Island. Before leaving the Lamaline area, turn south onto Allan's Island – no longer a true island because of the causeway connection. Several species of vagrant songbirds have shown up in the gardens and at the lighthouse on this little knob of rock, including Baltimore Oriole, Red-eyed Vireo and Rose-breasted Grosbeak. The high land at the centre of the "island" can be a good place to spot a couple of Whimbrel.

Lord's Cove. Manx Shearwater breeds on Middle Lawn Island, just off Sand Cove Head. Although there are no scheduled boat trips to this island, they may be arranged with local fishermen on a fee-for-service basis. Lord's Cove is the closest community to the island.

Lord's Cove to Salt Pond. The road from Lord's Cove to Salt Pond leads through a variety of habitats, from open barrens to conifer thickets and river valleys. Watch for Willow Ptarmigan in all seasons, and for Short-eared Owl and Northern Harrier in summer and fall. Several communities have small beaches and lagoons, and all can be checked for shorebirds in late summer. The old road from Lord's Cove to Roundabout may be passable – ask locally for directions. This road will give you better access to coastal vantage points, including Sand Cove Head, where you can scan the water for Manx Shearwater in all seasons except late fall and winter.

Salt Pond. Located at the head of Burin Inlet, Salt Pond is a good spot to find Lesser Yellowlegs. The small muddy area below the bridge where Route 220 and Route 222 converge seems a good place to find this species, as well as other shorebirds.

Marystown and Vicinity. The stretch between Burin and Marystown is typified by a network of roads and a maze of salt-water inlets and fresh-water ponds. It is difficult to pin down exact birding locations here, so be on the watch all the time! Many odd species have been recorded in this area, including White Pelican and Great Egret. Shorebirds will be found throughout the area in late summer and early fall. The Marystown area is the most developed part of the Burin Peninsula and offers plenty of accommodations, grocery stores, restaurants and other services.

Winterland. This is a small agricultural area at the intersection of Route 210 and Route 222. It can produce a wide variety of local songbird species and has potential as a vagrant hot spot.

JOHN PRATT

The Avalon Peninsula

Although it might be argued that the Avalon Peninsula is not the best birding area of Newfoundland, there can be no doubt that it is the area that is best understood. Most of the active birders in Newfoundland live in and around St. John's and have built up a good knowledge of the bird life within 150 km of the city. The result is evident from the relative wealth of information available for this fairly small area.

Placentia to Branch. Placentia is the old French capital of Newfoundland and was captured by the British in 1692. Surrounded to the north and east by high hills, the town is exposed to the waters of Placentia Bay to the west. During the summer, the ferry from North Sydney, Nova Scotia, docks at Argentia about 6 km to the north. You reach Placentia by taking Route 100 south from the Trans-Canada Highway.

Birding Features
Placentia is really a "jumping-off point." Drive south to Point Verde, where Arctic and Common Terns can be seen in summer. If the shearwaters are close to shore, Point Verde can be a good place to watch for them. Greater, Sooty and Manx Shearwaters are all possible during the summer. Parasitic and Pomarine Jaegers have also been seen on rare occasions. Common Loons are likely to be seen in any season, and in winter, you should be looking for Red-throated Loon, Red-necked Grebe, Surf Scoter, Black Scoter and White-winged Scoter. Common Eider and Oldsquaw are also possibilities in winter.

By continuing south on Route 100, you will eventually arrive at Cape St. Mary's Seabird Sanctuary. On the way, check the various coves and bays for sea ducks, alcids, loons, grebes, gulls and terns. The whole coastline is good for Bald Eagle at any time of year. Watch for Double-crested Cormorant flying by. The thick, dry spruce forests can be good places to listen for Gray-cheeked Thrush in spring. Cuslett is an interesting farming community. The valley along Cuslett River can be a good place to look for sparrows. Northern Shrike is seen there occasionally, especially in winter. The marsh near the mouth of the river commonly shelters a Common Snipe or two well into the winter, and Sora has been seen there as well. The harbour at St. Bride's can often produce sea ducks, alcids, loons and Red-necked Grebes. It is also most productive in winter, when visitors should look for Dovekie and Thick-billed Murre.

Cape St. Mary's Seabird Sanctuary. Cape St. Mary's is the site of one of eastern Canada's most important, spectacular and accessible seabird colonies. The road is paved all the way to the interpretation centre, where you will find various permanent and temporary displays, a knowledgeable staff of nature interpreters, and a well-stocked gift shop specializing in bird-related merchandise. An admission fee is charged at the interpretation centre, which is open through the summer months. Access to the trails leading to the seabird colonies is free. After April, visit "the Cape" to observe the thousands of nesting Northern

Gannets, Common Murres and Black-legged Kittiwakes. Razorbills, Black Guillemots and Thick-billed Murres nest in smaller numbers. Atlantic Puffins can occur in small numbers. Other species commonly seen at Cape St. Mary's include Great Cormorant and Bald Eagle. There is a Great Cormorant colony near Brierly Head, on the Placentia Bay side of the reserve.

When shearwaters are near land, look for Greater, Sooty and Manx Shearwaters, Pomarine and Parasitic Jaegers, and Northern Fulmar.

In late summer, flocks of Whimbrels show up, followed by numbers of American Golden-Plovers. Buff-breasted Sandpipers are known to accompany the plovers. Migrating raptors can include Northern Harrier, Sharp-shinned Hawk, Rough-legged Hawk, Merlin and Kestrel. Short-eared Owls sometimes breed in the area and are seen occasionally in migration. Peregrine Falcons are seen rarely throughout the fall and into the winter.

In winter, the cape is a good place to find Harlequin Duck, Common Eider, Oldsquaw, Common Loon and Red-necked Grebe. King Eider occurs occasionally mixed in with the Common Eider flocks. Thick-billed Murre and Dovekie can be seen. The road to the lighthouse is a good place to watch for Willow Ptarmigan.

Note: The road to Cape St. Mary's is not ploughed regularly in winter, and the interpretation centre is closed. The lighthouse is unmanned. Do not attempt to travel on the road to Cape St. Mary's without first confirming that the road is open for traffic, and that no heavy snowfall is anticipated during your visit. If snow starts unexpectedly, head back to St. Bride's as soon as possible. Carry survival equipment (blankets, candles, water, food, shovel) in your car. Cape St. Mary's is *not* currently within cellular telephone range.

Point Lance. This tiny, off-the-beaten-path community boasts a long sandy beach, where shorebirds and gulls can be found. Common Black-headed Gulls are seen here in small numbers in winter. Lance Cove can be a good place to look for loons, grebes and all three species of scoters. The grassy patches at the back of the beach may shelter the occasional stray sparrow or warbler, so remember to scuff through those spots.

Branch to North Harbour. From Branch, head north towards North Harbour along Route 92. On the way, watch for Willow Ptarmigan in the open country, especially in fall and winter. This is also a good stretch of road to seek out Pine Grosbeak, White-winged Crossbill, Common Redpoll, Gray Jay and Black-backed Woodpecker. Moose and woodland caribou may be seen from the roadside. Sea ducks, notably Greater Scaup and Red-breasted Merganser, are often noted at North Harbour. After you leave North Harbour, you may choose to head in many directions – back to Placentia via Route 91 (a dirt road), out to the Trans-Canada Highway through Whitbourne on Route 81 (also a dirt road), or on to St. John's on Route 91 and Route 93. Whichever way you go, consult the other sections of this chapter to identify the points at which your chosen route and other suggested birding routes intersect.

Southeast Avalon – Point La Haye to Portugal Cove South. Southeast Avalon is a particularly good destination in the late summer and fall, when seabird activity and then migrant songbird activity are at their most interesting. Take Route 90 south through St. Catherines and St. Joseph's. At Point La Haye there is a long gravel beach. Turn at the sign directing you to the Point La Haye Natural Scenic Attraction. One point of clarification – the sign is actually located inside the town of St. Mary's! Inside the beach look for nesting Common Terns in summer, and flocks of Snow Buntings in winter. The grassy meadows nearby are good places to look for American Pipit. From the low point, look for rafts of sea ducks in fall, winter and spring. Common Eiders are often seen here, as are all three species of scoters, and the occasional Harlequin Duck or King Eider. Oldsquaw is also to be expected. Onshore storms in summer can produce shearwaters and fulmars, and perhaps a few Parasitic or Pomarine Jaegers. The beach is unbroken and can be walked from one end to the other.

A similar, but much longer, beach will be found at St. Vincent's. Here, sea ducks are less likely to be seen, but shearwaters and other pelagic seabirds are often found during strong onshore storms in summer. This is also an excellent place to watch for humpbacked whales. Gull flocks should be checked for possible strays. Laughing Gulls have been recorded here on at least three occasions in summer.

Follow Route 10 to the intersection for St. Shott's. If you have time, turn south towards this small community, and if you have more time still, make a side trip to Cape Pine. At Cape Pine, you can get quite close to Atlantic Puffins, Razorbills and Black Guillemots, all nesting on a nearby cliff face. Go to the east of the lighthouse and then head north along the cliffs, keeping a careful watch as you go. Whales and shearwaters are often seen offshore from this vantage point.

At St. Shott's, you can also look for pelagic seabirds in season. A large sod farming operation attracts shorebirds in fall. If you wish to visit the sod farm, make sure to obtain permission first, as it is a private, working farm. The farm, called Emerald Isle Sod Farm, is on the west side of St. Shott's River, at the end of a narrow dirt road. You will find large patches of bright green grass growing on the open barrens. These patches attract American Golden-Plover, possibly accompanied by Hudsonian Godwits, one or two Buff-breasted Sandpipers or a few Pectoral Sandpipers. Similar flocks can be found on the barrens along the St. Shott's road, where Willow Ptarmigan, Rough-legged Hawk and Northern Harrier may also be spotted.

Trepassey is a large and spread-out community. Take the road through the town and head out towards Powles Point. If the tide is low, watch for small gulls, including Common Black-headed and possibly even Bonaparte's, roosting on the kelp-covered boulders in the inner harbour. Sea ducks can be seen from the point itself in winter.

Biscay Bay is a good destination in winter when sea birds seem attracted to this broad and shallow inlet. Common and Red-throated Loons, Red-necked Grebe, all three scoters, Greater Scaup, Oldsquaw, and both Common and Red-breasted Merganser may be found here (although to find all of these species in one visit would be exceptional!). A walk to Portugal Point should produce Purple Sandpiper in winter. In late summer, the roadside lagoons and grassy ponds abound with shorebirds. Park your car and walk through this area, checking each little puddle as you go. Lesser Yellowlegs, Short-billed Dowitcher and Dunlin have been seen here among other species. The outer beach is also good for Sanderling.

Portugal Cove South is the turnoff point for Cape Race, but it is also a worthwhile birding stop. Check the bay for loons, alcids, sea ducks and grebes, and the inner sandy dunes for shorebirds and sparrows in fall. Swallows are often seen on the wires along the roads in the community. Portugal Cove South has a couple of small grocery stores, so if you forgot your sandwiches this is the last place to buy some lunch before you head for Cape Race.

The Cape Race Road. Cape Race is a destination unto itself. This is largely due to the condition of the dirt road leading from Portugal Cove South. Although there are hopes that it will be upgraded, it is currently a very unreliable dirt road. Cars with low clearance are advised to use extreme caution, and everyone should check their spare tire before heading out.

The above having been said, Cape Race is a very fine birding destination. As you drive, scan the roadsides in late summer for flocks of American Golden-Plovers and herds of caribou. In winter, watch for Snowy Owls. Along the way, there are a few important stops.

The Drook. In Newfoundland terms, a "drook" is a steep-sided, wooded valley with a small watercourse meandering through. Although the local development committee has put up a sign to tell you when you reach The Drook (about 4.5 km southeast of Portugal Cove South), you won't have a hard time identifying it, especially after you descend the incredibly steep hill leading to the bottom. Before you do go down, park your car at the top of the hill and walk down over the open barrens towards the cliff edge. Be careful – the cliffs are steep and unforgiving, and can be treacherous in winter. Find a comfortable vantage point and scan the water with telescope or binoculars. In winter, this is an excellent place to find small flocks of Red-necked Grebes out off the rocky point on the north side of the cove. Sea ducks, including Common Eider and Oldsquaw, congregate here. In late summer, strong onshore gales can produce spectacular showings of Greater, Sooty and Manx Shearwaters, Northern Fulmars, Parasitic and Pomarine Jaegers, and even South Polar or Great Skuas, on very rare occasions. In fall this is a good place to encounter migrating Peregrine Falcons or Rough-legged Hawks. Check the beach for Sanderling and other shorebirds. Common Snipe is usually found in the grassy ponds on either side of the road. The small fenced meadows sometimes produce the most surprising rarities in fall and are worth a good look. The cove can be scanned from the promontory on the south side, as well.

Long Beach. There was once a small community at Long Beach, and apart from the Drook, it is the only place on the Cape Race road where you will see houses (which are now used as summer cottages). A broad, grassy meadow about 13 km from Portugal Cove South is bordered by a stream, the road and a shingle beach. In late summer, look around the grassy area for stray sparrows and songbirds, and for shorebirds as well. If there has been a recent storm, there will probably be deep beds of reddish seaweed on the beach. These are favoured by shorebirds, and you ought to observe them carefully. This may be easiest if you climb up on the embankment on the north side of the stream, so that you can look down on the beach. This also provides a good vantage point from which to scan for sea ducks and pelagic birds.

Cape Race. The actual lighthouse is about 20 km from Portugal Cove South. It is a place of great historic significance, and would be worth visiting for that reason alone. However, the birding can be of "historic" proportions, too!

As a major landfall, Cape Race attracts storm-driven vagrants throughout the year. Newfoundland's first records for Connecticut Warbler and Swainson's Hawk come from this headland. Stray warblers can almost be expected in late summer and early fall. Vagrant grassland birds such as Bobolink and Dickcissel may be found there at the same time. Scuff the tall, unkempt grasses around the buildings and along the cliff edges to flush out skulking sparrows and warblers. Late summer storms may also produce good showings of shearwaters and other pelagics (see "The Drook" for a complete description of species that might occur). In winter, scan the sea for Common Eider, remembering to check eider flocks for King Eider. Razorbills are usually present year-round in the surf just to the east of the lighthouse. Oldsquaw, Red-breasted Merganser, all three species of scoter, Red-necked Grebe, and Common and Red-throated Loons are seen in late fall and winter.

Note: The Cape Race Road also is not ploughed regularly in winter. Do not attempt to travel on the road unless you have first confirmed that it is open for traffic, and that no heavy snowfall is anticipated during the time when you plan to visit. If snow does start unexpectedly, head back to Portugal Cove south as quickly as possible. Carry survival equipment (blankets, candles, water, food, shovel) in your car. This area is *not* currently within range of cellular telephones. In an emergency, assistance may be available from the lighthouse keeper at Cape Race itself.

Portugal Cove South to Chance Cove Provincial Park. This extremely barren stretch is a good place to watch for Willow Ptarmigan in winter. Migrating raptors can occasionally be spotted along here in fall, and Short-eared Owls have been seen on several occasions in summer and fall. In winter, Snowy Owl is possible.

Chance Cove Provincial Park. Chance Cove is the site of a long-abandoned community and is now a provincial park. There are no formal campsites, but the park can accommodate tenting and travel trailer camping. A steeply sloping meadow leads down to a long shingle beach. In late summer, check for shorebirds. Baird's Sandpiper has been recorded here on a few occasions from mid-August to mid-September. Sea ducks favour this cove. Look for scoters, eiders, scaup and mergansers in late fall. Vagrant passerines including Lark Sparrow and Indigo Bunting have been recorded in September. The park is seasonal, and you should check with the appropriate government office in St. John's before planning to visit any later than September 1, or before June 1. If you are a real keener, you can walk or ski from the highway to the cove, but since this is a distance of about 7 km one way, it is not to be undertaken lightly! The intersection for Chance Cove Park is about 12 km south of Cappahayden on Highway 10.

Bear Cove. This shallow cove is located immediately beside the highway about 2 km north of Cappahayden. It is a very popular late summer and fall destination for Newfoundland birders. A wide variety of vagrant warblers, vireos and sparrows have been "pished" out of the thick alder beds at Bear Cove.

Note: Depending on the version of road map you are using, the town of Cappahayden may appear in the wrong place. Cappahayden is located at a sharp bend in Highway 10, immediately south of Burnt Point (not north of Burnt Point, as is shown on some maps).

Renews. Renews has become a major birding destination. In summer, visit to find breeding Arctic Tern and Common Tern, which can be seen on an island in the inner lagoon. In late summer and fall, the beaches at Renews produce many species of shorebirds. The "north" side of the harbour should be checked. Take the easterly turn at the north end of the long bridge, then turn south at the four-way intersection. Check the small lagoon behind the barrier beach for shorebirds. Two small puddles in meadows on the north side of the road can produce vagrants, as well as common migrants. Farther along the road, you can visit the fish plant. There may be significant gull activity if the plant is operating. This is also the way to the road to Bear Cove Point (not to be confused with Bear Cove). You may need to ask locally for specific directions to this road.

On the "south" side of the harbour, check the sideroad leading along the lagoon from the southern end of the bridge. You will see a fairway tower on your left. Stop here and scan among the boulders for Greater and Lesser Yellowlegs, Semipalmated Plover and other shorebirds. Farther along you will re-join Highway 10. Continue south, stopping to check the long beach leading towards the opening that leads from the outer harbour to the inner lagoon. This beach is a good shorebird location. The top of the beach will produce Savannah Sparrow from spring to fall, and in fall you should find Mourning Dove here too. Double-crested Cormorant is common in the harbour except in winter.

Bear Cove Point. A dirt road leads north from Renews to the Bear Cove Point lighthouse. Finding the start of the road is tricky, because it is not marked. To save time, ask locally for assistance. The road has become "sacred" to Newfoundland birders who go there every year in late summer and fall in search of vagrant songbirds. The alder-lined shoulders regularly produce disproportionate numbers and varieties of vireos and warblers. By patiently walking the 3.5 km road, checking through the alder thickets, you could well be rewarded with similar good fortune. If you aren't interested in "alder bashing," continue to the end of the road, where Bear Cove Point affords a good view of the ocean. You can watch for sea ducks in winter, shearwaters, kittiwakes, gulls and gannets through the summer, and alcids year-round. This is a nice picnic spot, if you are looking for a place to have lunch, and in the fall you can pick your fill of raspberries, blueberries and blackberries, too.

Ferryland. History buffs should visit Ferryland, the site of Lord Baltimore's Newfoundland colony, which was settled in 1621. A museum and interpretive centre houses artifacts from archaeological digs, and tours of the site are available seasonally. Birding can be good in the fall, when vagrant passerines, including Dickcissel and Cliff Swallow, have been recorded. Check the low, wet fields near the wharves on the north side of the harbour. Ferryland Head, where the lighthouse is located, provides good sea-watching opportunities, but unfortunately the road is not in good shape. If you are truly "gung ho," it is a nice walk.

Cape Broyle. Red-necked Grebe shows up here in winter, and Red-throated Loon has been recorded occasionally. There are many feeders in Cape Broyle, making it a hot spot for overwintering sparrows, including Fox, White-throated, Song, Swamp, Savannah and Lincoln's. A Grasshopper Sparrow was found here on a Christmas Count one year, and an Eastern Towhee appeared on another. Common Grackles, Mourning Doves and Northern Mockingbirds have also overwintered here. The lagoon is a good place for shorebirds in late summer and fall. Common Teal have been seen here in winter on many occasions. At that season, park your car near the post office and walk the many sideroads and laneways, checking feeders and hedges for flocks of birds. The road to Admiral's Cove on the north side of the harbour can also be productive in winter. If cone crops are good, watch for White-winged and Red Crossbills, Pine Siskin and Purple Finch.

Witless Bay Ecological Reserve. This is one of the most well-known seabird colonies in eastern Canada and has been given official reserve status by the Government of Newfoundland. Activities on and around the islands are subject to special regulations.

There are three main islands in the reserve. Gull Island is the most northerly. Green Island is the small one to the south of Gull Island. Great Island is the largest and most southerly of the three. Together, they host hundreds of thousands of breeding seabirds, which begin to arrive in April. Species nesting in the reserve include Atlantic Puffin, Common Murre, Thick-billed Murre, Razorbill, Black Guillemot, Herring Gull, Great Black-backed Gull, Black-legged Kittiwake and Northern Fulmar. Ironically, the most common of the nesting species, Leach's Storm-Petrel, is also the most difficult to see. Although census work on the huge colonies of these birds found on Gull and Great Islands suggests that as many as three-quarters of a million pairs are present, their nocturnal habits mean that they are rarely seen by casual birders.

The reserve is located about 33 km south of St. John's on Route 10. Various companies offer seabird and whale-watching tours from the communities adjacent to the reserve. Check the Yellow Pages or the "Birding Resources" section at the end of this chapter.

Note: Birders without the time or inclination to take a boat trip might want to visit Burnt Cove, St. Michael's and Bauline East. Spear Island and Pebble Island (sometimes called "Pee Pee Island") can be observed from the land. Both islands support seabird colonies. Pebble Island hosts several pairs of nesting Northern Fulmars. The nests can be seen on the steep, dark cliff faces at the southern end of the island.

Winter birding features of the Witless Bay area include large flocks of Common Eiders, Oldsquaw, Black-legged Kittiwakes (especially in onshore storms), Thick-billed Murres, Dovekies and Black Guillemots. Black-headed Gull may be found in Bay Bulls Harbour by checking among the flocks of larger gulls, which will probably include Iceland, Glaucous, Herring and Great Black-backed. Birders should also be alert for the occasional Lesser Black-backed Gull in winter.

JOHN PRATT, BRUCE MACTAVISH AND PAUL LINEGAR

St. John's

St. John's is the capital city of Newfoundland. It has a population of about 110,000 and is the major centre for services and commerce. Most provincial and federal government offices are located here. The city is served by Torbay International Airport, which is only about a 10-minute drive from the city core. St. John's boasts that it is the oldest European city in the New World and displays a certain "Old World" charm with its colourful row houses, bustling harbour and mixture of architectural styles. The city is located on the northeastern arm of the Avalon Peninsula, a mere 15 km from Cape Spear, the most easterly point in North America.

Birding Features
St. John's is blessed with two features that make birding a pleasure. One is natural, the other is man-made. The naturally occurring proliferation of streams, rivers and lakes (or "ponds," as they are known to Newfoundlanders) attracts many nesting and migratory bird species. An extraordinary network of trails connects these bodies of water, and other good birding habitat around the city. These trails are the work of many agencies, both public and private. A master plan connecting all the trails is known as The Grand Concourse. It is the work of the Johnson Family Foundation, a philanthropic organization that has contributed greatly to the city trail system. Visitors should obtain a map of this system which will prove to be an excellent companion for those birding in St. John's. The guide is available as an inexpensive map, or as a more expensive and highly detailed book.

The various ways in which you might combine trails and water bodies to make up a day of birding are endless, and it is well beyond the scope of this book to attempt to suggest itineraries. By comparing the city map (or Grand

Concourse map) with the following information, you will be able to plan your birding efforts quite effectively.

Oxen Pond Botanic Park. This unique park displays natural and cultivated plants in an exquisite setting. Traditional gardens and an exceptional "alpine house" are worth the visit. Birding outings have been offered regularly on Sunday mornings for many years. If you are new to east coast birding, this might be a good way to get a quick introduction to our avifauna. The park is located on Mount Scio Road and is not within easy walking distance of downtown. However, you can get there from Long Pond (see below) along Grand Concouse trail 22. A checklist of the birds of the park is available. There is a small admission fee. Call (709) 737-8590 for information.

Long Pond. Long Pond is on the north side of the Memorial University of Newfoundland campus, behind the National Research Council Building and the Engineering Building. A trail (Grand Concourse 17) goes all the way around the pond and passes through conifer forest, old-field, and riparian habitats. Resident species include Brown Creeper, Golden-crowned Kinglet, Boreal and Black-capped Chickadees, American Crow, Purple Finch and Pine Grosbeak. In spring, look for Blackpoll Warbler, Northern Waterthrush, Yellow-rumped Warbler, White-throated Sparrow and other eastern boreal forest nesters. In the riparian habitats you will find Yellow Warbler and Swamp Sparrow. Savannah Sparrow can be found in both riparian and old-field habitats. The pond itself hosts American Bittern, Sora and several species of breeding dabblers, including American Black Duck, Green-winged Teal, Northern Pintail and Mallard. In winter, the western end of the pond often hosts a small flock of Common Teal. Ospreys are common in summer, and Sharp-shinned Hawks and Merlins are often seen. In spring and fall, look for vagrant herons and egrets here.

The stream leading in to the pond flows out of a smaller pond in front of the Health Sciences Centre, a large hospital associated with the university. This small pond often attracts dabbling ducks in winter. Eurasian Wigeon is often seen here.

Burton's Pond. This small pond is on the university campus and can be found along Grand Concourse trail 21. A bubbler system keeps the ice away from a corner of the pond, even in the coldest winter. Aside from the resident dabblers, Burton's Pond often attracts overwintering divers. Tufted Ducks often alternate between Burton's Pond and Quidi Vidi Lake (see below).

Kent's Pond. A trail goes all the way around Kent's Pond, which is located at the intersection of Portugal Cove Road and Prince Phillip Drive. The trail (Grand Concourse 15) leads through conifer forest, with some deciduous breaks. Look for dabblers on the pond in spring, summer and fall. A few Greater Yellowlegs will probably appear in late summer. Typical nesting species include Boreal and Black-capped Chickadees, Blackpoll Warbler, Northern Waterthrush and Fox Sparrow. Yellow Warbler, American Redstart and Yellow-bellied Flycatcher can be found in deciduous stands.

Kenny's Pond. This unimposing little pond is located behind the Holiday Inn at the same intersection as Kent's Pond (see above). Grand Concourse trail 14 circles the pond. In spite of its modest appearance, this pond should be checked for diving ducks in fall, including Ring-necked and Tufted. Dabblers, notably Mallards, dominate the pond. Black-headed Gulls are seen here on occasion.

Quidi Vidi Lake. Quidi Vidi is the largest lake in St. John's. A trail (Grand Concourse 7) goes all the way around, but the best birding is at the upper end at the intersection of Carnell Drive and Lake Avenue/Clancey Drive. Check for diving ducks in fall and winter, including Tufted Duck, Greater and Lesser Scaups, Ring-necked Duck and occasional Bufflehead. Dabblers are regular. Check the winter flock for Eurasian and American Wigeons. In any season, check the gull flocks carefully. Black-headed, Herring, Great Black-backed and Ring-billed Gulls can be found here at almost any time. The peak time for Black-headed Gull is late November when upwards of a hundred may be seen. Mew Gulls occur almost every winter. Other occasional visitors include Lesser Black-backed Gull in winter, Laughing Gull in summer and fall, and Bonaparte's Gull in fall and winter. When the lake freezes over, huge gull flocks roost on the ice. Hundreds of Great Black-backed and Herring Gulls share the lake with large numbers of Iceland and Glaucous Gulls in winter. The very rare Yellow-legged Gull has been seen at Quidi Vidi in December and January. Peregrine Falcons and Gyrfalcons hunt at the lake in winter. Bald Eagles also put in regular appearances. The arrival of any large raptor is met by a mass "lift-off" of gulls. The soccer and rugby pitches on the north side of the lake are popular roosts for gulls. Virginia River enters the lake on the north side, and its banks should be checked in winter for sheltering sparrows.

Mundy Pond. This is a truly urban pond, located in the centre of the city. A trail through brushy deciduous thickets and tall grasses (Grand Concourse 24) goes around the pond. The western end has some mudflats that attract shorebirds. Gulls and terns like to roost on the rocky shore of a small island at the same end of the pond. Look for Black-headed and Lesser Black-backed Gulls in the flock, especially in fall and winter. Dabblers and diving ducks are often found here. Ospreys fish at the pond regularly in summer. In late summer, look for shorebirds, including Greater and Lesser Yellowlegs; Pectoral, Least, White-rumped and Semipalmated Sandpipers; Semipalmated Plover; Black-bellied Plover; American Golden-Plover; and Common Snipe. Hudsonian Godwit has been recorded on the grassy banks on the north side of the pond adjacent to Mundy Pond Road.

Rennie's River Trail. The Rennie's River Trail (Grand Concourse 18) leads from Long Pond to Quidi Vidi Lake. It passes through a variety of habitats, from conifer forest and wetland at the Long Pond end, to deciduous forest in the middle and "back yard" terrain at the lower end. Many vagrant and migrant warbler and vireo species have been recorded here in late summer and throughout the fall. Check the large willows from Elizabeth Avenue all the way to King's

Bridge Road. Where the trail crosses Portugal Cove Road (at the Riverdale Tennis Club), you may want to take a quick detour. Go north along Portugal Cove Road, keeping the soccer pitch to your right, until you reach Winter Avenue. This tree-lined street will deliver you out to King's Bridge Road, at the same place where the trail crosses. You can thus do a "loop" down Winter Avenue and back up the trail again. The lower section of the trail will take you past Wyatt Park and King George V soccer field, to the shore of Quidi Vidi Lake. These fields often host small gulls, including Black-headed, Ring-billed, Mew, and possibly Laughing Gull in spring, summer and fall.

St. John's Harbour. The harbour attracts many gulls, especially in winter. Unfortunately, the main attraction has always been the untreated sewage that has been pumped into the harbour at various points. With plans afoot to clean up the harbour and reduce or eliminate the release of untreated sewage, this dubious attraction may soon disappear and, with it, the gulls! For now, check the eastern corner of the harbour near the National Harbours Board building, where Iceland and Glaucous Gulls can be seen in winter along with Black-headed and possible Lesser Black-backed and Mew Gulls. Black-legged Kittiwake may occur here or at the mouth of the harbour during storms. Take Grand Concourse trail 8E to reach the mouth of the harbour, or 8N to check out the waterfront itself.

Waterford River. The lower stretch of Waterford River (Grand Concourse trail 25) is a good place to search for vagrant warblers and lingering sparrows in late fall and early winter. It also hosts gulls and dabbling ducks. The trail leads all the way to Bowring Park (see below).

Virginia River. Grand Concourse trail 12 follows Virginia River from Quidi Vidi Lake to Virginia Lake. In winter, this is a good trail to check for winter finches and overwintering sparrows.

Virginia Lake. This large lake is somewhat inaccessible because it is ringed by private property. It can be viewed from various vantage points along Grand Concourse trail 12, or from the roadside of Kensington Drive or Regent Street. The lake seems to attract diving ducks in winter, including Greater Scaup.

Bowring Park. Bowring Park is a large municipal park in west-central St. John's. Its many attributes are attractive to birds and birders, including planted gardens, natural conifer forests, many exotic and non-native trees and flowering shrubs, two rivers flowing through, an abundance of shelter, and food from natural and human sources. The Swan Pond often attracts dabbling ducks in winter, including Eurasian and American Wigeon. Wander the trails, especially those that cut through the old fields at the west end of the park, in search of vagrant warblers and sparrows in late summer and fall. The neighbourhood adjoining the west end of the park, including Squires Avenue, Midstream Place, McNab's Lane, and Waterford Heights North and South, has many bird feeders where finches, woodpeckers, Mourning Doves and sparrows can be found in winter.

The Outskirts of St. John's. St. John's is surrounded by good birding locations. The most reliable are reported here, but check with local birders for information on other hot spots.

Cochrane Pond Road. In late June or early July, take Ruby Line west from Route 10 to the intersection of Back Line Road. Turn south onto Back Line Road and proceed to Cochrane Pond Road. Turn west again and follow Cochrane Pond Road across the Goulds By-pass Road to a sharp left turn. From this point, you can drive or walk along the gravel farm road in search of nesting songbirds including Mourning, Wilson's and Magnolia Warblers; Yellow-bellied Flycatcher; Pine Grosbeak; Gray Jay; Hermit and Swainson's Thrushes; Boreal Chickadee; Golden-crowned Kinglet; and other northeast boreal species. On a good morning, this road can get your Newfoundland list off to a great start!

Forest Pond. Take Route 10 south to Petty Harbour Road, and turn east. Forest Pond is less than a kilometre down this road. In June it can be an excellent place to check for Tree, Barn and Bank Swallows, and possible Purple Martin (a rare visitor, not to be expected annually). Dabbling ducks frequent the pond.

Cape Spear and Black Head. Take Blackhead Road to Cape Spear, following the signs that advertise the National Historic Park. On the way, you can check Black Head, especially in late summer, for vagrant warblers, sparrows and icterids. Baltimore Orioles are often seen here in September mixed into the robin flocks. At Cape Spear, check the alder beds in late summer for a mix of local warblers, finches and sparrows, and possible vagrant songbirds including Red-eyed Vireo. At Cape Spear itself, check in all seasons for seabirds. Water Pipits and Savannah Sparrows nest here. Strong onshore storms can be tough on your optics, but rewarding in other ways. Greater, Sooty and Manx Shearwaters and Northern Fulmars are possible throughout the summer. Black-legged Kittiwake, Northern Gannet, Black Guillemot, Atlantic Puffin and Common Murre are to be expected from April to September. In late summer and fall storms, check for Leach's Storm-Petrel, Pomarine and Parasitic Jaegers from the point. On very rare occasions, skuas may be seen from here. By December, you should be looking for Purple Sandpipers on the rocks to the west of the point, and sea ducks including Oldsquaw, White-winged Scoter and Common Eider off the point itself. Lapland Longspurs sometimes show up in flocks of Snow Buntings in winter. Black Head and Cape Spear are stops along the East Coast Trail.

Cape St. Francis. Take Route 20 north from St. John's to Pouch Cove. Drive north through the community. The paved road ascends a steep hill and gives way to gravel. The road to Cape St. Francis is about 4 km long and can be deeply rutted at times. During gales from the northeast in any season, check here for sea birds. Species to be expected are similar to those reported for Cape Spear (see above). Cape St. Francis is also an excellent place to observe whales when they are close to shore. It is a stop on the East Coast Trail (see Birding Resources).

Conception Bay. West of St. John's is a large, north-facing inlet of the ocean called Conception Bay. In recent years, several reliable birding destinations have been identified along its heavily populated shores.

Kelligrews Point. Take Highway 2 west to Manuels, and turn left to keep the bay on your right. Follow the Conception Bay Highway (Route 60) south to Kelligrews. Find Pond Road, which is just south of a small stream that crosses under Route 60. Drive out this road to the end. You can actually drive out to the point itself, if you want. In fall, visit in search of seabirds, including Leach's Storm-Petrel and jaegers during onshore storms. Small gulls including Bonaparte's and Black-headed occur regularly in any season. Common Terns are present through the summer.

Spaniard's Bay. Take Route 1 (Trans-Canada Highway) west to Roache's Line (Route 70). Go north on Route 70. Divert onto the Carbonnear By-pass Road and follow it to the Bay Roberts exit. Turn off towards Bay Roberts, then turn left at the lights and re-join Route 70. Go north through Bay Roberts business area, staying on Route 70 North to Spaniard's Bay. The shingle beach and lagoons on both sides of the road are superb shorebird locations in late summer. Look for White-rumped and Semipalmated Sandpipers, Semipalmated and Black-bellied Plovers, Ruddy Turnstone, Sanderling, Red Knot, and Greater and Lesser Yellowlegs. Rare waders including Baird's Sandpiper (two occurrences), Buff-breasted Sandpiper and Curlew Sandpiper (one occurrence each) have been found here. Dunlin may occur in early Fall. Black-headed Gulls are often present in fairly large numbers at any time of year.

Harbour Grace. Follow the directions for Spaniard's Bay, but go all the way to Harbour Grace on the By-pass Road. (*Note*: At the time of printing, this road was not completed. Some readers may find that they have to divert through Bay Roberts. In that case, follow Route 70 North to Harbour Grace.) At Riverhead, just south of Harbour Grace, check the intertidal flats for shorebirds in late summer and fall. Species may include Greater and Lesser Yellowlegs, White-rumped and Semipalmated Sandpipers, Semipalmated and Black-bellied Plovers, and Ruddy Turnstone. Black-headed Gulls occur throughout the year. Riverhead was the site of Newfoundland's only record of Common Greenshank.

JOHN PRATT, BRUCE MACTAVISH AND PAUL LINEGAR

Coastal Seabird Colonies

Newfoundland has many coastal seabird colonies. Most are on islands or islets accessible only by boat. No one is allowed to land at any of these colonies without a permit, but it is possible to sail around the islands to observe the nesting birds. Regular commercial boat trips visit the Witless Bay Islands (see Witless Bay Ecological Reserve), and Cape St. Mary's is accessible from the land (see Cape St. Mary's Ecological Reserve). Together, these two colonies allow observation of almost all of the nesting seabird species found in

Newfoundland. Birders with a special interest in seabirds should review the *Researcher's Guide to Newfoundland Seabird Colonies* by David Cairns, Richard Elliott, William Threlfall and William Montevecchi (Memorial University of Newfoundland Occasional Papers in Biology, No. 10, 1986) where they will find a wealth of information on the seabird colonies surrounding the island of Newfoundland.

JOHN PRATT

Birding Resources★

Information on Birding in Newfoundland
Currently there is no specific text on the birds of Newfoundland. Enthusiasts and book collectors will be familiar with *The Birds of Newfoundland* by Peters and Burleigh, and may even know about *Birds of the Labrador Peninsula* by Todd. While both books are excellent additions to any birder's library, they are out of print, out of date and expensive. Today's birders will find these books of little use in planning a birding trip to Newfoundland, without further reference to the more modern field guides. Anyone planning to go birding in Newfoundland should avail themselves of a current official highway map, a current checklist of the birds and an appropriate field guide for the area. Any of the mainstream guides will be satisfactory. Birders visiting in spring and fall may wish to pack a guide to the birds of western Europe, just in case.

The *Telegram* is Newfoundland's only province-wide daily newspaper. John Pratt writes a weekly birding column in *The Telegram* called "Winging It." *The Telegram* can be viewed on the Internet, where back issues of "Winging It" can also be accessed (see Internet Resources below).

The Newfoundland Government publishes an excellent map book covering the entire island of Newfoundland at 1:250,000 scale. It can be obtained from the Lands Branch, Department of Government Services and Lands, Howley Building, P.O. Box 8700, St. John's, Newfoundland A1B 4J6. In western Newfoundland, check at Barnes Sporting Goods Store, 16 Humber Road, Corner Brook, for topographic maps of the area.

Gear
Stores devoted to birdwatching are a rarity, although The Bird House and Wild Things in St. John's both cater to birders. Most major centres have camera stores and bookstores where essentials can be purchased. Larger department stores and hardware stores tend to carry inexpensive but serviceable binoculars. Binocular and camera repair services may be difficult to find, especially outside the St. John's or Corner Brook areas.

Most major towns and cities will have clothing stores where "emergency" clothing can be purchased, but the best plan is to bring what you need – and to figure that out, you might want to visit one of the weather Web sites noted. Newfoundland has a marine climate. Be prepared for cold and wet in all

★All information in this section is current to October 1999.

seasons, and remember that this precaution applies to your optics as well as yourself! This may be especially important for birders planning pelagic outings or visits to exposed coastal sites such as Cape St. Mary's or Cape Race.

Internet Sites

If you can access the Internet, check Birding in Canada on the Internet at http://www.web-nat.com/bic/index.html This excellent site is updated regularly. It includes names and e-mail addresses of Newfoundland birders and is a valuable source of up-to-date information on rarities.

Newfoundland Birding News is at http://www.interlog.com/~gallantg/canada/newfound.html

The Natural History Society of Newfoundland and Labrador maintains a Web site at http://www.nhs.nf.ca You can download the current Newfoundland checklist and get information on upcoming society events at this site.

Newfoundland birders exchange information through a newsgroup called nf.birds. This newsgroup is worth a visit, since it will disclose the most current news and issues relating to Newfoundland birding.

Here are other valuable Internet sites:

The Telegram – www.thetelegram.com
East Coast Trail Association – http://www.ecta.nf.ca
National Parks – www.parkscanada.pch.gc.ca
Environment Canada – www.ec.gc.ca

Transportation and Accommodations

Scheduled air travel with national or regional carriers is available to various centres on the island and in Labrador, and to St. Pierre and Miquelon. Charter air service is available for those wishing to visit less accessible locations, particularly on the Labrador coast.

Ferries from North Sydney, Nova Scotia, travel to Port aux Basques year-round, and to Argentia from June to September. Coastal boat services are available in parts of Newfoundland and from Newfoundland to Labrador, but schedules change annually. Information can be obtained from Marine Atlantic by calling 1-800-341-7981.

There are no trains, but buses service most major centres on the island. Local medium-distance bus services are also available on a regular scheduled basis. Most major towns and cities offer a variety of car rental services. Specialty vehicles such as large vans should be booked well in advance of your arrival.

Hotels, motels and bed-and-breakfasts can be found throughout the province. Information on accommodations can be obtained from Tourism Newfoundland and Labrador at the Internet address above, or c/o Government of Newfoundland Box 8700, St. John's, Newfoundland A1B 4J6.

JOHN PRATT

YUKON TERRITORY

1   Watson Lake
2   Whitehorse
3   Alaska Highway South and
    the Tagish Birding Tour
4   Haines Junction and Kluane
    National Park
5   Klondike Highway
6   Tintina Trench
7   Dawson City
8   Dempster Highway (Dawson City
    to Inuvik)
9   Yukon Coastal Plain and Ivvavik
    National Park
10 Herschel Island–Qikiqtaruk

10 Herschel Island
9
IVVAVIK
NAT'L PARK

Inuvik

Arctic
Red River
Mackenzie River

Eagle Plains

8

Dawson
City   7

Klondike Hwy

5

Faro
Ross River
6

Haines Junction
Kluane
KLUANE
NAT'L PARK   4

2   Whitehorse

3

1   Watson Lake

YUKON TERRITORY

L and of the Midnight Sun, the Yukon contains arctic and subarctic species of birds on their breeding grounds. Recently, some far northwestern birds, including mainly Eurasian species, have been spotted. Key breeding birds include Brant on the coast; Greater White-fronted Goose on Eagle River; Common and King Eiders on the coast; Tundra Swan on the coast, Old Crow Flats and possibly south of there; Trumpeter Swan in Kluane National Park, southeastern Yukon, and perhaps centrally and north to the coast; Rough-legged Hawk north of latitude 67°; Ruddy Turnstone, probably on the coast; Semipalmated, Pectoral and Buff-breasted Sandpipers, also inland on the North Slope; Red Phalarope, Parasitic Jaeger and Glaucous Gull, on the coast; Black Guillemot on Herschel Island on the coast; a few Snowy Owls on the coast; Great Gray Owl along the Ogilvie, Peel and Porcupine Rivers; Boreal Owl, quite common; Siberian Tit, which most likely breeds in the far north, has provided a few records widely spread over the Yukon; Yellow Wagtail on the coast. Other rarities that have been seen include Ivory and Ross's Gulls and Bluethroat. The late Robert Frisch discovered Surfbirds in the Richardsons and Ogilvies, those mountains west of Dawson at the U.S. border, and in the Dawson Range near Carmacks.

Travel through southern and central Yukon Territory offers opportunities to view both alpine and boreal birds. Southeast Yukon boasts species that are typically eastern as well as western but that are seldom found east of the Cordillera. If your budget allows travel to the more remote areas of northern Yukon, you may encounter a couple of arctic species that are not found east of the Yukon.

The 482,515 km² that make up the Yukon contain fewer than 25,000 people. Key habitats consist of subarctic to arctic alpine, together with the North Slope and arctic maritime, including Herschel Island. Subarctic taiga forests are found in the valleys north of latitude 65°. Typical boreal forests cover the valleys throughout the Territory.

The best time to visit is from mid-May through June for migrants and breeders. Spring migration lasts from late April to early June and is more striking everywhere than fall migration. Spring migration on the far northern coast peaks in early June.

The top birding spot for arctic-subarctic terrain in the Yukon (the top such spot in North America, some say), and certainly rivalling Churchill, is the Dempster Highway. This road leads smack through the best area in the entire Yukon, south of the extreme northern fringe, and takes you near to the Arctic Ocean, the only road in North America to do so.

Other key spots to visit include Marsh Lake, southeast of Whitehorse, just off the Alaska Highway, for spring migrants; Lake Laberge, just north of Whitehorse, for spring migrants including nesting Short-billed Dowitcher; Kluane National Park and the adjacent Burwash Uplands, for typical south Yukon mountain birds; Yukon Coastal Plain for high-arctic species, such as Yellow Wagtail. If you wish to make a river trip for birds, try the Ogilvie, Peel and Old Crow through Old Crow Flats; and the Nisling, White and Yukon Rivers to Dawson.

Time restraints are always hard to satisfy. You could get a taste of the Yukon Coastal Plain in a full day. Kluane Park and the adjacent Burwash Uplands take two to three days to sample. A motorist with up to a week to spend should take the Dempster Highway, both for representative and key species. The really keen lister would be best satisfied on the Coastal Plain, where a single day may suffice for a good sample, but it will be an expensive day. The Dempster road is probably the number one site because of such special birds as Surfbird, Wandering Tattler, Northern Wheatear, Rock Ptarmigan, Long-tailed Jaeger, Gyrfalcon, Siberian Tit and others.

The Yukon Bird Club, founded in 1993, is dedicated to promoting awareness, appreciation and conservation of Yukon birds and their habitats. Regular field trips, led by skilled and enthusiastic birders, give local and visiting naturalists opportunities to explore the Yukon's diverse habitats and bird life. Each winter, the club hosts a series of evening slide shows, seminars and workshops covering a wide range of topics including bird identification. The regular publication *Yukon Warbler* highlights the club's events and local sightings, and contains a variety of articles on the Territory's bird life. For a schedule of field trips and events contact them (see below).

There are no bird alert numbers to call. For special tips, contact Helmut Grunberg of the Yukon Bird Club.

Local contacts

Yukon Bird Club, Box 31054, Whitehorse, Yukon Y1A 5P7; phone (867) 667-4630. E-mail: ybc@yknet.yk.ca; Web site: www.yukonweb.com/community/ybc/

Yukon Conservation Society, Box 4163, 302 Hawkins Street, Whitehorse, Yukon Y1A 3T3; phone (867) 668-5678. E-mail: ycs@polarcom.com

Canadian Wildlife Service, 91782 Alaska Highway, Whitehorse, Yukon Y1A 5B7; phone (867) 667-3931.

Helmut Grunberg, Whitehorse (867) 667-6703

Yukon Web site: www.yukonweb.com

Kluane Country Web site: www.yukonweb.com/community/kluane/

Yukon's Territorial Parks Web site: www.yukonweb.com/notebook/tparks.
html
Yukon National Parks Kluane: www.harbour.com/parkscan/kluane/
Vuntut Web site: www.harbour.com/parkscan/vuntut/
Ivvavik Web site: parkscanada.pch.gc.ca/parks/Yukon/ivvavik/ivvavik_e.htm

Yukon Tourism Information

May be obtained from Tourism Industry Association of the Yukon, 1109 – 1st
Avenue, Whitehorse, Yukon Y1A 5G4; phone (867) 668-3331; or Wilderness
Tourism Association, Box 3960 Whitehorse, Yukon Y1A 3M6; phone (867)
668-3180.

Further reading

Eckert, C., H. Grunberg, and P. Sinclair. 2000. *Checklist of the Birds of Herschel Island.* Yukon Bird Club, Whitehorse, Yukon.
Eckert, C., H. Grunberg, G. Kubica, L. Kubica, and P. Sinclair. 1998. *Checklist of Yukon Birds.* Yukon Bird Club, Whitehorse, Yukon.
Eckert, C., H. Grunberg, G. Kubica, L. Kubica, and P. Sinclair. 1995. *A Checklist of the Birds of Whitehorse, Yukon.* Yukon Bird Club. Whitehorse, Yukon.
Frisch, R. 1987. *Birds by the Dempster Highway.* Revised edition. Morriss Printing Co. Ltd., Victoria, British Columbia.
Grunberg, H. 1994. *Birds of Swan Lake, Yukon.* Keyline Graphics. Whitehorse, Yukon.
Yukon Conservation Society. 1995. *Whitehorse and Area Hikes and Bikes.* Lost Moose Publishing Ltd., Whitehorse, Yukon.

Travel on Yukon roads will lead you to some fairly isolated areas. If you
choose remote travel routes, be prepared for all weather conditions, and take
the precautions that you would for any wilderness travel.

ROBERT FRISCH
Revised by Cameron Eckert and Wendy Nixon

Watson Lake

Watson Lake, the first stop in the Yukon on the Alaska Highway, is the point
at which east meets west for many avian species. White-throated Sparrow,
American Redstart, Magnolia Warbler and Western Tanager are relatively
common in the area – but are seldom found farther west. Western species such
as Varied Thrush can be heard in the older spruce forest and Hammond's and
Least Flycatchers in the Balsam-Poplar forest. Evening Grosbeaks tend to
wander into this area in winter, the northern limit of their range. In the town
of Watson Lake there is a well-maintained walking trail around First Wye Lake.
Here you will often see Red-necked Grebe nesting, Pacific Loon and
Common Loon on the lake, and Violet-green and Tree Swallows feeding over
the open water. In the older forested areas around the town, you may
encounter one of the few Pileated Woodpeckers known to occur in the Yukon.
The eastern warblers (American Redstart and Magnolia) can often be seen

around Half Moon Lake or along the Liard River, west of Watson Lake, or in the lush growth of shrubs along the Liard. Shrubby wetlands in this area are home to Swamp Sparrows, also at the eastern limits of their range. With luck you may spot a Brewer's Blackbird at Half Moon Lake or other wetlands in the area – the northern extent of its range.

WENDY NIXON

Whitehorse

As capital of the Yukon, Whitehorse is *the* thriving community of northwestern Canada. Golden Eagles nest within 8 km of the city. The Harlan's Hawk (a colour morph of the Red-tailed) is the most common bird of prey in the valley. Gyrfalcons and Peregrine Falcons are seen regularly during migration. Yukon species are well documented in the Whitehorse area. In spring, Northern Shrike, Red-tailed Hawk, Bald Eagle and Northern Harrier can regularly be seen on migration through the Yukon River valley. On the Yukon River in downtown Whitehorse, Arctic Terns are a regular attraction in summer, and American Dipper can usually be spotted in open water below the Whitehorse Dam in winter.

At the time of the '98 Gold Rush, thousands of prospectors journeyed up from the south by boat to Skagway, Alaska, then climbed the rugged mountain passes to reach the Yukon River and a natural waterway to Dawson. Whitehorse was born on the banks of the Yukon at the head of the steamboat travel. Stern-wheeler boats were soon plying between Whitehorse and Dawson – two days down and five days return. Rails were needed to speed up the journey from Skagway; construction on the White Pass and Yukon Railway commenced in May 1898 with the 177 km line through to Whitehorse opening in 1900. When the war between the U.S.A. and Japan began, men and machines flocked in to build the Alaska Highway. Military and civilian workers pushed through 2200 km over a great variety of terrain in eight months (a feat that was estimated would take five years) to open the highway on November 20, 1942. Today the population of nearly 17,000 caters to government personnel as the headquarters of the Yukon, and to many summer visitors searching for that elusive Klondike spirit.

Daily air services to Vancouver and Alaska are provided. Buses run along the Alaska Highway year-round. Rental cars are available in Whitehorse, but book ahead in summer.

Whitehorse, at Kilometre 1480 on the Alaska Highway, has a wide collection of motels, hotels and campgrounds, and all the amenities of a southern city.

Birding Features

Set in the valley, near a major river and lake, the city has varied habitats, attracting a wide collection of birds. Trumpeter Swans pass through to nest not far away. Numerous birds of prey use the Yukon Valley as a migration funnel; a high concentration of these birds nest in the surroundings. Five areas to search during a stay include the following:

The Yukon River Trail: Rotary Peace Park to Schwatka Lake. Rotary Peace Park, adjacent to the historic riverboat S.S. *Klondike*, is located in downtown Whitehorse at the Riverdale Bridge. This is an ideal location to begin a bird walk along the Yukon River. In spring and fall, scan the exposed gravel bars and mudflats for shorebirds and various waterfowl. Watch for Harlequin Duck. In spring and summer Arctic Tern and Mew and Herring Gulls are plentiful. Flocks of Lapland Longspurs and Snow Buntings may be found along the river in early spring and fall. Check the bushes at the river's edge for various warblers and sparrows. Bald Eagles, Belted Kingfishers and various swallows are around too.

A birding walk from Rotary Peace Park can take three directions:

1. Stay on the downtown side of the river and use the newly constructed Robert Service Way walkway to stroll upstream along the river to Robert Service Campground.

2. Stay on the downtown side of the river and walk downstream towards the old shipyards.

3. Cross the bridge to Riverdale and the Yukon River Trail, which runs upstream along the Yukon River to Schwatka Lake.

All three paths offer interesting birds and a pleasant stroll.

To reach the Yukon River Trail, cross the bridge from downtown to Riverdale and take the path immediately to the right where the bridge ends. This track follows the river for a few kilometres to the Whitehorse Fish Ladder and the power dam at Schwatka Lake. The path, which winds through mixed Lodgepole Pine, White Spruce and Trembling Aspen, occasionally forks, but the forks all follow a similar flow, making it difficult to get lost. Watch for Bohemian Waxwing, Boreal and Black-capped Chickadees, Warbling Vireo, Ruby-crowned Kinglet, flycatchers and warblers. Take any opportunity to scan the river. In summer, the islands host large Mew Gull breeding colonies with a few pairs of Arctic Terns. There is a small Herring Gull colony at the power dam. In spring and fall watch for Pacific and Common Loons and perhaps a rare Yellow-billed Loon. American Dipper, most common in winter, is often found along the river below the dam. A few ducks may linger through the winter. Beavers and Muskrat are common along here.

Schwatka Lake. Schwatka Lake, which serves as the water supply for Whitehorse, is more of a widening in the Yukon River than an actual lake. It is the best downtown site for water birds that are usually associated with larger lakes. There are two ways to access Schwatka Lake:

1. Continue along the Yukon River Trail past the dam and the Whitehorse Fish Ladder to the very end (south) of the trail. To reach this location by car, simply drive through Riverdale to the Whitehorse Fish Ladder.

2. Start at Rotary Peace Park and take the South Access Road leading out of downtown, past the Robert Service Campground and take the first left past the Yukon Electric Station. This road follows the lake for a couple of kilometres to a fork where the paved road swings back up to the Alaska Highway via Miles Canyon. A dirt road continues along the lake another few hundred metres to a dead end.

During spring and fall migration, Schwatka Lake hosts a wide variety of loons, grebes and diving ducks. While Common and Pacific Loons are most common, Red-throated and Yellow-billed (especially fall) also occur here. Occasionally, large numbers of American Wigeons with the odd Eurasian Wigeon are found on the lake in spring. Tundra and Trumpeter Swans often touch down here in fall. Mew, Herring and Bonaparte's Gulls sometimes rest in good numbers on the lake. Check the adjacent woods for Townsend's Solitaire, Red-breasted Nuthatch, Golden and Ruby-crowned Kinglet, Boreal Chickadee, Pine Grosbeak, White-winged Crossbill and Three-toed Woodpecker.

McIntyre Creek Wetlands. McIntyre Creek wetlands are the largest in the City of Whitehorse and provide extremely important habitat to a diverse community of birds and other wildlife. The area is well known to local birders as one of the best places in the city to find species difficult to find elsewhere. To reach McIntyre Creek wetlands, take the Alaska Highway north from Two Mile Hill and turn left onto Fish Lake Road. The main wetlands are about 4 km along this road (adjacent to the Icy Waters Fish Farm). From the Alaska Highway, the Fish Lake Road follows McIntyre Creek for a kilometre, then climbs through Lodgepole Pine, past the Pumphouse Pond (on the left at about 3 or 4 km), and onto wetlands at the junction of Fish Lake and Copper Haul Roads (no signpost). En route to the wetlands, check Pumphouse Pond for grebes, ducks and swallows (in spring).

The main wetlands associated with McIntyre Creek are located on the opposite side of Fish Lake Road from the Icy Waters Fish Farm. Park at the overlook area on the Copper Haul Road, just off the Fish Lake Road, and explore this area by foot. The wetlands provide exceptional nesting habitat for a diverse and abundant songbird community. Listen for Boreal Chickadee, Alder and Hammond's Flycatchers, Golden-crowned and Ruby-crowned Kinglets, Swainson's Thrush, Bohemian Waxwing, Blackpoll Warbler, Northern Waterthrush, Common Yellowthroat, Townsend's and Wilson's Warblers, Lincoln's Sparrow, Rusty and Red-winged Blackbirds, and Red and White-winged Crossbills. During spring and fall migration, American Pipits are common, and a variety of sparrows are found, including White-crowned, Golden-crowned and American Tree and small flocks of Lapland Longspurs. Rarities have included American Redstart, Tennessee and MacGillivray's Warblers, and the Yukon's first Western Kingbird in May 1996.

This is perhaps the Yukon's best location for swallows. Throughout May, watch for the rare Northern Rough-winged among the feeding frenzy of Tree, Violet-green, Bank, Cliff and Barn. Displaying shorebirds include Common Snipe, Lesser Yellowlegs and Solitary Sandpiper. In early spring, the drumming Three-toed Woodpecker and the soaring vocals of American Dipper may be heard.

Fish Lake. Fish Lake ranks high among the many spectacular natural areas found in the Whitehorse area. Here you have the opportunity to experience the area's unique birdlife in a truly inspiring setting. To reach Fish Lake, continue on from McIntyre Creek wetlands to the end of the Fish Lake Road (about 15 km). In spring and summer, check out the wetland meadow along Fish Creek, listening for a variety of songbirds. Keep an eye skyward for soaring Golden Eagle, Northern Goshawk and Northern Harrier. Shorebirds occur along the edge of the lake and in the adjacent marshy areas. Scan for loons, grebes, waterfowl, Bonaparte's and Mew Gulls, and Arctic Tern. In winter, small coveys of Willow Ptarmigan inhabit the dense willows around the lake; American Dipper is common along Fish Creek, which generally remains open through the winter.

McIntyre Mountain. Ptarmigan are among the most sought-after birds by visitors to Whitehorse, and McIntyre Mountain is the best place to find them. The view from McIntyre Mountain puts Whitehorse in context. A good guide for reaching McIntyre Mountain and similar alpine areas is *Whitehorse and Area Hikes and Bikes* published by the Yukon Conservation Society (YCS). Copies are available from YCS (see above).

Directions to McIntyre Mountain: Take the Alaska Highway south from Robert Service Way (set your odometer to 0 km) and go right onto Lobird Road (0.4 km); take the first left turn off Lobird Road (0.8 km) and continue to a gravel pit (3.3 km); stay left through the gravel pit and then turn left again on Copper Haul Road (4.0 km); continue for 100 m, turn right (4.1 km) and then continue to a second gravel pit (4.9 km); follow the road through the gravel pit, at which point the road becomes quite steep and continues up the mountain to the treeline (9.2 km). Keep going past three drainages (at 12.2 km, 12.4 km, 12.6 km) to the top at 15.4 km. The little dipsy-doodle through the first gravel pit, across the Copper Haul Road and then on to the second gravel pit is a bit confusing. If you get slightly lost, try again and remember you should be going up in elevation.

Drive slowly, stopping often to bird along the way. Townsend's Warblers are scattered through the mid-elevation forests and, in 1999, Yellow-bellied Flycatchers were found for the first time in the Whitehorse area, near the junction of the Copper Haul Road and the gravel pit road.

All three species of ptarmigan occur on McIntyre Mountain. Willow Ptarmigan are most common and inhabit shrubs at the treeline and at lower elevations in winter. Rock Ptarmigan may be found in the higher elevation dry and rocky tundra. White-tailed Ptarmigan are restricted to the more inaccessible higher elevation rocky areas. In winter all three species may occur at lower elevations. In addition, in winter, Willow Ptarmigan may occur anywhere along the Fish Lake Road.

Songbirds include Townsend's Solitaire, Orange-crowned Warbler, Hermit Thrush and Fox Sparrow. Dusky Flycatcher is found in the taller dense shrubs that fill the drainage gullies on the mountain. In particular, check the three drainages noted above. As you move higher through subalpine habitat, the shrubs are reduced in height to about waist level and are the favoured breeding habitat of Golden-crowned and American Tree Sparrows. As the shrubs become even more reduced, listen for the exhilarating song of the Timberline subspecies of Brewer's Sparrow. Finally, with the trees far behind and the shrubs reduced to their most diminutive forms, you are free to explore the open alpine tundra. In spring, Savannah Sparrows sing from the tundra grasses while Horned Larks and American Pipits perform full-flight songs overhead. Check the rocky areas for Say's Phoebe and pika, and watch for soaring Golden Eagles. Hoary Marmots can be found in the area near the radio tower, and an occasional Woodland Caribou or Red Fox may be observed.

Haeckel Hill. Lying 915 m above Whitehorse, Haeckel Hill provides a splendid view of the city and also hosts a variety of alpine bird species. To get there, take the Fish Lake Road from the Alaska Highway for about 4 km, then turn right at the junction of the Fish Lake Copper Haul Roads (the first right before the fish farm). This rough gravel road (which is probably not passable in winter) continues approximately 6.5 km to the top, which is the site of a wind turbine. Rock Ptarmigan may be found here in late winter, and Willow Ptarmigan breed throughout this area. Golden and Bald Eagles often cruise by, and if you are lucky you may spot a Gyrfalcon.

Lower McIntyre Creek (Old Dump Site). The area where lower McIntyre Creek flows into the Yukon River is also know as the "Old Dump" as it was once the site of the Whitehorse landfill. It's hard to imagine the logic behind establishing a dump at this unique and scenic natural area. The Yukon Conservation Society did a tremendous job of cleaning up the area in 1992; however, rusting car bodies and chrome bumpers still loom from the hillside and serve to remind us that our garbage will similarly haunt our children. To reach this area from the Alaska Highway, take the Two Mile Hill towards downtown Whitehorse and turn immediately left onto Range Road and continue 1.8 km to the lights at Mountain View Drive. (If you are coming from downtown Whitehorse, simply take Mountain View Drive north to the same intersection.) Continue on Range Road for another 1.5 km, then go straight on a small dirt road as Range Road swings left. This small dirt road ends (about 200 m) with a spectacular view of lower McIntyre Creek and the Yukon River. You can also park at the junction of the small dirt road and Range Road and walk about 400 m farther on Range Road to another small trail on the right side which follows McIntyre Creek to its outflow at the Yukon River. When you're looking for this trail, if you cross the small bridge (culvert) on Range Road over McIntyre Creek, you have gone about 200 m too far.

During spring migration (April-May) this area hosts good numbers of waterfowl, including Tundra and Trumpeter Swans, Canada and Greater White-fronted Geese, Common and Barrow's Goldeneye, Canvasback, various dabblers, including an occasional Eurasian Wigeon and Gadwall. The site is also good for raptors such as Northern Harrier, Red-tailed Hawk, Bald Eagle, Gyrfalcon and Northern Shrike (usually in April). Watch for shorebirds in spring when the mudflats are exposed. The island in the middle of the Yukon River is a favoured gull roost and by late April hundreds of Herring Gulls and lesser numbers of Mew Gulls may be present. Search among them for rarer species such as Glaucous-winged. Common Ravens roost along the cliffs and often play in the updrafts rising off the river; it is not unusual to see one carrying away a golf ball from the nearby course. Like the upper reaches of McIntyre Creek, this area is an excellent place to watch swallows, with Violet-green, Tree, Cliff and Bank Swallows being most common. A male Purple Martin was an exceptional find here in May 1996. Regular passerines include Townsend's Solitaire, Mountain Bluebird, Savannah Sparrow and Lapland Longspur.

Swan Lake. Helmut Grunberg has been meticulously studying and documenting the birdlife of Swan Lake for the past 25 years. This spot, with its rich forest and wetland habitats, is very deserving of such attention. In 1994, Grunberg published the book *Birds of Swan Lake, Yukon*, which details the seasonal occurrence, breeding status and habitat use for 157 species. Since 1994, Eared Grebe, Brant, Whimbrel, Glaucous Gull and Caspian Tern have been documented in the Swan Lake area. The site hosts a variety of shorebirds, waterfowl raptors and songbirds. As well, many rarities have been found. We recommend that any birder who is interested in visiting Swan Lake purchase Grunberg's book, which is available at local bookstores. The book is available also at the Whitehorse Public library.

The road to Swan Lake (about 25 km) can be rather poor at any time of year. Travel with care and if road conditions appear questionable, don't proceed. It is best to let others know of your plans, including an expected return time. Consider contacting Helmut Grunberg (refer above) or other local birders for accurate directions or guidance.

To reach Swan Lake, start in downtown Whitehorse and cross the bridge to Riverdale; take the first left onto Hospital Road, then take the first left again onto the road to Long Lake. Continue past Long Lake and around the new Whitehorse sewage lagoons, staying on the main dirt road and on towards Swan Lake. Once there, explore the area by foot or, better yet, bring a canoe and paddle the lake. Take notes on the birds you see while at Swan Lake (species, numbers and breeding observations) and send them to the Yukon Bird Club (refer above).

Lake Laberge. Lake Laberge, made famous by Robert Service's "Cremation of Sam McGee" on its marge, is a wonderful birding destination. For river travellers making the trip from Whitehorse to Dawson, it represents a significant stretch of open water. The habitats along the lake consist of dry rugged hills and open forests with a few patches of dense White Spruce and Trembling Aspen. One of the best birding locations is the Lake Laberge Campground. To reach the campground, drive west from Whitehorse on the Alaska Highway for about 12 km and turn north on to the North Klondike Highway (Mayo Road). Continue for about 32 km, passing the rodeo grounds (at Kilometre 12 check for Upland Sandpiper in summer), then past Shallow Bay Road, Horse Creek Road and on to Deep Creek Road (watch for signs to the campground). Turn right on Deep Creek Road and continue about 3 km to its end at the campground.

From the campground, scan the open water for grebes, loons and various diving ducks, especially Oldsquaw, Surf and White-winged Scoters. In fall, watch especially for Yellow-billed Loon. Spruce Grouse inhabit the dense spruce stands, while Townsend's Solitaire frequents the open dry forests, and Yellow-bellied Sapsucker and Least Flycatcher occur in the Trembling Aspen forests.

During the summer months, a very pleasant outing is to canoe from the campground across the bay to Richtohofen Island. This is the best Yukon location for Double-crested Cormorant; a couple of pairs breed among the Herring Gulls on the small rocky islands just off Richtohofen Island. Arctic Terns are often seen here during summer and fall, and Herring and Glaucous Gulls linger on Lake Laberge into early November long after they have departed most other Yukon locations. Local rarities have included a Long-tailed Jaeger in June 1999. With careful searching, one may even encounter the spirit of Sam McGee, who is never without his field guide and spotting scope.

Whitehorse Landfill. The Whitehorse landfill, known locally simply as "the dump" versus "the old dump" (see above), offers little in the way of scenery, natural habitats or any other aesthetically redeeming features. It is, however, the best place for gull enthusiasts to find a variety of Yukon gull species. To reach the landfill, travel north along the Alaska Highway from Two Mile Hill and take the first left past Fish Lake Road. Stop at the gatehouse and explain to the attendant that you are there to look at the birds. As the sign says, "This is not a playground" so please stay well clear of any large trucks or heavy equipment.

In spring, the first gulls arrive in mid-April. Scan the hundreds of Herring and Mew for rarer species such as Ring-billed, California, Glaucous-winged and Glaucous. Thayer's Gulls are seen only in fall, with the first adults arriving in late August followed by the first juveniles in mid-September. Glaucous Gulls are regular in fall. Other rarities have included Iceland, Lesser Black-backed and Slaty-backed Gulls. Hybrids (Glaucous×Herring and Glaucous-winged×Herring) are fairly common in the Whitehorse area. Birders should be careful when identifying Glaucous-winged or Thayer's Gulls. Non-larids to expect include Bald Eagle, Common Raven, Black-billed Magpie, flocks of American Pipits and Rusty Blackbirds in fall, and a variety of sparrows, including the odd flock of Lapland Longspurs. It's always worth checking the composting area for sparrows and an occasional European Starling. For gull watchers, the show is usually over by the first week in November, but it may still be worth checking for late lingering gulls, eagles or dump-bound vagrants.

CAMERON ECKERT AND DAVID MOSSOP

Alaska Highway South and the Tagish Birding Tour

Diverse boreal forest and wetland habitats make for very interesting birding along the Alaska Highway south of Whitehorse. During migration, Marsh Lake and its associated wetland areas offer some of the best birding in southern Yukon. A popular day trip, known locally as the "Tagish Tour," is to drive in a loop (196 km) from Whitehorse south along the Alaska Highway to Jake's Corner, turning west on the Tagish Road to Tagish, then on to Carcross and back north to Whitehorse via the South Klondike Highway. The tour, extremely scenic, covers most of the habitats and associated birdlife found in the Whitehorse area.

Wolf Creek Campground. Wolf Creek Campground offers both day use and overnight camping and is an excellent place to see species associated with southern Yukon's rich White Spruce forests. To reach the site, take the Alaska Highway south from Whitehorse (Robert Service Way) about 11 km and watch for the left turn into the campground.

Park in the day-use parking area and wander through the campground. A variety of songbirds is found in the White Spruce and deciduous shrub habitat. Watch for Boreal Chickadees, Red and White-winged Crossbills, Bohemian Waxwings, Pine Grosbeak and Pine Siskin. Mountain Chickadees have also been seen here. Listen for the soft tapping of a Three-toed Woodpecker. In winter, watch for American Dipper along fast-flowing open-water stretches of Wolf Creek. At the south end of the campground, a trail leads to the Yukon River, with one branch of the trail running along Wolf Creek. The trail head is a good place to listen for Three-toed Woodpecker. Spruce and Ruffed Grouse may be seen in this area. Listen for Hammond's Flycatcher, Golden-crowned Kinglet and White-winged Crossbill along Wolf Creek. In spring and fall, Trumpeter and Tundra Swans and a variety of waterfowl may be seen along the Yukon River.

Lewes Marsh. The rich habitats of Marsh Lake offer some of the Whitehorse area's most exceptional birding opportunities. Three locations in particular are worth noting: Lewes Marsh, M'Clintock Bay, and Army Beach are regularly frequented by local birders, who are rarely disappointed by a trip to Marsh Lake. To reach Lewes Marsh, take the Alaska Highway south from Whitehorse (Robert Service Way) about 26 km to the Yukon River Bridge. Continue over the bridge and take the first left to a rest area and boat launch. From here walk north along the river to the dam. Alternatively, turn left immediately before crossing the bridge and view the river from the other side. To explore Lewes Marsh, turn right immediately before crossing the bridge. This road, known locally as "Gunnar's Road," runs along Lewes Marsh for about 7 km and leads to Gunnar Nillsson's sawmill. Birders can either walk or drive along the road, stopping at the many openings in the shrubs and mixed forest that border Lewes Marsh.

Lewes Marsh and the area around the Yukon River bridge is an excellent place to find a variety of water birds, especially during spring and fall migration. Trumpeter and Tundra Swans are common from mid-April through May. It's a good spot for uncommon ducks such as Redhead, Gadwall, Eurasian Wigeon and Harlequin Duck. The Yukon's first Wood Ducks, a pair, were found at Lewes Marsh on May 10, 1997. It's also a good place to look for Yellow-billed Loons in fall. In winter, check the open water around the dam for Common Goldeneye, Common Merganser and American Dipper.

During spring migration, Lewes Marsh area is excellent for shorebirds, especially uncommon species such as Western and White-rumped Sandpipers, Dunlin and Hudsonian Godwit. Even Wandering Tattler has occurred here! In fall, high water levels make the Lewes Marsh area unsuitable for shorebirds, but loons, grebes and waterfowl are still plentiful. Regular raptors include Red-tailed Hawk, Northern Harrier, Osprey and Bald Eagle. Golden Eagles are occasionally observed soaring overhead. During spring migration, the shrubs along the edge of Lewes Marsh can come alive with migrating passerines. Watch for a variety of warblers, Ruby-crowned Kinglet and Warbling Vireo. Other common spring migrants include swallows, American Pipits, Say's Phoebes and a variety of sparrows, including Lapland Longspur. Listen for Three-toed and Black-backed (rare) Woodpeckers and Golden-crowned Kinglets in the older White Spruce forests near Nillsson's sawmill. Mountain Chickadees are seen near the start of Gunnar's Road. A winter walk along Gunnar's Road will generally turn up Black-capped and Boreal Chickadees, . Three-toed Woodpecker, Gray Jay, White-winged Crossbill, Spruce Grouse and perhaps a Hairy Woodpecker.

M'Clintock Bay. To reach M'Clintock Bay, continue on the Alaska Highway south for 11 km from the Lewes Marsh area (37 km south of Robert Service Way) and turn right on the North M'Clintock Road. The road follows the M'Clintock River for a few kilometres. Take any opportunity to scan the river. The road leads to a waterfowl viewing facility known as Swan Haven. During spring migration (April-May) a nature interpreter is on hand with spotting scopes.

In spring, M'Clintock Bay is the site of one of North America's most spectacular concentrations of migrating swans. The first Trumpeter Swans reach M'Clintock Bay by mid- to late March and usually peak between April 22 and 28 at 2500 birds. Through late April, hundreds of Tundra Swans also arrive at M'Clintock Bay. The Trumpeters are destined for breeding grounds in central Alaska, although as many as a few hundred breed in the Kluane area. The Tundra Swans are believed to be headed for breeding grounds in the Kotzebue area of northwestern Alaska. The area is also excellent for migrating waterfowl. Eurasian Wigeon is regular here. In spring the mudflats along the M'Clintock River and at Swan Haven can be sensational for shorebirds. From mid- to late May all of southern Yukon's common shorebird species are regularly here, as well as many uncommon and rare ones such as Black-bellied Plover, Whimbrel, Sanderling, Western Sandpiper, Upland Sandpiper, Dunlin, Stilt Sandpiper and Hudsonian Godwit. The odd Sandhill Crane may be seen during migration. The forested habitats around M'Clintock Bay support Bohemian Waxwing, Red and White-winged Crossbills, Boreal Chickadee, Three-toed Woodpecker and Golden-crowned Kinglet.

Swan Haven's year-round bird feeder attracts Boreal and Black-capped Chickadee, Pine Grosbeak, Red-breasted Nuthatch and redpolls.

Army Beach and Marsh Lake Campground. To reach Army Beach, continue south on the Alaska Highway from M'Clintock Bay about 2.5 km (39.5 km south of Robert Service Way) and turn right onto the Army Beach Road. Continue along the road for a few hundred metres and as the road swings to the right, turn left and park at the Army Beach day-use area. To reach Marsh Lake Campground, you can either walk across the small creek at the Army Beach day-use area or continue south along the Alaska Highway for a few hundred metres and take the next right after the Army Beach Road. Army

Beach and the adjacent Marsh Lake campground offer fine views of Marsh Lake as well as mature White Spruce forest with some areas of tall shrubs. A small creek between Army Beach and Marsh Lake campground adds to the diverse habitats found at this location. Scan for loons, grebes and waterfowl. A breeding plumage Yellow-billed Loon was seen here in May 1989, and it's a very good location for these birds in fall. In spring, the outflow of the small creek attracts a variety of shorebirds, including the Yukon's only documented Willet. In spring, Bonaparte's Gulls and Arctic Terns are common. The surrounding shrubs and spruce forest are home to Ruby-crowned Kinglet, Bohemian Waxwing, Blackpoll Warbler, White-winged and Red Crossbills, and Pine Grosbeak. In fall, these shrubs attract various migrant sparrows. Check the large White Spruce for Three-toed Woodpeckers. The most spectacular birding feature associated with Army Beach is the fall passage of Golden Eagles. Significant movements noted in 1996 and 1997 indicated that Army Beach could serve as a top-notch raptor watch location. There is clearly a great opportunity here for a birder with a keen interest in raptors to coordinate a migration watch.

Jake's Corner. Jake's Corner, located on the Alaska Highway about 37 km south of Army Beach (77 km south of Robert Service Way), offers a restaurant, gas station and an unusual assortment of antique outboard engines and vintage road equipment. As such, it ranks highly among four-year-olds. A year-round bird feeder attracts the common Yukon feeder birds, as well as an occasional Mountain Chickadee, and flocks of Snow Buntings and Lapland Longspurs during spring migration. This feeder hosted a flock of up to 140 Gray-crowned Rosy Finches during late winter and early spring in 1999. Cliff Swallows nest in abundance on artificial nest platforms. Scan the hills beyond Jake's Corner for Golden Eagles and other raptors during migration.

Tagish Road Pond. From Jake's Corner, turn right (approximately west) on the Tagish Road for about 7 km to the "Tagish Road pond" located on the right-hand (north) side of the road. During spring migration, the pond hosts small numbers of waterfowl, shorebirds, an occasional American Coot, Lapland Longspur in the grassy areas, and perhaps a Mountain Bluebird perched on one of the fence posts. Bald or Golden Eagles and Red-tailed Hawk may be seen soaring overhead, and Ruffed Grouse may be heard drumming. During the recent dry years, the pond has lost much of its water but this may change with a few wet seasons. Melanistic (jet black) Arctic Ground Squirrels occur along the stretch of Tagish Road between Jake's Corner and the pond.

Tagish. To reach Tagish (located about 98 km from Whitehorse), travel west along the Tagish Road from Jake's Corner for about 20 km (13 km past the Tagish Road Pond). In Tagish check the campground for migrant songbirds, Three-toed Woodpeckers and Mountain Chickadees. Tagish's main birding attraction is Tagish Narrows, which is the connection between Tagish Lake to the south and Marsh Lake to the north. The Tagish Road crosses the Narrows via a bridge. In spring, there are extensive mudflats on both sides of Tagish

Narrows where it flows into Marsh Lake. However, the mudflats on the north-east side of Tagish Narrows are rather difficult to access, and the mud itself makes it a very hard slog. Most birders simply look from the parking area on the southwest side of the Tagish Narrows bridge. From here you can view Marsh Lake to the north and Tagish Narrows to the south. Scan the open water or walk a few hundred metres north (downstream) along the water's edge towards Marsh Lake for a better view of the mudflats. If something sparks your interest, you can consider putting on rubber boots and braving the mud. During spring migration (especially early to mid-May), the birding at Tagish Narrows can be spectacular. Many thousands of waterfowl cover the mudflats. Eurasian Wigeon is regular in spring. As well, the shorebirding can be phenomenal. Tagish Narrows remains open throughout the year and is a good place to find wintering Common Merganser and Common Goldeneye. A first-winter Ivory Gull discovered here on November 21, 1999, provided the Yukon's first well-documented record.

Carcross and Montana Mountain. To reach Carcross, drive west on the Tagish Road about 53 km from Jake's Corner (about 33 km past Tagish). To complete the loop to Whitehorse, drive north on the South Klondike Highway (stopping at Rat Lake), about 51 km back to the Alaska Highway and north another 15 km to Whitehorse. A trip south along the South Klondike Highway from Carcross takes you over the Chilkoot Summit to Skagway, Alaska, which in itself makes for an excellent day trip. Carcross is located between Bennett Lake immediately to the south and Nares Lake immediately to the north and is exceptionally beautiful. During spring migration, expansive mudflats along Nares Lake serve as an important staging area for waterfowl, shorebirds and gulls. Spectacular concentrations of migrant Mew Gulls have been noted here in early May. Bennett Lake does not tend to be as rich but is certainly worth checking for loons, grebes and waterfowl. For a pleasant walk from the Carcross townsite, cross the footbridge located at the Carcross interpretive centre and walk south along the train tracks, checking the open waters of Bennett Lake for water birds and the adjacent forests for songbirds.

The main birding attraction at Carcross is Montana Mountain. A very energetic birder could do the whole "Tagish Birding Tour" and Montana Mountain in one day. However, it is more reasonable to plan a full day (or at very least a half-day) to make the most of Montana Mountain. With a combination of driving and moderate hiking, birders can access very remote habitats that support species like White-tailed Ptarmigan, Blue Grouse, Dusky Flycatcher, "Timberline" Brewer's Sparrow and Gray-crowned Rosy Finch, which are very difficult to find elsewhere in the Whitehorse area. To reach Montana Mountain, start at Carcross and head south on the South Klondike Highway (towards Skagway, Alaska), which immediately takes you across the bridge over Nares River. Take the first right after the bridge onto a dirt road and continue a short distance to a T junction, where a right turn takes you back down to Nares River and a left turn begins the assent up Montana Mountain. The road may have impassable snow patches until late May but is usually clear by early June. Road conditions are generally poor, but with care it is possible to drive to the treeline with an ordinary car. At the treeline, a wash-out makes it impossible to drive farther. At this point it is safest to park and continue on foot. A hike along the road takes you past a Buddhist temple (an old water tower), an old mining camp, past the crumbling remains of stone houses to the top of the main road (the saddle). From here you can wander off in almost any direction in search of high alpine species.

The Subalpine Fir forests at the treeline are home to Blue Grouse. Dusky Flycatcher, Wilson's and Orange-crowned Warblers, and Golden-crowned Sparrow are found in the tall shrubby habitat at the treeline, while Townsend's Solitaire and Hermit Thrush can be heard singing from the open coniferous forests along an adjacent creek. Brewer's Sparrow favours dense low shrubs and may be seen anywhere along the road above the treeline. Willow Ptarmigan are common in this area. Continue along the main road to the old Buddhist temple and check for Say's Phoebe. Continue along the main road past the temple to a fork in the road; stay left to keep on the main road or go right to make a small detour down to an old mining camp. Say's Phoebes nest here in the old buildings and Brewer's Sparrows can be found in the low shrubs around the camp. Return to the main road and continue on to the remains of the stone houses. White-tailed Ptarmigan are regularly seen in this area, and Gray-crowned Rosy-Finch also occurs here. Just beyond the stone houses, the main road ends and trails radiate off in various directions. Any of the rocky slopes likely offer suitable habitat for White-tailed Ptarmigan and Gray-crowned Rosy-Finch. The ptarmigan do tend to call so don't ignore any obscure grouse-like noises. These sounds may also be coming from Pika, which also inhabit the myriad rocky crevices. Listen for Horned Lark and American Pipit, and scan the skies frequently for Golden Eagle.

Rat Lake. Rat Lake is located 30 km north of Carcross on the left (west) side of the South Klondike Highway and is worth checking on the return trip to Whitehorse. The lake's marshy habitats support American Coot and Red-necked Phalaropes. The Yukon's first breeding record for Pied-billed Grebe was found here. Wilson's Phalarope may also occur.

CAMERON ECKERT

Haines Junction and Kluane National Park

Haines Junction. Haines Junction, population 850, is located at the foot of the St. Elias Mountains and enjoys world-class scenery and outdoor recreational opportunities. The town, named for its position at the junction of the Alaska Highway and the Haines Road to Haines, Alaska, is fully serviced with restaurants, gas stations, motels, a bakery and grocery stores. The Kluane National Park Visitor Centre, located in Haines Junction, is a great source of information about the national park and other natural features around Haines Junction. The habitats and associated birdlife found in the Kluane region are different from those of the Whitehorse area, and the relatively sparse coverage of this area by birders means that much remains to be discovered.

Dezadeash River Trail. This moderate yet scenic trail is located right in Haines Junction and meanders through a variety of rich riparian habitats. The trail head is located at the northwest side of the bridge over the Dezadeash River at the start of the Haines Road. Numerous songbirds may be encountered, including Northern Waterthrush, Lincoln's Sparrow and Western Wood-Pewee. Check the taller Trembling Aspen groves for Warbling Vireo and Least Flycatcher, which are near the western limit of their ranges here.

Pine Lake Campground. Pine Lake Campground is located along the Alaska Highway about 10 km east of Haines Junction. It offers both day use and overnight camping. A trail at the campground runs through diverse habitats, including old-growth White Spruce, small shrubby creeks and marshy areas, with views of the open lake. Expect to encounter many of the birds associated with these habitats, including Three-toed Woodpecker, Boreal Chickadee, Gray Jay, Golden-crowned Kinglet, Blackpoll Warbler and White-winged Crossbill. In recent years, Brown Creeper, very rare in the Yukon, has been reported from Pine Lake. Mew and Bonaparte's Gulls are seen along the lake shore, while Red-necked Phalarope may be found in the marshy areas.

Kluane National Park. More than half covered by snow and ice year-round, and containing Mount Logan, Canada's highest peak, Kluane National Park also hosts over 180 species of birds. There are 88 species confirmed as nesters, with an additional 23 probables. Trumpeter Swans are likely breeders with Tundra passing through. Golden and Bald Eagles, Gyrfalcon, Peregrine Falcon, the three ptarmigan species – Willow, Rock and White-tailed – are all confirmed nesters, as are Wandering Tattler, Northern Hawk Owl, Gray-cheeked Thrush, Mountain Bluebird, Northern Wheatear and Snow Bunting. The largest sub-species of Moose in North America is quite common in the wooded valleys, and Dall Sheep graze the slopes of Sheep Mountain. Other mammals to be watched for include Grizzly and Black Bears, Wolf, Coyote, Red Fox, Wolverine, Lynx, Marmot and Arctic Ground Squirrel.

The oldest archaeological evidence of man in this area has been dated to 8000 to 10,000 years ago, near the end of the last ice age. Early explorers noted that according to legends, some of the native villages have been occupied continuously for at least 1000 years. The Kluane area was not explored by white men until late in the 1800s, with recorded history not beginning until 1890. The Gold Rush of 1898 and later discoveries in the park in 1903 at Sheep and Bullion Creeks, near the south end of Kluane Lake, brought hordes of people. Some of the buildings of this once-active Silver City may still be seen at the east end of the lake. Other discoveries of gold and copper in the park area resulted in several roads, now used as hiking trails.

The Alaska Highway opened up the region. During its completion in 1942, a recommendation was made to set aside Kluane as a park. On December 8, 1942, a protected reserve of 16,000 km² was established for the protection of wildlife. Two years later, lands around Kluane Lake and potential mineral-producing properties along the highway were deleted, with some other land added as compensation. Later the same year, mineral explorations were allowed and mining rights granted in the park. To provide for the ever-increasing numbers of people who wanted to live in the area "away from civilization," a strip 309 m wide along the west side of the highway was withdrawn in 1962, to allow for settlement. Finally, in 1972, a block of land 13,500 km² became a National Park Reserve.

To mountaineers, Kluane means adventure and challenge; several peaks are over 5000 m, and Mount Logan soars to 5959 m. The first reference to these heights was made by Bering, the famous Russian explorer, to a European audience in 1741, when he described Mount St. Elias. Finally in 1897, an Italian, H.R.H. Prince Luigi Amedeio Dei Savoia, Duke of Abruzzi, challenged Mount St. Elias. Canadian climbers ascended Mount Logan in 1925 and other peaks have been "conquered" since.

Haines Junction hosts the park administration office and the main visitor centre. Located at the junction of the Alaska and Haines Highways, the two main arteries connecting the Yukon to Alaska and southern Canada, this community at Kilometre 1640 is a good base, providing most visitor services. Other commercial accommodation and campgrounds occur on both highways, north and south.

Weather is a major factor restricting outdoor activity. Suitable times for camping and hiking occur between May 15 and September 15. Ski touring and winter camping are possible; however, take the usual precautions regarding clothing and emergency gear.

Approximately 200 km of hiking trails are provided, some leading to remote areas and others ideal for day trips. A map showing these and other interpretive features is available from the main office. Suggested trips are listed under birding features.

For further help, write Kluane National Park, Box 5495, Haines Junction, Yukon YOB 1LO; phone (403) 634-2251 or call the visitor centre at (867) 634-7207. More information on this spectacular park can be found in *Kluane: Pinnacle of the Yukon*, ed. J. B. Theberge (Toronto: Doubleday, 1980). This 175-page book contains a chapter on birds.

Birding Features

Valleys in the park are at about 590 m (Haines Junction is 588 m) above sea level.

The park includes three main vegetation zones: montane, consisting of White Spruce forest in the lower valleys and up to 800 to 1100 m; subalpine, with tall shrubs, mostly willow with scattered individual White Spruce, extending up to 1400 m; and a lower alpine zone of small shrubs, extending upward into the alpine tundra with dwarfed plants.

Beginning at Haines Junction, one trail begins from park headquarters; several other trails start a minimum of 8 km away from town. Obtain a map from the information office. Before starting out, check with the park staff at headquarters in Haines Junction. Staff sometimes lead hikes throughout July and August. They will also show you the most productive birding trips and tell you what recent sightings have been made. Guided trips are available through local tour operators.

Most of the hikes are along valleys. Special birds to look out for are a possible Trumpeter Swan, which likely nests, and a variety of breeding ducks, including both goldeneyes. Watch for soaring Golden and Bald Eagles, both nesting here. You may be lucky and spot a Gyrfalcon or Peregrine Falcon, as they also breed in the park. On your trip up to the higher country, look for all three species of ptarmigan, which nest. Shorebirds around lakes and on the tundra during the breeding season include American Golden-Plover, Wandering Tattler and Red-necked Phalarope. Long-tailed Jaegers may be harassing the smaller birds seeking food for their own young. The forests contain nesting Northern Hawk Owl, and probably Great Gray and Boreal. Breeding thrushes include Gray-cheeked, Mountain Bluebird and the elusive Northern Wheatear. Listen for Orange-crowned Warbler in the woods, as well as for the Blackpoll. Gray-crowned Rosy-Finches breed high up in the hills, whereas American Tree Sparrows are lower down. Smith's Longspur and Snow Bunting are also breeding on the tundra.

STAFF OF KLUANE NATIONAL PARK
Revised by Cameron Eckert and Kluane National Park

Tintina Trench

In the spring or as the colours change in the fall, a drive north from the Alaska Highway up the Canol Road to Ross River is well worth the trip. The migration of Sandhill Cranes through the Tintina Trench is a spectacular sight for those visiting the Faro or Ross River area. Tens of thousands of cranes can be seen overhead in late April to early May en route to breeding sites in Alaska. Their return from late August to mid-September is equally spectacular set against a backdrop of fall colours. A variety of waterfowl also use the Trench on migration. If you travel the Campbell Highway (east-west near Ross River and Faro) through a remote stretch of road in southeast Yukon, stop in at the arboretum in Faro. The interpretive signs highlight local birds.

WENDY NIXON

Dawson City

Headquarters for the famous Gold Rush of 1898, Dawson City has now been restored in places to recapture the flavour of '98. Visitors flock to this northern community, once touted as "the largest city west of Chicago and north of San Francisco." These lands had been explored very little until gold was found on August 17, 1896, in Bonanza Creek, a tributary of the Klondike River. News leaked out to a world deep in depression, and when, in the summer of 1897, miners from Dawson arrived in Portland, Oregon, and San Francisco with nearly $2 million (1897 dollars!), the rush was on. By the following spring, about 60,000 women and men had passed through Dawson on their way to hoped-for riches at the Klondike. Dawson City sprang up at the confluence of the Yukon and Klondike Rivers. By summer's end in 1898, some 30,000 people called it home. By the following spring, all creeks in the area were staked. Between 1896 and 1904, creeks in the area produced more than $100 million in gold. Jack London, Robert W. Service and others wrote colourful tales of their personal experiences. Later, Pierre Berton, raised there, added to these stories. Today, an actor gives readings from Service's works daily in the original cabin each summer. Several historical buildings have been restored by the National Historic Sites Service, which operates them with daily shows, productions and activities all summer. Interpreters of human history are located at various centres in the community throughout the summer. The post office, built in 1900, serves as the interpretive centre for Klondike Gold Rush International Historic Park.

Most visitors arrive via the Alaska Highway to Whitehorse, then the Klondike Highway No. 2 northwest for 481 km; alternatively, take the Alaska Highway into Alaska to the Tetlini Junction and proceed northeast 201 km into Dawson. The latter road is closed in winter. Regular bus service departs Edmonton twice a week year-round. Major airlines fly daily into Whitehorse with smaller lines flying from there into Dawson. Campgrounds are available along the highways and near Dawson. Commercial accommodation is often at a premium in July and August; book ahead.

Much has been written about the Klondike, particularly regarding the Gold Rush. Information may be obtained from The Interpretive Service, Klondike Gold Rush International Historic Park, Dawson City, Yukon YOB 1GO.

Birding Features

Klondike Highway. Driving Yukon Highway 2, the Klondike Highway, from Whitehorse to Dawson, stop and check wetlands and lakes along the way. They often have Common and Pacific Loons and several species of waterfowl. Ndu Lake, at Kilometre 442, usually hosts nesting American Coot, seldom seen elsewhere in the Yukon.

Within the town limits, abandoned lots with shrubs provide rich habitats for an abundance of birds. The town's Common Ravens are always entertaining, with a pair utilizing a nest in a cottonwood by the museum in the city core. Forests, meadows and mountainsides outside the city are host to many birds.

Owls are calling in April; a Northern Hawk Owl has nested near the airport. Later in April, Rough-legged Hawks appear. The Harlan's colour morph of the Red-tailed Hawk is not uncommon nesting in the valleys, as is the Northern Harrier. At this time, some Northern Shrikes pass through along the Klondike Highway. May is the migrant month and also the time when nesting species come in numbers. Check the Yukon River for Red-throated Loon and especially Kilometre 694 of the Klondike Highway, where sloughs and flooded hayfields draw Sandhill Crane; Tundra Swan; the small race of Canada Geese; American Golden-Plover; Whimbrel; Pectoral, Baird's and Least Sandpipers; Long-billed Dowitcher; and Semipalmated Sandpiper. From early May you will find numerous Hammond's Flycatchers; Alder Flycatchers arrive to breed in late May. Say's Phoebes pass through from mid-May to early June. The downstream end of town and also the "Slide" from late April onward are places to locate a Townsend's Solitaire that stays to breed. American Pipits are common in spring. American Tree and Fox Sparrows are plentiful in town during May.

One of the best birding locations at Dawson is the Yukon River campground on the west side of the river from Dawson. Townsend's Warbler breeds right in the campground. Viewing the river from the campground is one of the best places for Peregrine Falcon. Dom Hill is another really good place to look for songbirds.

In June to mid-July, breeding populations are most dense. Within the community, you should have no trouble finding such species as Violet-green and Cliff, the most common swallows; Tree and Bank Swallows are also present. Townsend's Solitaires are still on territory. While in the downstream end of town, check out the numerous Fox Sparrows, mainly in this area. Look in spruce woods wherever you find them, for Varied and Swainson's Thrushes, and Yellow-rumped and Townsend's Warblers. Hermit Thrushes are likely to be ferreted out in the aspen bluffs around town; listen also for Orange-crowned and Yellow Warblers. You may sight a Wilson's Warbler migrating through. Common Redpolls breed in or very near town. White-winged Crossbill is usually found breeding most years. Lincoln's Sparrows are common, the most active singer in the "night." The most common sparrow, White-crowned, adds to the diversity.

Outside of Dawson in June and early July, watch the Klondike River for Red-throated Loons and a fair number of Common Mergansers. Ducks are not too numerous, with Bufflehead the only common species in the Klondike Valley. The American Kestrel is the most common breeding raptor throughout the area.

In fall, late July to October, Sandhill Cranes and Canada Geese pass through.

ROBERT FRISCH
Revised by Cameron Eckert and Wendy Nixon

Dempster Highway (Dawson City to Inuvik)

The ribbon of gravel that runs from the boreal interior of the Yukon, across the Arctic Circle, to the Mackenzie Delta on the edge of the vast arctic tundra, is the only road in North America which gives access to this representative section of our subarctic. Over 160 bird species have been sighted. The contrasting landforms and vegetational diversity are remarkable in any context, passing from mountains and highlands in the Yukon to the flat forests of the delta; rich, wooded valleys alternate with bare, rock-strewn slopes and alpine barren; timberline is rarely far from the road; tundra ponds, numerous creeks and several major rivers add to the diversity. This trip allows you to see, here on their breeding grounds, the far northern birds you've watched on migration. Most of them are observed from the car window. Along the way look for Pacific and Red-throated Loons, numerous Golden Eagles, Gyrfalcon, Willow and Rock Ptarmigans, American Golden-Plover, Surfbird, Upland Sandpiper, Wandering Tattler, Baird's Sandpiper, Long-tailed Jaeger, Northern Hawk Owl, Gray-cheeked Thrush, Northern Wheatear, Harris's Sparrow, Lapland and Smith's Longspurs, and a few pairs of Snow Bunting. Watch for Siberian Tit. You will pass near a major Dall Sheep lambing range and possibly even spot a Grizzly going rapidly away.

The 721 km good gravel road begins 40 km east of Dawson City, or 481 km north of the Alaska Highway, just west of Whitehorse. A bus runs several times a week from Whitehorse to Dawson. Five government-operated camp-sites are along the way: Tombstone Mountain at Kilometre 74.5; Engineer Creek at Kilometre 195; Richardson Mountains at Kilometre 465; Nutuiluie Campground and Information Centre at Kilometre 543; Happy Valley at Inuvik. Commercial accommodation can be found at Eagle Plains Hotel and Campsite at Kilometre 368. The country is very fragile, with camping at other than designated spots discouraged. Gasoline may be purchased at Kilometre 0 (turn-off), Kilometre 368 (Eagle Plains Hotel), Kilometre 556 (Fort McPherson), and at the end, at Inuvik at Kilometre 721.

Keep in mind the special conditions this far northern drive may present. Weather can change rapidly – generally for the worse – as you move from a mountain range to a valley or back into plateau country. From early June to mid-August snowfall is rare, except above 1370 m, and usually melts almost immediately. The snow cover is gone by mid- to late May at the highway level. Persistent snow cover returns in mid-September to October. The ice on the Peel and Mackenzie Rivers usually goes out in mid-May and on the Ogilvie and Blackstone Rivers in late April to early May. There are several year-round open water spots on the Blackstone and North Klondike Rivers. Warm Creek at Kilometre 212 is the most prominent creek that remains unfrozen for long periods even at −40°C. The mosquito season runs from mid-June to early August, with greatest numbers in July. They are not very thick in the Southern Ogilvie Mountains at that time, but come in hordes north of there, even on high ridges. Stay on the road is the best advice for walking in vegetation stirs them up. Black flies appear in late July but are never too bad except across in the Mackenzie Valley and sometimes in the Richardson Mountains.

Traffic and services are sparse along this route. Make certain you have a good spare tire, extra gasoline, oil, a spare fan belt, as well as a good set of tools that you know how to use! Extra food and a first-aid kit are musts. A parka, hat, wool pullover sweater, warm footwear, mitts, rainwear and mosquito repellent should be carried. Plastic headlight covers should be acquired. The road is open all year, so if you travel on it in winter have a full complement of winter outdoor clothing and a sleeping bag for each person.

Hiking in the lower country off the road can be a hazard, particularly in the hummocks and tussocks of the upland tundra. Progress is 1 to 2 km per hour. Most birds can be seen from the road anyway. Alpine hiking is easier. Several of the high-country birds can be seen only away from the road. On your walks, look for Rock Ptarmigan; White-tailed Ptarmigan and Surfbird are found only away from the road; Baird's Sandpiper, Horned Lark, Northern Wheatear, American Pipit, Gray-crowned Rosy-Finch, Golden-crowned Sparrow and Snow Bunting are all seen best on territory away from the highway in the breeding season.

Caution regarding the animals. The slopes above North Fork Pass are crit-ical to the lambing of Dall Sheep. Don't climb there until after mid-June when the sheep have withdrawn deeper into the mountains. The Porcupine herd of Caribou herd crosses the highway each spring and fall in migration to and from the Arctic Ocean coast. Some traffic control is undertaken at this time. If you see the Caribou, stay well away so as not to frighten them. Stay away from the several Golden Eagle eyries in your hikes. There are a few Peregrine Falcons ranging the high country. Because of the danger these birds are in from DDT still being used in the southern countries where they winter, leave them alone if you spot one.

The government has imposed a no-hunting zone of 8 km on either side of the highway. This 16 km strip allows the observer a chance to birdwatch and still avoid any conflict with hunters.

The information for this major route has been borrowed from an excellent, comprehensive and thoroughly interesting booklet, *Birds by the Dempster Highway*, by Robert Frisch, 1987. This guide includes a great number of helpful hints, ranging from how to identify small birds on the wing, to breeding areas (he has noted extensions north and south from the usual published accounts). His list of "Dempster Specials" illustrates the uniqueness of this road, with many wanted birds easily available. Included also is a detailed species account for the 164 birds to be found. Anyone planning the trip should obtain a copy ($3.50 plus postage) to supplement the information supplied here. Write Yukon Conservation Society (see above) or Dawson Museum, Dawson City, Yukon Territory, YOB 1GO.

Birding Features

The road crosses a great variety of habitat. Several far northern breeders nest along it, particularly in the bare tussock-hummock tundra. If you are short of time and don't wish to make the whole trip, a drive north as far as the Blackstone Uplands, from Kilometre 87 to Kilometre 132 in the Southern Ogilvie Mountains, will provide most of the boreal, alpine and arctic species. Bird activity along the highway peaks in late May to early June. At that time the breeders are on territory and the species that nest far to the north are still passing through. By mid-May spring is well on its way, and by the end of June to early July bird activity falls off sharply. Mosquitoes are also few in number from mid-May to mid-June, when they increase. In fall, from mid-August to mid-September, the country is beautiful, with yellows and reds predominating, but there are few birds except along the Peel and Mackenzie Rivers, where large numbers pass through. Shorebirds come in August, with waterfowl in September.

Tintina Valley or Trench along the Lower North Klondike River, Kilometres 0 to 50, elevation 460 to 885 m. The habitat includes boreal forest of spruce, poplar and birch, including muskeg forest. There are extensive burns and willow thickets. A bird of note here is Sharp-tailed Grouse. Near the river, tall White Spruce and Balsam Poplar with willow thickets prevail. Sloughs and swamps lie near the Klondike River. From Kilometre 25 onward, look for the spurs of the Ogilvie Mountains. This is the only typical boreal forest with pronounced aspen succession that you will encounter, so check it out. A number of forest birds reach their northern breeding limits here, including Ruffed Grouse, Yellow-bellied Sapsucker, Hairy Woodpecker, Western Wood-Pewee,

Hermit Thrush, Townsend's Warbler and Common Nighthawk. Boreal Owls are year-round residents in tall dense spruce in the valley bottom. Listen for the call from midwinter to mid-April. Hammond's and Alder Flycatchers are common in the deciduous woods and thickets. Violet-green and Tree Swallows are around clearings and habitations. In winter, American Dipper is found on the open water of the North Klondike River at Kilometre 10. Orange-crowned Warbler is common from Kilometre 0 to Kilometre 73 at the timberline. Look for it in deciduous trees and tall shrubbery. Lincoln's and Fox Sparrows are also found in this area.

Upper North Klondike River Valley, Kilometres 50 to 72, elevation 885 to 1035 m. This stretch is in montane spruce forests with a few aspen and scrub birch in the understory. The forests grade into the treeline of scrubby trees and bushes at Kilometre 68. The public campsite is situated in the last woods at Kilometre 72. You'll begin encountering birds of the subarctic mountains, such as Wilson's Warbler and American Tree Sparrow. With luck, you may spot Wandering Tattler. The Northern Goshawk is often sighted south of here and along the valley to the timberline. The old-growth stands of spruce here, and those to the south, often have Three-toed Woodpeckers. American Dipper occurs in the Upper Klondike River and its tributaries. Fox Sparrows are fairly common in the valley.

Southern Ogilvie Mountains – North Fork Pass, Kilometres 72 to 87, elevation 1035 to 1310 m. Vegetation consists of scrubby tundra with some bare tussock tundra. Ponds are found in the East Blackstone valley. You are near the alpine tundra; look up from the highway above 1370 m for the rich meadows, heath and tussocks. The pass forms the divide between the Klondike-Yukon River systems of the Pacific, and the Blackstone-Peel River systems of the arctic watersheds. To the east rise the Sheep Mountains, where you may spot Dall Sheep. West of the road is the Cloudy Range. You have entered the richest alpine birding area on the route, the Southern Ogilvie Mountains. To reach this "birders' dreamland," from the pass at Kilometres 80 to 83, hike up the west flanks of Sheep Mountain, which the road skirts. These mountains rise another 610 m; though rather steep, they are climbed easily. These slopes are the lambing grounds of Dall Sheep, so stay off until the second week of June. Look for all the alpine birds, regularly located here, and also Surfbird and Baird's Sandpiper, which are seen only occasionally. The Golden Eagle is a regular sight along the highway. Willow and Rock Ptarmigans are spotted higher up. This is the best area in which to find White-tailed Ptarmigan, but you'll have to go into these mountains east or west of the pass. In ponds you should see Red-necked Phalaropes, which are common. Northern Wheatears are most common in these Southern Ogilvie Mountains. Look for them in cliffs and rock rubble on the Sheep Mountains to the east of the pass. Townsend's Solitaires occur on rocky slopes. The Northern Shrike is most often seen here, especially in the valley to the west, near the source of the East Blackstone River. You will encounter redpolls. There is a problem of identification between Common and Hoary in this country, so don't be surprised if you're confused about which you are watching. The "experts" are not sure either! American Tree and White-crowned Sparrows are common to abundant. You should spot a Golden-crowned Sparrow in the shrubby gullies above Kilometres 81 to 82 as this is the most likely spot on the route. The Fox Sparrow is common in bushy areas lower down in valleys. On your hike east and west of the pass, look for Snow Bunting in rock debris near remnant snowbeds. Nesting sites of these birds in the Sheep Mountains are within an easy one-day's excursion from North Fork Pass. To get there, hike up the valley east of about Kilometre 90 and then up a tributary valley from the south. On the trip you should be able to locate Golden Eagle, Rock and White-tailed Ptarmigans, Wandering Tattler, Northern Wheatear, American Pipits and Gray-crowned Rosy-Finch, together with Arctic Ground Squirrel, Pika, marmot and some sheep.

Blackstone Uplands, Kilometres 87 to 132, elevation 915 to 1035 m. The landscape consists of bare tussock and shrubby tundra, with some fen. There are many lakes and ponds, including Moose Lake at Kilometre 105; Chapman Lake at Kilometre 120 and some kettle ponds at Kilometres 120 to 125. The rivers include the East, West and Main Blackstone, with wide gravel pans. There are groves of spruce and Balsam Poplar along the river. This site is the climax of the trip for numbers and diversity of birds. Here you may spot nesting Red-throated Loon, Oldsquaw, Golden Eagle, Gyrfalcon, Willow and Rock Ptarmigan, American Golden-Plover and other shorebirds, Long-tailed Jaeger, Short-eared Owl, redpolls (mainly Common), and Smith's and Lapland Longspurs. Many breeding woodland species are also in the treeline and groves of willows along the Blackstone River. The adjacent mountains contain nesting Townsend's Solitaire on rocky slopes, Surfbird, American Pipit, Gray-crowned Rosy-Finch, Golden-crowned Sparrow and Snow Bunting. Spring migrants, particularly water birds, come in large numbers. Moose Lake, at Kilometre 105, is usually ice-free by late May, with Chapman Lake, at Kilometre 120, icebound until early June. In both bodies and other smaller ones, there is usually open water along the edges from early May on. Such habitat draws in water birds like a magnet.

The Red-throated Loon nests by ponds and smaller lakes in open country around Blackstone Forks at Kilometre 117. This is probably the most accessible

American Golden-Plover

spot in Canada at which these birds can be seen on territory. The Tundra Swan is seen regularly in spring at Moose Lake. The Oldsquaw is a regular breeder on the numerous ponds near the Upper Blackstone River, east and west branches. The Golden Eagle is usually around from late March onward. Northern Harrier swoops low in the Upper Blackstone valleys. Gyrfalcon will be back up in the mountains, hunting low down, or perched on a tussock. Willow and Rock Ptarmigans are common, with Willow the more numerous. An American Golden-Plover is usually noticed from the road as it defends a territory. The Whimbrel nests in open tundra along valleys and on low ridges. It is usually spotted between Kilometres 90 and 100. An Upland Sandpiper may be spotted from clearings in open taiga forest to tussock tundra with some shrub and a few spruce. At Kilometre 132, Cache Creek, check carefully for a Wandering Tattler in the gravel along the creek, or for an American Dipper on the water. You may sight a Pectoral Sandpiper on migration. Many of the ponds should have a Red-necked Phalarope spinning around as it feeds. The Long-tailed Jaeger is fairly common in the open tussock tundra. Mew Gull, the common gull along here, breeds by braided streams and tarns. Bonaparte's Gull has a breeding site in trees just west of Kilometres 119 to 122 by the ponds lined with spruce. Arctic Terns also breed here in braided stream areas near the Blackstone River at Kilometre 118. The Short-eared Owl flits its wings as it flies by. Near the treeline, look in tall willows for a Gray-cheeked Thrush. In the mountains nearby, you'll find Northern Wheatear in the cliffs and rock rubble. The highland warbler singing in the bushes is probably a Wilson's.

West of here some 100 km, Dr. Theo Hotmann found six Siberian Tits in August 1982. His group drove to Kilometre 119 and then paddled upstream on the Blackstone River to 65°42' north latitude and 137°25' west longitude; they then climbed a ridge about 457 m above the river to find the birds in a very open stand of spruce fairly close to the treeline. The spot is about 20 km from the highway as the crow flies (from the point where the road runs north of the Ogilvie River, about 100 km south of Eagle Plains). Use maps 116H and 116G and F of Mines and Technical Surveys. Refer to *Birdfinding in Canada*, Vol. 3, No. 3, May 1983.

Common Redpolls occur along the road as fairly common summer residents throughout the subalpine shrubs. You may also spot a Golden-crowned Sparrow. The Lapland Longspur is an abundant bird in bare tussock tundra in the highlands and mountains.

Northern Ogilvie Mountains, Kilometres 132 to 197, elevation 610 to 1005 m. This stretch consists of discontinuous subarctic taiga forest of White Spruce, with Balsam Poplar along streams up to the timberline around 915 m. You'll also see much Black Spruce muskeg grading into tussock tundra. The main streams are the Blackstone River and Engineer (Big) Creek. There are no lakes and only one pond at Windy Pass, Kilometre 155. Your second choice of campsites is at Kilometre 195. These mountains are known more for their beautiful scenery than as a birding area. Townsend's Solitaire is common at the treeline. The Wandering Tattler breeds at Windy Pass. There is a known Baird's Sandpiper breeding site close to and south of the highway at Windy Pass. As

Lapland Longspur

you drive, watch for a Gyrfalcon. You may spot a Willow or a Rock Ptarmigan too. Check the treetops for Northern Hawk Owl, seen from here north. As in the previous sites, the Wilson's Warbler is the typical highland species.

Ogilvie River Valley, Kilometres 197 to 248, elevation around 610 m. The valley contains taiga-type forest with much cottonwood and some Tamarack. Extensive willow thickets occur with no open tundra near the highway. There are several creeks, including Warm Creek at Kilometre 212, which are open year-round. Check this valley for a nesting Great Gray Owl. Warm Creek hosts the American Dipper in winter.

Eagle Plains, Kilometres 248 to 410, elevation 610 to 915+ m. The lands are covered with continuous low hummocky Black Spruce taiga, which thins northward to Black Spruce–Tamarack forest tundra. Taller White Spruce and Balsam Poplar are along the Eagle River with open tundra ridge tops at Kilometres 255 to 280 and northeast of Eagle River. No lakes are found, but there are oxbow ponds along the river. The one hotel and service stop on the route, Eagle Plains, is at Kilometre 368. This is the area of the fewest birds, including a virtual absence of eagles. A few woodland species occur, including the odd Spruce Grouse, Northern Hawk Owl, Gray Jay, Gray-cheeked Thrush, Yellow-rumped Warbler and a very few Blackpoll Warblers. The one consolation is that the Eagle Plains are the driest for rainfall on the Yukon side. Rock Ptarmigans occur on bare ridges on the southern rim from Kilometres 265 to 280. Swainson's Hawk may breed near Kilometre 280. The Gray-cheeked Thrush is quite common from here north, both at the treeline and in shrubby taiga.

Southern Richardson Mountains and Foothills, Kilometres 410 to 450, elevation 460 to 760 m. The highway cuts through hummock-tussock tundra with intermittent woods along streams and a few patches elsewhere. Many creeks are located here, with the main ones Rock, at Kilometre 433, and Cornwall, at

Kilometre 448. No lakes are found. Aside from the lack of waterfowl and a few missing species of shorebirds, these mountains are prime birding territory. This area just north of the Arctic Circle is the best place to study Rock Ptarmigan, American Golden-Plover, Long-tailed Jaeger, Gray-cheeked Thrush and Smith's Longspur. Back in the mountains you'll find Surfbirds. Watch for Gyrfalcons as you drive, and Upland Sandpipers may be spotted if you are lucky. Short-eared Owls occur along here. Gray-crowned Rosy-Finches are fairly common in the high alpine rocky area. Near Rock River at Kilometre 437, look for Golden-crowned Sparrow at the timberline. At Kilometre 448 on the Cornwall River, look for a Harlequin Duck on the water and a nearby Lapland Longspur.

Northern Richardson Mountains, Kilometres 450 to 492, elevation 460 to 915 m. The road approaches the mountains through bare tussock-hummocky tundra. It crosses into the Northwest Territories on the crest at Kilometre 467. Tundra occurs in the mountains with much rocky terrain. There are no woods, except in the gullies of Cornwall River and its tributaries. The lower courses of the creeks are deeply incised with gorges, including James Creek at Kilometre 480. There are some lakes and ponds on the NWT side. This is the area most arctic in character, with continuous permafrost present. A campground occurs at Kilometre 465. Horned Larks, American Pipits and Northern Wheatears are best observed along here at the border and around Kilometre 490. Baird's Sandpiper is also found at the border in saddles along the mountain spine. The high country from Kilometres 467 to 490 is probably the most convenient along the route for alpine birding. There are no steep ascents and the country is the nearest to the arctic you will see along the route. Most mountain species occur here, as do Northern Wheatears. Scan the hills and roadside for Willow Ptarmigan, American Golden-Plover, Baird's Sandpiper west of Kilometre 480, Long-tailed Jaeger, Gray-crowned Rosy-Finch and Lapland Longspur.

Peel Plateau, Kilometres 492 to 541, elevation 90 to 610 m. The plateau consists of a partially wooded sloping upland dissected by many streams. The land is covered with sparse hummocky taiga and hummock-tussock tundra. Taller spruce, birch and poplar grow in the valleys. The two streams, Vittrekwa River and Stony Creek, are steeply incised and muddy. Many lakes and ponds occur. On open ridges, look for Willow Ptarmigan. In streamside thickets in the uplands you should spot a Wilson's Warbler. The woods from timberline into shrubby tundra may produce a Gray-cheeked Thrush. At Kilometre 510, Halfway Lake is the spot to locate both a Harris's and a Golden-crowned Sparrow. As you drive east towards the Peel River, watch the lakes and ponds for Tundra Swan. The woods usually have Blackpoll Warbler. As you approach the Peel River, scan any water for a Pacific Loon.

Peel River Valley, Kilometres 541 to 543. This river bench contains a White Spruce forest; birch grow on the valley slopes with a dense willow-alder understory. The banks and river are muddy. There are many oxbow lakes. Free ferry services are available from spring to fall. The NWT government operates a campground and information centre on the east side of the river. Nearby Fort

McPherson was established by the Hudson's Bay Company in 1848, and trappers continue to use it today as their home base. There are no services at Fort McPherson. Look for Pacific Loons on the river and Sandhill Cranes on the east side. The luxuriant vegetation in the valley is alive with bird song in late May and early June. See what you can locate. Migrants use the valley, particularly shorebirds in August and waterfowl in September.

Peel River to Mackenzie River, Kilometres 543 to 609, elevation around 90 m. The habitat is mainly low muskeg taiga, with White Spruce and birch on better-drained sites and ridges. There are many lakes and a few creeks, such as Frog Creek at Kilometre 590. Scan the lakes and shores for Pacific Loons, Sandhill Cranes and Semipalmated Plovers. The latter is often found in gravel pits along the highway and by the Peel and Mackenzie Rivers. A Blackpoll Warbler should be heard in the woods along here.

Mackenzie River Valley, Kilometres 609 to 615. Some moderately tall White Spruce and birch grow on the slopes. High, steep banks occur in places such as the Lower Ramparts. The small community of Arctic Red River lies at the crossing of the Mackenzie. Arctic Red River was first settled permanently as a Catholic mission in 1868; a trading post followed shortly thereafter. Free ferry service is available across the Mackenzie from spring to fall. The Blackpoll Warbler sings in nearby woods, and Lincoln's Sparrow occurs near the river crossing in tall dense shrub. This is the last known sighting of the bird. Herring, Mew and a few Glaucous Gulls may be seen along the river.

Mackenzie River to Inuvik, Kilometres 615 to 726, elevation 10 to 90 m. This last stretch tends to be low muskeg-thin taiga, swampy and shrubby. Watch for Sharp-tailed Grouse. There are a few creeks; the largest, Rengleng River, lies near Kilometre 650. Lakes occur along the highway, particularly near the northern end. Some rocky scarps and hills are found near Inuvik, including the Campbell Hills. There are several public campsites near Inuvik. Birdlife is similar to that reported at Inuvik (see below in NWT). Look for Harris's Sparrow in the discontinuous Black Spruce taiga as you approach town.

Birds by the Dempster Highway AND ADDITIONAL
UNPUBLISHED NOTES BY ROBERT FRISCH
Revised by Cameron Eckert

Yukon Coastal Plain and Ivvavik National Park

The strip of land from the mountains down to the coast at the northern edge of the Yukon has produced 122 species of birds with nearly 60 nesting. As the main fall staging area for the Snow Goose of the western Canadian Arctic, the North Slope also plays host to far western species, including the Northern Wheatear, Bluethroat and Yellow Wagtail. Pacific and Red-throated Loons nest too.

Until very recently, knowledge of this land was limited to the coast. With the advent of helicopters and wide-tired aircraft, plus the need to assess the impact on wildlife by the proposed construction of a major pipeline, detailed studies have now been done on this unique strip of northern Canada. Northern and eastern range extensions have thus been established.

Access to these plains is by air, usually from Inuvik. To arrange a trip, check with tour companies in Inuvik, wilderness tour operators based in the Yukon, and Parks Canada, regarding access to Ivvavik National Park. As in all Yukon travel, be prepared for winter conditions even in summer.

The best landing spots are Stokes Point, midway between Alaska and the Mackenzie Delta; Herschel Island, farther west; and Clarence Lagoon on the far western boundary, adjacent to Alaska.

Information for this section was obtained with the help of Tom Barry and from a major article, "Distribution and Abundance of Birds on the Arctic Coastal Plain of Northern Yukon and Adjacent Northwest Territories 1971–1976," by Richard F. Salter, Michael A. Gollop, Stephen R. Johnson, William R. Koski and C. Eric Tull in *Canadian Field-Naturalist*, Vol. 94, No. 3, July–September 1980, pp. 2190–237. The Yukon Bird Club and Canadian Wildlife Service have a great deal of information about this area. Check with them.

Birding Features

The North Slope plains occur as low arctic tundra north of the mountains, adjacent to the Beaufort Sea. Birds to be found include those inhabiting northern woodlands, tundra and marine habitats. The flat landscape contains a few incised river valleys and is underlain by continuous permafrost. Polygonal ground and permafrost-related features are everywhere. Small lakes abound, particularly on the eastern side and near the coast. The vegetation consists of a mosaic of dry tussock, wet sedge and low willow shrubbery. Tall bushes grow along rivers and some lakes.

The low, sandy and silty cliffs and narrow beaches of the Beaufort Sea coast are separated by river deltas, barrier islands, spits and lagoons. There are two permanent settlements, Komankuk, 30 km from the Alaska border, and Shingle Point (DEW line sites), near the west side of the Mackenzie Delta. Herschel Island (see elsewhere), 3 km off the coast, was a major whaling base in the early 1900s and until recently an RCMP outpost.

Open water appears as early as mid-May on some of the deltas. Lakes begin to have some meltwater by late May, with most of them ice-free by late June. Coastline open water first shows in late May or early June, with cracks in the sea ice opening up by mid-June. The ice pack leaves the shore area by mid-July and returns by October to November.

Mid-June would be the best time to come, since all breeding birds are on territory and a few far northern species are still coming through. Search for the four loon species: Common and Yellow-billed are very rare but may be seen; Pacific and Red-throated breed along here. The Tundra Swan nests near tundra lakes. Brant pass through in early June and again in September. The Coastal Plain is the major fall staging site for the Snow Goose of the western Arctic. They begin arriving in mid-August and quickly build up to numbers often exceeding 200,000. Departure is around mid-September. The Oldsquaw is the most numerous duck on the plain. Common Eider is a breeder on the barrier beaches. King Eider is a migrant from mid-May to mid-June.

Rough-legged Hawk and Golden Eagle may be seen nesting farther inland on river cliffs. Gyrfalcon and Peregrine Falcon are fairly numerous, with the former remaining all year. Willow Ptarmigan is the more abundant, but Rock Ptarmigan also is fairly plentiful in the more barren areas. Breeding shorebirds are fairly common and include Semipalmated Plover, American Golden-Plover, Whimbrel, Pectoral Sandpiper, Semipalmated Sandpiper, Long-billed Dowitcher, Stilt Sandpiper and Buff-breasted Sandpiper. American Golden-Plover, Red Phalarope, Lapland Longspur, Snow Bunting and Northern Wheatear are among the northern breeders that flock to this subarctic tundra to take advantage of the brief summer to nest and raise their young. Pomarine Jaeger is a migrant. Parasitic and Long-tailed Jaegers are very common breeders. Glaucous Gulls raise young here as do Arctic Terns. Black Guillemot is limited to the coast, on, and west of Herschel Island. Look in the buildings on the island for some nests. Snowy Owl is a confirmed breeder with numbers highly erratic. Short-eared Owls breed throughout the area. Northern Wheatear is found nesting. The Bluethroat is a rare inhabitant of shrubby draws. The Yellow Wagtail is relatively common on the tundra near the coast; Red-throated Pipit has occurred. American Tree and White-crowned Sparrows breed, as do Lapland Longspur and Snow Bunting.

REVISED BY WENDY NIXON

Herschel Island – Qikiqtaruk

Herschel Island lies 5 km off the Yukon coast. As a result of the Inuvialuit Final Agreement, the 112 km² island is a Yukon territorial park. The site is rich in arctic flora, permafrost features, arctic mammals, birds and marine life, with a history of commercial whaling, trading, missionaries and police, and Inuvialuit use which continues today.

The island is renowned among birdwatchers as a special place to view arctic breeders such as eiders, numerous shorebirds, jaegers and longspurs. It is home to the western arctic's largest breeding colony of Black Guillemots and one of the densest breeding populations of Rough-legged Hawks in North America. Workboat Passage, the protected body of water between the island and the mainland, is a migration corridor and moulting area for seabirds and ducks, and a key fall staging area for Oldsquaw and scoters.

Situated on the edge of the coastal migration path, the island boasts several rare bird records, including Yellow-headed Blackbird, the Yukon's first Ross's Gull and Canada's second record of Wood Sandpiper. Ninety-four bird species have been recorded on Herschel Island, with breeding status confirmed for 40. The Yukon Bird Club in Whitehorse has prepared a checklist for the birds of Herschel Island. To obtain a copy, see above.

To access the island, air charters are available from Inuvik, NWT. A number of Inuvialuit operators may be available for boat tours along the coast. They can be accessed through the Aklavik Hunters and Trappers Association, (867) 978-2723. Other outfits to contact for travel and tour information include

Arctic Tour Company in Inuvik, (867) 777-4100 and Go Wild Tours in Whitehorse, (867) 668-2411.

Birders who are planning an extended trip to the island should contact the Herschel Island Territorial Park office in Inuvik.

ADAPTED BY CATHERINE McEWEN FROM
Checklist of the Birds of Herschel Island

Winter Birding in the Yukon

While many birders dream of a world in which the last two weeks in May remain for 12 months, winter is a reality, and in the Yukon it is hard to ignore. Winter birding is relatively limited here; however, many birders will be surprised to learn that nearly 60 species have been documented in the Yukon from December 1 to February 28. In any given year 35 to 40 species are reported and the Whitehorse Christmas Bird Count usually turns up 20 to 25 species. Most numerous are Common Raven, Black-billed Magpie and Gray Jay. As in most winter sites across Canada, feeder-watching is best to find a variety of birds. Bulk numbers tend to be low in December, but usually pick up considerably through January and February. Most common at feeders are Black-capped and Boreal Chickadees, Common and Hoary Redpolls (usually at a ratio of about 100:1), Pine Grosbeak, and more rarely Red-breasted Nuthatch, Mountain Chickadee, Dark-eyed Junco and Red Crossbill. Evening Grosbeak is a Watson Lake winter specialty. Suet feeders usually attract Downy and Hairy Woodpeckers. Farther afield, check open water areas for Mallard, Common Goldeneye, Bufflehead (rare), Common Merganser and American Dipper. Ruffed and Spruce Grouse may be seen along roadsides. Sharp-tailed Grouse occurs in southwestern and central Yukon. Check mature spruce forests for Three-toed Woodpecker and White-winged Crossbill. Other regulars include Bald and Golden Eagles, Gyrfalcon, Northern Goshawk, Northern Hawk Owl, Great Horned and Boreal Owls (usually detected only by call in late winter), Bohemian Waxwing and more rarely Northern Shrike (early and late winter), American Robin (early winter) and Snow Bunting. Winter rarities have included Canvasback, Barrow's Goldeneye, Hooded Merganser, Great Gray Owl, Short-eared Owl, Black-backed Woodpecker, Horned Lark, Steller's Jay, European Starling, Fox Sparrow, Rusty Blackbird, Gray-crowned Rosy Finch, House and Purple Finches, Pine Siskin and House Sparrow. Indeed, there are many surprises even during this most quiet of seasons, so dress warmly and don't breathe on your binoculars.

CAMERON ECKERT

11C
12B

No. 1
No. 2

Sachs
Harbour   BANKS ISLAND

6
Tuktoyaktuk
5   Anderson
Inuvik   11A   River   11B
Cape Parry

VICTORIA

7
Rendezvous
Lake

12A

ISLAND   N U N A V U T

Cambridge
Bay
9

Great Bear Lake

4
Bathurst Inlet   8   QUEEN MAUD GULF
11E

BIRD SANCTUARY

Tungsten

3   N O R T H W E S T

T E R R I T O R I E S   THELON GAME

Fort Simpson   11H
Nahanni   SANCTUARY
Butte
Fort Liard   Fort
Providence   Yellowknife
2
Great Slave
Lake

Hay River

1
Fort Smith
WOOD

BUFFALO

NAT'L PARK

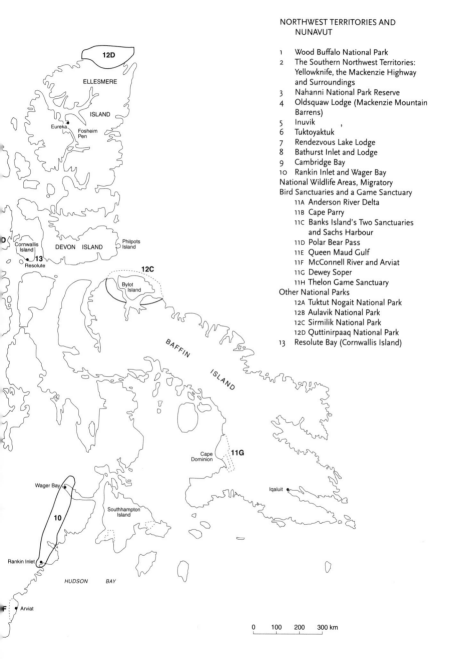

NORTHWEST TERRITORIES AND
NUNAVUT

1   Wood Buffalo National Park
2   The Southern Northwest Territories:
    Yellowknife, the Mackenzie Highway
    and Surroundings
3   Nahanni National Park Reserve
4   Oldsquaw Lodge (Mackenzie Mountain
    Barrens)
5   Inuvik
6   Tuktoyaktuk
7   Rendezvous Lake Lodge
8   Bathurst Inlet and Lodge
9   Cambridge Bay
10 Rankin Inlet and Wager Bay
National Wildlife Areas, Migratory
Bird Sanctuaries and a Game Sanctuary
    11A Anderson River Delta
    11B Cape Parry
    11C Banks Island's Two Sanctuaries
        and Sachs Harbour
    11D Polar Bear Pass
    11E Queen Maud Gulf
    11F McConnell River and Arviat
    11G Dewey Soper
    11H Thelon Game Sanctuary
Other National Parks
    12A Tuktut Nogait National Park
    12B Aulavik National Park
    12C Sirmilik National Park
    12D Quttinirpaaq National Park
13 Resolute Bay (Cornwallis Island)

409

NORTHWEST TERRITORIES AND NUNAVUT

Since the first edition of this book was written, the Canadian north has undergone significant changes. Foremost is the establishment of two territories where only the Northwest Territories (NWT) used to exist. On April 1, 1999, the Nunavut Territory officially covered 2.12 million square kilometres of the former NWT, leaving 1.17 million square kilometres for the western territory. The new territory is demarcated on modern maps of Canada and includes all the islands of Hudson and James Bays. The other significant changes include a tremendous increase in the tourism industry of the north and a number of new, formally protected areas. The result for birders is that information on birds in the north is easier to obtain, and places to see them are easier to find and get to.

The Northwest Territories' capital is Yellowknife (pop. 17,000), located on the north arm of Great Slave Lake. The NWT is now home to over 39,000 people and is steadily growing. It has all the forested habitat of the two territories, two of the world's largest fresh-water lakes, the Mackenzie Delta and a portion of the high arctic islands. The opportunities to see the range of birds that occupy boreal and tundra regions are excellent. Expect to find everything from Canada and Bay-breasted Warblers to Red Phalarope and American Golden Plover if you start in the south and end up on the tundra.

The capital of Nunavut is Iqaluit (pop. 4500), an ocean-front community on southeastern Baffin Island. Most of the 25,000 inhabitants of this territory are Inuit, spread out across the region's 24 other settlements. Interestingly, there are no roads outside of communities in Nunavut, so if you plan to visit, you will arrive by airplane or ship. Nunavut contains the full variety of arctic habitats, from taiga forests just north of Manitoba to the expansive beauty of tundra lowlands and polar ice fields on the arctic islands. Within the territory is an impressive number of seabird colonies of gulls, murres, fulmars, etc., together with rapidly expanding populations of Snow Geese. Nunavut is the only place in Canada where you will see nesting birds such as the Common Ringed Plover and the Ivory Gull.

The north offers opportunities to see birds on their breeding grounds that you cannot find in other parts of Canada. It simultaneously offers the chance to see more biting insects than most people are aware exist! When travelling to the north, preparation is important.

A trip to either territory requires careful planning of your itinerary, making sure you bring enough and proper clothing, supplies if you are travelling independently, and plenty of bug repellent and/or bug clothing. Cellular phones do not work in almost all areas of the north, but the new hand-held satellite telephones work well if you cannot use a normal phone (all communities have normal phone service) and can be rented for your trip, giving excellent insurance in case of difficulty.

Arriving at your birdwatching location of choice is relatively straightforward. In the west, you can drive from northern British Columbia into the NWT via Fort Liard, following the Liard River, then east along the Mackenzie River towards Fort Providence, Yellowknife, Hay River and the other communities accessible by road from northern Alberta. Two major airlines service the largest centres in the north on a daily basis and include jet flights several times a week to locations as far north as Cambridge Bay and Resolute. If you would like to venture farther afield, many local airlines service smaller communities at scheduled times. For those without budgetary restrictions, charter aircraft can take you almost anywhere you desire. Once you get to the community at or near your destination, local guides and outfitters are almost always available to take you "out on the land."

Since the mid-90s, the cruise-ship industry has been steadily growing, and in many instances caters directly to birdwatchers. These cruises often pass through either Lancaster or Jones Sounds, south and north of Devon Island respectively. They often go by some of the most spectacular seabird colonies in the high Arctic. This represents one of the best ways to see a species such as Ivory Gull. Some of the Ivory Gull colonies are restricted because the species is sensitive to human intrusions, while others are inaccessible except at great cost. Birders on the cruise ships often see the Ivory Gull in a pelagic setting where they are not being disturbed, along with other species not normally seen on land (such as Dovekie). Some of the companies giving tours include Zegrahm Expeditions and Quark Expeditions, though there are others. With the increase in the tourism industry, the number of companies providing accommodation and services is too great to list here (but we've provided an update to the two lodges from the last edition). Rest assured that almost every community provides somewhere to stay, however small and expensive.

Several excellent resources will provide all the up-to-date information you require. In the west, try the NWT Explorer's Guide (www.nwttravel.nt.ca) available from NWT Arctic Tourism, Box 610, Yellowknife, Northwest

Territories, X1A 2N5; phone (867) 873-7200. For the east, try The Nunavut Handbook (www.arctic-travel.com) or contact Nunavut Tourism, P.O. Box 1450, Iqaluit, Nunavut, X0A 0H0; phone 1-800-491-7910 or (867) 979-6551. You will find interesting and useful information from both sources to make your birding trip fulfilling. To maximize your birding, plan on arriving some-time between late May and mid-July, depending on how far north you plan to go. Many migrants are back in the southern areas by late May, but there will usually be snow patches on the ground well into July if you head north to the islands. The shorebird mating rituals tend to peak before July 1, so if watch-ing hooting flights of the Pectoral Sandpiper is on your "must see" list, head out early. Don't forget to leave some extra time in your travel schedule in case of weather problems — fog and snow can prevent a scheduled aircraft from landing at its destination, making a day or two wait possible.

Birdwatching in the north is unlike anything farther south. Most people who are used to getting a hundred species in a hard day of birding will be very dis-appointed at the relatively low density and species richness of the bird commu-nities in the north. Furthermore, if the small mammal populations are at a low in their cycle, raptor sightings can be few and far between on the tundra. Each year is different. But birding trips to the north often mean a host of peripheral benefits — fantastic wildlife viewing of non-bird species, the chance to see true wilderness and the joy of living life at a slower pace. So come prepared to see new bird species, but expect to have a much more holistic birding adventure!

There are no bird clubs in the Northwest Territories or Nunavut at this time, but bird information is being collected by the Canadian Wildlife Service (CWS) with a program called the Northwest Territories Bird Checklist Survey. The program will soon be revised to accommodate Nunavut, but nothing else will change. Visit the Web site for more information (www.NWTChecklist.com) or find it on the Environment Canada Web site for the prairie and northern region under the Nature heading (www.mb.ec.gc.ca). CWS operates offices in both Iqaluit and Yellowknife and must be contacted for permits to enter the bird sanctuaries and national wildlife areas that are in the north. If you plan

Ross's Gull

to visit an area before June 1, you must have your permit application in before the end of January. If you plan to visit an area after June 1, you must apply before the end of March of the same year. Contact them in the west at Canadian Wildlife Service, Environment Canada, Suite 301, 5204-50th Avenue, Yellowknife, Northwest Territories X1A 1E2; phone (867) 669-4700, or in the east at CWS, Environment Canada, Box 607, Iqaluit, Nunavut X0E 0H0; phone (867) 979-2062.

Now that the Internet has become so accessible and information quality is constantly improving, significant resources are available to help plan your birding trip. Although some of the highlights have been captured in this book, an excellent all-round resource to find out more information is a site called "Links River, North of Sixty" (www.denendeh.com/linksriver/index.html). Knowing that Internet sites sometimes come and go without notice, we have included only a few addresses. General searches using keywords of the site you want to visit will often help turn up useful information.

Northern Canada covers a huge area of land and water – trying to see much more than a tiny piece on a birding trip is very difficult and often expensive. To highlight some of the information in this chapter, here are some of the top recommendations:

– If you only want to build a large Nunavut "list," and you are in Ontario, go out onto the James Bay Islands.

– If it is your wish to see the most boreal species, but aren't concerned with arctic species, go to Fort Liard.

– The least expensive place to see some arctic species is Yellowknife, followed by Inuvik.

– The least expensive place to see exclusively arctic species such as northern nesting shorebirds is Cambridge Bay.

– If you want to see seabirds, take a cruise ship.

– If it's Peregrine Falcons you want, head to Rankin Inlet.

– If it's a desire to inform your friends that you have seen more Snow Geese than one can imagine, canoe through the Queen Maud Gulf Sanctuary.

– If you'd like to be somewhere isolated, but don't want to fuss with logistics, visit a birding lodge.

– If you are one of those few people who really want a unique and eternally memorable arctic birding experience, charter an aircraft and stay out on the tundra for a couple of weeks. You'll have the freedom of true wilderness and will be able to watch birds 24 hours a day!

CRAIG MACHTANS

Wood Buffalo National Park

Home of the Wood Buffalo, nesting grounds for the Whooping Crane and host to over a million swans, geese, and ducks during migration, this park is one of the largest and most special in the world. All four of the continent's major migration flyways overlap here. Of the 227 species of birds noted within its boundaries, 142 nest, with only 25 species overwintering. Forty-six mammal species have been recorded, including Moose, Woodland Caribou, Black Bear and Wolf. Several species of frogs and the Canadian Toad are present. The most northerly hibernacula of the Red-sided Garter Snake in North America are found in the karst topography of the Salt River area.

Soon after glaciers receded, about 9000 years ago, humans moved in. Native peoples speaking the Cree, Chipewyan and Beaver languages still inhabit the area today. The first European recorded to have arrived here was Samuel Hearne, in the winter of 1771–72. He considered the buffalo to be "plentiful." Fort Chipewyan is the oldest continuously inhabited settlement in Alberta. Established in 1788, "Fort Chip" was the centre for the extensive fur trade in the entire northwest. Within 134 years, the park was established as a way to protect the bison, and quickly had to be enlarged when the bison started using areas south of the Peace River. Today the park is the largest piece of protected boreal wilderness in Canada and is recognized internationally with a UNESCO designation as a World Heritage Site.

Coincidentally, Wood Buffalo National Park (WBNP) also happened to contain another disappearing species. The search for the nesting grounds of the Whooping Crane had been going on for years. These birds once numbered several thousand and were spread across the plains of North America. Land clearing and hunting reduced the population to less than 100 by the 1920s. By the early 1940s, the bird appeared to be headed for extinction. From 1922 until 1954, not a single active nest was found. In 1937, the United States government established a wildlife refuge at Arkansas, Texas, to protect the last wintering grounds of these birds. Men scoured the country to discover where the few remaining birds nested during the summer. On a helicopter trip during forest fire suppression activities in 1954, G. M. Wilson, superintendent of forestry at Fort Smith, spotted two adult white birds and a young one in an area south of Great Slave Lake. The next day, Dr. W. A. Fuller, then the regional biologist for the Canadian Wildlife Service and now a retired professor of biology from the University of Alberta, identified them as Whooping Cranes. The nesting grounds were confirmed after a very difficult ground search in 1955. Their nesting territory lies between the headwaters of the Nyarling, Sass and Klewi Rivers in the northeast corner of the park.

CAUTION! You are not allowed directly into the area from spring until fall, but Whoopers can sometimes be seen from vantage points that are accessible. A 600 m height restriction exists for aircraft flying over the park north of Highway 5, as further protection for the birds. As of 1999, the birds have made a substantial recovery. There are currently around 183 adults, and 17 young were produced in that year. A population of 1000 individuals is the current management goal.

As one of the largest parks in the world, WBNP covers 48,807 km², straddling the Northwest Territories and Alberta border. Fort Smith, the park headquarters, sits just north of the Alberta border on Highway 5, in the NWT. Fort Smith, serviced by airlines if you wish to avoid the long drive from the south, is 30 km by road from the park. To reach the park by car, take one of the several roads in Alberta to the town of Peace River, then drive west 21 km to Highway 35 and north on 35 into the NWT. Proceed east on Highway 5 to Fort Smith and south into the park.

The Peace–Athabasca Delta is the best park birding area (even though it is in Alberta!). Access is difficult. By car, drive 145 km south from Fort Smith on a gravel and dirt road; take a canoe or powerboat up the Peace River for 8 km; hike about 15 km down an old road to get to the best areas. Or start from Fort Chipewyan and go into this and other delta areas. It is best to get local information and a local guide when you get to Fort Smith or Fort Chipewyan, but it is worth it! For detailed directions, a map and a list of professional guides and tour companies, contact the park staff. In the delta, a guide is almost indispensable. Several gravel roads provide ready access to parts of the park. Hiking trails have been constructed to allow additional exploration. The roadways, trails, rivers and lakes to explore are shown on special brochures available at the park office and information outlets.

No commercial accommodation exists within the park; however, Fort Smith contains hotels, as does Fort Chipewyan near the southeast end of the park (accessible only by boat from the NWT or by highway in Alberta). Pine Lake, a lovely spot 66 km south of Fort Smith, has a 36-site campground and a group site. Tenting and other primitive camping are allowed anywhere in the park as long as the site is beyond 1.5 km from Pine Lake or any road or trail. There is a campsite in the town of Fort Smith.

Park staff have prepared a checklist of the birds of Wood Buffalo, together with several brochures. For copies, write The Superintendent, Wood Buffalo National Park, Box 750, Fort Smith, Northwest Territories X0E 0P0; phone (867) 872-7900. Park staff are on duty all year to offer assistance.

Birding Features

Most of the park is boreal forest, but access will allow you to visit a variety of habitats. There are only a couple of roads in the entire park, so the specific spots you can go to are few and will be impossible to miss when you arrive in the park. Check out the most northerly area to see American Avocet at Grosbeak Lake or the portion of the salt plains that falls out of the park. Recent bird sightings of note include a Broad-winged Hawk near Hay Camp, a Mourning Dove at the Salt River and Upland Sandpiper at Parson's Tower.

The Peace–Athabasca Delta is one of the largest inland deltas in the world. Waters from the Peace, Athabasca and Birch Rivers converge here. Serious birders should endeavour to travel into it. This biologically rich area attracts hundreds of thousands of migrating birds from all four North American flyways each year. No other area in the park can compete with the delta for sheer numbers and variety of birdlife. Look for Great Blue Heron, almost all of the northern nesting species of geese, ducks, Golden and Bald Eagles, Osprey, Peregrine Falcon and owls, including Short-eared and Hawk. The recommended time to come to the delta, in fact to the whole park, is the last two weeks of May, before the bugs and leaves are out, alternatively the middle weeks of September. The most northerly colony of American White Pelican in North America occurs on rocky islands in the Slave River, near the town of Fort Smith.

BOB LEWIS
Revised by Craig Machtans

The Southern Northwest Territories: Yellowknife, the Mackenzie Highway and Surroundings

Yellowknife is the only city in the NWT. Owing to its large size, it has excellent services and amenities from which to base any birding trip. The immediate area is excellent for waterfowl, with both Great Slave Lake and countless other water bodies within driving, boating or hiking distance.

The first recorded visit by Europeans to the area was by Samuel Hearne in 1771. Gold was discovered on the shores of Great Slave Lake in 1934 and the city was born as a boom town. The population crashed during World War II, when six of the operating mines closed. A second major gold discovery in 1945 started another gold rush. Two gold mines still operate in the city limits, and the diamond industry is rapidly taking hold northeast of Yellowknife. However, it doesn't take more than 20 or 30 minutes of travel to feel like you are in relatively undisturbed wilderness.

Road access is via the Mackenzie Highway north from Peace River, Alberta. The road is paved all the way except the last 100 km, which is currently being upgraded to a straighter, paved road. Numerous territorial parks and campgrounds can be found along the way to break up the trip and start birdwatching before you get to Yellowknife. Alternative access is from northern B.C. via the (gravelled) Liard and Mackenzie Highways to Fort Providence. Buses to Edmonton depart daily, and scheduled daily air service links Edmonton directly to Yellowknife. A traveller into the area should carry extra gasoline, tires, fan belt and sleeping bag, since service centres are far apart.

Yellowknife has several hotels, and excellent restaurants with northern fare are found in several venues. Fred Henne Territorial Park, immediately adjacent

Parasitic Jaeger and Red-necked Phalarope

to the city, provides a camping place. A worthwhile stop in town is the Prince of Wales museum. Information on the area is available by writing NWT Tourism (see introduction).

Birding Features

Yellowknife. When you arrive in Yellowknife, you cannot miss Common Ravens, the official bird of this city. In spring and summer, mostly nonbreeders remain in town. When the adults and young arrive, later, is the best time to observe their antics. Take a stroll around Niven or Frame Lake, within the city, any time of year. Niven is especially good in spring when migrating shorebirds and waterfowl are drawn to the shallow, rich lake. If you are in town quite late in the fall or quite early in spring, interesting species tend to turn up around the open water near the power generating station on Jackfish Lake. In spring, the water at the bridge across the Yellowknife River tends to open early and draw in large flocks of birds. Also in spring, a small area called Willow Flats down by the big lake right in Yellowknife is often a fantastic spot for spring migrants. Throughout the spring and summer you can see breeding pairs of Red-necked Grebes on most local lakes. The Ingraham Trail is a gravel road that heads east of Yellowknife to several local cottage lakes and popular day hikes, such as Cameron Falls and Big Hill Lake. An excellent reference book on the local area is *Shield Country: Life and Times of the Oldest Piece of the Planet* (Red Deer Press). It was written by local naturalist Jamie Bastedo and has a bounty of information visitors will enjoy. He also recommends nearby David Lake as a good spot for birdwatching. Here you can expect to see four or five gull species.

When you arrive in town, stop at the Northern Frontier Visitors' Association, just off Highway 3, on the way into Yellowknife, near the Prince of Wales Northern Heritage Centre and the Legislative Assembly of the Northwest Territories. Here you will find everything you need to prepare for your stay, including maps, pamphlets, interpretive exhibits, souvenir merchandise and a reservation service for local tour operators.

Use Yellowknife as a base for boat trips such as down the Thelon River (see below).

West Mirage Islands, north arm of Great Slave Lake. The Mackenzie Highway enters the Precambrian Shield country of rocks and lakes near Rae and Edzo on the north arm of Great Slave Lake. All areas east of the lake are in shield country. Twenty-one kilometres south-southwest of Yellowknife, the West Mirage Islands are accessible from the city by boating out through Yellowknife Bay onto the "big lake." These 97 rocky outcrops contain a variety of terrestrial and lake habitats that result in a wide diversity of breeding birds. Sixty-five species have been reported from these islands. The cold waters of Great Slave Lake result in low arctic conditions, encouraging more northerly species to occur. Look for Greater Scaup, Red-breasted Merganser, Red-necked Phalarope, Parasitic Jaeger and Arctic Tern. California Gull and Caspian Tern occur here at the northern limit of their ranges. The big lake is one of the very few places where you can see four species of loons in one day: Pacific, Common, Arctic and Yellow-billed, though only the first three are confirmed breeders. A special cautionary note: Many of the species you'll see in these areas are ground nesting and highly sensitive to human disturbance. Exercise some restraint and try not to disturb the birds by spending time on the islands among their nests. For some extra information, see the brochure on Great Slave Lake from CWS on the page (www.mb.ec.gc.ca) under the Ecosystem heading.

Liard Highway and Fort Liard. This gravel road south to Fort Nelson, B.C., leaves the Mackenzie Highway just south of Fort Simpson and follows the Liard River. Along the way you will drive through progressively more impressive forests, until you think you are somewhere much farther south. Stop at Blackstone Provincial Park for a great place to see and hear many forest songbirds right from your tent and enjoy views of Nahanni Butte. Camping facilities are first rate. About 100 km farther south is the small community of Fort Liard. A newer hotel and general store provides amenities for the traveller. This area is the most species rich in the entire NWT. So far, over 150 different birds have been positively identified here, with the potential for at least another 10 and many migrants. Look for the most northerly presence of Barred Owl, Canada and Magnolia Warblers, Western Tanager and maybe a Broad-winged Hawk (six were seen in the summers of 1998 and 1999). Boreal species like the Palm Warbler, crossbills and Northern Hawk Owl are not difficult to find. The local forests, up to 35 m tall, will yield dozens of species, including at least 19 wood warblers for anyone willing to tromp through some alders. If you get taken into some of the local lakes, there is a chance to see Trumpeter Swans. While you are in Fort Liard, take a walk around Hay Lake, just outside the hamlet. A trail circumnavigates the lake and will treat you to the common birds of the area. Fort Liard seems to draw in the vagrants too. In 1998 a Northern Mockingbird stayed for the summer (by himself), and every year there seems to be at least one odd sighting, including Mourning Dove in 1999. Keep your eyes peeled for the unexpected. The town is undergoing a resource boom in recent years, so hotel space may be at a premium. Make sure you call ahead for a reservation to the Liard Valley General Store and Motel, (867) 770-4441.

Fort Providence. This community lies on the north bank of the Mackenzie River. Cross on the ferry in summer and on an ice bridge in winter. From Fort Providence you can take a canoe, boat or a bush road west, downstream to Mills Lake, at the junction of the Horn River. Mills Lake, a widening of the Mackenzie River, contains a large marsh and willow clumps on the north bank. In spring, depending on how much water is around (hope for low water levels), large groups of waterfowl congregate. You might see up to several thousand ducks, geese, swans and shorebirds on a good day. Depending on the spring, mid-May is often near the migration peak. In early spring, simply crossing on the ferry will turn up a few good birds – shorebirds often hang out on the pans of ice moving down the river and aren't too deterred by the ferry. In August and early September fall warblers abound; waterfowl arrive in September and October on their way south.

East from Fort Providence by boat, you can reach Beaver Lake and the beginning of the Mackenzie River at Great Slave Lake. This eastward trip should produce Red-necked Grebe and other water birds, Bald Eagle and Osprey. Concentrations of migrant Tundra Swan, Canvasback and other diving ducks gather at Beaver Lake and Deep Bay of Great Slave Lake in September and early October.

T. W. BARRY
Revised by Craig Machtans

Nahanni National Park Reserve

This valley of legends contains 91.5 m high Virginia Falls and hosts at least 170 species of birds (including migrants), of which 22 are year-round residents. A few Trumpeter Swans nest in the park, as do Golden and Bald Eagles; Gyrfalcon; Spruce, Blue and Ruffed Grouse; White-tailed Ptarmigan; and Northern Hawk Owl. Boreal Owls and both species of three-toed wood-peckers are permanent residents. Thirty-one mammal species have been recorded in the park. Grizzly and Black Bear are common; moose occur in the valleys; Dall Sheep are found sporadically in the alpine tundra areas with the densest population around Deadmen Valley; Woodland Caribou occupy the upper valleys of both the Flat and South Nahanni Rivers.

The park was established in 1971 and covers 4766 km² of the Northwest Territories, just east of the Yukon border. Access is by boat or float plane. Charter planes fly out of Fort Simpson, NWT (308 km east of Rabbit Kettle Lake), Fort Liard (see below), Watson Lake, Yukon (224 km southwest), and Fort Nelson, B.C., straight south. Information on these charter companies and outfitters operating in the park may be obtained by writing the park superin-tendent (see below).

Canoeing the South Nahanni and Flat Rivers has become a popular activ-ity. To assist hardy, adventuresome people, Parks Canada has prepared an excel-lent booklet dealing with the 300 km section of the South Nahanni that lies within the park. This material also describes a 128 km section of the Flat River from Seaplane Lake to its junction with the South Nahanni. Brief notes are provided on the human history, natural history and river characteristics such as gradients and canoeing grade.

Several hot springs, with accompanying beautiful tufa deposits and exotic vegetation, enhance the picture. Mean water temperatures in these pools are around 21°C, with seasonal variations. The Kraus Hot Springs beside Clausen Creek, near the eastern boundary of the park, contain two source pools where water as hot as 35° or 36°C bubbles up through fine mud.

Hiking trips in the park are increasing in popularity. Excursions range from a one-day outing to a week or more. Almost any tributary creek valley can be taken to explore wilderness. Higher elevation explorations can also be made. High-country trips include the tundra-like Tlogotsho and Nahanni plateaus and ridge walking, with the latter being some of the finest in Canada. Visitors also take the excellent excursion to Sunblood Mountain.

Park staff have prepared a brochure and bird list on the park. For this infor-mation, a list of outfitters and boating guides operating in the park, together with a list of charter companies to fly you in, write to The Superintendent,

Nahanni National Park, P.O. Box 348, Fort Simpson, Northwest Territories XOE ONO; phone (867) 695-3151.

Birding Features
The Nahanni contains birds from the more southerly Great Plains and foothills, such as Blue Grouse and Black Tern, and northern species such as Gyrfalcon and Arctic Tern. Trumpeter Swans have nested at Yohin Lake. Look for Bald Eagle near this lake too. You may also spot Arctic and Red-throated Loons, a wide variety of ducks, including such prairie species as Northern Shoveler and Redhead. Both goldeneye species are seen together with Osprey, and four species of grouse (Spruce, Blue, Ruffed and Sharp-tailed) nest here. Boreal species that breed in the park include Northern Hawk Owl and Boreal Owl, both species of three-toed woodpeckers, Common Raven, Boreal Chickadee and Gray-cheeked Thrush. When travelling through or near the deep canyons, watch for Peregrine Falcon and Black Swift, which are noted regularly. American Dipper can be spotted around white water. If you are only canoeing down the river, you will not be treated to so many species. Try to get to some areas of clearer water where raptors do more fishing and you'll be in other habitats.

Park wardens have recently begun regular bird surveys as part of a monitoring scheme. As a consequence, bird information for the park has steadily improved in recent years. Confirmed breeding records have recently been obtained for Mew Gull, Red-breasted Merganser and Townsend's Solitaire. New sighting records for the park include Canvasback, Dowitcher, Harlequin Duck, Whimbrel, Short-eared Owl and Tundra Swan. Much of the recent survey work has been in the Rabbitkettle Lake area, where 87 species were recorded in 1996. Contact park staff for recent bird information.

REVISED BY CRAIG MACHTANS

Oldsquaw Lodge (Mackenzie Mountain Barrens)

Over 130 species of birds have been recorded at this naturalist lodge beside the Canol Heritage Trail, including such northern specialties as Gyrfalcon, Long-tailed Jaeger, Smith's and Lapland Longspurs, Wandering Tattler, Willow, Rock, and White-tailed Ptarmigan, and of course the vocal Oldsquaw duck, from which the lodge draws its name.

Accessible by chartered flight from Whitehorse, this exclusive wilderness lodge caters to naturalists, birdwatchers, artists and photographers. Guided hikes are offered daily, catering to small groups and customized to accommodate different interests and abilities. The emphasis is on quality, coziness and personal attention in a serene environment. For more information, contact Oldsquaw Lodge, Box 10461, Whitehorse, Yukon Y1A 7A1; e-mail nbarichello @polarcom.com; phone (867) 668-6732; fax (867) 667-4769.

Birding Features
Set on a lake-dotted tundra plateau, known as the Mackenzie Mountain Barrens or Dechenla (Kaska Dena name meaning "land at the end of the

Gyrfalcon

sticks"), against a backdrop of peaks rising to 3000 m, the lodge is north of the 63rd latitude and 32 km northeast of the Yukon border. As a high elevation wetland underlain by permafrost, the Mackenzie Mountain Barrens emulate the arctic tundra, which is much farther north, and as such supports an impressive diversity of arctic birds, as well as the more typical subarctic nesters. It is noteworthy that this area is also home to the largest herd of woodland caribou in the world.

ROBERT FRISCH
Revised by Barb and Norman Barichello

Inuvik

Near the mouth of the Mackenzie River on the northern edge of the boreal forest and adjacent to arctic tundra, Inuvik certainly has a diversity of birdlife. Species usually spotted not too far away include Rough-legged Hawk, Golden and Bald Eagles, Peregrine Falcon, six gull species and Northern Hawk Owl; Northern Wheatear and Yellow Wagtail nest to the west and sometimes come into Inuvik; redpolls and Lapland Longspur are usually around. The abundant shrubby habitat in and near town is usually full of Yellow Warblers and White-crowned Sparrows.

The Mackenzie Delta has long been a meeting place for the Dene and Inuit peoples, who searched for food, and later for furs to fill the needs of the white traders. Inuvik means "place of the people" in the language of the local Inuit, the Inuvialuit. The first permanent settlement, Aklavik, was established on the west side of the delta in 1915 at the opening of a fur-trading post. However, because of unstable soil conditions, a new community, Inuvik, was carved out of the wilderness in 1955. The site, originally called East-3, had many factors in its favour: good river access, flat upland suitable for an airport, freedom from flooding, low ice content or permafrost in the soil, a good gravel deposit for road building and ready availability of fresh drinking water. Today the community is a government centre, base for oil exploration in the delta and Beaufort Sea, a transportation and communication centre, and the terminal point of the Dempster Highway, the first North American public road to cross the Arctic Circle. Utility lines are all above ground in a large boxlike structure called a utilidor.

The community of nearly 3300 people is one of the largest in the NWT. Flights come from Edmonton, via Yellowknife and Norman Wells, with daily service. The small community has all the amenities you would expect from a much larger centre, including numerous hotels and restaurants that cater to the tourist crowd. Other charter services fly into various communities from Inuvik. Boats can come down the Mackenzie River via the "east branch" of the delta. The hardy can arrive via the Alaska and Dempster highways via Whitehorse (1253 km away) – a definite adventure and a great way to see the north. Many companies operate from the community in the summer, so book well in advance if you require accommodation. In-town and near-town campgrounds offer alternative resting places for the hardy who wish to combat mosquitoes and black flies. These warriors come out in late June and are very aggressive until September, after the first frost.

Further information and help are available from the Western Arctic Regional Visitor's Centre, (867) 777-4727.

Inuvik can function as the jumping-off point for the far western Arctic, including Sachs Harbour with the two Banks Island bird sanctuaries, about 525 km northeast; Cape Parry Bird Sanctuary 410 km northeast; Anderson River Delta Bird Sanctuary about 240 km northeast (see below for descriptions); and, of course, the Yukon Arctic coast to the west, with several Asiatic nesting species (refer to the Yukon chapter). If you plan to visit any of the above, except the Yukon coast, you must have a permit from the Canadian Wildlife Service. Contact them in Yellowknife (see introduction).

Birding Features
Inuvik sits near the northern treeline in the Mackenzie Valley, with tundra close by. The valley acts as a migration corridor for northern species. A variety of habitats, including the open green spaces within the town and vicinity, attracts the birds. Visitors are usually impressed with the antics of the Common Raven, probably the most obvious bird year-round and the most abundant in winter. Visit the town dump at the east end, off the airport road in May and early June to check the six gull species: Glaucous, Herring, Thayer's, Mew, Bonaparte's and Sabine's. A trip to the sewage lagoon at the west end of town should produce 20 or more different species of shorebirds, especially in late May and June. Along the waterfront, from the "in town" airstrip next to the sewage lagoon, upstream of the commercial docks, you should expect a variety of large and small land birds. Many of these species are near the northern limit of their range. Varied Thrush and White-crowned and Fox Sparrows are heard here in spring.

Hike to the tundra above the northeast side of town for Hoary and Common Redpolls and Lapland Longspur nesting sites. Take a cab or convince a local birder to take you along the airport road and out to the Dempster Highway, then to Campbell Lake and beyond, even to Arctic Red River, 132 km south, for Northern Goshawk, Rough-legged Hawk, Golden and Bald Eagles, Peregrine Falcon, Merlin and Northern Hawk Owl.

With the delta so near the arctic coast, Alaska and Asia, there is an excellent chance of seeing rarities. In the past, species reported have included Ruff, Bar-tailed Godwit, Yellow and White Wagtail and the Northern Wheatear. Refer to Dempster Highway and Yukon coast accounts for these species and others.

T. W. BARRY
Revised by Craig Machtans

Tuktoyaktuk

Situated on the Arctic coast, Tuktoyaktuk (Tuk) allows a visitor to observe two, and sometimes three, loon species, numerous geese and ducks, including Common (Pacific race) and King Eiders, abundant shorebirds in spring, three species of jaeger, a variety of gulls and a diverse collection of land birds.

Tuk was established by "free traders," who eventually sold out to the Hudson's Bay Company. Located just east of the Mackenzie Delta, Tuk has an excellent harbour. Transportation companies long recognized the advantage of bringing goods down the Mackenzie River on barges and then transferring them to sea-going ships servicing the Arctic coast communities. With the construction of the DEW line site, and the school and nursing station in the mid-1950s, families from the region moved into the village. Oil exploration brought a boom economy, when Dome Petroleum, Esso Resources Canada and Gulf Canada set up their base camps here to explore the Beaufort Sea. Since then things have quieted down a bit, but there is still excellent potential for natural gas developments in the area. Today the community contains about 1000 people. There are two hotels in town, the Tuk Inn, (867) 977-2381, or the Pingo Park Lodge, (867) 977-2155. For local information, call the hamlet office, (867) 977-2286. Airplane is generally the way in, via scheduled service from Inuvik, though you could arrive via an ice road in the winter or boat in the summer. Guides and boats for a charter trip along the Beaufort Sea coast or into the Mackenzie Delta are available through the president of the Tuktoyaktuk Hunters and Trappers Association in Tuk. Local people still hunt the beluga or white whale during July and August.

Birding Features

The area in and around Tuk represents coastal tundra. Come in late May through the first three-quarters of June to observe both migrants and local breeders at their peak. The sea ice generally goes out in late June. Prior to that time, the tundra ponds are filled with meltwater, as are most of the lagoons along the beaches. Shorebirds arrive in their full breeding plumage then. You can witness their elaborate aerial courtships and hear them call, using sounds heard only on the breeding grounds – an experience never to be forgotten. Ponds and lakes hold Arctic and Red-throated Loons, with the occasional Yellow-billed Loon offshore to add to your list. Tundra Swan, geese and a variety of ducks are also present. Pomarine, Parasitic and Long-tailed Jaegers; Glaucous and Sabine's Gulls; and Arctic Tern are all observed moving through and around Tuk. From a charter plane or helicopter, you can spot Common and King Eiders along the edge of the shore-fast ice, migrating in May and June.

Buildings away from town are sometimes used for nesting by Rough-legged Hawk, an occasional Gyrfalcon and Common Raven. June and July are best for tundra-nesting land birds. Check for the "common" species, including Willow Ptarmigan, Semipalmated Plover, Whimbrel, Pectoral and Semipalmated Sandpiper, Hudsonian Godwit, Hoary and Common Redpolls and Lapland Longspur. Ponds around Tuk accumulate moulting waterfowl in July and August. Lagoons and ponds next to the airport often have Tundra Swan. Coastal lakes and lagoons near Toker Point, north of Tuk, host scaup, Oldsquaw and White-winged and Surf Scoters.

By early August, fall migration is well under way. Some species, such as American Golden-Plover and Pectoral Sandpiper, migrate east along the coast; Red Phalaropes move west instead. Late August and September bring Brant and Snow Geese past Tuk, on their way to staging areas in the Mackenzie and farther west to the Yukon coast.

T. W. BARRY
Revised by Craig Machtans

Rendezvous Lake Lodge

Located a few hundred kilometres east of Inuvik, just inside the treeline, is a new lodge that promises an excellent birding trip. Lac Rendezvous and area contain a mixture of species from the forests and the tundra, and boast a list of 132 species, 104 of which breed here! Special highlights include the facts that the lodge is in the only known breeding ground of the Eskimo Curlew, which may not yet be extinct; Short-billed Dowitchers are a very common nesting bird right behind the lodge; and there are 34 species of waterfowl, 26 species of shorebirds and 18 species of raptors, including tree-nesting Gyrfalcon. The local area also has significant opportunities for other wildlife viewing, including Wolverine, Grizzly Bear and Barren-ground Caribou. Access to the lodge is via a chartered aircraft from Inuvik (see above). Contact either Billy Jocobson at Box 182, Tuktoyaktuk, Northwest Territories XOE ICO; phone (867) 977-2406 or Joachim Obst at Box 1888, Yellowknife, Northwest Territories XIA 2P4; phone (867) 669-7084.

CRAIG MACHTANS

Bathurst Inlet and Lodge

This lodge is part of a tiny (and very traditional) Inuit community located north of the Arctic Circle in Canada's central Arctic. The Inuit residents of Bathurst Inlet and the Warner family have owned and operated the lodge for 30 years and continue to be on site every summer. You will be housed in comfort at one of the finest wilderness lodges in the world, and one of the first to specialize in ecotourism and natural history programming. A professional naturalist is on site. A pontoon boat tours the inlet, stopping often at favoured birding habitats. Regularly observed birds include nesting Peregrine Falcon; Gyrfalcon (some years); Golden Eagle; Rough-legged Hawk; Yellow-billed, Red-throated and Pacific Loons; jaegers; Common and sometimes King Eiders; Glaucous and Thayer's Gulls; Oldsquaw; and Tundra Swan. Short hikes near the boat or from the lodge usually reveal nesting Lapland Longspur, Horned Lark, Harris's Sparrow, Snow Bunting, Gray-cheeked Thrush, Red-necked Phalarope, Willow and sometimes Rock Ptarmigan, Hoary and Common Redpolls, and the Gamble's subspecies of White-crowned Sparrow, Baird's and Least Sandpipers; and Semipalmated Plover. Mammals you are likely to see include Barren-ground Caribou, Muskox, Arctic Wolf and Barren-ground Grizzly.

Complete lists of flora and fauna will be supplied on request. Contact Bathurst Inlet Lodge, P.O. Box 820, Yellowknife, Northwest Territories X1A 2N6; phone (867) 873-2595, fax (867) 920-4263; e-mail enquiry@ bathurstinletlodge.com; Web site www.bathurstinletlodge.com.

GLENN AND TRISH WARNER AND ESTHER BRADEN
Revised by Glen and Trish Warner

Cambridge Bay

The small town of Cambridge Bay is gaining popularity among birders. Probably owing to its ease of access (direct jet service from Yellowknife), the area is becoming more recognized as a good stop. Cambridge Bay is on the south-eastern tip of Victoria Island. The local area is arctic tundra, and a large variety of shorebirds breed here. This is the easiest location in the high Arctic to visit and find sites that have quite good birding. Look for Gryfalcon, Ruddy Turnstone, Baird's Sandpiper, Black-bellied Plover, Buff-breasted and Pectoral Sandpipers, Red and Red-necked Phalaropes, Semipalmated Plover and Sandpiper, Stilt Sandpiper and Whimbrel. There is potential for several other species as well. Iceland Gulls have been reported by one observer, as well as Sabine's Gulls, Yellow-billed Loons and other typical arctic species. As noted above, access is via jet from Yellowknife on a direct flight. Information for the local area, accommodations, etc., can be obtained from the Arctic Coast Visitor Centre in town, (867) 983-2224.

CRAIG MACHTANS

Rankin Inlet and Wager Bay

Rankin Inlet is a small community on the west coast of Hudson Bay. For the past 15 years, researchers here have been studying one of the densest popula-tions of tundra Peregrine Falcons in the world. The birds are easily viewed when in the area and are quite common at several other spots along the west shoreline of Hudson Bay. Other birds in the area making the trip worthwhile include Black Guillemot, Baird's Sandpiper, Common Eider, Dunlin, Semipalmated Plover, Rock Ptarmigan, Tundra Swan and many other water-fowl species. Access to Rankin Inlet is very easy. Major airline flights leave directly from Yellowknife in the west or go through Rankin Inlet on their way to Yellowknife from the east. Accommodations are available at the Siniktarvik Hotel, (867) 645-2807.

Rankin Inlet is also one access point for Wager Bay, an area currently expected to become another national park before long. The area was chosen to represent the Central Tundra Natural Region and is another good spot to see Gyrfalcons and peregrines. There is a well-regarded tourist lodge in the area, Sila Lodge, that can be reached in Manitoba, (204) 949-2050. Birders regularly turn up 10 to 15 species in an afternoon, including three loon species, both eiders, both falcons, Rough-Legged Hawk, Sandhill Crane, Black Guillemot and three gull species. CWS has records for Thick-billed Murre for the area as well.

CRAIG MACHTANS

National Wildlife Areas, Migratory Bird Sanctuaries and a Game Sanctuary

The Canadian Wildlife Service (CWS) (Department of the Environment) has the federal responsibility for protecting and managing migratory bird species. In the Canadian north, one way CWS does this is to protect important areas used by birds. Currently there are 15 sanctuaries in the NWT and Nunavut, and two National Wildlife Areas, with one more nearing the final stages of negotiation. You can be guaranteed of seeing many birds at each of these sites, though in some you might see tens of thousands of one species (like at a seabird colony on Coburg Island), or many individuals of several species (such as at Polar Bear Pass). Below is a quick list of some of the protected areas and the birds you will find if you have the opportunity to travel to these remote sites. Some of these spots are visited by cruise ships, whose staff arrange permits and all other logistical considerations, and usually provide a birding expert on board. If you are adventurous and wish to visit one of these places yourself, you will need a permit. For that and other information about the area you want to visit, contact the CWS office in the territory you will be visiting (see introduction for contact information and application deadlines).

For more information about the sanctuaries and National Wildlife Areas, go to the CWS regional home page (www.mb.ec.gc.ca) and look under the Wildlife Habitat Conservation area (www.mb.ec.gc.ca/ENGLISH/LIFE/ MIGBIRDS/SANCTUARIES). Alternatively, you can access the site via Environment Canada's Web site at www.ec.gc.ca

Birding Features

These sanctuaries lie either on the Arctic coast or on the Arctic islands. From west to east they include the following:

Anderson River Delta Bird Sanctuary. Lying about 240 km northeast of Inuvik, at the mouth of the Anderson River, the area contains the nesting grounds of an excellent collection of waterfowl and other water birds. These include Arctic and Red-throated Loons, Tundra Swan, Greater White-fronted Goose,

Snow Goose, Brant, and a variety of ducks, including Oldsquaw. Land birds include Rough-legged Hawk, Golden and Bald Eagles, Gyrfalcon, Harris's Sparrow, Thayer's Gull and Willow Ptarmigan. Shorebirds have ideal breeding habitat and include Hudsonian Godwit, Stilt and Least Sandpipers and Whimbrel. The European Starling first reached the Arctic coast at this site in 1963. You will see several species here at the northern edge of their ranges, such as American Robin, Northern Flicker and Green-winged Teal. The search for the probably extinct Eskimo Curlew continues here, but as yet there have not been any sightings. The hiking is quite difficult, so, like other remote areas, only the prepared should plan a trip here. Check out the account for Lac Rendezvous for an easier place to get to with similar species.

Cape Parry Bird Sanctuary. Approximately 400 km north and mainly east of Inuvik, the site lies out on the end of the cape. The area protects a colony of Thick-billed Murre, the only colony known in the western Canadian Arctic. So, if you cannot get to the eastern Arctic, this is the only location to see these birds on their nesting grounds. Birds appear to be attracted here because of the breakup of sea ice in June near the nesting cliffs. The open water also draws in migrating loons, Oldsquaw and eiders.

Banks Island's Two Sanctuaries and Sachs Harbour. The one on the west side is the larger sanctuary, the one at the north end being a thin sliver (now wholly contained within Aulavik National Park). These two sanctuaries, 480 km north of the Arctic Circle, host a large number of waterfowl species similar to those at Kendall Island and Anderson River. The community of Sachs Harbour (pop. 135) is a perfect base to search for nesting Snow Geese (the population of geese within the lower sanctuary is currently about a half million birds), three jaeger species, Sandhill Crane and Snowy Owl. Ross's Geese also occur in the area in low numbers. Common mammals include Polar Bear, Muskox (nearly 50,000 roam the island), Arctic Fox and Wolf. Peary Caribou are becoming extremely rare in the area, so do not expect to see them. If you are interested in plants, the flora north of the 72nd parallel is unsurpassed. Local guides can take you out on the land from Sachs Harbour, and unless you charter an air-craft, this is probably the best way to see areas farther away from town. Excellent accommodations are available at Kuptana's Guest House, (867) 690-4151. Sachs Harbour is serviced by scheduled air flights from Inuvik. Contact Aklak Air for schedule information, (867) 777-3777.

Polar Bear Pass National Wildlife Area. Created in 1986, this NWA has had a long history of research. The National Museum of Canada started operating a research station here in 1968. The now abandoned structure still stands on the northern bank of the pass, overlooking the wetland where many bird species may be found. So far, 54 species have been seen here, including 30 known to breed. Depending on the year, it can be a fantastic spot to see Snowy Owls – from one spot in 1998 there were 12 visible! The wetlands generally contain a large variety of waterfowl, including Red-throated Loon and King Eider. Sixteen species of shorebirds have been recorded, including Black-bellied

Plover, Ruddy Turnstone, Red Knot, Sanderling, Purple Sandpiper and Red Phalarope. Of special interest is that you may be viewing birds from European populations or from Central and South American populations. Banding returns indicate both areas are used by birds in Polar Bear Pass.

Access is via a chartered aircraft from Resolute (see below), some 120 km away – a short flight and probably one of your best bets for a relatively accessible high arctic visit. Because of the local topographic relief, the area is quite stunning and numerous interesting spots are accessible by half-day hikes, including some interesting prehistoric reef remnants that look like standing stones. For large mammals, Bathurst Island has some Muskox, but the population of Peary Caribou has declined to near extinction in recent years.

Queen Maud Gulf Bird Sanctuary. Sitting on the coast nearly 1000 km northeast of Yellowknife, this 62,000 km² wetland of international importance contains several extensive nesting colonies of breeding Snow and Ross's Geese. Approximately 99% of the world's population of Ross's Geese nest here; the latest estimate was that the birds numbered close to a million. There is no shortage of the rapidly expanding Snow Geese either, recently estimated at about 2 million birds! When the first edition of this book was released, the population was estimated to be less than 50,000. The presence of such a large population is affecting the local habitat rather substantially, and more news is available by searching the Web. Forty-seven bird species and six mammal species have been spotted. The Ellice River area on the west side is a critical calving site for the Bathurst herd of Barren-ground Caribou. The site is only 75 km south of Cambridge Bay (see above), so access would be by charter from that community. The current operator is Adlair Aviation, (867) 983-2569.

McConnell River Bird Sanctuary and Arviat. Located on the west central shore of Hudson Bay, about 90 km north of the Manitoba border, this reserve of 32,800 ha is only 27 km south of Arviat and 230 km north of Churchill. Arviat is the home of the Inuit Cultural Institute, established to preserve Inuit culture. The small community is still rich in tradition. Locally, before going to the bird sanctuary, you can expect to see a number of species, including Common Eider, a large variety of shorebirds and other waterfowl. In fact, any of the communities along the west shore of Hudson Bay will provide rewarding birding experiences. The Snow Goose colony at McConnell River has undergone rapid growth. First reports of geese nesting here were in 1930; in 1975 their numbers were estimated at 320,000 breeding birds and the current estimate is that after more increases, the population has since decreased. Other abundant nesting species include Oldsquaw and Common and King Eiders; Willow Ptarmigan breed and Rock Ptarmigan are winter migrants; all three jaegers are common breeders; several other land birds nest, including Lapland Longspur and Snow Bunting. Access to the area is via Rankin Inlet (see above). The scheduled flights into Rankin from the west are three days per week, and from there you can get to and from Arviat on scheduled service. Local accommodation in Arviat is available at the Padlei Inns North, (867) 857-2919 or Ralph's Bed and Breakfast, (867) 857-2653.

Dewey Soper Bird Sanctuary. Sitting on the southwest side of Baffin Island, this 815,900 ha reserve is named after the man who first found the nesting grounds of the blue phase of the Snow Goose. The reserve lies about 340 km north-west of Iqaluit. This is another area where some of the largest colonies of geese in the world exist. Make the trip here after the birds have completed nesting and are moving around to feed and build up strength for their southern flight. Mid-July is the time to arrive. You won't disturb their nesting, but rather will see the families feeding on the plateau. At the same time, you will observe what is probably the most important nesting area for Brant in the eastern Arctic. Other numerous species include the Canada Goose, Oldsquaw, eiders and several species of shorebirds. They are concentrated on the west side of the sanctuary around Cape Dominion. Some of the other birds to look for include Arctic and Red-throated Loons, Tundra Swan, both eiders, Willow and Rock Ptarmigans, a variety of shorebirds, including Purple Sandpiper, three jaeger species and the normal upland birds as mentioned in other spots above.

Thelon Game Sanctuary. Located northeast about 600 km from Yellowknife, this sanctuary can be travelled through by canoe. The river is one of the country's most desired paddles. On a trip on the river in late June and July, if you are lucky, you may spot all four species of loon. In addition, you should be able to locate Tundra Swan, the larger and smaller races of Canada Goose, Greater White-fronted Goose, both the white and blue colour phases of Snow Goose, Rough-legged Hawk, Golden and Bald Eagles, Gyrfalcon, Peregrine Falcon, Merlin, Snowy and Short-eared Owls, and possibly American Kestrel. A sur-prisingly wide variety of tundra and treeline bird species are also observed on such a voyage. Several companies cater to trips along the Thelon, one of which is Air Thelon. Contact them in Yellowknife at (867) 920-7110 or e-mail them at tundra@thelon.com This area is not a Migratory Bird Sanctuary, so no permit is required from CWS for access.

T. W. BARRY
Revised by Craig Machtans

Other National Parks

Since the previous edition, five new national parks or reserves have been created: Quttinirpaaq (Ellesmere Island), Auyuittuq (eastern Baffin Island), Sirmilik, (northern Baffin Island) in the east and Aulavik (northern Banks Island) and Tuktut Nogait (mainland coast) in the west. None of these areas were created specifically because of fantastic birds, but they all offer excellent opportunities to see birds and other wildlife. And since there are now parks where there weren't, you can expect to find more information about the areas and a certain amount of infrastructure or on-site staff depending on where you are or when you travel. In short, the creation of these areas has made them a natural destination for anyone wishing to see arctic wildlife. In addition, several new parks are currently being proposed, including ones at Wager Bay (see account in this chapter) and northern Bathurst Island. A brief explanation of some of the highlights of these new parks is offered below. Anyone planning on visiting in the eastern Arctic can contact the regional warden office in Pangnirtung at (867) 473-8828, e-mail nunavut_info@pch.gc.ca or snail mail at Box 353, Pangnirtung, Nunavut X0A 0R0. For the other parks in the west, contact information is provided below.

Before planning a trip to any of these areas, it is advisable to contact the local warden office for the most up-to-date information. Good information on all the northern parks can be found on the Parks Canada Web site (parkscanada.pch.gc.ca)

Tuktut Nogait National Park. This new park is over 400 km east of Inuvik, near the community of Paulatuk. Some of the species in the park are the same as those described under the Anderson River Sanctuary account, but the more easterly location of the park moves it above treeline. As a result, tundra-nesting species can be found in the park, as are raptors including Gyrfalcon and Peregrine Falcon, Golden Eagle, Tundra Swan, Least Sandpiper and Horned Lark. The park is not known as a birding hot spot, except for peregrine on the cliffs of the Hornaday River. Access is via charter from Inuvik (see above) or by boat from the community. Parks Canada also suggests that you may hike the 45 km to the park, though you will be crossing private lands and should seek permission for such passage from the Inuvialuit Land Administration. Contact Parks Canada for details in Paulatuk, (867) 580-3233.

Aulavik National Park. Located on the north end of Banks Island, this national park also encompasses a CWS Migratory Bird Sanctuary. The sanctuary was created to protect moulting areas of Snow Geese and Brant. Seeing the large groups of flightless birds running along the tundra is always amazing – there is little doubt that they could outrun almost anyone. Over 40 species of birds have been recorded in the sanctuary area. Recent surveys by park wardens indicate that some of the most common species include Rough-legged Hawk, Glaucous Gull, Black-bellied Plover, Sandhill Crane, Lapland Longspur and Yellow-billed Loon. Travellers to the park usually canoe down the Thompson River, notable as Canada's most northerly navigable river. Access to the park is via Inuvik (see above) and then by charter aircraft, as the aircraft has to be able to land without a formal airstrip (the scheduled service to Sachs Harbour cannot take you to the park and there are no air companies locally). The park office in Sachs can be contacted at (867) 690-3904.

Sirmilik National Park Reserve. The new park would include portions of northern Baffin Island east of Borden Peninsula and all of Bylot Island. Coincidentally, Bylot Island is already a Migratory Bird Sanctuary administered by CWS. Bylot Island has large colonies of Thick-billed Murres (hundreds of thousands) and Black-legged Kittiwakes (tens of thousands), and in the lowlands supports a large population of Snow Geese. Thirty bird species breed on the island, and another 20 have been seen there. Plan on spotting Northern Wheatear, Northern Fulmar, Red Knot and many other shorebird species. This island is a typical stop for the arctic cruise ships that were mentioned in the introduction. CWS has records of Dovekie for the area, reported by cruise-ship staff.

Quttinirpaaq National Park Reserve. This park contains one of the true high arctic oases, Lake Hazen and the adjacent areas. Surrounded by rugged mountains and ice caps, the largest lake in the high Arctic forms a thermal oasis where vegetation and, consequently, animal life is much richer than in nearby other regions. Spectacular is an understatement.

For birds, you can expect to see only those hardy species willing to make a go of it near the top of the world. The park species list is currently at 30, including those you may see such as Common-Ringed Plover, Red Knot, Gyrfalcon, Arctic Tern, Sanderling and Glaucous Gull. Access to the area is via a chartered aircraft from Resolute (see below). Parks Canada estimates the average cost of the drop-off and pick-up to be about $27,000 (if one person paid the whole cost), so the price is reasonable only if you have a large group (up to 10 can fit in the aircraft) or if you do not have financial constraints.

CRAIG MACHTANS

Resolute Bay (Cornwallis Island)

Resolute, the nearest community to the north magnetic pole, served as a harbour during the Franklin searches of the mid-1800s. A joint U.S.–Canadian airstrip and weather station was opened in 1947. Inuit were relocated from other parts of the Arctic to this site in 1953. Today the community of 200 people serves as a staging area for oil and gas exploration and scientific expeditions in the arctic islands. Ivory and Ross's Gulls have nested near Resolute Bay. A trip here, when combined with chartering a plane for exploration, is very expensive. If money is no problem, you can come and see large numbers of Northern Fulmar, Greater Snow Goose, Thick-billed Murre, Glaucous and Thayer's Gulls, Black-legged Kittiwake and Black Guillemot.

Perhaps the most striking feature of Resolute for first-time visitors is the starkness of the landscape. The settlement is located in an area that is dominated by gravel, so much so that green plants and vegetated tundra are not within easy walking distance. Unless you are arriving here only to say you have been this far north, plan on paying for a charter to take you to a more lush and bird-rich area – there are several nearby (see below). If you are only able to fly to a northern community with regular jet service because of budgetary restrictions, you might do better to shorten the trip and spend your time around Cambridge Bay or another arctic community with better local birding.

There are several places to stay in Resolute, some out at the airport in the industrial section of town (Narwhal Hotel, [867] 252-3968), and some right in the hamlet, some 10 km away (Qausuittuq Inns North, [867] 252-3900 and South Camp Inn, [867] 252-3737). The Quasuittuq Inn is the newest, but all are very good places to stay. The local territorial wildlife officer is often a good contact for information about the area, (867) 252-3879, but you are very apt to run into birders or people with interest in birds through staff at your hotel or at the research base (Polar Continental Shelf) near the airport. The community has a small store if you need some essentials, but it would be best to arrive completely prepared for your whole trip. Access to Resolute has recently been reduced to a single airline, First Air. Flights are only once or twice per week, depending on whether you connect via Yellowknife or Iqaluit.

Birding Features

The birding right in and around Resolute is not that spectacular, as the site description above might indicate. If you are constrained to the very local area, try going north of the airport, and just west of the garbage dump to Allen Bay. There you can see species that include Black-legged Kittiwake, jaegers, Glaucous Gull, Sanderling, Purple Sandpiper, Baird's Sandpiper and Oldsquaw. Otherwise, you are mainly restricted to birding along the ocean-front near the community which can be highly variable for the effort put in.

To view the uniqueness of the high Arctic, charter an aircraft and visit the seabird colonies, east on Lancaster Sound. The closest site to Resolute Bay, Prince Leopold Island, lies about 160 km east and a bit south, off the north-eastern coast of Somerset Island. Sheer cliffs on Prince Leopold contain colonies of Northern Fulmar, Black-legged Kittiwake and Thick-billed Murre; talus slopes are the nest sites for Black Guillemot; crests of cliffs contain Glaucous and Thayer's Gulls. Then fly south to Creswell Bay on nearby Somerset Island where Greater Snow Goose breed. The expansive sedge lowlands on the north side of the bay are rich with shorebird species, including Pectoral, White-rumped and Buff-breasted Sandpipers; both large plovers; and Red Phalarope. Additionally, you might see Red Knot, Rough-legged Hawk, Ruddy Turnstone, Sabine's Gull and lots of Lapland Longspurs. Creswell Bay is also fairly well known for its concentration of Polar Bears when the bay is still iced over. After the ice clears, whale-watching charters visit the area, and if they land, there are significant archaeological sites to visit and a great run of Arctic Char at the head of the bay in the Union River.

Resolute is also the access point for Polar Bear Pass National Wildlife Area described previously.

T. W. BARRY
Revised by Craig Machtans

APPENDIX

CHECKLIST OF THE BIRDS OF CANADA

B – Breeding
X – Present and usually migrant
★ – Vagrant, accidental or very few records
La = Newfoundland but Labrador only

	BC	AB	SK	MB	ON	PQ	NB	NS	PEI	NF	YK	NWT	NU
Number of Species	481	383	371	377	471	421	391	441	337	371	278	268	181
Red-throated Loon	B	B	B	B	B	B	X	X	X	B	B	B	B
Pacific Loon	B	B	X	B	B	B	★	★	★	★	B	B	B
Common Loon	B	B	B	B	B	B	B	B	B	B	B	B	B
Yellow-billed Loon	X	★	★	★	★	★					X	B	B
Pied-billed Grebe	B	B	B	B	B	B	B	B	B	★	B	B	
Horned Grebe	B	B	B	B	B	B	X	X	X	★	B	B	B
Red-necked Grebe	B	B	B	B	B	B	X	X	X	★	B	B	
Eared Grebe	B	B	B	B	B	★		★			★	B	
Western Grebe	B	B	B	B	★			★			★		
Clark's Grebe	B	B	B	B									
Yellow-nosed Albatross						★	★	★					
Black-browed Albatross								★	★				
Laysan Albatross	★												
Black-footed Albatross	X												
Short-tailed Albatross	★												
Northern Fulmar	B				★	X	X	X	★	B		B	B
Mottled Petrel	★												
Murphy's Petrel	★												
Black-capped Petrel					★			★					
Cory's Shearwater								X		★			
Pink-footed Shearwater	X												
Flesh-footed Shearwater	X												
Greater Shearwater					★	X	X	X	X	X		★?	★?
Buller's Shearwater	X												
Sooty Shearwater	X					X	X	X	X	X		★?	★?
Short-tailed Shearwater	X												
Manx Shearwater						X	X	X		B			
Black-vented Shearwater	★												
Audubon's Shearwater					★			★	★				

433

	BC	AB	SK	MB	ON	PQ	NB	NS	PEI	NF	YK	NWT	NU
Little Shearwater								★					
Wilson's Storm-Petrel					★	X	X	X	X	★		★?	★?
White-faced Storm-Petrel								★					
European Storm-Petrel								★					
Fork-tailed Storm-Petrel	B												
Leach's Storm-Petrel	B				★	B	B	B	X	B			
Band-rumped Storm-Petrel				★									
White-tailed Tropicbird								★					
Red-tailed Tropicbird	★												
Brown Booby								★					
Northern Gannet				★	★	B	X	X	X	B		★	★
American White Pelican	B	B	B	B	B	★	★	★	★	★		B	
Brown Pelican	X				★	★		★					
Brandt's Cormorant	B												
Double-crested Cormorant	B	B	B	B	B	B	B	B	B	B	B		B
Great Cormorant					★	B	X	B	B	B			
Red-faced Cormorant	★												
Pelagic Cormorant	B												
Anhinga					★								
Magnificent Frigatebird	★				★			★		★			
American Bittern	B	B	B	B	B	B	B	B	B	B		B	B
Least Bittern	★		★	B	B	B	B	★	★	★			
Great Blue Heron	B	B	B	B	B	B	B	B	B	★	X	B	★
Great Egret	★	★	B	B	B	B	X	X	★	★		★	★
Little Egret						★	★	★		★			
Snowy Egret	★	★	★	X	B	★	X	X	★	★		★	★
Little Blue Heron	★	★	★	★	X	★	★	X	★	★			
Tricolored Heron		★		★	X	★	★	X		★			
Reddish Egret													
Cattle Egret	X	★	B	X	B	★	X	X	★	★		★	★
Green Heron	B	★	★	★B	B	B	X	X	★	★			
Black-crowned Night-Heron	B	B	B	B	B	B	B	B	★	★			

	BC	AB	SK	MB	ON	PQ	NB	NS	PEI	NF	YK	NWT	NU
Yellow-crowned Night-Heron		★		★	X	★	★	X	★	★			
White Ibis				★	★	★	★	★		★			
Glossy Ibis				★	★	★	★	X	★	★			
White-faced Ibis	★	B	★	★	★	★							
Wood Stork	★				★	★	★						
Greater Flamingo							★	★		★			
Black Vulture	★				★	★	★	★	★	★La	★		
Turkey Vulture	B	B	B	B	B	B	B	X	★	★	★		
Black-bellied Whistling-Duck					★	★		★					
Fulvous Whistling-Duck	★				X	★	★	★	★				
Bean Goose						★					★		
Pink-footed Goose						★				★			
Greater White-fronted Goose	X	★	X	X	X	★	★	★	X	★	B	B	B
Emperor Goose	X												
Snow Goose	X	★	X	B	B	X	X	X	X	★	B	B	B
Ross's Goose	X	★	X	B	B	X	★					B	B
Canada Goose	B	B	X	B	B	B	B	B	B	B	B	B	B
Brant	X	★	★	X	X	X	X	X	X	★	B	B	B
Barnacle Goose						★		★		★			★
Mute Swan	B			★	B	★B	★						
Trumpeter Swan	B	B	B	X	★	★					B	B	X
Tundra Swan	X	B	B	B	B	B	★	★	★	★	B	B	B
Whooper Swan	★					★							
Wood Duck	B	B	B	B	B	B	B	B	B	X	★		★
Gadwall	B	B	B	B	B	B	B	B	B	★	B	B	★
Falcated Duck	★												
Eurasian Wigeon	X	X	X	X	X	X	X	X	X	★	X	★	
American Wigeon	B	B	B	B	B	B	B	B	B	B	B	B	B
American Black Duck	B	B	B	B	B	B	B	B	B	B			B
Mallard	B	B	B	B	B	B	B	B	B	X	B	B	B
Blue-winged Teal	B	B	B	B	B	B	B	B	B	B	B	B	X
Cinnamon Teal	B	B	B	X	★B	★	★	★			X		
Northern Shoveler	B	B	B	B	B	B	B	B	B	B	B	B	B
Northern Pintail	B	B	B	B	B	B	B	B	B	B	B	B	B

	BC	AB	SK	MB	ON	PQ	NB	NS	PEI	NF	YK	NWT	NU
Garganey	★	★		★	★	★	★	★	★	★			
Baikal Teal	★												
Green-winged Teal	B	B	B	B	B	B	B	B	B	B	B	B	B
Canvasback	B	B	B	B	B	X	★	★	★	★	B	B	
Redhead	B	B	B	B	B	B	★	★	B	★	B	B	X
Ring-necked Duck	B	B	B	B	B	B	B	B	B	B	B	B	X
Tufted Duck	X			★	★	★	X	★	★				
Greater Scaup	B	X	B	B	B	B	B	X	B	B	B	B	B
Lesser Scaup	B	B	B	B	B	B	X	X	X	★	B	B	B
Steller's Eider	★					★							
Spectacled Eider	★												
King Eider	★	★	★	B	B	B	X	X	★	★	B	B	B
Common Eider	★		★	B	B	B	B		X	B	B	B	B
Harlequin Duck	B	B	★	X	X	B	B	X	X	B	B	B	★
Surf Scoter	B	B	B	B	B	B	X	X	X	X	B	B	X
White-winged Scoter	B	B	B	B	B	B	X	X	X	X	B	B	X
Black Scoter	X	★	★	B	X	B	X	X	X	B	★		X
Oldsquaw	B	X	★	B	B	B	X	X	X	X	B	B	B
Bufflehead	B	B	B	B	B	B	X	X	X	X	B	B	B
Common Goldeneye	B	B	B	B	B	B	B	B	X	B	B	B	X
Barrow's Goldeneye	B	B	X	X	X	B	X	X	X	X	B	B	X
Smew	★			★		?							
Hooded Merganser	B	B	B	B	B	B	B	B	B	B	X	★	B
Common Merganser	B	B	B	B	B	B	B	B	B	B	B	B	B
Red-breasted Merganser	B	B	B	B	B	B	B	B	B	B	B	B	B
Ruddy Duck	B	B	B	B	B	B	B	B	X	★	B	B	
Osprey	B	B	B	B	B	B	B	B	B	B	B	B	B
Swallow-tailed Kite					★			★					
White-tailed Kite	★												
Mississippi Kite			★		★			★					
Bald Eagle	B	B	B	B	B	B	B	B	B	B	B	B	B
Northern Harrier	B	B	B	B	B	B	B	B	B	B	B	B	B
Sharp-shinned Hawk	B	B	B	B	B	B	B	B	B	B	B	B	
Cooper's Hawk	B	B	B	B	B	B	B	B	X	★			
Northern Goshawk	B	B	B	B	B	B	B	B	B	B	B	B	
Red-shouldered Hawk			★	X	B	B	B	X	★				
Broad-winged Hawk	B	B	B	B	B	B	B	B	B		★	B?	
Swainson's Hawk	B	B	B	B	★	★		★	★	★	X	X	
Zone-tailed Hawk								★					
Red-tailed Hawk	B	B	B	B	B	B	B	B	B	★	B	X	
Ferruginous Hawk	B	B	B	B	★								
Rough-legged Hawk	X	X	X	B	B	B	X	X	X	B	B	B	B
Golden Eagle	B	B	B	X	B	B	X	X	★	★	B	B	X

	BC	AB	SK	MB	ON	PQ	NB	NS	PEI	NF	YK	NWT	NU
Crested Caracara					★								
Eurasian Kestrel	★						★	★					
American Kestrel	B	B	B	B	B	B	B	B	B	B	B	B	B
Merlin	B	B	B	B	B	B	B	B	B	B	B	B	B
Gyrfalcon	B	X	X	X	X	B	X	X	X	X	B	B	B
Peregrine Falcon	B	B	B	B	B	B	B	B	X	X	B	B	B
Prairie Falcon	B	B	B	X	★								
Chukar	B		B										
Gray Partridge	B	B	B	B	B	B	★	B	B				
Ring-necked Pheasant	B	B	B	B	B	★B	B	B	X				
Ruffed Grouse	B	B	B	B	B	B	B	B	B	B	B	B	
Sage Grouse		B	B										
Spruce Grouse	B	B	B	B	B	B	B	B		B	B	B	B
Willow Ptarmigan	B	B	★	B	B	B				B	B	B	B
Rock Ptarmigan	B		★	X	★	B		★		B	B	B	B
White-tailed Ptarmigan	B	B									B	B	
Blue Grouse	B	B									B	B	
Sharp-tailed Grouse	B	B	B	B	B	B			B		B	B	
Greater Prairie-Chicken			★										
Wild Turkey	B	B	B	B	B	B							
Mountain Quail	★												
California Quail	B												
Northern Bobwhite					B	★							
Yellow Rail	★	B	B	B	B	B	B	★	★			B	B
Black Rail					★			★					
Corn Crake								★		★			★
Clapper Rail							★	★		★			
King Rail				★	B	★	★	★	★	★			
Virginia Rail	B	B	B	B	B	B	B	B	B	B		X	
Sora	B	B	B	B	B	B	B	B	B	B	B	B	
Purple Gallinule					★	★	★	★		★			
Common Moorhen	★			★	B	B	B	B	X	★			
Eurasian Coot						★				★			
American Coot	B	B	B	B	B	B	B	B	B	★	B	B	
Limpkin								★					
Sandhill Crane	B	B	B	B	B	B	★	★	★	★	B	B	B
Common Crane		★				★					★		
Whooping Crane	★	B	X	X	★							B	
Northern Lapwing						★	★	★	★	★			★

	BC	AB	SK	MB	ON	PQ	NB	NS	PEI	NF	YK	NWT	NU
Black-bellied Plover	X	X	X	X	X	X	X	X	X	X	X	B	B
European Golden-Plover						★		★		★			
American Golden-Plover	B	X	X	B	B	X	X	X	X	X	B	B	B
Pacific Golden-Plover	★	★											
Mongolian Plover	★	★			★								
Snowy Plover	★	★	★		★						★		
Wilson's Plover					★			★	★				
Common Ringed Plover						★		★	★	★		B?	B
Semipalmated Plover	B	B	B	B	B	B	X	B	B	B	B	B	B
Piping Plover		B	B	B	B	B	B	B	B	B			
Killdeer	B	B	B	B	B	B	B	B	B	B	B	B	B
Mountain Plover		B	★										
Eurasian Oystercatcher										★			
American Oystercatcher					★	★	★	B	★				
Black Oystercatcher	B												
Black-necked Stilt	★	B	★	★	★		★	★	★	★			
American Avocet	B	B	B	B	B	★	★	★	★			★	
Common Greenshank						★		★		★			
Greater Yellowlegs	B	B	B	B	B	B	X	B	X	B	X	B	X
Lesser Yellowlegs	B	B	B	B	B	B	X	X	X	X	B	B	X
Common Redshank										★			
Spotted Redshank	★				★			★		★			
Wood Sandpiper	★									★	★		
Solitary Sandpiper	B	B	B	B	B	B	B	X	X	★	B	B	B
Willet	X	B	B	B	X	★	B	B	B	B	★	★	
Wandering Tattler	B	★		★	★						B	B	
Spotted Sandpiper	B	B	B	B	B	B	B	B	B	B	B	B	B
Terek Sandpiper	★												
Upland Sandpiper	B	B	B	B	B	B	B	X	B	★	B	B	
Eskimo Curlew					★			★	★			B?	
Whimbrel	X	X	X	B	B	X	X	X	X	X	B	B	X
Little Curlew										★			
Bristle-thighed Curlew	★												
Far Eastern Curlew	★												
Slender-billed Curlew					★								
Eurasian Curlew						★		★		★			
Long-billed Curlew	B	B	B	X	★	★	★	★	★				
Black-tailed Godwit					★	★			★	★			
Hudsonian Godwit	B	X	X	B	B	X	X	X	X	X	X	B	B
Bar-tailed Godwit	★					★		★		★	★		
Marbled Godwit	X	B	B	B	B	X	★	★	★	★	★	★	B

	BC	AB	SK	MB	ON	PQ	NB	NS	PEI	NF	YK	NWT	NU
Ruddy Turnstone	X	X	X	X	X	X	X	X	X	X	B		B
Black Turnstone	X										★	B	

	BC	AB	SK	MB	ON	PQ	NB	NS	PEI	NF	YK	NWT	NU
Surfbird	X	★									B		
Great Knot	★												
Red Knot	X	X	X	X	X	X	X	X	X	X	★	B	X
Sanderling	X	X	X	X	X	X	X	X	X	X	X	B	B
Semipalmated Sandpiper	X	X	X	B	B	B	X	X	X	X	B	B	B
Western Sandpiper	X	X	X	X	X	★	★	X	X	★	X	X	
Red-necked Stint	★	★				★							
Little Stint	★				★		★	★			★		
Temminck's Stint	★												
Least Sandpiper	B	B	B	B	B	B	X	B	X	B	B	B	B
White-rumped Sandpiper	★	X	X	X	X	X	X	X	X	X	X	B	B
Baird's Sandpiper	B	X	X	X	X	X	X	X	X	★	B	B	B
Pectoral Sandpiper	X	X	X	B	B	X	X	X	X	X	B	B	B
Sharp-tailed Sandpiper	X	★			★	★					X		
Purple Sandpiper			★	★	X	X	X	X	X	X		B	B
Rock Sandpiper	X		★										
Dunlin	X	X	X	B	B	X	X	X	X	X	X	B	B
Curlew Sandpiper	★	★	★	★	★	★	★	★	★	★			
Stilt Sandpiper	X	X	X	B	B	X	X	X	★	★	B	B	B
Spoonbill Sandpiper	★	★											
Buff-breasted Sandpiper	X	X	X	X	X	X	X	X	X	★	B	B	B
Ruff	★	★	★	★	★	X	★	X	★	★			

	BC	AB	SK	MB	ON	PQ	NB	NS	PEI	NF	YK	NWT	NU
Short-billed Dowitcher	B	B	B	B	B	B	X	X	X	X	B	B	
Long-billed Dowitcher	X	X	X	X	X	X	X	X	★		B	B	

	BC	AB	SK	MB	ON	PQ	NB	NS	PEI	NF	YK	NWT	NU
Jack Snipe										★La			
Common Snipe	B	B	B	B	B	B	B	B	B	B	B	B	B

	BC	AB	SK	MB	ON	PQ	NB	NS	PEI	NF	YK	NWT	NU
Eurasian Woodcock										★			
American Woodcock			★	B	B	B	B	B	B	B			

	BC	AB	SK	MB	ON	PQ	NB	NS	PEI	NF	YK	NWT	NU
Wilson's Phalarope	B	B	B	B	B	B	B	X	X	★	B	B?	
Red-necked Phalarope	B	B	B	B	B	B	X	X	X	X	B	B	B
Red Phalarope	X	X	★	X	X	B	X	X	★	X	B	B	B

	BC	AB	SK	MB	ON	PQ	NB	NS	PEI	NF	YK	NWT	NU
Great Skua						?	★	X	★	X			
South Polar Skua	★						★	X		X			
Pomarine Jaeger	X	★	★	X	X	B	X	X	X	X	X	B	B
Parasitic Jaeger	X	X	★	B	B	B	X	X	X	X	B	B	B
Long-tailed Jaeger	X	★	★	X	★	B	★	★		X	B	B	B

	BC	AB	SK	MB	ON	PQ	NB	NS	PEI	NF	YK	NWT	NU
Laughing Gull	★			★	X	★	X	X	★	★			

	BC	AB	SK	MB	ON	PQ	NB	NS	PEI	NF	YK	NWT	NU
Franklin's Gull	B	B	B	B	X	★	★	★		★	★	B	
Little Gull	★	★	★	B	B	★B	X	★	X	★	★		
Black-headed Gull	★			★	X	★B	X	X	X	B			
Bonaparte's Gull	B	B	B	B	B	B	X	X	X	★	B	B	X
Heermann's Gull	X												
Black-tailed Gull								★		★			
Mew Gull	B	B	B	B	★	★	★	X	★	★	B	B	
Ring-billed Gull	B	B	B	B	B	B	B	X	B	B	★	B	B
California Gull	B	B	B	B	B	★	★	★			★	B	
Herring Gull	B	B	B	B	B	B	B	B	B	B	B	B	B
Yellow-legged Gull						★				★			
Thayer's Gull	X	X	X	X	X	★		★	★	★	X	B	B
Iceland Gull	★	★	★	X	X	B	X	X	X	X	★	B	X
Lesser Black-backed Gull	★		★	X	X	X	X	X	★	★	★	★	
Slaty-backed Gull	★		★		★	★				★			★
Western Gull	X												
Glaucous-winged Gull	B	★		★							X	★	
Glaucous Gull	X	X	X	X	X	B	X	X	X	X	B	B	B
Great Black-backed Gull	★		★	X	B	B	B	B	B	B		★	★
Sabine's Gull	X	X	★	X	X	X	★	★	★	★	★	B	B
Black-legged Kittiwake	X	★		★	X	B	B	B	X	B	★	B	B
Red-legged Kittiwake	★									★			
Ross's Gull	★			B	★	★		★		★	★	B	
Ivory Gull	★			★	★	X	★	★	★	X	★		B
Gull-billed Tern						★	★	★					
Caspian Tern	B	B	B	B	B	★B	X	X	X	B	★	B	B
Royal Tern					★		★	★	★	★			
Elegant Tern	★												
Sandwich Tern					★	★	★	★		★			
Roseate Tern						★B	★B	B	★				
Common Tern	X	B	B	B	B	B	B	B	B	B			
Arctic Tern	B	★	B	B	B	B	B	B	B	B	B	B	B
Forster's Tern	B	B	B	B	B	★	★	★	★	★		B	
Least Tern			★	★	★		★	★	★	★			
Aleutian Tern	★												
Bridled Tern										★			
Sooty Tern					★	★	★	★					
White-winged Tern				★	★	★	★						★
Black Tern	B	B	B	B	B	B	B	B	★	★	B	B	B?
Black Skimmer					★	★	★	★	★	★			
Dovekie				★	★	X	X	X	X	X			★
Common Murre	B					B	B	X	X	B			★

	BC	AB	SK	MB	ON	PQ	NB	NS	PEI	NF	YK	NWT	NU
Thick-billed Murre	B				★	B	X	X	X	B	★	B	B
Razorbill					★	B	B	B	★	B		★	B
Black Guillemot		★	★	X	B	B	B	B	B	B	B	B	B
Pigeon Guillemot	B												
Long-billed Murrelet		★			★	★				★			
Marbled Murrelet	B												
Kittlitz's Murrelet	★												
Xantus's Murrelet	★												
Ancient Murrelet	B	★	★	★	★	★					★		
Cassin's Auklet	B												
Crested Auklet													
Parakeet Auklet	★												
Least Auklet												★	
Crested Auklet	★												
Rhinoceros Auklet	B												
Atlantic Puffin					★	B	B	B	★	B			B
Horned Puffin	B												
Tufted Puffin	B												
Rock Dove	B	B	B	B	B	B	B	B	B	B	B	★	
Band-tailed Pigeon	B	★	★	★	★	★	★	★					
Oriental Turtle-Dove	★												
White-winged Dove	★	★		★	★	★	★	★		★La			
Eurasian Collared-Dove			★		★								
Mourning Dove	B	B	B	B	B	B	B	B	B	X	X	X	★
Inca Dove					★								
Common Ground-Dove					★			★					
Black-billed Cuckoo	X	X	B	B	B	B	B	B	B	★			
Yellow-billed Cuckoo	★	★		★B	B	★B	X	X	X	★			
Groove-billed Ani					★								
Barn Owl	B	★	★	★B	B	★	★	★	★	★			
Flammulated Owl	B												
Western Screech-Owl	B	★	B										
Eastern Screech-Owl		★	B	B	B	B	★	★	★				
Great Horned Owl	B	B	B	B	B	B	B	B	B	B	B	B	
Snowy Owl	X	X	X	B	X	B	X	X	X	X	B	B	B
Northern Hawk-Owl	B	B	B	B	B	B	B	B	★	B	B	B	B
Northern Pygmy-Owl	B	B											
Burrowing Owl	B	B	B	B	★	★	★						
Spotted Owl	B												

	BC	AB	SK	MB	ON	PQ	NB	NS	PEI	NF	YK	NWT	NU
Barred Owl	B	B	B	B	B	B	B	B	B			B	
Great Gray Owl	B	B	B	B	B	B	★	★	★	★La	B	B	
Long-eared Owl	B	B	B	B	B	B	B	B	B	★		X	
Short-eared Owl	B	B	B	B	B	B	B	B	B	B	B	B	B
Boreal Owl	B	B	B	B	B	B	X	X	X	B	B	B	
Northern Saw-whet Owl	B	B	B	B	B	B	B	B	B	X	★		
Lesser Nighthawk					★								
Common Nighthawk	B	B	B	B	B	B	B	B	B	★	B	B	B
Common Poorwill	B	★B	B		★								
Chuck-will's-widow					B	★	★	★		★			
Whip-poor-will			B	B	B	B	B	B	★				
Black Swift	B	B										★	
Chimney Swift			B	B	B	B	B	B	X	X			
Vaux's Swift	B	★B											
White-throated Swift	B	★	★										
Green Violet-ear		★			★								
Broad-billed Hummingbird					★		★						
Xantus's Hummingbird	★												
Ruby-throated Hummingbird	★	B	B	B	B	B	B	B	B	B		★	
Black-chinned Hummingbird	B	★			★			★					
Anna's Hummingbird	B	★	★										
Costa's Hummingbird	★	★											
Calliope Hummingbird	B	B	★										
Broad-tailed Hummingbird	★												
Rufous Hummingbird	B	B	★	★	★	★	★	★		★	X		
Belted Kingfisher	B	B	B	B	B	B	B	B	B	★	B	B	
Lewis's Woodpecker	B	B?	★	X	★								
Red-headed Woodpecker	★	★	B	B	B	★B	X	X	★	★			
Acorn Woodpecker	★												
Red-bellied Woodpecker			★	X	B	X	★	X	★				
Yellow-bellied Sapsucker	B	B	B	B	B	B	B	B	B	B	B	B	
Red-naped Sapsucker	B	B	B										
Red-breasted Sapsucker	B	★									★		
Williamson's Sapsucker	B	★	★										
Downy Woodpecker	B	B	B	B	B	B	B	B	B	B	B	B	
Hairy Woodpecker	B	B	B	B	B	B	B	B	B	B	B	B	

	BC	AB	SK	MB	ON	PQ	NB	NS	PEI	NF	YK	NWT	NU
White-headed Woodpecker	B												
Three-toed Woodpecker	B	B	B	B	B	B	B	B	★B	B	B	B	B
Black-backed Woodpecker	B	B	B	B	B	B	B	B	B	B	B	B	
Northern Flicker	B	B	B	B	B	B	B	B	B	B	B	B	B
Pileated Woodpecker	B	B	B	B	B	B	B	B	B		B	B	
Olive-sided Flycatcher	B	B	B	B	B	B	B	B	B	B	B	B	
Western Wood-Pewee	B	B	B	B	★						B	B	
Eastern Wood-Pewee			B	B	B	B	B	B	B	★			
Yellow-bellied Flycatcher	B	B	B	B	B	B	B	B	B	B	X	B	
Acadian Flycatcher	★				B	★	★	★					
Alder Flycatcher	B	B	B	B	B	B	B	B	B	B	B	B	B
Willow Flycatcher	B	B	B	B	B	B	B	★	B				
Least Flycatcher	B	B	B	B	B	B	B	B	B	X	B	B	
Hammond's Flycatcher	B	B									B	B	
Gray Flycatcher	B	★		★									
Dusky Flycatcher	B	B	B		★			★			X	B?	
Pacific-slope Flycatcher	B	B											
Cordilleran Flycatcher	★	?											
Black Phoebe	★												
Eastern Phoebe	B	B	B	B	B	B	B	B	B	★	★B	B	
Say's Phoebe	B	B	B	B	★	★	★	★		★	B	B	
Vermilion Flycatcher					★			★					
Ash-throated Flycatcher	X				★		★						
Great Crested Flycatcher	★	B	B	B	B	B	B	B	B	★			
Sulphur-bellied Flycatcher					★		★	★		★			
Variegated Flycatcher					★								
Tropical Kingbird	★				★	★							
Couch's Kingbird					★			★					
Cassin's Kingbird					★			★					
Thick-billed Kingbird	★												
Western Kingbird	B	B	B	B	B	★	★	X	★	X	★		
Eastern Kingbird	B	B	B	B	B	B	B	B	B	B	X	B	★
Gray Kingbird	★				★			★					
Scissor-tailed Flycatcher	★	★	★	X	X	★	★	★					
Fork-tailed Flycatcher			★		★	★	★	★		★			
Brown Shrike								★					
Loggerhead Shrike	X	B	B	B	B	★B	★	★	★				
Northern Shrike	B	B	X	B	B	B	X	X	X	X	B	B	B

	BC	AB	SK	MB	ON	PQ	NB	NS	PEI	NF	YK	NWT	NU
White-eyed Vireo			★	★	B	★	★	★		★			
Bell's Vireo					X								
Black-capped Vireo					★								
Yellow-throated Vireo			B	B	B	B	★	★	★	★			
Plumbeous Vireo					★			★					
Cassin's Vireo	B	B	B			★							
Blue-headed Vireo	B	B	B	B	B	B	B	B	B	B	X	B	
Hutton's Vireo	B												
Warbling Vireo	B	B	B	B	B	B	B	★	★	★	B	B	
Philadelphia Vireo	B	B	B	B	B	B	B	X	B	X	X	B	
Red-eyed Vireo	B	B	B	B	B	B	B	B	B	B	X	B	
Gray Jay	B	B	B	B	B	B	B	B	B	B	B	B	B
Steller's Jay	B	B	★			★					★		
Blue Jay	B	B	B	B	B	B	B	B	B	B			
Western Scrub-Jay	★			★									
Clark's Nutcracker	B	B	★	X	★						★	B	
Black-billed Magpie	B	B	B	B	B	★	★	★		★	B		
Eurasian Jackdaw				★	★		★	★	★				
Pied Crow					★			★					
American Crow	B	B	B	B	B	B	B	B	B	B	★	B	B
Northwestern Crow	B												
Fish Crow					★			★					
Common Raven	B	B	B	B	B	B	B	B	B	B	B	B	B
Sky Lark	B												
Horned Lark	B	B	B	B	B	B	B	B	B	B	B	B	B
Purple Martin	B	B	B	B	B	B	B	B	X	★	★		
Tree Swallow	B	B	B	B	B	B	B	B	B	B	B	B	B
Violet-green Swallow	B	B	B	★	★			★			B	B	
N. Rough-winged Swallow	B	B	B	B	B	B	B	X	★	★	X		
Bank Swallow	B	B	B	B	B	B	B	B	B	B	B	B	
Cliff Swallow	B	B	B	B	B	B	B	B	★	★	B	B	B
Cave Swallow					★	★		★					
Barn Swallow	B	B	B	B	B	B	B	B	B	B	B	B	
Carolina Chickadee					★								
Black-capped Chickadee	B	B	B	B	B	B	B	B	B	B	B	B	
Mountain Chickadee	B	B									B	★	
Chestnut-backed Chickadee	B	★											
Boreal Chickadee	B	B	B	B	B	B	B	B	B	B	B	B	B
Gray-headed Chickadee											★		
Tufted Titmouse					B	B	★	★					

	BC	AB	SK	MB	ON	PQ	NB	NS	PEI	NF	YK	NWT	NU
Bushtit	B												
Red-breasted Nuthatch	B	B	B	B	B	B	B	B	B	B	B	B	B
White-breasted Nuthatch	B	B	B	B	B	B	B	B	B				
Pygmy Nuthatch	B												
Brown Creeper	B	B	B	B	B	B	B	B	B	B	★		
Rock Wren	B	B	B	★B	★			★					
Canyon Wren	B												
Carolina Wren		★		★	B	★B	★	★					
Bewick's Wren	B				B		★	★					
House Wren	B	B	B	B	B	B	★B	X	★	★		★	
Winter Wren	B	B	B	B	B	B	B	B	B	B	X		B
Sedge Wren			B	B	B	B	B	★	★	★			
Marsh Wren	B	B	B	B	B	B	B	B	★	X	★	B?	
American Dipper	B	B	★								B	B	
Golden-crowned Kinglet	B	B	B	B	B	B	B	B	B	B	X	B	B
Ruby-crowned Kinglet	B	B	B	B	B	B	B	B	B	B	B	B	B
Arctic Warbler													
Blue-gray Gnatcatcher	★	★	★	★B	B	B	X	X	X	★			
Siberian Rubythroat					★								
Bluethroat											X		
Northern Wheatear	★	★		X	X	B	★	★		★	B	B	B
Stonechat							★						
Blue Rock–Thrush	★												
Eastern Bluebird		★B	B	B	B	B	B	B	B	★			
Western Bluebird	B	★B											
Mountain Bluebird	B	B	B	B	★	★	★	★		★	B	B	
Townsend's Solitaire	B	B	B	X	★	★	★	★	★	★	B	B	
Veery	B	B	B	B	B	B	B	B	B	B			
Gray-cheeked Thrush	B	B	B	B	B	B	X	★	X	B	B	B	
Bicknell's Thrush					★	B	B	B	B				
Swainson's Thrush	B	B	B	B	B	B	B	B	B	B	B	B	B
Hermit Thrush	B	B	B	B	B	B	B	B	B	B	B	B	B
Wood Thrush		★	★	B	B	B	B	B	★	★			
Eurasian Blackbird					★	★				★			
Dusky Thrush	★												
Fieldfare					★	★	★	★		★			
Redwing								★		★			
American Robin	B	B	B	B	B	B	B	B	B	B	B	B	B
Varied Thrush	B	B	X	X	X	★	★	★		★	B	B	
Gray Catbird	B	B	B	B	B	B	B	B	B	B			

	BC	AB	SK	MB	ON	PQ	NB	NS	PEI	NF	YK	NWT	NU
Northern Mockingbird	B	B	*B	B	B	B	B	B	B	B		★	
Sage Thrasher	B	*B	*B	★	★		★						
Brown Thrasher	★	B	B	B	B	B	B	X	X	★			★
Curve-billed Thrasher		★		★									
European Starling	B	B	B	B	B	B	B	B	B	B	B	B	★
Crested Myna	B												
Siberian Accentor	★												
Yellow Wagtail	★										B	B	
White Wagtail										★			
Black-backed Wagtail	★												
Red-throated Pipit	★										★		
American Pipit	B	B	X	B	B	B	X	X	X	B	B	B	B
Sprague's Pipit	B	B	B	B	★								
Bohemian Waxwing	B	B	B	B	B	X	X	X	X	X	B	B	
Cedar Waxwing	B	B	B	B	B	B	B	B	B	B	B	B	B
Phainopepla					★								
Blue-winged Warbler		★	★	★	B	★	★	X	★	★			
Golden-winged Warbler		★		B	B	B	★	★		★			
Tennessee Warbler	B	B	B	B	B	B	B	B	B	B	B	B	B
Orange-crowned Warbler	B	B	B	B	B	B	X	X	★	★	B	B	B
Nashville Warbler	B	B	B	B	B	B	B	B	B	B	★		
Virginia's Warbler					★			★		★La			
Northern Parula	★	★	★	B	B	B	B	B	B	★			
Yellow Warbler	B	B	B	B	B	B	B	B	B	B	B	B	B
Chestnut-sided Warbler	B	B	B	B	B	B	B	B	B	★			
Magnolia Warbler	B	B	B	B	B	B	B	B	B	B	B	B	B
Cape May Warbler	B	B	B	B	B	B	B	B	B	B	X	B	B
Black-throated Blue Warbler	★	★	★	X	B	B	B	B	B	★			
Yellow-rumped Warbler	B	B	B	B	B	B	B	B	B	B	B	B	B
Black-throated Gray Warbler	B	★	★		★	★	★	★	★	★			
Black-throated Green Warbler	B	B	B	B	B	B	B	B	B	B			
Townsend's Warbler	B	B	B	★			★			★	B	★	
Hermit Warbler	★			★	?	★	★			★			
Blackburnian Warbler	★	B	B	B	B	B	B	B	B	B			
Yellow-throated Warbler	★		★	★	X	★	★	X	★	★			
Pine Warbler		★	★	B	B	B	B	X	★	★			
Kirtland's Warbler					B	★							
Prairie Warbler	★		★	★	B	★	X	X	★	★			
Palm Warbler	B	B	B	B	B	B	B	B	B	B	X	B	B
Bay-breasted Warbler	B	B	B	B	B	B	B	B	B	B	B	B	

	BC	AB	SK	MB	ON	PQ	NB	NS	PEI	NF	YK	NWT	NU
Blackpoll Warbler	B	B	B	B	B	B	B	B	X	B	B	B	
Cerulean Warbler				★	B	B	★	★		★			
Black-and-white Warbler	B	B	B	B	B	B	B	B	B	B	B	B	
American Redstart	B	B	B	B	B	B	B	B	B	B	B	B	
Prothonotary Warbler				★	B	★	★	★		★			
Worm-eating Warbler				★	★	★	★	★	★	★			
Swainson's Warbler					★	★		★					
Ovenbird	B	B	B	B	B	B	B	B	B	B	B	B	
Northern Waterthrush	B	B	B	B	B	B	B	B	B	B	B	B	
Louisiana Waterthrush					B	★	★	★					
Kentucky Warbler		★		★	X	★	★	★		★			
Connecticut Warbler	B	B	B	B	B	B	★	★		★		★	
Mourning Warbler	B	B	B	B	B	B	B	B	B	B	X	B	
MacGillivray's Warbler	B	B	B		★						B	★	
Common Yellowthroat	B	B	B	B	B	B	B	B	B	B	B	B	B
Hooded Warbler	★	★	★	★	B	★	★	X		★			★
Wilson's Warbler	B	B	B	B	B	B	B	B	B	B	B	B	B
Canada Warbler	B	B	B	B	B	B	B	B	B	★	X	B	
Painted Redstart	★				★								
Yellow-breasted Chat	B	B	B	X	B	★	★	X	★	★			
Hepatic Tanager						★							
Summer Tanager		★	★	X	X	★	★	X	X	★			
Scarlet Tanager	★	★	B	B	B	B	B	B	X	★			
Western Tanager	B	B	B	X	★	★	★	★		★	B	B	
Green-tailed Towhee	★	★	★	★	★	★		★					
Spotted Towhee	B	B	B	★	★	★	★	★	★				
Eastern Towhee		★	B	B	B	B	X	X	★	★			
Cassin's Sparrow		★			★			★					
Bachman's Sparrow					★								
American Tree Sparrow	B	X	B	B	B	B	X	X	X	B	B	B	B
Chipping Sparrow	B	B	B	B	B	B	B	B	B	B	B	B	B
Clay-colored Sparrow	B	B	B	B	B	B	X	X	★	★	★	B	
Brewer's Sparrow	B	B	B	★				★		B			
Field Sparrow			B	B	B	B	X	X	★	★			
Vesper Sparrow	B	B	B	B	B	B	B	B	B	★			
Lark Sparrow	B	B	B	B	B	★	X	X	★	★	★		
Black-throated Sparrow	★	★			★	★							
Sage Sparrow	★		★					★					
Lark Bunting	★	B	B	B	★	★	★			★			
Savannah Sparrow	B	B	B	B	B	B	B	B	B	B	B	B	B
Grasshopper Sparrow	B	B	B	B	B	B	★	X	★	★			
Baird's Sparrow	★	B	B	B	B								
Henslow's Sparrow					B	★		★					
Le Conte's Sparrow	B	B	B	B	B	B	★	★			X	B	B

	BC	AB	SK	MB	ON	PQ	NB	NS	PEI	NF	YK	NWT	NU
Nelson's Sharp-tailed Sparrow	B	B	B	B	B	B	B	B	B	★		B	
Seaside Sparrow							★	★					
Fox Sparrow	B	B	B	B	B	B	B	B	B	B	B	B	B
Song Sparrow	B	B	B	B	B	B	B	B	B	★B	B	B	B
Lincoln's Sparrow	B	B	B	B	B	B	B	B	B	B	B	B	B
Swamp Sparrow	B	B	B	B	B	B	B	B	B	B	B	B	B
White-throated Sparrow	B	B	B	B	B	B	B	B	B	B	B	B	B
Harris's Sparrow	X	X	B	B	B	★	★	★		★		B	B
White-crowned Sparrow	B	B	B	B	B	B	X	X	X	B	B	B	B
Golden-crowned Sparrow	B	B	★	★	★			★			B	B	
Dark-eyed Junco	B	B	B	B	B	B	B	B	B	B	B	B	B
McCown's Longspur	★	B	B	★									
Lapland Longspur	X	X	X	B	B	B	X	X	X	X	B	B	B
Smith's Longspur	B	X	X	B	B	★		★			B	B	★
Chestnut-collared Longspur	★	B	B	B	★		★	★		★			
Rustic Bunting	★												
Snow Bunting	X	X	X	X	B	B	X	X	X	X	B	B	B
McKay's Bunting	★												
Northern Cardinal		★	★	B	B	B	B	B	X	★			
Rose-breasted Grosbeak	B	B	B	B	B	B	B	B	B	B	X	B	
Black-headed Grosbeak	B	B	B	X	★	★	★	★					
Blue Grosbeak	★				X	★	★	X	★	★			
Lazuli Bunting	B	B	B	X	★						★	★	
Indigo Bunting	B	B	B	B	B	B	B	X	X	★			
Varied Bunting					★								
Painted Bunting	★				★	★	★	★					
Dickcissel	★	★	★B	B	B	★	X	X	★	★			
Bobolink	B	B	B	B	B	B	B	B	B	B		★	★
Red-winged Blackbird	B	B	B	B	B	B	B	B	B	B	B	B	B
Eastern Meadowlark			★	B	B	B	B	★	★				
Western Meadowlark	B	B	B	B	B	★B	★	★		★B			
Yellow-headed Blackbird	B	B	B	B	B	★	★	★	★	★	★	X	★
Rusty Blackbird	B	B	B	B	B	B	B	B	B	B	B	B	B
Brewer's Blackbird	B	B	B	B	B	★	★	★			★	B	
Common Grackle	B	B	B	B	B	B	B	B	B	B	★	B	
Great-tailed Grackle	★				★			★					
Shiny Cowbird						★							
Brown-headed Cowbird	B	B	B	B	B	B	B	B	B	B	B	B	
Orchard Oriole	★		★B	B	B	★	X	X	★	★			
Hooded Oriole	★				★	★							
Baltimore Oriole	B	B	B	B	B	B	B	B	B	★	★		
Bullock's Oriole	B	B	B		★			★					

	BC'	AB	SK	MB	ON	PQ	NB	NS	PEI	NF	YK	NWT	NU
Scott's Oriole					★								
Common Chaffinch							★	★		★			
Brambling	★	★	★	★	★	★		★			★		
Gray-crowned Rosy Finch	B	B	X	X	★	★					X	B	
Pine Grosbeak	B	B	B	B	B	B	B	B	B	B	B	B	B
Purple Finch	B	B	B	B	B	B	B	B	B	B	B	B	
Cassin's Finch	B	B			★								
House Finch	B	★B	B	B	B	B	B	B	B		★		
Red Crossbill	B	B	B	B	B	B	B	B	B	B	B	B	
White-winged Crossbill	B	B	B	B	B	B	B	B	B	B	B	B	B
Common Redpoll	B	B	B	B	B	B	X	X	X	B	B	B	B
Hoary Redpoll	X	X	X	B	X	B	X	X	★	★	B	B	B
Pine Siskin	B	B	B	B	B	B	B	B	B	B	B	B	B
Lesser Goldfinch	★				★								
American Goldfinch	B	B	B	B	B	B	B	B	B	B	★		★
Evening Grosbeak	B	B	B	B	B	B	B	B	X	B	X	B	
House Sparrow	B	B	B	B	B	B	B	B	B	B	★	B	
Eurasian Tree Sparrow				★B	★								

INFORMATION PROVIDED BY:

BRITISH COLUMBIA: Gary Davidson and *Pocket Checklist of B.C. Birds* by Wayne Campbell, August, 1999, Wild Bird Trust of B.C. Trust, B.C.

ALBERTA: Jocelyn Hudon, Chair, Alberta Bird Record Committee

SASKATCHEWAN: Martin Bailey

MANITOBA: Rudolf Koes

ONTARIO: Margaret Bain and *Field Checklist of Ontario Birds*, 1999, FON and OFO

QUEBEC: Pierre Bannon and *Liste commentée des oiseaux du Quebec*, 1996, by N. David

NEW BRUNSWICK: David Christie

NOVA SCOTIA: Jim Wolford and Blake Maybank

PRINCE EDWARD ISLAND: Dan McAskill and *Field Checklist of Birds*, 6th edition

NEWFOUNDLAND: John Pratt and *Checklist of the Birds of Insular Newfoundland and Its Continental Shelf Waters*

NWT: Craig Machtans and *Birds of NWT*, 2nd ed., 1996; Sirois and McRae

NUNAVUT: Anthony W. White, Craig Machtans and Sirois and McRae, 1996 (refer above)

YUKON: *Checklist of Yukon Birds*, 1999 by Cameron Eckert, Helmut Grujnberg, Greg Kubica, Lee Kubica and Pam Sinclair

NOTES